THE DOG LOVER'S COMPANION TO NEW ENGLAND

By JoAnna Downey and Christian J. Lau,

with Beth Rogers

AVALON
TRAVEL

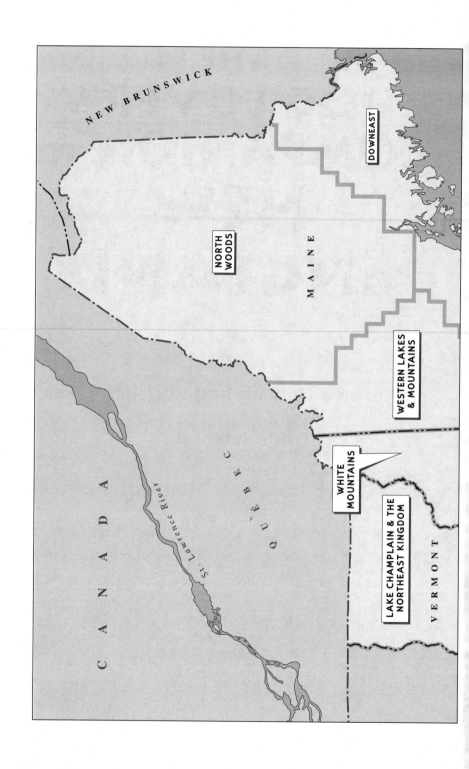

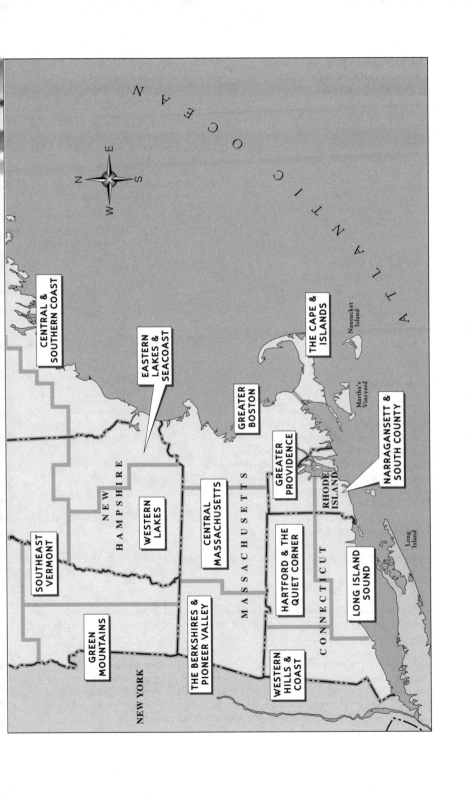

THE DOG LOVER'S COMPANION TO NEW ENGLAND

First Edition

JoAnna Downey and
Christian J. Lau

Published by
Avalon Travel Publishing
5855 Beaudry Street
Emeryville, CA 94608, USA

Please send all comments,
corrections, additions,
amendments, and critiques to:

**THE DOG LOVER'S COMPANION
TO NEW ENGLAND
AVALON TRAVEL PUBLISHING
5855 BEAUDRY ST.
EMERYVILLE, CA 94608, USA
EMAIL: INFO@TRAVELMATTERS.COM
WWW.TRAVELMATTERS.COM**

Printing History
1st edition—June 2001
5 4 3 2 1

ISBN: 1-56691-288-1
ISSN: 1531-4243

Editors: Helen Sillett, Marisa Solís
Series Manager: Angelique Clarke
Copy Editor: Donna Leverenz
Graphics Coordinator: Erika Howsare
Production: Amber Pirker, Marcie McKinley
Map Editors: Michael Balsbaugh, Naomi Dancis, Mike Ferguson
Cartography: Kat Kalamaras, Mike Morgenfeld
Index: Vera Gross

Cover and Interior Illustrations: Phil Frank

Distributed in the United States and Canada by Publishers Group West

Printed in USA by R.R. Donnelley

CONTENTS

INTRODUCTION

"Dogs are our link to paradise. They don't know evil or jealousy or discontent. To sit with a dog on a hillside on a glorious afternoon is to be back in Eden, where doing nothing was not boring—it was peace."

—Milan Kundera

In an increasingly hectic world of cell phones, beepers, emails, voice mail, and technologically driven everything, where everyone wants a piece of you and wants it NOW!, it is hard to remember that there is one creature in your life that asks for nothing more than to be with you. Whether you're going to the grocery store, the car wash, the beach, or on vacation, all your dog asks is to come along. In fact, in all our years of knowing dogs, we have never been turned down when we asked the question "You want to come?" Put it like that, and our dogs will jump up, wag their tails eagerly, and be out the door in a flash.

Never once have they said suspiciously, "So where are you going?" before making their decision. Never once have they answered, "Naw, I think I'll just stay here and take a nap." No, even if you asked your faithful friend to go to hell and back with you, their answer would be the same: "Can we go now?"

But as the world gets more crowded and patience grows thinner, it becomes harder to take your dog even when your schedule allows. Parks have become a turf battle between dog owners and those who think canines occupy a place only slightly above a rodent. Hotels and restaurants raise a horrified eyebrow when you ask if your dog can come in. As deep as the human-dog bond goes, you just stop expecting your dog to be welcome and, instead, leave her behind watching reruns of *Home Alone.*

But our dogs, George and Inu, don't let us off that easily. In fact, they are master guilt-meisters. When George, a shaggy, 30-pound bearded collie/terrier mix, gets the bad news that he has to stay at home, he tortures JoAnna by hiding behind the potted plant in the front hall. He slinks into the corner right by the front door, looking oh so pitiful, but refusing to disappear into the bedroom, thereby forcing JoAnna to pass him on her way out. And there he sits, peering pathetically between the scrawny branches, ears down and eyes mournful, silently pleading with her to change her mind. Inu, a golden retriever, uses a different tactic. He curls into a tight little ball and sinks way down onto the floor so that only his sad puppy-dog eyes can be seen. The message is clear: How can you go out and have all that fun without me?

To avoid this doggy guilt, we've adapted our lifestyles to include our dogs whenever possible. We tend to rent videos instead of going to the movies. We take our dogs to the post office, the nail salon, the pharmacy, and wherever else we can get away with it. We set out to learn which places in our neighborhood are dog friendly, and with this book we've taken things even further.

When we wrote *The Boston Dog Lover's Companion,* we tried to discover the best of everything you can do with your dog in the Greater Boston area, all the way out to Cape Cod, Martha's Vineyard, and Nantucket. With *The Dog Lover's Companion to New England* we've gone way beyond Beantown to find the best parks, ponds, paths, and peaks in all six states of New England—Connecticut, Rhode Island, Massachusetts, Maine, New Hampshire, and Vermont. Along the way we've met people and dogs we never would have known, talked to folks in jobs we never knew existed, discovered trails and towns that were once only names on a map, and, best of all, allowed our dogs to lead us, instead of the other way around. George and Inu always seemed to know that out on the trail it was their job to teach us the hidden joys a particular park had to offer. We would never have experienced these places in the same way without them.

Although this is a vast and diverse geographical area, all six states share a passionate interest in preserving both their historical roots and their natural resources. Wonderful conservation organizations act as watch dog and guard dog over the beautiful forests in this region. And equally fascinating town centers offer historical walking tours so you and your curious canine can bone up on a little history on your daily stroll. You'll find hidden swimming holes, beautiful beaches, leash-free dog parks, and more than a few mountains where you can sit in peace with your pooch. You'll enjoy dozens of diversions where your canine pal can join you. Go on a harbor cruise, catch an outdoor movie, march in a pets-only parade, take a trip on a scenic railroad, all with your dog showing the way. You can explore the little-known parks tucked away in each town and travel in style at the many hotels, restaurants, and outdoor cafés that welcome you and your dog. Our hope is that after reading this book you'll find it even harder to close your door on that lovable little mug of hers; we also expect your dog's tail will be wagging on a regular basis. And, along the way, we hope you'll learn things about New England you never knew. We know we did!

THE PAWS SCALE

At some point we've got to face the facts: Humans and dogs have different tastes. We like eating spinach and smelling lilacs and covering our bodies with soft clothes. They like eating roadkill and covering their bodies with horse manure.

The parks, beaches, and recreation areas in this book are rated with a dog in mind. Maybe your favorite park has lush gardens, a duck pond, a few acres of perfectly manicured lawns, and sweeping views of a nearby skyline. But unless your dog can run leash free, swim in the pond, and roll in the grass, that park doesn't deserve a very high rating from a pooch's perspective.

The very lowest rating you'll come across in this book is the fire hydrant symbol 🔥. When you see it, that means the park is merely "worth a squat." Visit one of these parks only if your dog just can't hold it any longer. These parks have virtually no other redeeming qualities for canines.

Beyond that, the paws scale starts at one paw 🐾 and goes up to four paws 🐾🐾🐾🐾. A one-paw park isn't a dog's idea of a great time. Maybe it's a tiny park with few trees and too many kids running around. Or perhaps it's a magnificent-for-people park that bans dogs from every inch of land except paved roads and a few campsites.

Four-paw parks, on the other hand, are places your dog will drag you to visit. Some of these areas come as close to dog heaven as you can get on this planet. Many have water for swimming or zillions of acres for hiking. Some four-paw parks give you the option of letting your dog off leash. Others have restrictions, which we'll detail in the descriptions.

You will also notice a foot symbol 👣 every so often. The foot means the park offers something extra special for the humans in the crowd. You deserve something for being such a good chauffeur.

This book is not a comprehensive guide to all of the parks in New England. We've tried to find the best, largest, and most convenient parks. Some areas have so many wonderful parks that we found ourselves getting jaded. What would have been a four-paw park in one area looked like a mere two- or three-paw place after seeing so many great spots in another area. Other cities had such a limited supply of parks that, for the sake of dogs living and visiting there, we ended up listing parks that wouldn't be worth mentioning otherwise.

Since street signs and signposts are often confusing in this neck of the woods, we've given specific directions to all the parks. When you ask a Yankee how to get somewhere, you'll most often get a look that says, "If you have to ask, you shouldn't be going there." Or you'll get scrambled and vague directions that result in your becoming hopelessly lost. Although we've tried to make it as easy as possible for you, we highly recommend picking up a detailed street map before you and your dog set out on your adventures.

TO LEASH OR NOT TO LEASH

That is not a question that occupies a dog's mind. Ask just about any normal, red-blooded American dog if she'd prefer to visit a park and be on leash or off, and she'll say, "Arf!" (Translation: "Is this a trick question?") No doubt about it, most dogs would give their canine teeth to be able to frolic without that dreaded leash.

When you see the running dog symbol 🐕 in this book, you'll know that under certain circumstances your dog can run around in leash-free bliss. The rest of the parks demand leashes. We wish we could write about the places where dogs get away with being scofflaws, but those would be the first parks the animal-control patrols would hit. We can't advocate breaking the law, but, if you're going to, please follow your conscience and use common sense.

And just because dogs are permitted off leash in certain areas, that doesn't necessarily mean you should let your dog run free. In state forests and large tracts of land, unless you're sure your dog will come back to you when you call or will never stray more than a few yards from your side, you should keep her leashed. A deer or rabbit that crosses your path could mean hours of searching for your stray dog. And an otherwise docile homebody can turn into a savage hunter if the right prey is near. In pursuit of a strange scent, your dog could easily get lost in an unfamiliar area.

Be careful out there. If your dog really needs leash-free exercise but can't be trusted in remote areas, she'll be happy to know that several beaches permit well-behaved, leashless pooches, as do a growing number of beautiful, fenced-in dog exercise areas.

THERE'S NO BUSINESS LIKE DOG BUSINESS

There's nothing appealing about bending down with a plastic bag or a piece of newspaper on a chilly morning and grabbing the steaming remnants of what your dog ate for dinner the night before. It's disgusting. Worse yet, you have to hang on to it until you can find a trash can. And how about when the newspaper doesn't endure before you're able to dispose of it? Yuk! It's enough to make you wish your dog were a cat.

But as gross as it can be to scoop the poop, it's even worse to step in it. It's really bad if a child falls in it, or—gasp!—starts eating it. And have you ever walked into a park where few people clean up after their dogs? The stench could make a hog want to hibernate.

Unscooped poop is one of a dog's worst enemies. Public policies banning dogs from parks are enacted because of it. At present a few good New England parks and beaches that permit dogs are in danger of closing their gates

to all canines because of the negligent behavior of a few owners. A worst-case scenario is already in place in several communities—dogs are banned from all parks. Their only exercise is a leashed sidewalk stroll. That's no way to live.

If we had a nickel for every dog constable that listed violations of the pooper-scooper laws as the thing that made their job most difficult, let's just say we could quit our day jobs. Almost everyone we spoke to named unscooped poop as their number-one headache—and the thing most likely to make their towns ban dogs from public parks. Several town leaders told us the biggest pressure they have right now is what to do about the "dog problem" complaints they receive from local residents.

Just be responsible and clean up after your dog everywhere you go. Stuff plastic bags in your jackets, your purse, your car, your pants pockets—anywhere you might be able to pull one out when needed. Or if plastic isn't your bag, newspapers do the trick. If it makes it more palatable, bring along a paper bag, too, and put the used newspaper or plastic bag in it. That way you don't have to walk around with dripping paper or a plastic bag whose contents are visible to the world.

If you don't enjoy the squishy sensation, try one of those cardboard or plastic bag pooper-scoopers sold at pet stores. If you don't feel like bending down, buy a long-handled scooper. There's a scooper for every preference.

We've tried not to lecture about scooping throughout the book, but it does tend to be JoAnna's pet peeve. To help keep parks alive, we should harp on it in every park description, but that would take another 100 pages, and you'd start to ignore us anyway. And if we mentioned it in some parks and not others, it might convey that you don't have to clean up after your dog in the descriptions where it's not mentioned. Trust us. *Every* park has a pooper-scooper law!

ETIQUETTE REX:
THE WELL-MANNERED MUTT

While cleaning up after your dog is your responsibility, a dog in a public place has his own responsibilities. Of course, it really boils down to your responsibility again, but the burden of action is on your dog.

Etiquette for restaurants and hotels is covered in other sections of the introduction. What follows is some very basic dog etiquette. We'll go through it quickly, but if your dog's a slow reader, he can go over it again: No vicious behavior; no jumping on people; no incessant barking; no leg lifts on backpacks, human legs, or any other personal objects you'll find hanging around beaches and parks. Dogs should come when they're called and should stay on command.

Everyone, including dogs, makes mistakes, but you should do your best to remedy any consistent problems. It takes patience and it's not always easy. For instance, George considers it his doggy duty to bark at weird people—at least those he thinks are weird (and we hate to say it, but he's usually right). But that's no excuse. Strange folk or not, your dog shouldn't be allowed to bark at others unless they're threatening you or breaking into your house.

And Inu has this selective hearing problem. He only pays attention to commands when the wind is blowing a certain way (at least that's his explanation). Tell him to come one day, and he's right there. But when the breeze is blowing toward a certain great smell. . . well, it seems to cloud his usual good hearing. But "under voice control" means all the time. If your dog won't obey you, fix the problem or put him on a leash. There are certain public behaviors that should not be tolerated in a dog. George and Inu are constantly learning their boundaries the hard way, and we're constantly learning to avoid situations that might make our sweet dogs look like canine delinquents. There's a limit to the "dogs will be dogs" adage.

SAFETY FIRST

A few essentials will keep your traveling dog happy and healthy. When planning a trip with your dog, know his limitations. Some dogs are perfectly fine in a car; others get motion sickness. Some dogs happily hop in their kennel cab for airline flights; others are traumatized for hours. Only you know your dog's temperament. Here are some guidelines to consider before you hit the road:

HOT DOG

If you must leave your dog alone in the car for a few minutes, do so only if it's cool out and if you can park in the shade. Never, ever, ever leave a dog in a car with the windows rolled up all the way. Even if it seems cool, the sun's heat passing through the window can kill a dog in minutes. Roll down the window just enough for your dog to get air, but so there's no danger of his getting out or someone breaking in. Make sure he has plenty of water.

You also have to watch out for heat exposure when your car is in motion. Certain cars, such as hatchbacks, can make a dog in the backseat extra hot, even while you feel OK in the driver's seat.

Try to take your vacation so you don't visit a place when it's extremely warm. Dogs and heat don't get along, especially if the dog isn't used to heat. The opposite is also true. If a dog lives in a hot climate and you take him to a freezing place, it may not be a healthy shift. Check with your vet if you have any doubts. Spring and fall are usually the best times to travel.

DRINK UP!

Water your dog frequently. Dogs on the road may drink even more than they do at home. Take regular water breaks, or bring a heavy bowl (the thick clay ones do nicely) and set it on the car floor so your dog always has access to water. When hiking, be sure to carry enough for yourself and a thirsty dog. When at the beach, remember that if you don't offer your pal fresh water, he may help himself to the salt water. This won't be a pretty picture, we assure you.

Rest stops: Stop and unwater your dog. There's nothing more miserable than being stuck in a car when you can't find a rest stop. No matter how tightly you cross your legs and try to think of the desert, you're certain you'll burst within the next minute. But think of how a dog feels when the urge strikes and he can't tell you the problem. There are plenty of places listed in our book to allow your dog to relieve herself.

How frequently you stop depends on your dog's bladder. If your dog is constantly running out the doggy door at home to relieve himself, you may want to stop every hour. Others can go for significantly longer without being uncomfortable. Watch for any signs of restlessness and gauge it for yourself.

CAR CRUISING

Even the experts differ about how a dog should travel in a car. Some suggest doggy safety belts, available at pet supply stores. Others firmly believe in keeping a dog kenneled. They say it's safer for the dog if there's an accident, and it's safer for the driver because there's no dog underfoot. Still others say you should just let your dog hang out without straps and boxes. They believe that if there's an accident, at least the dog isn't trapped in a cage. They say that dogs enjoy this more anyway.

We tend to agree with the latter school of thought. Inu and George travel very politely in the backseat and occasionally love sticking their snouts out of the windows to smell the world go by. The danger is that if the car kicks up a pebble or annoys a bee, their noses and eyes could be injured. So we usually open the window just enough so our dogs can stick out a little snout.

Whichever way you choose to travel, your pet will be more comfortable if he has his own blanket with him for the duration. A veterinarian acquaintance uses a faux-sheepskin blanket for his dogs. At night in the hotel, the sheepskin doubles as the dog's bed.

FLYING FIDOS

Air travel is even more controversial. Many people feel it's tantamount to cruel and unusual punishment to force a dog to fly in the cargo hold like a piece of luggage. And there are dangers to flying that are somewhat beyond your control, such as runway delays—the cargo hold is not pressurized when on the ground—and connecting flights that tempt the wrong-way fates.

JoAnna and George have racked up some serious frequent flyer miles in George's eight years of life, without ever having a problem. But they don't leave this to chance. There are some very specific rules you can follow to ensure your dog's safety. For example, always book nonstop flights. Don't take the chance that your dog could be misdirected while changing planes.

And always inform the flight crew you are traveling with your pet. That way they can inform you when your dog has boarded the plane safely and will take extra precautions when on the runway. Also, make sure you schedule takeoff and arrival times when the temperature is below 80 degrees and above 35 degrees Fahrenheit. And don't forget to consult the airline about their regulations and required certificates. Most airlines will ask you to show a health certificate and possibly proof of a rabies vaccination.

The question of tranquilizing a dog for a plane journey is a difficult one. Some vets think it's insane to give a dog a sedative before flying. They say a dog will be calmer and less fearful without taking a disorienting drug. Others think it's crazy not to afford your dog the little relaxation he might not otherwise get without a tranquilizer. We suggest discussing the tranquilizer issue with your vet, who will take the trip's length and your dog's personality into account.

On their first flight together, JoAnna gave George a very mild sedative. He was very dehydrated afterward, so on the return leg he went without the drug. He was just fine and has not been sedated since. Flying is not his favorite activity, but it's better than being left at home, so he trusts JoAnna to make sure he's treated well.

THE CARRY-ON

Your dog can't pack her own bags, and, even if she could, she'd probably fill them with dog biscuits and chew toys. It's important to stash some of those in your dog's vacation kit, but here are some other items to take along: bowls, bedding, brush, towels (for those muddy days), first-aid kit, pooper-scoopers, water, food, prescription drugs, tags, treats, toys, and, of course, this book.

Be sure your dog wears her license, identification tag, and rabies tag. On a long trip you may even want to bring along your dog's rabies certificate. Some parks and campgrounds require rabies and licensing information. You never know how picky they'll be.

It's a good idea to snap one of those barrel-type IDs on your dog's collar, too, showing the name, address, and phone number of where you'll be vacationing. That way if she should get lost, at least the finder won't be calling your empty house. Carrying a picture of your dog, in case the two of you become separated, is also not a bad idea.

Some people think dogs should drink only water brought from home so their bodies don't have to get used to too many new things. We've never had a problem feeding our dogs tap water from other parts of the state, nor has anyone else we know. Most vets think your dog will be fine drinking tap water in most other U.S. cities.

PEST CONTROL

Chances are that your adventuring will go without a hitch, but you should always be prepared to deal with trouble. Make sure you know the basics of animal first aid before you embark on a long journey with your dog.

The more common woes—ticks, burrs, poison ivy, and skunks—can make life with a traveling dog a somewhat trying experience.

Ticks are hard to avoid in New England. They can carry Lyme disease, so you should always check yourself and your dog thoroughly after a day in tick country. In fact, it's a good idea to keep checking for a day or two after you've been out. Ticks are crafty little critters, and it's not unusual to find ticks on your dog two, three, or four days after your walk in the woods. Don't forget to check ears and between the toes.

If you find a tick that is unattached, you can remove it from your dog with your hands, but tweezers are best. If you find an attached tick (it's usually swollen and looks like a dark corn kernel), use tweezers to grasp it as close to your dog's skin as possible and pull it straight out. If you are unable to grasp the tick close to the skin, try twisting it counterclockwise, "unscrewing" the tick's head. Frequently they will let go. Avoid leaving any tick mouth parts embedded under your dog's skin. Disinfect the area before and after removing the pest.

The tiny deer ticks that carry Lyme disease are difficult to find. Consult your veterinarian if your dog is lethargic for a few days, has a fever, loses her appetite, or becomes lame. These symptoms could indicate Lyme disease. If you spend a lot, or even a little, time in Rhode Island, Connecticut, or the islands of Cape Cod, Martha's Vineyard, Nantucket, or Block Island, or, for that matter, any of the woodlands in the other states, we urge you to have your dog vaccinated. Lyme disease can be deadly, and the reported cases become more widespread every year.

Burrs—those round pieces of dry grass that attach to your socks, your sweater, and your dog—are an everyday annoyance. But, in certain cases, they can be lethal. They can stick in your dog's eyes, nose, ears, or mouth and work their way in. Check every nook and cranny of your dog after a walk if you've been anywhere near dry grass. Be vigilant.

Poison ivy is also a common menace. Dogs don't react to poison ivy, but they can easily pass its oils on to people. If you think your dog has made contact with poison ivy, avoid petting her until you can get home and bathe her (preferably while wearing rubber gloves). If you do pet her before washing her, make sure you don't touch your eyes, and wash your hands immediately.

If your dog loses a contest with a skunk (and she always will), rinse her eyes first with plain warm water, then bathe her with dog shampoo. Towel her off, then apply tomato juice. If you can't get tomato juice, you can also use a solution of one pint of vinegar per gallon of water to cut through the stink.

BONE APPÉTIT

In Europe dogs enter restaurants and dine alongside their folks as if they were people, too. (Or at least they sit and watch and drool while their people dine.) Not so in America. Rightly or wrongly, dogs are considered a health threat. But many health inspectors will say they see no reason why clean, well-behaved dogs shouldn't be permitted inside a restaurant.

Ernest Hemingway made an expatriate of his dog, Black Dog (aka Blackie), partly because of America's restrictive views on dogs in dining establishments. In "The Christmas Gift," a story published in *Look* magazine in 1954, he describes how he made the decision to take Black Dog to Cuba, rather than leave him behind in Ketchum, Idaho:

This was a town where a man was once not regarded as respectable unless he was accompanied by his dog. But a reform movement had set in, led by several local religionists, and gambling had been abolished and there was even a movement on foot to forbid a dog from entering a public eating place with his master. Blackie had always tugged me by the trouser leg as we passed a combination gambling and eating place called the Alpine where they served the finest sizzling steak in the West. Blackie wanted me to order the giant sizzling steak and it was difficult to pass the Alpine. . . . We decided to make a command decision and take Blackie to Cuba.

Fortunately, you don't have to take your dog to a foreign country in order to eat together at a restaurant. New England has many restaurants with outdoor tables, and these establishments welcome dogs to join their people for an alfresco experience.

The law on patio-dining dogs is somewhat vague, and you'll discover different versions of it. But, in general, as long as your dog doesn't go inside a restaurant (even to get to outdoor tables in the back) and isn't near the food preparation areas, it's probably legal. The decision is then up to the restaurant proprietor.

The restaurants listed in this book have given us permission to tout them as dog-friendly eateries. But keep in mind that rules can change and restaurants can close, so we highly recommend phoning before you get your stomach set on a particular kind of cuisine. Also, even if they are listed here as allowing dogs, as a courtesy you should politely ask the manager if your dog may join you on that particular day. Remember, it's the restaurant owner, not you, who will be in trouble if someone complains.

Some basic restaurant etiquette: Dogs shouldn't beg from other diners, no matter how delicious their steak looks. Dogs should not attempt to get their snouts (or their entire bodies) up on the table. They should be clean, quiet, and as unobtrusive as possible. If your dog leaves a good impression with the management and other customers, it will help pave the way for all the other dogs who want to dine alongside their best friends in the future.

A ROOM AT THE INN

Good dogs make great hotel guests. They don't steal towels, and they don't get drunk and keep the neighbors up all night. In the years between writing *The Boston Dog Lover's Companion* and now, we have seen a drastic and, thankfully, positive change in attitude from many innkeepers. Hotel proprietors are realizing that allowing dogs is good business, and they tell us some of their best guests are those who travel with their pets. This book lists dog-friendly accommodations of all types, from motels to bed-and-breakfast inns to elegant hotels. But the basic dog etiquette rules are the same.

Dogs should never, never, NEVER be left alone in your room. Leaving a dog alone in a strange place is inviting serious trouble. Scared, nervous dogs can tear apart drapes, carpeting, and furniture, or injure themselves. They can also bark nonstop and scare the daylights out of the housekeeper. Just don't do it.

Only bring a house-trained dog to a lodging.

It helps if you bring your dog's bed or his blanket. He'll feel more at home and won't be tempted to jump on the bed. If your dog sleeps on the bed with you at home, bring a sheet and put it on top of the bed so the hotel's bedspread won't get furry or dirty.

After a few days in a hotel, some dogs come to think of it as home. They get territorial. When another hotel guest walks by, it's *"Bark! Bark!"* When the housekeeper knocks, it's *"Bark! Snarl! Bark! Gnash!"* Keep your dog quiet, or you'll both find yourselves looking for a new home away from home.

For some strange reason, many lodgings prefer small dogs as guests. All we can say is, *"Yip! Yap!"* It's really ridiculous. Large dogs are often much calmer and quieter than their tiny, high-energy cousins. (Some hotel managers must think small dogs are more like cats. Wrong.) If you're in a location where you can't find a hotel that will accept you and your big brute, it's time to try a sell job. Let the manager know how good and quiet your dog is (if he is). Promise he won't eat the bathtub or run around and shake the hotel. Offer a deposit or sign a waiver, even if they're not required for small dogs. It helps if your sweet, soppy-eyed dog is at your side to convince the decision maker.

You could always sneak your dog into a hotel, but we don't recommend that you attempt to do so. The lodging might have a good reason for its rules. Besides, you'll always feel as if you're going to be caught and thrown out on your petard. You race in and out of your room with your dog as if ducking sniper fire. It's better to avoid feeling like a criminal and move on to a more dog-friendly location. For a sure bet, try a Motel 6, Red Roof Inn, or Howard Johnson. Most of these establishments allow you to bring your dog with you. Some have more lenient pet rules than others.

The lodgings described in this book are for dogs who obey all the rules. Rates listed are for double rooms, unless otherwise noted.

HE, SHE, IT

In this book, whether neutered, spayed, or *au naturel*, dogs are never referred to as "it." They are either "he" or "she." We alternate pronouns so no dog reading this book will feel left out.

A DOG IN NEED

"A dog is the only thing on this earth that loves you more than he loves himself."
—Josh Billings

If you don't currently have a dog but could provide a good home for one, we'd like to make a plea on behalf of all the unwanted dogs who will be euthanized tomorrow and the day after that and the day after that. JoAnna adopted George from an animal shelter and Chris saved Inu from inattention at the hands of his previous owners. We believe in and support all efforts to control the existing dog population (spay or neuter your dogs!) and to assist the dogs who currently and desperately need homes. Animal shelters and humane organizations are overflowing with dogs who would devote their lives to being your best buddy, your faithful traveling companion, and a dedicated listener to all your tales of bliss and woe.

For more information, contact your local shelter or the National Humane Education Society (521-A East Market Street, Leesburg, VA 20176; (703) 777-8319), a nonprofit organization that teaches people about the importance of being kind to animals and maintains the Peace Plantation Animal Sanctuary for dogs and cats. In New England, contact the MSPCA at 350 South Huntington Avenue, Boston, MA 02130, (617) 522-7400.

Need a nudge? Remember these words by writer Lloyd Alexander: *"I had no particular breed in mind, no unusual requirements. Except the special sense of mutual recognition that tells dog and human they have both come to the right place."* Don't wait. Save a dog's life today!

CONNECTICUT

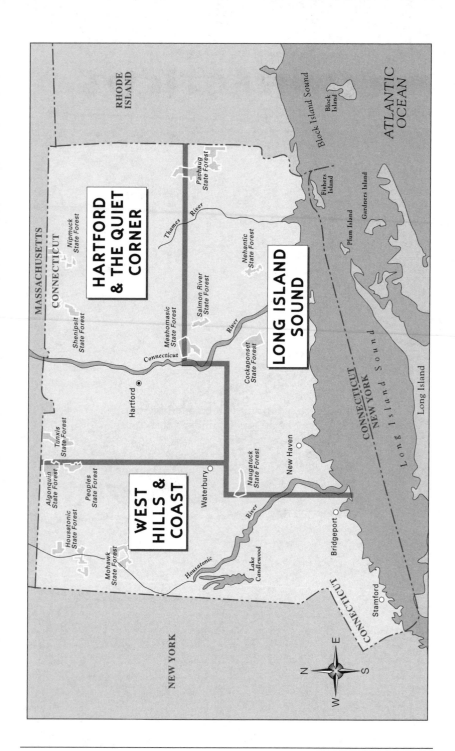

CONNECTICUT

Connecticut is the gateway to New England and a great place to get acquainted with the charm of this region. It's the third-smallest state in the Union and has over three million people in its 5,000 square miles. Even with those daunting density numbers, much of the state is still open land—forests, farms, and parks. The mountains here are molehills compared to the ranges in Connecticut's northern neighbors, but lower elevations make summit views easier to reach. With 90 miles of coastline on Long Island Sound and the Connecticut River, New England's central water thoroughfare, the Constitution State can also boast some of the best water spots anywhere in New England.

Blue Trails: Connecticut has some 700 miles of hiking trails. Many of the trails run through state and town park property, but most are on private lands, maintained and mapped by the Connecticut Forest and Park Association, a private, nonprofit group. The Association, founded in 1929, calls this system of loosely connecting trails the Blue Trails and identifies them with familiar blue-blazed markers.

The majority of the Blue Trail hikes are only a mile or two in length, but a few are quite long; the Tunxis Trail, for example, is 21 miles in length. Obviously, we can't describe all of them—the Association's *Connecticut Walk Book* does that—but we do include the significant hikes either with a separate listing or with a mention in the particular park the trail runs through.

As far as trail rules go, your pup will be anything but blue. While on the Blue Trails your dog may be off leash if under voice control. However, if the Blue Trail runs across state-owned land (like a forest or a park), then the leash rules of that park trump that of the Blue Trail. The same principle applies to the trail hours. They are open dawn to dusk, unless park rules are different.

For more information and/or for a copy of the *Connecticut Walk Book,* the guide to the Blue Trails, contact the Connecticut Forest and Park Association at 16 Meriden Road, Rockfall, CT 06481, (860) 346-2372; www.ctwoodlands.org.

Mattabesett Trail: This combination of three trails covers over 50 miles of central Connecticut terrain with the longest portion being 35 miles in length. The trail covers some of the more mountainous regions of Middlesex County and is a great way to explore the many parcels of the Cockaponset State Forest. The Mattabesett is part of Connecticut's Blue Trail network and is managed by the Connecticut Forest and Park Association. The best places to access the trail are at Millers Pond State Park in Durham and Guifridda Park in Meriden. (860) 346-2372.

Airline State Park Trail: This 49-mile recreation trail runs from Windham to Putnam in the north and from East Hampton to Willimantic in the south. The two sections break at Willimantic. This easy to moderate hike along the old Airline railroad bed will take you along a grassy graveled trail through the back doors of several towns. The access points are along U.S. Route 44 in Pomfret, State Route 97 in Hampton, State Route 203 in Windham, State Route 2 in

Colchester, and State Routes 85 and 207 in Hebron. Dogs must be leashed on the trail. (860) 424-3200.

Farmington Canal Linear Park Trail: This trail offers a wonderful walk with an amazing history. Now part of the National Rails-to-Trails Conservancy, it was originally part of the 83-mile Farmington Canal that transported freight and passengers. In fact, you can still visit Lock 12 and the lockkeeper's house, as well as see parts of the canal as you traverse the approximately three-mile paved path in Cheshire and Hamden. Hopefully you and your dog don't have allergies, because you'll find enough flora and fauna along the way to impress even the most discriminating naturalist. Call the Rails-to-Trails Conservancy at (202) 331-9696.

Dogs must stay on leash. There are four entrances to the trail with parking lots: on Cromwell Avenue, Mount Sanford Road, and North Brooksvale Road in Cheshire, and in Brooksvale Park in Hamden. Open sunrise to sunset. (860) 424-3200.

Farmington Valley Greenway: The Greenway is part of a statewide effort to reclaim former canal and rail land and create recreational green space. The flat, paved Greenway runs for 25 miles, from Farmington to East Granby, following the former train line. Along the way you will be treated to views of canal locks, historic buildings, and stone archways.

Future plans include extending the trail to the Massachusetts border, as well as connecting this trail system to Farmington Canal Linear Park Trail (see above).

Dogs must be leashed. The best access is at Stratton Brook State Park in Simsbury. Open dawn to dusk.

The Greenway is managed collectively by the towns and parks along the route.In Avon, (860) 409-4332; in Simsbury, (860) 424-3200, in Granby, (860) 653-8947.

Metacomet Trail: This Blue Trail runs from Meriden to Suffield and the Massachusetts state line, all the way up to Mount Monadnock in New Hampshire. In New Hampshire it becomes the Monadnock Trail. The Connecticut portion is 51 miles in length, and runs along a striking traprock ridge, with a number of mountain summits. It is named for Metacomet, better known as King Philip, the famous Indian chief who supposedly ordered the burning of Simsbury from these hills.

Two good access points for the trail are at Hubbard Park in Meriden and Talcott Mountain State Park in Simsbury. The Connecticut Forest and Park Association administers the entire trail system. (860) 346-2372.

Tunxis Trails: The Tunxis Trail system is part of the Blue Trail network and covers much of the upper Connecticut River Valley. The main route, running from the Massachusetts state line in Hartland to Burlington, is 21 miles long and passes through some of the more remote wilderness in Connecticut on the eastern side of the Barkhamstead Reservoir. The primary access point for this Blue Trail is in Tunxis State Forest in Hartland. For more information, contact the Connecticut Forest and Park Association at (860) 346-2372.

1

HARTFORD & THE QUIET CORNER

This section of Connecticut mixes the bright lights of Hartford's big city with the stillness of the northeastern part of the state, known as the Quiet Corner.

A strict sect of puritans, seeking to escape the more liberal ways of Massachusetts, established the first pilgrim settlements along the Connecticut River in 1633. With forefathers like these, we are not surprised at the all-business personality of Hartford today. As both the state capital and the insurance center of the United States, Hartford is a vibrant city, but it is still trying to find itself when it comes to recreation and entertainment (despite Mark Twain's efforts).

No matter what your opinion is about the pace of Hartford, everyone agrees on the peaceful beauty of the Quiet Corner. This area is dotted with stunning woodlands, historic towns dating back to the 17th and 18th centuries, and mill villages on the Quinebaug and Shetucket Rivers.

AVON

PARKS, BEACHES, AND RECREATION AREAS

• Sperry Park/Farmington Valley Greenway 🐾 See **1** on page 18.
This is a small green space, but from here you can access the Farmington Valley Greenway (see page 16). Located at the center point of the Greenway, you can go north or south from Sperry Park. There is one other outstanding feature here, but only on nice days and only at lunch. A portable trailer called "The Dog House" serves hot dogs and more at the park entrance. The rest of Sperry is for the pigeons. And squirrels. And ants.

Dogs must be on leash in the park and on the Greenway.

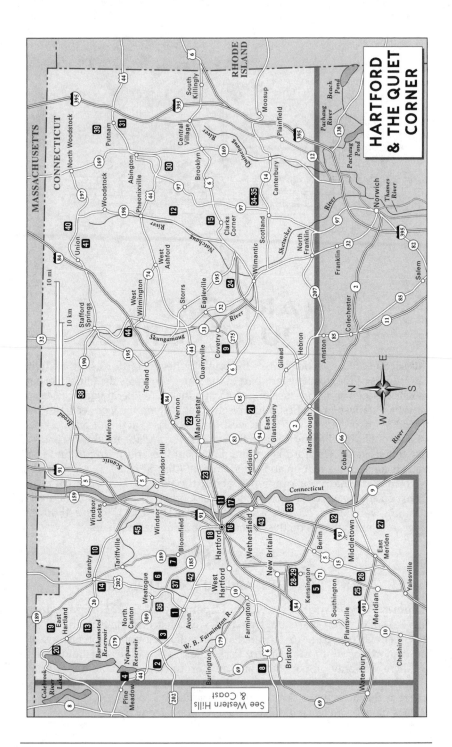

HARTFORD & THE QUIET CORNER

From U.S. Route 44, take State Routes 10/202 north for a quarter mile. The park is on the right. Open dawn to dusk. (860) 409-4332.

RESTAURANTS

Harry's Big Tomato Pizza: The big tomato pizza got a big tomato welcome from our dogs. We carried the pizza to the patio tables outside where our waiting crew was doing its imitation of Pavlov's dogs. Riverdale Farms Plaza, State Route 10, Avon/Simsbury line. (860) 409-0707.

Kevin Charles Smokehouse: This restaurant specializes in all things smoked, including our dogs' all-time favorite: smoked pig ears. A big bin of these treats is available for canine visitors, plus a variety of smoked lunch meats, salads, grilled selections, and homemade soups for human visitors. Get your order to go and settle into one of the outdoor tables with your pooch. 427 West Avon Road; (860) 673-6696.

PLACES TO STAY

Avon Old Farms: This antique red barn turned inn is just a jaunt up the road from the Metacomet Trail access in West Hartford and the Talcott Mountain Reservoir, making it the perfect spot for Spot. Pets are welcome in some of the rooms, with rates from $89 to $275, including continental breakfast. 279 Avon Mountain Road (U.S. Route 44), Avon, CT 06001; (860) 677-1651, (800) 836-4000; www.avonoldfarmshotel.com.

DIVERSIONS

Pick a peck of pickled peppers: And you and Sparky can do it, too, at the Pickin Patch at Woodford Farm, a pick-your-own-produce place (the produce varies seasonally). This family farm has been in operation since 1666, making it one of the oldest working farms in the country. Woodford Farm is open May through December and is located on Nod Road. (860) 677-9552.

Row, Row, Row Your Boat: Huck Finn Adventures rents canoes on the Farmington River. This is a quiet stretch of water, so there's no chance of losing Muttley in the rapids. (860) 693-0385.

BARKHAMSTED

PARKS, BEACHES, AND RECREATION AREAS

• **American Legion State Forest** 🐾 🐾 🐾 See **2** on page 18.
The 782-acre American Legion Forest hugs the west bank of the Farmington River, and most folks come here to enjoy the fast-moving flow. Although we love the water, we come for the Henry R. Buck Trail, part of Connecticut's Blue Trails system, which runs through this forest. Starting at the old bridge site off West River Road, the trail leads through the forest to the appropriately named Tremendous Cliffs. Spectacular wildflowers bloom along the path, and park rangers lead guided walks in the spring to showcase the flowers. Although you and your dog are welcome to join these walks, there's no need to wait for them—just do as we do, and hit the trail.

There are 30 wooded sites in the Austin F. Hawes Campground, right in the middle of the forest and just a short walk from the Farmington River. You are permitted one leashed pet per campsite. Camping is permitted mid-April through Labor Day. There is a $10 fee per night. For camping reservations call 1-877-668-CAMP.

Dogs must be kept on leash in the forest.

From the intersection of State Routes 181 and 318, take West River Road north for 1.5 miles into the park. Open from dawn until dusk. (860) 379-2469.

• Lake McDonough Recreation Area 🐾🐾🐾 See ❸ on page 18.

Lake McDonough is located on 446 acres of woodlands, water, and trails. Although this is usually enough of a reason to come here, this park also offers one of the more unusual trails we've come across: the Braille Trail.

This fully accessible, self-guided nature trail runs along the shores of Lake McDonough. The path, opened in 1994, is designed for people with physical impairments, and comes complete with Braille signage, a guide rope, and a system of ramps and railings to assist you on your way. The quarter-mile trail, located on the west side of Lake McDonough just a few hundred yards from Goose Green Beach, features more than 30 signposted natural landmarks allowing visitors to read about—and touch—many of the trees and rocks that are indigenous to Southern New England. Although it is a fascinating sensory experience to try to walk this trail without using your sight, you probably won't want to; the views over the lake from here are truly gorgeous. The trail is not open during the winter.

The recreation area is part of the greater Hartford park system, the Metropolitan District Commission. The MDC has row boats and paddle boats available for rent at Lake McDonough, which is the only way you'll enjoy the water since dogs are not permitted on the beaches. Dogs must be on leash.

From U.S. Route 44, take State Route 318 east for two miles. Turn right onto Goosegreen Road and make an immediate left into the recreation area. Open daily from 8 A.M. to 8 P.M., from April 1 until October 29. (860) 379-0938.

• Peoples Forest 🐾🐾🐾🐾 🐾 See ❹ on page 18.

This 2,954-acre forest has a myriad of color-coded, interconnected trails that will keep you and Muttley busy for hours and days. With trails running along the Farmington River and through the adjoining woods, there's something for everyone here, including history hounds!

Near the main parking area you'll find the ancient burial ground from the long-gone 1700s settlement known as Barkhamsted Light. The grave markers at the head and foot of the graves are known as manitou stones, coming from the Native-American word for spirit.

The orange-blazed Jessie Gerard Trail leads to the open ledges of Overlook and Chaugham Lookout, offering excellent birds-eye views of the Farmington Valley below. The "299 steps," an infamous stone staircase at the start of the trail, run up alongside a cascading brook. It's a short but difficult climb, worth taking to get to the rest of the trail. The route passes a waterfall and then, after a mile, reaches the Overlook and our favorite views of the hike. Continue on for a half mile to Chaugham Lookout for a great view of the Berkshire Hills. Don't miss it in fall—the foliage viewing is fantastic.

If you continue farther, you'll reach the Veeder boulders, two glacial erratics left here from the last ice age. From here, you can either circle endlessly or head back the way you came.

Helpful trail maps are available at the state forest office and museum. Dogs are permitted on leash.

From State Route 181, take Pleasant Valley Road (State Route 318) east for three-quarters of a mile. Turn left onto East River Road for 2.5 miles into the state forest. Open 8 A.M. to sunset. (860) 379-2469.

RESTAURANTS

The Village Sweet Shoppe: Right in the middle of Riverton, this sweet, sweet shop dishes out homemade ice cream, candy, and drinks. You can sit a spell outside on the white benches and watch the world—or at least Riverton—go by. 3 Riverton Road; (860) 379-7250.

The Yellow Victorian: This place garners kudos from all reviewers, including our picky canine critics. This period 1880s Victorian (yes, it's yellow) serves up some amazing continental cuisine, and you can dine on one of the few porch tables with your dog nearby. This place is only for well-mannered pooches, and reservations are recommended. 6 Riverton Road; (860) 379-7020.

PLACES TO STAY

American Legion State Forest camping: See pages 19–20.

Old Riverton Inn: This quaint, historic inn is in the middle of the even-quainter little town of Riverton. Open since 1796, it is on the National Register of Historic Places. Plan ahead for your best advantage: they permit pets in one room only. The room rate is $125 a night. Open Wednesday through Sunday. State Route 20, Box 6, Riverton, CT 06065; (860) 379-8678, (800) 378-1796.

Rose and Thistle B&B: Little dogs rule! This small two-room inn rests on 10 acres, overlooking a pond for the swimmers in the pack. The inn is intimate and tucked away, just as we wanted it to be. Dogs are accepted with prior approval. Rates range from $95 to $105, including a full breakfast. 24 Woodacres Road, Barkhamstead, CT 06065; (860) 379-4744.

BERLIN

PARKS, BEACHES, AND RECREATION AREAS

• **Ragged Mountain Preserve** 🐾 🐾 🐾 See 5 on page 18.

There is nothing ragged about Ragged Mountain. It's a wonderful spot, with volcano cliffs and excellent fall-foliage viewing. This is also a premier rock-climbing site, but, unless your dog is part mountain goat, you'll probably be happier on the path below.

The main trail extends from the gate for a six-mile loop to the ridge. It's marked with blue and red, and then connects with the blue-blazed Metacomet Trail about two miles in. After the ridge, with its views of Hart Pond and expansive meadows, keep a sharp eye out for your turn back onto the Ragged Mountain Preserve Trail, as the Metacomet Trail continues north.

Dogs on leash only.

From State Route 372, take State Route 71A south for 1.5 miles. Turn right onto West Lane for a half mile to the park gate and parking area. Open dawn to dusk. (860) 346-2372.

PLACES TO STAY

Hawthorne Inn: Rooms come equipped with their own refrigerator here, so you can keep your dog's water icy cold. Rates are from $70 to $85, including an excellent continental breakfast. 2387 Wilbur Cross Parkway, Berlin CT 06037; (860) 828-4181; www.hawthorne-inn.com.

BLOOMFIELD

PARKS, BEACHES, AND RECREATION AREAS

• Penwood State Park 🐾🐾🐾 See 6 on page 18.

Across the road from its better known cousin, Talcott Mountain State Park, this park may not have a four-state view to offer visitors, but it's no slouch when it comes to parks.

You can access the blue-blazed Metacomet Trail from this park, or you can try the white Nature Trail. Rocks and glacial erratics, as well as some side trails and old logging roads, are waiting to be explored. Lake Louise also makes a nice destination, and, although dogs are not permitted at the main swimming beach, there are other access points around the lake for doggie dips.

When you get to the park, don't stop at the front parking lot. Take the winding, narrow road through the woods until you reach the hidden meadows tucked surreptitiously in the trees. Park there for easy access to the trails. It's worth the bumpy ride.

Dogs must be on leash.

From State Route 178, take State Route 185 west for 1.2 miles. The park is on the right. Open 8 A.M. to sunset. (860) 566-2304.

• Wilcox Park 🐾🐾🐾 See 7 on page 18.

This 218-acre park is a wonderful city park. Combining recreation areas with a scenic woodland that rings the park, you'll find plenty to do here. There is a fairly extensive, although short, trail system—most woodland paths branch off from the main access road—so you can steer clear of the summer day camp in July and August. The flies and ticks, however, are a little less easy to avoid, so come prepared.

During the winter you won't have to contend with the bugs or the crowds; the trails are easy to follow in all seasons.

Trail maps are available at the town hall. Dogs must be on leash.

From Blue Hills Avenue (State Route 187), take Tunxis Avenue (State Route 189) south for one-half mile. Turn right onto Adams Road for one mile, then make a right onto Hoskins Road to the end and a small parking lot. Open 8 A.M. to sunset. (860) 243-2923.

BURLINGTON

PARKS, BEACHES, AND RECREATION AREAS

• Sessions Woods Wildlife Management Area 🐾🐾 See 8 on page 18.

This 455-acre wildlife management area appears as advertised—full of wildlife. We found beaver ponds, deer tracks, and a lot of smells for the dogs to explore.

For an unusual, if limited, trail try the Beaver Pond Trail. This quarter-mile boardwalk will take you out over the beaver pond and includes several wildlife demonstration sites along the way.

For a longer extension, you can access the Tree Identification Trail from here, which offers a more traditional woodland walk along East Negro Hill Brook to a fire tower with terrific views. A waterfall and another beaver pond are thrown in for good measure.

The trail forms a loop, so you can take either fork—unless you want to join with the Tunxis Trail, in which case you should take the right fork.

Dogs must be leashed, and hunting is allowed from October through February.

From State Route 4, take State Route 69 south for four miles. The park entrance road is on the right. Open dawn to dusk. (860) 675-8130.

CANTERBURY

RESTAURANTS

The Baker's Dozen: Wake up and smell the coffee! The outdoor picnic tables at this scrumptious bakery invite you to enjoy mornings with your pup. There is also a drive-through window to make acquiring your caffeine fix even easier. 5 Westminster Road; (860) 546-9814.

CHESHIRE

NATURE HIKES AND URBAN WALKS

Cheshire Historical District Walking Tour: Cheshire is a well-preserved New England town where you can walk streets that date back over 200 years. Start the walking tour at the Town Green on Main Street, head south down to the Foote House at Main Street and Cornwall Avenue, and then back up Main Street to the Seth Johnson House at Horton Avenue. Most of the houses you pass were built between 1740 and 1840. A tour brochure is available from the Central Connecticut Tourism Bureau; contact them at (860) 225-3901.

DIVERSIONS

Apple Pie Puppy: At Bishop Farms, a 200-year-old working farm, you can pick your own apples in the fall, and dogs can come along. The dogs' only comment was that apple picking was rewarding but "no walk in the park." 500 South Meriden Road; (203) 272-8243.

COVENTRY

PARKS, BEACHES, AND RECREATION AREAS

• **Nathan Hale State Forest** 🐾 🐾 🐕 See **9** on page 18.

The main attraction in this forest is Nathan Hales's childhood home. Although not his actual birthplace (he was born in 1755 and the house was rebuilt in 1776), it's close enough to boast a museum and a forest named after Connecticut's Revolutionary War hero. Your dog probably won't give two sticks for a visit to the museum (where she isn't allowed anyway) but will probably be interested in the rest of the 1,219 acres here.

Starting at the homestead just off South Street, you can take a 1.5-mile trail that leads through an open meadow and up onto a small ridge above Bear Swamp. The trail is quite lovely and follows a fairly flat, easy route the entire distance, ending at Bear Swamp Road where there are picnic tables for the weary hiker.

Dogs must be leashed.

From U.S. Route 6 near the Andover town line, take South Street east for 4.5 miles into the park. Open 8 A.M. to sunset. (860) 742-6917.

PLACES TO STAY

Mill Brook Farm B&B: This cozy 1850 farmhouse is in the center of historic Coventry, and, with just two guest rooms, you will feel like family. Rates range from $50 to $89. Breakfast is served. 110 Wall Street, Coventry, CT 06238; (860) 742-5761.

CROMWELL

PLACES TO STAY

Comfort Inn: Pets are welcome for no additional fee at this 75-room hotel. Rates range from $89 to $109, including continental breakfast. 111 Berlin Road, Cromwell, CT 06416; (860) 635-4100, (800) 4-CHOICE; www.comfortinn.com.

EAST GRANBY

PARKS, BEACHES, AND RECREATION AREAS

• Peak Mountain 🐾🐾 See 🔟 on page 18.

At 673 feet, this molehill barely qualifies as a mountain. But if you're looking for an easy walk with some good views, this will be one molehill you'll enjoy making into a mountain. The outlook can't really be called a summit, but the sunsets are beautiful up here. For a longer walk, continue along the ridge or double back.

Dogs must be leashed.

From State Route 187, take State Route 20 west for one mile. Turn right onto Newgate Road. The turnout is on the right. Open dawn to dusk. (860) 346-2372.

EAST HARTFORD

PARKS, BEACHES, AND RECREATION AREAS

• Great River Park and Boat Launch 🐾🐾 See 🔟 on page 18.

Boats and dogs seem to go together, and this tiny riverside park is always full of local dogs. One added bonus of taking a walk here—you've got the best view of the Hartford skyline (don't laugh!). Although the park and boat launch are not very big, it's a great place to socialize with other dogs (and their owners) in the midst of the city. A few walking trails and a large outdoor amphitheater are available.

Leashes are required.

From State Route 2, take Exit 3 to Pikin Street west for a quarter mile. The park is at the intersection with East River Drive. Open 8 A.M. to 10 P.M. (860) 722-6524.

PLACES TO STAY

Holiday Inn: Pets can stay with you for a $10 fee. Room rates range from $99 to $129. 363 Roberts Street, East Hartford, CT 06108; (203) 528-9611, (800) 465-4329; www.holiday-inn.com.

EAST WINDSOR

PLACES TO STAY

Best Western Colonial Inn: This 121-room, full-service hotel is a convenient and comfortable place to stay while on the road. Rates range from $50 to $125 including breakfast. An additional deposit of $25 is required for your pet. 161 Bridge Street, East Windsor, CT 06088; (860) 623-9411; www.bestwestern.com.

EASTFORD

PARKS, BEACHES, AND RECREATION AREAS

• **Natchaug State Forest** 🐾🐾🐾 See **12** on page 18.

Natchaug means "and between rivers" and, in this case, that would be the Bigelow and Still Rivers. With over 12,935 acres to explore, this forest will keep you busy for many visits.

For an easy walk, take the Forest Road Loop, accessible from Kingsbury Road, a short distance from the parking area. From here you can connect to a myriad of trails. A map is advisable if you want to make sense of where you're going.

The Natchaug Trail runs north about 6.5 miles starting from the parking area. About a mile into the trail you will pass through the Nathaniel Lyon Memorial Park, commemorating the first Union general to die in the Civil War.

Maps are available at the main entrance. Dogs must be leashed.

From U.S. Route 44, take State Route 198 south for a half mile. Turn left onto General Lyon Road, then immediately right onto Pilfershire Road for 1.8 miles. Turn right onto Kingsbury Road and into the park. Open 8 A.M. to sunset. (860) 974-1562.

ENFIELD

PLACES TO STAY

Motel 6: Small dogs only, please. One pet per room. Rates range from $37 to $49 per night. 11 Hazard Avenue, Enfield, CT 06082; (860) 741-3685, (800) 4-MOTEL6; www.motel6.com.

Red Roof Inn: If you just can't get started in the morning without your caffeine fix, this hotel provides complimentary coffee in the lobby each morning.

Rates range from $35 to $75 per night. 5 Hazard Drive, Enfield, CT 06082; (860) 741-2571, (800) THE-ROOF; www.redroof.com.

Super 8 Motel: Get out the scale, because if your dog is under 30 pounds, he is welcome here. Rates range from $44 to $62 per night, with a $10 pet fee. 1543 King Street, Enfield, CT 06082; (860) 741-3636; www.super8.com.

FARMINGTON

RESTAURANTS

Ann Howard Cookery, Inc: It's a big name for a little place, but what a wonderful little place it is. Essentially a catering company that sells breads and muffins to people who walk in, you can preorder a picnic that will make your dog drool. 767 Brickwalk Lane; (860) 678-9486.

Ice Cream and Yogurt Parlor: This yummy café serves ice cream and frozen yogurt, and you can plop down on the picnic tables on the porch to enjoy it. On our last visit, they were dreaming up a new flavor called Dog Dish, which might be on the menu when you get there. 1048 Farmington Avenue; (203) 677-0118.

PLACES TO STAY

The Centennial Inn: This 112-room, suite-style hotel is situated on 12 acres—enough room for our dogs to stretch their legs inside and out. Rates range from $85 to $250, including a continental breakfast, plus a $10-per-pet fee. 5 Spring Street, Farmington, CT 06032; (860) 677-4647, (800) 852-2052; www.centennialinn.com.

Farmington Inn: This inn offers luxury service, and reserves two of its 74 rooms for pooches. Rates range from $99 to $169 per night. 827 Farmington Avenue, Farmington, CT 06032; (860) 677-2821, (800) 684-9804; www.farmingtoninn.com.

Homewood Suites: These 132 apartment-style rooms are perfect for the long-stay traveler. Each has a kitchenette. Rates range from $125 to $160 a night, plus a $125 room-cleaning fee for pets. 2 Farm Glen Boulevard, Farmington, CT 06032; (860) 321-0000; www.hilton.com.

Marriott Hotel: This is a quintessential suburban Marriott hotel, with one exception. They welcome pets! There are 375 rooms, with a path for morning walks just behind the hotel. Rates range from $100 to $175. 15 Farm Springs Road, Farmington, CT 06032; (860) 678-1000; www.mariott.com.

GRANBY

PARKS, BEACHES, AND RECREATION AREAS

• **Enders State Forest** 😗 😗 See **13** on page 18.

This state forest was once a private farm. Now a wildlife management area, it is best known for the lovely woodland trail that runs along the West Branch Salmon Brook. Along the way are several waterfalls (best seen in the springtime) and natural swimming pools. Access the trail from the parking area and wander as far as your dog will lead you.

The rest of the 453 acres feature unblazed trails in fairly dense woods. Dogs must be leashed.

From State Route 20, take State Route 219 south for 1.5 miles into the park. Roadside pullouts are on both sides of the highway. Open 8 A.M. to sunset. (860) 379-2469.

• McLean Game Refuge 🐾🐾🐾 See **14** on page 18.

Senator George McLean established this 3,400-acre parcel as a wildlife preserve in 1932. Senator McLean wished the refuge to be "a place where some of the things God made may be seen by those who love them as much as I have loved them and who may find in them the peace of mind and body that I have found." His wish has come true. There are miles and miles of trails here that everyone will love.

To give ourselves a destination, we walked the short path to scenic Trout Pond. Pick a trail; they almost all lead to the pond. Your dog will probably want to stay awhile. If you keep going on the trail, you will pass Senator McLean's log cabin, which overlooks the pond.

The Summit Loop Trail is also a good choice. Leading to an overlook of Barndoor Hills, you'll enjoy your walk through a meadow, along Bissell Brook, and up to the scenic vista overlooking a pastoral farmland spread out below. The entire loop is about three miles.

A helpful map of the trail system is posted at the parking area. Dogs must be leashed at all times.

From State Route 20, take U.S. Route 202 south for one mile. The park entrance road is on the right. Open 8 A.M. to 8 P.M. (860) 653-7869.

HAMPTON

PARKS, BEACHES, AND RECREATION AREAS

• James L. Goodwin State Forest 🐾🐾🐾 See **15** on page 18.

This wildlife sanctuary was given to the town of Hampton by James L. Goodwin. Located on over 2,171 acres, the state forest has three man-made ponds plus areas that have been cleared and cultivated to encourage wildlife.

From the Conservation Center at the parking area, you can take a loop trail around Pine Acres Lake. The short trail leads over the dam and to Governor's Island, a small spit of land on the lake for nesting birds.

The Black Spruce Pond Trail, a moderately easy walk, boasts a beaver lodge and tons of wildflowers. A portion of the path is an interpretive trail, highlighting the diversity within the forest.

As with all state forests, leashes are required.

From State Route 198, take U.S. Route 6 east for three miles. Turn left onto Potter Road and into the park. Open 8 A.M. to sunset. (860) 455-9534.

HARTFORD

"There's enough Charter Oak here to build a plank road from Hartford to Salt Lake City."
—Mark Twain

Over the years, Hartford has had a number of well-known residents, including Mark Twain, J.P. Morgan, and Harriet Beecher Stowe. Hartford's most famous resident, however, is not a person but a tree: the Charter Oak. When England revoked Hartford's independence in 1687, the throne demanded the return of the Royal Charter declaring the colony's freedom. Instead of returning it, the charter was hidden for years in an oak tree—the now infamous Charter Oak. A storm brought the tree down in the 19th century, and the salvageable wood was used to make a few objects. But, like the "Washington slept here" signs, today everything in Hartford claims to be made from the Charter Oak.

PARKS, BEACHES, AND RECREATION AREAS

• Bushnell Park 🐾 🐾 See 16 on page 18.

You can grab the brass ring in this park in the center of Hartford. Boasting an antique carousel, this Victorian-era park hearkens back to another time. Dogs are not allowed inside the carousel building, but we admit we like the thing just the same.

David Bushnell, the park's namesake, was a student at Yale and the inventor of the first submarine, which was launched in Old Lyme. What's even more impressive is that he completed this invention in 1775, in time for use during the Revolutionary War.

One of the first public parks in the U.S., this lovely spot is located right across from the State House and is home to several war memorials, expansive manicured lawns, and outdoor Bushnell Pavilion.

No dogs are allowed in the swimming and picnic area.

The park is located downtown between Elm Ford and Jewel Streets. Open dawn to dusk. (860) 722-6514.

• Charter Oak Landing 🐾 🐾 See 17 on page 18.

This narrow stretch of riverfront park has a boat launch and fly-fishing grounds, and, although there aren't a lot of trails, this is a great example of Hartford's commitment to reclaiming the waterfront for use as a recreation area.

Dogs must be on leash.

The park is located at the intersection of State Route 2 and U.S. Route 5 at the Connecticut River and the Charter Oak Bridge. Open dawn to dusk. (860) 713-3131.

• Elizabeth Park 🐾 🐾 🦴 See 18 on page 18.

This 102-acre park, the site of the country's first municipal rose garden, is a mecca for rose and flower lovers. Donated to the city by Charles Pond, a wealthy industrialist, and named for his deceased wife, Elizabeth, the park was designed by Frederick Law Olmsted and features countless gardens, lawns, winding pathways, a pond, and flowers, flowers, everywhere.

On the edge of Hartford and West Hartford, this gorgeous city park isn't for either the clumsy-footed or the frisky pup who needs his leash-free freedom. This is a serene and contemplative place, and we include it here mostly because it is one of Hartford's most beautiful parks and will be enjoyed by nature lovers everywhere. Just be sure you keep your dog on leash! The best rose-viewing time is June and July.

Elizabeth Park is at the corner of Asylum and Prospect Avenues on the Hartford/West Hartford town line. Open dawn to dusk. (860) 722-6514.

NATURE HIKES AND URBAN WALKS

Mark Twain House/Harriet Beecher Stowe House: These neighboring houses are now museums to their respective former owners. And while your dog can't go inside with you, leashed dogs are welcome to stroll the grounds. Mark Twain spared no expense in decorating his house—his decorator was Louis Comfort Tiffany. Be sure to check out the striking brick pattern and fanciful Victorian architecture on the outside. Just past both houses are wooden stairs down to an expansive lawn perfect for a romp. Dogs must be on leash.

The two museums are in downtown Hartford on Farmington Street. Open 8 A.M. to dusk. Contact (860) 493-6411 for the Mark Twain House, and (860) 525-5105 for the Harriet Beecher Stowe House.

Wading at Wadsworth Athenaeum: If you're downtown in Hartford looking for a walk that is as stimulating to you as it is to your pooch, take the Connecticut Freedom Trail and head for the Athenaeum grounds at the corner of Gold and Main Streets. The property has some great outdoor sculptures, including a huge steel work called "Windamajig" that moves with the wind. Dogs are not permitted inside. (860) 278-2670.

RESTAURANTS

Heidi's: Hightail it to Heidi's for breakfast or lunch. The take-out deli opens early, which is just perfect for you crack-of-dawn dog walkers. 221 Main Street; (860) 247-8730.

Hot Tomatoes: Across from Bushnell Park, near the train station, the smell of Italian food will draw you to Hot Tomatoes. There's a rash of innovative Italian dishes served up here, and, in the warm months, it's all served on the patio, too. Your dog can join you there, where he'll drool for a bite of the famous cheese garlic bread. One Union Place; (860) 249-5100.

PLACES TO STAY

The 1895 House: Located in the historic district near the University of Connecticut Law School, this bed-and-breakfast is for the most discriminating canines. There are just two double rooms and a suite, but all are luxurious. Rates range from $60 to $85 per night, including breakfast. 97 Girard Avenue, Hartford, CT 06105; (860) 232-0014.

Capital Hill Ramada Inn: You can't get much more in the thick of it in Hartford than here. This Ramada accepts pets for a $25 fee; room rates range from $80 to $110 per night. 40 Asylum Street, Hartford, CT 06103; (860) 246-6591, (888) 298-2054; www.ramada.com.

Crowne Plaza: Little dogs rule here—there is a size limit for canine guests. Rates range from $90 to $255, plus a $25-per-night-per-pet fee. 50 Morgan Street, Hartford, CT 06120; (860) 549-2400; www.basshotels.com.

Days Inn: Dogs are welcome here. Rates range from $39 to $99 per night. 207 Brainard Road, Hartford, CT 06103; (800) DAYS-INN, (860) 247-3297; www.daysinn.com.

FESTIVALS

Annual Festival of Light: On Constitution Plaza, the city powers over 200,000 lights from the day after Thanksgiving until the first week in January. Santa arrives by helicopter on November 26 to illuminate the lights, angels, and fountains. For more information, call (860) 728-3089.

DIVERSIONS

Tunnel of Love: If you get tired of seeing Hartford from above ground, check it out from below the city. The Park River was buried for two miles to prevent floodwaters from the Connecticut River from backing up into the city. The folks at Huck Finn Adventures will lead you and your well-behaved pooch on an underground canoe trip. This trip goes through darkened tunnels, so all canoeists get lighted head gear, but your dog will have to rely on you to light his way. Trips leave from the Charter Oak Landing. (860) 693-0385.

HARTLAND

PARKS, BEACHES, AND RECREATION AREAS

• **Horace B. Clark Woods** 🐾 🐾 🐕 See **19** on page 18.

These woods were the first of the New England Forestry Foundation forests established in Connecticut. This stretch of wilderness near the Massachusetts border, like most of the land in this area, was once cleared farmland, but it is now covered with pine trees and dense underbrush. Hiking is only available on a few short forest roads that bisect the 432-acre plot. On the bright side, your dog is permitted leash free. The park is surrounded by the Tunxis State Forest, where your hiking and exploring options are almost unlimited.

From State Route 20, take State Route 179 (Granville Road) north for two miles. Turn right onto Fuller Road for a half mile. The park and a small road-side parking area are on the left. Open dawn to dusk. (978) 448-8380.

• **Tunxis State Forest** 🐾 🐾 🐾 See **20** on page 18.

This is arguably the most beautiful and undisturbed woodland in the state. You can access the forest primarily via the Tunxis Trail, part of the Blue Trail system, which runs for miles through dense forests and quiet streams.

This part of the Tunxis Trail is the most remote and least hiked of the Blue Trails. Once used for smuggling contraband across the state border, this forest was referred to as Satan's Kingdom. Today it's used for more upstanding purposes, and, when we crossed the border, we were only smuggling dog treats, which hasn't been a crime for ages.

From Old Route 20 (Walnut Hill Road), begin at the blue-blazed Tunxis Trail into the woods. You'll soon cross a lovely brook, followed by yet another brook. Your dog will enjoy the wide flat walking paths, and you may even wish to picnic along the brook in solitude. You can continue the full two miles to State Route 20 and back or return to the parking area from here.

Another interesting destination here is a matrix of boulder hideaways called the Indian Council Caves. Native Americans considered the caves spiritual places, and they were used by the Council as a place of power and connection between this world and the next. Some of the stony nooks are big enough to explore, and others are home to small furry woodland creatures. The caves, nestled in a soft pine forest, are at the Barkhamstead end of the park and also accessible via the Tunxis Trail.

Dogs must be on leash.

From State Route 179, take State Route 20 west for three miles into the park. There are numerous trailheads and roadside pullouts along the highway. Additional access is on Walnut Hill Road. Open 8 A.M. to sunset. (860) 424-3200.

RESTAURANTS

Mountaintop Country Store: You have precious few choices way up here, so we were pretty excited when we found this place. It's not fancy, but at least we were able to get lunch and an ice-cream novelty from the cooler by the counter. Outdoor picnic tables are available. 180 North Hartland Road; (860) 653-2405.

HEBRON

PARKS, BEACHES, AND RECREATION AREAS

• **Gay City State Park** 🐾🐾🐾 See **21** on page 18.

This park has a regular Hatfield and McCoy history. It was named Gay City after the surprising result of a bitter feud between two prominent founding families of this long-lost town, the Sumners and the Gays; the animosity between the two was so intense that it finally destroyed the town. Ironically, when the last remaining members of the Sumner family donated their land to the state of Connecticut, they stipulated that it be called Gay City, after the other family.

This 1,569-acre park centers around the remains of that 18th-century abandoned mill village, long gone in the pursuit of progress. As you wander the old roads through the woods, stone foundations can be spotted, along with other reminders of the village that once was.

There are a number of colored trails in the park, but they can loosely be characterized as either the "outer loop" to the north or the "Gay City loop" to the south.

Despite the name, it's not so gay for dogs, for they have to stay on leash. There is a fee of $8 for non–state residents and $5 for state residents on weekends and holidays. To avoid the fee, park in a small parking lot just north of the park entrance on State Route 85 and walk in.

From State Route 94, take State Route 85 north for three miles into the park. Open 8 A.M. to sunset. (860) 424-3200.

MANCHESTER

PARKS, BEACHES, AND RECREATION AREAS

• **Case Mountain Open Space** 🐾🐾 See **22** on page 18.

This property, maintained by the Manchester Conservation Commission, is located in the middle of urban sprawl, but you will feel miles away from the rush of the city here. For a two-mile walk on gently curving paths, take the Lookout Trail to a partially cleared area overlooking Hartford.

From the parking area, go past the gate to the white-blazed Carriage Road. Almost immediately you will reach the red trail intersection and a sign reading, "Trail to Lookout." After a mile of several twists and turns, you and your leashed pup will find yourselves kings of the hill and all you survey.

From Interstate 384, take Exit 4 to Highland Street west for a quarter mile. Turn right onto Spring Street for a quarter mile. The park and a parking area are on the left. Open dawn to dusk. (860) 647-3084.

•Wickham Park 🐾🐾🐾 See **23** on page 18.

The lawns in this park are every homeowner's dream—wide, grassy, green expanses, punctuated by stunningly maintained shrubbery. Clarence Wickham left his estate for the enjoyment of the public after his death, and do we ever enjoy it!

This park has all kinds of interesting sights on its 250 acres: ponds, picnic areas, an aviary, a petting zoo, and a Japanese tea garden. The aviary and zoo are off-limits to dogs, but they will enjoy the walking/biking path and fitness trail. A trek to the highest point is advised, where a replica log cabin at the pinnacle of the park offers a panoramic view.

The John Bissell Greenway (see below) can be accessed here.

Keep the pooch on leash here. There is $2 day-use fee.

From Interstate 84, take Exit 60 to U.S. Routes 6/44 west for a quarter mile. The park is on the right. Open 9:30 A.M. to sunset from April through October. (860) 528-0856.

NATURE HIKES AND URBAN WALKS

Charter Oak/John Bissell Greenways: Connecticut has a series of bike trails linked together in a system called the Greenway. The Charter Oak section is six miles long, stretching from Forbes Street in East Hartford to Main Street (State Route 83) in Manchester; at the midway point, it intersects with the John Bissell Greenway, which runs eight miles to the Bissell Bridge in Hartford. A favorite with cyclists, expect to see quite a few of them on the path.

Dogs must be leashed on the path. Trailheads and parking lots are available at Wickham Park and at the intersection of Main Street and Charter Oak Street. Open 6 A.M. to 10 P.M. (860) 527-5200.

PLACES TO STAY

Clarion Suites Inn: This simple suite-style hotel offers several surprising amenities, including fireplaces in each room. Rates range from $89 to $175 per night, with a $10 fee per night per pet. 191 Spencer Street, Manchester, CT 06120; (860) 643-5811; www.clarion.com.

Manchester Village Inn: Pooches are welcome at this 44-room inn in the center of town. Rates range from $52 to $77 per night. There is a $5-per-pet fee. 100 Center Street, Manchester, CT 06120; (860) 646-2300.

DIVERSIONS

Summer Concert Series: A summer series of free outdoor concerts is offered for your enjoyment at the Manchester Bicentennial Band Shell. The Band Shell is on the grounds of Manchester Community College at 60 Bidwell Street. For more information or to request a schedule, call (860) 647-8811.

MANSFIELD

PARKS, BEACHES, AND RECREATION AREAS

• Mansfield Hollow State Park/Mansfield Hollow Lake Project 🐾🐾🐾 See **24** on page 18.

This is a busy, active state park—lots of people out jogging, walking their dogs, and playing with their children. There are the usual picnic and recreational facilities you'd expect in an oft-used park, but the main attraction in this 2,328-acre park is the 500-acre dam project.

Mansfield Hollow Lake offers plenty of recreation options for the sporty dog. Although four-legged friends are not permitted at the main swimming area, with 500 acres of shoreline to explore, you'll still find plenty of access points. Canoe and boat rentals are also available if you want to get out on the water.

Within the state park, dogs must be leashed.

From State Route 89, take State Route 195 south for a half mile, then turn left onto Bassett Bridge Road for a mile into the park. Open 8 A.M. to sunset. (860) 424-3200.

RESTAURANTS

University of Connecticut Dairy Bar: This place has a college degree in Dairy—the homemade ice cream is some of the best we've tasted. On a hot day there's a line, but it's worth the wait. 3636 Horsebarn Road; (860) 429-2534.

DIVERSIONS

Mansfield Drive-In: This is one of the few remaining drive-in theatres east of the Connecticut River, and it offers first-run movies on three screens. Since dogs get in free, you'll never have a reason to leave your dog home alone again. Double features nightly at dusk. $6.50 per person; dogs are free. Call for schedules. 228 Stafford Road; (860) 456-2578.

MERIDEN

PARKS, BEACHES, AND RECREATION AREAS

• Hubbard Park 🐾🐾🐾 See **25** on page 18.

Hubbard Park is an 1800-acre stretch of hiking heaven. The hike to Castle Craig, a replica of an ancient castle, is a fairly easy three-mile trek on the Metacomet Trail. The goal is to make it to the castle high atop a cliff 1,000 feet above sea level, where you will have panoramic views of Meriden below. Double your distance by going on to West Peak, but it's a whole lot tougher.

The striking traprock cliffs here are known as the Hanging Hills of Meriden, a popular state landmark. Less well known is the legend of the black dog that haunts the trails. He has been spotted passing hikers on the trail, leaving no footprints, and hikers farther along the trail report no sighting of any dog. Legend states that the first time you see the black dog you will have good luck. The next time you see him, it is a warning. Your third view of the ghost dog signals an untimely demise. Lucky for us, the only black dog we saw was George, who is most assuredly not a ghost.

Real dogs permitted on leash, although the rules don't cover ghost dogs. Dogs are not permitted in the castle.

You can also drive up to Castle Craig from Mirror Lake, making a visit here a short stroll instead of a hike.

Hunting is allowed in season unless otherwise posted.

From U.S. Route 691, take Exit 4 to West Main Street east for one mile. Turn left onto Hubbard Park Drive into the park. Open sunrise to sunset. (203) 630-4259.

•Guifridda Park 🐾🐾🐾 🐕 See **26** on page 18.

This park is on the small side, but it rates a plus in our book because dogs can run leash free here. So romp and roll as you please, and, if you need a longer walk, Lamentation Mountain and Chauncey Peak, via the Mattasebett Trail, are accessible from here.

The park is at the corner of Bee and Baldwin Streets near the golf course. Open sunrise to a half an hour before sunset. (203) 630-4259.

PLACES TO STAY

East Inn: This 72-room hotel, formerly a Days Inn, offers what you would expect: comfortable rooms in a basic setting. Rates range from $45 to $90 per night, including continental breakfast. 900 East Main Street, Meriden, CT 06450; (203) 238-1211.

Ramada Inn: George loved to fetch the complimentary *USA Today* from our doorstep here. This property has been recently renovated, and the rooms are equally fetching. Rates range from $69 for a regular room to $150 for a suite. 275 Research Parkway, Meriden, CT 06450; (203) 238-2380, (888) 298-2054; www.ramada.com.

FESTIVALS

Festival of Lights: Meriden lights up around Thanksgiving, stringing over 300,000 lights in and around Hubbard Park on West Main Street. It's a lovely time to walk around the park and enjoy the holiday season. The lights stay up until January 15. (203) 630-4259.

MIDDLEFIELD

PARKS, BEACHES, AND RECREATION AREAS

•Wadsworth Falls State Park 🐾🐾🐾 See **27** on page 18.

This 285-acre state park has fairly easy hikes, but the name hints at the special surprise in store for you here: waterfalls. Two sets of them, actually. There are three trails to pick from here: the Little Falls Trail marked in blue, the White Birch Trail marked in white, and the Main Trail in orange.

The Main Trail runs a touch over three miles, and you will pass by both sets of falls. You'll come to Little Falls in under a mile, a very pretty spot where the

Coginchaug River cascades down rocky ledges. Continue on the trail for about half a mile, until you reach a paved road. Follow the paved road to a parking area, and then just follow the sound of the falls to find the next big kahuna—Wadsworth Falls. It is an impressive column of water dropping straight down. All your choices traverse fairly easy, flat paths.

Dogs permitted on leash. Parking fee of $5 for in-state and $8 for out-of-state cars, from Memorial Day through Labor Day. Access is free the rest of the year.

From State Route 66, take State Route 157 south for two miles. The park is on the left. Open 8 A.M. to sunset. (860) 424-3200.

NEW BRITAIN

PARKS, BEACHES, AND RECREATION AREAS

•Walnut Hill Park 🐾 🐾 See **28** on page 18.

This tiny 90-acre jewel sits in the middle of New Britain. It's a park with a pedigree, having been designed by Frederick Law Olmsted, the famous designer of New York's Central Park and Boston's Emerald Necklace of city parks. If this park were a dog, it would win Best of Breed.

There are walking paths, monuments, and a band shell here. A walk to the crest of the park provides some lovely views of the town. Dogs must be on leash in the park.

The park is located between Hart, Main, and Vine Streets. Open dusk to dawn. (860) 826-3360.

•Stanley Park 🐾 🐾 See **29** on page 18.

This 360-acre city park supports a gamut of recreational activities, with most of the park surrounding the town golf course. There is enough green space to appease your dog, and the half-mile, crushed-gravel path around the pond is quite nice.

Dogs need to be leashed.

Stanley Park is located at the intersection of Stanley Street (state Route 71) and Glover Boulevard. Open dawn to dusk. (860) 826-3360.

NEW HARTFORD

RESTAURANTS

Chatterly's Café: The tables on the enclosed sidewalk patio are just perfect for lunch or dinner al fresco. A wide selection of salads is offered, and, for the hungry bunch, the grilled baby lamb chops are perfection. Sit outside for a great meal and view of Main Street. 2 Bridge Street; (860) 379-2428.

DIVERSIONS

Down the lazy river: Bring your dog along when you rent a canoe at Main Stream Canoe Corporation. They even have doggie-sized life jackets. (860) 693-6791.

NEWINGTON

RESTAURANTS

Doogie's: "Home of the 2-Foot Hot Dog" may not be the classiest joint but will probably be the only place your dog is intimidated by another dog—these wieners are bigger than most small pups! Outdoor seating is available. 2525 Berlin Turnpike; (860) 666-1944.

PLAINVILLE

PLACES TO STAY

Ramada Inn: This recently renovated hotel offers the standard amenities you would expect from a reliable chain. Pets are welcome in smoking rooms. Rooms range from $60 to $86, while suites range from $180 to $210 per night. 400 New Britain Avenue, Plainville, CT 06062; (860) 747-6876, (888) 298-1054; www.ramada.com.

POMFRET

PARKS, BEACHES, AND RECREATION AREAS

• **Mashamoquet Brook State Park** 🐾🐾🐾🐾 See **30** on page 18.
This beautifully named park means "stream of good fishing," and although our tongues trip over the Native American pronunciation, there is nothing else we want to change about this park. Its diversity makes it an especially attractive place to spend a day.

The park encompasses 860 acres and features wooded hillsides, several brooks, and at least one really interesting legend. In 1742 Israel Putnam, of Revolutionary War fame, tracked down and shot the last known wolf in the state of Connecticut. Today there is a plaque on the Wolf Den, the cave where this poor wolf met her untimely end.

To reach Wolf Den and Table Rock, a large flat boulder that looks like a table, head for the bridge over the Mashamoquet Brook and follow the blue blazes. The "No Dogs" sign refers to the campground, so don't let this confuse you. Dogs are allowed on the trails.

Along this three-mile round-trip, you'll wander on flat, easy, pine-covered trails past glacial boulders and open hillsides. Our dogs give it a big paws up!

From the parking area take the well-marked trail a half mile to the den. Dogs need to be leashed.

Park entrances are on U.S. Route 44 and Wolf Den Drive (off State Route 101). Open 8 A.M. to sunset. (860) 928-6121.

RESTAURANTS

The Vanilla Bean Café: Paws down, this was one of our dogs' favorite places. The Bean Café, as it is referred to by the regulars, serves lunch and dinner every day, breakfast on weekends. The huge outdoor patio welcomes well-behaved dogs to dine with their masters, and there is even a distant picnic table under a nearby tree for those less social hounds. Lunch options cover a very large chalkboard above the counter, where you place your order and head outside to await its delivery. Dinner includes full wait service, and recent yummy selections have included Black Fish Provençal, salmon poached in white wine with asparagus dressing, and Smoked Mozzarella and Basil Ravoli. The Café often has live music at night, and the newsletter called "Bean Soup" keeps regulars and regular-wannabes informed. 450 Deerfield Road; (860) 928-1562.

PUTNAM

PARKS, BEACHES, AND RECREATION AREAS

• **Putnam River Trail/Robert Miller Park** 🐾🐾🐾 See **31** on page 18.
Starting at Robert Miller Park, the Putnam River Trail, a newly completed rail trail, currently runs three miles along the Quinebaug River to a pedestrian-only bridge. The path crosses the river and returns along the other side to Putnam Center. Dedicated in 1999, there are long-range plans to one day connect this path all the way to Rhode Island's trail system.

The flat, gravel recreational path has been a bona fide hit. Used by walkers, joggers, bikers, and dogs, and lit by old gas lamps in the evening, this is an especially scenic river walk—one that can be enjoyed in all seasons at any time of the day. Dogs must be leashed.

The park and start of the river trail is at the junction of State Route 171 and Kennedy Drive. Open dawn to 10 P.M. (860) 928-1228.

RESTAURANTS

The Bar-B-Q Hut: This hut is nothing fancy, but if you're looking for some good, down-home barbecue, stop in for takeout and a guaranteed paw-licking meal. 1 Mechanics Street (State Route 12); (860) 928-6499.

Corner Café: This eclectic café offers a large menu and is just the spot to enjoy sandwiches, salads, dessert, and ice cream. Inside, the furnishings could compete with the nearby antique stores. Outside, there are a few tables on the sidewalk that provide a place to stop and watch the world go by. 88 Main Street; (860) 928-4885.

Nikki's Dog House: Brightly colored picnic tables outside give you a chance to enjoy a dog with your dog. 35 Main Street; (860) 928-0252.

The Vine Bistro: The outdoor café seating makes this a pleasant stop for lunch or dinner. The menu includes soups, salads, and pastas, all of which are delicious. As you might guess from the name, there is also an extensive wine list, so you can enjoy a glass of vino with Fido. 85 Main Street; (860) 928-1600.

PLACES TO STAY

King's Inn: This 40-room, motel-style lodge has a special surprise for water-loving hounds: there's a pond on the property, and they can dive right in. There are a few suites available with efficiency kitchens. Rates range from $56 to $120; there is no extra fee for Fido. 5 Heritage Road, Putnam, CT 06260; (860) 928-7961.

ROCKY HILL

PARKS, BEACHES, AND RECREATION AREAS

• Elm Ridge Park 🐾 See 32 on page 18.

This 26-acre park doesn't have any walking trails. Mostly, it's ballparks and swimming pools, but Elm Ridge's claim to fame is its many organized outdoor activities for the town of Rocky Hill. As a destination itself, the park doesn't offer a lot for dogs, but there is talk of an expansion that may add some walking trails.

Dogs must be leashed.

From Main Street (State Route 99), take Elm Street (State Route 160) west for a half mile. The park is on the left. Open dawn to 11 P.M. (860) 258-2784.

• Quarry Park 🐾🐾 See 33 on page 18.

This 84-acre park was once, as the name states, a quarry for traprock. In fact, the many boulders here give Rocky Hill its name. There are 45 acres of woods, but the most striking feature is the vertical cliffs and structural remains of the quarry operation. Trails cross through the park, mixing woods with quarry exploration.

Dogs must be leashed.

From Interstate 91, take Exit 24 to State Route 99 south (Silas Deane Highway) for a quarter mile. Turn left onto Marshall Road for two blocks into the park. Open dawn to dusk. (860) 258-2772.

DIVERSIONS

Cookout Concert Series: We go for the free music, but our dogs focus on the cookout portion of the activities. Whether it's dinner or dancing you are interested in, this summer series of concerts offers great bands and an on-site barbecue to provide the perfect picnic dinner. Held every Wednesday night in July and August, from 6 to 8:30 P.M. at Elm Ridge Park. (860) 258-2784.

Dog Day at the Pool: How many times have we seen Inu, standing forlornly, looking longingly at our local pool, just wishing he could be invited in for a dip? The folks who run the outdoor pool in Elm Ridge Park have seen one too many sad pooches, and they decided that after the outdoor pool closes for the season, there's no reason to keep those sad puppy dogs from getting their wish. So, for one August afternoon, dogs can go swimming at the pool. There's a $2 donation to support local animal shelters. For more information, call (860) 258-2784.

Fetch me a Ferry: You can take the short but fun ferry ride from Rocky Hill to Glastonbury. The ferry folk are dog people, and George and Inu didn't have to beg for pats. The ride across costs $2.25 per vehicle and driver; $.75 for each additional human passenger; no charge for Rover, and it's only a 10-minute ride. The ferry runs from May 1 to October 31. For information and a schedule, call (860) 443-3856.

Movies in the Park: Every Friday night in the summer, a strange thing happens. The popcorn consumption spikes up just as the free outdoor movie starts in Elm Ridge Park. All movies start at 9 P.M., and it's strictly family fare. Leashed dogs are welcome. For a schedule, call (860) 258-2784.

SCOTLAND

PARKS, BEACHES, AND RECREATION AREAS

• **James V. Spignesi Jr. Wildlife Management Area** 🐾 🐾 See **34** on page 18.

This park, formerly Pudding Hill Management Area, was renamed for conservation officer James Spignesi, who dedicated his career and life to fostering the enjoyment of nature. He was killed in the line of duty on November 20, 1998, while enforcing Connecticut's fish and game laws, and this park honors his memory.

A trailhead is easily accessible from the parking lot, and heads into the woods before splintering into smaller trails. Some of the paths abut farmland, so keep an eye open for cows, especially if your dog has any herding tendencies, like one Shetland sheepdog we know.

Dogs must be leashed, and hunting is permitted from October through February.

From U.S. Route 6 in Hampton, take State Route 97 south for four miles into Scotland. The parking lot is on the left. Open dawn to dusk. (860) 642-7239.

• **Rock Spring Wildlife Refuge** 🐾 🐾 🐾 See **35** on page 18.

This is 445 acres of pure beauty. Managed by the Nature Conservancy, this was once farmland that has reverted back to wilderness.

From the very tiny parking area, head downhill and pass through a break in the stone wall, where you will find a trail map posted. There are basically two trails: the white trail and the yellow trail. The white trail passes through diverse terrain and will lead you to the banks of the Little River. You can also visit Indian Spring, which is the springhead of the Old Bar One Indian Spring, a former natural water supply for Native Americans.

The yellow trail heads to a lookout with views of the Little River. Both trails are well maintained and easy to follow.

Dogs must be leashed here.

From U.S. Route 6 in Hampton, take State Route 97 south for 3.5 miles into Scotland. The small park sign and pullout are on the left. Open dawn to dusk. (860) 344-0716.

SIMSBURY

PARKS, BEACHES, AND RECREATION AREAS

• **Stratton Brook State Park** 🐾 🐾 See **36** on page 18.

This state park is heavily developed as state parks go, which will curb your dog's hiking enjoyment. The park has replicated a cute covered bridge, making it a perfect photo op, but your best bet for a hike is to access the Farmington Valley Greenway which runs through here.

From State Route 167, take State Route 309 west for 1.5 miles. The park entrance is on the left. Open 8 A.M. to sunset. (860) 424-3200.

• **Talcott Mountain State Park** 🐾 🐾 🐾 🐾 See **37** on page 18.

Heublein Tower at the top of Talcott Mountain is a popular hiking destination, due in no small part to the 360-degree views of four states that await you here. Gilbert Heublein, who called this place home every summer until 1937, built the tower in 1914. The 557 acres and tower were donated to the state so people—and dogs—everywhere could share Gilbert's panoramic views.

Take the blue-blazed Metacomet Trail less that two miles round-trip from the parking area, and you'll be 1,000 feet above sea level when you arrive. You'll walk along several woods roads before you reach the ridge ascent—just stick to the paint and you'll be fine.

For hearty hikers and hounds, the trails here also connect through to the West Hartford Reservoir in West Hartford; expect to hike eight or nine miles to get there and back.

You can also reach the tower via the Tower Trail which is accessible from the Lifestar landing pad at the far end of the parking area. The trail leads to King Philip's Cave, a hideaway for the famous Native American leader, before ascending to the tower. Dogs are permitted on leash.

From State Routes 10 and 202, take State Route 185 east for 1.5 miles. The park is on the right. Open 8 A.M. to sunset. (860) 424-3200.

RESTAURANTS

French Onion Cocktail Lounge and Gourmet To Go: This purebred wins best in show by making outstanding gourmet food and letting you share it with your dog. Muttley can enjoy lunch and dinner with you on the front porch. 570 Hopmeadow Road, no phone.

October Farms: Nothing cools down our hot dogs like ice cream, and the ice cream here is cool, cool, cool. The big green clapboard house serves chocolate chip flurries and frozen yogurt nonstop in the warm weather. The picnic tables next to the shop provide the perfect spot to share a cone with your pooch. 544 Hopmeadow Street; (860) 651-5950.

Simsbury Deli: This place offers what you'd expect from a deli and does a good job satisfying your expectations. Take your food out to the picnic tables on the side for an open-air lunch. 566 Hopmeadow Road; (860) 658-7359.

PLACES TO STAY

Iron Horse Inn: This is a lovely spot for Spot. You can take in the view from your own private balcony or cook up a feast in your own small kitchenette. Pets are welcome with a $15-per-pet fee. Rates range from $79 to $160 per night. 696 Hopmeadow Street, Simsbury, CT 06070; (860) 658-2216; www.iron-horseinnofsimsbury.com.

Simsbury 1820 House: This 34-room inn is listed on the National Historic Register. The main house was constructed in 1820 by Elisha Phelps, a former member of Congress. Dogs are welcome in the antique-filled carriage-house rooms. This hotel is just a hop, skip, and a jump from nearby Talcott Mountain and Penwood State Parks. Rates range from $85 to $125. 731 Hopmeadow Street, Simsbury, CT 06070; (860) 658-7658, (800) 879-1820; www.simsbury1820house.com.

SOMERS

PARKS, BEACHES, AND RECREATION AREAS

• **Shenipsit State Forest** 🐾🐾🐾 See **38** on page 18.

We may not be able to pronounce it, but we love it. This forest stretches over 6,126 acres in the towns of Somers, Ellington, and Stafford, and offers some great hiking opportunities.

For a wonderful walk to the summit of Soapstone Mountain, take the blue-blazed Shenipsit Trail. Although a fairly steep one-mile climb, once you arrive you can see all the way to Mount Monadnock and Mount Greylock on a clear day. The fire tower is marked with graffiti and other debris, marring the otherwise beautiful view, so we advise you keep your eyes on the extended scenery. The 33-mile Shenipsit Trail is part of the Blue Trail network and sporadically runs from East Hampton to Somers.

Within this park are countless other forest trails to explore, all of them lined with maple and hardwood trees, making this forest a scenic splendor in the autumn. The trails are easy to follow but, other than the Blue Trail, not many are marked. Make sure you bring water on a hot day—there aren't any lakes or streams to help you or your pup cool down.

Dogs must be leashed in the state forest.

From State Route 30, take State Route 190 west for three miles. Turn left onto Sodam Road for two miles, then turn right onto Soapstone Road into the forest's parking area. Open from 8 A.M. to sunset. (860) 424-3200.

SOUTH WINDSOR

DIVERSIONS

Pin a pup on me: The Yellow Dog Collection is an art gallery that has gone to the dogs! You'll find jewelry, "wearable" art, and clocks in the shapes of dogs' noses. 395 Buckland Road; (860) 648-2056.

SOUTHINGTON

PLACES TO STAY

Motel 6: You'll find free coffee and HBO here, so you can keep yourself awake while you stay up late watching movies in one of the 126 rooms at this clean, comfortable hotel. No frills, but, at rates of $45 a night, it's a bargain. One dog per room, please. 625 Queen Street, Southington, CT 06489; (860) 621-7351, (800) 4-MOTEL6; www.motel6.com.

DIVERSIONS

Citizen Canine: The Southington Drive-in is one of a handful of drive-in movie theatres left in the United States, so catch a movie here while you still can. This twin-screen drive-in features first-run movies at dusk most summer evenings. Admission is $6.50 per person. Dogs are free! For a schedule, call (860) 628-2205.

Fly me to the Moon: Or at least to West Hartford. Charter a mini-sightseeing plane ride, and your dog can come along. There's even a window that opens for your pooch to feel the wind in her face, although you might not want her to stick her head out as you're going 120 miles per hour. Prices vary depending on plane and time. Interstate Aviation, 62 Johnson Avenue, Southington, CT 06062; (860) 747-5519.

Pup, Pup, and Away: Berkshire Balloons will take you up, up, and away in their beautiful balloon, and your dog can come too. Travel over the scenic Farmington River Valley on an early morning flight. A couple of caveats: your dog will be a paying passenger, so it can get pricey. In addition, the noise from the balloon is very loud, and some dogs may find the whole experience a bit frightening. But if you and your pup are game, then what a game it is!

Balloon pilot extraordinaire Robert Zerpolo recommends a "test run" a morning or two before your actual flight; you bring the dog out to the launch in advance to check out his reaction before you plunk down your cash for a ticket for your pup. Rates rise higher than the balloon at $250 per man or beast. For more information, call (203) 250-8441.

THOMPSON

PARKS, BEACHES, AND RECREATION AREAS

• **West Thompson Lake Recreation Area** 🐾 🐾 See **39** on page 18.
This lake was created in 1965 by the West Thompson Dam on the Quinebaug River. The U.S. Army Corps of Engineers owns and manages the 1,700 acres of land that surrounds the lake. Several trails weave around the lake and dam, including a half-mile interpretive trail next to the dam.

Camping is available at 27 simple but neat campsites, all located on the lake and offering solitude and a chance to see the many birds that flock here during the summer. Sites are $10 per night on a first-come, first-served basis and are available from May to September. Dogs must be leashed.

From Interstate 395, take Exit 98 to State Route 12 south for one mile. Turn right onto West Thompson Road for a half mile, then turn right onto Reardon Road for a half mile. The park is on the left. Open 8 A.M. to dusk. (860) 923-2982.

RESTAURANTS

Coaches Corner at Quaddick Pond: This market and deli will tempt you with an assortment of sandwiches, burgers, and pizza, all of which you can share with your canine compadre at one of the outdoor picnic tables. In the summer months, there is an ice cream take-out window that is sure to please your pooch's palate as well as yours. 1105 Quaddick Town Road, (860) 928-0102.

PLACES TO STAY

West Thompson Lake Recreation Area camping: See above.

UNION

PARKS, BEACHES, AND RECREATION AREAS

• **Bigelow Hollow State Park/Nipmuck State Forest** 🐾 🐾 🐾 🐾 See **40** on page 18.

This park has run amok with wild white flowering bushes, and, try as we might, we could not determine if they were wild azaleas or wild rhododendrons. Either way, the walks and trails that cross this 500-acre park are adorned with these captivating flowering bushes at every turn.

There are a number of water destinations, including Bigelow, Breakneck, and Mashapaug Ponds. The Bigelow Pond Trail leads about 1.5 miles around the edge of the water, and your dog should find plenty of dive-in spots. Just watch out for the many anglers who flock to these clear, fresh ponds.

If you'd like to keep going, pick up the Nipmuck Trail from the parking area, a Blue Trail that runs south for some 30-plus miles and gives you access to neighboring, leash-free Yale Forest.

Dogs must be leashed in the state park and forest. On summer weekends and holidays, the state park has a day-use fee of $5 for state residents and $8 for out-of-staters.

From Interstate 84, take Exit 74 to State Route 171 east for four miles. The parks are on the left. Open 8 A.M. to sunset. (860) 424-3200.

• **Yale Forest** 🐾 🐾 🐾 🐕 See **41** on page 18.

This privately owned forest is used by Yale University for study and field work. It's also used by dogs looking for a leash-free romp.

The Nipmuck Trail, one of Connecticut's Blue Trails, gets its degree by going to school—the trail runs to and through this forest for nine miles, plus an additional three miles of other trails are nearby to explore.

Along your walk you will stumble upon the ruins of a sawmill, cross Bigelow Brook, and wander through stands of white birches. Best of all, Yale doesn't require your dog to be leashed, or have a degree, to hike here. The Yale forestry folks do run forest experiments in what they call the Research Camp, and dogs are not permitted in the posted area.

From Interstate 84, take Exit 74 to State Route 171 east for four miles. The park is on the right. Additional access is in Ashford on Boston Hollow and Eastford Roads. Open sunrise to sunset. (203) 432-5137.

VERNON

RESTAURANTS

Rein's New York Style Deli-Restaurant: No matter where you are headed, everyone agrees that the place to take a break is at Rein's. Not only is this deli one of the few "real" Jewish delis found outside of New York City, but it's also out of this world. The menu is packed with delicacies like cheese blintzes, knishes, corned beef, and egg creams.

You can get it all to go or take advantage of some of the picnic tables on the side. Located right off of Interstate 84 at Exit 65. 435 Hartford Turnpike; (860) 875-1344.

Howard Johnson: You and your small dog are welcome here, but there is an $8-per-pet fee. Rates range from $45 to $65. 451 Hartford Turnpike, Vernon, CT 06066; (860) 875-0781, 800-I GO HOJO; www.hojo.com.

WEST HARTFORD

PARKS, BEACHES, AND RECREATION AREAS

• **Talcott Mountain Reservoir/West Hartford Reservoir** 🐾🐾🐾 See **42** on page 18.

Talcott Mountain Reservoir, commonly known as West Hartford Reservoir, is a nature lover's paradise. It features 3,000 acres of beautiful forestland, more than 30 miles of paved and gravel roads for joggers and bicyclists, and hiking trails for you and Rover—all just a short distance from downtown Hartford.

West Hartford Reservoir provides drinking water to 400,000 Hartford-area residents daily, and, although you can't swim here, there are trails galore.

The eight-mile gravel loop trail encircling the reservoir provides stunning water vistas, with plenty of side trails and woods roads to explore, including a trip through a Revolutionary War campsite. You can even connect to the 51-mile-long Metacomet Trail that passes through the park. This area tends to be very popular for all kinds of outdoor activity, so keep an eye out for anglers and mountain bikers.

There are maps posted throughout the area to help you find your way.

Dogs must be leashed.

From State Route 218, take U.S. Route 44 west for three miles. The park and parking area are on the right. Open from 8 A.M. to 8 P.M., mid-April to late October, and 8 A.M. to 6 P.M. in the off-season. (860) 278-7850.

PLACES TO STAY

Nutmeg Bed-and-Breakfast Reservation Service: This clearinghouse organization matches visitors to bed-and-breakfasts throughout Hartford and surrounding areas. They have an ever-updated list of small B&B's that accept pets. Call with your itinerary and preferred towns, and they'll take it from there. P.O. Box 1117, West Hartford, CT 06127; (800) 727-2792; www.bnb-link.com.

WETHERSFIELD

PARKS, BEACHES, AND RECREATION AREAS

• **Wintergreen Woods** 🐾🐾 See **43** on page 18.

Winter green or summer green, Wintergreen Woods makes a great antidote to urban sprawl. This 120-acre plot adjoins the Wethersfield Nature Center and offers a scenic woodland walk within minutes of the city.

The main trails here are marked in white and blue, with the spur trails blazed in red. There's also a trail that leads along Folly Brook, which is easily navigated from the parking lot.

The Blue Trail is the most commonly traveled trail; it also starts at the parking lot and is paved with wood chips. It's only about a half mile long, so if you want a longer hike, you might want to continue on to the white trail when you come across it.

Keep the pooch on leash here.

From Interstate 91, take Exit 24 to State Route 99 north for two miles. Turn left onto Nott Street for a mile, then make the second right onto Folly Brook Boulevard for one block. Turn right onto Greenfield Street and park at the nature center. Open from 8 A.M. to sunset. (860) 721-2953.

RESTAURANTS

The Spicy Green Bean Deli: When in the middle of Wethersfield's historic district and dying for breakfast or lunch, head here. This place serves up simple but tasty fare, as well as a variety of bakery goods. 285 Main Street; (860) 563-3100.

PLACES TO STAY

Motel 6: They say they'll leave the light on, and they live up to that promise here. Nothing fancy, just clean and convenient. Rates from $45 per night. 1341 Silas Deane Highway, Weathersfield, CT 06109; (860) 563-5900, (800) 4-MOTEL6; www.motel6.com.

Ramada Inn: This chain hotel doesn't offer any surprises, but it is clean and comfortable and welcomes well-behaved pets. Rates range from $55 to $85 per night, with no fee for pets. 1330 Silas Deane Highway, Wethersfield, CT 06109; (888) 298-2054; www.ramada.com.

WILLINGTON

PARKS, BEACHES, AND RECREATION AREAS

• Nye-Holman State Forest 🐾 🐾 See **44** on page 18.

This state forest borders the Cole W. Wilde Trout Management Area, so, yep, there's a river running through it. It's catch and release here, but don't be fooled: anglers take their fishing very seriously, so keep your dog from interfering with the free flow of fish and the fishermen who love them.

A gravel road winds through the woods, and some unmarked trails veer off along the way. As you explore, you may come across the William Chambers Shepard Memorial. He was devoted to promoting the wise use of forests, and helped establish the Natural Resources Council of Connecticut. Also look for picnic tables dotting the road.

Leashes are required.

From Interstate 84, take Exit 69 to State Route 74 east for 1.5 miles. The entrance is on the left. Open dawn until dusk. (860) 424-3200.

RESTAURANTS

Track 9 Diner: The dog-biscuit jar on the counter clued us in to the fact that this diner was dog friendly. The food is standard diner fare but, on a nice day, you can sit on the patio and keep your dog on the sidelines. 12 Tolland Turnpike; (860) 487-1619.

WINDHAM

RESTAURANTS

Paradise Eatery & Market: One outdoor table is available from which to enjoy the delicious ethnic foods here. You can romp all over the globe—from Spain to Greece to Russia and back. You won't even break a sweat, and your taste buds will thank you. 713 Main Street; (860) 423-7682.

WINDSOR

PARKS, BEACHES, AND RECREATION AREAS

• **Northwest Park and Nature Center** 🐾🐾🐾 See **45** on page 18.
This 473-acre park is the jewel of the town of Windsor. The park has over eight miles of trails, showcasing a wide variety of wildlife habitat, from wetlands to ridge walks.

The half-mile Braille Trail is worth a mention here. A rope guide lines the trail to help blind hikers navigate through the bog. If you are up for more of a challenge, check out the 1.5-mile Yellow Trail, which treks through the wetland. And, if you want a really strenuous trail, check out the mile-long Hemlock Trail, which departs from the Bog Trail/Braille Trail.

Dogs must be on leash, and there is a dog tie-up area if you want to visit the nature center.

From Interstate 91, take Exit 38 to State Route 75 north for 1.5 miles. Turn left onto Prospect Hill Road for one mile, then turn right onto Lang Road into the park and the nature center. Trails are open dawn to dusk. (860) 285-1886.

NATURE HIKES AND URBAN WALKS

Windsor Center River Trail: This trail runs along the river on 43 acres of woods and waterways. Although just 1.25 miles long, you'll follow a gentle slope over two bridges that cross the brook and marshland. The main entrance is on Mechanic Street behind Town Hall. Open dawn to dusk. (860) 285-1990.

PLACES TO STAY

Residence Inn by Marriott: This apartment-like hotel has outdoor picnic areas and grassy spots for a morning "walkie." However, the hotel requires a $100 pet fee per stay, which is pretty steep for just a night or two. Breakfast is included. Rates range from $89 to $169. 100 Dunfrey Lane, Windsor, CT 06095; (860) 688-7474 or (800) 331-3131; www.marriott.com.

WINDSOR LOCKS

NATURE HIKES AND URBAN WALKS

Windsor Locks Canal: This towpath between Suffield and Windsor Locks runs along the banks of the Connecticut River. Once part of the locks system that provided power to move barge traffic down the river, today you and your dog can enjoy a four-mile scenic river walk.

The path is closed from November to April so as not to disturb the nesting birds. Leashes are required. Towpath access and parking are on Canal Street off of State Route 159 in Suffield. Open dawn to dusk. (860) 527-5200.

PLACES TO STAY

Baymont Inn: Pets are welcome in some of the rooms in this 110-room hotel. Rates range from $80 to $100 per night. 64 Ella de Grasso Turnpike, Windsor Locks, CT 06096; (860) 623-3336, (800) 301-0200; www.budgetel.com.

Bradley Ramada Inn: Located close to the airport, you won't find any surprises here. The rooms are simple but comfortable, and dogs are welcome on approval. Complimentary breakfast is included. Rates range from $78 to $105 per night. 5 Ella de Grasso Turnpike, Windsor Locks, CT 06096; (860) 623-9494, (800) 2-RAMADA; www.ramada.com.

Homewood Suites Hotel: This all-suite hotel provides mini-apartments when you need a home away from home. Dogs are permitted only if you are staying for a week or longer. Rates range from $99 to $169 per night. 65 Ella T. Grasso Turnpike, Windsor Locks, CT 06096; (860) 627-8463.

Motel 6: This chain of economy motels accepts small pets, one per room. Rates range from $35 to $49. 3 National Drive, Windsor Locks, CT 06096; (860)627-5311, (800) 4-MOTEL6; www.motel6.com.

Sheraton Hotel: If you ever get stuck on a layover at Hartford, this is the closest choice for you and your pet. Rates range from $85 to $325 per night. Bradley International Airport, 1 Bradley Airport Road, Windsor Locks, CT 06096; (860) 627-5311; www.sheraton.com.

WOLCOTT

PLACES TO STAY

Wolcott Motor Inn: This small family-owned inn has 27 rooms, four with Jacuzzis. All they ask is no dogs in the tub. Rates range from $45 to $80. 1273 Wolcott Road, Woolcott, CT 06716; (203) 879-4618.

WOODSTOCK

RESTAURANTS

Fox Hunt Farms Gourmet & Café: This hearty deli has everything you could want, plus a French bakery, to boot. Take out and head out. 292 State Route 198; (860) 928-0714.

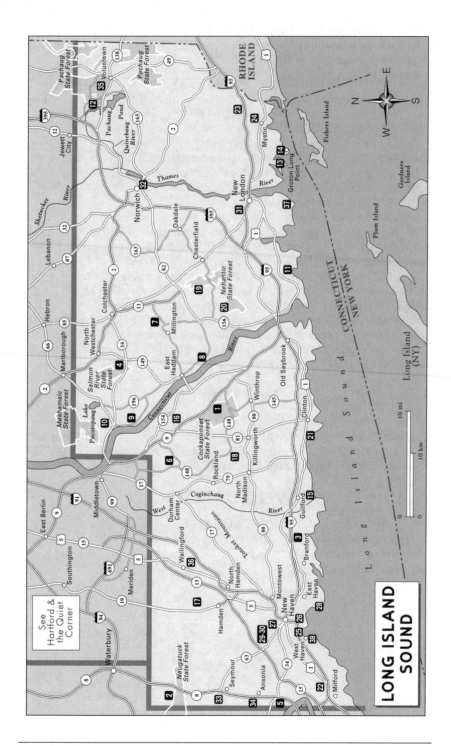

LONG ISLAND SOUND

2
LONG ISLAND SOUND

Much of Connecticut's history, personality, economy, and recreational opportunities are based on its rivers and access to the sea. This is especially true for the cities along Long Island Sound between New Haven and New London. From Mystic's rich whaling history to New London's Navy port to New Haven's critical role in the American Revolution, these towns historically offered a way for Connecticut to prosper and emerge from the shadow of New York and Massachusetts. Today they are economic linchpins and define this 90-mile coastline.

Surprisingly enough, the Constitution State's most important waterway, the Connecticut River, doesn't have a coastal port city because of the sandy terrain and shallow water, leaving Lyme and Saybrook as quaint seaside villages with much of the land still open and undeveloped for you and your pup to enjoy.

•Cockaponset State Forest 🐾 🐾 🐾 🐾 See ❶ on page 48.
Our dogs never get tired of these 15,652 acres of wooded fun. There are countless trails to choose from, and the forest is parceled out through nine towns in both New Haven and Middlesex Counties, including Chester, Durham, Haddam, and Killingworth.

Your first stop should be the ranger station in Haddam for park maps and information. From here, travel to our favorite neck of the woods in Chester on the Cockaponset Trail. Seven miles long, it's one of the park's longest routes, taking you past the Pataconk Reservoir into some of the deepest woods in the state forest.

The Mattabesett Trail, part of the Blue Trail system, also runs through the forest. A popular portion of this trail takes you to Bear Rock, named for the large bear-shaped boulder here. A shorter loop trail in Durham off Harvey Road also leads to this destination.

But don't let us curb you. Pick up a map and let your dog be your guide.

Dogs must be leashed here.

From State Route 154, take Jail Hill Road north for three-quarters of a mile. Turn right onto Beaver Meadow Road for a half mile and then left onto the access road into the parking area and ranger station. Open 8 A.M. to sunset. (860) 345-8521.

BEACON FALLS

PARKS, BEACHES, AND RECREATION AREAS

• Naugatuck State Forest 🐾🐾 See ❷ on page 48.

This untamed, 2,600-acre wilderness begged for the once-over sniff from our dogs. Offering miles of unmarked trails, there are several points of interest here including the High Rock Grove and Spruce Brook Ravine and Falls. Both are easily reachable using the main access road, Cold Spring Road. A road walk doesn't sound very exciting, but traffic is rare and the path is wide.

Another hiking possibility is the Naugatuck Trail. This five-mile path is part of the Blue Trail system. The route is dotted with rocky outcroppings that provide fine views.

Leashes are required.

From the bridge in downtown Beacon Falls, turn right onto Lopus Road and cross the overpass. Turn right onto Cold Spring Road for a half mile to the end of the pavement and roadside park. Open dawn to dusk. (860) 424-3200.

NATURE HIKES AND URBAN WALKS

Beacon Mill Village: Stroll down Main Street to the once thriving, now abandoned mills that are a testament to this town's history. Listed on the National Historic Register, you will find old mill buildings, canals, and walkways that make for interesting exploring. Maps are available at the town offices on Main Street.

Take State Route 8 south to exit 24. Take a right at the end of the exit ramp. Mill Complex is the first building on your left. (203) 729-8254.

BRANFORD

PARKS, BEACHES, AND RECREATION AREAS

• Youngs Pond 🐾🐾🐾 🐕 See ❸ on page 48.

We nicknamed this pond Inu's Pond, because swimming here made him young again. This irresistible swimming hole had so many dogs fetching balls in the water it was practically a golden retriever Olympics. Dogs can also practice their 50-yard dash in the field because in this area only, dogs may be off leash.

Dogs must be leashed on the trails.

The park is on State Route 146 (Blackstone Avenue) at the intersection of Totoket Road. Open dawn to dusk. (203) 488-8394.

RESTAURANTS

Carmela's Trattoria and Pastry: Everything here looked, and smelled, amazing. Even better, it tasted better than amazing. This take-out homestyle Italian cuisine was a big hit with our canine taste testers, too. 576 Main Street; (203) 481-3599.

PLACES TO STAY

B&B By the Sea: The owner, Cindy Brown, is a real dog lover, and her two big black dogs will welcome your pooch to this lovely B&B. It's only a block up from the Long Island Sound, and it's the seaside house you've always dreamed of owning. Rates range from $75 to $110. 1 Maltby Street, Branford, CT 06405; (203) 483-5938, (800) 434-2985; www.sweetbyandby.com.

Days Inn: This standard hotel offers modern rooms in comfortable surroundings. Rates range from $65 to $75. 375 East Main Street, Branford, CT 06405; (203) 488-8314, (800) 255-9296; www.daysinn.com.

Motel 6: Dogs under 30 pounds are welcome here. One dog per room, please. Rates range from $42 to $52. 320 East Main Street, Branford, CT 06405; (203) 483-5828, (800) 4-MOTEL6; www.motel6.com.

CHESTER

PLACES TO STAY

Inn at Chester: This 43-room farmhouse dates back to the founding year of our great American democracy—1776. It's wonderfully maintained and boasts surprisingly modern amenities for a house that has been standing since George Washington was president. Rates range from $100 to $275 and include a continental breakfast. 318 Main Street, Chester, CT 06412; (860) 526-9541, (800) 949-STAY; www.innatchester.com.

DIVERSIONS

Fetch me a Ferry: You can take the short, fun ferry ride from Chester to Hadlyme. An added bonus: this is the oldest still-operating ferry service in the country, having first started ferrying pups in 1655. Rates are $2.25 for car and driver, $.75 per human passenger, with no charge for dogs. The ferry crosses the Connecticut River at the edge of Gillette Castle State Park and runs from April 1 to November 30. For information and a schedule, call (860) 443-3856.

COLCHESTER

PARKS, BEACHES, AND RECREATION AREAS

• **Day Pond State Park/Salmon River State Forest** 🐾 🐾 🐾 See **4** on page 48.

This park dates back to the 18th century when the Day Family built a pond to support their sawmill. Today you'll find several winding trails on 180 acres of beauty.

One unique trail, the Comstock Bridge Connector, leads from Day Pond to the covered Comstock Bridge, one of only three historic bridges still in existence in Connecticut. The bridge is closed to traffic now so you and your dog will enjoy walking over it. The trail, accessible from the South Loop, tracks through the woods and then heads up to a ridge providing views of the Salmon River.

For a longer hike, take the Salmon River Trail into Salmon River State Forest which surrounds the state park. These 6,115 acres take the prize for water-based activities. The Salmon River is one of the finest fishing rivers in the state, and your dog will enjoy taking the plunge at several access points. Several trails also cross the forest leading through stands of hemlock, stone walls, and the remains of several colonial settlements.

Dogs must be on leash in state parks and forests.

From State Route 16, take State Route 149 north for three-quarters of a mile. Turn left onto Day Pond Road into the park. Open 8 A.M. to sunset. (860) 424-3200.

RESTAURANTS

New England Soft Serve: The name says it all—cones, root beer floats, frozen yogurt, everything you need to cool down on a hot day. 56 School Road; (860) 537-5459.

DERBY

PARKS, BEACHES, AND RECREATION AREAS

• Osbornedale State Park 🐾🐾🐾 See 5 on page 48.

This state park has both a park and museum on its 350 acres. Hiking and horse trails are available, as well as grassy rolling hills and bucolic views. This place is the perfect spot to chase a ball or kick up your heels.

Adjacent to the open meadows and rolling hills of the park, the museum is located on the grounds of the former Francis E. Osborne Kellogg Estate. Built as a farmhouse in 1850, it has evolved into the impressive federal structure it is today. You can enjoy the landscaped formal gardens, but not the museum's interior, with your dog.

The Kellogg Environmental Center, adjacent to the park, is an impressive natural science and environmental educational facility operated by the Department of Environmental Protection, Office of Communications, Education, and Publications. The Center uses the state park's meadows, streams, old pastures, and wooded hills as a setting for its programs.

Dogs must be leashed.

From U.S. Route 8, take Exit 15 to State Route 34 west for two miles. Turn right onto Lakeview Terrace for a quarter mile, then right onto Hawthorne Avenue for a half mile. Fork left onto Chatfield Street for a half mile. The park is on the left. Open 8 A.M. to sunset. (203) 735-4311.

RESTAURANTS

Roseland Pizza: The pizza is amazing here, but what else would you expect from a place that has been tossing pizzas since 1935? No boring pepperoni here; look for white pizza topped with a variety of seafood, or chicken and sausage pizza. Takeout is available from the back door lit with the neon sign

"Orders to Go." Then you can head to nearby Osbournedale State Park for an outdoor picnic or sit down in front of the restaurant at one of the benches. 350 Hawthorne Avenue; (860) 735-0994.

Sundaes by the River: This is how our dogs would like to spend every Sundae. Right on the banks of the Housatonic River, where as many people arrive by water as by car. Get your cones to go, head down the stairs, and enjoy the view. 418 Roosevelt Drive; (860) 736-9238.

DURHAM

PARKS, BEACHES, AND RECREATION AREAS

• Millers Pond State Park Reserve 🐾🐾🐾 See 6 on page 48.

This 231-acre undeveloped state park reserve is very pretty, thanks to the mountains of mountain laurel that blossom here. When in bloom, you'll understand how this lovely plant earned its position as the state flower of Connecticut. For a waterside walk, take a hike along Miller's Pond or head to the dam, less than a mile from the pond. The Mattabesett Trail also cuts through here, offering another 35 miles of trail to explore.

Dogs must be leashed on state lands.

From State Route 9 in Haddam, take Candlewood Road west for four miles. Turn right onto Foothills Road for two miles. The park is on the left. Open 8 A.M. to sunset. (860) 424-3200.

EAST HADDAM

PARKS, BEACHES, AND RECREATION AREAS

• Devil's Hopyard State Park 🐾🐾🐾🐾 See 7 on page 48.

This state park encompasses 860 scenic acres and miles of trails to explore. Named for the unusual pothole formations that dot Chapman Fall's splash pool, it is said that they were made by the devil's hooves as he hopped from one rock to another. The heat from the hooves melted the rock, forming these indentations.

Turns out, you can anticipate more than a good story here. The highlight of any visit to this park is the above-mentioned Chapman Falls. Cascading over three tiers totaling a 60-foot drop, you can reach these beautiful falls easily from the main parking area.

From the falls, we recommend taking the orange-blazed Vista Trail on a 2.5-mile loop that leads by an old covered bridge up to a scenic overlook and along the Eight Mile River.

Dogs must be leashed in the state park.

From State Route 82, take Hopyard Road north for three miles into the park. Open 8 A.M. to sunset. (860) 424-3200.

• Gillette Castle State Park 🐾🐾🐾 See 8 on page 48.

They say that every man's home is his castle and, in this case, it used to be true. Gillette Castle is the former home of William Gillette (better known as the actor who once played Sherlock Holmes). Although the house is off-limits to pooches, you can admire it from the outside and enjoy the stunning views of the Connecticut River Valley while hiking the several trails in this 184-acre park.

One of the most enjoyable hikes runs along the former rail bed of the Seven Sister Shortline Miniature Railroad—an actual down-sized train that was William Gillette's favorite toy.

Dogs must be on leash.

From State Route 148, take River Road north for 1.75 miles. The park entrance is on the left. Open 8 A.M. to 7 P.M., Memorial Day through Columbus Day and weekends in December. (860) 526-2336.

RESTAURANTS

Bagels, Etc.: There's a lot of "etc." here, like sandwiches, wraps, and other yummy stuff. And for those early risers, both canine and human, this place opens at 5:30 A.M., so you can get your java fix early. 347 Moodus Road; (860) 873-2234.

EAST HAMPTON

PARKS, BEACHES, AND RECREATION AREAS

• Hurd State Park 🐾🐾🐾 See 🖸 on page 48.

Located on the banks of the Connecticut River, this state park has much to offer visitors looking for a workout. Encompassing 884 acres, there are four main color-coded trails: red, white, blue, and green. For expert hikers, the red trail is the one for you—it has the highest grade. For us mere mortals, the blue trail offers views of the Connecticut River, while the 3.5-mile white loop trail provides access to the river and Split Rock, a ledge that overlooks the river and valley below.

There is a convenient map board at the parking area to assist you in your choices. Dogs must be on leash.

From State Route 149, take State Route 151 north for 5.5 miles. Turn left onto Hurd Park Road for a half mile. The park is on the left. Open 8 A.M. to sunset. (860) 424-3200.

• Meshomasic State Forest 🐾🐾🐾 See 🔟 on page 48.

This 6,691-acre forest stretches across the Bald Hill Range of mountain peaks in the northwest corner of East Haddam. It also has the distinction of being the state's first protected forest. The "high" point, both literally and figuratively, is the Great Hill that offers views of Great Hill Pond and the Connecticut River Valley from its quartz ledges. To get there from the parking area, take the yellow-blazed Shenipsit Trail just under two miles to the top. You'll have to content yourself with a view of the pond because you can't get there from here!

Dogs must be on leash.

From the intersection of State Routes 66 and 151, take Depot Hill Road north for a mile. Turn right onto Gadpouch Road. The parking area is on the right. Open dawn to dusk. (860) 424-3200.

PLACES TO STAY

Nelson's Family Campground: Dogs are welcome here, but you have to keep them on a leash. This campground offers lots of family activities, including bingo and mini-golf. The fee is $27 per night. 71 Mott Hill Road, East Hampton, CT 06424; (860) 267-5300.

EAST LYME

PARKS, BEACHES, AND RECREATION AREAS

• **Rocky Neck State Park** 🐾🐾 See **11** on page 48.

This is a good news, bad news park. The bad news is that although the park is right on the water, dogs are not allowed on the beach. And because everyone else comes here for the lake, the good news is that you and your dog will have the rest of the 708 acres mostly to yourselves.

You have many multicolored trail choices here. The yellow trail leads to the blue trail, and both run along the Four Mile River (which is longer than four miles!). If you want a longer hike, hit the red trail from the parking lot; it exits onto State Route 156 or loops back into the parking lot.

If you head toward the beach, you'll pass a marshy area where you can catch blue crabs.

Keep the dogs on leash. There's a $5 parking fee for Connecticut residents and an $8 fee for out-of-state cars.

From Interstate 95, take Exit 72 to State Route 449 south for a mile. Turn right onto State Route 156 for a quarter mile to the park entrance. Open 8 A.M. to 8 P.M. (860) 739-5471.

PLACES TO STAY

Motel 6: This nice, clean hotel has rates that range from $49 to $66, and it's easy on and easy off Interstate 95. One pet per room. 269 Flanders Road, Niantic, CT 06357; (860) 739-6991, (800) 4-MOTEL6; www.motel6.com.

Starlight Motor Inn: This motel-style inn isn't fancy, but it's clean and comfy. Rates range from $40 to $99. 256 Flanders Road, Niantic, CT 06357; (860) 739-5462.

ESSEX

PLACES TO STAY

The Griswold Inn: This inn, located right in town, dates back to the 1700s. Relax on your four-poster bed or curl up by the fire with your faithful companion. Dogs are allowed in select rooms. Rates range from $95 to $195 per night, including breakfast. 36 Main Street, Essex, CT 06426; (860) 767-1776; www.griswoldinn.com.

GRISWOLD

PARKS, BEACHES, AND RECREATION AREAS

• **Hopeville Pond State Park** 🐾🐾 See **12** on page 48.

This pond, originally a mill pond for a former wool mill, always harbored great potential for recreational use. Today that potential has been realized, even if we can still smell the distant odor of sheep. The Federal Government bought the land in 1930, and the Civilian Conservation Corps soon went to work on the park. Although there aren't many trails for walking, there are roads, a tree farm, and day-use facilities on the 544 acres here.

The Nehantic Trail, one of Connecticut's blue-blazed trails, can be accessed here for a 13-mile hike into nearby Pachuag State Forest.

Dogs must be leashed. On weekends and holidays there is a $8 fee for out-of-state cars and $5 for in-state vehicles.

From State Route 138, take State Route 201 north for 2.5 miles to the park entrance on the left. Open 8 A.M. to sunset. (860) 424-3200.

PLACES TO STAY

Homespun Farm B&B: Fresh flowers and fruit await your arrival at Homespun Farm. This 260-year-old farmhouse has adapted well to its new life as an inn. The rooms are cozy, quaint, and comfortable. Rates range from $65 to $110; a $50 refundable pet deposit is required. 306 Preston Road, Griswold, CT 06351; (860) 376-5178; www.homespunfarm.com.

GROTON
PARKS, BEACHES, AND RECREATION AREAS

• **Bluff Point Coastal Reserve State Park** 🐾🐾🐾🐾 🐾 See **13** on page 48.

While all the city beaches refuse to allow your dog to set paw on their shores, Long Island Sound beckons from this 800-acre coastal reserve. Located right on the water, there are beaches and water access points throughout. There is also a 100-acre tidal marsh, and visitors can hike out onto the sea wall for an even better view of the sound.

The Bluff Point Trail, a 4.5-mile loop trail, starts near the upper parking area and runs along the Poquonok River for much the way, out to Bluff Point, which rests on the sound. From here you'll have fabulous views of the water and marshes; you can even take a spur trail along a sandy peninsula before heading back inland.

This is a protected area so dogs must be on leash.

From State Route 117, take U.S. Route 1 west a quarter mile. Turn left onto Depot Road for a quarter mile. The park is on the right. Open 8 A.M. to sunset. (860) 424-3200.

• **Haley Farm State Park** 🐾🐾🐾 🐾 See **14** on page 48.

This is one scenic spot you won't want to miss. As you enter the park, you'll be greeted by green rolling hills dotted with stone walls and old buildings. Once inside, you and your dog can putter around the ponds, romp through meadows, and sniff the many Indian artifacts in this 198-acre state park.

Other trails will take you to Canopy Rock, an interesting rock formation, and Palmer Cove, where there is water access and swimming opportunities for your pooch.

Dogs must be leashed.

From U.S. Route 1, take State Route 215 east for a half mile. Turn right onto Brook Street for a half mile, and then right onto Haley Farm Road into the park. Open 8 A.M. to sunset. (860) 424-3200.

NATURE HIKES AND URBAN WALKS

Fort Griswold Battlefield/Fort Griswold State Park: On September 6, 1781, the British forces, commanded by our own Benedict Arnold, captured this fort from Colonel William Ledyard and massacred the soldiers of the Continental Army. As one of the best-preserved Revolutonary-era forts, history buffs will appreciate a walk around the grounds. Even if history isn't your thing, the view from the fort to the harbor and the Thames River are more than worth a visit.

Dogs have to be on leash. The battlefield is at the intersection of Park and Smith Streets. Park along Park Street. Open 8 A.M. to sunset. (860) 445-1729.

PLACES TO STAY

Benham Motel: This is standard motel-style lodging, with rates from $39 to $85. 107 Benham Road, Groton, CT 06340; (860) 449-5700.

Clarion Inn: Dogs are welcome at this 69-room hotel. You will need to have a credit card on file, just in case Fido decides to have the curtains for dinner. Rates range from $90 to $175. 156 Kings Highway, Groton, CT 06340; (860) 446-0660, (800) 443-0611; www.clarioninn.com.

Morgan Inn and Suites: Of the 56 rooms, three are pet friendly, so book early. In the summer, rates range from $99 to $125; $69 to $89 in the winter. There is a $10 pet fee. 135 Gold Star Highway, Groton, CT 06340; (860) 448-3000, (800) 280-0054.

Thames Inn and Marina: This inn on the water offers rooms with kitchenettes. Well-behaved pooches are welcome with permission. Rates range from $99 to $149 with a pet fee of $25. 193 Thames Street, Groton, CT 06340; (860) 445-8111; www.visitmystic.com/thamesinn.

GUILFORD

PARKS, BEACHES, AND RECREATION AREAS

• **West Woods** 🐾🐾🐾 See **15** on page 48.

West Woods is 1,000 acres of cooperation in action. The State of Connecticut owns a piece, the Guilford Land Trust owns a part, and the rest is under private ownership. However, everyone has worked together to insure that all of the land and the 40 miles of trails are open to hikers.

A sophisticated system of trail markings helps you identify where you are and where you want to be. Circle markers identify north-south trails, and rectangles mark east-west trails.

From the parking area, we suggest taking the white, green, and blue trails (in that order) on a three-mile loop through a hemlock forest, swampland, and several ridges that provide an overlook of the entire area. You'll even traverse a boardwalk over the marsh on your return to the parking area.

Keep dogs on leash here.

From State Route 77, take State Route 146 west for 1.4 miles. The parking area and trailheads are at the intersection with Sam Hill Road. Open dawn to dusk. (203) 453-9677.

PLACES TO STAY

B&B at B: There are three rooms at this cozy B&B, so you will feel like family. Rates range from $79 to $125, including a full breakfast. 279 Boston Street, Guilford, CT 06437; (203) 453-6490.

HADDAM

PARKS, BEACHES, AND RECREATION AREAS

• **Haddam Meadows State Park** 🐾🐾🐾 See **16** on page 48.
This park is basically a large meadow—175 acres, to be exact—on the Connecticut River flood plain, and it was in full bloom when we last visited. The display of brilliantly colored wildflowers are a springtime must-see.

The best way to experience the meadow without disrupting the ecosystem is on the access road, which loops around the entire area. We met lots of local dogs on our visit; apparently the park gets the sniff of approval from the local pooches. There is plenty of room to romp and socialize, and you can access the Connecticut River for a cooling dip.

Dogs on leash only.

From State route 81, take State Route 154 south for three miles. The park is on the left. Open 8 A.M. to dusk. (860) 454-3200.

RESTAURANTS

Everyday Gourmet: Cakes, ice cream, and specialty foods abound. There are outdoor tables looking out over the back of an industrial park near the bridge between Haddam and East Haddam. Gourmet food with roadside views. 95 Bridge Street; (860) 345-9234.

HAMDEN

PARKS, BEACHES, AND RECREATION AREAS

• **Sleeping Giant State Park** 🐾🐾🐾🐾 See **17** on page 48.
While you might be tempted to let sleeping dogs lie, you definitely want to wake up them up for a trip to Sleeping Giant State Park. This 1,439-acre park gets its name from the shape of the park's foothills, which, from a distance, resemble a large sleeping man. Sleepwalking or not, you'll find over 30 miles of hiking trails that showcase the best of Connecticut's forests.

The Quinnipac Trail, which leads from the parking lot to a stone fire tower, is a three-mile loop trail on a fairly easy incline. Along the way you'll pass an old quarry, climb the "giant's" head, and enjoy views of New Haven and the Long Island Sound. During our last visit, we ran into Bella, a Pomeranian, with her owner, Deana. They love this park so much they come regularly all the way from Rhode Island.

All the trails are well marked, and there are enough of them that you might not see any other hikers. An intermittent stream runs through the interior of the park, depending on the amount of rainfall.

Dogs must be on leash. There is an $8 parking fee for non-Connecticut residents and $5 for residents.

From State Route 10, take Mount Carmel Avenue east for a quarter mile. The park is on the left. Open 8 A.M. to sunset. (860) 424-3200.

RESTAURANTS

Wentworth Ice Cream: Wow! An ice-cream place that caters to canines. You can select from dozens of flavors, and your dog has a flavor all her own: Canine Crunch, a low-dairy, doggie-treat ice cream designed especially for canine customers. Sit outside on the porch or in the gazebo in the side garden to enjoy your treat. 3697 Whitney Avenue; (203) 281-7429.

KILLINGWORTH

PARKS, BEACHES, AND RECREATION AREAS

• Chatfield Hollow State Park 🐾🐾🐾 See 18 on page 48.

Scheeder Pond, built in the 1930s by the Civilian Conservation Corps, dominates the 355 acres of this state park. Although it is off-limits to doggie paddlers, you can head out on one of the eight trails within the park, ranging from a short stroll to two miles in length.

Expect to find heavily wooded areas, where natural caves and rocky ledges once provided shelter for Native Americans. A popular route is the white trail up to the Lookout, a rocky clearing.

You can also access the Chatfield Hollow Trail from here. Part of the Blue Trail system, this scenic four-mile hike leads to the "Fat Man Squeeze," a large crack in a rocky cliff with panoramic vistas.

Dogs must be on a leash. There is a parking fee of $8 for out-of-staters and $5 for in-state cars.

From State Route 81, take State Route 80 west one mile. The park entrance is on the right. Open 8 A.M. to sunset. (860) 424-3200.

LEDYARD

PLACES TO STAY

Abbey's Lantern Hill Inn: You will find country-quaint comfort at this eight-room inn. Rates range from $89 to $149. 780 Lantern Hill Road, Ledyard, CT 06339; (860) 572 -0483; www.abbeyslanternhill.com.

Applewood Farms Inn: This 1820s-era inn, set on 33 acres, boasts a putting green, if you feel the need to brush up on your game. Stay in any of the five rooms, all decorated Martha Stewart style. Rates range from $75 to $185, including a full breakfast. 528 Colonel Ledyard Highway, Ledyard, CT 06339; (203) 536-2022; www.visitmystic.com/applewoodfarms.

Mares Inn: Of the five guest rooms, pets are permitted only in the suite, so you will stay in style here. Suite rates start at $125. 333 Colonel Ledyard Highway, Ledyard, CT 06339; (860) 572-7556.

LYME

PARKS, BEACHES, AND RECREATION AREAS

• **Hartman Park** 🐾🐾🐾 See **19** on page 48.

This lovely woodland park was donated to the city by the Hartman family and offers over 10 miles of trails for you and your pup to enjoy.

Take the orange-blazed Heritage Trail from the parking area for a hike that traverses beautiful woods, historic farm remains, fields of flowers, wetlands, and a scenic ridge. This four-mile loop takes you by several stone foundations from a 17th-century farm and up to Three Chimneys Ridge. The three points here are rumored to be the remains of one of a series of forts built in 1634 by the Puritan colony of Saybrook. Built to protect the colony in case the tensions in England worsened, the forts were returned to farmland once Oliver Cromwell quelled the unrest across the sea.

Maps are available at the town hall. Dogs must be leashed.

From State Route 82 in East Haddam, take State Route 156 south into Lyme for two miles. Turn left onto Beaver Brook Road for 2.5 miles, then left onto Gungy Road for a mile. The park is on the right. Open dawn to dusk. (860) 434-7733.

• **Nehantic State Forest** 🐾🐾🐾🐾 See **20** on page 48.

Burn, baby, burn. The Connecticut Department of Forestry has borrowed a page from the Native Americans' playbook here by setting fires every few years to clean out the woody undergrowth in the forest. By burning away the thick undergrowth, the first Americans encouraged more delicate grasses and ferns to grow freely, attracting game such as deer and turkey and making the forest easier to navigate. Now restored to its precolonial appearance—the way it looked when the Europeans first landed here—you and your pup will find the forest eerily sparse and open, which makes it very interesting to explore.

In the eastern section, you'll see stone walls, meadows, trees, and a yellow-blazed trail leading to Chapman Ridge, known locally as a tough climb.

The western section is named for an Indian tribe that once hunted here; the name probably means "point of land on a tidal river." We like to think it means "lovely woods with great walks for dogs." The Nayantaquit Trail loops through the forest and is just under three miles long.

Leashes are required.

From State Route 156, take Beaver Brook Road east for three miles. Turn right onto Keeny Road for two miles into the park. Open 8 A.M. to sunset. (860) 873-8566.

MADISON

PARKS, BEACHES, AND RECREATION AREAS

• **Hammonasset Beach State Park** 🐾🐾 See **21** on page 48.

This park consists of 919 acres of salt marshes, fields, and a beach that stretches out for a good two miles along the Long Island Sound. Sadly, the park does not allow dogs on the beach or in the campground. But don't turn around just yet. The park has several pleasant trails and nature walks through its diverse habitats.

In the west end of the park is the Willard's Island Nature Trail with a boardwalk and viewing platform. The park also has a bike path adjacent to the beach and numerous fields where you can play catch with your dog.

Dogs must be leashed in state parks. There is an $8 parking fee for nonresidents and $5 for residents.

From Interstate 95, take Exit 62 to Hammonasset Connector south for a mile into the park. Open 8 A.M. to sunset. (203) 245-2785.

PLACES TO STAY

Madison Beach Hotel: This 35-room hotel is right on the beach, and the rocking chairs on the porch make it the perfect spot to relax. The hotel's history stretches almost as far as the view: it was a boarding house for whalers in the 1800s. Rates range from $85 to $225. Dogs are an additional $20 per night. 94 West Wharf Drive, Madison, CT 06443; (203) 245-1404; www.madisonbeachhotel.com.

MILFORD

PARKS, BEACHES, AND RECREATION AREAS

• **Eisenhower Dog Park** 🐾🐾 🐕 See **22** on page 48.

This large park hides a secret known to local dogs—there is a fenced-in area within the park where dogs can play off leash. They must be on leash everywhere else, and park regulars make sure to point that out to visitors. The park is on North Street (State Route 121). Open dawn to dusk. (203) 783-3201.

MYSTIC

PARKS, BEACHES, AND RECREATION AREAS

• **Denison Pequotsepos Nature Center** 🐾🐾🐾 See **23** on page 48.

This 125-acre nature center includes a wildlife sanctuary and seven miles of trails through woodlands, meadows, and wetlands. The trails are color coded, but color-blind canines don't rely on color, they follow their noses.

For those less nosey, the red trail leads you from the parking area past two ponds. To take a loop through the entire preserve, we suggest connecting to the yellow trail where the red trail ends. This will lead you through a marsh, along the Pequotsepos Brook, and to a wide-open meadow before returning you to the parking area. Maps are available at the nature center or at brochure kiosks along the trails.

Make sure to check out the birds of prey in their cages; there are five injured owls under the care of the nature center. These birds did not seem the least bit fazed by our dogs peering in at them. Probably thought they were really big mice.

Dogs must be on leash. Admission is $4; members of the center get in free. From Interstate 95, take Exit 90 to State Route 27 north for a quarter mile.

Turn right onto Jerry Brown Road for a mile, and then right onto Pequotsepos Road for a half mile. The Nature Center is on the left. Grounds are open Monday through Saturday, 9 A.M. to sunset, and Sunday, 10 A.M. to sunset. (860) 536-1216.

• **Mystic River Park** 🐾 **See 24 on page 48.**
Near downtown, this small park hugs the edge of the Mystic River. It is not really a destination on its own, but it makes a lovely break for a stroll of downtown Mystic. This park has benches where you can rest your paws and watch the river. One welcome accessory is a poop bag dispenser for easy cleanups.
    Dogs must be on leash.
    The park is downtown on West Main Street. Street parking is available. Open dawn to dusk. (860) 441-6777.

NATURE HIKES AND URBAN WALKS

Aye, Aye Captain: Mystic Seaport is one of Connecticut's best-known destinations. Wander through this re-created 19th century maritime community dedicated to shipbuilding and whaling. Dogs are not permitted in any of the buildings, but there are plenty of boats to explore and wharves to sniff. (888) 9-SEAPORT.

RESTAURANTS

Christine's Heart and Soul Café: This place has variety, as well as heart and soul. Where else can you get a smoothie and Coquille St. Jacques at the same place? You'll have to take out here, as there is no outdoor seating, but you can walk down to Mystic River Park for a picnic. 4 Pearl Street; (860) 536-1244.

Mystic Drawbridge Ice Cream Shop: This place claims to make the best ice cream, and we were willing to put them to the test. While we each might differ on the definition of "best," we can tell you this is pretty darn good. There are freshly baked cookies and brownies, coffee, and all sorts of usual and not-so-usual flavors of ice cream. 2 West Main Street; (860) 572-7978.

Mystic Pizza: Yes, this is the *Mystic Pizza* of the movie fame. You remember, the movie that made Julia Roberts a star? The screenplay was penned after the author visited this spot for lunch, so there's no telling what could happen to you after you have lunch here. They say the pizza is a "slice of heaven"—you decide. 56 West Main Street; (860) 536-3737.

Somewhere in Time: This bookstore, eatery, and coffeehouse is a good choice for take-out fare. Try the specialty sandwiches, with names like the John Wayne and the Judy Garland. We really knew these guys had their hearts in the right place when we saw the "Free Puppies" sign at the counter. 3175 Goldstar Highway; (203) 536-1985.

PLACES TO STAY

Amerisuites: This comfortable chain hotel is within walking distance of the Aquarium and Mystic Seaport. The rooms are all mini-suites, with kitchenettes and separate sleeping and living areas. Rates range from $69 to $199 per night. 224 Greenmanville Avenue, Mystic, CT 06355; (860) 536-9997, (800) 833-1516; www.amerisuites.com.

The Harbour Inne and Cottage: Located on the water in historic downtown Mystic, this seven-room inn offers a beautiful view of the river. Some rooms have fireplaces, and one has a Jacuzzi. Rates range from $49 to $250, including breakfast. There is a $10 fee for Fido. 15 Edgemont Street, Mystic, CT 06355; (860) 572-9253; www.harbourinn-cottage.com.

The Howard Johnson Inn: You'll be in the thick of things at the seaport here. Rates range from $49 to $139 per night. 179 Greenmanville Avenue, Mystic, CT 06355; (860) 536-2654, (800) 544-2465; www.hojo.com.

The Inn at Mystic: This inn is located on 13 acres of wooded hillside, with some stunning landscaped gardens. The decor is a mix of antique elegance in the main house, with more moderate accommodations in the outer buildings. Rates from $75 to $275, depending on season and type of room. P.O. Box 216, Mystic, CT 06355; (860) 536-9604.

FESTIVALS

Mystic May Day Festival: Held the first Saturday in May, this outdoor festival runs the length of Main Street in Mystic. There's music and food, and a not-to-be-missed Maypole dance. The Annual Bed Race features participants racing their beds down Cottrell Street. For more information, call the Mystic Chamber of Commerce at (860) 572-9578.

Unbearable Lightness of Mystic: Every December, Old Mistick village lights up—literally. Some 4,000 lights adorn the walks and streets of Old Mistick, in honor of the Christmas holiday. On top of that, you'll find carolers, live music, and holiday-themed events. The action starts at dusk during the last two weeks of December. (860) 434-5542.

DIVERSIONS

Easter Bonnets and Bones: Every Easter season, Old Mistick Village hosts an Easter Parade for pooches on the Green. Dogs of all shapes and sizes don their Easter bonnets and strut their stuff. There's even a canine twist on the traditional Easter Egg hunt, with dog treats instead of colored eggs. Believe us, this one's a howl! Proceeds go to great animal causes, and it's a lot of fun to see the dogs all decked out. (860) 536-2280.

NAUGATUCK

NATURE WALKS AND URBAN HIKES

Naugatuck Green: Take a walk through historic Naugatuck and view the many architectural wonders here. Start on the Green at the Civil War Monument, erected here in 1885, and view the McKim, Mead, and White fountain, which was built in 1894. (These architects are better known for some of their other designs, including the Metropolitan Opera House, Columbia University, and Old Penn Station in New York City.) Continue to Meadow Street north to Hillside Avenue, and make a left. This stretch of road has original cobblestones, so watch your paws. Continue up the hill to Fairview Avenue, where there is a delightful vista and some outstanding Victorian mansions. From here you can loop back to the Green again to complete your walk. (203) 777-8550.

NEW HAVEN

Too many people never get past their first impression of New Haven, which is one of factories and dockside warehouses. For those that go beyond it, they find this coastal town on the Quinnipiac River is a city of many parks, the home of elite Yale University, and a historic downtown of ivy-covered brick homes and churches.

PARKS, BEACHES, AND RECREATION AREAS

• East Rock Park 🐾 🐾 See **25** on page 48.

East Rock Summit, on the New Haven–Hamden town line, towers over the surrounding city neighborhood and beckons even the most urban city dwellers to its trails. A steep main trail to the summit rewards hikers with views of Long Island Sound.

If a climb is not in the cards, there are 10 miles of trails to choose from, as well as a self-guided nature walk.

The park also contains the Pardee Rose Gardens. A walk through the gardens is filled with the fragrance of flowers, and you won't need a dog's keen nose to smell them. Fifty varieties of roses are found here, with peak blooming time in June and July.

Dogs are permitted on leash and need to remain on the paths in the gardens.

From Interstate 91, take Exit 6 to State Street north; drive a half mile to the park entrance. Trail maps are available at the ranger station, on the corner of Orange and Cold Spring Streets. Open 8 A.M. to sunset from April to November. (860) 946-6086.

• East Shore Park/Nathan Hale Park 🐾 🐾 🐾 See **26** on page 48.

These two neighboring parks, on the eastern end of New Haven Harbor, offer amazing views of the city and the active waterfront. East Shore Park alone is 82 acres of waterfront property with plenty of hiking trails. Nathan Hale Park offers restored Revolutionary War displays.

Even if your dog isn't a history hound, she will still enjoy a walk here, especially around Black Rock and Nathan Hale Forts. The forts were used to defend the harbor during the fight for independence. Once you're finished sniffing around the cannons, you can wander over to surrounding East Shore Park, where the dogs have a little bit more play room.

The parks have an active ranger and naturalist staff offering guided walks. Dogs need to be leashed.

From Interstate 95, take Exit 50 to Woodward Avenue south for a half mile. The park is on the right. Open daily Memorial Day to Labor Day, from 8 A.M. to sunset. Nathan Hale Park, (203) 946-8790; East Shore Park, (203) 946-6086.

• Edgewood Park Dog Run 🐾 🐾 🐾 🐕 See **27** on page 48.

This 123-acre park offers an interpretive nature trail but not much else in the way of hiking options. Most dogs come for the off-leash dog run and some romping and rolling with their pals. Although not a large space, on any given day there are plenty of hometown canines here to show you the ropes.

Dogs need to be leashed outside the run.

From U.S. Route 1, take State Route 10 north for a half mile. The park is on the left. Open dawn to dusk. (203) 946-8028.

•Lighthouse Point Park 🐾 🐾 See **28** on page 48.
This park and bird sanctuary on the East Haven peninsula offers amazing views of Long Island Sound and New Haven Harbor. This park allows your dog water access and a quiet stroll along a nature trail. An antique carousel may be fun to look at, but unfortunately it's off-limits to dogs. Dogs need to be leashed.

From U.S. Route 1, take Townsend Street south for 2.5 miles. Turn right onto Lighthouse Road into the park. Open Memorial Day to Labor Day, 6 A.M. to sunset. (203) 946-8005.

•West Rock Nature Center 🐾 🐾 🐾 See **29** on page 48.
In most nature centers, the rarest of all species is the *Canine familiaritis*—more commonly known as the dog. Not so here at West Rock. You can enjoy the facilities and check out the scenic setting with your leashed dog.

Take the path to the lovely Wintergreen Falls Overlook. The trails take you past ponds, glacial boulders, and a variety of other native flora and fauna. In the winter, there are areas set aside for sledding and, as long as your dog is on leash, he is welcome to join you.

From State Route 15 (Merritt Parkway), take Exit 59 to Whalley Avenue south for a mile. Turn left onto Fitch Street for a mile, then left onto Wintergreen Avenue for 1.25 miles. The center is on the right. Open from 10 A.M. to sunset year-round except Sundays and holidays. (203) 946-8016.

•West Rock Ridge State Park 🐾 🐾 🐾 See **30** on page 48.
A favorite trail here is the Regicides Trail, known almost as much for its history as for its stunning cliff walks. This trail is named for the two judges, or regicides, who signed the death warrant of King Charles I of England in 1649. After the ascension of King Charles II in 1660, they were forced to flee for their lives. They came to the American colonies and were hidden by friends in the "Judges Cave" here on West Rock.

The six-mile trail follows the crest of the West Rock ridge and can be difficult in sections. If you find the footing too tough for you or your pooch, try paved Baldwin Drive, which follows the same route and crosses the Regicides Trail several times. The drive is only open in the summer.

Dogs must be on leash.

From State Route 15 (Merritt Parkway), take Exit 59 to Whalley Avenue south for a mile. Turn left onto Fitch Street for a mile, then left onto Wintergreen Avenue for 1.25 miles. The park is on the left. Open dawn to dusk. (860) 424-3200.

NATURE HIKES AND URBAN WALKS
New Haven Green: This green in the heart of New Haven is located on one of nine squares laid out in the city's original 1628 plan. As you walk around, you'll pass three historic churches, all built between 1812 and 1815, plus excellent examples of Gothic, Federalist, and Georgian architecture styles. The *Amistad* Memorial is here, commemorating the slave ship whose involuntary

passengers won their freedom after taking control of their ship. Dogs are permitted in the park on leash. Located on Church Street. (203) 777-8550.

Yale Campus Walking Tour/New Haven First Tour: Yale University educates all comers. Students lead the one-hour free walking tour on the Yale Campus. If you miss the scheduled walk times, you can take the audio-guided walking tour for a $2 fee; pick up the cassettes at the Yale Information Center, 149 Elm Street. (203) 432-2300.

RESTAURANTS

Louis' Lunch: This diner is reported to be the site of the first hamburger, and they are still using the same grill as they did back then. The hamburgers are made fresh, cooked to perfection, and then served on toast, just like the original. The building is equally historic; it's on the National Register of Historic Places. 263 Crown Street; (203) 562-5507.

Pepe's Pizzeria: This claims to be the first pizza made in America. We don't know if it's the first or the last, but it is a New Haven institution. People line up here, and the choices are dizzying. Open for lunch and dinner, you will have to take it to go in order to share with your hound. 157 Wooster Street; (203) 865-5762.

PLACES TO STAY

Motel 6: Leave the light on for us here. Rates run from $49 to $69. 270 Foxon Boulevard, New Haven, CT 06513; (203) 469-0343, (800) 4-MOTEL6; www. motel6.com.

Residence Inn by Marriott: This apartment-style hotel accepts pets, with a $10 fee. Rates range from $150 to $210. 3 Long Wharf Drive, New Haven, CT 06511; (800) 331-3131; www.marriott.com.

FESTIVALS

International Festival of Arts and Ideas: Trust Yale University to come up with this great idea. In late June or early July there is a schedule of events celebrating the humanities, including concerts on the Green, and performance and visual arts in the streets. Dogs are welcome at all outdoor events. (203) 498-1212.

Lights on a Lighthouse Point: Visit Lighthouse Point Park for the Annual Fantasy of Lights. In the evenings from mid-November through New Year's you can drive through an amazing exhibit of lights. Some displays are 30-feet tall, and many are animated. All proceeds benefit worthy charities. For information, call (860) 777-2000, extension 603.

NEW LONDON

PARKS, BEACHES, AND RECREATION AREAS

• **Connecticut College Arboretum** 🐾🐾🐾🐾 🐕 See **31** on page 48. Send us back to school if it means getting to hang out in this arboretum. Established in 1931, this is a lovely stretch of well-manicured grounds surrounding the Connecticut College campus. Best of all, Leashes 101 is not a required course here. Dogs are allowed off leash, but neither they—nor you—are allowed to trample on any of the well-maintained shrubbery here, so you may want to leash up in some of the more delicate areas.

The grounds are divided into a western portion and an eastern portion, on respective sides of campus. The western portion is larger, more interesting to explore, and contains the Bolleswood Natural Area, as well as wetlands and ponds. The main trail, which starts at the entrance, will take you on a loop past formal plantings, forested wetlands, the marsh pond, a stand of white pine, and the outdoor theatre. At the preserved natural areas, take an elective course: optional loop trails lead through the marshes and shrubbery.

From State Route 32, take Williams Street north for a mile into the campus and arboretum. Street parking is available. Open sunrise to sunset. (860) 439-5020.

RESTAURANTS

Fred's Shanty: This local dive has been a favorite since it opened in 1972. With blue awnings shading picnic tables right next to the water, you can order your take-out sandwiches or seafood and then pick your seat. There's an ice cream–only window if you can't wait for dessert. 272 Pequot Avenue; (860) 447-1301.

Thames River Greenery: We'll have a coffee, with a side of roses. This combined coffee shop/plant store has outdoor tables where you can have your coffee and your dogwood, too. 62 State Street; (860) 443-6817.

PLACES TO STAY

The Red Roof Inn: Safe, comfortable—everyone knows what to expect here. Rates range from $39 to $99 per night. 707 Coleman Street, New London, CT 06320; (860) 444-0001; www.redroof.com.

DIVERSIONS

Block Island Dogs: For a day trip or a weekend adventure, dogs and their well-behaved people can take the ferry from New London to Block Island, a jewel of an island off the coast of Rhode Island (see page 133). Two- and four-footed folks can stroll on, but cars need reservations. Nelseco Navigation, seasonal ferry. (401) 783-4613.

Sound Hounds: Go from New London to Orient Point on Long Island every hour on the hour on Cross Sound Ferry Services. Dogs on leashes are welcome to hit the open seas. (860) 443-5281.

NORTH HAVEN

PLACES TO STAY

Holiday Inn: This 140-room hotel offers standard Holiday Inn–style convenience and comfort. Rates range from $95 to $170. 201 Washington Street, North Haven, CT 06473; (800) 528-2121; www.holiday-inn.com.

NORTH STONINGTON

PLACES TO STAY

Arbor House: This hilltop estate comes with its own winery and stocked fishing pond, not to mention spectacular views of the sound. Rates range from $85 to $145. 75 Chester Maine Road, North Stonington, CT 06359; (860) 535-4221; www.arborhouse.com.

NORWICH

PARKS, BEACHES, AND RECREATION AREAS

• **Howard T. Brown Memorial Park** 🐾 🐾 See **32** on page 48.

This riverfront park is party central for Norwich—it seems that all the special events in Norwich take place at this restored waterfront park. The park itself is not that big a place, but the gazebo and Chelsea Landing work overtime. Relax with a picnic or wait for the next band to come by. If your dog insists on a walk, head for the Heritage Walk, a 1.5-mile river trail that is part of Connecticut's Greenways system and can be accessed from this park. The trail follows the Yantic River and passes by not one, but two, waterfalls.

Dogs are permitted on leash and are allowed at most of the events.

The park is located downtown on Shetucket and Water Streets. Open 24 hours. (860) 823-3759.

NATURE HIKES AND URBAN WALKS

Walking Tours of Norwich: Norwich does not allow dogs in many of its parks, but city streets are still fair game. There are several walking tours with educational brochures put together by the tourism bureau. There are several options, including one that takes you past Benedict Arnold's birthplace. Maps are available from the Tourist Bureau on Main Street. (860) 886-4683, (800) 4-NORWICH.

PLACES TO STAY

Ramada Inn: This hotel is a short (and complimentary) ride from both casinos in Connecticut. If you are not the gambling type, you can hike in the Pachaug State Forest to pass the time. Rates range from $79 per room to $250 for a suite. 10 Laura Boulevard, Norwich, CT 06360; (860) 899-5201, (888) 298-2054; www.ramada.com.

OLD LYME

RESTAURANTS

Hallmark Drive In: The Hallmark is the hallmark of Old Lyme—the place all hungry hounds head for. We make it our regular stop for sandwiches, grinders, ice cream, and fried seafood. Fried dough is a menu highlight, too, and, if you haven't experienced it, make a special trip. 113 Shore Road; (860) 434-1998.

Pizza Plus: The menu of pizza, grinders, salads, and pasta goes on and on. Take your pick, and then pick a red or green picnic table outside. 284 Shore Road; (860) 434-3282.

PLACES TO STAY

Old Lyme Inn: This 13-room restored 1850s inn is a treat for the eyes and the body. Feather beds with brass fixtures and Victorian furnishings await you. Some rooms have fireplaces. There is an on-site restaurant for convenience. Rates range from $78 to $200. 85 Lyme Street, Old Lyme, CT 06371; (860) 434-2600, (800) 434-5352; www.oldlymeinn.com.

OXFORD

RESTAURANTS

The European Shoppe: They offer flavored coffees, fresh pastries, and bistro lunches. Bon appétit! 109 Playhouse Corner; (203) 262-1500.

SALEM

PLACES TO STAY

Witch Meadow Lake Campground: We were bewitched by the nature trails running over 120 acres of property. Nice touch for a campground. Dogs are welcome but must be kept at your campsite—no wanderers. $28 per night. 139 Witch Meadow Road, Salem, CT 06420; (860) 859-1542.

SEYMOUR

PARKS, BEACHES, AND RECREATION AREAS

• French Park 🐾🐾 See **33** on page 48.

The centerpiece here is a Civil War memorial. That, and the view of the Naugatuck Valley. The park is stately and quiet with a few short paths that run through the park. Your dog won't be panting after a visit here, but it makes for a nice quick stop. Leash laws are enforced.

From U.S. Route 8, take Exit 22 to State Route 67 south for a quarter mile. Turn left on Garden Street for one block, then left onto Spruce Road. Open dawn to dusk. (203) 888-2511.

• Little-Laurel Lime Ridge Park 🐾🐾 See **34** on page 48.

For a park with a name like a nursery rhyme, this park is anything but. We rate it for explorers only. There are no trail maps, so it'll be a test of your orienteering skills. Even Mary's Little Lamb might have a hard time finding its way.

If you're game, however, the lush forest contains dramatic views of the Housatonic River Valley.

From U.S. Route 8, take Exit 19 to State Route 334 (Great Hill Road) north. Turn left onto Laurel Lane to the end. Open sunrise to sunset. (203) 888-2511.

DIVERSIONS

Back to school night: Every Tuesday night in July and August, the Bungay Elementary School hosts a free concert from 6:30 to 8:30 P.M. Canine music lovers welcome on leash. For performance details, call (888) 588-7880.

VOLUNTOWN

PARKS, BEACHES, AND RECREATION AREAS

• Pachaug State Forest 🐾🐾🐾 See **35** on page 48.

Pachaug State Forest is the largest state forest in Connecticut. At 22,938 acres, there are countless options to explore. Designated a National Natural Landmark, it also contains the most extensive Atlantic white cedar swamp left in the state.

There are no less than three Blue Trails that cross this forest. To climb to Mount Misery, follow the Nehantic Trail, which starts at Hopeville Pond State Park and runs for 13 miles to Green Fall Pond. Most of the trail leads through pine forests, with a short climb to the rocky summit.

The Narrangasett Trail offers 16 miles of wooded paths, punctuated by stunning views of the Atlantic Ocean. The Bullet and High Ledges are two oft-visited overlooks that provide some of the best views of both Lake Wyassup and the ocean beyond.

Finally, the Pachaug Trail adds another 28 miles of woodland scenery to the hiking choices here. There's a rhododendron sanctuary with a stunning stand of old growth bushes that shouldn't be missed. They bloom from mid-June to mid-July.

Camping is available at the Green Falls Campground or the Mount Misery Campground. One leashed dog allowed per campsite. Rates range from $9 to $10 per night. For reservations, call (860) 376-4075.

It's a state park, so leash 'em up.

From State Routes 138/165, take State Route 49 a half mile into the park. Open 8 A.M. to sunset. (860) 424-3200.

PLACES TO STAY
Pachuag State Forest camping: See pages 69–70.

DIVERSIONS
Head for the Hay: This is one time that being called a "hayseed" is a compliment. Davis Farm conducts fall pumpkin-picking runs in horse-drawn carriages, and there is room for your dog on the hayride. Rides are held in October. (860) 599-5859.

WALLINGFORD

PARKS, BEACHES, AND RECREATION AREAS

• **Wharton Brook State Park** 🐾 🐾 See **36** on page 48.
This 96-acre state park started out as a traveler's wayside, the precursor to today's Interstate rest stops. Located on wooded, sandy knolls, visitors are presented with a selection of short, moderately easy hikes on a combination of open green space and wooded terrain. There is a swimming beach on Wharton Brook, but dogs are not permitted.

State park rules require dogs be on leash.

From I-91, take Exit 13 to U.S. Route 5 south a quarter mile.

Parking fee of $5 for in-state cars; $8 for out-of-state cars in the summer. Open 8 A.M. to sunset. (203) 269-5308.

DIVERSIONS
And the band played on: Every Thursday, at the Masonic Geriatric Healthcare Center at 22 Masonic Avenue, there are free concerts. The band plays on from 6:30 to 8:30 P.M. in July and August. (203) 284-3980.

WATERFORD

PARKS, BEACHES, AND RECREATION AREAS

• **Harkness Memorial State Park** 🐾🐾🐾 See **37** on page 48.
Having made their money in Standard Oil, the Harkness family donated their 235-acre estate to the state of Connecticut. Dogs are welcome on the grounds, and there's a special treat for little dogs. The park staff will let you take your dog with you on the mansion tour, provided you can carry her. So, in this case, terriers rule and Labradors drool.

Somehow we think Labs are more interested in the wide-open grassy lawns of the estate anyway. A paved path also loops through the middle of the park, formal gardens, leading to a great view of the Long Island Sound from the picnic areas. The only place dogs are not permitted is the beach.

Leashes are required here. The parking fee is $5 for state residents and $8 for others.

From U.S. Route 1, take State Route 213 south for 3.5 miles. The park is on your right. Open 8 A.M. to sunset. (860) 443-5725.

NATURE HIKES AND URBAN WALKS

Millstone Nature Trail: The Millstone Nuclear Power Plant has installed a short, self-guided nature hike on its property, running right along the water overlooking the Long Island Sound. We realize a nature trail at a nuclear power plant sounds like an oxymoron, but we promise your dog will only glow with enjoyment. Dogs must be leashed. The plant and trail is on Rope Ferry Road off of State Route 156. Open dawn to dusk. (860) 691-4670.

PLACES TO STAY

Lamplighter Motel: Pets are accepted by arrangement with the owner, so get ready to sing your pup's praises as a well-behaved houseguest. There are 38 motel-style rooms with cable TV and a pool. Rates range from $75 to $120 per night. 211 Waterford Parkway North, Waterford, CT 06385; (860) 442-7227.

DIVERSIONS

Hark, all ye music lovers: Harkness Memorial State holds a classical summer concert series called Summer Music. Weekly weekend concerts are held in July and August at an outdoor tent near the mansion. There is lawn seating as well, and leashed Beethovens are welcome. Tickets can be purchased at the park and are $16.50 per person; dogs are free. For more information, call (860) 442-9199.

WEST HAVEN

PARKS, BEACHES, AND RECREATION AREAS

• **Bradley Point Park and Promenade** 🐾🐾 See **38** on page 48.
Locals walk, swim, rollerblade, bike, and just generally hang out in this park and on its 3.5-mile long promenade. The main draw is the view of Long Island Sound, which is hard to beat on a sunny summer day. Dogs are not allowed

on the beach; you'll just have to enjoy it from the walkway. The daily parking fee for nonresidents is $10 all day and $4 after 4 P.M.

Dogs must be on leash.

From Interstate 95, take Exit 42 to State Route 162 south for 1.5 miles. The park is on the left. Open dawn to dusk. (203) 937-3651.

DIVERSIONS

Outdoor Summer Concerts: West Haven's Center Green comes alive with music every Friday evening from June to August. The bands take the stage at the John C. Ireland Bandstand at 7 P.M.; the music changes weekly. For details, call (203) 937-3534.

WESTBROOK

PLACES TO STAY

Maple's Motel: Pets are welcome at this 18-room motel, and you can fix a midnight snack in your kitchenette. Rates range from $40 to $75. 1935 Boston Post Road, Westbrook, CT 06498; (860) 399-9345.

WETHERSFIELD

PLACES TO STAY

Motel 6: Small dogs are permitted here; one dog per room. Room rates range from $35 to $49 per night. 1341 Silas Deane Highway, Wethersfield, CT 06109; (860) 563-8900, (800) 4-MOTEL6; www.motel6.com.

Ramada Inn: Rates range from $55 to $85 per night, with no extra charge for the pup. 1330 Silas Deane Highway, Wethersfield, CT 06109; (860) 563-2311, (800) 2RAMADA; www.ramada.com.

3
WESTERN HILLS AND COAST

We may very well be the first folks to use Litchfield and Fairfield in the same sentence; these two neighboring counties are worlds apart.

Litchfield County, or, as it's better known, the Litchfield Hills, is considered the remote, mountainous region of Connecticut. In 1694, Benjamin Wadsworth, one of the first settlers to the area, called it "a hideous, howling wilderness." Visitors today will find it anything but hideous, but the wilderness description still fits. Nothing is as quintessentially New England as the small towns in this northwest corner of the state, where the main activities are farming, antiqueing, and hiking the Appalachian Trail.

Coastal Fairfield County couldn't be more different. Home to some of the richest communities in the United States, these part-city, part-suburban towns live by the clock.

Towns like Stamford, Norwalk, Westport, and Fairfield operate in the "commuter corridor" of New York City; we wouldn't call this a "canine corridor," however, for the urban sprawl has not been kind to dogs or nonresidents. Most urban parks are for residents only, and many no longer allow dogs at all. Additionally, dogs are prohibited on the beaches in the summer and, in most cases, year-round.

But this is an expansive state, and we have still found plenty of spots you can take Spot. So whether you are trying to catch the next train or make it over the next ridge, city and country blend together to form this region known as Western Connecticut.

Appalachian Trail: This 2,100-mile national trail runs through the northwest corner of Connecticut over the Taconic Mountains and along the Housatonic River. The Appalachian Trail enters Connecticut in Sherman on the New York border and takes a 50-mile journey through the most beautiful section of the state to the Massachusetts line in Salisbury.

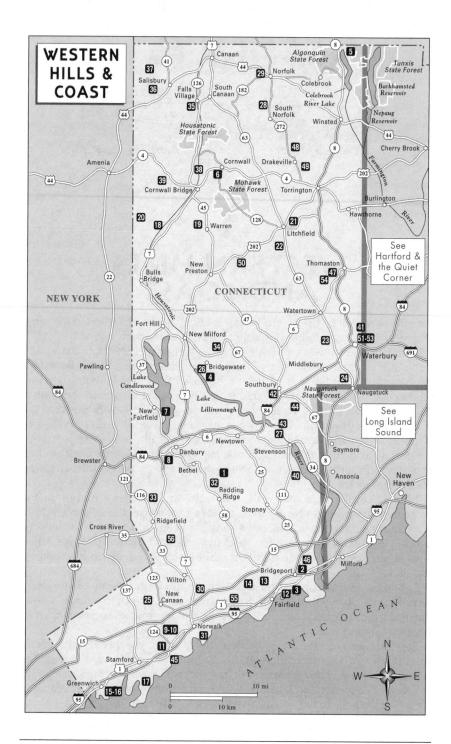

WESTERN
HILLS &
COAST

Salisbury
37
36
41
Canaan
44
Falls
Village
126
South
Canaan
182
35
Housatonic
State Forest
44
Amenia
4
Cornwall Bridge
39
38
6
Cornwall
Mohawk
State Forest
20
18
45
Warren
19
128
44
NEW YORK
22
Bulls
Bridge
7
New
Preston
202
CONNECTICUT
Fort Hill
Housatonic
202
New Milford
34
Pawling
37
Lake
Candlewood
26
4
Bridgewater
84
7
New
Fairfield
7
Lake
Lillinonaugh
6
Newtown
Danbury
Brewster
84
8
Bethel
32
1
Redding
Ridge
121
116
33
58
Stepney
Cross River
Ridgefield
35
56
33
684
7
123
Wilton
30
137
25
New
Canaan
55
1
124
9-10
Norwalk
31
15
11
Stamford
45
1
Greenwich
17
15-16
95

Algonquin
State Forest
8
5
Norfolk
29
Colebrook
Colebrook
River Lake
Tunxis
State Forest
Barkhamsted
Reservoir
Nepaug
Reservoir
28
South
Norfolk
Winsted
272
44
Cherry Brook
Drakeville
48
8
49
4
Torrington
202
Burlington
Hawthorne
Farmington River
21
Litchfield
22
202
50
63
Thomaston
47
54
See
Hartford &
the Quiet
Corner
Watertown
8
84
47
6
23
41
51-53
Middlebury
Waterbury
691
24
Southbury
42
Naugatuck
State Forest
Naugatuck
44
67
See
Long Island
Sound
43
27
Stevenson
Seymore
40
Ansonia
New
Haven
34
8
25
111
25
95
15
1
46
Bridgeport
2
Milford
14
13
12
3
Fairfield
ATLANTIC OCEAN
N
W   E
S
0   10 mi
0   10 km

Dogs can be off leash on the trail but must be under voice control. This section of the trail is administered by the Connecticut Forest and Park Association. (860) 356-2372.

Walking Weekends: Every October on Columbus Day weekend the Northeast Connecticut Visitors District sponsors a Walking Weekend in the 25 towns in Northeast Connecticut, which is sometimes referred to as the Heritage Corridor. While the planned activities make this weekend anything but quiet, a sponsored walk is a great way to introduce yourself to the stunning natural landscape found here. Your leashed dog is welcome at most of the outdoor activities, especially the guided walking tours. For information on the events scheduled, call (860) 928-1228.

BETHEL

PARKS, BEACHES, AND RECREATION AREAS

• **Collis P. Huntington State Park** 🐾🐾🐾 See ❶ on page 74.

This 878-acre park was a gift from Archer and Anna Hyatt Huntington, in memory of Archer's stepfather, Collis P. Huntington. The setting is ideal for a quiet stroll through well-kept woods.

This place is off the beaten path, which helps maintain its favored-park status with locals. None of the trails are marked, but the paths are fairly easy to follow. From the parking area, you can take the main loop trail, which runs for 5.5 miles through the entire park, passing by several wooden bridges, two ponds, several streams, and flowering trees in a hardwood forest. The lovely statues here are all the work of renowned sculptress Anna Hyatt Huntington.

Dogs must be on leash.

From State Route 302, take State Route 58 south for a mile. Bear left and then right onto Sunset Hill Road for two miles. Turn left onto Dodgingtown Road and the park. Open 8 A.M. to sunset. (860) 424-3200.

BRIDGEPORT

PARKS, BEACHES, AND RECREATION AREAS

• **Beardsley Park** 🐾🐾 See ❷ on page 74.

Beardsley Park, the home of Beardsley Zoo, is a little like Rome—all roads lead to it. Resplendent in its Victorian detailing, this park is a popular and busy city centerpiece. Although dogs are prohibited from the zoo itself, you won't mind making do in the park surrounding the zoo. There is a wide, paved path running throughout, and, if you can avoid the Canadian geese who seem to be trying to become permanent fixtures, you'll enjoy your walk.

Of course beauty isn't everything. While dogs in the 19th century would have had the run of the park, their modern-day descendants are relegated to ho-hum leashed walks on the gravel path.

Dogs must be on leash.

From U.S. Route 8, take U.S. Route 1 north for a mile. Turn left onto Nobel Avenue for a half mile. The park is on the left. Another entrance is off East Main Street. Open 8 A.M. to sunset. (203) 576-7233.

• **Seaside Park** 🐾🐾 See **3** on page 74.
Established in 1865, this 370-acre park retains much of its Victorian feel, giving visitors a glimpse of life over 100 years ago, when seaside parks were *the* places to see and be seen.

Although the highlights are a Ferris wheel and some other amusements your dog won't get too worked up over, a wide grassy path that runs alongside the no-dogs-allowed beach is considered fair game. The multiuse recreation path gets its fair share of paw prints as well.

Leashes are required, and, with the many picnickers this park attracts, we actually wanted to keep our dogs close by. Rocky tends to see picnics as a moveable feast spread out for his pleasure.

From U.S. Route 1, take Park Avenue south for two miles to the intersection with Waldemere Road and the park entrance. Open 8 A.M. to sunset. (203) 576-7233.

RESTAURANTS
Auntie Babe's Ice Cream: We all wished we had an Auntie Babe like this when we were growing up—the ice cream and grilled food is heaven to a 10-year-old. Or a dog. Make that a corn dog. There's a take-out window and benches. 4191 Main Street; (203) 365-0294.

PLACES TO STAY
Holiday Inn: Just across the street from the courthouse, this hotel is centrally located in town, but be wary of late-night walks. There are 234 rooms, with rates from $119 to $139, plus a $50 refundable pet deposit. Small dogs under 20 pounds are welcome. 1070 Main Street, Bridgeport, CT 06604; (203) 334-1234; www.holiday-inn.com.

DIVERSIONS
Hounds Head for the Hamptons: On a fine summer day, taking the Long Island ferry from Bridgeport to Port Jefferson is the most relaxing way to avoid the inevitable rush-hour traffic to the beaches. Pack your dog, your swimsuit, your sunscreen, and make a weekend of it. For schedules and rates, call (888) 4-FERRY or (516) 473-0286.

BRIDGEWATER

PARKS, BEACHES, AND RECREATION AREAS

• **Sunny Valley Preserve** 🐾🐾🐾🐾 See **4** on page 74.
This 1,850-acre preserve is a rare gem. Nestled along the Housatonic River, this Nature Conservancy property offers many trails for dogs of all sizes and tastes.

Our favorite trail is the Lakeside Trail. Although there really isn't a "lake" to be found, the trail does access Lake Lillinoah, which is actually just a dammed section of the river. Our dogs don't care what we call it. They just want to know if they can swim. (Yes, George and Inu, you can!)

From the parking area, follow the flat, wide, blue-blazed trail into a rich forest of maple, oak, and other hardwoods. Autumn is a breathtaking time to visit when all the trees are ablaze. Continue through the woods until you reach the red trail, which is the Lakeside Trail. This heads down to the river while traversing woods, hills, and an overlook of the river below.

For a 3.5-mile loop, take the entire Lakeside Trail and return on the Silver Mica Trail to the parking area. This is one of the truly special hikes in this area and a place you will want to revisit again and again.

A map board is posted in the parking area to guide you. Dogs must be on leash.

From State Route 202 in New Milford, take State Route 67 south three miles. Go south for one mile on State Route 133 and turn right onto Hat Shop Hill Road. Continue a half mile to a rotary; go around the rotary to Hemlock Road for 1.8 miles. The gravel parking area is on your left at end of road. Open dawn to dusk. (860) 344-0716.

BROOKFIELD

PLACES TO STAY

Twin Tree Inn: Well-behaved dogs are welcome at this 46-room country home. The deluxe suites have sliding glass doors that open onto the back lawn, making midnight walks a snap. Rates start at $75, plus a $10 pet fee. 1030 Federal Road, Brookfield, CT 06804; (203) 775-0220; www.travelhero.com.

CANAAN

RESTAURANTS

Collins Diner: Welcome back to 1941. That's when this railroad car diner opened, and not much has changed since then. Collins serves typical diner fare, all of which you can get to go—including the blue-plate special. You and your dog can dine outdoors at the concrete tables and benches in front. Railroad Plaza (U.S. Route 7); (860) 824-7040.

Falls Village Inn Pizza and Restaurant: Get your pizza to take out to the big wrap-around porch, and you can share your crusts with your pooch. 33 Railroad Plaza (U.S. Route 7); (860) 824-4910.

PLACES TO STAY

Lone Oak Campsites: This 500-site campground is not only the largest in the state, but also one of the nicest we've seen. Full services and lots of extras—including two hot tubs, nature walks, and plenty of family activities. Leashed dogs are permitted, but not in the cabins or rental tents. There is a dog walk area, too. Tent sites are $30 per night. U.S. Route 44, East Canaan, CT 06024; (860) 824-7051, (800) 422-CAMP.

COLEBROOK

PARKS, BEACHES, AND RECREATION AREAS

• **Colebrook River Lake Dam/West Branch Reservoir** 🐾🐾🐾 See **5** on page 74.

Located on the West Branch of the Farmington River, this 6500-acre project is part of the system of reservoirs that controls the flow of flood waters in the Connecticut River Valley. The lake and its 388 surrounding acres are maintained as a multipurpose recreational area. Best of all, the dam provides amazing views, so take a quick trek across it.

For hiking fun, head into the woods along the lakeshore on a narrow path beside the water's edge. You can pick up the trail near the blue U.S. Army Corps of Engineers Station on the access road.

The park is jointly managed by the U.S. Army Corps of Engineers and the Metropolitan District Commission. Dogs need to be leashed, and hunting is permitted in some areas October through February.

From State Route 20 in Winchester, take U.S. Route 8 north for four miles. The dam entrance is on the right. Open 7:30 A.M. to dusk. (860) 379-6925.

CORNWALL

PARKS, BEACHES, AND RECREATION AREAS

• **Mohawk Mountain State Park/Mohawk State Forest** 🐾🐾🐾 See **6** on page 74.

This park is comprised of acre after acre of woods—3,351 of them, to be precise—deep in the heart of Litchfield Hills. This property, managed by the Nature Conservancy, encompasses one of the last remaining old-growth forests, called Cathedral Pines, which was severely damaged in a series of tornadoes in 1989. Although much of the forest is as pristine as it was hundreds of years ago, other sections give testimony to nature's mercurial moods.

Take the Mohawk Trail for the best look at this National Natural Landmark. Unfortunately the walk is marred by the many great tree trunks littering the trail. Our dogs took these as a challenging obstacle course, but you might feel a little depressed by the sight of these fallen giants.

Once you get through the first section you will climb a small hill and then head downward to wander along a stream. About a mile and a half into your walk, you'll access the Mattatuck Trail which leads to a fire tower atop Mohawk Mountain and a lovely overlook. The whole walk is a little less than four miles.

For a shorter, easier route, the interpretive bog trail and boardwalk is a popular walk. The path, which begins at the park headquarters, is lined with mountain laurel and sundew.

Dogs must be on leash.

From State Route 43, take State Route 4 east for two miles. The state forest is on the right. The state park and Cathedral Pines are off of Great Hollow Road, south of State Routes 4 and 43. Open 8 A.M. to sunset. (860) 672-6100.

NATURE HIKES AND URBAN WALKS

Covered in Connecticut: Connecticut has just three remaining covered bridges, and one of those is just off U.S. Route 7, about five miles from the intersection of State Route 4. The Cornwall Bridge crosses the Housatonic River on State Route 128, and you can stop and enjoy the view from the other side. (860) 672-2709.

PLACES TO STAY

Cornwall Inn: The Cornwall Inn is a cozy, historic inn, with creature comforts like a fireplace where you can warm yourself during the chilly winter. Pets are restricted to select guest rooms in the adjacent mountain lodge, but these rooms are as lovely, if a bit more rustic, as the main inn. Rates range from $79 to $149 per night. 270 Kent Road, Cornwall Bridge, CT 06754; (860) 672-6884, (800) 786-6884; www.cornwallinn.com.

DANBURY

PARKS, BEACHES, AND RECREATION AREAS

• Bear Mountain Park 🐾🐾 See **7** on page 74.

The local federal correctional institution donated this land to Danbury, and has the distinction of being one of the only places where you start your walk at the higest point and head downhill. Begin at the top of Bear Mountain, 888 feet above sea level; from here you can mosey down to Lake Candlewood.

Along the way you'll get some excellent views of the water and pass through a lovely wooded forest. But, remember, although it's a fairly easy walk down the wooded trail, it'll be uphill on the way back with your leashed Lassie.

Dogs are not allowed to swim in the lake.

From Interstate 84, take Exit 6 to State Route 37 north for 3.5 miles. Turn right onto Bear Mountain Road into the park. Don't be confused by some signs that read "Kennedy Trails"; that is also Bear Mountain. Open dawn to dusk. (203) 743-0546.

• Tarrywile Park and Mansion 🐾🐾🐾 See **8** on page 74.

We love to tarry awhile in Tarrywile, this former estate turned city park. Purchased by the city in 1985, there are currently 636 acres of woods and meadows to explore, but that number keeps going up as the city acquires more land.

Visitors can choose a short 1.5-mile hike or spend a half day exploring the longer trails. All in all, there are seven miles of trail choices, taking you through old orchards and gorgeous flowering trees en route to several ponds. The most popular destinations include Parks Pond, Tarrywile Lake, and the picnic area in the fruit orchard. Maps are available at the mansion headquarters.

Dogs are permitted on leash in the park, but they are not allowed to swim here.

From U.S. Route 7, take Wooster Heights east for a mile. Turn right onto Southern Boulevard for one mile. The park and mansion entrances are on the right. Open sunrise to sunset. (203) 744-3130.

RESTAURANTS

Cor's: This place is open for breakfast and lunch every day, and everything is homemade. The menu specials rotate, but our dogs give the meatloaf and grinders a special paws up. You can take out, but there's no outdoor seating. 65 West Street; (203) 792-9999.

J.K.'s Restaurant: J.K's serves up something called Original Texas Hot Wieners—short fat dogs, smothered with either chili or mustard. A Danbury institution for the past 75 years, one bite will tell you why. Our dogs wanted to be smothered with their dogs. They also have hamburgers and other grilled grub to go. No outdoor seating, but it's good enough to eat standing up. 126 South Street; (203) 743-4004.

PLACES TO STAY

Hilton and Towers: This 115-room, full-service hotel welcomes dogs. All the usual modern amenities are available, including an on-site restaurant. Rates range from $99 to $185, plus an additional $10 fee for your pup. 18 Old Ridgebury Road, Danbury, CT 06810; (203) 794-0600, (800) HILTONS; www.hilton.com.

Holiday Inn: Don your bonnets because this Holiday Inn has a hat theme. This hotel celebrates the fact that Danbury was the home of the first American hat and is the center of the hat industry in the U.S. The hotel prefers smaller dogs, and they'll do a quick security sweep after check out. Rates range from $115 to $129. 80 Newtown Road, Danbury, CT 06810; (203) 792-4000, (888) 452-4772; www.holiday-inn.com.

Ramada Inn: Dogs are welcome at this 180-room hotel, conveniently situated on the edge of town. Rates range from $59 to $125. Route 84, Danbury, CT 06810; (203) 792-3800, (888) 298-2054; www.ramada.com.

DARIEN

Darien parks are less than dog friendly, especially if you are a dog from out of town. You must be a Darien resident to use the parks and, even then, with the exception of one leash-free park, the town officials are not extremely happy to see dogs on their paths. Also, dogs are not allowed on any Darien beaches year-round. It's enough to make us want to hightail it out of there (which is, we suspect, exactly the idea).

PARKS, BEACHES, AND RECREATION AREAS

• **Cherry Lawn Park** 🐾🐾🐾 🐕 See 🄳 on page 74.

This place is awesome, but you have to have a Darien permit to officially use the parking area. So, unless you are willing to buy a house or befriend a resident, you can't set paw into this park. But, since it's the only leash-free park in the city, if you can find a way to get here, do.

The park has wide grassy areas leading to a pond for swimming. A mile-long trail beats a flat, wide path into the woods from the pond; local dogs gather here for regular romps, so your pooch is likely to make a friend if you visit.

This park is also home to the Darien Nature Center, which is open year-round and hosts a number of guided walks in the park.

From U.S. Route 1, take Brookside Road north for a quarter mile. The park and parking lot are on the right. Darien Nature Center is open 9 A.M. to 2 P.M.; (203) 655-7459. The park is open dawn to dusk; (203) 656-7325.

• **Tilley Pond Park** 🐾🐾 See 🄴 on page 74.

This park is a little on the small side, but it provides a great place to take a break from shopping in Darien. The manicured grassy stretches and paved walks in the park and woods provide room to roam. But make sure to accessorize with a matching leash, as they are mandatory here.

From U.S. Route 1, take Mansfield Street north one block to the park. Open dawn to dusk. (203) 656-7325.

•Woodland Park Nature Preserve 😺 😺 😺 See **11** on page 74.
Thanks to a resident, Walter Irving, who sold his land to Darien in 1959, this park has been a delight for 40 years. You are likely to catch sight of some unusual birds and lovely wildflowers here. Local hounds haunt this park, so this is your chance to run with the home dogs.

The marked trails in the park offer a pleasant and beautiful woodsy walk. We recommend the one-mile white trail or the 1.5-mile yellow trail; both lead through the mature pine forest. Dogs must remain on leash on all the trails.

From U.S. Route 1, take Hollow Tree Ridge Road north for a half mile. Turn left onto Middlesex Road for a quarter mile. The park is on the left. Open dawn to dusk. (203) 656-7325.

RESTAURANTS
Uncle's Deli: This place rocks for breakfast or lunch, and you can take your food outside to the picnic table. This green and white deli is practically a fixture in Darien. Our dogs love the roll-ups as much as the locals do. 1041 Post Road; (203) 655-9701.

FAIRFIELD
Although there are city parks in Fairfield, none of them welcome you and your dog. Apparently, in these parts, parks are to be seen but not enjoyed. They are for Fairfield residents only, and dogs—even dogs living in Fairfield—do not qualify as residents. However, there is a bright spot: land designated as open space and managed by the Conservation Department does allow dogs—even nonresident dogs—and for the most part, leashes are not required on open space.

PARKS, BEACHES, AND RECREATION AREAS
• Ash Creek Open Space 😺 😺 🐾 See **12** on page 74.
The focus of this 25-acre park is the preservation of Fairfield's history and salt marshes. Once the site of the Penfield grist mills, today the park's short nature trails permit you to explore the salt marsh on a peninsula in Ash Creek, taking you through a wildflower meadow on the way. You can also get up close to the mills' foundations and other remnants of this park's former life, all while overlooking Ash Creek.

Dogs must be leashed and are not permitted in the playground or picnic areas.

From U.S. Route 1, take Old Post Road south for a block. Turn left onto Turney Road; the parking area is directly on the left. Open dawn until one hour after sunset. (203) 256-3071.

• Brett Woods Conservation Area 😺 😺 🐕 See **13** on page 74.
This 185-acre stretch is one of the largest parks we've found in Fairfield. A few rough hiking trails run through a variety of woodlands and streams and even

some wetlands, but be careful of the ticks. An unmaintained former town road leads into the woods from the lot, and several north-south spur trails run from it. If you go south, the trails lead through wooded terrain to the former Treasure Road and a secondary parking area. If you head north, you—and your dog— will run smack into Brett Woods Pond, where your dog can cool off with a dip.

Your dog can forgo the leash if she obeys voice commands.

From Merritt Parkway, take Black Rock Turnpike north for a half mile. Turn left onto Hemlock Road for a quarter mile, then right onto Burr Street for a quarter mile. Turn left onto North Street for a mile to the park entrance. Open dawn until one hour after sunset. (203) 256-3071.

• Lake Mohegan Open Space 🐾🐾🐾 🐕 See **14** on page 74.

Local dogs beg to be taken here, and we can see why. The 167 acres contain miles of wooded trails, but the locals come for the swimming. Lake Mohegan, Mill River, and North Pond are all options for a dip, and Inu was eager to try them all.

You can take a loop trail around most of the lake, plus several spur trails lead along the river and into the woods. Dogs need to stay away from the designated swimming holes at Lake Mohegan, but there are plenty of other swimming options along its shores.

Dogs must be under voice control.

From the Merritt Parkway, take Black Rock Turnpike south for a mile, then turn left onto Tahmore Drive for a half mile into the parking area. Open dawn until one hour past sunset. (203) 256-3071.

RESTAURANTS

Firehouse Deli: The blackboard is the cue to what's fresh and what's hot at this historic red firehouse-turned-deli. The outdoor tables fill up quickly at lunch, so get fired up, grab a sandwich, and slide over to a perch at this great people-watching place. 22 Reef Road; (203) 255-5527.

Pizza Works: Pizza by the slice, an East Coast tradition, is alive and well here. On a nice day, there are plastic chairs lining the front of the store. Nothing fancy, but it's quick, cheap, and good. 1512 Post Road; (203) 255-0303.

DIVERSIONS

And the band played on. . . : Have a howling good time every Sunday, Wednesday, and Thursday evenings at 7 P.M. for a series of summer concerts on the Sherman Green throughout July and August. For performance schedules, call (203) 256-3144.

GREENWICH

If you're a dog in Greenwich, you are restricted to leashed walks on your neighborhood sidewalk. If you're visiting here, don't even bother trying to find a place to walk your dog. It doesn't exist. After trying to get the park rules and regulations from city officials, we were told firmly that although residents can walk their dogs in some of the parks in Greenwich, they'd really rather they didn't. The officials didn't even want their parks to appear in a book that "advertised" places for dogs. So what can we say? The following parks "tolerate" your pet, but, if the city never saw a dog in a Greenwich park again, we feel certain they would be thrilled.

PARKS, BEACHES, AND RECREATION AREAS

• **Grass Island** 🐾 🐾 See **15** on page 74.
This is one of the two parks in the Greenwich inner harbor, and the main attraction here is the view. There are picnic tables, grass, and, uh, did we mention the view? Look out over the harbor at all those yachts and just imagine how the other half lives. Inquiring dogs want to know.

Dogs must be on leash. You must have a resident sticker to park here.

The park is located off of Shore Road in the village of Belle Haven. Open dawn to dusk. (203) 622-7830.

• **Roger Sherman Baldwin Park** 🐾 🐾 See **16** on page 74.
Walk along the boardwalk here and breathe in the salt air. This small park does not have trails; the walk along the water and the view of the sound are pretty much it—but they are enough to lure us back. Although not a large space, there is a concert pavilion on the grounds, so stroll by on a summer evening for a little night music.

Dogs must be on leash.

From U.S. Route 1, take Greenwich Avenue south for a mile. Turn right onto Arch Street. The park is on the left. Open dawn to 10 P.M. (203) 622-7830.

• **Greenwich Point Park** 🐾 🐾 See **17** on page 74.
The fee for this peninsula park on Tod's Point is steep: to get into the park during the summer, you have to buy a house in Greenwich. Or know somebody who can smuggle you in, as we did.

If you live in town, you'll find a beachfront, picnic areas, and walking and biking paths. Our dogs liked exploring the foundations of the old cannon turrets, remnants of the old fort that once stood its ground here. And when George fetched the newspaper, all he brought back was the real estate section. Mmm. . .

Dogs must be leashed.

From Interstate 95, take Exit 5 to Sound Beach Avenue south for two miles. Turn right onto Shore Road to the end and a small parking area. Open dawn to dusk. (203) 622-7830.

DIVERSIONS

Pups in the Park: Pop on down to hear a little night music at the open air concert series by the Greenwich Pops every Wednesday night at Baldwin Park. Both choral and symphonic concerts are featured at the Pappas Pavillion. The concerts run from 7:30 to 9 P.M. For performance schedules, call (203) 622-7830.

KENT

PARKS, BEACHES, AND RECREATION AREAS

• **Appalachian Trail—Caleb's Peak** 🐾 🐾 🐾 🐾 🐾 See **18** on page 74.
This section of the Appalachian Trail is really worth a special mention. The three-mile stretch that runs from Kent along the Housatonic River is one of the

most pleasant and scenic walks we have ever taken. This gently sloping path runs north along the river where wildflowers and waterfowl abound.

Heading southwest from the parking area you'll soon reach Saint John's Ledge and Caleb's Peak, both with fine views of the river. The ridge is easy to traverse, although there is a brief steep and rocky section before reaching the summit.

If you'd prefer a shorter walk, pick up the section that connects to the Bull's Bridge Scenic Loop, a two-mile trek near waterfalls and covered bridges. Apparently George Washington slept here—or at least, fished his horse out of the river. No one seems to know which.

From U.S. Route 7, take State Route 341 west for a half mile crossing the Housatonic River. Turn right onto Skiff Mountain Road for a mile, and then bear right onto River Road (dirt road) for 1.6 miles to the parking area. Open 24 hours. (860) 356-2372.

•Kent Falls State Park 🐾🐾🐾 See **19** on page 74.
The falls, the falls, the falls—we loved them! You can't avoid them here, because as you enter the park you can see—and hear—them. A trail runs alongside the cascading water, providing great views the whole way up and back. The trail is just over a quarter of a mile in length, but it's a near-vertical scramble, so pups will be panting. Other paths lead off into the 295 acres of the park, if you can tear yourself away from the water.

Dogs need to be on leash in the state park.

From State Route 341, take U.S. Route 7 north for six miles. The park entrance is on the right. Open 8 A.M. to sunset. (860) 927-3238.

•Macedonia Brook State Park 🐾🐾🐾 See **20** on page 74.
A multitude of trails wind up and around the 1,000-foot hills clustered within the boundaries of this 2,300-acre park. From the parking lot, take the white-blazed Cobble Mountain Trail. About a mile in, it intersects with the Macedonia Ridge Trail which takes you to the summit of Cobble Mountain. The open ledges offer panoramic views west toward the Catskills.

If you continue on the Macedonia Ridge Trail, you will reach the top of Pine Hill, where you can look east this time. To get back to the parking area, turn right on the old grassy access road, then back to the Cobble Mountain Trail.

Maps are available at the ranger station. Dogs must be on a leash.

From U.S. Route 7, take State Route 341 west for two miles. Turn right onto Macedonia Brook Road for two miles into the park. Open 8 A.M. to sunset. (860) 927-3238.

RESTAURANTS
Kent Market: This is really a grocery store, but it's worth a visit to say hi to the resident Jack Russell terriers. Sidney and Phantom live in the window of the market, keeping an eye on their world. They love visitors, so stop in to stock up on supplies. 12 North Main Street; (860) 927-3089.

Stosh's Ice Cream: This converted railcar is great fun, dog friendly, and, if you can delay your demand for ice cream, has a food menu, too. The food selections focus on Dazzle Dogs, a variety of hot dogs smothered with everything you can imagine—and some things you can't. Try the Appalachian Trail Cookies made especially for hungry hikers who come off the trail nearby. Our dogs got their own bowl of ice cream topped with a milk bone. Kent Station Square; (860) 927-4495.

Stroble Baking Company: This family-owned bakery offers gourmet food such as Pizza Rustica and Shrimp with White Beans and Tarragon. Sit out at the tables in front of the bakery to enjoy your meal. There is also a mouthwatering display of cakes and pies if you can save some room. 14 North Main Street; (860) 927-4073.

LITCHFIELD

PARKS, BEACHES, AND RECREATION AREAS

• Topsmead State Forest 🐾 🐾 🐾 See 21 on page 74.

This lovely estate was a gift by Edith M. Chase, who lived here until her death in 1972. It was Miss Chase's wish that the property be open for quiet visitation and passive recreation. There are two formal gardens and four acres of groomed lawns on more than 500 acres surrounding an English Tudor–style house. The grounds include hiking paths and an ecology trail.

As on all state property, dogs must be leashed.

From U.S. Route 202, take State Route 118 east for two miles. Turn right onto East Litchfield Road for a mile, and then right onto Buell Road into the park. Open 8 A.M. to sunset. (860) 567-5694.

• White Memorial Conservation Center 🐾 🐾 🐾 See 22 on page 74.

It's a big one. A real big one. At 4,000 acres, this conservation center is larger than any state park in all of Connecticut. And it's hard to top for natural beauty. The Center was founded by Alain and Mary White, a brother-and-sister team who wanted to preserve Connecticut's flora, fauna, and wildlife.

There are over 35 miles of trails here, as well as a nature sanctuary and natural history museum. Check out the 1.2-mile long boardwalk which encircles Little Pond over marshes that would otherwise be too wet to wander. Hike all the way around Little Pond, or take the shorter loops around Duck Pond and Mallard Marsh. We should warn you—these ponds are named for ducks for a reason. Unless you want your dog and car to smell "just ducky," we suggest you follow the leash law.

Maps are $2.50 at the bookstore near the parking area, and we highly recommend making the investment. There is no fee to use the trails, but donations are appreciated.

From State Route 63, take U.S. Route 202 west for two miles. Turn left onto Bissell Road for a half mile, then left onto Whitehall Road. The parking area is on the right. Trails are open dawn to dusk. (860) 567-0857.

NATURE HIKES AND URBAN WALKS

Downtown Litchfield Center: It's hard to imagine a more picture postcard–perfect New England town than Litchfield. Surrounded by rolling hills with stunning vistas, this town is nestled in the heart of some of the most beautiful country in the region.

Start at the Visitor Center on the Green, where you can pick up a map to guide you. Along the way you'll see the Congregational Church, which was built in 1828 and claims to be the most-photographed church in New England. When its architectural style fell out of favor in 1873, the church was moved and began a career as a movie theatre, a dance hall, and even a roller skating rink! When the town began its historical revival efforts in 1929, the church was moved back to its former home on the Green. You can also visit the birthplace of Harriet Beecher Stowe. (860) 567-4506.

RESTAURANTS

Aspen Garden: Mama Mia—this place is fantastico! At lunchtime, pizzas, calzones, and grinders rule, but dinner expands to include steak, seafood, and pasta dishes. You can top it all off with a dish of ice cream, and who wouldn't want to? The patio seating is first come, first served, and here your dog can join you on your culinary trip to the Mediterranean. 51 West Street; (860) 567-9477.

Bohemian Pizza: This cozy cedar-shingled shack dishes up some amazing pizza, with a host of the usual and not-so-usual toppings. We must say, this is the first time we've seen fiddlehead greens and prosciutto on a pizza. You'll have to take out, but this place is just up the road from White Memorial Conservation Center (see page 85). 342 Bantam Road; (860) 567-3980.

Country Life Whole Foods Grocer: This is a grocery store for the healthy, clean-living pooch. In our bunch, that would be George. Rocky is too much of a biscuit hound, and Inu has a taste for junk food. However, all were satisfied with our selections here. This wonderful pit stop is good and good for you, and the outdoor picnic tables make this a great spot for Spot. 383 Torrington Road; (860) 567-4435.

Litchfield Grocer: We couldn't decide if this was an old-fashioned village grocer or the latest trend in upscale eateries. Everything is so fresh you should slap it, as Beth's mother would say. Meat counters with deli people just waiting to make the sandwich of your dreams beckon to hungry shoppers. Be sure to stop by the fresh produce counter and bakery, too. Dogs line up impatiently at the door, waiting for their owners to come out with the goods. 33 West Street; (860) 567-4882.

PLACES TO STAY

Tollgate Hill Inn: This 1745 inn is on the National Registry of Historic Places, and it is a wonderful place. Much of the original building is intact, and the 20 rooms feature four-poster beds. Rates range from $110 to $189 per night, including continental breakfast. U.S. Route 202, Litchfield, CT 06759; (860) 567-4545, (800) 445-3903; www.litchfieldcty.com/dining/tollgate.

DIVERSIONS

Start your wine-ing: We were thrilled to find Haight Vineyards, because we love tasting wine and hanging out with our dogs, and rarely do we mix the two. There was no whining, just some very tasty wine-ing on our visit here. Outside tables are perfect for a picnic. 29 Chestnut Hill Road; (860) 567-4045.

Summer singing: If you're here on a Wednesday in June, July, or August, head to the Green for the town's summer concert series. Leashed dogs are welcome to enjoy the music with their owners. The free concerts run from 7 to 9 P.M. (860) 567-4506.

MIDDLEBURY

PARKS, BEACHES, AND RECREATION AREAS

• Hetzel Refuge 🐾 🐾 See **23** on page 74.

This place is a pristine, wooded wildlife refuge with enough solitude to make stressed out souls breathe again. Located on 66 acres, the short trails crisscross the refuge, offering prime wildlife observation areas.

Dogs need to be on leash to protect the wildlife. The park contains the Flanders Nature Center, but dogs are not permitted in the building.

From Interstate 84, take Exit 17 to State Route 63 north for two miles. The park is on the left. Open dawn to dusk. (203) 263-3711.

• Hop Brook Lake and Recreation Area 🐾 🐾 See **24** on page 74.

The functional reason for this 538-acre park is flood control, but until Noah and the ark arrive this recreation area will be swimming with people and their pooches. Seven and a half miles of trails run through wetlands, woods, and water, water everywhere. You can access all the trails from the parking areas.

Dogs must be leashed and are not permitted at the swimming beach, but there are plenty of access points along the lake. Currently there is no fee, but that may change in the future.

The gates for the parking area are open from April to October, but you can hike into the park year-round. This recreation area is also the parking area for the Trolley Greenway (see below), which runs to Middlebury.

From Interstate 84, take Exit 17 to State Route 63 south for one mile. The park is on your left. Open 8 A.M. to sunset. (203) 729-8840.

NATURE HIKES AND URBAN WALKS

Trolley Greenway/Larkin Bridle Path: Mail was delivered along this route via trolley service from 1908 to 1929, but after the demise of the trolley the stretch was converted to a walking and biking greenway. A connecting 10-mile section of former railway was donated to the city and is now known as the Larkin Bridle Path. Both paths are multiuse, and you will find this a perfect place for a good stroll with Rover.

Access is via the Hop Brook Recreation Area (see above) and from Kettletown Road in Southbury. Open dawn to dusk. (888) 588-7880.

NEW CANAAN

PARKS, BEACHES, AND RECREATION AREAS

• New Canaan Nature Center 🐾 🐾 🐾 See **25** on page 74.

One visit here and you'll know you've arrived in the land of Canaan. Located on 40 gorgeous acres, you'll find two miles of crisscrossing paths traversing meadows, two ponds, woodlands, dense thickets, an old orchard, and a cattail marsh. You can even walk across a marsh on a 350-foot boardwalk.

Don't miss the northern corner of the park, where the butterfly field is located. It is really a ticket back to your childhood—or puppyhood, as the case may be. George gave up chasing his usual tennis ball in favor of hightailing after a butterfly.

Dogs are permitted on leash. There is no fee, but donations are requested.

From the center of town on State Route 106, take State Route 124 north a half mile. The park is on the left. Grounds are open dawn to dusk. (203) 966-9577.

NEW MILFORD

PARKS, BEACHES, AND RECREATION AREAS

• Lovers Leap State Park Reserve 🐾🐾 See 26 on page 74.

No, this park didn't get its name from moony-eyed high schoolers. Apparently, Native American Chief Waramaug had his home on the cliff overlooking the lake and the falls here, back when white settlers were few and far between. His beautiful daughter, Lillinoah, for whom the lake on the Housatonic River is named, came upon a white man in the forest one day, and soon they were in love. The young man had to leave for the winter but promised to return and marry Lillinoah in the spring. He was late returning and, in order to stop his daughter's tears, Chief Waramaug arranged for her to marry another man. Little did he know the ways of the heart, for Lillinoah, refusing to marry any but her true love, donned her wedding dress, grabbed her canoe, and headed for the falls. Her lover, choosing this moment to return, raced to find her. From the overlook, he saw Lillinoah in her canoe, and she saw him. Without hesitation he leapt into the water, she bailed out of the canoe, and they embraced—just before they both fell over the 120-foot drop of the Great Falls.

Today there is a tower at the top of the cliff, and a one-mile trail that runs along the base of the falls.

Dogs must be leashed.

From U.S. Route 202, take State Route 67 south a quarter mile. Turn right onto Grove Street for three miles. The park is on the left. Open 8 A.M. to sunset. (860) 424-3200.

RESTAURANTS

Grand Patisserie: Stop in and get some gourmet to go here. You'll choose from amazing pastries (as the name implies), specialty coffees, and a lunch selection that changes daily. 27 Main Street; (860) 354-4525.

PLACES TO STAY

Heritage Inn: This historic 1870 inn features 20 rooms with country-quaint furnishings. Dogs are welcome with prior approval. Rooms range from $75 to $110, including continental breakfast. 34 Bridge Street, New Milford, CT 06776; (860) 354-8883, (800) 311-6294.

NEWTOWN

PARKS, BEACHES, AND RECREATION AREAS

• Paugussett State Forest 🐾🐾🐾 See 27 on page 74.

You can take the high road or the low road in this 1,935-acre park, which is divided into two sections.

In the 794-acre "upper" section, we recommend the Lillinoah hiking trail. It is a six-mile loop through a pine forest and part of the statewide Blue Trails system. Sections of this trail are closed from December 15 to March 15, however, so as not to disturb nesting bald eagles who winter here.

The lower portion of this forest hugs the Housatonic River and is accessible via the Zoar Trail. This 6.5-mile loop trail runs through the forest and back, along the banks of Lake Zoar. About a mile in, you will find a small beach, if your dog doesn't find it first. Doggie paddlers are permitted. The remainder of the trail follows a series of ups and downs, climbs to lake overlooks, then back down and up again.

Dogs must be leashed. The forest is open to hunting from October through February.

From the intersection of State Routes 34 and 111, take Great Quarter Road north for 1.5 miles to a parking area turnaround. Open from 8 A.M. to sunset. (860) 424-3200.

RESTAURANTS

Newtown General Store: For over 200 years, this store has served the needs of hungry travelers. They serve up breakfast, lunch, and ice cream. Judging by the crowd gathering for morning coffee, Newtown is still an early-to-bed, early-to-rise kind of place. 43 Main Street; (203) 426-9901.

DIVERSIONS

Wine Not: The family-owned McLaughlin Vineyards, on the Connecticut Wine Trail, is delightfully dog friendly. Dogs are welcome for hiking and picnicking on the estate, which slopes down to the Housatonic River. Even without the chance to sample some of the grapes' finest, this place is worth a visit. Alberts Hill Road; (203) 426-1533.

NORFOLK

PARKS, BEACHES, AND RECREATION AREAS

• Dennis Hill State Park 🐾🐾🐾 See 28 on page 74.

This 240-acre park is a gift from Doctor Fredrick Shepard Dennis to the state, and we say thank you to the good doctor. At the very tippy top of the park—that's Dennis Hill—stands a pavilion that was part of the Dennis summer residence. Climb the cupola to the roof and, at 1,627 feet, you'll enjoy a panoramic view of Litchfield Hills.

An easy loop trail called Romantic Ramble, a two-mile stroll, ought to be taken with a loved one—of any species. Keep dogs on leash in the state park.

From U.S. Route 44, take State Route 272 south for two miles. The park is on the left. Open 8 A.M. to sunset. (860) 424-3200.

• Haystack Mountain State Park 🐾🐾🐾 See 29 on page 74.

On a clear day you can see forever. . . or at least as far as the Berkshires in one direction and Long Island Sound in the other. For a quick, half-mile climb to 1,716-foot-high Haystack Mountain and the observation tower at its peak, your best bet is to take the access road and drive to the top parking area. From there you can hike the mile-long summit trail.

Enjoy these 224 acres with your dogs on leash.

From U.S. Route 44, take State Route 272 north for a mile. The park is on the left. Open 8 A.M. to sunset. (860) 424-3200.

RESTAURANTS

The Real Food Company: The dogs got to hang out on the back deck, while we fetched for them for a change. The friendly staff dishes up gourmet to go, with a nice selection of fruit, veggies, snacks, and health foods in this immaculate shop. And yes, the food is totally real. 32 Greenwoods Road; (860) 542-1999.

NORWALK

PARKS, BEACHES, AND RECREATION AREAS

• **Cranbury Park** 🐾 🐾 See **30** on page 74.
This 130-acre preserve has a variety of hiking and walking trails, and, sadly, a leash restriction. But beggars can't be choosers because most of the parks in Norwalk don't allow dogs at all. This former estate still features the mansion and the manicured lawns and gardens. The trails meander through the property, among shade trees and open, grassy spaces. A bike path and a concert pavilion are also on-site.

From U.S. Route 7, take Kennsett Avenue east for a half mile to Gruman Avenue and the park. Open 7:30 A.M. to 8 P.M. (203) 854-7806.

• **Taylor Farm** 🐾 🐾 🐾 🐾 🐕 See **31** on page 74.
This big strip of a leash-free park is the exception to the rule in Norwalk. One of the few parks that allows dogs at all, we think it's doggone civilized that it also happens to be a leash-free property. And since this is the obvious hot spot for the locals, you'll always meet up with a pack of happy canines on a visit here. Fortunately, the natives are friendly in these parts and eager to show you around.

In addition to the large play field, which is perfect for throwing balls, there are some short trails in the park for a more solitary stroll. The field is fenced, for those dogs with wandering paws.

From Interstate 95, take Exit 16 to East Avenue south for a quarter mile. Bear left on Gregory Boulevard for a half mile, then bear left onto Calf Pasture Beach Road to the end. Turn left onto Beach Road to the park. Open 7:30 A.M. to 8 P.M. (203) 854-7806.

RESTAURANTS

Swanky Franks: Well, you only need one restaurant listing when it's a place as famous as this one. Listed on every top-roadside-eatery list, this place knows how to put on the dog. Swanky doesn't mean lace tablecloths, but it does mean tasty grilled food, sandwiches, and seafood. You can sit outside at the rainbow-colored picnic tables to enjoy your lunch or dinner. Be prepared to wait on hot summer days. This place is one very popular doghouse! 182 Connecticut Avenue; (203) 838-8969.

PLACES TO STAY

Silvermine Tavern: This is paws down Rocky's favorite place to hang his leash in Connecticut. This historic landmark permits pets in the 12 rooms above the

Country Store, and the rooms are lovely and delightfully television free. You and your pooch are welcome to pass the evening in front of the fireplace in the main building. Rates range from $80 to $120 per night. 194 Perry Avenue, Norwalk, CT 06854; (203) 847-4558; www.silverminetavern.com.

FESTIVALS

PAWS Adopt-a-Pet Fest: Bring a dog, or pick one up here at the PAWS annual Adopt-a-Pet Fest. Even if you have your hands full with your current pooch, you can check out the vendor booths specializing in all things canine. There is even food and music for the two-legged contingent. Held every September on the Norwalk Green. (203) 750-9572.

DIVERSIONS

Strings under the Stars: The summer brings music to the two-acre Norwalk Green. The city sponsors a couple of concerts a month, usually held from 3 to 5 P.M. on weekends. Leashed, well-heeled pooches are welcome. (203) 854-7746.

PLEASANT VALLEY

DIVERSIONS

Pleasant Valley Drive-In: This place is like a trip back to our childhood, and we loved every minute of it. The dogs liked the complimentary biscuits the movie operator gave them on the way in. Movies play at dusk on Friday, Saturday, and Sunday. Admission is $6.50 per person. State Route 181; (860) 379-6102.

PLYMOUTH

RESTAURANTS

Country Store and Fudge Factory: Look for the big red barn near the center of Plymouth. It is home to a country store and attached ice-cream parlor. Sit outside on multilevel decks and enjoy your cone. 655 Main Street; (860) 283-8888.

Riders Grill and Ice Cream: If you miss the sign, look for the display of Harley Davidson motorcycles that marks this diner. The grill serves up hot dogs, hamburgers, and fried seafood, which you can enjoy at the picnic tables outside or take with you as you drive into the sunset. 2627 Waterbury Road (State Route 262); (203) 753-4745.

REDDING

PARKS, BEACHES, AND RECREATION AREAS

• **Putnam Memorial State Park** 🐾🐾🐾 See **32** on page 74.

Connecticut thinks of Putnam Memorial State Park as its very own Valley Forge, for this is where General Israel Putnam spent the winter of 1778–79 with his revolutionary war soldiers. Valley Forge was no picnic that winter, so just imagine how much colder and more brutal the winter was 250 miles north, here in Redding.

This is a perfect spot for those inclined to mix a history lesson with a walk in the park. In the eastern half of the 252-acre park a road winds past a number of memorial sites, including the encampment site, the cemetery, and the officers' barracks. More rustic trails and Lake Putnam are waiting to be explored across the road, in the western section of the park. Although you can't swim here, a scenic trail winds along the water.

Dogs must be on leash.

The park is just north of the intersection of Black Rock Turnpike and Putnam Park Road (State Route 107) on Putnam Park Road which divides the park. Parking is available on both sides of the road. Open 8 A.M. to sunset. (860) 424-3200.

RIDGEFIELD

PARKS, BEACHES, AND RECREATION AREAS

• **Seth Low Pierreport State Park Reserve** 🐾🐾🐾 See **33** on page 74.
As Inu can attest, a wet dog is a happy dog, and boy, oh boy, was he happy here. The parking area for this park doubles as a boat launch, and dogs are free to swim here as long as they stay out of the way of the boats. So, before we started our trek into the 300-acre woods, the dogs hopped into the clear clean lake for a dip.

Once you do drag your dog away from the water, a great outlook and vista of Lake Naraneka await, accessible via a short hike up from the parking area. Several other short trails weave their way through this reserve, but no maps or markings are available to guide you.

Dogs must stay on leash.

From State Route 35, take State Route 116 north for three miles. Turn right onto Barlow Mountain Road (follow boat launch signs) to the parking area on the right. Open 8 A.M. to sunset. (860) 454-3200.

NATURE HIKES AND URBAN WALKS

Walking Tour of Ridgefield: This exceedingly well-preserved New England town dates back to 1708 and features such famous past residents as Benedict Arnold and Eugene O'Neill. Main Street is located on a 750-foot-high ridge where mansions, parks, and restaurants share the stage with the unique geology. The Housatonic Valley Tourism Office on Main Street provides a brochure detailing the history of the town and the buildings. (203) 743-0546.

RESTAURANTS

Country Corners: This deli/bakery/general store combo is right on the corner of State Routes 35 and 116, making it the perfect place to watch the world go by. Grab a sandwich or deli delight inside, then settle in at the outdoor tables and chairs. 622 Main Street; (203) 438-8465.

ROXBURY

PARKS, BEACHES, AND RECREATION AREAS

• **Mine Hill State Park Reserve** 🐾🐾 See **34** on page 74.
This may be undeveloped state park land, but it has extremely well-developed ruins of the former blast furnace that once occupied this site. A nature

trail just under a mile long and a 3.5-mile loop trail wind past many of the mines and ruins.

Dogs must be leashed, especially if they might get curious about the mine shafts.

From State Route 199, take State Route 67 north for two miles. Turn right onto Mine Hill Road. The dirt road has a parking area on the right. Open 8 A.M. to sunset. (860) 424-3200.

SALISBURY

PARKS, BEACHES, AND RECREATION AREAS

• Prospect Mountain/Housatonic River Trail 🐾🐾🐾🐾 🐕 See 35 on page 74.

This is not just a place to launch a canoe, it's also a place to have a picnic, visit a historic site, take a nature walk, and hike the Appalachian Trail. All of those activities are available to you on this stretch of the Housatonic River, courtesy of the local water utility company.

You will first pass through the Ames Iron Works Historic Site, a quarter-mile walk around kiosks that detail the history of this place. If you cross the road at the canoe launch, you can pick up the Appalachian Trail. Look for the white blazes and a sign reading "Footpath—No Bikes."

The Appalachian Trail runs two miles from the parking area to the summit of Prospect Mountain, which overlooks the valley. Don't stop here; the best view is from a spot called Rand's View. Continue on the trail another half mile until it intersects a blue-blazed trail. A sign points to the right for Rand's View, just a few feet farther down the Appalachian Trail. From this overlook, you can gaze north into New England and, on a clear day, you'll be able to see Mount Greylock 50 miles to the north.

Leashes are not required here.

From U.S. Route 7 in Canaan, take State Route 126 north for a quarter mile. Turn left onto Point of Rocks Road, then right onto Water Street and across the bridge into Salisbury. Make the immediate right onto Housatonic River Road for a half mile. Parking and the trailhead are on the right. Open 24 hours. (860) 346-2372.

• Appalachian Trail—Lions Head/Bald Peak 🐾🐾🐾 🐕 See 36 on page 74.

A ridge connects Bear Mountain and Lion's Head, and, while hikers pour onto Bear Mountain, the overlook at Lion's Head to the south has an equally good view with a shorter overall climb are far fewer visitors. We should warn you, however, that although this is one of the most beautiful spots along the Appalachian Trail, it is also one of the most difficult sections of the trail in the state of Connecticut. If you go all the way to Bald Peak, your round-trip will be 7.5 miles.

For hounds willing to risk a few tired paws for a fantastic view, take the white-blazed trail from the parking area, which will connect with the Appalachian Trail. Two miles in, you will see blue blazes marking the path to

Lion's Head. Along the way you'll have fine views and access to hills, meadows, wildflowers, and plenty of lovely forestland. Continue north a half mile to reach the Bald Peak Trail.

On the Appalachian Trail, dogs need to be under voice control but not necessarily leashed.

From U.S. Route 44, take State Route 41 north for one mile to the small parking area on the left. Open 24 hours. (860) 346-2372.

• **Mount Riga State Park Reserve** 🐾🐾🐾 See **37** on page 74.

The 276-acre Mount Riga State Park Preserve, in the northwest corner of Connecticut, is the best place to access Mount Frissell, the highest point in the Nutmeg State. The summit is actually in Massachusetts, but the ridge leading to the top is still the highest elevation in Connecticut. The path weaves through a wonderfully dense and wild forest offering panoramic views with a surprisingly moderate ascent.

From the parking area, you'll follow an old logging trail until it connects with the South Taconic Trail along the ridge. At the top, you will be 2,435 feet above sea level, and this is only one-tenth of the mountain's original size 445 million years ago. Along the way, the trails weaves in and out of New York, Massachusetts, and Connecticut, so keep an eye out for the century-old tri-state stone marker. You'll have to retrace your steps for the return trip to the parking area, so bank on a five-mile round-trip hike.

Dogs must be leashed.

From U.S. Route 44, take State Route 41 north for four miles. The park is on the right. Better access for the peak is from the U.S. Route 44/State Route 41 intersection. Take Factory Street/Mount Riga Road west six miles to a dam. Turn right onto Mount Washington Road. The parking area is on the left. Open 8 A.M. to sunset. (860) 424-3200.

RESTAURANTS

Harvest Bakery: Bring in the harvest—it's delicious. This bakery serves up soups and salads, as well as fresh-baked breads, cookies, and cakes. Outdoor picnic tables are available. Closed Mondays. 10 Academy Street; (860) 435-1302.

On the Run Coffee Shop: This yellow-and-blue Victorian house serves as java central for Lakeville. They advertise fine fast food to go, and they were not kidding. After agonizing over our many muffin choices, one bite made us wish we had gotten one of every flavor. They do breakfast and lunch here, starting as early as 5:30 A.M. You can share your goodies with your pup at the outdoor picnic tables in front. 4 Ethan Allen Street; (860) 435-2007.

Oscar's Ice Cream and Candy: After all the hiking options available in Salisbury, we needed a place to rest and take stock. And what better way than with a cone from Oscar's? They boast over 100 varieties of candy, too. 19 Main Street; (860) 435-8800.

PLACES TO STAY

Inn at Iron Masters: Size doesn't matter here but age does. Large dogs don't have to worry about a "small dogs only" rule, but young pups may be disappointed to find this inn only accepts dogs a year old or older. The rooms are motel style, with comfortable loungers in front of the TV set—just like at home. Rates range from $85 to $145, including breakfast. There are designated pet rooms, so you will need a reservation to guarantee a spot. 229 Main Street, Lakeville, CT 06039; (860) 435-9844; www.innatironmasters.com.

SHARON

PARKS, BEACHES, AND RECREATION AREAS

• Housatonic Meadows State Park/Housatonic State Forest
🐾🐾🐾 🐕 See **38** on page 74.

Take the Pine Knob Loop Trail for a lovely woodland walk along the Hatch Brook. You'll traverse water, hills, and an open valley, making this an extremely scenic and popular walk. The trail is flat and open, and, although you will climb a little, for the most part it is an easy and perfect walk for dogs of all sizes.

The 2.5-mile trail loops through the 451-acre state park and forest. From the parking lot at the Housatonic River, take the blue-blazed trail along the brook for about a mile until it intersects the Appalachian Trail. Climb another quarter mile to several rocky ledges and an overlook.

We can't say enough about the variety of terrain you'll see on this short walk. Mountain laurel, birch, maple, and hemlock trees, glacial outcroppings, gorgeous views, and a bubbling brook. Doggie heaven!

Dogs need to be leashed.

From State Route 4, take U.S. Route 7 north one mile into the park. The trail starts across the road from the park entrance. Open 8 A.M. to sunset. (860) 927-3238.

• Sharon Audubon Center 🐾🐾🐾 See **39** on page 74.

Usually, Audubon Centers have a "no pets" policy, so we applaud Sharon's Audubon Center for their experimental program. Leashed dogs are allowed on some of the 11 miles of trails on this 890-acre property. In order to keep our four-legged friends in good standing here, visitors need to be extra careful about following the rules.

Dogs are not allowed on all the trails. Check out the map board at the parking area to see your options, which are clearly marked. Our favorite choice is the Ford/Borland Trail, a three-mile loop that begins at the parking area.

Cross the wooden bridge over Herrick Brook and turn right onto the Deer Trail, which will lead you along Ford Pond and to Bog Meadow Pond. This walk takes you by stone walls, a rock dam, peaceful ponds, and open grasslands. From the pond you'll want to follow the Hazelnut Trail to finish your loop, or you may also wish to access the Lower Hal Borland Trail, the steepest and most challenging option. If you still feel the need to go on, the Appalachian Trail cuts through here and can be accessed about a half mile from the entrance on State Route 4.

Dogs must be on leash here. There is a $3 fee per person, and $1 per dog, unless you are an Audubon member, in which case your entrance is free.

From U.S. Route 7, take State Route 4 west for 5.5 miles to the entrance. Open dawn until dusk. (860) 364-0520.

SHELTON

PARKS, BEACHES, AND RECREATION AREAS

• **Indian Well State Park** 🐾🐾🐾 See **40** on page 74.

The trail system in this state park is comprised of short, scenic hikes though forests and meadows, including one to a waterfall, and the longer—and even more scenic—Paugussett Trail. This trail runs along the beautiful Housatonic River all the way to Stevenson Dam, then on to the town of Monroe. The first 3.5 miles are the most scenic and certainly the most pleasant for walking; when we hit the 100-foot-high ledge that required us to climb straight up, the dogs looked at us as if to ask, "Did we sign up for this?"

For a short walk to the scenic waterfalls, take the trail leading from the main parking area.

Leash rules are a little tricky here. Within the borders of the state park, dogs must be on leash. However, some of this trail runs over private lands, and so the Blue Trails network rules apply—dogs must be under voice control but not necessarily leashed.

From U.S. Route 8, take State Route 110 north for 2.3 miles. The park is on the right. Continue north about one mile farther for access to the Paggussett Trail. Open 8 A.M. to sunset. (203) 924-5907.

• **Riverview Park** 🐾🐾 See **41** on page 74.

This tiny park is a lovely jewel with a name that describes its stunning view of the Housatonic River. Just a hop, skip, and a jump from Indian Well State Park, this much smaller cousin is more laid-back and less crowded than its well-developed neighbor.

Dogs must be on leash.

From U.S. Route 8, take State Route 110 north one mile. The park is on the right.

Open dawn to dusk. (203) 925-8422.

PLACES TO STAY

Amerisuites: Chihuahuas only need apply; this hotel accepts pets that are 10 pounds or under. If you make the cut, rates range from $109 to $154 a night. 695 Bridgeport Avenue, Shelton, CT 06484; (203) 925-5900; www. amerisuites.com.

Ramada Hotel: This newly renovated Ramada welcomes you and your pup to its 155 rooms. Rates range from $69 per room to $155 for the suites. 780 Bridgeport Avenue, Shelton, CT 06484; (203) 929-1500, (888) 298-2054; www.ramada.com.

Residence Inn by Marriott: This is mainly an extended-stay hotel, and the rooms have small kitchenettes. At $20 per day, the pet fee is pretty steep. Room rates depend on length of stay but start at $115 per night. 10001 Bridgeport Avenue, Shelton, CT 06484; (203) 926-9000; www.marriott.com.

SOUTHBURY

PARKS, BEACHES, AND RECREATION AREAS

• Southbury Dog Park 🐾🐾🐾🐾 🐕 See 42 on page 74.

Southbury has set aside 12 acres on the Pomperaug River just for dogs, dogs, dogs. This off-leash area has about 1,000 feet of river frontage for swimming, and big grassy meadows for ball fetching and tail chasing. A small section of woodlands on privately owned property is available for walking, but hiking is not the draw here—losing the leash is!

From Main Street (U.S. Route 6), take Roxbury Street (State Route 67) north for a quarter mile to the river and the park. Open dawn to dusk. (203) 262-0633.

• Kettletown State Park 🐾🐾🐾 See 43 on page 74.

Manhattan was purchased from the Native Americans for a handful of beads, and this lovely 492 acres was purchased for a brass kettle. As usual, the natives got the short end of the deal, for this park offers some of the most varied and numerous woods trails of any state park in Connecticut.

The Pomperaug Trail, one of the Blue Trails, cuts through here and leads to Lake Zoar on the Housatonic River. If you take the Brook and Crest Connector Trails, you'll form a 3.5-mile loop entirely within the state park. Oxford Loop is an option that spurs off at the end of the Pomperaug Trail and takes you along the eastern shore of Lake Zoar, adding another 1.5 miles to your hike. The Stevenson Dam is found here as well.

The only drawback is that dogs have to stay on leash. On summer weekends there is a $5 in-state and $8 out-of-state fee.

From State Route 188 in Oxford, take Barry Road west for a mile. Turn right onto Good Hill Road for a mile, then right onto Maple Tree Hill Road for a half mile. Turn left onto Georges Hill Road into Southbury; the park entrance is on the left. Open 8 A.M. to sunset. (203) 264-5678.

• Southford Falls State Park 🐾🐾 See 44 on page 74.

This 120-acre park along the Eight Mile River is the former home of the Diamond Watch Company. And watch is exactly what we did—we watched the falls, the covered bridge, and the old gristmill. These hiking destinations got all our paws moving along the small trail system.

Dogs must be leashed.

The park is four miles southwest of Southbury on State Route 188. Open 8 A.M. to sunset. (203) 264-5169.

STAMFORD

PARKS, BEACHES, AND RECREATION AREAS

• Cove Island Park 🐾🐾 See 45 on page 74.

This park is mostly about water—the Long Island Sound, to be exact. For Stamford residents, it's open year-round, but the park is off-limits to nonresidents from June through August. What you'll find when you do visit is lots of grassy areas and perfect picnic spots overlooking the sound.

Locals concerned about Long Island Sound sponsor occasional clean-up days, and dogs are welcome if kept on leash. In fact, the last clean-up day resulted in a small mound of unclaimed tennis balls, to which happy canine helpers helped themselves. For more information, call (888) SAVE-LIS.

A parking permit must be purchased at Terry Conners Ice Rink.

From Boston Post Road, take Weed Avenue until it ends. The entrance is on the left. Open dawn to dusk. (203) 977-5217.

RESTAURANTS

Brasitas Restaurant: Ole! This place is not just for dogs south of the border, as our salsa dogs can attest. Take your pick of Latin specialties such as Camarones al Ajillo (shrimp tossed with fresh tomatoes, garlic, and chardon-nay)—and enjoy it all at the restaurant's outdoor tables. We washed it all down with tropical Latin fruit smoothies. 954 Main Street; (203) 323-3176.

Planet Pizza: Dig into a dish of pizza plus updated Italian specialties here. The outdoor tables are the perfect spot for dinner with your dalmatian. 920 Summer Street; (203) 357-1101.

Pat's Hubba Hubba: The dog tails start wagging just as soon as we pull up to this hot-pink, retro 50's–style diner in the middle of Stamford's downtown area. We get fries for the whole pack, and you can also order dogs (hot dogs, that is), burgers, and fried seafood dinners. 189 Bedford Street; (203) 359-1718.

PLACES TO STAY

Holiday Inn Select: This holel's 383 rooms are just waiting for you and your canine. A refundable pet deposit of $75 to $150 is required, so make sure your pooch is on his best behavior. Rates start at $205. 700 Main Street, Stamford, CT 06901; (203) 358-8400; www.holiday-inn.com.

STRATFORD

PARKS, BEACHES, AND RECREATION AREAS

• **Boothe Memorial Park and Museum** 😊 😊 See **46** on page 74.

This National Historic landmark makes an excellent backdrop for wedding photos, as we discovered on our last visit. We stumbled on a bridal party in full regalia. Rocky, thrilled with the prospect of hors d'oeuvres, nearly jumped into the limo with the bride, where he was about as welcome as a muddy dog in church.

After dragging him away from the fun, we discovered why so many brides make this the backdrop of choice. This 32-acre homestead has a single path that leads through a charming rose garden, clock tower, barn, picnic areas, and ice house.

Dogs must be leashed.

From the Merritt Parkway, take Exit 53 to State Route 110 south. Make an immediate left onto Main/Putney Street for a half mile to the entrance on the left. Open 7 A.M. to dusk. (203) 381-2046.

DIVERSIONS

An Affair to Remember: Dog Affair is hosted by New Leash On Life, a local group committed to placing homeless dogs into new adoptive homes. Since all our pooches came to us from previous homes, we heartily support this excellent cause. The day of fun and frolic includes games, adventures, and even a pet psychic. Held in early June at Boothe Memorial Park, there is a $5 admission fee for humans; your pup gets in free. For dates and details, call (203) 944-0171.

THOMASTON

PARKS, BEACHES, AND RECREATION AREAS

• **Northfield Brook Lake and Dam** 🐾🐾 See **47** on page 74.
The Army Corps of Engineers was busy in the mid-1960s—they built seven dams on the Naugatuck River to help prevent flooding of the river valley. It seems to have worked, since this 216-acre area is a flood-free zone for happy hikers and their dogs.

As you pull in past the stone gates that guard the entrance, slow down and look for the trailhead, which starts from this access road. The parking area is just a quarter mile ahead, so you'll want to walk back to pick up the 1.7-mile hiking trail that leads along the dam.

Dogs must be leashed and are not permitted on the beach.

From U.S. Route 6, take State Route 254 north for two miles. The entrance is on the right. Open from 8 A.M. to 8 P.M. (860) 283-5540.

TORRINGTON

PARKS, BEACHES, AND RECREATION AREAS

• **John A. Minetto State Park** 🐾🐾 See **48** on page 74.
This 678-acre state park, formerly known as Hall Meadow, is located on the site of the first house constructed in town. The house is long gone, but not the gentle rolling hills and quiet woods you and your dog will discover on a visit here.

We loved the well-marked hiking trails available here but so, apparently, do the geese and ducks. This park has several ponds just perfect for those feathered friends flying south for the winter—or those who are looking for the perfect summer home. We were lucky enough to spot a breeding pair and their young ones, although they spotted George and Inu first and headed for the water.

The Hall Meadow Dam, built by the U.S. Army Corps of Engineers, is also accessible from here. You can walk out onto the dam and then take the steps down to pick up the trail system.

Dogs must be leashed.

From State Route 4, take State Route 272 north for 5.5 miles. The entrance is on the right. Open 8 A.M. to sunset. (860) 283-5540.

• **Burr Pond State Park/Paugnut State Forest/Sunny Brook State Park Reserve** 🐾🐾🐾 See **49** on page 74.

"Keep close to nature's heart, and break clear way, once in a while, and climb a mountain or spend a day or week in the woods."

John Muir uttered those eloquent words more than a hundred years ago, and we couldn't agree more. In his honor, the 1,642-acre Paugnut State Forest named a trail for this explorer, naturalist, and writer who served several presidents in the arena of forest management and was a major force behind the establishment of the national park system.

Although the state forest can be accessed from the Sunny Brook State Park at one end and the Burr Pond State Park at the other, there is another entrance into the forest that we prefer since we are usually headed for the John Muir Trail, which is part of Connecticut's Blue Trail network. This trail, which can be accessed off Newfield Road, is the fastest way to reach the summit of Walnut Mountain, a four-mile trek from one state park to the other.

Burr Pond State Park is named for Milo Burr who built a rock dam here, creating the pond that bears his name and a source of power for a fledgling company called Borden. Borden used to make condensed milk here, but there is nothing condensed about this 426-acre park. Our favorite walk is circling the banks of 88-acre Burr Pond.

Sunny Brook State Park Reserve has several unmarked trails, but you should only explore if you really know where you're going.

Dogs must be leashed.

To get to Burr Pond State Park from U.S. Route 8, take Exit 46 to Pinewoods Road west for a quarter mile. Turn left onto Winstead Road for one mile, then turn right onto Burr Mountain Road for a half mile into the park. To get to the Sunny Brook and state forest entrances from State Route 4, take Main Street north for a mile. Turn left onto Newfield Road for two miles to Sunny Brook or for three miles to the state forest and the John Muir Trail. Open 8 A.M. to sunset. (860) 482-1817.

RESTAURANTS

Alfredo's Deli: Next to the tracks that pass through Torrington you will find Alfredo's Deli. The menu of pizza and sandwiches can be enjoyed at the outdoor tables in front of the deli, if you don't mind a little diesel with your deli. 168 Water Street; (860) 482-1888.

Central Lunch: Central Lunch dishes up Italian food just the way Beth's mama used to make it. Nothing fancy, mind you, just good old-fashioned cooking. 31 Hungerford Street; (860) 496-0297.

Rickie's Drive In: This would have been a blast from the past, one of those '50s-era drive-up restaurants, except that all the picnic tables were painted bright multicolors, reminding us we were in the new millennium. The menu features American favorites like burgers and dogs. 1150 East Main Street; (860) 749-3917.

TRUMBULL

Trumbull parks are lovely, but the people at the Parks and Recreation Department aren't so friendly. In fact they refused to give us any information about their parks and requested we not include any descriptions in this book. What we can tell you is this: Trumbull parks are for Trumbull residents only; cars need a resident parking sticker, and they do check. All parks require leashes and are open dawn to dusk. For residents, the parks with trails are Old Mine

Park, Indian Ledge Park, and Beach Memorial Park. If you would like directions or more information, you may call (203) 452-5060, but we suggest you keep on moving to friendlier parts.

DIVERSIONS

Concerts on the Green: On Tuesday evenings in July and August you can catch some catchy tunes in Trumbull. The fun begins at 7 P.M. every Tuesday on the Green in the center of Trumbull. Dogs are welcome as long as they don't try to sing harmony. For more information, call (203) 452-5060.

Dancing Dachshunds: The Trumbull Arts Festival kicks off the week after Labor Day each year and celebrates the arts, including music, dance, drama, and literature. Held on the Trumbull Green, it also celebrates the most delicious art of all—food! For more information, call (203) 452-5065.

RESTAURANTS

Trumbull Inside Scoop: This place beats the heat by dishing up some delicious ice cream. Oh, and they serve grilled food, too. 926 White Plains Road; (203) 459-4780.

WASHINGTON

PARKS, BEACHES, AND RECREATION AREAS

• Mount Tom State Park 🐾🐾 See **50** on page 74.

Mount Tom is one of the oldest parks in the Connecticut state park system and is named for the mountain contained within its boundaries. Climb the 1,325-foot summit on a simple and easy one-mile trail that ascends 500 feet to a stone tower. On top you'll enjoy 360-degree views of the rolling hills and valleys of western Connecticut.

This hike doesn't get a lot of traffic even though the mountain is 125 feet higher than its more famous Massachusetts counterpart. Clearly the better-known mountain to the north had a much better press agent.

As with all state parks, leashes are required. A $2.50-per-day use fee is charged during the summer.

From State Route 47, take U.S. Route 202 east for five miles. The park is on the right. Open 8 A.M. to sunset. (860) 424-3200.

WATERBURY

PARKS, BEACHES, AND RECREATION AREAS

• Bucks Hill Park 🐾 See **51** on page 74.

This park, on the edge of Waterbury, looks to all the world like a suburban recreation area. Head back behind the ball fields, however, and the view changes. Woods and wetlands fan out from here with a small network of trails. It would be hard to walk for more than a mile or two in the woods without retracing your steps, but it will do when Spot needs some green space.

Dogs must be on leash.

The park is on Montoe Road off of North Main Street. Open 7 A.M. to 8 P.M. (203) 574-6793.

- **Lewis Fulton Park** 🐾🐾 See **52** on page 74.

Mr. and Mrs. William Fulton donated this land to the city in the 1920s in honor of their son Lewis. The park was designed in 1924 by the firm of Frederick Law Olmstead and is listed on the National Register of Historic Places. The paved paths are made for meandering, so wander and enjoy the greenhouse, romantic groves, and unusual plants and shrubs.

Dogs must be leashed.

The park is on Cooke Street off Main Street in downtown Waterbury. Open dawn to dusk. (203) 574-6793.

- **Library Park** 🐾🐾 See **53** on page 74.

This park was designed by Frederick Law Olmstead II, the son of the famous landscape architect. Although it's no Central Park—it's just a slip of green in the middle of the city—the park is pretty and big enough for a stroll. The land was the site of an early burial ground before being donated for park use. If you walk around the lower wall of the park, you can still see the grave markers.

Dogs must be on leash.

This park is on the corner of Grand and Meadow Streets in downtown Waterbury. Open dawn to dusk. (203) 574-6793.

RESTAURANTS

Cross Roads Cantina: The best hamburgers in Waterbury, say the local pundits. The closed-in outdoor deck means your pooch can join you as long as he stays outside of the rail. 210 Meadow Street; (203) 573-9458.

PLACES TO STAY

Courtyard by Marriott: You are close to the action here in this 206-room, suite-style hotel. Rates range from $99 to $125, with no additional pet fee. 63 Grand Street, Waterbury, CT 06702; (203) 596-1000; www.marriott.com.

House on the Hill Bed-and-Breakfast: This newly renovated 1880s Victorian mansion has five rooms, all with modern amenities added in 1998. Dogs are welcome but not smokers. Rates range from $100 to $150, including a full breakfast. 92 Woodlawn Terrace, Waterbury, CT 06710; (203) 757-9901.

Sheraton Hotel: Small dogs are welcome here in the heart of Waterbury. Rates range from $99 to $129 per night. 3590 East Main Street, Waterbury, CT 06795; (888) 625-5144; www.sheraton.com.

WATERTOWN

PARKS, BEACHES, AND RECREATION AREAS

- **Black Rock State Park/Mattatuck State Forest** 🐾🐾🐾 See **54** on page 74.

In this park you'll find a "cave" named for a guy called Old Leatherman, who wandered for 31 years in leather clothes, supposedly as a self-inflicted punishment for a failed business and broken engagement. Like clockwork, he showed up in the same place at the same time every 34 days for the entire 31 years, staying in the cave here when passing through Watertown. Boy, talk about being tough on yourself!

You can reach this cavelike jumble of large boulders from the parking area by hiking a two-mile section of the blue-blazed Mattatuck Trail. You'll walk along rolling countryside before connecting to a red spur trail leading to Crane Lookout, a cliff that stands 800 feet above the rocky caves and overlooks the valley below. In fact, Leatherman's Cave was formed from the boulders that fell from the cliff above.

From the lookout, backtrack slightly and return to the blue-blazed trail down to the caves.

Dogs must be leashed.

From U.S. Route 8, take U.S. Route 6 west for a mile into the park. Open 8 A.M. to sunset. Daily fee. (860) 677-1819.

PLACES TO STAY

Addington's B&B: This 1840 former dairy farm is now a comfortable inn that allows pets "within limits." This means with prior approval and as long as there are no other dogs staying there on your visit. Rates range from $95 to $125. 1002 Middlebury Road, Watertown, CT 06795; (860) 274-2647; www.inweb.com.

WESTPORT

PARKS, BEACHES, AND RECREATION AREAS

• Winslow Park 🐾🐾🐾🐾 🐕 See **55** on page 74.

If the dogs could create their own park, this place would be it. Over 75 percent of the park is off leash, and the rolling hills, streams, poop bag dispensers, and park benches make this park inviting for everyone. Local owners have even supplied the park with a communal water bowl to refresh parched pooches. With a place this fabulous, you know the local dogs flock here, so a drop-in doggie play group always seems to be in full swing.

The off-leash area is in the back of the park, behind the split log fence. You must keep your dog leashed until you get to the leash-free zone. Behind the fence is acre after acre of open fields, wooded trails, and a beckoning stream.

The park is at the intersection of Compo Beach Road (State Route 136) and U.S. Route 1. Open dawn to dusk. (860) 454-5188.

RESTAURANTS

The Chefs Table: After tasting this chef's food, you will want to beg at his table. This place does gourmet everything, with homemade soups and good-for-you meals such as fat-free turkey burritos. Take out and head for the back patio seating, where your dog can join you. 42 Church Street; (203) 226-3663.

Woodies Roadhouse: Formerly Swanky Franks (not to be confused with its sister store in Norwalk, although the ownership is still the same), Woodies offers a smorgasbord of choices for breakfast, lunch, and dinner. If ribs are your dog's delight, you'll want to make this a must-stop on your way into your pup's good graces. They make a mean hot dog, too, and the new breakfast menu makes this an all-purpose road stop. Picnic tables in the summer months mean your dog can sit by your side as you sup and slurp. 1050 East Post Road; (203) 226-5355.

Tacos or What: This yummy Mexican take-out place has the one thing all burrito-loving hounds look for: an outdoor table to get under and catch everything that drops. So take out your tacos, tamales, and quesadillas and make your pooch a happy hound. 1550 Post Road; (203) 254-1725.

WILTON

PARKS, BEACHES, AND RECREATION AREAS

•**Woodcook Nature Center** 🐾 🐾 🐾 See 56 on page 74.

About half of this 146-acre preserve is wetlands, created by dams in the Spectacle Creek Watershed. The other half is scenic woodlands and boulder-strewn trails—all perfect for an afternoon walk with your favorite four-legged pal.

There are four color-coded trails here, all named in honor of former directors of the Nature Center. Your best bet is to start with the yellow trail which takes you along the outer edges of the preserve, passing through forests and overlooks—although the overgrown shrubs tend to obscure the view. The wetlands are best seen from the swamp boardwalk.

A map board will point you in the right direction, and information is available at the center itself.

This is a not-for-profit center and donations are welcome, but there is no fee to access the trails.

From the intersection of State Routes 116 and 102, take State Route 102 west for 2.5 miles. Take a left onto Nod Road at the major fork in Route 102. Continue for 1.5 miles south until you see signs on the right. Turn right onto Deer Run Road and follow it for approximately one mile to the entrance of the Nature Center on the left. Go through the gates and proceed to the small parking area. Open from dawn until dusk. (203) 762-7280.

NATURE WALKS AND URBAN HIKES

Weir Hill Farm National Historic Site: J. Alden Weir was an American Impressionist painter who had a summer home and studio here in Wilton. The immaculately preserved buildings and grounds are part of the Connecticut Impressionist Art Trail. No dogs are allowed in the buildings, but the grounds are open to visitors (canine and otherwise) year-round.

Periodic guided walking tours of the estate are offered. Leashes are required. The site is located on Old Branchville Road off State Route 102. Grounds are open dawn until dusk. (203) 834-1896, or Weir Farm Trust at (203) 761-9945.

RESTAURANTS

The Inside Scoop: We have the inside scoop on the Inside Scoop. Hot dogs and hamburgers are on the menu, as well as some salads for hounds hankering for something healthful. But the best part of all are the buckets of ice-cream flavors. Convenient picnic tables surround this roadside eatery. 951 Danbury Road; (203) 544-9677.

DIVERSIONS

Wilton Courtyard Concerts: The Wilton Library holds a free summer concert series, where live bands do their level best to entertain the lunch crowd. No one shushes you here, despite the abundance of librarians in attendance. Bring your lunch and your dog to the steps of the courtyard at 137 Old Ridgefield Road. (203) 762-3950.

WOODBURY

RESTAURANTS

The Skinny Dog Gifts and Café: There's no way a dog could stay skinny on the fare they dish up here—gourmet soups, sandwiches, cappuccinos, lattes, and Italian ices. The dogs would have sampled the whole menu if we had let them. You will have to get your order to go, but they are awfully nice about special requests for any waiting pooches. 428 Main Street South; (203) 266-4775.

RHODE ISLAND

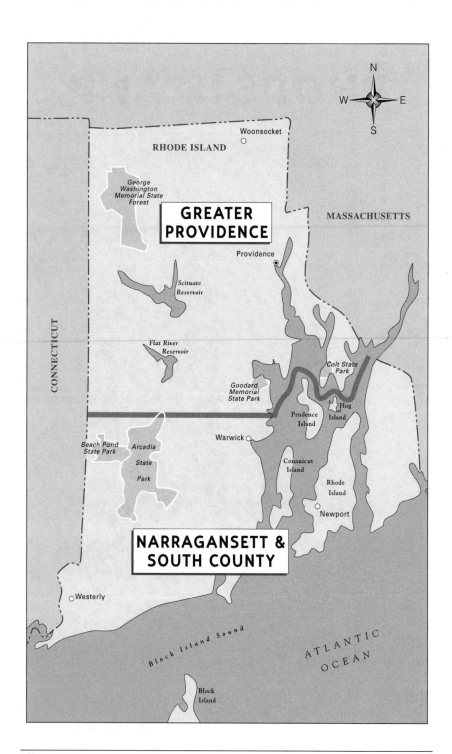

RHODE ISLAND

Rhode Island is the smallest state in the union but the most densely populated. Because of its size, many New Englanders consider it somewhat of a pesky little brother to the other larger states. That is until summer time, when all of New England flocks to the Ocean State's impressive seacoast. The state is only 1,200 square miles but enjoys over 400 miles of sandy coastline on the Atlantic Ocean and Narragansett Bay.

If you were wondering about the name, it goes back to the explorer Giovanni da Verrazano who first saw "Aquidneck," as the Narragansetts called the area, and thought it looked like the Greek isle of Rhodes—hence Rhode Island. After that, not much changed until founder Roger Williams came here in 1636. Fleeing Puritan persecution in Massachusetts, he established Rhode Island as a model of religious tolerance and, as the state's motto claims, a place of "Hope."

North South Trail: This trail runs north and south (where else?) for the entire length of Rhode Island, a little over 72 miles from the Massachusetts border to Block Island Sound. Actually, the route is still being completed, but you can hike many portions through some of the best woods in the Ocean State. The trail winds through eight western towns, with its northern terminus in Buck Hill Management Area in Burrillville and its southern end in Charlestown at Ninigret Conservation Area at the Atlantic Ocean. The northern part of the trail connects to Massachusetts's Midstate Trail in Douglas, Massachusetts, continuing north to the New Hampshire border. For information, contact the North South Trail Council at (401) 781-8117.

State Parks and Wildlife Management Areas: Unlike other New England states, some of the best parks in the Ocean State are located in Wildlife Management Areas. The good news is that dogs are allowed off leash from August 15 to March 1st. The bad news is that hunting is permitted from October through February; all visitors, including pets, are required to wear 200 square inches of fluorescent orange (that's a hat or vest) during this time. Frankly, we don't think you should visit during hunting season. But, if you're determined, make sure you're visible and don't look anything like a deer.

The state parks are not as dog friendly. The rules state that pets are welcome, but they must be leashed. The state park beaches are typically off-limits to dogs. For information, contact the Rhode Island Division of Parks and Recreation at (401) 277-2632.

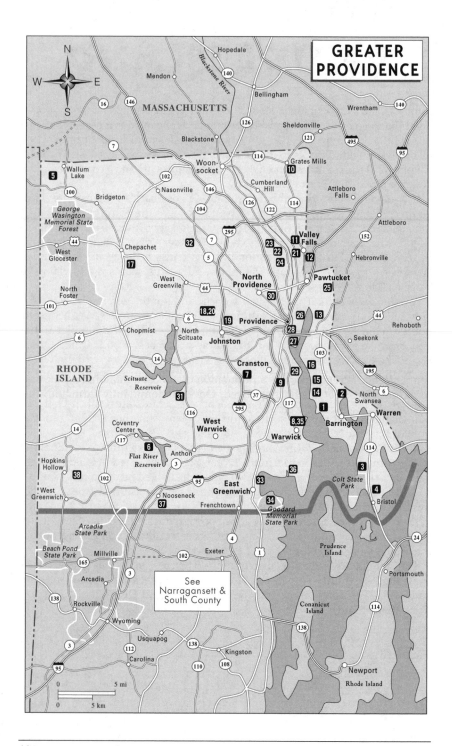

GREATER PROVIDENCE

4
GREATER PROVIDENCE

The towns around the state's capital combine rural simplicity with urban sophistication. Providence has a population of almost a million, and the surrounding areas are equally populated. Once predominantly farmland, this area has also been closely involved with the sea; during the Revolution it was a privateering port and one of the first colonies to balk against Britain's ban on shipping.

Today the farmland has turned to parks, and the privateering has turned into commercialism. Both can be enjoyed by you and your dog—one for its recreation, the other for its entertainment.

Blackstone River Valley National Heritage Corridor: In 1986, the Blackstone River Valley National Heritage Corridor was created by the National Park Service to oversee the preservation of the birthplace of the American Industrial Revolution. It was in this corridor, from Providence, Rhode Island, to Worcester, Massachusetts, that the United States began to change from a nation of farmers to an industrial power. Today, there are a number of state and town parks, bike paths, and historical mill sites jointly dedicated to this important era in American history. The National Park Service does not own any land in the corridor but helps the states and towns coordinate the management of individual properties. For additional information, maps, and a list of parks, visit or call the Blackstone Valley Visitor's Centers in Pawtucket at 175 Main Street, (401) 724-2200; or in Woonsocket at 1 Depot Square, (401) 762-0250).

East Bay Bike Path: Rhode Island is one of the leading states when it comes to building bike paths. One of the best examples, the East Bay Bike Path, runs along the Naragansett Bay from Providence at India Point Park to Independence Park in Bristol, for a distance of 15 miles through two counties.

Of course, you and your dog don't have to be cycling fanatics to enjoy the path. You can walk along the many hills, coves, and marshes of the bay as the path passes through a number of picturesque parks and bayside villages. Dogs must be on leash. Open sunrise to sunset. For more information, call the Rhode Island Intermodal Department at (401) 222-4203.

BARRINGTON

PARKS, BEACHES, AND RECREATION AREAS

• Haines Memorial State Park 🐾🐾 See ❶ on page 110.

These 102 acres along the Bristol County line and Narragansett Bay were donated to the public in 1911 in honor of Dr. George Haines. Today the state park is a popular destination for ballplayers, picnickers, and boaters who come here to use the boat ramp, playgrounds, and picnic areas. The park also has a few acres of open fields, woods, and short trails that make it a respectable doggie destination.

Dogs need to be on leash on all state property.

From State Route 103, take Washington Road for a quarter mile. The park is on the right. Plenty of parking is available. Open from sunrise to sunset. (401) 253-7482.

• Osamequin Nature Trails and Bird Sanctuary 🐾🐾🐾 See ❷ on page 110.

The three miles of walking trails through the wetlands of the Hundred Acre Cove is one of the most popular hiking areas this side of the Narragansett Bay. The park has four intertwining paths. Each trail is under a mile long and follows a dry route through meadows, lowland shrubs, and scattered patches of pine forests. A map display at the park entrance will help get you started. Dogs must be leashed.

From the intersection of State Routes 103 and 114, take State Route 114 north for three-quarters of a mile. The park and parking are on the right. Open dawn to dusk. (401) 247-1925.

BRISTOL

PARKS, BEACHES, AND RECREATION AREAS

• Colt State Park 🐾🐾🐾 See ❸ on page 110.

This beautiful park features 464 acres of spacious, manicured lawns and gardens surrounded by the sparkling, airy waters of the Narragansett Bay. It was previously owned by Colonel Samuel Pomeroy Colt, nephew of Samuel Colt who invented the Colt revolver.

Your dog may like to know that most water dogs head to the far, rocky end, called North Point, for a dip. Mill Gut Inlet is another favorite spot, or you can wander through the many fruit trees and flowering gardens remaining from the park's farming days. The East Bay Bike Path passes by the park entrance, and over 400 picnic tables are scattered throughout the property.

Dogs need to be leashed on all state property. Summer campsites are also available.

From State Route 114, take Asylum Road west for a half mile into the park. Plenty of parking is available at numerous points within the park. Open from sunrise to sunset. (401) 253-7482.

•Independence Park 🐾🐾🐾 See ◪ on page 110.

You've probably noticed that we mention the East Bay Bike Path often, but no reference is as important as this one: Independence Park is where it all begins. From here the path heads north to Providence following the eastern shore of Narragansett Bay.

Independence Park allows year-round ocean access for your pet. Granted, it doesn't compare to Maui (much of it is rocky, and you'll have to contend with fishermen and bay cruisers using the boat ramp), but the water is cool and clear, and your dog can get to it. You'll also find a well-maintained lawn and plenty of park benches here for kicking back and enjoying the waterfront view.

From State Route 114, take Thames Street south for one-tenth of a mile. The park and parking is on the right. Open sunrise to sunset. (401) 253-7482.

NATURE HIKES AND URBAN WALKS

Coggeshall Farm Museum: On your next dog walk, take a step back in time to the 1790s. Coggeshall Farm is a working farm and museum dating back to the 18th century where you and your well-behaved dog can walk through acres of rustling corn and pastures plowed by oxen. Or stop by the blacksmith shop or barn to see the everyday tasks that kept a farm going 200 years ago.

Throughout the year, the museum hosts special events of yesteryear. Our favorites are the October Pumpkin and Corn Sale (the authentic cider really has a kick to it) and the May sheep shearing (somehow Inu is always a little bit better behaved after we point out what happens to "bad pets"). Call the museum for a complete schedule of events (see number below).

Dogs need to be leashed and under control around the farm animals. There is a $1 admission charge.

From State Route 114, take Poppasquash Road east for 1.25 miles. Turn right onto Colt Road into the park. Open 10 A.M. to 5 P.M. October through February and to 6 P.M. March through September. (401) 253-9062.

RESTAURANTS

Café LaFrance: We're sadly accustomed to bumping into "No Dogs Allowed" signs at parks throughout New England, but we were surprised to hear that dogs may soon not be allowed on the sidewalks of Bristol. Delicious coffee, soups, and sandwiches right in downtown make Café LaFrance the most popular sidewalk café in town, especially with dog owners. And apparently the number of dogs left unattended or sitting with their owners on the busy sidewalk is a town concern. At press time, town officials and Café LaFrance were discussing the issue. In the mean time, the coffee is still flowing. 483 Hope Street; (401) 253-0360.

Quito's Restaurant: Spend any time on Narragansett Bay and you quickly get a hankering for seafood. When that happens, it's time to head for Quito's and the best seafood takeout on the waterfront. Clam chowder, fish sandwiches, lobster rolls, and calamari are the menu highlights. 411 Thames Street; (401) 253-4500.

PLACES TO STAY

Reynolds House Inn: This 17th-century National Historic Landmark offers six quaint rooms in a traditional bed-and-breakfast setting. All have private baths and most welcome your pet. Rooms range from $90 to $165 per night; full breakfast is included. 956 Hope Street, Bristol, RI 02809; (800) 754-0230, (401) 754-0230.

FESTIVALS

Patriotic Pup: There is no better way to celebrate the Fourth of July than with a parade, and Bristol should know; they've been doing it since 1785, making this the oldest Independence Day parade in the country. The parade forms at Chestnut and Hope Streets and begins at 10:30 A.M. Patriotic exercises start at 8:30 A.M. For more information, call (401) 253-0445.

DIVERSIONS

Airdales A'Sail: How about a morning or afternoon of island hopping? Climb aboard the Prudence Ferry, mate, for a trip out to Prudence Island or Hog Island. By far the best way to experience the islands and the majestic Narragansett Bay, a one-hour round-trip to Prudence Island and a half-hour excursion to Hog Island ar both offered.

Sea dogs need to be leashed and under control. The ferry runs daily from the Church Street Wharf, and a one-way ticket is under $3. For more details and latest departure dates and times, contact the Prudence Ferry at (401) 253-9808.

Animal Angel: We all know your pet is an angel, but you just may want to make sure things are in order by coming to the Blessing of the Animals at Coggeshall Farm. The ceremony, normally held in early August, is for the farm museum's animals and any visiting pets. A donation to the museum is requested. For exact date and more details, call Coggeshall Farm at (401) 253-9062.

Common Canines in Concert: Make a "concerted" effort to join the fun at the Bristol Common for the summer concert series. Held on Thursday evenings at 7 P.M. from July to early September, performances range from jazz to classical to pop to "we're not sure what's going to happen." Call (401) 253-7000 or (401) 253-8106 for appearance schedule.

BURRILLVILLE

PARKS, BEACHES, AND RECREATION AREAS

• **Buck Hill Management Area** 🐾🐾🐾 🐕 See **5** on page 110.

What better way to corner off the state than with 2,049 acres of pristine woodlands? This remote area, managed by the Rhode Island Department of Environmental Management, abounds with forests, meadows, wetlands, and, if you can believe it, hills.

Buck Hill, Badger Mountain, and Bensen Mountain will take you to the highest point in the state accessible to the public. (The state's official high point, Jerimoth Hill at 812 feet, is on private land and is off-limits to the public.) The hiking routes are primarily on the park's forest roads and cover a good portion of the park. There are also a number of small ponds and a few undeveloped footpaths to explore.

The Management Area is also home to one of the few completed portions of the North South Trail (see page 109). The three miles of hiking trail here make up the northern terminus of the in-progress, border-to-sea state path.

Dogs need to be on a leash from April 1 to August 15, and under voice control the rest of the year.

To get to the main entrance from U.S. Route 100, take Buck Hill Road west for 1.25 miles. The park entrance, a dirt road, is on the right. A parking area and trailhead are a quarter mile in. Open 5 A.M. to a half hour after sunset. (401) 789-3094.

RESTAURANTS

Sharon's Country Kitchen and Creamery: Whether you are looking for a pre- or post-hiking meal (or Rocky's favorite, a mid-couch snooze snack), Sharon cooks up just what you need. Order appetizing fish-and-chips, burgers, chowder, salads, and ice cream from the take-out windows and enjoy your meal at the picnic tables. South Main (U.S. Route 100); (401) 568-6998.

PLACES TO STAY

Buck Hill Family Campground: This campground, with 98 sites for tents and RVs, has its own pond, plus it's next door to the spacious Buck Hill Management Area. The campground is open May through October. Dogs must be kept on leash. Sites range from $19 to $29 per night. 464 Wakefield Road, Pascoag, RI 02859; (401) 568-0456.

COVENTRY

PARKS, BEACHES, AND RECREATION AREAS

• Coventry Greenway 🐾🐾🐾 See ⑥ on page 110.

We are happy to say that Rhode Island is adding bike paths faster than we can list them. One of the newest and biggest projects is the East Coast Greenway, an impressive route that will someday go from Florida to Maine. A 55-mile section of the trail is planned for Rhode Island, with the southern portion running from the Connecticut border through Coventry along an old railroad bed.

As of this writing, the entire Coventry Greenway section is open, but not completed. A paved portion runs along a three-mile stretch from the West Warwick border to the Flat River Reservoir. West of the reservoir, the railroad-bed trail extends another five miles to the Connecticut border; this portion is not paved, which may actually be preferred by most dog walkers.

To get to the Coventry Recreation Community Center from State Route 116, take State Route 117 west for a half mile. The center is on the right. Parking is available. Open dawn to dusk. (401) 822-9107.

RESTAURANTS

Deciantis Ice Cream: Ice cream is irresistible any time, any place, but when it's available right along the Conventry Greenway, there is no stopping us. And, if you follow Inu's creed, a step or two on a bike path qualifies as enough exercise to justify an extra scoop. Plenty of outdoor tables are available, and, since Deciantis is also a market, drinks and other simple snacks are available before or after your walk. 1373 Main Street (State Route 117); (401) 823-9160.

CRANSTON
PARKS, BEACHES, AND RECREATION AREAS

• **Meshanticut State Park** 🐾🐾 See **7** on page 110.

This park will make you loopy. The entire state park is the duck-dominated lake and Meshanticut Drive, a paved roadway, that circles it. So the only thing to do here is join the countless number of local walkers who make the half-mile loop around Meshanticut Lake. On any given day, you are sure to find numerous walkers, many with dogs, doing laps and trying to keep count of them.

Dogs must be on leash.

From the intersection of State Routes 5 (Atwood Avenue) and 12 (Phenix Avenue), take State Route 5 south for a third of a mile. Turn right onto Cranston Street for a half mile then right onto Dean Street into the park. Open sunrise to sunset. (401) 277-2632.

• **Stillhouse Cove Park** 🐾🐾 See **8** on page 110.

Location, location, location. This is a very small, grassy piece of parkland, but waterfront property is worth its weight in gold to any canine longing for a swim. The lawns are well maintained, the water looks refreshing, and the cove is home to two yacht clubs, so harbor views are picturesque. Dogs must be on leash.

From U.S. Route 1A, take Narragansett Boulevard south for a half mile. The park is on the left. Limited street parking is available. Open 24 hours a day. (401) 461-1000.

• **Washington Secondary Bicycle Path** 🐾🐾 See **9** on page 110.

This section of the state's extensive bike path system is a five-mile, rails-to-trails route from the West Warwick border to the village of Knightsville near the Providence border. A wide, paved path, you'll find yourself sharing it with cyclists, joggers, roller bladers, and other dog walkers.

From State Route 37, take Exit 3 to Pontiac Street. The trail is accessible at points north or south off Pontiac Street. For more information, call the Rhode Island Intermodal Department at (401) 222-4203.

PLACES TO STAY

Days Inn: This standard hotel has 60 rooms and is conveniently located off Interstate 95 for quick trips to Providence. Room rates range from $79 to $99 with an additional $25 refundable deposit required for Rover. 101 New London Avenue, Cranston, RI 02920; (401) 942-4200.

CUMBERLAND
PARKS, BEACHES, AND RECREATION AREAS

• **Diamond Hill State Park** 🐾🐾 See **10** on page 110.

We won't say the best thing about this park is the ice-cream shop across the street, but. . . we're thinking it just might be.

Diamond Hill State Park serves the local residents well enough as a picnic area, amphitheater, and home of the town ball fields, but it lacks much appeal for the dogs of Cumberland. The park has one litter-strewn (the day that we visited) trail that leads up Diamond Hill. The view's good, but this park is no diamond in the "ruff." Dogs must be leashed.

From Interstate 295, take Exit 11 to Diamond Hill Road (State Route 114) north for about three miles. The park entrance and plenty of parking are on the right. Open dawn to dusk. (401) 728-2400.

• The Monastery 🐾🐾🐾 See **11** on page 110.

These grounds are the local dog hangout even though dogs have to be on leash and the property is not very big. In fact the 1.5-mile Monastery Trail just about covers the entire perimeter of this Trappist enclave, now owned by the town. The path works its way through woods, fields, some pavement, and over a footbridge. For a completely paved route, try the Sri Chinmoy Peace Mile. It follows the loop road through the grounds.

From Interstate 295, take Exit 11 to Diamond Hill Road (State Route 114) south for a little over a mile. The entrance and parking are on the right at 1464 Diamond Hill Road. Open dawn to dusk. (401) 728-2400.

• Valley Falls Heritage Park 🐾🐾 See **12** on page 110.

This park, part of the Blackstone River Valley National Corridor, is a former mill site. Most of the structures, built between 1813 and 1934, are long gone. Today, there are great views of the river and falls, a picnic area, and one of the most elaborate spiraling walkways you can find. There are limited grassy areas, and dogs need to be on leash.

From the intersection of Broad and Mill Streets, take Mill Street east for a quarter mile. The park and a parking lot are on the right. Open dawn to dusk. (401) 728-2400.

RESTAURANTS

Ice Cream Machine: It takes a machine to satisfy the summer crowds that gather at Ice Cream Machine for shakes, cones, and splits. A couple of picnic tables are available out front, but most people take their tasty delights over to Diamond Hill State Park (across the street) to indulge. Open April to October. 4288 Diamond Hill Road; (401) 333-5053.

EAST PROVIDENCE

PARKS, BEACHES, AND RECREATION AREAS

• Bold Point Park 🐾🐾 See **13** on page 110.

This park is only two acres in size, but its location on Narragansett Bay makes it feels much roomier. Most of the park is comprised of an open lawn, seawall, and benches. Your dog can access the water if he or she desires, but you are better off enjoying the view of the Providence Harbor and waterfront.

Keep an eye out for boat launchers and fishermen who share the park with you. Dogs are allowed on leash only.

From Veterans Memorial Drive, take Warren Avenue west. Turn left onto Pier Road into the park. Parking is available. Open dawn to 9 P.M. (401) 435-7756.

•Carousel Park 🐾🐾 See **14** on page 110.

This park may not have the fun and excitement it did back in the 1890s when it was the Crescent Amusement Park, a popular summer destination for the people of Providence, but at least it is now open to dogs.

The amusement park is long gone (the Looff Carousel, built about 1895, still remains). Replacing it is an open public space that's still a popular destination for many. Around the carousel are trails, landscaped lawns, and promenades.

Dogs must be on leash. The carousel only runs during the summer, Wednesday through Sunday.

From State Route 103, take Crescent View Avenue west for three-quarters of a mile. The park is on the left. Plenty of parking is available. Open dawn to 9 P.M. (401) 435-7756.

•Sabin Point Park 🐾🐾 See **15** on page 110.

What this park lacks in size is offset by what it offers in the way of views and cool breezes. Jutting out into Narragansett Bay at the mouth of the Providence Harbor, the park is no more than five acres, but it attracts many visitors on any given weekend.

The park offers a boat launch, pier, playground, picnic tables, two small beaches, open lawns, and a few shade trees. A dog can certainly find his way into the water here—just beware of the fishermen's lines. Dogs are allowed on leash only.

From State Route 103, take Bullocks Point Avenue south for a mile. Turn right onto Shore Road for a half mile into the park. Parking is available. Open dawn to 9 P.M. (401) 435-7756.

•Squantum Woods State Park 🐾🐾 See **16** on page 110.

Don't expect to run into a park ranger here—or anyone else, for that matter. This is one of those small, out-of-the-way pieces of land that seems to make up a good portion of the Rhode Island State Park system. As you park, you'll see a meadow for ball throwing. Beyond that, a trail runs through the woods for a half mile to the Providence Harbor and the East Bay Bike Path. Dogs must be on leash.

From Pawtucket Avenue (State Route 103), take Veterans Memorial Parkway north for a half mile. The park is on your left. Open 9 A.M. to 9 P.M. (401) 277-2632.

RESTAURANTS

Dari Bee: Looking to cool off on a hot summer's day? Then this is the place to Bee. Dari Bee's soft serve, cones, and shakes really hit the spot. The menu also offers burgers and fries. And the outdoor seating along the East Bay Bike Path makes for some good dog watching. Bullocks Point Avenue; (401) 433-1931.

PLACES TO STAY

New Yorker Motor Lodge: This small motel offers comfortable rooms on the western side of Providence. Well-behaved dogs are welcome in most rooms. Rates range from $60 to $70. 400 Newport Avenue, East Providence, RI 02916; (401) 434-8000.

GLOCESTER

PARKS, BEACHES, AND RECREATION AREAS

• **Heritage Park** 🐾 🐾 🐾 See **17** on page 110.

Heritage Park is the perfect place for a quiet walk in the woods. Padding paws on pine needle–covered paths, babbling brooks, and scurrying chipmunks are the only sounds you'll hear.

The park is 127 acres of pine trees scattered amongst rocky outcroppings with a 1.5-mile loop trail. Off of the loop trail are a number of cutoffs to make your walk shorter or varied. Fitness stations mark your way, if you are feeling energetic and can keep your dog from trying to romp down the trail without you. A trail map is displayed at the parking lot to help you plan your route. Dogs need to be on leash.

From the intersection of U.S. Route 44 and State Route 102, take U.S. Route 44 east for two miles. Turn right onto Chestnut Oak Road for a quarter mile. The park and a parking lot are on the left. Open 6 A.M. to 9 P.M. (401) 568-6206.

PLACES TO STAY

Holiday Acres Campground: For a water dog, this really is a holiday; the campground is situated on a wooded lakefront. For those pups that don't want to get wet, you can rent canoes and paddleboats, too. Dogs must be leashed. Nightly rates for both tents and RVs are $19 to $29. 591 Snake Hill Road, North Scituate, RI 02857; (401) 934-0789.

RESTAURANTS

Brown & Hopkins Country Store: This colonial building, in the historic village of Chepachet, dates back to 1799, and they've been selling goods here since 1809. Some of the items for sale have changed since then, but not much else. Oh, and the coffee and pastries are pretty good, too. Get it to go. Closed Monday through Wednesday. 1179 Putnam Pike (U.S. Route 44); (401) 568-4830.

JOHNSTON

PARKS, BEACHES, AND RECREATION AREAS

• **Dame Farm** 🐾 🐾 🐾 See **18** on page 110.

Located on the far western side of Snake Den State Park, the Dame family farm, first started around 1780, is an actual working farm that is now part of the state park system. The farm is open to the public, and an interpretive trail leads you through the pastures, orchard, and family cemetery. Along the way you'll see displays of some of the farm equipment used in yesteryear. Remember, this is a working farm, and today's farm equipment has the right-of-way.

Dogs must be on leash.

From U.S. Route 44, take State Route 5 south for a half mile. Turn right onto Brown Avenue for three-quarters of a mile. The farm is on the left. Open dawn to dusk. (401) 222-2632 or (401) 949-3657.

• **Johnston Town Forest** 🐾 🐾 See **19** on page 110.
Even though you never get far enough away from the drone of Interstate 295 and the surrounding residences, this hike offers a pleasant two miles of walking trails. A single trail follows a series of small ponds through woods and fields. At the second pond, a good place for a dip on a hot summer day, the trail splits and leads into two separate short loops. The loop to the left circles a large field where you can break out the Frisbee.

Dogs need to be on leash and are not permitted in neighboring Johnston War Memorial Park (except for parking).

From the intersection of State Routes 5 and 6A, take State Route 6A east for a quarter mile. Turn right onto Memorial Avenue. The park and trailhead are on the left, and parking is on the right in Johnston War Memorial Park. Open dawn to 10:30 P.M. (401) 272-3460.

• **Snake Den State Park** 🐾 🐾 🐾 ◀● See **20** on page 110.
Don't let the name keep you from visiting this undeveloped state park. In fact, the snake den is what brings people and their dogs here. Forty feet deep, 50 feet wide, and 300 feet long, the canyon abruptly appears in an otherwise rolling, wooded landscape in central Rhode Island.

Beyond the snake den, via the main canyon trail, is an expansive forest, noteworthy in its own right. The unorganized trail system snakes its way north/south for about two miles through varied woods and rock-filled fields.

Dogs are required to be on leash in all state parks.

To get to the main parking area from U.S. Route 44, take State Route 5 south for a half mile. Turn right onto Brown Avenue for a quarter mile. Parking and the trailhead are at the roadside pullouts. Open sunrise to sunset. (401) 277-2632.

LINCOLN

PARKS, BEACHES, AND RECREATION AREAS

• **Blackstone River Bike Path/Blackstone River State Park** 🐾 🐾
See **21** on page 110.
A more descriptive name for this park might be the Blackstone Canal State Bike Path. It's not really a park in the general sense of the word and it's not really along the river. It's actually on the towpath of the canal. But no matter what you call it, you are sure to enjoy this new park, uh, path on the river, uh canal.

This newly opened paved path currently runs three miles from Lonsdale Village in the south to Quinville Village in the north. Along the way you'll find remnants of old red-bricked mills, dams, and bridges.

Dogs must be on leash.

From State Route 146, take Breakneck Road (State Route 123) east for a half mile onto Great Road (State Route 123). Continue onto Front Street (State Route 123) for a half mile; the park entrance and parking are on your left. Open dawn to dusk. (401) 334-7773.

• Chase Farms Park 🐾🐾🐾🐾 See **22** on page 110.

By now, with the kids still in school and the bills piling higher and higher, you realize you can't quite quit that unrewarding office job in the city. You're going to have to delay your dream of getting back to your roots, of getting back to "The Land." Yes, reality hurts, but you can still get a taste of what "The Land" would be like by herding up the dogs and heading on out to Chase Farms Park.

From the entrance, the dogs will be biting at the bit to get out into those fields of tall grass and rolling meadows, but, no, not you. You're going to need a minute to take it all in.

Hunkering on up to the fence post, you slip a blade of grass into your mouth and imagine endless fields of wheat and corn and yourself working "The Land," plowing and planting those fields, your fields. Your team of oxen is out in front of you working hard. It feels good to use your muscles, to get your hands dirty, to sweat.

And boy, are you sweating. The sun is just beating down on you and your rock-filled, dust-bowl land. You're breaking your back out here behind these stinking animals. "Where is the water cooler!" Then you remember. There is no water cooler. That's back at the office. And maybe that squeaky office chair and presentation due next week in a temperature-controlled environment isn't so bad after all.

No matter what your dreams are, rest assured you'll enjoy a visit to Chase Farms Park. It once really was a working farm belonging to the Chase family from 1867 to 1979, when they donated it to the state as conservation land.

The acres upon acres of open grasslands and rolling hills are now a wonderful place for dog walking. There are also about three miles of trails or former tractor paths. And, if that isn't enough, in the center of it all is a fantastic pond surrounded by shade trees to cool off under after your walk.

All leashed dogs are welcome.

From State Route 146, take Breakneck Road (State Route 123) east for a half mile onto Great Road (State Route 123). Continue on Great Road for almost half a mile. The park and a parking lot are on the left. Open dawn to 9 P.M. (401) 762-0250.

• Lime Rock Preserve 🐾🐾🐾 See **23** on page 110.

This isolated park is only a short drive from populated Providence, but a world away when you are looking to escape but don't have a lot of time to do it.

The park's name comes from the limestone found throughout the area. This attractive mineral fosters many unique and rare species of plants—some found nowhere else in Rhode Island. A springtime walk, when wildflowers abound, is a must. These mineral deposits are also attractive to commercial ventures. Luckily, the property is now owned, managed, and preserved by the Nature Conservancy, protecting it from further development.

The main hiking thoroughfare is an abandoned electric rail bed that once ran from Providence to Woosocket. To get to the pond in the middle of the property, follow the rail bed for about a half mile and take the first footpath on the right. The path circles the pond (about a mile around) and crosses a dam. The other paths loop through much of the wooded areas teeming with ferns and wildflowers.

Dogs need to be on leash. Note that the rail bed and trails in the lower elevations get flooded during wet weather.

From State Route 146, take State Route 123 west for 1.7 miles. Turn right onto Wilbur Road for a half mile to an unmarked, dirt road on the right. Look for a small billboard and parking area off Wilbur Road. Open dawn to dusk. (401) 331-7110.

• Lincoln Woods State Park 🐾 🐾 🐾 See **24** on page 110.

Lincoln Woods State Park is the biggest and most widely used park in northeast Rhode Island—and with good reason. It has 627 acres of woods, miles of bridle and hiking trails, and hidden coves on sparkling Olney Pond.

The park gets a lot of use during the summer season, but there is still plenty of room for an energetic dog. And in winter the crowds are gone and many of the park roads are closed to vehicle traffic, giving you and your pooch plenty of space. Depending on when you visit, you can use the access road, Table Rock Road, to reach Olney Pond or the trails along its edge. Pick anywhere on the northern shores, except at the designated beach area, and you'll find a great spot for you and your pal to enjoy the pristine waters.

Dogs must be leashed.

A word of caution: The park rangers point out that dog droppings are becoming a big problem, and they are considering not allowing dogs in the park. We can't say it enough. . . pick up after your dog.

From State Route 146, take Breakneck Road (State Route 123) east for a half mile onto Great Road (State Route 123). Continue on Great Road for almost half a mile. The park entrance is on the right at Manchester Print Works Road. Open sunrise to sunset. (401) 723-7892.

RESTAURANTS

Lincoln Creamery: Lincoln Creamery has all our favorite flavors. When you're out park hopping with a big group like ours, it's tough to find a lunch stop everyone agrees on. Lincoln Creamery makes it easy. It has all our favorite ice-cream flavors, plus burgers and fries. The outdoor seating has room for the whole pack. 270 Front Street; (401) 724-1050.

NORTH SMITHFIELD

NATURE HIKE AND URBAN WALKS

Slatersville Walking Tour: Slatersville played an important role in the American Industrial Revolution, and with one walk through the village you can see why. The walking tour is about a mile long and includes the town cemetery, several 17th-century mills, and historic government buildings. All are remnants of the first planned industrial village designed and built by John Slater, young brother to the same Samuel Slater who built the first mill in Pawtucket. It begins at the Slatersville Reservoir near the intersection of Main Street and State Route 5. For additional information and a map, visit the Blackstone Valley Visitor's Center in Pawtucket (corner of Main Street and Roosevelt Avenue), or call (401) 762-0440 or (401) 762-0250.

DIVERSIONS

At the Movies: Not only are movie mutts welcome at the Rustic Drive-in Theatre, but the theatre has three screens showing double-features on each. You are bound to get two paws up from your canine critic.

The drive-in is open from April through September. For showings and information, call (401) 769-7601. Louisquisset Pike (State Route 146).

PAWTUCKET

PARKS, BEACHES, AND RECREATION AREAS

• **Slater Memorial Park** 🐾🐾 See **25** on page 110.
When it comes to covering all the bases, Slater Memorial Park is the park of parks. If you can't find something to do here, you are in big trouble. The park has a zoo, carousel, ball fields, concession services, a duck pond, playgrounds, plenty of parking, and, more importantly for visiting dogs, a bike path, hiking trails, open fields, and woods to explore.

The park along the Ten Mile Long River has been a haven for local recreation since the city of Pawtucket purchased the Daggett Farm in 1894. The original Daggett House, built in 1685, is still there.

Dogs must be leashed and are not permitted on any of the ball fields.

From Interstate 95, take Exit 29 to State Route 15 and Armistice Boulevard east for 1.5 miles. The park is on your right after crossing State Route 1A. Plenty of parking is available. Open 6 A.M. to 9 P.M. in summer and 6 A.M. to 8 P.M. in winter. (401) 728-0500.

NATURE HIKES AND URBAN WALKS

Pawtucket Walking Tour: Okay, those of you who think that the only thing going on in this city is the Paw Sox can stop chuckling. Yes, Pawtucket does play second fiddle to its sister city, Providence, but those in the know will tell you it does have an important history of its own. The Pawtucket Walking Tour is a good way to find it. The tour circles around the Blackstone River on Main and Exchange Streets and includes City Hall and Slater Mill. It was here on the Blackstone River in 1793 that Samuel Slater built the first water-powered mill, and similar mills soon followed, starting the American Industrial Revolution throughout the Blackstone River Valley and the U.S.

For a map or more information, contact the Pawtucket Preservation Society at (401) 725-9581 or the Blackstone Valley Visitor Center at (401) 724-2200.

PROVIDENCE

This capital city is also the third largest urban center in New England. Located along Narragansett Bay, it was a major shipping port in the 18th and 19th centuries. Today it is the home of Brown University, historic College Hill, and an impressive canal system that runs through the city. It is currently going through an exciting revitalization of its waterfront, making this a great stop on any tour through New England.

PARKS, BEACHES, AND RECREATION AREAS

• Blackstone Park 🐾🐾 See **26** on page 110.

This hilly and undeveloped 40-acre park overlooks the Seekonk River. It's a simple neighborhood park with a few hiking paths and clearings. You'll find most visitors on the sidewalk of the outer eastern perimeter of the park along East River Drive. Park users are generally walkers and joggers enjoying the river views on one side and the park's woods and salt marshes on the other.

The park is located in the East Side neighborhood between East River Drive, South Angell Street, and Irving Avenue. Street parking is available on East Rive Drive. Open 7 A.M. to 9 P.M. (401) 785-9450.

• India Point Park 🐾🐾 See **27** on page 110.

Wide green lawns and panoramic views of the Providence Harbor make these 18 harborside acres an attractive stop for you and your pet. The park also attracts many cyclists, as it is the northernmost point along the East Bay Bike Path (see pages 111–112) which runs south to Bristol.

You can saunter the bike path or the walkway at the water's edge or kick back on the lawns and benches overlooking the busy harbor.

Dogs on leash, please.

From the Point Street Bridge, take South Water Street south for two blocks. Turn left onto India Street for three blocks. The park is on the right. Open 7 A.M. to 9 P.M. (401) 785-9450.

• Kennedy Plaza 🐾🐾 See **28** on page 110.

Normally a park this size doesn't get much attention, but, when it's located between City Hall and the State House you know it's going to be teeming with people, and that's just the kind of park Inu enjoys. That's not to say he doesn't like to chase a ball in a big field, but most days he prefers to join the crowds here at Kennedy Plaza, talking politics or watching the skaters at the new skating rink. Dogs need to be on leash.

The park is located in the Financial District between the Exchange Terrance, Exchange Street, Dorrance Street, and Kennedy Plaza. Limited street parking is available. Open 7 A.M. to 9 P.M. (401) 785-9450.

• Roger Williams Park 🐾🐾🐾 See **29** on page 110.

In most major cities there is a park that defines its identity—whether it is the Boston Common, New York's Central Park, or Roger Williams Park here in Providence. This beautifully designed 430 acres at the southern end of the city features well-maintained, spacious, and rolling lawns, monuments and statues, eight lakes, gravel walkways, bike paths, and countless species of trees and flowers. The roomiest points in the park are towards the south away from the zoo and other park amenities.

Dogs are allowed on leash only.

For local residents, there are numerous access points into the park loop roads from State Routes 12 and 117. From outside Providence, visitors can take Interstate 95 to Exit 16 and State Route 10 east for a half mile to the park. Ample parking is available throughout the park. Open 7 A.M. to 9 P.M. (401) 785-9450.

• Wanskuck Park 🐾 🐾 **See 30 on page 110.**

This small, locals-only park is a pleasant surprise in the diverse northwestern corner of Providence, but the lack of parking makes it a difficult stop for those who live outside the Wanskuck neighborhood. Parking is not permitted on the surrounding streets. So, if you can get here, 18 acres of lush lawns and shady trees await you. Dogs must be on leash.

From State Route 146, take Branch Avenue west. Make an immediate right onto Woodward Road for a half mile. Open 7 A.M. to 9 P.M. (401) 785-9450.

NATURE HIKES AND URBAN WALKS

Blackstone Boulevard: This former rail-line-turned-bikeway/footpath probably gets more traffic servicing bikers, joggers, and walkers than it ever did when trolleys transported passengers through the East Side. The paved path runs down the middle of tree- and mansion-lined Blackstone Boulevard from Hope Street in the north to Butler Avenue at its southern terminus. That's a total distance of a 1.5 miels, and you'll find plenty of dogs strutting their stuff up and down the stately boulevard.

The path is a public sidewalk and open 24 hours a day; (401) 785-9450.

Roger Williams National Memorial: This park, just across the Moshassuck River from the State House, commemorates founder Roger Williams who, in 1636, founded Rhode Island after suffering religious persecution in Massachusetts. This 4.5-acre park is believed to be part of the original settlement. Dogs are permitted on leash. Open 9 A.M. to 4:30 P.M.; (401) 521-7266.

Waterplace Park and River Walk: Waterplace Park and the accompanying River Walk located in the center of Providence is an impressive example of the city's on-going revitalization. Built on the convergence of the Moshassuck and Woonasquatucket Rivers, Providence is now using the rivers to restore the forgotten downtown, bringing in thousands of visitors and creating an inspired urban setting.

Waterplace Park features four acres centered around a tidal basin on the Woonasquatucket—a Native American phrase meaning "the river where the tide ends." Moshassuck, which joins the Woonasquatucket two blocks south of the basin to form the Providence River, means "river where the moose water." You probably won't see a moose along any of the rivers, but you will enjoy the river sights nonetheless. Around the basin are an amphitheater, restaurants, shops, and manicured lawns. Festivals, concerts, Waterfire (see DIVERSIONS—Smoke On The Water), paddleboats, and water taxis keep the park and rivers teeming with activities enjoyable for both you and your pet.

With at least two miles completed, it's from here that the River Walk follows both sides of the rivers on an ever-expanding walkway. The brick-and-cobblestone path is lined with massive granite blocks from nearby old Union Station, and numerous Venetian-style footbridges cross the waterways. Indeed, with or without a gondola ride, you might think you are in Venice. Open 7 A.M. to 10:30 P.M. (401) 621-1992.

RESTAURANTS

Geoffs On Thayer: Looking for some of the best sandwiches in town? Well, look no further. If you can think of a combination, Geoffs can make it with a wide assortment of breads, rolls, meats, cheeses, spreads, and toppings. And don't forget the pickle. The outdoor corner seating makes it easy to enjoy lunch and watch the action on Thayer Street. 178 Angell Street; (401) 751-9214.

Maxmillians Ice Cream Outlet: Located on trendy Thayer Street, Maximillians is Inu's favorite place to sample the local flavor. 241 Thayer Street; (401) 273-2736.

Starbucks Coffee: We try not to promote chain stores and restaurants, but, with the great outdoor seating at Wayland Square, we don't want you to miss out. Besides, George is kind of hooked on the whole latté scene anyway. 468 Angell Street; (401) 831-9481.

PLACES TO STAY

Caddy House: This three-room 1839 Victorian inn welcomes well-behaved dogs in their apartment suite. With a separate entrance and full kitchen facilities, you will enjoy the freedom to come and go at will. Make your reservations in advance as the dog-friendly room is often occupied. Rooms range from $80 to $90. 127 Power Street, Providence, RI, 02903; (401) 273-5398.

The Westin Providence: Although many Westin Hotels allow pets, don't let your dog expect the red carpet treatment here. In fact, most dogs are not permitted because there is a 10-pound limit. There is also a $100 deposit, only $50 of which is refundable, and dogs must enter and exit the hotel in a crate. One West Exchange Street, Providence, RI 02903; (401) 598-8000.

FESTIVALS

Partying Providence Pup: If your dog is anything like Inu, we'll be sure to see you at Providence's First Night celebration. Inu doesn't like to miss a party and this is a big one. Dogs are not permitted inside any of the venues, but the city is alive on New Year's Eve, and there are plenty of outdoor performances and exhibits. For more information, call (401) 521-1166.

DIVERSIONS

Fandango Fridays: Friday nights at the outdoor Waterfront Park Amphitheater are filled with a world of free music. Every summertime Friday night from 7 P.M. to 11 P.M., Riverwalk visitors are entertained with country, jazz, folk, blues, and an array of musical talent from around the world. For more information, call (401) 621-1992.

Four on the Floor: Get your walking shoes on for the Annual Pet/Pledge Walk held in September at Roger Williams Park. Walk 3.5 miles with other owners and their pets. Each walker is asked to raise $25 in pledges. The day also includes prizes, raffles, a canine obstacle course, animal-related vendors and displays, and pet contests. For more information and registration, contact the Providence Animal Rescue League at (401) 421-1399.

Woof in the Season: Join the Providence Animal Rescue League for the holidays. Paws For Christmas is an open-house weekend in December where pets and their owners are invited to get their picture taken with Santa (a $5 donation), decorate the "Hope Tree," and enjoy holiday treats. For more information, contact the Providence Animal Rescue League at (401) 421-1399.

Smoke on the Water: Quickly becoming one of the premier events in New England, Waterfire is not to be missed by man nor beast. On numerous, if unscheduled, evenings (mostly on Saturdays) from spring to autumn, Providence's extensive riverways are set aglow with 100 floating blazing cauldrons. But there is more glowing than the river. The entire city comes to life with the spectacle of water, fire, and music. (401) 272-3111.

Paddle Providence: George loves trotting along the River Walk, but where he really longs to be is on the water. Others must agree because the easy flowing waters of Woonasquatucket River are a popular downtown canoeing spot. And, since the city rents canoes and kayaks, you and your pet can join in, too. Of course, you'll feel like a simple hired hand when your dog kicks back in the middle of the boat and dangles his paws in the water.

Canoe and kayak rentals are available from April through October at Waterplace Park in downtown. Rates are $12 per hour and $35 per day. For more information, call Paddle Providence at (401) 453-1622.

SCITUATE

PARKS, BEACHES, AND RECREATION AREAS

• **Scituate Reservoir and Gainer Dam** 🐾🐾🐾 ◄● See **31** on page 110.

If you want to get a sense of how the little boy with his finger in the dike felt, take a hike to Gainer Dam. The massive, earth-covered dam holds back the Pawtuxet River creating the Scituate Reservoir, the largest body of fresh water in the Ocean State.

The dam and access roads are open to pedestrians and their pets. The roads are paved, so it's an easy and popular walk through the woods and along the base of the massive structure.

Dogs need to be leashed and are not permitted in the reservoir—it's the public water supply for Providence.

From the intersection of State Routes 12 and 116, take State Route 116 (north Road) south for a quarter mile. The trailhead and parking are on the right. Open dawn to dusk. There is no contact.

RESTAURANTS

Famous Creamery & Grille: This place isn't modest, but they make up for their boast of fame with some great ice cream and burgers. Hartford Pike (junction of State Routes 6 and 116); (401) 934-0278.

Suzy Q's Place: "Oh, Suzy Q, we love you, Suzy Q. . . " Burgers, ice cream, and plenty of tables in a roomy outdoor setting make everyone love Suzy Q's. 208 Plainfield Pike (junction of State Routes 14 and 116); (401) 647-9070.

SMITHFIELD

PARKS, BEACHES, AND RECREATION AREAS

• **Mowry Conservation Area** 🐾🐾🐾 See **32** on page 110.

This town conservation property is a beautiful 26-acre site dominated by a tall, white pine forest and the Woonasquatocket River. Years ago, this was the site of a forge, but little remains of it today. Now, it's just a great place for a hike. The single, pine needle–covered trail crosses the Woonasquatocket River via a bridge and loops through a forest, rocky outcroppings, and hills for about a mile. There's even a scenic picnic spot along the river. Dogs must be on leash.

From the intersection of State Routes 5, 104, and 116, take State Routes 5 and 104 north for one mile. Turn left onto Old Forge Road for a quarter mile. The park is on the right, and roadside parking is on the left. Open 6 A.M. to 9 P.M. (401) 233-1017.

RESTAURANTS

Christopher Matthews: Great sandwiches and breakfast treats make this a delicious stop before or after an outing in the woods. You can get your turkey and cheese to go or enjoy it at the shady picnic area. 21 Smith Avenue; (401) 949-4567.

Powder Mill Creamery & Coffee Roasters: The menu here offers ice cream and yogurt, coffees, fresh baked goods, burgers, and sandwiches. Sit at one of the picnic tables that overlook the Waterman Reservoir. 777 Putnam Pike (U.S. Route 44); (401) 949-3040.

WARWICK

PARKS, BEACHES, AND RECREATION AREAS

• Arnold's Neck Park 🐾🐾🐾 See **33** on page 110.

You'll find George's hidden corner of Warwick when you come out to Arnold's Neck. Tucked into Apponaug Cove alongside Apponaug Harbor, this is a small, little-known park right on the water. The park itself is only about three acres of grass, but it offers a good beach for dogs and great views of the peaceful harbor and the many water birds that have also discovered our hideaway.

Dogs must be on leash.

From U.S. Route 1, take Arnolds Neck Drive east to the end. Parking is available. Open sunrise to sunset. (401) 738-2000.

• Goddard Memorial State Park 🐾🐾🐾 See **34** on page 110.

Do 14 miles of trails and a two-mile shoreline sound inviting? Our dogs love visiting this state park on the Potowomut peninsula between Greenwich Cove and the Potowomut River.

The park is 489 acres in size and has open meadows, thick pine forests, and beaches. Remarkably, the woods are relatively new to the area. Beginning in 1874, a 50-year tree planting program was put into motion by the owners of the land, Henry Russell and Colonel Goddard, who turned a barren sand dune into what you see today.

The park has almost 400 picnic tables where you and Spot can enjoy a lunch break. Dogs must be on leash.

From U.S. Route 1 (Main Street) in East Greenwich, take Forge Road into Warwick. Turn left onto Ives Road for two miles. The park is on the left. Open sunrise to sunset. (401) 884-2010.

• Slater Grove Memorial Park 🐾🐾🐾 See **35** on page 110.

This recently renovated park on the northern end of Narragansett Bay is a great place to explore—especially for dogs that like the water. The park is comprised of a series of rolling, rocky hills with some woods and open fields along the bay. For adventurous souls, there is a thin seawall that you can traverse (depending on the tide) out to Rock Island, a quarter mile spit of land that doesn't really offer anything except the experience, which is good enough for us.

Dogs must be on leash.

From U.S. Route 1A and State Route 117, take Post Road east for half a mile. Turn right onto Narragansett Parkway for half a mile. The park is on the left. Parking is available. Open sunrise to sunset. (401) 738-2000.

• Warwick City Park 🐾🐾🐾 See 36 on page 110.

Warwick packs a lot into this 126-acre park. While the park meets much of the city's demand for ball fields and playgrounds, it also protects much of the natural beauty on this peninsula between Brush Neck and Buttonwoods Coves. In addition to the recreational fields, miles of hiking trails are available, such as the three-mile bike path and boardwalk along Brush Neck Cove.

Dogs must be on leash. From Memorial Day to Labor Day there is a nominal entrance fee on weekends.

From West Shore Road (State Route 117), take Long Street east onto Asylum Road for 1.5 miles into the park. Plenty of parking is available. Open sunrise to sunset. (401) 737-3272.

PLACES TO STAY

Comfort Inn Airport: If you and your pet are flying in or out of Providence, this is the closest accommodation to T.F. Green Airport, the largest airport serving Rhode Island. The hotel also offers free airport parking and/or complimentary shuttle to the airport. Room rates range from $50 to $100. 1940 Post Road, Warwick, RI 02886; (800) 221-2222.

Crowne Plaza at the Crossings: The Crowne Plaza was the site of the 1999 National Yankee Golden Retriever Club Conference, and it hosts many other dog club conferences. So you know they like dogs. A stay here does require a $50 deposit. Room rates range from $139 to $209. 801 Greenwich Avenue, Warwick, RI 02886; (401) 732-6000 or (800) 465-4329.

Master Hosts Inns: This comfortable hotel offers rooms and deluxe suites for you and your pet. Located just minutes away from both Providence and Newport, it makes a convenient stop off Interstate 95. Room rates range from $109 to $170. Dogs cannot be left unattended. 2138 Post Road, Warwick, RI 02886; (401) 737-7400; www.masterhosts.com.

Motel 6: All Motel 6 locations allow dogs, as long as you don't leave your pet unattended. This Motel 6 has just renovated its rooms. Room rates are from $60 to $80. One dog is welcome per room. 20 Jefferson Boulevard, Warwick, RI 02888; (401) 467-9800, (800) 4-MOTEL6; www.motel6.com.

FESTIVALS

Gaspee Days: One of the sparks that ignited the American Revolution was the 1722 sinking of the British ship, the HMS *Gaspee*. Perhaps even more historic is the celebration Warwick puts on in commemorating the event. Most of the month-long festivities, a parade, fair, concerts, and colonial encampment, take place in historic Pawtuxet Village. Gaspee Days begin in early May and end in mid-June with a reenactment of the *Gaspee* burning in Pawtuxet Cove. For more information and dates, call (800) 4-WARWICK.

WEST GREENWICH

PARKS, BEACHES, AND RECREATION AREAS

• Big River Management Area 🐾🐾🐾🐾 🐕 See **37** on page 110.
The Big River isn't the only thing that's big here in Kent County. With 8,600 acres, everything in this state property is bigger than life, including rivers, trails, and miles and miles of logging roads. Most of them appear to have no clear direction and a few are unmarked, but no one seems to mind. "Eventually, you come out somewhere," was a carefree comment from a mountain biker we passed a couple of miles in. So you many not know where you are going, but you'll see plenty of things along the way including wildlife, stone walls, and ancient cemeteries.

The trails around Tarbox Pond are popular because of the varied terrain and scenic pond, but other trails branch off Burnt Sawmill Road and New London Turnpike.

Dogs must be on leash from March 1 through August 15 and under voice control at other times.

To get to the western side of the park from Interstate 95, take Exit 6 to State Route 3 south for a quarter mile. Turn left onto Burnt Sawmill Road. Continue straight into the park. There are numerous turnouts for parking (avoid the private homes along the way). The main parking area is a half mile past the dam.

To get to Tarbox Pond from Interstate 95, take Exit 6A to Hopkins Hill Road south for 1.5 miles. The pond is on your left, and roadside pullouts are on both sides. Open 5 A.M. to a half hour after sunset. (401) 539-2356.

• Wickaboxet Management Area 🐾🐾🐾 🐕 See **38** on page 110.
This state-run park has 678 acres of thick woodlands and wetlands and is only a small part of a vast wilderness area in western Rhode Island. Adjoining the park are pristine lands belonging to the National Audubon Society, the University of Rhode Island (both are off-limits to dogs), and the Acadia Management Area.

Because of limited development in the area, you have a better chance of seeing some wildlife along the trail. One morning, we surprised a ruffed grouse in a thicket just off the trail. Deer, fox, and other birds can also be found along the crisscrossing forest roads and footpaths in Wickaboxet Management Area.

Dogs must be on leash from March 1 through August 15 and under voice control at other times.

From Interstate 95, take Exit 5 to State Route 102 north for three miles. Turn left onto Plain Meeting House Road for three miles. The park entrance and a parking lot are on the right. Open 5 A.M. to a half hour after sunset. (401) 539-2356.

PLACES TO STAY

Oak Embers Campground: This is a nice place to stay, but, with Acadia Management Area right next door, it's a dog paradise. Open November through September, there are 60 tent and RV sites. Dogs must be kept on leash. Sites range from $19 to $24 per night. 219 Escoheag Hill Road, West Greenwich, RI 02817; (401) 397-4042.

WEST WARWICK

NATURE HIKES AND URBAN WALKS

Washington Secondary Bike Path: As we go to press, the blacktop is just hardening on the first segment of West Warwick's half of the Washington Secondary Bike Path. The path is shared with neighboring Cranston, which has already opened its portion. Once completed, the path will connect Cranston to the Coventry Greenway. For updates, call West Warwick Department of Recreation at (401) 822-9260 or the Rhode Island Department of Environmental Management at (401) 222-2632.

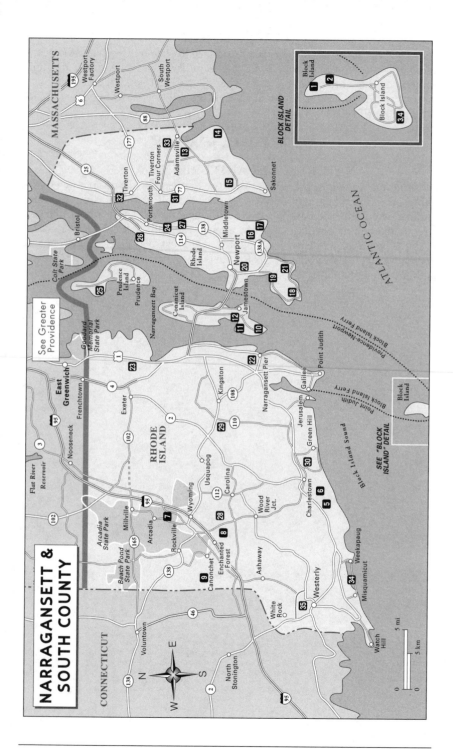

NARRAGANSETT & SOUTH COUNTY

5
NARRAGANSETT AND SOUTH COUNTY

Narragansett Bay, unarguably Rhode Island's most dominant natural feature, extends 28 miles inland, almost dividing the tiny state in half. The towns on its east, Newport and Little Compton, consist of some of the wealthiest lands in the state and have long been summer playgrounds for New England's well-to-do. The towns on the other side of the bay, or South County as it's called, are dominated by industry and urban life. This large bay, long-time home of the America's Cup, has some of the best harbors and beach access in New England and, we are happy to say, many of the beaches allow dogs.

BLOCK ISLAND (NEW SHOREHAM)

Block Island gets its name from the Dutch navigator, Adrian Block, who in 1614 explored the New England coastline and discovered the 11-square-mile island, called "one of the 12 Last Great Places in the Western Hemisphere" by the Nature Conservancy. Fortunately, they believe in putting their money where their mouth is. The Nature Conservancy owns and preserves 30 percent of Block Island.

Island Bound Hound: Year-round ferry service is available from Point Judith Galilee State Pier in Narragansett. The one-hour-and-10-minute ride costs $10 per person, $3 per bike, and $30 per car. Dogs are free but must be on a leash. There is summer-only ferry service from Newport and Providence; the trip is about two hours and cars are not permitted. For information and reservations, call Interstate Navigation Inc. at (401) 783-4613 or (860) 442-7891.

PARKS, BEACHES, AND RECREATION AREAS

• **Block Island National Wildlife Refuge** 🐾 🐾 🐾 🐾 See ❶ on page 132.

Sandy Point, a 46-acre beach on the northern tip of the island, is home to impressive coastal dunes and shifting, sandy, white beaches. The beach offers endless seaside opportunities and stunning views, complete with a lighthouse.

If you're here for beachcombing, Settler's Rock is the first thing you should find. The monument marks the spot where the first island settlers landed in 1661. A mile west up the beach is North Light. The lighthouse was built in 1867 and is now a maritime museum (considered the most remote museum in the country).

The refuge is recognized as an important bird-nesting area and migratory stop. Dogs must be leashed and are not permitted on the dunes or beach grass areas.

From Old Harbor, take Corn Neck Road north for four miles to a parking area at Sachem Pond/Settler's Rock. Walking west on the beach takes you into the refuge. Open dawn to dusk. (401) 364-9124.

• **Clay Head Trail and The Maze** 🐾 🐾 🐾 🐾 See ❷ on page 132.

We like to think the descriptions in the *Dog Lover's Companion to New England* are pretty comprehensive, but this is one place where you get no help from us. You're on your own in The Maze, a series of crisscrossing trails through shrubs, fields, and wetlands to the Clayhead Bluffs on the northeastern corner of the island. This might be a good time to test out your dog's heightened sense of direction. Either that, or bring a compass.

The one coherent trail starts at Corn Neck Road and winds its way to the coast. There is a small beach where the trail reaches the rocky shoreline, and then it winds north along high coastal bluffs to the wildlife refuge. This main trail and maze of paths leading from it provide a wonderful walking and bird-watching opportunity along with views of farms, ponds, and the coast. The 200-acre property is protected by the Nature Conservancy. Dogs must be on leash.

From Old Harbor, take Corn Neck Road north for 3.5 miles. Turn right onto the dirt park access road for a half mile to the trailhead. Open a half hour before sunrise to a half hour after sunset. (401) 466-2129.

• **Mohegan Bluffs** 🐾 🐾 🐾 🐾 See ❸ on page 132.

Marking the southeast corner of Block Island, the Mohegan Bluffs are 200-foot, multicolored cliffs abruptly rising out of the Atlantic Ocean. You can enjoy the spectacular views from the top, including distant Long Island, or venture down the bluffs' steep staircase to the beach below where you have miles of seashore to explore.

The cliffs are named after the local Manisses, tribe which defeated the attacking Mohegans here years ago.

The Nature Conservancy requires dogs to be leashed.

From the ferry landing, take Water Street south onto Spring Street, then onto Mohegan Trail and onto Lakeside Drive for a total distance of four miles. Turn left onto Cooneymus Road for a half mile then left on dirt Black Rock Road for a quarter mile to the parking area and trailhead. Open a half hour before sunrise to a half hour after sunset. (401) 466-2129.

• Rodman's Hollow 🐾🐾🐾🐾 **See 4 on page 132.**
Arguably Block Island's most captivating natural feature, Rodman's Hollow is a glacial outwash basin or "a big hole in the ground."

Several miles of trails here include a great loop through the stream- and pond-filled hollow with a return route atop rolling, shrub-covered hills. Along the way you'll have excellent ocean views. Other trails allow you and your pet access over the bluffs to the southern coast beachhead.

This conservation land, managed by the Nature Conservancy and the Block Island Conservancy, is beautiful any time of year but especially in mid-May when the vegetation is in bloom. Dogs must be on leash.

From the ferry landing, take Water Street south onto Spring Street, then onto Mohegan Trail and onto Lakeside Drive for a total distance of four miles. Turn left onto Cooneymus Road for a half mile then left on dirt Black Rock Road for a quarter mile to the parking area and trailhead. Open a half hour before sunrise to a half hour after sunset. (401) 466-2129.

NATURE HIKES AND URBAN WALKS

The Greenway: Although any one of the parks on Block Island is sure to keep you busy for the afternoon, this extensive 25-mile network of paths connects many of the parks. Most of the routes are in the southern half of the island and are accessible from Center, Old Mill, Beacon Hill, and West Side Roads. (401) 466-5200.

RESTAURANTS

Aldo's: Playing island tourist is hard work. Luckily you and your dog can plop down at Aldo's patio almost anytime for a full breakfast, donuts, pastries, or any one of their 32 flavors of ice cream. Weldon's Way; (401) 466-2198.

The Daily Market: Not only is this deli and natural food market the place to get a wide variety of soups and sandwiches (how about roast beef and horseradish or a hummus and veggie wrap), but they also offer plenty of smoothies, coffee, and fruit to be enjoyed at their outdoor tables. 457 Chapel Street; (401) 466-9908.

PLACES TO STAY

Eastgate House: Eastgate is an elegant escape-to destination on the scenic, southern end of Block Island. The two-room bed-and-breakfast has luxury bathrooms and expansive porches overlooking the ocean. Only one room is set aside for guests with pets. Well-behaved dogs, with prior permission, are welcome. The room rate is $250 plus an additional $25 a night for your dog. Spring Street, Block Island, RI 02807; (401) 466-2164; www.eastgatehouse.com.

FESTIVALS

Arf Art: Experience the distinctive flare of the Block Island Arts Festival. Dog friendly and artistically impressive, the event is held annually in mid-August at Esta's Park. For more information, call (800) 383-2474.

CHARLESTOWN

PARKS, BEACHES, AND RECREATION AREAS

• **Ninigret National Wildlife Refuge** 😺 😺 See **5** on page 132.
This wildlife refuge on marshy Ninigret Pond is located on the former site of a World War II airport, used to test planes and train pilots before both went overseas. Although the airstrips are now slowly being removed, some of the pavement still exists as the marshes try to reclaim their natural state.

Pick any point or cove along Ninigret Pond and you will quickly see why it deserves national protection. The land is covered with numerous beach shrubs, trees, and sandy trails. The pond is a spacious mixture of fresh and salt water.

Plenty of parking is available.

Dogs are required to be on a leash and to stay on designated trails in all National Wildlife Refuges.

From U.S. Route 1, take Old Post Road north for a quarter mile. Enter Ninigret Park on the right. Follow the park road to the end for the refuge parking area and trailheads. Open dawn to dusk. (401) 364-9124.

• **Ninigret Park** 😺 😺 See **6** on page 132.
This 227-acre town park encompasses ball fields, tennis courts, and playgrounds, but there are also some open fields and nature trails for your dog to enjoy. Located next to neighboring Ninigret National Wildlife Refuge, the trails start beyond the nature center and pond beach. Dogs need to be on leash and are not permitted on the ball fields or in the playground areas.

From U.S. Route 1, take Old Post Road north for a quarter mile. The park entrance is on the right. Plenty of parking is available. Open 7 A.M. to sunset. (401) 364-1222.

RESTAURANTS

Hitching Post: No need to leash your dog up here. Once they see the menu, they're not going anywhere but the counter. And why not? Burgers, seafood, and ice cream, that's why not! Get it to go or enjoy it at the outdoor seating area. 5402 Post Road (U.S. Route 1); (401) 364-7495.

EXETER

PARKS, BEACHES, AND RECREATION AREAS

• **Acadia Management Area** 😺 😺 😺 😺 🐕 See **7** on page 132.
Ask anyone in Rhode Island, and they all say the same thing: Head for Acadia!

With 14,000 acres, it has something for everyone, including happy trail hounds.

This state-managed park is blanketed by a dense forest, dotted with numerous ponds, and cut by rivers and brooks. A number of roads and a state highway also run through it, so you can literally pull off the road almost anywhere and find a trail or forest road leading to a fantastic hike.

One of our favorite destinations is a hike up to Mount Tom Cliffs. This relatively easy, three-mile loop trail has magnificent views from Mount Tom. You may want to keep your dog under restraint on the cliffs and near the trailhead where there are giant anthills (it's true; some of them are a foot high).

Another area that dogs really fall for is Stepstone Falls. The well-named falls are formed by a series of rock ledges over which the Falls River, a large brook, gradually cascades. Take the Ben Utter Trail for an easy 1.5-mile walk.

Dogs must be on leash from March 1 through August 15 and under voice control at other times. Maps are available at the park headquarters.

To get to the park headquarters from the intersection of State Routes 3 and 165, take State Route 165 west for 1.5 miles. Turn left onto Acadia Hill Road for 2.5 miles, then turn left at the end of the road for half a mile. The headquarters and parking are on the right.

The headquarters is open Monday to Friday 8:30 A.M. to 4 P.M., and the park is open every day 5 A.M. to a half hour after sunset. (401) 539-2356.

RESTAURANTS

Middle Of Nowhere Diner: Western Washington County may very well be the middle of nowhere, but at least you won't go hungry. The Middle Of Nowhere Diner cooks up countless platters of tasty pancakes, burgers, and daily specials morning, noon, and night. Order it to go and enjoy a hearty meal at the outdoor picnic tables. 222 Nooseneck Hill Road; (401) 397-8855.

HOPKINTON

PARKS, BEACHES, AND RECREATION AREAS

• **Black Farm Management Area** 🐾🐾 🐕 See 🎱 on page 132.
This 245 acres of hardwood forest and marshes features Plain Pond at its center and Wood River marking its eastern border. Mainly used for hunting, there are plenty of safe times throughout the year to enjoy the forest with your dog. A single trail runs from the parking area to Plain Pond and the Wood River.

Dogs must be on leash from March 1 through August 15 and under voice control at other times.

From Interstate 95, take Exit 2 to Townsend Road south onto Woodville Alton Road for a mile and a quarter. The park, parking, and trailhead are on the left. Open 5 A.M. to a half hour after sunset. (401) 539-2356.

• **Long and Ell Ponds Nature Area** 🐾🐾🐾🐾 See 🎱 on page 132.
This area in western Rhode Island occupies a beautiful far-off corner of the state. The two ponds, Long and Ell, are engulfed by a series of rocky ridges and cliffs covered with pine trees, giant rhododendrons, and mountain laurels, making swimming here impossible. Your walk will require a combination of

strolling, rock climbing, and swamp wading. But the area is unique and gorgeous, making a visit here highly recommended.

Most of the property is owned and managed by The Nature Conservancy; the state of Rhode Island and the Audubon Society are other managers. Dogs must be on leash.

Note that dogs are not permitted at nearby Ashville and Blue Ponds.

From State Route 3, take Canonchet Road north for 2.5 miles. The Long Pond parking lot and trailhead are on the left. For the main trailhead, continue on Canonchet Road for another half mile then turn left onto North Road for a mile. The trailhead and parking are on the left. Open a half hour before sunrise to a half hour after sunset. (401) 331-7110.

JAMESTOWN

PARKS, BEACHES, AND RECREATION AREAS

• Beavertail State Park 😊 😊 😊 See 🔟 on page 132.
This breathtaking park at the southern tip of Jamestown Island in Narragansett Bay is the place for any sea dog. Because of the rocky shore, water access is limited and even dangerous, but the views and sea breezes are simply stunning. Picnicking on the grassy ground is popular, too.

The 153 acres are also home to the Beavertail Lighthouse. The original light was built in 1749, making it the third oldest lighthouse in the country. The present light was erected in 1856.

Dogs are required to be on leash in all state parks.

From U.S. Route 138, take North Main Road south for 2.5 miles into downtown. Turn right onto Southwest Avenue and onto Beavertail Road. Continue 2.5 miles into the park. Open sunrise to sunset. (401) 423-9941.

• Fort Getty Recreation Area 😊 😊 See 🔟 on page 132.
Fort Getty sits on Fox Hill, a rocky peninsula jutting out from Jamestown into Narragansett Bay. Although there aren't many shade trees to help escape the sun and sea, the rocky terrain and shoreline offer plenty of places to explore and sniff.

Dogs must be on leash and are not permitted in the Fox Hill Salt Marsh, the adjacent Audubon Society of Rhode Island property. In season (Memorial Day to October 2), the day-use fee is $8. There is no charge in the off-season.

You and your dog will also enjoy camping here. The 118 sites for tent campers are available from May 18 to October 1. Rates range from $19 to $24.

Dogs must be on leash in the campground and cannot be left unattended.

From U.S. Route 138, take North Main Road south for 2.5 miles into downtown. Turn right onto Southwest Avenue and onto Beavertail Road. Turn right onto Fort Getty Road for a half mile into the park. Open sunrise to sunset. (401) 423-7211.

• Mackerel Cove Beach 😊 😊 See 🔟 on page 132.
This is a nice flat beach on a land bridge between the two islands that make up Jamestown. The waves roll in a bit easier here than in most beaches because Mackerel Cove is so long and shallow.

Dogs must be leashed and are not permitted on the beach in season (Memorial Day to October 2) from 9 A.M. to 5 P.M. Note that dogs are not permitted in the Sheffield Cove Marsh, the Audubon Society of Rhode Island property across Beavertail Road.

From U.S. Route 138, take North Main Road south for 2.5 miles into downtown. Turn right onto Southwest Avenue onto Beavertail Road. The beach and parking are on the left. Open sunrise to sunset. (401) 423-7211.

PLACES TO STAY

Fort Getty Recreation Area camping: See page 138.

LITTLE COMPTON

PARKS, BEACHES, AND RECREATION AREAS

• Simmons Pond Management Area 😾 😾 🐕 See **13** on page 132.

Once the hunters have gone away, the 400 acres around Simmons Pond are a great area for your dog to enjoy a tranquil walk in the woods. In addition to the pond, the property is divided by Cole Brook and covered with a thick wood and wetlands. In total, there are about five miles of trails and roads, some of which can get a little marshy in the spring.

Dogs must be on leash from April 1 through August 15 and under voice control at other times.

From State Route 77, take Peckham Road east for 1.75 miles. Turn left onto Long Highway for a quarter mile the right onto Colebrook Road for two-tenths of a mile. The park and a parking lot are on the right. Open 5 A.M. to a half hour after sunset. (401) 222-2632.

• South Shore Town Beach 😾 😾 😾 🐕 See **14** on page 132.

This beach doesn't exhibit picture-postcard perfection, but it also doesn't have a leash law or ban dogs at anytime. The half-mile peninsula sits between the Atlantic Ocean and Tuniper's Pond and is mostly covered with washed up stones, but there is certainly plenty of sand here, too.

From State Route 77, take Swamp Road onto Browell Road for two miles. Turn right onto South Shore Road for a mile into the park. There is a nonresident, summertime parking fee of $10. Open sunrise to a half hour after sunset. (401) 635-2311.

• Wilbur Woods 😾 😾 😾 🐕 See **15** on page 132.

You may not be able to afford to build a house here in beautiful Little Compton—there's a two-acre lot minimum—but you can walk like a big dog in this hidden stretch of forest along the meandering Dundery Brook. The refreshing stream is a nice place to cool off, and the forest road that circles through the park makes for an easy one-mile trip through a heavily wooded, 75-acre area.

Dogs must be under voice control.

From State Route 77, take Swamp Road east for a half mile. The park entrance, a gravel road, is on the left. Look for a hidden sign in the trees. Parking is available throughout the park. Open 5 A.M. to a half hour after sunset. (401) 635-4400.

DIVERSIONS

Rhode Island Red or White: In this part of the Ocean State, it seems everything is named after the Rhode Island Red, the popular chicken breed first bred in 1854 in a nearby village. But cultivated dogs know it really refers to the wine at Sakonnet Vineyards. Whether your choice is red or white, a visit to the winery will be a bubbly time for both you and your leashed dog. All visitors are invited to enjoy a picnic on the stately grounds or a vineyard walk. Sam, the vineyard's resident retriever, may even come out to lead a tour.

On most summer weekends, the vineyard also plays host to a variety of events including music and hot-air balloon festivals. Call for dates and details. 162 West Main Road; (401) 635-8486.

MIDDLETOWN

PARKS, BEACHES, AND RECREATION AREAS

• Gardiner's Pond 🐾🐾🐾 See 16 on page 132.

Gardiner's Pond is the centerpiece of five parks and beaches on Sachuest Point. Dogs are not permitted at most of the parks, but they can take this rather interesting walk around the town reservoir on top of high, wide, earthen walls. Almost 1.25 miles around, the water level on the north side often prevents visitors from making a complete loop.

Dogs must on leash and are not permitted in the reservoir.

From the intersection of State Routes 114 and 138, take Miantonomi Avenue east a half mile onto Green End Avenue. Continue one mile. Turn right onto Paradise Avenue for 1.3 miles then left onto Hanging Rock Road for a half mile. Just after Hanging Rock Road turns left, you'll find the pond's dirt parking area on the right. Open dawn to dusk. (401) 847-1993.

• Sachuest Point National Wildlife Refuge 🐾🐾🐾 See 17 on page 132.

Sachuest Point is a breathtaking peninsula where the Sakonnet River and the Atlantic Ocean meet to form a diverse area teeming with wildlife. Within the park's 242 acres are three miles of trails through salt- and freshwater marshes, rocky shorelines, and upland areas of beach shrubs and grasses.

Maps are available at the visitor center. Dogs are required to be on a leash and stay on the designated trails.

From the intersection of State Routes 114 and 138, take Miantonomi Avenue east a half mile onto Green End Avenue. Continue one mile then turn right onto Paradise Avenue for 1.3 miles. Turn left onto Hanging Rock Road for a half mile. Continue straight onto Sachuest Road for a half mile into the park. Parking is available. Open a half hour before sunrise to a half hour after sunset. (401) 847-5511.

RESTAURANTS

Flo's Clam Shack: Flo's delicious seafood brings in all kinds of patrons. Bikers, beachcombers, dog owners, and even owners of a sixty-two-foot yacht all drop anchor here to enjoy almost any kind of seafood imaginable. They have great burgers and shakes, too. The outdoor picnic table makes it easy to share with your pup. 4 Wave Avenue; (401) 847-8141.

PLACES TO STAY

Bay Willows Inn: This newly renovated motel has 21 cheerful rooms with plenty of amenities. Some suites are available with efficiencies. Room rates range from $60 to $110. 1225 Aquidneck Avenue, Middletown, RI 02842; (401) 847-8400, (800) 838-5642; www.baywillowsinn.com.

Howard Johnson Inn—Newport: This full-service hotel offers modern amenities in a convenient location. Pets are welcome in most rooms. Room rates range from $79 to $189. 351 West Main Road, Middletown, RI 02842; (401) 849-2000 or (800) 654-2000; www.hojo.com.

Newport Ramada Inn: This standard hotel allow pets in four pet-friendly rooms on the basement level. At least it's not out in the car! Room rates are $85 to $190 plus a $10 pet fee per night. 936 West Main Road, Middletown, RI 02842; (401) 846-7600, (800) 846-8322; www.newenglandramadas.com.

NEWPORT

Located on a point overlooking Narragansett Bay, this lovely harbor was known to the Native Americans as "Aquidneck." By the mid–19th century it was the summer home to America's wealthiest families who built palatial mansions along Ocean and Bellevue Drives, many of which still stand today. One eccentric millionaire used to host champagne and caviar parties for his guests and their dogs—all of whom ate at the same table. We wish we could say that Newport is still a dog-loving town, but times change; why, even the America's Cup is no longer held here.

PARKS, BEACHES, AND RECREATION AREAS

• Brenton Point State Park 🐾 🐾 🐾 See ⓲ on page 132.

This park occupies the site of one of the many elegant oceanfront Newport mansions that was once off-limits to you and me. Luckily, today it is Brenton Point State Park, 89 acres of breathtaking waterfront property open to the public.

William Brenton, for whom the park is named, was the first estate owner back in the 17th century. After a number of other distinguished, wealthy owners (and a number of law suits over the land), the property was commandeered in 1941 by the United States Army, its richest tenant to date. The property was used as a defensive position in case of an attack on Narragansett Bay. You can still see some remains of both the former mansions and fortresses in the park, which opened in 1976.

There are plenty of grassy areas for picnickers and also plenty of water access, although it is a very rocky coastline; no sand beach here. The park gets very crowded on summer weekends. Dogs are required to be on leash.

From U.S. Route 114 and State Route 138, take Broadway south into downtown and Spring Street. Follow Spring Street onto Coggeshall Avenue. Turn right onto Ocean Avenue for 3.5 miles into the park. Parking is available. Open sunrise to sunset. (401) 847-2400.

• King Park 🐾 🐾 🐾 See ⓳ on page 132.

The views from this small, harborside park are fit for a king. Located right on the water, you can see the entire harbor, Newport Bridge, and the Newport

Waterfront. Plenty of grass, trees, sitting areas, and even some good water-access points make this a good stop.

Dogs must be on leash, and they are not permitted at the ball fields or playgrounds.

The park is located on Wellington Avenue just west of Thames Street. Parking is available. Open 6 A.M. to 9 P.M. (401) 847-2400.

•Miantonomi Memorial Park 🐾 🐾 See **20** on page 132.

This small city park memorializes World War I veterans. On the top of Miantonomi Hill is a memorial tower, now listed on the National Historic Register. Most of the park is one wide grassy lawn; the rest of it is a tree-covered hill with some trails leading up to the monument. Dogs must be on leash.

The park is located at the intersection of State Route 138 and Hillside Avenue. Parking is available. Open 6 A.M. to 9 P.M.; (401) 847-2400.

•Rovensky Park 🐾 🐾 See **21** on page 132.

This is a scenic, well-maintained park in one of the more exclusive Newport neighborhoods. Approximately the size of two city blocks, it is decorated with many flowering shrubs, trees, and gardens. There is also plenty of grass for urban dogs tired of the concrete. The property is managed by the Preservation Society of Newport County. Dogs must be on leash.

The park is located at the intersection Bellevue and Rovensky Avenues. Limited, resident-only parking is available. Open dawn to dusk. (401) 847-2400 or (401) 847-1000.

RESTAURANTS

Bob & Gerry's Ice Cream: Everyone's trying to be like Ben & Jerry, but, hey, if you've got the goods, we don't care what you call yourself. The ice cream is pretty good, especially after a hot walk down happenin' Thames Street. 438 Thames Street; (401) 849-6904.

Sandwich Board Deli: This sidewalk café is close enough to all the harbor action, but just enough out of the way to enjoy some peace and quite—plus some great sandwiches and pastries—with your dog at an outside table. 397 Thames Street; (401) 849-5358.

PLACES TO STAY

Inn On Bellevue: Well-behaved dogs with their own blankets are welcome with prior approval on ritzy Bellevue Avenue. The inn is open May through November. Room rates range from $140 to $175. 30 Bellevue Avenue, Newport, RI 02480; (401) 848-6242.

Motel 6: All Motel 6 locations allow dogs as long as you don't leave your pet unattended. One dog is welcome per room. Rates are $60 to $100. 249 JT Connell Highway, Newport, RI 02840; (401) 848-0600, (800) 4-MOTEL6; www.motel6.com.

Murray House Bed-and-Breakfast: Located between the exclusive Bellevue Avenue and scenic Almy Pond, Murray House offers three private, colonial homes with private guest rooms, some with private baths and some with shared baths. A light breakfast is included. Prices range from $65 to $150.

Advance reservations are required. 1 Murray Place, Newport, RI 02840; (401) 846-3337; www.bbonline.com/ri/murray.

Sanford-Covell Villa Marina: This elegant 1869 historical landmark offers a rare glimpse of wealthy Newport in the last century. Originally built as a "summer cottage," this bed-and-breakfast still features a grand staircase rising 35 feet from floor to ceiling, sumptuous wood banisters and balconies, and a sunset view of Narragansett Bay. Some cottage!

The Villa has seven guest rooms and two guest suites. Breakfast is included. Rooms range from $65 to $295; not all rooms are available to pets. 72 Washington Street, Newport, RI 02840; (401) 847-0206.

NARRAGANSETT

PARKS, BEACHES, AND RECREATION AREAS

• Canonchet Farm 🐾 🐾 🐾 See **22** on page 132.

Canonchet Farm is a living museum that invites people and dogs to explore the workings of an 18th-century farm. Our dogs jump back and forth between having no interest in the farm to being "waaayyyy" too interested in the animals. So, on our visits, we head right for the trails. There are 170 acres here, and the barnyard only takes up five of them. The rest are farm animal–free and include hiking paths, fields, woods, streams, and ponds.

The museum is open May through September, Wednesday through Saturday, 11 A.M. to 4 P.M., and there is a $3.50 admission fee. The trails are free and open year-round. Dogs must be on leash and are not permitted in the buildings or barns.

From State Route 1A, take Strathmore Road north for a quarter mile into the farm. Open dawn to dusk. (401) 738-5400.

NATURE HIKES AND URBAN WALKS

Ocean Road and The Towers: This is a popular waterside walk along the Ocean Road seawall and walkway. It runs from the center of town (at U.S. Route 1A) and the Narragansett Pier and Pavilion to Tucker's Dock, a distance of eight-tenths of a mile. In between you'll pass by The Towers, the last remains of the Victorian-era Narragansett Casino. Open 24 hours a day. (401) 782-0658.

PLACES TO STAY

Long Cove Marina Campsites: This coastal campground is right on Point Judith Pond and Love Cove. Open May to October 15, it has 180 tent and RV sites, many right on the water. Dogs must be kept on leash. Sites range from $16 to $20 per night. 325 Old Point Judith Road, Narragansett, RI 02882; (401) 783-4902.

RESTAURANTS

Coffee Bean: Whether you need a simple cup of coffee or a delicious, imaginative sandwich, the Coffee Bean has it. Plenty of outdoor seating, too, so you won't have to dine alone. Woodruff Avenue; (401) 782-6226.

DIVERSIONS

Captain Canine: It's all aboard for sea dogs, first mates included. Leashed and well-behaved dogs are welcome aboard the Southland Riverboat cruises. The riverboat steams around scenic Point Judith Pond for a 1.75-hour sightseeing tour or a 2.5-hour sunset tour. Voyages depart from the State Pier in Galilee on weekends in the spring (May–June) and fall (September–October), and daily in the summer (July–August). Cruises are $8 to $12. For more information, call (401) 783-2954.

NORTH KINGSTOWN
(INCLUDING THE VILLAGE OF WICKFORD)

The little village of Wickford and its harbor on Narrragensett Bay is a busy port of call. It's been that way ever since the 18th century hey days as an important shipping channel between the mainland and Newport and other bay islands. Today, the island goods are delivery via the many bay bridges, but Wickford is still active with plenty of pleasure crafts and visiting tourists.

PARKS, BEACHES, AND RECREATION AREAS

•**Wilson Park** 🐾🐾 See **23** on page 132.
Wilson Park is North Kingstown's 75-acre recreation area and that means it is mainly ball fields and playgrounds, all of which are off-limits to George, Inu, and Rocky. But they all enjoy the park for the 1.5-mile bike path, attracting bikers, walkers, bladers, and joggers. It's not perfect, but it's all you get in North Kingstown. Dogs must be on leash.

From the intersection of U.S. Route 1 and State Route 102, take State Route 102 east for a quarter of a mile. The park is on the left. Plenty of parking is available. Open dawn to dusk. (401) 294-3331.

NATURE HIKES AND URBAN WALKS

Wickford Walk: Giving your dog some fresh air and exercise doesn't always require a 10-mile trek through the woods. Sometimes a stroll through town is a refreshing change of pace, and what better place than in the village of historic Wickford? This seaside harbor village tips the scales of New England quaintness. In fact, Main Street has been selected as one of the top 10 Main Streets in the country. The prime strolling areas are the shop-lined streets and bridges around Wickford Cove. For information on events and other town activities, call (401) 295-5566.

RESTAURANTS

Brown Street Deli: Stop by this little deli for a great sandwich to go. Soup, salad, sandwiches, and coffee are part of the full menu. 85 Brown Street; (401) 295-1150.

Pastry Gourmet: It's been said (we're not sure by whom) that you can burn more calories strolling down Main Street for the afternoon than an hour of hiking down the trail. And since we don't want to be responsible for your wasting away to nothing, you had better make a stop at this tasty bakery for something sweet. Kick back on the comfortable benches out front—you've earned it. 45 Brown Street; (401) 295-8400.

PLACES TO STAY

Budget Inn of North Kingstown: This comfortable little motel isn't fancy, but it offers clean, modern rooms at affordable prices. Dogs are welcome in most rooms. Room rates range from $40 to $120 plus a $10 charge per pet. 7825 Post Road, North Kingstown, RI 02852; (401) 294-4888.

FESTIVALS

Festive Fido: A walk in Wickford is a special treat any time of year, but it is especially enchanting during the Wickford Festival of Lights. The historic district, decorated with thousands of white lights, becomes a winter wonderland. The annual December celebration on Main and Brown Streets includes seasonal entertainment and food, a tree-lighting ceremony, and many festive visitors and dogs. For more information and dates, call (401) 295-5566.

PORTSMOUTH

PARKS, BEACHES, AND RECREATION AREAS

• **Glen Park** 🐾 🐾 See **24** on page 132.

Glen Park is the town recreation area, so you'll run into many a soccer mom in the parking lot, but once you reach the hiking and equestrian trails, things get a lot quieter. The park has a good-sized picnic area and nice views of the nearby Sakonnet River. Dogs must be on leash.

From State Route 138, take Glen Road east for a quarter mile. The park is on the right. Parking is available. Open sunrise to sunset. (401) 683-1990.

• **Heritage Foundation of Rhode Island Park (Prudence Island)** 🐾 🐾 🐾 See **25** on page 132.

The state of Rhode Island owns over 1,000 acres of this scenic island in Narragansett Bay on both the northern and southern tips. Each portion offers great natural beauty, beaches, and many forest roads for hiking. Yes, it is a bit of a journey out to Prudence Island, but, if you have the time, it is well worth the effort.

Dogs need to be leashed and ticks are a problem on the island. Also, even though half of the island is residential, there are no services, so bring plenty of food and water.

To get to the park, take the ferry from Bristol to Prudence Island and Homestead Dock. Take Narragansett Road north 2.5 miles to the northern portion, or go south on Narragansett Road for a mile and then turn right onto Broadway into the park. Open 5 A.M. to a half hour after sunset. Call (401) 683-4236 for the park and (401) 253-9808 for the Prudence Ferry.

• **Melville Pond Nature Preserve** 🐾 🐾 🐾 See **26** on page 132.

This secluded park, just off the beaten path of Newport and the local naval base, is a great place to escape for a walk. The heavily wooded preserve is 150 acres in size, has four miles of hiking trails, two ponds, and some closed-to-vehicles roads (once used by the Navy) for easy walking.

Your pup must be on a leash.

From State Route 114, take Stringham Road west. Turn right onto Dupont Street into the Melville Recreation Area. Turn left at the end of the road (at the campground) and take the first right to the parking area. Open dawn to 7 P.M. (401) 683-3255.

• **Sandy Point Beach** 🐾🐾🐾🐾 See **27** on page 132.
This fantastic beach is about a half mile long and forms a point in the Sakonnet River. The wide-open spaces make it a great place for a walk or a swim, even in the summer when the tail-wagging ban is in high season.

Dogs must be on leash, and from 9 A.M. to 5 P.M., Memorial Day to Labor Day, dogs need to be kept to the right end of the beach.

From State Route 138, take Sandy Point Avenue east for one mile to the park. Limited parking is available. Open sunrise to sunset. (401) 683-1990.

RESTAURANTS

Shiver Me Timbers: When the crew needs a good meal fast, the best way to prevent a mutiny is a stop at Shiver Me Timbers. They offer bakery items, pastries, ice cream, and plenty of specialty sandwiches for the most discriminating of tastes. Don't get Inu started on the brownies! 954 East Main Road; (401) 683-6338.

PLACES TO STAY

Melville Pond Campground: This wooded, 123-site campground is conveniently located near Newport and has spots for both tents and RVs. Nightly rates are $16 to $29. Open April 1 through November 1. Dogs must be leashed and cannot be left unattended. 181 Bradford Avenue, Portsmouth, RI 02871; (401) 849-8212.

DIVERSIONS

Take a Walk on the Wild Side: Join the Heart and Sole Walk for the Animals fund-raiser. It's a one-mile stroll or a three-mile strut in Glen Park. The walk is held each spring (May/June) featuring stupid pet tricks, a pet/owner lookalike contest, and plenty of other fun activities. Participants are asked to locate sponsors or make a $10 donation.

The walk is presented by the Potter League for Animals (in Middletown) as a fund-raiser for the Newport County shelter. For more information and exact dates and times, call (401) 846-8276.

RICHMOND

PARKS, BEACHES, AND RECREATION AREAS

• **Carolina Management Area** 🐾🐾🐾 🐕 See **28** on page 132.
This 2,359-acre management area is a real mix of forests, open fields, swamps, ponds, and rivers. The diversity is spectacular, but what is even more amazing is that you'll have the place to yourself most of the year. Of course, October through February the hunters come out of the woodwork, but in the spring and summer the park is yours.

The primary trail here is the North South Trail that runs the length of the park and the state. There are also other minor trails and crisscrossing forest roads.

Dogs must be on leash from March 1 through August 15 and under voice control at other times.

From Interstate 95, take Exit 3 to State Route 138 east for 2.5 miles. Turn right onto State Route 112 south for 2.5 miles then right onto Pine Hill Road. Proceed one mile or 1.25 miles to two parking areas for access to the southern portion of the park. Open 5 A.M. to a half hour after sunset. (401) 798-0281.

PLACES TO STAY

Sun Valley Motel: This no-frills motel isn't fancy, but they have set aside one room for traveling pets. A $25 returnable deposit is required. Room rates range from $50 to $70. 1219 Main Street, Richmond, RI 02898; (401) 539-8485.

SOUTH KINGSTOWN

PARKS, BEACHES, AND RECREATION AREAS

• **Great Swamp Management Area** 🐾🐾🐾🐾 🐕 See **29** on page 132.

This 3,349 acres, bordered by the Chipuxet and Pawcatuck Rivers, the Chickasheen Brook, and Morten Pond, is an amazingly scenic and diverse watery wilderness. In between all this water is an expansive system of ebbing and flowing marshes and swamps that are forever changing and teeming with life. Through it all are miles and miles of dry, unpaved forest roads that provide great hiking opportunities.

Dogs must be on leash from March 1 through August 15 and under voice control at other times.

From the intersection of State Routes 110 and 138, take State Route 138 west. Make an immediate left onto Liberty Lane for one mile. At the end of the road, turn left onto dirt Great Neck Road into the park. Open 5 A.M. to a half hour after sunset. (401) 277-3075 or (401) 798-0281.

• **Trustom Pond National Wildlife Refuge** 🐾🐾🐾 See **30** on page 132.

This federally protected property sure packs a lot into 642 acres. There is a beach, sand dunes, marshes, fresh- and saltwater ponds, grasslands, and forests. And it's all connected by three miles of trails. Look for the osprey platforms on the dunes, but don't get too close!

The beach is closed April to August for the nesting season, and dogs are required to be on a leash and stay on designated trails.

From State Route 1, take Moonstone Beach Road south for one mile. Turn right onto Matunuck Schoolhouse Road for three-quarters of a mile. The park and parking are on the left. The beach entrance (open in the off-season) is at the end of Moonstone Beach Road. Open dawn to dusk. (401) 364-9124.

NATURE HIKES AND URBAN WALKS

South County Bicycle Path: This latest addition to the Rhode Island bike path system runs 11 miles from the magnificently restored West Kingston train station to the village of Peace Dale. Along the way it parallels the Great Swamp Management Area via an old railroad line. Future plans include extending the path southward to Narragansett Beach. Dogs must be on leash.

Street parking is available at the southern terminus in Peace Dale at State Route 108 and High Street. Open dawn to dusk. For more information, contact the RI DOT Bicycle Program Coordinator at (401) 222-4203, extension 4042.

PLACES TO STAY

Larchwood Inn: This 160-year-old, three-story, 18-room country inn is located in the historic village of Wakefield. Most rooms have private baths and are decorated in a colonial style. Room rates range from $35 to $140 plus a $5-per-night charge for your pet. Pet cannot be left unattended. 521 Main Street, Wakefield, RI 02879; (401) 783-5454, (800) 275-5450.

Worden Pond Family Campground: The 200-site campground gives you great access to Worden Pond, the Great Swamp Management Area, and the South Kingstown Bike Path. Open May to October 15. Dogs must be kept on leash. Sites range from $19 to $24. 416A Worden Pond Road, Wakefield, RI 02879; (401) 789-9113.

DIVERSIONS

Doggie Dash: A word of warning to those owners who exercise their pets by driving to the local doggie hot spot and letting Rover run with the big dogs while you sip coffee and chat. You are running the risk of being labeled the weak link at this year's Doggie Dash, the annual two-mile run held at South Kingstown Junior High School. Picture the disappointment on your dog's face as he drags you across the finish line for 29th place. If you can't bear that, start training now or aim for the one-mile fun walk or silly pet trick competition.

For more information and exact date, call the Animal Rescue League of Southern Rhode Island at (401) 295-7872.

Caruso for Canines: Marina Park is the musical spot for Spot on Thursdays in July and August. The free concerts are scheduled from 6:30 to 8 P.M. and cover a wide variety of musical tastes. Our dogs are hoping for an appearance by Three Dog Night, but we have a hunch they're in for a long wait. For more information, call (401) 789-9301.

TIVERTON

PARKS, BEACHES, AND RECREATION AREAS

• **Fogland Marsh Preserve** 🐾 🐾 See **31** on page 132.
Although we know you love your dog, you might wish for a little less dogginess after a visit to this beautiful salt marsh on Sakonnet River. Protected by the Nature Conservancy, there are no trails here but you can walk on the "beach"—the open coastal access that varies in size and murkiness depending on the tides and the most recent storm. If your dog is anything like ours, during low tide she'll be doing an imitation of the *Creature From the Black Lagoon* after a romp here. Most of the time, the beach is about a quarter mile long. The rest of the time, bring a towel.

Dogs must be on leash.

From the intersection of State Routes 77 and 179, take State Route 77 south for 1.5 miles. Turn right onto Pond Bridge Road for a half mile then left onto

Neck Road. Make a right onto Fogland Road for a half mile and then turn left onto High Hill Road. The park is at the end of the road. Parking is available. Open a half hour before sunrise to a half hour after sunset. (401) 331-7110.

• Fort Barton/Fort Barton Woods 🐾🐾🐾 See **32** on page 132.

Fort Barton, a series of ancient earthen mounds and ridges overlooking the Sakonnet River, is the gateway to the Fort Barton Woods.

The fort dates back to the Revolutionary War when it served as a staging area for the colonists' invasion of Aquidneck Island, Newport, and the Battle of Rhode Island. On the site is a historic cemetery and an open observation deck offering impressive views of the river, the distant Narragansett Bay, and much of Newport County.

From the rear of the fort grounds you can follow a quarter-mile easement trail to the dense forest and hills of the Fort Barton Woods.

Trail maps are available at the Town Hall across the street from the fort entrance. Dog are allowed on leash only.

From U.S. Route 24, take State Route 77 south for three-quarters of a mile. Turn left onto Highland Road for three-quarters of a mile. The fort and parking are on the left at the intersection with Lawton Avenue. Open sunrise to sunset. (401) 625-6700.

• Weetamoo Woods 🐾🐾🐾 See **33** on page 132.

This town forest offers more than 450 acres of woodlands, cedar swamps, mountain laurel, ponds, streams, and rocky outcroppings. In addition, you'll find four miles of trails and remnants of the farms and mills that once occupied this land. The map at the trailhead marks numerous hiking destinations in the park. June is a good time to visit when the mountain laurel is in bloom.

From State Route 77, take East Road (State Route 179) east for three-quarters of a mile. The park's entrance is on the left. Follow the dirt road a quarter mile to the parking area and trailheads. Open sunrise to sunset. (401) 625-6700.

RESTAURANTS

Evelyn's Drive-In: Not only are the seafood sandwiches and clam rolls delicious, but the shaded, outdoor seating right on Nannaquaket Pond is the perfect and popular setting for dining with a hungry hound. 2335 Main Road; (401) 624-3100.

WESTERLY

PARKS, BEACHES, AND RECREATION AREAS

• Quonochontaug Barrier Beach 🐾🐾🐾 See **34** on page 132

When you are a dog, beach access is a hard thing to find, especially in Westerly where those "keep out" signs can really get a doggie down. Even at Quonochontaug Barrier Beach, dogs are restricted during the summer. This two-sided sandy peninsula lies between the Atlantic Ocean and Quonochontaug Pond, offering a mile-long beach on both sides. You even get to choose your water conditions: the warm calmer inland side or the livelier ocean side.

Dogs are not permitted from Memorial Day through Labor Day and must be leashed at other times. Everyone is required to stay off the dunes and beach grass.

From U.S. Route 1, take Langworthy Road south onto Weekapaug Road then onto Wawaloam Drive for a total distance of two miles. Turn right onto Spring Avenue for a half mile into the park. Parking is available. Open 7:30 A.M. to 9 P.M. (401) 596-2877.

•Wilcox Park 🐾 🐾 See 35 on page 132.

For a town green, this one's a big one. Offering 18 acres of manicured lawns, gardens, and shaded pathways, you'll find plenty of space for your dog to kick up her heels.

The park is located at the intersection of U.S. Routes 1, 1A, and 2. Parking is available. Open dawn to 9 P.M. (401) 596-2877.

PLACES TO STAY

Sea Shell Motel: Sure, most of the beaches are off-limits to dogs here in Westerly, but, when you stay at this family-oriented motel, you'll gain access to beautiful Winnapaug Pond. The motel has 10 rooms. Rates range from $50 to $100 plus a $10 pet charge per stay. The motel is open May through September. 19 Winnapaug Road, Westerly, RI 02891; (401) 348-8337; www.seashell-motel.com.

MASSACHUSETTS

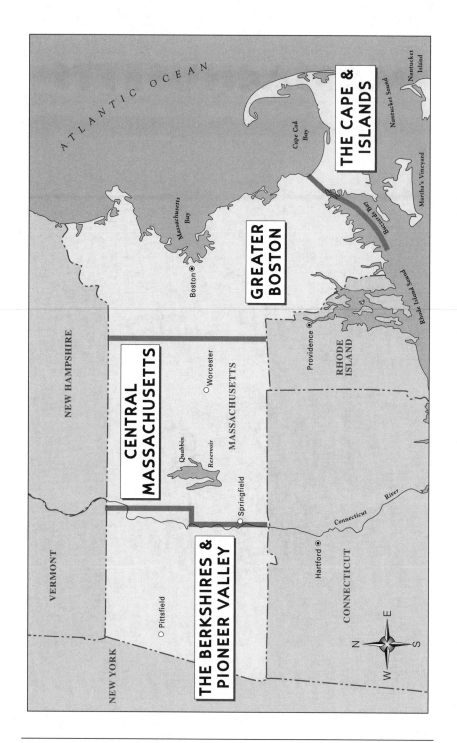

THE CAPE & ISLANDS

Nantucket Island

Nantucket Sound

Martha's Vineyard

Cape Cod Bay

Buzzards Bay

ATLANTIC OCEAN

Massachusetts Bay

Boston

GREATER BOSTON

Rhode Island Sound

Providence

RHODE ISLAND

Worcester

MASSACHUSETTS

CENTRAL MASSACHUSETTS

NEW HAMPSHIRE

Quabbin Reservoir

Springfield

Connecticut River

Hartford

CONNECTICUT

THE BERKSHIRES & PIONEER VALLEY

VERMONT

Pittsfield

NEW YORK

N E S W

MASSACHUSETTS

New England's earliest settlements were located in Massachusetts, and, since the time the Pilgrims first established Plymouth Colony in 1620, Massachusetts has been leading the way. The birthplace of American independence, Boston and the entire state played a vital leadership role in the early years of our new nation.

For 200 years, the eastern part of the Commonwealth earned its living by the sea. Whaling was predominant along the seacoast towns of Gloucester and New Bedford, and on the island of Nantucket. In the west, farming was the occupation of choice, and many of the naturally dense forests were removed to serve the agricultural needs of the population.

Today these forests are returning, just as the whales return to the sea. Instead of whale hunts, we have whale watches. Instead of forest destruction, citizens support forest management and conservation. For you and your dog this is good news, for it is on the conservation lands that you will find some of the best parks and, even better, most of them are leash free.

State Parks and State Forests: In Massachusetts, dogs must be leashed on all state property. The parks are good areas for walking your dog, although pets are not permitted on recreational beach areas during the summer. The state forests have more relaxed rules and are typically better spots to walk Spot. However, be aware that hunting is allowed in the state forests between October and February. For more information, contact the Massachusetts Department of Environmental Management Office of Public Information, 100 Cambridge Street, 19th Floor, Boston, MA 02202; (617) 626-1250; www. state.ma.us/dem.

The Trustees of Reservations: Founded more than a century ago by Boston Parks' founder Charles Eliot, this preservation organization manages more than 75 properties on nearly 18,000 acres throughout the Commonwealth. Most of the lands have been given in trust through private donations, and, although all are beautiful, we've only listed the parks that both welcome dogs and are appropriate for you and your pet. Dogs must be leashed on most Trustees properties with a few exceptions which are noted. For more information or to become a member, contact 572 Essex Street, Beverly, MA 01915; (978) 921-1944.

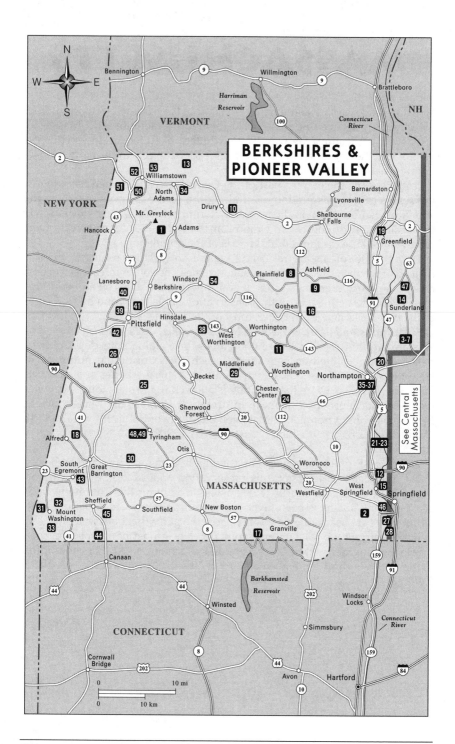

BERKSHIRES &
PIONEER VALLEY

6
THE BERKSHIRES AND PIONEER VALLEY

The westernmost area of Massachusetts, affectionately known as "The Berkshires," features small 19th-century mill towns and lush vacation resorts known for their pastoral settings. Bordered to the east by the Berkshire Mountains and to the west by the Housatonic River, this lovely area was once home to the Native American tribes the Mohegans and the Mohawks. Since the 17th century, however, European settlers have lived and played here. Such diverse residents as Norman Rockwell, Nathaniel Hawthorne, and Andrew Carnegie all had summer homes here; today you and your dog can enjoy exploring the history and beauty of this special place.

The Pioneer Valley, known as the "western frontier" until well into the 18th century, gets its name from the many 17th-century settlements located along the Connecticut River. Today the "pioneer" towns are the college towns of Amherst, Northampton, and Hadley which add an eclectic mix of small-town living and hip intellectualism to the area. Dwarfed by Mount Tom and Holyoke Reservations, these areas offer many hiking opportunities for you and your pup.

Appalachian Trail: Over 80 miles of the Appalachian Trail pass through Massachusetts' Berkshire Mountains and Housatonic Valley. The trail enters the Commonwealth in the southwestern corner at Mount Everett State Reservation in Mount Washington and departs into Vermont at Clarksburg State Park in Clarksburg.

Dogs need to be leashed on the trail, which is open 24 hours a day. For information about the Appalachian Trail in Massachusetts, call the Appalachian Mountain Club at (413) 442-8928.

Metacomet-Monadnock Trail: The MM Trail, as it is nicknamed, is one of three routes that run north and south across the entire state. It is 117 miles in length following the Holyoke Range and the Connecticut River from the Connecticut state line into New Hampshire and Mount Monadnock. Although dogs are not permitted on Mount Monadnock, that's New Hampshire's choice. In Massachusetts, you and you four-legged trail mate can hike the entire portion in the Commonwealth, about 98 miles from Southwick to Northfield. Other access points are in Hadley, Holyoke, and Wendell. Dogs must be leashed.

For more information, call the Massachusetts Department of Environmental Management (DEM) at (617) 727-3180.

Norwottuck Rail Trail: This state-run, paved trail runs for 10 miles from Amherst to Northampton through Hadley. The bike path was originally a railway built in 1887 that connected Northampton and Boston. You can still see some of the posts along the route that indicated when the train should sound its whistle. The highlight of the bike path is the crossing of the Connecticut River on a half-mile-long former railroad bridge. Eventually the path will connect to the Northampton Bikeway, only a block away from Northampton terminus.

Dogs must be leashed in all state parks. Parking and access is at Connecticut River Greenway State Park in Northampton, Mountain Farms Mall (off State Route 9) in Hadley, and at Station Road in South Amherst. For brochures and more information, call (413) 586-8706.

Robert Frost Trail: This 33-mile trail, named for the poet who once taught at Amherst College, was built and is maintained by the Amherst Conservation Commission. It runs from the Mount Holyoke Range to Mount Toby, linking many of the Amherst conservation properties, as well as state parks and forests in Hampshire County. You can recognize the trail by the orange blazes on trees and rocks. Occasionally the trail overlaps with the Metacomet-Monadnock Trail. The trail begins at the Notch Visitor's Center in the Holyoke Range State Park. For a $4 trail map and more information, contact the Amherst Conservation Commission at the Amherst Town Hall. (413) 256-4045.

ADAMS

PARKS, BEACHES, AND RECREATION AREAS

•**Mount Greylock State Reservation** 🐾 🐾 🐾 🐾 See ❶ on page 154.
This spectacular park in the Berkshires lays claim to many notable distinctions. Mount Greylock, at 3,491 feet, is the highest point in the Commonwealth and offers views of five states. The reservation became Massachusetts's first state park in 1898. And transcendentalists Herman Melville and Henry David Thoreau found inspiration in these woods and mountains. The Appalachian Trail passes through the reservation and is part

of an elaborate 45-mile trail system. In all, the 12,500-acre park has something for everyone.

At the summit of Mount Greylock (which you can drive to) is the War Memorial, Bascom Lodge (open daily from 7 A.M. to 10 P.M., mid-May to mid-October), and views of three states. The Hopper, a ravine of old-growth spruce trees, and March Cataract Falls, a 30-foot cascade, are popular hiking destinations. Either location can be easily reached on one-mile hiking paths. We suggest you stop by the Visitor's Center on Rockwell Road for free maps and trail information to reach the countless spots you and Spot will love.

Happy campers will be pleased to know your leashed dog is welcome in the campground. There are 35 sites for tents and RVs (no hookups); primitive toilets are provided. Rates are $5 to $6 per night. Open Memorial Day to mid-October. For reservations, call (877) 422-6762.

As in all Massachusetts state parks, dogs must be kept on leash.

From U.S. Route 7 in Lanesborough, take North Main Street north for a half mile. Turn right onto Quarry Road (Greylock Road), then left onto Rockwell Road and into the park. Note that Rockwell Road is closed in the winter. Open sunrise to a half hour after sunset. (413) 499-4262.

PLACES TO STAY
Mount Greylock State Reservation camping: See page 156.

DIVERSIONS
Ramblin' Man and Dog: All of western Massachusetts comes out for the Mount Greylock Ramble. The Columbus Day hike up the highest mountain in the Commonwealth is an annual tradition going back 40 years. It's also part of the northern Berkshires' annual Fall Foliage Festival that takes place the first week in October. The climb is rated moderate, and each person that reaches the top receives a certificate to recognize the achievement (be sure to share it with your trail hound). For exact time and more information, call (413) 663-3735.

AGAWAM

PARKS, BEACHES, AND RECREATION AREAS

• Robinson State Park 🐾🐾🐾 See 🔢 on page 154.
This 800-acre park, created in 1934 from a generous donation by a farmer named Robinson, serves as a major day-use area for the Springfield area. This long stretch of forest with five miles of frontage on the Westfield River offers many options for the urban pooch who longs for a little adventure.

Take your dog on the two-mile walk along the river trail. Or, if you're looking for more than a swim, take a three-mile hike on flat easy trails that run over Miller Brook and through the quiet forest. This trail starts at the end of the parking area; you'll enter the woods on a path which turns into a footbridge that leads over the brook. Your dog can cool herself in the water here before proceeding through the forest. Follow the blue markers to stay on the trail.

Dogs must be on leash.

From State Route 57, take State Route 187 (North Westfield Street) north for three-quarters of a mile. Turn right onto North Street. The park is on the left. Open 8 A.M. to 8 P.M. (413) 786-2877.

AMHERST

As this book goes to press, Amherst has a "flexible" leash law—meaning dogs under voice control may go without their leashes. However, this law stands in jeopardy, and we can't assure you that it will still stand by the time you read this. So although most of the parks are listed as leash free, you may want to check on the current restrictions.

PARKS, BEACHES, AND RECREATION AREAS

• **Amethyst Brook Conservation Area** 🐾🐾🐾🐾 🐕 See **3** on page 154.

This is *the* place for dogs in Amherst. During the 5:30 to 6:30 P.M. "rush hour," you and your dog will meet up with plenty of other happy dogs romping in the meadow or splashing in Amethyst Brook.

Although there are several loop trails that weave through the forest here, the main trail follows the Robert Frost Trail which runs through the heart of the conservation area and continues another 26 miles north. You can either make this park your destination (as most people do) or take a longer hike on the Frost Trail.

If Amethyst Brook is your destination, you can hike a short two-tenths of a mile to the meadow and a clean, cool diversion canal at the entrance to the woods. Many people never get farther than this popular spot, but, if you continue on in the forest, you'll traverse a lovely woodland walk along the northern branch of Amethyst Brook on flat, easy trails. A hike of the entire property covers about two miles.

From Amherst Center, take Main Street east for one mile onto Pelham Road. The parking area and trailhead are on your left. Open dawn to dusk. (413) 256-4045.

• **Groff Park** 🐾🐾 See **4** on page 154.

This recreational park is mainly composed of large, well-maintained ball fields, but a wooded picnic area with some short trails is along the western side. Mutt mitts are available at the parking area, and local dogs make this a popular dog-walking spot. You won't get a great workout, but you will meet plenty of other tail-waggers. Dogs must be leashed.

From Amherst Center, take State Route 116 south for one mile. Turn left onto Mill Lane. The park is on your left. Open 8:30 A.M. to 8:30 P.M. (413) 253-0700.

• **Larch Hill Conservation Area** 🐾🐾🐾 🐕 See **5** on page 154.

This wonderful conservation are, offers 27 acres of beautifully manicured nature trails. Once part of a family estate, the area has been preserved since the 1970s and is home to the Hitchcock Center for the Environment, an educational organization that offers nature walks and conservation programs to area schools. The mixture of historical gardens, landscaped pools, and maple and larch trees makes a visit here peaceful, unusual, and fun. You can walk here from town, which makes it a popular destination, but you will think you're a hundred miles away from civilization. A detailed map is available at the Hitchcock Center.

Dogs must be on leash on the nature trail but may be off leash under voice control on other trails.

From Main Street, take Pleasant Street (State Route 116) south for a half mile. The park entrance is on the right. The center is open from 9 A.M. to 4 P.M. The trails are open dawn to dusk. (413) 256-6006.

• Mill River Recreation Area 🐾🐾🐾 🐕 See ⑥ on page 154.

This recreation area offers something for everyone. Although there are mostly ball fields at the main park entrance, if you proceed through the woods beyond, you'll walk along quiet Mill River to Puffer Pond, a popular swimming hole. From here you can swim, hike the pond trail, play in the meadow on the northern end of the pond, or branch off into the Pulpit Hill Woods to the north. In all, there are over 200 acres to explore, and all of them will be loved by your dog.

In the summer, dogs are not allowed on the southern side of Puffer's Pond off State Road. Dogs are allowed to swim on the northern side of the pond before 10 A.M. and after 6 P.M. Dogs must be leashed at the parking areas and around the pond; they may be off leash on the trails.

To reach the main parking area from Main Street, take North Pleasant Street north for three miles. Turn right onto Pine Road to where the road splits. Take the right split onto State Route 63, and turn almost immediately into the park on your right. The trails start behind the ball fields.

To reach Puffer's Pond, continue past the main entrance on State Route 63. Turn right onto Pulpit Hill Road and then take another right onto Mill Road. The northern parking area will be on your left at the junction of Summer Street. The parking gate closes at 7:30 P.M. Trails are open dawn to dusk. (413) 256-4045.

• Holyoke Range State Park 🐾🐾🐾 See ⑦ on page 154.

Although Mount Holyoke and its famous Summit House is the most well-known peak in this range, Mount Norwottuck is actually the highest peak at 1,106 feet. There are many trails for you and your dog to explore at this 2,252-acre park, and you'll probably return again and again to do so. Both the Robert Frost Trail and the Metacomet-Monadnock Trail run through this park, and Rattlesnake Knob, a scenic vista, is a popular destination. For a trail map, stop by the Notch Visitor Center, open Monday to Thursday from 8 A.M. to 4 P.M., at the parking entrance.

From Main Street, take Pleasant Street (State Route 116) south for five miles. The Visitor Center and park are on your left. Open 8 A.M. to 8 P.M. (413) 586-0350.

RESTAURANTS

Amber Waves: Take your dog to the Far East—or at least as far east as Main Street. This popular Asian café will satisfy your hunger pangs with dishes like Sichuan Peanut Sauce Noodles or Vietnamese Vermicelli Rice Salad. Eat at one of the small tables outside. 63 Main Street; (413) 253-9200.

Amherst Brewing Company: Plenty of outdoor seating is available at this festive local watering hole. Standard pub fare is served, but the street scene makes it a fun place to dine. 24–36 North Pleasant Street; (413) 253-4400.

Bart's Homemade: An espresso bar and ice-cream shop (with some sandwiches and salads mixed in for those who can't live on caffeine and sugar alone), this Pleasant Street café has a great outdoor seating area from which to watch the world drift by. Try one of the many coffee and ice-cream blended drinks, and your dog will need to leash you for the rest of the day. 103 North Pleasant Street; (413) 253-9371.

The Black Sheep Bakery Café: For the best baked bread in the Pioneer Valley, get your picnic supplies at this café. Or just about any other meal you wish. Sandwiches like Holy Guacamole, Smokey Joe's, or *C'est la Brie* are available to go or to eat at one of the outdoor tables. 79 Main Street; (413) 253-3442.

La Veracruzana: This Mexican grill offers unique southwestern and Mexican cuisine at reasonable prices. Try a sincronizada with cactus leaf or chorizo. (Then say that three times fast!) Outdoor tables overlook the town common. 63 South Pleasant Street; (413) 253-6900.

PLACES TO STAY

Lord Jeffery Inn: This elegant 48-room inn located in the heart of Amherst will be a welcome pleasure for you and your pup. Dogs are allowed in smoking rooms only, but the staff is very hospitable, and you'll love staying here. All the rooms are spacious and furnished with antiques. An on-site restaurant provides room service for all meals including your complimentary breakfast, if you wish. Rooms range from $79 to $139; suites range from $129 to $89. Dogs are $15 per night. 30 Boltwood Avenue, Amherst, MA 01002; (413) 253-2576, (800) 742-0358; www.pinnacle-inns.com.

ASHFIELD

PARKS, BEACHES, AND RECREATION AREAS

• **Bear Swamp Reservation** 🐾🐾🐾 See 🖳 on page 154.

Maybe the name discourages folks, but this little-visited reservation is much more than a "swamp." Managed by the Trustees of Reservations, these 266 acres are like a well-guarded secret offering three miles of trails and an abundance of wildlife. The well-marked trails take you past 150-year-old stone walls (set up by farmers to mark old property lines), lovely woodlands, a small brook, and even an active beaver dam on Beaver Pond. The whole loop on four different trails is about 2.5 miles, and you and your leashed dog will be rewarded with a scenic walk away from the crowds. Maybe we should keep it a secret after all!

Dogs need to be leashed.

From State Routes 112 and 116, take Hawley Road west for 1.5 miles. The park entrance is on the left. Open sunrise to sunset. (413) 684-0148.

• **Chapelbrook Reservation** 🐾🐾🐾🐾 See 🖳 on page 154.

This 143-acre park is owned by the Trustees of Reservations, and, once you enter the woodland and hear the sound of cascading water, you'll know you're in for a treat. You have the choice of two lovely hikes—a short seven-tenths-of-a-mile walk along Chapel Brook, or a one-mile route up Pony Mountain.

From the parking area, you can view the falls along the road, then proceed down a dirt road along the brook until it dead-ends at private property. This walk offers cool forest shade, and your dog will enjoy refreshing herself in the waters. For those who prefer a little more exercise, go across Williamsburg Road from the parking area and take the main Summit Trail up Pony Mountain. The trail can be steep in places, but it is well worth the effort.

Dogs must be leashed.

From State Route 112, take State Route 116 east for 1.5 miles. Turn right onto Williamsburg Road for two miles. The park entrance is on the right at the bridge. Open sunrise to sunset. (413) 684-0148.

CHARLEMONT

PARKS, BEACHES, AND RECREATION AREAS

• Mohawk Trail State Forest 🐾🐾🐾🐾 See **10** on page 154.

The 6,457 acres in this state forest on the Mohawk Trail has been called "one of the most scenic woodland areas of Massachusetts," and, after a visit, it's hard to argue with the Commonwealth's visitors guide. The rich, dense forest of pine, maple, birch, and oak, mixed with fields of wild flowers and mountain laurel, is a haven of natural beauty. The highlight of the forest, and the numerous hiking routes through it, is the grove of old-growth trees on Clark Ridge.

Other hiking destinations lead to the peaks of Clark and Todd Mountains and the many rivers, streams, and ponds found in the park. For maps and information, stop by the forest headquarters at the main parking area.

Dogs must be on leash in all state parks.

From State Route 8A, take U.S. Route 2 (Mohawk Trail) west for 3.75 miles. The park entrance is on the right. Plenty of parking is available. Open 9:30 A.M. to 7:30 P.M. (413) 339-5504.

NATURE HIKES AND URBAN WALKS

Mohawk Park: This small park along U.S. Route 2, better known as the Mohawk Trail, is home to the "Hail to the Sunrise" Memorial—a monument to the famous Indian trade path and the tribes that used it. The park is only a few grassy acres, but it's a good place for a break when you are traveling this historic route. The Mohawk Trail dates back thousands of years. The actual paved road opened in 1914, becoming the first scenic road in New England. Open 24 hours a day. (413) 773-5463.

PLACES TO STAY

Charlemont Inn: This no-frills, 16-room motor inn allows well-behaved dogs. Rooms range from $39 to $69. Box 316, Charlemont, MA 01339; (413) 339-5796.

Hilltop Motel: This seven-room motel along the Mohawk Trail looks out over the valley below. Although these aren't luxury digs, you'll find the rooms clean and comfortable with great views. Rooms range from $30 to $79. 2023 Mohawk Trail (U.S. Route 2) Charlemont, MA 01339; (413) 625-2587.

Mohawk Trail State Forest: This state forest campground has five cabins (each sleeps up to four) and 56 sites for tents and RVs (no hookups) along the Cold River. Dogs must be on leash and cannot be left unattended. Nightly rates are $10 to $12 for campsites and $25 to $35 for the cabins. Open year-round except for the tent sites, which are open May through Columbus Day. P.O. Box 7, Route 2, Charlemont, MA 01339. Call (413) 339-5504 for information or (877) 422-6762 for reservations.

CHESTERFIELD

PARKS, BEACHES, AND RECREATION AREAS

• Chesterfield Gorge 🐾🐾🐾 🐾 See **11** on page 154.

You won't find any place quite like this 166-acre property, owned by the Trustees of Reservations. The gorge itself, formed by glacial movement and then thousands more years of rivers smoothing the stone, has a 100-foot drop and is nothing short of spectacular. Dogs must be on leash here for their own protection.

At the upper end of the Gorge are the remains of High Bridge, a historic crossing built in 1739 as part of the Boston-Albany Post Road. British troops crossed the bridge following their defeat at Saratoga in 1777.

The property abuts the Gilbert Bliss State Forest, so for a longer hike you can enter the forest and trails there. A $2 entrance fee is charged to non–Trustee of Reservations members.

From State Route 143, take Ireland Street south for one mile. Turn left onto River Road for a quarter mile. The park is on the left. Open sunrise to sunset. (413) 684-0148.

CHICOPEE

PARKS, BEACHES, AND RECREATION AREAS

• Chicopee Memorial State Park 🐾🐾🐾 See **12** on page 154.

This 575-acre park has two ponds, a swimming beach, and a wide network of trails for you and your dog to enjoy. Although you can't romp with the other sunbathers at Cooley Reservoir, your dog can swim along the back shore and in Cooley Brook, which runs along the two-mile Big Foot Trail through the northern section of the park.

Canoes are also popular on Cooley Reservoir and are available to rent for a day or half day. For details and reservations, call (413) 534-2352

Leashed dogs are welcome at the picnic shelters and on the trails. A map is available at the main parking area. There is a $2 day-use fee.

From the Massachusetts Turnpike (Interstate 90), take Exit 6 to Johnny Cakes Hollow Road north. The park is on the left. Open 9 A.M. to 8 P.M. (413) 594-9416.

PLACES TO STAY

Motel 6: All Motel 6 locations allow one dog per room, as long as he is not left unattended. Rates are $59 per room. Burnett Road, Chicopee, MA 01020; (413) 592-5141, (800) 4-MOTEL6; www.motel6.com.

CLARKSBURG

PARKS, BEACHES, AND RECREATION AREAS

• **Clarksburg State Park** 🐾🐾🐾 See **13** on page 154.

It has been said that there is no better place to view the fall foliage than in New England. And New Englanders head to the Berkshires and the Pioneer Valley to view the best of the autumn spectacle. A popular spot for leaf peeping is here in the town of Clarksburg near the Vermont border.

The park is home to a rich and dense forest of pines and maples surrounding a popular swimming hole, Mauserts Pond. Around the pond is a short footpath that is good for viewing the leafy display and providing access points to the water.

Camping is available here at 47 wooded sites for tents and RVs. Rates are $10 to $12 per night. Open mid-May to mid-October. Call (877) 422-6762 for reservations.

Dogs need to be leashed in all state parks. There is $2 day-use fee.

From U.S. Route 8, take Middle Road west for a quarter mile. The park is on your right. Parking is available. Open sunrise to a half hour after sunset. (413) 663-8469.

PLACES TO STAY

Clarksburg State Park camping: See above.

CUMMINGTON

NATURE HIKES AND URBAN WALKS

" This little rill, that from the springs,
Of yonder grove its current brings,
Plays on the slope awhile, and then
Goes prattling into groves again. . . "

William Cullen Bryant Homestead: Cullen wrote the above words to "The Rivulet" while at this home in 1823. Now a property of the Trustees of Reservations, you can walk along Rivulet Brook and see the brook that inspired those lines. On this short one-mile path you and your dog will enjoy a tranquil spot to spend an hour. No admission fee is charged to use the trails, which are open all year. There is a charge to visit the house, but dogs aren't allowed inside anyway.

Dogs must be on leash.

From State Route 9, take State Route 112 east for 1.5 miles to Bryant Four Corners. The homestead is on your left with a small parking area on your right. Open sunrise to sunset. (413) 684-0148.

DEERFIELD

PARKS, BEACHES, AND RECREATION AREAS

• **Mount Sugarloaf State Reservation** 🐾🐾 🐾 See **14** on page 154.

Mount Sugarloaf is only 652 feet high, but it rises quickly out of the Pioneer

Valley and has no nearby rivals when it comes to height. So there are, literally, drop-dead views from the steep cliffs at the summit.

Although dogs may appreciate the cooling breezes carrying all sorts of scents at the top, the park does not offer them much more. You can hike one short trail to the summit, but it is fairly difficult because it climbs Mount Sugarloaf via a rocky route. An easier way to the summit is to drive up the reservation's Mountain Road.

Dogs must be leashed in all state parks.

From Interstate 91, take exit 24 to State Route 116 east for one mile. The park and Sugarloaf Mountain Road is on the left. Open sunrise to sunset. (413) 545-5993.

NATURE HIKES AND URBAN WALKS

Historic Deerfield: Deerfield dates all the way back to 1669 when it was a British outpost on the Deerfield River. And, if you take a walk down Old Main Street, or "The Street" as it is more commonly known, you'll see not much has changed since those pioneer days. The five-block historic district includes homes, shops, and farms from the 18th and 19th centuries. Contemporary canines are not permitted in the historic buildings. Parking is available. (413) 774-5581.

RESTAURANTS

Chandler's Tavern and Restaurant: This elegant restaurant on the grounds of the Yankee Candle Company is one of the best loved in the Pioneer Valley. The beautiful garden patio is open during the summer months, and you and your dog are allowed to dine on the outer tables. Serving lunch and dinner, you'll have a varied continental menu to choose from. At the intersection of State Routes 5 and 10; (413) 665-1277.

PLACES TO STAY

Motel 6: All Motel 6 locations allow dogs, as long as you don't leave your pet unattended. One dog is welcome per room. Rates are $59 per night. U.S. Route 5, South Deerfield, MA 01373; (413) 665-7161, (800) 4-MOTEL6; www. motel6.com.

EAST LONGMEADOW

PARKS, BEACHES, AND RECREATION AREAS

• **Heritage Park** 🐾 🐾 See **15** on page 154.

This 20-acre park will provide dogs with a short walk through a pine forest surrounding a grassy picnic area and a pond. Although the pond is only the type a duck could love, your own dog may decide ducky is just fine with him, so we suggest you abide by the leash law and keep your pup on leash. The woodland stroll and a shady lunch spot should make for a leisurely break on a summer day.

The park is at the intersection of State Route 83 and Dearborn Avenue. Open 5 A.M. to 9 P.M. (413) 525-5437.

EGREMONT

PLACES TO STAY

Baldwin Grange Bed-and-Breakfast Inn: This elegant 1803 Federal-style inn has been newly restored to its original wood-paneled glory. There are eight lovely rooms, each with a private bath and four-poster bed, some with fireplaces. Dogs are permitted in the off-season only, and your pet needs prior permission from the management. Off-season rates range from $90 to $120. P.O. Box 47, North Egremont, MA 01252; (413) 528-2808, (888) 770-8350; www.baldwingrangeinn.com.

Swiss Hutte: This charming chalet-style inn has 12 modern rooms in a cozy setting. Quiet brooks run across the property, and the rooms have all the amenities you could wish for. Rates range from $75 to $110 or $125 to $160 including breakfast and dinner. Advance notice is required for pets. State Route 23; (413) 528-6200; www.swisshutte.com.

FLORIDA

RESTAURANTS

Summit Café: This hillside restaurant lies high on a mountain ridge along State Route 2. You and your dog are welcome on the outdoor deck which overlooks the valley below. The menu features steak, fish, chicken, and scrumptious salads. The view is, well, amazing. U.S. Route 2; (413) 662-2625.

PLACES TO STAY

Whitcomb Summit Motel and Cottages: Dogs are not permitted in the motel, but they are welcome in the very rustic cottages. The cabins are heated and have running water and literally sit at the summit of Mount Whitcomb. Rates are $45 to $75. 229 Mohawk Trail, Florida, MA 01247; (413) 662-2625, (800) 547-0944; whitcombsummit.com.

GOSHEN

PARKS, BEACHES, AND RECREATION AREAS

• **Daughters of the American Revolution State Forest** 🐾 🐾 🐾 See **16** on page 154.

This state forest was created in 1922 from a land donation from the Daughters of the American Revolution (D.A.R.). The park totals over 1,600 acres, and, with more than 15 miles of trails, you'll find plenty of solitude here. Blue marks the spot for hiking, red for hiking and bridle, and orange for cross-country skiing.

The most popular area is the busy Upper Highland Lake recreation area. Your dog can't swim there in the summer, but if you head for Moose's Hill, you'll leave the crowds behind. At 1,697 feet it is the highest point in valley (we have no idea why it's a hill and not a mountain, but, hey, your dog won't care what they call it!).

Camping is allowed here, and the 50 sites fill up early. Nightly rates are $10 to $12 for campsites; reservations are recommended during the summer.

Open May to Columbus Day for tents and year-round for RVs. Call (877) 422-6762 for reservations.

There is a $2 parking fee at Upper Highland Lake in the summer. If you wish to avoid the fee, park at the Ludwig Road entrance. Dogs need to be leashed in all state parks.

From State Route 9, take State Route 112 north for one mile. The park entrance is on the right. To reach Ludwig Road from State Route 112 in Ashfield, take State Route 116 east for 2.5 miles. Turn right onto Williamsburg Road for three miles, then right onto Ludwig Road which will lead to the western boundary and a gate. Open sunrise to a half hour after sunset. (413) 268-7098.

PLACES TO STAY

Daughters of the American Revolution State Forest camping: See page 154.

GRANVILLE

PARKS, BEACHES, AND RECREATION AREAS

• **Granville State Forest** 🐾🐾🐾 See **17** on page 154.

With 2,397 acres in Granville State Forest alone plus the adjacent Tunix State Forest right across the border in Connecticut, endless opportunities await for your pup to download an abundance of pent-up energy.

This dense forest has surprisingly few visitors, even in the summer, so if you're looking for a getaway, this could be it.

For a fabulous swimming hole that allows dogs in the summer, try the falls at Hubbard Brook. It has a relatively safe "rock slide," a natural chute that shimmies over a short fall into a deep swimming hole along the Hubbard River. You can reach this glorious spot through the campground on a trail that hugs the brook. Along the way, you and your leashed pooch will enjoy the cool shaded path and many places to wallow in the water. Although the trails aren't marked, all of them all well traveled and easy to follow.

Campers will be pleased to know that there is a small 22-site campground with quite a few amenities. Rates are $12 per night, plus overnight parking fee. A discount is offered to Massachusetts residents. For reservations, call (877) 422-6762.

Dog must be on leash. There is a $2 day-use fee.

From State Route 57, take West Hartland Road south into the park. Open sunrise to a half hour after sunset. (413) 357-6611.

PLACES TO STAY

Granville State Forest camping: See above.

GREAT BARRINGTON

PARKS, BEACHES, AND RECREATION AREAS

• **Monument Mountain Reservation** 🐾🐾🐾 🐕 See **18** on page 154.

This towering mixture of majestic pines and oaks with medieval, rocky outcroppings is owned by the Trustees of Reservations and offers 503 acres and three miles of hiking trails. The actual climb to the top of Monument Mountain (1,735 feet at Squaw Peak) is steep in sections but can be accomplished by most dogs. Once at the top, you will be awed by the breathtaking views of the Housatonic Valley below and the Taconic and Hoosac Ranges in the distance.

Although it's a hike recommended at all the tourist stops, the trail does not get overly crowded, but you are bound to run into someone. In fact, in 1850 Herman Melville crossed paths with Nathaniel Hawthorne here. We wonder what they had to say to each other. The two literary geniuses probably just talked about the weather and moved on.

Dogs must be under voice command.

From the intersection of U.S. Route 7 and State Route 23 (State Road), take U.S. Route 7 north for 2.5 miles. The park and a dirt parking lot are on the left. Open sunrise to sunset. (413) 298-3239.

PLACES TO STAY

Chez Gabrielle: This small two-bedroom guest house offers all the comforts of home. The rooms are tastefully furnished and have fireplaces and small refrigerators. They even provide dog doors so your pet can go into the fenced-in yard easily! Continental breakfast is served. Rooms range from $90 to $125 per night, plus an additional $10 pet fee per night. 320 State Road, Route 23E, Great Barrington, MA 01230; (413) 528-0906.

Mountain View Motel: Prior permission is needed for your pet to stay at this standard motor lodge. Rates range from $45 to $175, plus an additional charge of $15 per night for your pet. 304 State Road (State Route 23), Great Barrington, MA 01230; (413) 528-0250.

The Turning Point Inn: This hilltop inn is on 2.5 acres next to the Appalachian Trail and the Butternut Ski Resort. Dogs are not permitted in the 1800 Federal Colonial inn, but they can stay with you in the two-floor, two-bedroom cottage with its own kitchen. Breakfast is included. Rates range from $210 to $230. 3 Lake Buel Road; Great Barrington, MA 01230; (413) 528-4777.

Wainwright Inn: Originally a tavern dating back to 1766, this elegant, eight-room bed-and-breakfast awaits tuckered travelers and pooped pups. All rooms have private baths and cozy furnishings. Dogs are allowed with prior approval and with a one night's refundable deposit. Rates range from $75 to $200 per night, including full breakfast. 518 South Main Street, Great Barrington, MA 01230; (413) 528-2062; www.wainwrightinn.com.

RESTAURANTS

Danico's Roadside Grill: It's said that there are more restaurants per person in the Berkshires than anywhere else in the United States, but that still doesn't keep the crowds from forming at Danico's. This souped-up roadside stand offers a broad menu of ice cream, burgers, fish and chips, and sausage and peppers, all to be enjoyed under the pines at their picnic tables. 935 Main Street (U.S. Route 7); (413) 528-5558.

Four Brothers Pizza Inn: It normally takes four brothers cooking 24 hours a day to keep our hungry lot fed, and Four Brothers does it with plenty of zesty taste. Enjoy anything off the Greek-style menu (pizza and pastas are the specialties) at their shady outdoor tables. Stockbridge Road; (413) 528-9684.

Sweet Peas: If hummus, alfalfa sprouts, or kalamatas are part of your daily diet, then you are sure to enjoy lunch at Sweet Peas. Actually, the creative wraps, sandwiches, chilis, salads, and soups are delicious enough to appease even the most finicky of eaters. If that fails, there is always the homemade ice cream. The outdoor patio helps too. 325 Stockbridge Road; (413) 528-7786.

FESTIVALS

A Taste of the Berkshires: Sure George, Inu, and Rocky like a nice outing on the trail, but what's number one in their book is food and more food. That's why Great Barrington's September smorgasbord of farm-fresh produce, restaurants' specialties, and caterers' delights is such a big hit. Workshops on farm life are offered too. The feast is held at the Band Stand Green the weekend after Labor Day. (413) 528-1947.

GREENFIELD

PARKS, BEACHES, AND RECREATION AREAS

• **Rocky Mountain and Highland Park** 🐾🐾🐾🐾 ◀🐾 See **19** on page 154.

Rocky is convinced they named this mountain for him, so please don't tell him that it was named long before he was born. In fact, this special park is managed by the town of Greenfield and features several scenic points—the Poet's Seat Tower, named for poet Frederick Tuckerman, a contemporary of Emerson, Hawthorne, and Dickinson, and Sachem Head, a rock formation that looks like a bear in profile. On the northern side of the park is Rocky Mountain; Highland Park and Temple Woods occupy the southern section.

Poet's Seat Tower sits atop the Rocky Mountain Loop Trail, and the overlook is magnificent. This trail is marked by red blazes and is well traveled. After Tuckerman's death in 1873, a small wooden tower was erected in his memory. That has since been replaced by a stone tower, and we're sure you'll agree this is a place to conjure creativity.

Follow the blue-blazed Pocumtuck Ridge Trail in the opposite direction from the parking area, and you'll wander through Temple Woods towards Sachem Head. You'll find an old bear cave to explore as you're looking for the "bear" profile along the cliffs of Sachem Head. In all, the two loops are two miles each—or you might wish to combine them for a leisurely afternoon's hike.

Dogs must be on leash.

From U.S. Route 5 (Federal Street), take Maple Street east for a half mile. Turn right onto Mountain Road. The park is on the left. Parking is available. Open 6 A.M. to 10 P.M. (413) 773-5463.

NATURE HIKES AND URBAN WALKS

Walking Tour of Historic Greenfield: Take this self-guided tour of downtown Greenfield and explore the many historical points of interest in this 300-year-old village. From stately Victorian homes to Civil War monuments to churches that date back over 200 years, you and your dog will enjoy exploring life as it was when Greenfield was a British outpost. Maps are available at the Court Square Town Common Information Booth on Main Street. (413) 774-2791.

RESTAURANTS

Laughing Goat Coffeehouse and Café: Enjoy all the action on Main Street plus a morning cup of coffee and bagel or a full lunch menu at this sidewalk café. 286 Main Street; (413) 774-3841.

PLACES TO STAY

The Brandt House: This eight-room bed-and-breakfast is located right in town. Dogs are allowed in select rooms with advance reservations. Rates range from $75 to $150 per night. Breakfast is included. 29 Highland Avenue, Greenfield, MA 01301; (413) 774-3329, (800) 235-3329.

Candlelight Inn: This 56-room motel is located right on State Route 2 and is definitely in the no-frills category. But if you really need a place for the night, this one will do. Rates range from $39 to $70. 208 Mohawk Trail, Greenfield, MA 01301; (413) 772-0101, (888) 262-0520.

Old Tavern Farm: This quaint bed-and-breakfast is located just outside of town on a working farm. They offer three comfortable rooms, and the proprietors will make you feel right at home. Dogs must be leashed on the property. Rates range from $75 to $149. Full country breakfast served each morning. 817 Colrain Road, Greenfield, MA 01301; (413) 772-0474.

FESTIVALS

A Classic Day in Greenfield: We don't know how many days are like this, but if every day were a Classic Day, your dog might never want to leave. This annual town celebration, held every May, features live music, food, entertainment, and activities for all ages. The event is held at the Town Common. Call for dates and details. (413) 773-5463.

HADLEY

PARKS, BEACHES, AND RECREATION AREAS

• **Joseph Skinner State Park** 🐾 🐾 See **20** on page 154.
Visitors have been coming to the Summit House on top of Mount Holyoke since the 1850s, and a structure has been on this site since 1821—making it the oldest mountain resort in America. From 1854 to 1942 a cable railway transported tourists to the top, and, although you can still drive to the summit, George thinks taking the easy way is for wimps. Real dogs walk!

From the rear of the parking area (which is sometimes gated in the colder months), take the Two Forest Trail to the summit. It's a mile to the 940-foot peak.

Dogs must be leashed in all state parks.

From State Route 9, take State Route 47 south for two miles. The park entrance is on the left. Open sunrise to a half hour after sunset. (413) 586-0350.

RESTAURANTS

Pete's Drive-In: For a blast from the past, stop by this nifty roadside diner for a great meal and a little retro economics, as well. In addition to the period decor, the two-burgers-for-two-bucks special makes dining here a true '50s experience. Plenty of shady picnic tables are available for your dog to share one of those burgers. Located conveniently on the Norwottuck Bike Trail. 287 Russell Street (State Route 9); (413) 585-0241.

PLACES TO STAY

Clark Tavern Inn Bed-and-Breakfast: This small bed-and-breakfast offers quiet hospitality in three charming rooms. A delicious breakfast is served each morning, and dogs are welcome in one of the rooms. Reservations are required. Rates range from $75 to $165. 98 Bay Road, Hadley, MA 01035; (413) 586-1900.

Howard Johnson Inn: This 100-room hotel is a comfortable, standard HoJo's. Full amenities and fairly large rooms are standard fare. Dogs are welcome in most rooms. Rates range from $50 to $129. 401 Russell Street, Hadley, MA; (413) 586-0114, (800) 654-2000; www.hojo.com.

HOLYOKE

PARKS, BEACHES, AND RECREATION AREAS

• **Holyoke Community College** 🐾🐾🐾 🐕 See **21** on page 154.
No more leashes, no more books, no more ranger's dirty looks! George loves going back to school when it's at Holyoke Community College. Because behind this little community college is a lovely old woods that backs up against the Holyoke Range with 1.3 miles of trails that lead through woods, cliffs, and overlooks. Tannery Brook runs through the center of the property. The trails started in 1975 as a class project, and a trail guide was produced in 1993. The guide can be obtained from the director of facilities at the college and is recommended when hiking here. Best of all, dogs are allowed off leash if under control.

From Interstate 91, take exit 16 and follow signs to State Route 202 south. One mile from the exit make a left onto Campus Road and follow the perimeter road to the back of the campus. Sign and parking area are on your left. (413) 538-7000.

• **Mount Tom State Reservation** 🐾🐾🐾🐾 See **22** on page 154.
With over 1,800 acres and 20 miles of hiking trails, this is a park to please every pup. According to legend, the peak got its name when the British explorers Elizur Holyoke and Rowland Thomas competed for which peak would be named after each. Holyoke picked neighboring Mount Holyoke and Thomas promptly announced his peak would be called Mount Tom. Like its neighbor, Mount Tom once had a hotel on top, but today it is in its natural condition.

Many different trails lead through the reservation and to the summit. One of our favorites is the Tea-Bag Trail which is marked by red blazes and leads beside several brooks and waterfalls on its way to the top. Lake Bray is also an excellent swimming spot; you can rent a canoe and explore its shores from the water. Your dog will probably find all the great spots, but picking up a trail map on your way into the park will probably make your search faster.

From Interstate 91, take exit 17A to U.S. Route 5 north for four miles. Turn left onto Reservation Road and into the park. (413) 527-4805.

• Springdale Park 🐾🐾 See **23** on page 154

This pleasant city park on the western side of the Connecticut River has plenty of grassy open spaces for ball throwing and an esker path that runs along the river. There is no water access, but the view is great. Dogs must be on leash.

Take Interstate 91 north to Exit 15, continuing to State Route 5 north. Where State Route 5 forks, stay to the right on Anderson Hill Road. The park is a mile north on the right. Open 8 A.M. to 8 P.M. (413) 534-2163.

RESTAURANTS

Schermerhorns Seafood Restaurant: Seafood is the specialty here, but there are many other things to choose from on this varied menu. A shady wooden outdoor patio is available where you and your dog can enjoy your meal. 224 Westfield Road;(413) 534-4528.

PLACES TO STAY

Holiday Inn: This 220-room hotel is located right off busy Interstate 93 for easy access to all the Pioneer Valley has to offer. The rooms are clean and comfortable with all the usual amenities. Pets are welcome with a $25 refundable deposit. Rates range from $85 to $165. 245 Whiting Farm Road, Holyoke, MA 01104; (413) 534-3311 or (800) 465-4329; www.holiday-inn.com.

HUNTINGTON

PARKS, BEACHES, AND RECREATION AREAS

• Knightville Dam Recreation Area 🐾🐾🐾 🐕 See **24** on page 154.

Take a beautiful hike along the Westfield River at this scenic dam project. Managed by the U.S. Army Corps of Engineers, this river has long provided an important gateway for salmon, beavers, and other wildlife in the Berkshires. In the 19th century much of the river was used for transportation and industry. Today you'll still find stone walls and old home foundations as you hike the woods here.

The Claude M. Hill Horse Trail follows the river and is accessible on the far side of the dam. Dogs must be under voice control.

From U.S. Route 20, take State Route 112 north for four miles. Turn right onto Knightsville Dam Road into the park. Maps are available at the dam office. Open 6:30 A.M. to 9 P.M. (413) 667-3430.

LEE

PARKS, BEACHES, AND RECREATION AREAS

• October Mountain State Forest 🐾🐾🐾 See **25** on page 154.

October Mountain State Forest is the largest state forest in Massachusetts. Its 16,127 acres are enough to keep you hiking for a year, let alone just a month in the fall.

The principal trail here and the easiest to find and follow is the Appalachian Trail which is accessible near the ranger station, the main entrance, and the camping area.

But there are far more opportunities to get out into the wilderness than just via the AT. In the backcountry, there are numerous multipurpose trails and forest roads that will lead your pack to places like October Mountain, Schermerhorn Gorge, Woods Pond, and Washington Mountain Marsh. Most of the trails can be reached from the western end of the park near Woodland and Schermerhorn Roads.

Maps are available at the main entrance.

Camping is available for tents and RVs (no hookups) at the simple 50-site campground. Nightly rates are $10 to $12 per night. Open mid-May to mid-October. RR 2, Box 193, Lee, MA 01238. Call (877) 422-6762 for reservations.

Dogs must be leashed in all state parks. There is a $2 day-use fee.

From U.S. Route 20, take Center Street east for a half mile. Turn left onto Greylock Street for one mile, then right onto Bradley Street into Woodland Road for a total of a half mile. The main entrance is on the right. For the backcountry trails, continue on Woodland Road (turning right at Woods Pond) for three-quarters of a mile. Turn right onto Schermerhorn Road where there are numerous pullouts and trailheads. Open sunrise to a half hour after sunset. (413) 243-1778.

NATURE HIKES AND URBAN WALKS

A Walking Tour of Lee: The entire downtown area of Lee is listed in the National Register of Historic Places, and you'll soon see why. Main Street looks like it came straight out of Central Casting. This half-mile walk includes all of the historic buildings on Main Street plus Sullivan Station, the train station built on the Housatonic River in 1893. Maps are available from the Chamber of Commerce at the start of the walk at Main and Park Streets. (413) 243-0852.

PLACES TO STAY

Devonfield: This country bed-and-breakfast is located on a 40-acre estate in the heart of the Berkshires. Dogs are permitted in the elegant cottage only, which is available with a king or twin beds. The popular cottage has its own Jacuzzi, fireplace, and kitchenette. A full breakfast is included. Room rates range from $155 to $260. 85 Stockbridge Road, Lee, MA 01238; (413) 243-3298, (800) 664-0880; www.devonfield.com.

October Mountain State Forest camping: See page 171.

LENOX

PARKS, BEACHES, AND RECREATION AREAS

• Kennedy Park 🐾🐾🐾 See 26 on page 154.

This town park provides a quick getaway to some great hiking and cross-country skiing trails. With 500 acres to sniff and a mix of meadows and thick forests, this is one of those rare town parks that actually offers a true parkland any dog could love. The five-mile trail system consists of a series of criss-crossing loops so you can pick and chose your distances and direction.

Dogs must be leashed.

From the northern intersection of U.S. Route 7 and State Route 7A, take U.S.

Route 7 north for half a mile. The park entrance is on the left. Open sunrise to sunset. (413) 637-3646.

PLACES TO STAY

Seven Hills Country Inn: This wonderful 52-room inn offers resort-style activities with bed-and-breakfast–style coziness. Located on 27 expansive acres, you and your pet will stay in spacious rooms with antique-filled charm. Pets are allowed in select rooms only. Room rates are $85 to $325, including full breakfast; pets are an additional $20 per night. 40 Plunkett Street, Lenox, MA 01240; (413) 637-0060, (800) 869-6518; www.sevenhillsinn.com.

Walker House Inn: This small bed-and-breakfast offers eight unique rooms, each with a different musical theme. First built in 1804, it features elegant hardwood rooms with four-poster beds and private baths. Well-mannered mutts are welcome. Rates range from $80 to $210. 64 Walker Street, Lenox, MA 01240; (413) 637-2387, (800) 235-3098; www.walkerhouse.com.

RESTAURANTS

Perfect Picnics: Your dog can't go to Tanglewood, but you can give her a taste of what everyone is eating there with a lunch from Perfect Picnic. The gourmet picnic baskets are a standard at Tanglewood and are sure to top the pops with you and your pet. So pick one up and head out to the local park accompanied by your favorite classical recording; it'll almost be like being there! Each lunch is $16. Open from Independence Day to Labor Day. 72 Church Street; (413) 637-3015.

LONGMEADOW

PARKS, BEACHES, AND RECREATION AREAS

• Longmeadow Flats 🐾🐾🐾 See **27** on page 154.

This 333-acre preserve is jointly managed by the Stebbins Wildlife Refuge and Longmeadow Conservation Land. Located on the old floodplain of the Connecticut River, this is a lovely place to walk with your dog. Bring your binoculars because this is a popular birding area, as well.

Three miles of trails on the property can be accessed from the parking area at the corner of Pond Side and Bark Haul Roads. From here you'll pass a small pond on your way to the Connecticut River. You will cross over the railroad tracks (which are still used), but most of the trail is flat and open, making an easy trek for pups of all sizes. Dogs must be on leash.

From Interstate 91, take Exit 1 to U.S. Route 5 south for three miles. Turn right onto Bark Haul Road to the end and the parking area. Open sunrise to sunset. (413) 786-9300.

• Turner Park 🐾🐾 See **28** on page 154.

This lovely city park has two ponds that you and your dog can stroll around. But you won't want to go swimming here, as they can only be described as "ducky," but the grassy pathways and lovely shade trees make this an enjoyable park to visit.

Dogs must be leashed.

From U.S. Route 5, take Bliss Road east for two miles. The park is on your right. Open 8 A.M. to 8 P.M. (413) 786-9300.

MIDDLEFIELD

PARKS, BEACHES, AND RECREATION AREAS

• Glendale Falls Reservation 🐾🐾🐾 See **29** on page 154.

The meadows, forests, and brooks here were once the home of the Glendale Farm dating back to the 18th century. Today, the wildflower-filled meadows and Glendale Brook and Falls, tumbling down over 150 feet, are great places for a romp. A short 1.2-mile hiking trail allows you to explore the falls. The 60-acre property is owned by the Trustees of Reservations which requires dogs to be leashed.

From State Route 143 in Worthington, take River Road south for 5.5 miles. Turn right onto Clark Wright Road for a half mile. The park entrance is on the right. Open sunrise to sunset. (413) 684-0148.

PLACES TO STAY

Strawberry Banke Farm Bed-and-Breakfast: A three-room bed-and-breakfast, this charming little inn provides cozy lodging for you and Rover. Each room is tastefully and comfortably furnished. Staying here feels like a home away from home. Rates range from $50 to $85 per night including breakfast. Skyline Drive, Middlefield, MA 01243; (413) 623-6481.

MONTEREY

PARKS, BEACHES, AND RECREATION AREAS

• Beartown State Forest 🐾🐾🐾 See **30** on page 154.

Like many state forests in the Berkshires, Beartown covers a vast area, but only a small portion of the park is developed. Picnic and camping areas, beaches, well-maintained and blazed hiking trails comprise only a portion of these 10,000 acres, and, not surprisingly, that's where the majority of the visitors go. The rest of the forest remains undeveloped except for dirt forest roads and secondary trail systems.

In Beartown, the developed area is at the main entrance and Benedict Pond. Around the scenic and swimmable pond is a 1.5-mile loop with plenty of marvelous viewing and access points. You can also access the Appalachian Trail from here.

Now think of us what you will (and we know you do), but we prefer the miles of solitary, muddy, rocky, and will-we-survive-it routes through the back country. Some of the middle-of-nowhere paths are the Bridle Trail and the Turkey and Wildcat Trails, which all roughly begin near Benedict Pond. Our dogs' enthusiasm for this wilderness is only bridled by the occasional equestrian who also has access to these trails.

Maps are available at the main entrance. Dogs must be leashed in all state parks. There is a $2 day-use fee.

From the intersection of U.S. Route 23 and State Route 57, take U.S. Route 23 east for two miles. Turn left onto Blue Hill Road for a half mile into the park. Parking is available. Open sunrise to a half hour after sunset. (413) 528-0904.

MOUNT WASHINGTON

PARKS, BEACHES, AND RECREATION AREAS

• Bash Bish Falls State Park 🐾 🐾 🐾 See **31** on page 154.

Splash splish at Bash Bish. The 200-acre Bash Bish Falls State Park lies within the boundaries of Mount Washington State Forest (see below), but given that the falls are probably the most impressive in the Commonwealth, they deserve special designation. The water, tumbling an estimated 80 feet over giant boulders in wooded and dark Bash Bish Gorge, is refreshing, but caution is needed, especially for dogs. The wet rocks are slippery and water levels can change quickly.

The falls are easily reachable via the short, quarter-mile walk from the parking lot. Addition trails connect to the Mount Washington State Forest trail system.

Dogs must be leashed in all state parks.

From U.S. Route 23 in Egremont, take U.S. Route 41 south. Make an immediate right onto Mount Washington Road into the town of Mount Washington, and continue straight on East Road for 3.5 miles. Turn left onto West Road for 1.25 miles, then turn right onto Falls Road into the park. Open sunrise to a half hour after sunset. (413) 528-0330.

• Mount Everett State Reservation 🐾 🐾 🐾 See **32** on page 154.

This impressive state property is home to many scenic wonders including Guilder Pond, the highest freshwater pond in Massachusetts, and Mount Everett. The 2,026-foot peak affords stunning three-state views over the southern Berkshires and Taconic Mountains. You can also find the Appalachian Trail within the park's 1,356 acres, plus numerous other hiking opportunities.

Dogs must be leashed in all state parks.

From U.S. Route 23 in Egremont, take U.S. Route 41 south. Make an immediate right onto Mount Washington Road into the town of Mount Washington and continue straight on East Toad for 3.5 miles. Turn left onto West Road for 1.25 miles, and then left onto Mount Everett Road into the park. Open sunrise to a half hour after sunset. (413) 528-0330.

• Mount Washington State Forest 🐾 🐾 🐾 See **33** on page 154.

If you think the entire town of Mount Washington is one big state park, you are not far from the truth. This town, representing the southwestern corner of the Commonwealth, is almost 40 percent parkland; Mount Washington State Forest and its 4,169 acres and 30 miles of trails make up a big piece of this green space.

The park is split into four different sections, so the best bet is to pick up a trail map at the park headquarters before starting your hike. The popular routes feature the Appalachian and Race Brook Trails in the eastern portion and the Alander Mountain Trail, a three-mile route to an open summit overlooking New York and Connecticut.

Dogs must be leashed in all state parks.

From U.S. Route 23 in Egremont, take U.S. Route 41 south. Make an immediate right onto Mount Washington Road into the town of Mount Washington and continue straight on East Road for seven miles. The park entrance and headquarters are on the right. To get to the eastern portion of the park from U.S. Route 23, take U.S. Route 41 south for five miles into Sheffield. A trailhead and parking lot are on the right. Open sunrise to a half hour after sunset. (413) 528-0330.

NORTH ADAMS

PARKS, BEACHES, AND RECREATION AREAS

• **Natural Bridge State Park** 🐾 🐾 ◀● See **34** on page 154.

Seashells are fun to collect, but you really have something when you mash them all together and give a few glaciers a couple of million years to do their thing. Then it might look like a giant deposit of marble, worn and eroded in spectacular fashion, like you'll see at Natural Bridge State Park. This natural bridge is a stream-cut opening in the massive white block. The chasm is 60 feet high and 475 feet long.

George, who is really part mountain goat, loves this place because showing up Inu, who has a more difficult time navigating boulders, is a full-time passion. But even rock-challenged pups will enjoy rocks as beautiful and diverse as these; the short trails are fenced in so you don't have to worry about taking a wrong step.

Dogs must be leashed in all state parks.

From U.S. Route 2, take U.S. Route 8 north for a half mile. The park entrance is on the left. Open sunrise to a half hour after sunset. (413) 663-6392.

PLACES TO STAY

Historic Valley Campground: This full-service campground offers 103 wooded sites for tents and RVs plus access to Windsor Lake. Rates range from $17 to $29, plus an additional pet charge of $2 per day. Dogs must be leashed. Open May 15 to October 15. 10 Main Street, North Adams, MA 01247; (413) 662-3198.

FESTIVALS

Fall Foliage Festival: Berkshire County's weeklong Fall Foliage Festival is the highlight of the autumn season. Most of the events, including a pet show, bazaar, and parade, take place on Main Street in October. For more information, call (413) 663-9204.

NORTHAMPTON

This funky little town offers the best in small-town living. A center for such diverse movements as Jonathan Edward's Great Awakening and the early suffragette movement, Northampton has always been on the cusp of new thinking. Surrounded by prestigious Smith College—a women's college established in 1875—but dying as an industrial town in the 1960s, Northampton has today rebounded to become a model of urban renewal.

PARKS, BEACHES, AND RECREATION AREAS

•Childs Memorial Park 🐾🐾 See **35** on page 154.

While bikers and skaters zoom by on the Northampton Bikeway, and boaters cruise the Connecticut River, the pace is a little slower at Childs Memorial Park. Anything more than a brisk walk through manicured lawns and gardens on tree-lined paths past statues and monuments seems a little strange. The three-city-block park requires dogs to be leashed.

From U.S. Route 5, take State Route 9 west for 1.25 miles. The park is on the right. Open dawn to dusk (gates are closed to vehicles at 7 P.M.). (413) 586-6950.

•Elwell Recreation Area/Connecticut River Greenway State Park 🐾🐾 See **36** on page 154

These two parks on the Connecticut River are mostly used for bike and foot access to the Northampton Bikeway and the Norwottuck Rail Trail and for boat access to the river. The parks do feature some green spaces and water access points for dogs to get some exercise.

Dogs must be leashed in all state parks.

From Interstate 91, take exit 19 to State Route 9 east for one-tenth of a mile. Turn left onto Damon Road. Park entrances are on the immediate right and a half mile up the road. Open sunrise to sunset. (413) 586-8706.

•Look Memorial Park 🐾🐾🐾 See **37** on page 154.

This beautiful 150-acre park is a wonderful gift from Fannie Burr Look to the people of Northampton. Not only did she donate the land, but she provided the funds to build all of the amenities and maintain the grounds for years to come.

The park includes a theatre, ball fields, tennis courts, picnic areas along the Mill River, a zoo, playgrounds, a steam train, mini-golf, and a mile-long bike/walking path. Obviously, dogs are not permitted in most of these areas, but it all adds up to a pleasant setting for a park. For exercise, the bike path and Mill River will provide plenty of options.

Dogs must be leashed. The day-use fee is $2 to $3 from April through October 15, and $1 in the off-season.

From U.S. Route 5, take State Route 9 west for three miles. The park is on the left. Open dawn to dusk. (413) 584-5457.

NATURE HIKES AND URBAN WALKS

Northampton Bikeway: One of the first bike paths in the Commonwealth, this path is 2.6 miles long and runs from Look Memorial Park through town to Elwell Recreation Area where it connects to the Norwottuck Rail Trail. Dogs must be leashed. Open dawn to dusk. (413) 586-6950.

RESTAURANTS

Cha Cha Cha!: You'll do the cha-cha and the tango once you taste the food at this great little Mexican grill. With an intriguing mix of Mexican and new-age cuisine, you'll find cilantro on your fajita and peanut sauce in your burrito. Truly delicious. A few secluded tables outside. 134 Main Street; (413) 586-7311.

Coolidge Park Café: This Noho institution has a relaxing outdoor patio where you and Fido can enjoy breakfast, lunch, or dinner. Breakfasts are especially popular here. The banana buckwheat pancakes would make Calvin Coolidge rise out of his nearby grave. 36 King Street; (413) 584-3100.

Fresh Pasta Company: Dine al fresco at this Italian trattoria. Two small full-service tables are available outside. Pizza, pasta, and seafood are just a few of the varied menu offerings. Corner of Main and Masonic Streets; (413) 686-5875.

Look Bakery and Restaurant: Located in Florence, this charming café has outdoor seating on the main drag. Sandwiches, burgers, vegetarian fare, and coffee are all served with a friendly word. Water is available for your pooch. 91 North Main Street; (413) 586-5221.

Tailgate Picnic: For box lunches and scrumptious food to go try this unique eatery. The sun-dried tomato sandwich is for dainty dogs and the orchard sandwich is for chow hounds. 159 Main Street; (413) 584-1882.

FESTIVALS

First Night: Join the fun on New Year's Eve for this annual town party celebrating the coming and passing of the year. Activities abound all day on Main Street and throughout the town. Dogs dig the fun at all the outdoor activities. (413) 584-7327.

PERU

PARKS, BEACHES, AND RECREATION AREAS

• **Dorothy Frances Rice Sanctuary For Wildlife** 🐾🐾🐾 🐕 See **38** on page 154.

We had just pulled off into the small parking area when we saw our tour guide coming down the lane. He sauntered over with the kind of grin, trot, and wagging tail that only a jolly Labrador can put together. After George and the Lab had a playful getting-to-know-you romp right there in the road, we followed him on our personal tour of the sanctuary. JoAnna's only wish was to be able to keep up with the eight legs trotting ahead of her.

The hiking trails on this remote conservation property are popular year-round. With three miles of level paths and 276 acres of fields, varied forests, ponds, and wetlands, you'll find plenty of terrific walks for you and your dog. We can't promise you'll have your own personal guide like we did, but you'll still find plenty here to satisfy any dog's taste. And since George marked all the trees with his own special "George was here" flag, your dog will probably know where to go.

The conservation property is owned and managed by the New England Forestry Foundation.

Dogs must be leashed in the parking areas and under voice control on the trails.

From State Route 143, take South Road south for one mile. After South Road turns left, the park's gated entrance is straight ahead. Park outside the gate. Open dawn to dusk. (978) 448-8380.

PITTSFIELD
PARKS, BEACHES, AND RECREATION AREAS

• **Burbank Park** 🐾🐾🐾 See **39** on page 154.

Although the mountains of Berkshire County are a big playground to many in western Massachusetts, the numerous lakes and ponds also attract many outdoor enthusiasts. Pittsfield boasts two watery havens, Onota Lake and Pontoosuc Lake.

A good way for the dogs to enjoy a day at the lake is a trip to Burbank Park on the eastern shore of Onota Lake. The shallow, three-quarter-mile shoreline has plenty of water access points for dogs, plus a short bike path to go with it. The surrounding woods also provide some brief hiking opportunities, but most visitors stick to the shore and the picnic areas in the park.

Dogs must be leashed.

From U.S. Routes 7 and 20, take West Street west for one mile. Turn right onto Valentine Road for one mile, then left onto Lakeview Drive into the park. Parking is available. Open dawn to dusk. (413) 499-9343.

• **Pittsfield State Forest** 🐾🐾🐾🐾 See **40** on page 154.

We've found far too many state forests are little more than a place for hunters and loggers, but that is not the case at Pittsfield State Forest. Park visitors are overwhelmed with its dense forest of majestic pines, 30 miles of trails, acres of wild berries and azaleas, and mountain ponds.

Not to be missed is Berry Pond. The alpine pond and its sparkling water is a popular swimming and camping destination. Lulu Pond is another park highlight. For mountain views, people head to Berry and Tower Mountains off the park loop road.

Some good hiking routes are the Parker Brook Trail, which follows the creek to Tilden Swamp, and the Lulu Brook Trail to Lulu Pond. Both are scenic paths and provide plenty of water breaks for your dog. The Taconic Crest Trail also runs the length of the park.

Dogs will be happy campers at the 31-site campground for tents and RVs (no hookups). Nightly rates are $5 to $12 and include flush toilets and hot showers. Open mid-May to mid-October for tents and year-round for RVs. Call (877) 422-6762 for reservations.

Dogs must be leashed in all state parks. There is a $2 day-use fee.

From U.S. Routes 7 and 20, take West Street west for two miles. Turn right onto Churchill Street for 1.5 miles, then tunr left onto Cascade Street into the park. Parking is available. Open sunrise to sunset. (413) 442-8992.

• **Springside Park** 🐾🐾🐾 See **41** on page 154.

Pittsfield residents have it easy when it comes to dog walking. Not only are they in the center of the Berkshire Mountains, but right in the middle of town lies the 237 acres of Springside Park. This diverse property supports numerous trails through wetlands, forests of tall pines, open meadows, and many ridges and hollows. The crisscrossing trail system let's you vary your walk with any number of possible loops.

Dogs must be leashed. Maps are available at the park entrance.

From State Route 9, take U.S. Route 7 north for three-quarters of a mile. The park entrance is on the right. Open dawn to dusk. (413) 499-9343.

•Wild Acres 🐾🐾🐾 See 42 on page 154.

This out-of-the-way town conservation property has an inviting, scenic pond and some good hiking trails through the surrounding pine woods that separate it from the Pittsfield Airport. The pond is a popular picnicking and fishing spot for kids, so watch out for your pet's favorite trick, the fish roll.

Dogs must be leashed.

From U.S. Routes 7 and 20, take South Mountain Road west for 1.25 miles. The park entrance is on the left. Open dawn to dusk. (413) 499-9343.

NATURE HIKES AND URBAN WALKS

Arrowhead: Arrowhead is the former family home of Herman Melville who lived here from 1850 to 1863. It was here that he completed *Moby Dick.*

Pets are not permitted in the historic house itself, but the 44-acre estate offers gardens and nature trails for you and your dog to explore. 780 Holmes Road; (413) 442-1793; www.mobydick.org.

PLACES TO STAY

Crowne Plaza: This first-class hotel is located right in downtown Pittsfield near the crossroads of Routes 7, 9, and 20. Offering 179 spacious full-service rooms, you and your dog will be very comfortable here. Pets are welcome with a $50 refundable deposit. The management reserves the right to remove any pet disturbing other guests. Rooms range from $99 to $250 per night. Berkshire Common, Pittsfield, MA 01201; (413) 499-2000, (800) 2-CROWNE; www.holiday-inn.com.

Pittsfield State Forest camping: See page 179.

RESTAURANTS

Bagels Too: North Street is a long way from its hey day, but you can still find a decent cup of coffee, a place for you and your dog to sit, and some of the best bagels in the Berkshires at this conveniently located café. 166 North Street; (413) 499-0119.

SHEFFIELD

PARKS, BEACHES, AND RECREATION AREAS

• Appalachian Trail—Shays' Rebellion 🐾🐾🐾 See 43 on page 154.

Most of the Appalachian Trail in the Berkshires runs through mountainous state forests, but this stretch of the trail is a refreshing change for most hikers. The route is flat and cuts through rolling farmlands between the Hubbard Willard Brook and the Housatonic River.

This was also the site of the last battle of Shays' Rebellion in 1787. Daniel Shays led an uprising of mostly poor farmers protesting taxation during the hard economic times after the American Revolution. They were squashed by the Massachusetts militia, and the leaders were tried for treason but later pardoned. Nothing that dramatic will shake up your walk here, but your dogs might enjoy playing hide-and-seek in the tall grasses.

Dogs must be leashed on the Appalachian Trail.

From U.S. Route 7, take Lime Kiln Road west onto Rebellion Road for a mile. Turn right onto Egremont Road for a quarter mile. The trailhead and parking is on the left and the monument is on the right. Open 24 hours a day. (413) 442-8928.

• Bartholomew's Cobble 🐾🐾🐾🐾 See 44 on page 154.

All it takes is one step onto this property and you immediately recognize the effort that goes into the lands managed by the the Trustees of Reservations. This impressive nonprofit land conservation organization protects over 75 properties in Massachusetts, and Bartholomew's Cobble is one of the finest.

The 278 acres on the Housatonic River offer rolling pastures, woodlands of birch and oak, babbling streams, and, of course, Bartholomew's Cobble, a rocky marble and granite outcropping of boulders and craggy ledges.

For hiking, there are 6.5 miles of trails, including the 1.5-mile interpretive Ledges Trail, plus paths along the river and the hayfield route to the top of Hurlburt's Hill where you'll enjoy stunning views.

Dogs must be on leash. For nonmembers, there is a $2 daily fee.

From the intersection of U.S. Route 7 and State Route 7A, take State Route 7A south for a half mile. Turn right onto Rannapo Road for 1.5 miles, then go straight onto Weatogue Road. The park entrance is immediately on the left. Open sunrise to sunset. (413) 229-8600.

NATURE HIKES AND URBAN WALKS

• Sheffield Covered Bridge 🐾🐾🐾 🐾 See 45 on page 154.

Here is your chance to take a short walk and a big trip back in time. Turn off busy Route 7, and you will immediately turn back the clock. Walking through the covered bridge is just one part of this time warp. Continue down the country lane (it's a dirt road, of course) for three-quarters of a mile along the river and picturesque farm pastures.

The bridge is an exact duplicate of the one built in 1854. That bridge was still open to auto traffic until 1974, but it burned down in 1994. There are also plenty of water access points around the bridge for your dog.

Dogs must be on leash.

The bridge is located just north of the center of town off of U.S. Route 7 at the intersection of Covered Bridge Lane and Cook Road. Open 24 hours a day. (413) 528-4006.

PLACES TO STAY

Ivanhoe Country House: Although a name like this conjures up visions of the Scottish highlands, this equally charming 1780s colonial house will delight you. Set on 25 beautiful acres, you and your dog will enjoy cozy rooms complete with hardwood floors and claw-foot tubs; some rooms even have fireplaces. Rooms range from $75 to $125; dogs are an additional $10 per night. 254 South Undermountain Road, Sheffield, MA 01257; (413) 229-2143.

Race Brook Lodge: This restored 19th-century inn is as scenic as it is special. Located in a restored barn, there are 15 country-quaint rooms, many of which allow dogs. Every third Sunday the inn offers a jazz session followed by a gourmet lunch. Rates range from $90 to $165 with an additional $25 pet fee per stay. There is a two-night minimum during the high season. 864 Under-mountain Road, Sheffield, MA 01257; (413) 229-2916, (888) 725-6343; www.rblodge.com.

SPRINGFIELD

Although Springfield is the largest town in Central Massachusetts, we can't say it's the most dog friendly. There are plenty of parks here, but almost all of them are covered with ball fields and recreation areas—two things that can really get a doggy down. So although there is a patch of green in every neighborhood, we didn't list them unless they were fit for Fido.

PARKS, BEACHES, AND RECREATION AREAS

• **Forest Park** 🐾🐾🐾 See **46** on page 154.
This beautiful 800-acre city park has countless trails that weave through pine forests and along manicured lawns. With four small lakes, a botanical garden, a nature trail, and historical sites, you and your dog will find plenty to do here. Trail maps are available at the information booth at the entrance off Summer Avenue, and we suggest you pick up one and head over to Porter Lake or to the trails to the right of the main access road.

History buffs will want to check out the Carriage House, the only surviving structure from a lavish estate built in 1882 by skate magnate Hosmer Barney. He donated over 110 acres to the city of Springfield which helped establish Forest Park as the park it is today. For a history of a different sort, visit King Phillip's Stockade in the far southwestern corner of the park.

Dogs must be on leash. There is a $2 day-use fee.

From Interstate 91, take Exit 2 to Longhill Street (State Route 21). Turn right onto Sumner Street for seven blocks. The park is on your right. Open 8 A.M. to dusk. (413) 787-6440.

RESTAURANTS

Blue Moon Café: You and your dog will visit this little café more often than once in a blue moon. Located on Summer Street, you can choose from a menu that offers coffee, bakery items, sandwiches, and dessert. Eat at the tables outside or take a picnic to Forest Park just down the street. Summer Street (State Route 21); (413) 737-4911.

Du Jour Café: Located downtown at the Civic Center Plaza, you will enjoy the European feel of this local café. The tables outside on the mall are nice on warm summer days. 1327 Main Street; (413) 732-3900.

Gus & Pauls: This popular Springfield establishment has the best outdoor seating in the city. Located on Main Street just west of the Civic Center, you'll be in the catbird's seat for people watching. Dogs like it for the water bowls they will receive from the friendly staff. 1500 Main Street; (413) 781-2253.

PLACES TO STAY

Holiday Inn: This standard Holiday Inn is located in the downtown hub near the train station. Most of its 244 comfortable rooms are dog friendly. Rates range from $70 to $109 per night. 711 Dwight Street; Springfield, MA 01104; (413) 781-0900; www.holiday-inn.com.

DIVERSIONS

Bright Lights, Big City: For an explosion of lights and eye-popping winter displays, come over to Forest Park for the annual Bright Nights at Forest Park. Over 350,000 light bulbs are used to create two miles of a winter wonderland. Walk or drive through the park from November through December to see this "electrifying" creation. (413) 748-6190.

Time Out for Movies: Take in the lights of Hollywood for free at your local Springfield park during July. A different movie is featured on an outdoor movie screen each week at five local parks. Free popcorn included. But don't let your dog hog it all! Activities start at 7 P.M.; the movie begins at 8 P.M. Call for times and locations. (413) 748-6190.

STOCKBRIDGE

NATURE HIKES AND URBAN WALKS

Berkshire Botanical Garden: This is more than a walk in the woods. The Berkshire Botanical Gardens are 15 acres of country landscapes featuring perennial and annual arrangements. Leashed, well-behaved dogs are welcome with permission from the management. The gardens are open every day 10 A.M. to 5 P.M., May through October, and are located at the intersection of State Routes 102 and 183; (413) 298-3926.

RESTAURANTS

Daily Bread Bakery: Give us this day our daily bread. And amen to that! Whether it's a Main Street stroll or an all-day hike in the mountains, the Daily Bread Bakery is the stop for delicious coffee, baked goods, and sandwiches. Main Street; (413) 298-0272.

Stockbridge General Store and Main Street Café: If you can't find what you need at the general store on Main Street, then you probably don't need it anyway. Between the café and the store you can get a dish of ice cream, a sandwich to go, or some drinks for the trail or road. Main Street; (413) 298-3060.

FESTIVALS

Main Street at Christmas: Like the chicken and the egg question, we're not sure which came first. Did Norman Rockwell's painting capture or create Stockbridge at Christmastime? Either way, the Main Street Christmas Celebration, held annually the first weekend in December, is straight out of Rockwell's painting. The event includes caroling, tree lighting, a luminaria walk on Saturday night (bring a candle or flashlight), and a re-creation of the famous painting on Main Street. For more information, call (413) 298-5200.

SUNDERLAND

PARKS, BEACHES, AND RECREATION AREAS

• **Mount Toby State Forest** 🐾🐾🐾 See **47** on page 154.
The Robert Frost Trail runs through this state forest, and you'll travel on part of it to reach the summit of Mount Toby, the tallest mountain in the Pioneer Valley at 1,269 feet. This is an often strenuous but very scenic hike that will

take you by waterfalls, through a maple grove, and up to gorgeous views. The state forest is over 1,500 acres so there are many trails you may wish to explore if you aren't planning a trek to the summit.

For those who want to tackle the 6.5-mile hike to the top, we suggest you take the Sugar Farms Trail which starts through the gate on the "blue route." For your hike to the summit, the trail will also be marked with orange for the Robert Frost Trail, but that veers off once you reach the top. Be sure to bring a picnic (and your camera!) to celebrate your arrival at the top. The view looking out over the Connecticut River is marvelous.

Dogs must be on leash.

From State Route 116, take State Route 47 north for four miles. Turn right onto Reservation Road for a half mile. The entrance is on your right. Open sunrise to sunset. (413) 545-5993.

TYRINGHAM

PARKS, BEACHES, AND RECREATION AREAS

• McLennan Reservation 🐾🐾🐾 See **48** on page 154.

This is another one of the great properties belonging to the Trustees of Reservations. These 594 acres on the eastern side of the Tyringham Valley are nestled along Camp Brook and Round Mountain.

The park features a scenic two-mile loop trail that runs through a rich forest of pine, hemlock, and maple trees around Hale Pond. The pond was created by beavers, and, if you are very quiet, you may see one or any of the other kinds of wildlife that inhabit the park.

Dogs must be on leash.

From the center of town, take Main Road east for two miles. Turn left onto Fenn Road (a dirt road). Park on Fenn Road and walk a third of a mile up Fenn Road to the park entrance. Open sunrise to sunset. (413) 298-3239.

• Tryingham Cobble 🐾🐾🐾 See **49** on page 154.

This Trustees of Reservations property on 206 acres is located across the valley from McLennan Reservation and is just as inviting. The cobble, otherwise know as Cobble Hill, is a wooded but rocky ridge rising 400 feet over the valley. A two-mile loop trail starts on the lower open slopes and ascends the ridge with plenty of viewpoints from the outcropping cliffs.

From Main Road in the center of town, take Jerusalem Road south for a quarter mile. The park entrance is on the right. Open sunrise to sunset. (413) 298-3239.

PLACES TO STAY

Sunset Farm Inn: This bed-and-breakfast is on a 300-acre former farm along the Appalachian Trail. Dogs are welcome to explore the endless hiking opportunities here, but they cannot be left unattended. Advance notice of your dog is required too. The inn has four rooms with rates of $85 per night. A full breakfast is included. 74 Tryingham Road, Tyringham, MA 01238; (413) 243-0730.

WEST SPRINGFIELD

PLACES TO STAY

Econo Lodge: Located just outside the downtown hub, this 58-room hotel isn't glamorous but will suffice for weary travelers passing through. Rates range from $49 to $69. 1533 Elm Street, West Springfield, MA 01089; (413) 734-8278.

Ramada Inn and Suites: This suite-style hotel offers 48 small efficiency rooms for you and your dog. Rooms range from $70 to $110. 21 Baldwin Street, West Springfield, MA 01089; (413) 732-1231.

Red Roof Inn: This clean and comfortable motel offers all the modern conveniences for you and your dog. Continental breakfast is included in the morning. Rates range from $59 to $79. 1254 Riverdale Street, West Springfield, MA 01089. (413) 731-1010; www.redroofinns.com.

WEST STOCKBRIDGE

RESTAURANTS

Caffe Pomo d'Oro: This combined coffeehouse, café, and bakery is in the former town train station. With delicious sandwiches, pastas, breads, pastries, and coffees plus a pleasant outdoor patio, it's easy to make it your next stop. 6 Depot Street; (413) 232-4616.

PLACES TO STAY

Shaker Mill Inn: Originally a stagecoach stop in the 1800s, this fabulous inn features nine suites, all with kitchenettes and balconies overlooking gorgeous gardens and hillside vistas. Dogs are welcome for an additional $25 fee per stay. Rates range from $145 to $250, breakfast included. State Route 102, West Stockbridge, MA 01266; (413) 232-4600; shakermillinn.com.

The Williamsville Inn: This 16-room inn offers the historical appeal of a country inn with the modern conveniences of a full-service hotel. Dogs are allowed in certain rooms and cannot be left unattended. Rates range from $120 to $195. State Route 41, Stockbridge, MA 02166; (413) 274-6118; williamsvilleinn.com.

WILLIAMSTOWN

PARKS, BEACHES, AND RECREATION AREAS

• **Clark Art Institute** 🐾 🐾 🐾 See **50** on page 154.
If you're looking for a dog walk that covers all the bases, then the woods and cow pastures of the Clark Art Institute are your masterpiece excursion.

The Stone Hill Clark Trail system begins and ends from the back parking lot of the museum and has two loops that overlap each other. The Pasture Loop is seven-tenths of a mile long and the Stone Bench Loop is 1.5 miles. They both start and end together, covering the same terrain, but the Stone Bench Trail runs farther out into the woods and the fields.

The woods are pleasant, but it's the hillside pastures that will make you ooh and aah. The sculptured trails are mowed so you can easily follow them through the grass. Be sure to take your time because it's a great place to sit and enjoy the artistic views of the Taconic Range and beautiful Williamstown below. Remember that this is a working pasture, so depending on when you visit there may actually be cows and their goopy "pies" in the fields.

And, since you asked, there *is* a stone bench on the Stone Bench Trail near the summit of Stone Hill.

From Williamstown center at the intersection of U.S. Routes 2 and 7 (Main Street) and South Street, take South Street south for a quarter mile. The museum is on the right and parking and the trailheads are behind it. Open dawn to dusk. (413) 458-9545.

• Field Farm 🐾🐾🐾🐾 🐕 See **51** on page 154.

This spectacular property of manicured, grass-covered trails, ponds, corn fields, caves, pastures, and woods is owned by the Trustees of Reservations and lies at the foothills of the Taconic Range.

The farm covers 300 acres and has about six miles of relatively flat trails over most of it. The cornfields and pastures are still in use, but you and your dog are welcome to walk through them. The pond, in the center of the farm near the parking lot, is a great place to cool off. Some small streams periodically cross the winding, looping trails. Trail maps are available at the parking lot/trailhead.

Visiting dogs must be under voice control at all times. For nonmembers, there is a $2 daily fee.

From the intersection of U.S. Routes 7 and 43, take U.S. Route 43 west. Make an immediate right onto Sloan Road for one mile. The park entrance is on the right. Open sunrise to sunset. (413) 298-3239.

• Hokins Memorial Forest 🐾🐾 See **52** on page 154.

These 2,430 acres are managed by Williams College and mark the very northwest corner of Massachusetts. The lush woods here are a popular place for bird-watching, hiking, and cross-country skiing. The park has some hiking trails, but many people stick to the forest roads that run through the property.

Dogs must be on leash.

From Williamstown center at the intersection of U.S. Routes 2 and 7 (Main Street) and South Street, take U.S. Route 7 north one block. Turn left onto Buckley Street. The park is at the end of the road. Open dawn to dusk. (413) 597-2346.

• Pine Cobble 🐾🐾🐾 See **53** on page 154.

This is a quick but very rewarding hike to the top of Pine Cobble, one of the more modest peaks of the Berkshire Hills. It's an easy climb through a wooded landscape with a round-trip distance of 3.5 miles. From the summit you can view the Housac Valley, Mount Greylock, and the Taconic Range. Dogs must be on leash.

From U.S. Route 7, take North Housac Road. Turn left onto White Oaks Road for one mile, then turn right onto Brooks Road for seven-tenths of a mile. Roadside parking and the trailhead are on the left. Open 24 hours a day. (304) 535-6331.

RESTAURANTS

Lickety-Split: Sooner or later, visitors to Williamstown make their way to Spring Street to see and be seen. What better way to stroll past the shops than with a dish of something smooth and creamy from Lickety-Split? 69 Spring Street; (413) 458-1818.

Robin's: For lunch or dinner, Robin's has a first-class menu for Chris and JoAnna's gourmet tastes, yet it's relaxed enough to allow the dogs to sit just off the patio. For a special treat, try the black lobster ravioli. Located at the end of Spring Street at 113 Latham Street; (413) 458-4489.

The Store at Five Corners: There's no outdoor seating for you and your dog, but this is the fanciest and most popular general store in New England. You can find all kinds of gourmet foods, wine, and cheese for a delightful picnic to go. Five Corners is at the junction of U.S. Route 7 and State Route 43; (413) 458-3176.

PLACES TO STAY

Cozy Corner Motel: Find your own cozy corner at this comfortable 12-room motel. All rooms are cheerful and clean. Rates range from $52 to $83, with an additional $5 fee for Muttley. 284 Sand Springs Road, Williamstown, MA 01267; (413) 458-8006.

Jericho Valley Inn: With your dog, your own cozy cottage, and 350 private acres nestled in the heart of the Berkshire Mountains in beautiful Williamstown, this is as good as it gets.

Dogs are permitted in the 12 colorful cottages scattered along the estate. The one- to two-bedroom units have full kitchens, fireplaces, and range from $118 to $258. P.O. Box 239, 2541 Hancock Road, Williamstown, MA 01267; (413) 458-9511, (800) 537-4246; www.jerichovalleyinn.com.

Old Stone Church B&B: This inn, once a 1830s church, now offers a single room for the blessed folks who are lucky enough to book it. Dogs are welcome with prior approval and one night's deposit. The room rate is $80 a night. 1213 Green River Road, Williamstown, MA 01267; (413) 458-2166.

The Villager Motel: Small pets are welcome at this 13-room motel. Rates range from $59 to $85. 953 Simonds Road, State Route 7N, Williamstown, MA 02167; (413) 458-4046.

Williams Inn: With its elegant colonial decor, 100 rooms, and a location right on the Green, the Williams Inn is the center of activity on any given weekend. Rates range from $80 to $150. There is a $5 fee per dog, and you must give advance notice that you are coming with your pet. On the Green, Williamstown, MA 01267; (413) 458-9371.

WINDSOR

PARKS, BEACHES, AND RECREATION AREAS

• **Notchview Reservation** 🐾🐾🐾🐾 See **54** on page 154.

This park is one of the largest conservation properties of the Trustees of Reservations. It covers 3,108 acres and has 15 miles of hiking trails. Not only is it big, but it'll take you and your leashed dog higher and higher. Most of the park's hardwood forests, pastures, orchards, ponds, and streams have an elevation over 2,000 feet. From the highest point, Judges Hill (2,297 feet), you can see Mount Monadnock in New Hampshire, the Green Mountains in Vermont, and the Catskills in New York.

There is a $2 entrance fee for nonmembers. Maps are available at the visitor center.

From the center of town at the intersection of State Routes 8A and 9, take State Route 9 east one mile. The park entrance is on the left. Open sunrise to sunset. (413) 684-0148.

7
CENTRAL MASSACHUSETTS

Central Massachusetts is squeezed between the two most well-known sections of the state: Boston and its scenic seacoast to the east, and the Berkshires to the west. In between, it's easy to forget the scenic and historical valleys that make up this central area. Home of the Shakers and the transcendentalists and the birthplace of the American Industrial Revolution, these towns contributed tremendously to the economic development of New England.

Although Quabbin Reservoir, the largest body of water here, is off-limits to dogs, plenty of dam projects, lakes, parks, and recreation areas allow your pooch in every season.

Blackstone River Valley National Heritage Corridor: In 1986, the Blackstone River Valley National Heritage Corridor was created by the National Park Service to oversee the preservation of the birthplace of the American Industrial Revolution. It was in this corridor, from Providence, Rhode Island, to Worcester, Massachusetts, that the United States began to go from a nation of farmers to an industrial power. Today, a number of state and town parks, bike paths, and historical mill sites in the river valley are jointly dedicated to this important time in American history. The National Park Service does not own any land in the corridor but helps the states and towns coordinate the management of the individual properties. For additional information, maps, and a list of parks, visit or call the Blackstone Valley Visitor's Center in Uxbridge, Massachusetts at 287 Oak Street; (508) 278-7604.

Midstate Trail: The Midstate Trail is just what you think. It runs border to border through the middle of the Commonwealth and Worcester County from Rhode Island's North South Trail to New Hampshire's Wapack Trail for a distance of 92 miles. Contact the Department of Environmental Management for more information. (617) 727-3180.

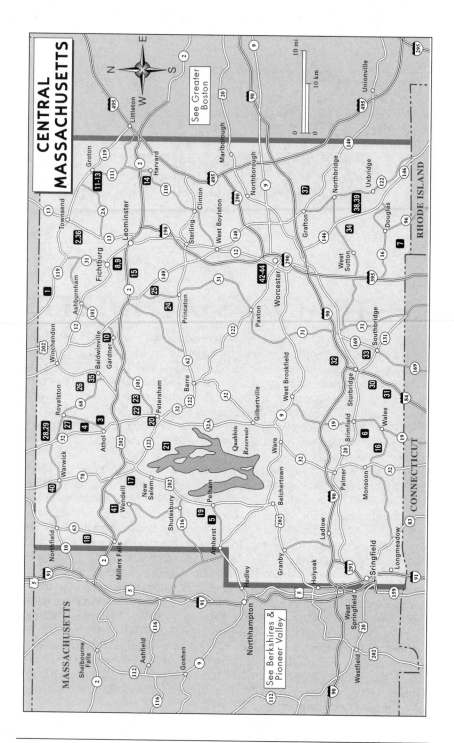

CENTRAL MASSACHUSETTS

See Greater Boston

See Berkshires & Pioneer Valley

MASSACHUSETTS

RHODE ISLAND

CONNECTICUT

10 mi

10 km

ASHBURNHAM

PARKS, BEACHES, AND RECREATION AREAS

• **Ashburnham State Forest and Mount Watatic Wildlife Management Area** 🐾🐾🐾 See **1** on page 190.

The Ashburnham State Forest is split up in little pieces all over Ashburnham. From the parking area, you have a choice of trails. The Blueberry Trail is just a quarter-mile long and leads into the rather dense forest for a trip to nowhere special (or maybe even Grandma's house, so watch out for wolves). The Wapack Cutoff Trail is three-quarters-of-a-mile long and connects to the Wapack Trail, with New Hampshire via the Midstate Trail just over a mile away. Take any of these paths for a woodland walk or continue on to the most popular destination, Mount Watatic, which locals love for its view. The mountain is also the official "beginning" of the Wapack Trail, a 21-mile trek to the Pack Monadnocks in Greenfield, New Hampshire.

Dogs must be leashed on state land.

From State Route 101, take State Route 119 west for 1.5 miles. The small, dirt parking lot is on the right. Open dawn to dusk. (617) 973-8700.

RESTAURANTS

Village Pizza: Nuzzle up to the take-out window for a classic selection of pizza, topped off with ice cream. This place is not trendy or fancy, but if you are hungry in these parts, this is the only option with outdoor seating for you and your dog. The tables outside are old booths that moved outdoors when the place was redone. 8 Gardner Road; (978) 827-1328.

PLACES TO STAY

Marble Farm: Our mutts wag their tails when we say we're headed to Marble Farm. It's a very cozy 18th-century farmhouse, found just a hop, skip, and a jump from the Midstate Trail in Ashburnham. The tail wagging starts at the acres surrounding the farmhouse and Marble Pond, a swimming hole that Inu makes a beeline for. The owners permit pets at their discretion, so make sure all are on their best behavior. Rates range from $65 to $75. Some rooms have shared baths. 41 Marble Road, Ashburnham, MA 01430; (978) 827-5423.

ASHBY

PARKS, BEACHES, AND RECREATION AREAS

• **Willard Brook State Forest** 🐾🐾🐾🐾 See **2** on page 190.

With over 2,380 acres to explore at this popular park, you and your dog will have plenty of leg room to hightail it through the woods and streams. Hugging the brook and State Route 119, this wooded state forest offers flat, pine needle–covered paths that weave through thick woodlands, several streams, and around two ponds. Swimming is allowed in Pearl Hill Pond, and Willard and Pearl Hill Brooks offer plenty of water to wallow in. Dogs must be leashed, and there is a $2 day-use fee. Maps are available at the main entrance.

From State Route 31, take State Route 119 east for 2.5 miles. The park is on the right. Open 10 A.M. to 8 P.M. (978) 597-8802.

RESTAURANTS

The Country Creamery: Inu and George pride themselves on being city slickers, but, when it comes to food, they yield to their country cousins. This local eatery, just outside Willard Brook State Forest, offers plenty of good country cookin', and our dogs know a good thing when they smell it. Serving standard diner fare and creamy, delicious ice cream. 4 Greenville (State Route 119); (978) 386-5800.

ATHOL

PARKS, BEACHES, AND RECREATION AREAS

• Bearsden Woods 🐾🐾 See 3 on page 190.

We have to think that Bearsden is so named because bears live here, so we kept looking over our shoulder. Maybe this name hearkens back to a time when bears were more common in the Commonwealth—at least, that's what we told ourselves. The 10 miles of hiking trails did help keep us occupied, and, if you head for the top of Roundtop Mountain, the hike will consume your energy and focus. From the parking lot, a dirt road continues to Millers River.

On state lands, leashes are required.

From Main Street (State Route 2A and 32), take Bearsden Road (near the Athol Memorial Hospital) north for two miles. Parking is on your right. Open dawn to dusk. (617) 973-8700.

• Tully Lake Project/Tully Dam 🐾🐾🐾 See 4 on page 190.

Most of the Tully Lake area is undeveloped, with old cart roads providing hiking access to the 1,250 acres of public land. Tully Lake was formed by damming the east branch of the Tully River. The U.S. Army Corps of Engineers maintains the area surrounding the dam, and the Trustees of Reservations run the associated campground.

The Tully Lake Hiking Trail is a four-mile loop around the lake, which also crosses over the dam. If that's not enough to tucker your pooch, head onto the new Tully Trail, a 20-mile hiking loop that connects much of the open recreational lands in Royalston, Warwick, and Orange. Dogs must be leashed on state park lands, but, if you take the Tully Trail to the properties owned by the Trustees of the Reservation, you can unleash.

Camping is permitted here on land managed by the Trustees of Reservations. The 30 campsites have access to the Tully Lake Hiking Trail and the 18-mile Tully Trail that runs up to Tully Dam. Rates range from $11 to $13. Leashed pets are permitted. For reservations call (877) 422-6762.

Dogs must be leashed at the dam's recreation area.

From U.S. Route 2, take exit 17 for State Route 32. Take State Route 32 north for six miles to near the Royalston town line. The parking is on the right past the dam. Open 7 A.M. to 8 P.M. (978) 249-9150.

PLACES TO STAY

Tully Lake Campground: See above.

AUBURN

PLACES TO STAY

Baymont Inn and Suites: This moderate hotel has regular rooms and suites, all of which welcome your any-old-sized pooch. The lobby breakfast is included. Rates range from $84 to $124, and a $50 pet fee is required. 446 Southbridge Street, Auburn, MA 01501; (508) 832-7000.

BARRE

PLACES TO STAY

Jenkins Inn: This 1800s-era Victorian house and well-manicured gardens welcome you and your dog. This town and inn are quiet and bucolic, compared with the bustling city of Worcester to the south. Rates range from $100 to $140. 7 West Street, Box 779, Barre, MA 01005; (978) 355-6444, (800) 378-7373.

BELCHERTOWN

PARKS, BEACHES, AND RECREATION AREAS

• **Cadwell Memorial Forest—Mount Lincoln** 🐾 🐾 🐕 See **5** on page 190.

Mount Lincoln stands at 1,240 feet, making it a great observation area. Obviously the city agreed because the top of this mountain looks like technology central. Towers, power lines, and radar mar the beautiful summit, but don't let that stop you from this hike. The woods surrounding it are quite lovely. Along the way you'll pass an old graveyard, an open glen, some waterfalls, and a rich and varied forest.

Cadwell Forest, at 1,900 acres, was given to the University of Massachusetts in 1951 by the widow of Fran Cadwell who had been the president of Amherst Savings Bank. The parking area is off Amherst Road; follow the white-blazed trail to the cemetery of the 27th and 35th Massachusetts Infantry. The winding gravel road that peels off from here is the actual road to the summit. This forest is managed by the Department of Forestry and Wildlife Management, and dogs are allowed off leash if under voice control.

From Amherst, take Main Street 4.3 miles (it turns into Pelham-Amherst Road). The park is on the left side just past Hawley Reservoir. Open sunrise to sunset. (413) 323-0419.

NATURE HIKES AND URBAN WALKS

McLaughlin Fish Hatchery: Walk through the largest fish hatchery east of the Mississippi. Although there aren't any formal "trails," dogs (and their humans) are welcome to wander through the miles of ponds, pools, and bricked pathways that lead through this fascinating place. See how efforts are underway to conserve the habitats of endangered fish in the wild and learn how hatcheries are helping to bring back species that have been overfished in the lakes and oceans. Dogs must be on leash, please. Open 9 A.M. to 5 P.M. (413) 323-7671.

BRIMFIELD

PARKS, BEACHES, AND RECREATION AREAS

• **Brimfield State Forest** 🐾🐾🐾 See **6** on page 190.
This heavily forested property has over 20 miles of roads and trails used primarily for hiking, walking, and horseback riding. Dean Pond Recreation Area, located in the western portion of the forest, has a beach and picnic facilities, but dogs are not allowed on the swimming beach in the summer. You can find a few access spots along the edge beyond the beach boundaries, but our suggestion is to stick to the trails and avoid the whole beach thing altogether. From State Route 19, take U.S. Route 20 west for 2.25 miles. Turn left onto Monson Road for a half mile, then left onto Sutcliffe (Dean Pond) Road for one mile into the park. Open sunrise to sunset. (413) 267-9687.

RESTAURANTS

Athen's Pizza: Well, it's not Greece, but the pizza is pretty darn good. Located right in town, this friendly little pizza and pasta restaurant has shaded outdoor tables overlooking the town green. North Main Street (State Route 20); (413) 245-9437.

DIVERSIONS

Something old, something new, something borrowed, something. . . : No, we aren't suggesting a wedding for your dog. Just a trip to the Brimfield Antiques Market, the world's largest antique show, held each July and September. This is a scene you have to see at least once, and, even if your dog can't tell a Chesterfield from an Ethan Allen, he'll probably enjoy tagging along with you at this outside antiques flea market. Miles of booths, stalls, food, entertainment, and just good old browsing fun is yours to enjoy. Call for exact dates and information. (413) 283-6149.

BOLTON

DIVERSIONS

A Loaf of Bread, a Jug of Wine, and Howl: The Nashoba Valley Winery in Bolton lets dogs join their wine-sipping owners here at the winery. Pooches must be leashed, but we wag our tail that dogs are welcome at all. The 50-acre farm has pick-your-own berries and fruit, as well as the winery. Bring a picnic, or pick up one at the restaurant here. If you would rather be waited on, the restaurant has outdoor seating in nice weather, and well-behaved dogs are welcome on the deck. 100 Wattaquadoc Hill Road; (978) 779-5521.

DOUGLAS

PARKS, BEACHES, AND RECREATION AREAS

• **Douglas State Forest** 🐾🐾🐾🐾 See **7** on page 190.
If you have been searching high and low for a place to spend a day in the woods, point your paws towards Douglas. Edging the state border with

Rhode Island, this 5,000-acre forest has enough to keep even the most active pup busy for a long, long time. There are miles of trails to explore, including the Midstate Trail, which starts in this forest. One item worth noting: This forest contains an Atlantic Cedar Swamp—rare for being this far north and inland. A boardwalk traverses the swamp, which has been designated a Massachusetts Wildland.

From State Routes 16 and 96, take Main Street southwest for a 1.25 miles. Turn left onto Wallum Lake Road. This is the main entrance and the closest access to the Cedar Swamp Boardwalk. Another small parking lot is on State Route 16 near the Webster town line, on the north side of the road. This lot is close to the Midstate Trail. Open sunrise to sunset. (508) 476-7872.

FITCHBURG

PARKS, BEACHES, AND RECREATION AREAS

• Coggshall Park 🐾🐾🐾 See 🎱 on page 190.

Referred to as the "Crown Jewel of Fitchburg," this place really sparkles. It's a Victorian-era charmer—a true green oasis in the middle of the bustling city. It all started with a 39-acre gift from Henry Coggshall over 100 years ago. We think he'd be pleased with how it all turned out. The heart of this jewel is Mirror Lake, which twinkles like a diamond in the sun and is home to a number of photogenic waterfowl. Every season has its charms, and this is the kind of place that draws visitors back again and again. A not-to-be-missed season is spring, when the 1,000 daffodils planted by local grade-school students bloom.

A free concert series takes place here on Sundays in the summer, and it's hard to imagine anything more relaxing than the music wafting across the water. The only flaw in this gem is that dogs must remain on leash.

From State Route 12, take Depot Road west. Turn left onto Franklin Road and then onto Electric Avenue. The park is on the left. Open 8 A.M. to dusk. (978) 345-9572.

• Parkhill Park 🐾🐾 See 🎱 on page 190.

Well, we found this park to be memorable but hope that no one else has quite the same memories as Beth and Rocky. Rocky found the heat to be too much the July day we visited, and, with all that sheltie hair, it's understandable. He overheated, threw up, and collapsed in the park, causing Beth to frantically wet him down, throw him into the air-conditioned car, and race back to the vet in Boston. He recovered just as they were pulling into the hospital parking lot, insisting he did not need to see the vet. He suffered no long-term consequences, but Beth had another scare. She dropped her Palm Pilot when she saw Rocky go down, but the honest and upstanding people of Fitchburg turned it in.

And, all in all, if she had to pick between her electronic life-minder and her dog, Beth would put Rocky first every time. So keep a careful eye on your dog on hot summer days, because they can overheat very quickly, and, trust Beth, it's a very scary experience.

After all that, it is hard to give this park great marks, as, truthfully, it has more facilities for sports activities than dogs. A paved bike and walking trail, leading off into the wooded part of the park near the baseball field, is the best choice for a dog walk.

Dogs must be on leash.

From State Route 12, take Beech Street south for two miles. Turn left onto Franklin Lane. The park is on the left. Open from 10 A.M. to sunset. (978) 345-9572.

RESTAURANTS

Lucky Dog: Next to City Hall at 718 Main Street is a parking lot that plays seasonal home to the restored red lunch wagon called Lucky Dog. A nearby outdoor tent with tables was a great place for our lucky dogs to enjoy their fare. This place is not permanent and has no phone—just great summer grilled food. 718 Main Street.

DIVERSIONS

Summer concerts on the Commons: Every summer music wafts across the Fitchburg Common. In July and August, the town hosts a music series, with concerts every Wednesday night from 6:30 P.M. to dusk. The music ranges from classical to ragtime, so there is something for everyone. For a schedule, call the Fitchburg Recreation Department at (978) 345-9572.

GARDNER

PARKS, BEACHES, AND RECREATION AREAS

• Dunn State Park and Gardner Heritage State Park 🐾🐾 See 🔟 on page 190.

The concept of a Heritage State Park is that these urban "parks" celebrate a city's heritage, including the industrial history. In Gardner, the Heritage State Park consists of a downtown Visitor's Center, with an interactive display, and Dunn State Park, less than a mile away. Dunn State Park has a pond and swim beach, where dogs are prohibited, and some grassy fields where you can play with your leashed pooch. There is one trail, just under a mile in length, that explores the woods near the pond. When in Gardner, this is the closest green space to downtown.

From U.S. Route 2, take Exit 24B to State Route 140 north for three-quarters of a mile. Turn left onto Betty Spring Road for two miles to the end, then make a right onto Pearl Street for a quarter mile. The park is on the right. Open 10 A.M. to 8 P.M. (508) 630-1497.

RESTAURANTS

Skip's Blue Moon Diner: Nearby Worcester has an unusual claim to fame as the town that made diner cars famous. The town used to crank out these railroad car look-alikes for use as dining spots throughout the country. One of these lunch cars serves as the building for Skip's Blue Moon Diner. It's family fare, and you can take out traditional diner food for a picnic. 102 Main Street; (978) 632- 4333.

PLACES TO STAY

Colonial Hotel: This cozy inn located near Dunn's Pond State Park allows small pets as long as they stay "contained." Rates range from $65 to $85 per night, plus a $10 pet fee. 625 Betty Spring Road, Gardner, MA 01440; (978) 630-2500.

GROTON

John Winthrop, a Boston founder and preacher famous for his "Boston is as a city upon a hill" comment, named this town Groton after his ancestral home in England. Today, it is a prosperous, well-preserved New England community and home to two of the best-of-the-best college prep schools: Lawrence Academy and Groton School.

PARKS, BEACHES, AND RECREATION AREAS

• Groton Place and Sabine Woods 🐾🐾🐾🐾 🐕 See 11 on page 190.

This place is as close to heaven as we have found, and bless the people at New England Forestry Foundation for making this memorial forest leash free. Groton Place and the attached Sabine Woods are over 200 acres of wooded pleasure along the sleepy Nashua River. One local pooch, Bailey, cued us into the best swimming access points, and Inu was happy for the advice.

The stone gates boast a sign that reads "Wildlife Sanctuary: For the benefit and pleasure of the people of Groton," and we are glad they let the rest of us in, too. Just inside the gate on the main loop trail is a memorial bench dedicated to the Groton Hunt, which used to take place on these grounds. The main loop is about two miles long, with offshoot trails at various points.

From State Route 111, take State Route 225 west for one mile. The park road and gate are on the left. Use roadside parking. Open dawn to dusk. (978) 448-8380.

• Hayes Woods 🐾🐾 See 12 on page 190.

The town of Groton takes conservation quite seriously, and hikers are all the better for it. Hayes Woods is a section of forest that Groton residents wanted to protect, so the Conservation Trust now owns and manages the land. The woods are lovely, dark, and deep, with lots of pine trees. This place is quietly serene, despite its proximity to houses. The trails are generally short, and dogs must be leashed.

From State Route 111/119 in Pepperell, take Shirley Street south for 1.5 miles into Groton. Turn left onto Maple Street, and then make an immediate right into the small dirt parking area. Open dawn until dusk. (978) 448-1106.

• Lawrence Woods 🐾🐾🐾 See 13 on page 190.

Groton is preserving its past for enjoyment in the future. This stand of town forest offers quiet reflection and hiking along the banks of the Nashua River. The trails run through woods, as well as along the river. Since this forest abuts Groton Place (see above), the sense of being alone in the wilderness is strong. You can get here by car or by canoe—it's your choice. Dogs must be leashed in this portion of conservation land.

From State Route 111, take State Route 225 west for one mile. These woods are across from Groton Place (see above) where parking is available. Open dawn to dusk. (978) 448-1106.

RESTAURANTS

Johnson's Drive-in Restaurant and Dairy Bar: In New England lingo, "dairy bar" means ice cream, usually homemade, always delicious, and drive in is not the same as drive through. You are expected to sit a spell, usually at outside tables, and get your grub from take-away windows like the one here at Johnson's. You can get more than ice cream here—they serve lunch and dinner as well—but it's the ice cream that brings us back. The outdoor tables are perfect for visiting dogs. 164 Boston Road, (978) 448-6840.

The Gourmet Bagel: Coming from the big city like we do, we are always suspicious of small town bagel shops, especially when they claim gourmet status. The offerings here are not what we city folk call gourmet bagels—the flavors of bagels and cream cheeses are pretty standard—but the quality is good and the service cheerful. The menu also includes smoothies and daily special quiches. You will have to take it to go. 159 Main Street, (978) 448-9634.

The Natural Market: Organic produce is used to fix fresh lunches like minestrone soup and sweets like gluten-free strawberry shortcake. Everything here is both good and good for you. The picnic table with the shady umbrella out front of the store called to Beth and Rocky, and that's where they had lunch. 148 Main Street, (978) 448-5075.

DIVERSIONS

Doggy Paddlers: The Nashoba Paddler offers seasonal canoe excursions on the Nashua and the Squaancock Rivers. From home base, you can head three to four hours by canoe in either direction, finding lovely preserved forests and stopping points along the route. They also offer special canoe events, like the full-moon guided tour. Dogs are welcome, and you can even get dog-sized life jackets. Open May through October. (978) 448-8699.

HARVARD

PARKS, BEACHES, AND RECREATION AREAS

•**Oxbow National Wildlife Refuge** 🐾 🐾 See **14** on page 190.
This place is dedicated to wildlife-viewing activities, and a lot of wildlife is out there to view. Much of the refuge is wetlands, however, so often the only wildlife you see are the man-eating mosquitoes heading straight for you. On the plus side, the wildflowers are stunning, if you can stop swatting the mosquitoes long enough to take in the flowers. To best see this refuge, take the woods road up to the start of the main trail. This park offers a series of interpretive programs, and your dog is welcome to attend too.

Dogs must be on leash.

From State Route 111, take State Route 110 west for two miles. Turn right onto Depot Street (at the Still River sign) to the end and parking. Open from a half hour before dawn to a half hour after sunset. (978) 443-4661.

NATURE HIKES AND URBAN WALKS

Fruitlands Museum: If all museums were like this, our dogs would be the most cultured hounds around. Although the indoor exhibits commemorate such diverse movements as the Shakers, the transcendentalists, and the Hudson School of Painting, your dog isn't allowed to put in his two-paws worth (or four paws, for that matter!) So you might think this place would be a yawn, but admittance to the grounds is a stellar treat indeed.

This stunning stretch of land overlooking the Nashoba Valley is always breathtaking, but never more so than in spring, when all the fruit trees are in bloom, or in fall, when the fall foliage colors appear. Trek down from the parking area to the start of the yellow trail, which heads through woods and onto former farmland. One note of caution: we are certain the bugs are big enough here to carry away small dogs, so bring the heavy-duty spray.

First-time visitors can pick up a brochure at the Fruitlands store which details the three-plus miles of walking trails on the property. Open 10 A.M. to 5 P.M., May through October. Grounds are open year-round to members; nonmembers pay $8. (978) 456-3924.

FESTIVALS

May Apple Blossom Festival: The wine makers at Nashoba Valley Winery hold an Apple Blossom Festival on the grounds in May, complete with music and wine tasting. As always, leashed dogs are welcome to join in the fun. (978) 779-5521.

DIVERSIONS

Strike up the Band: Fruitlands is the summer home of the Concord Band. They hold concerts on Thursdays at 7:30 P.M., and the grounds open at 5 P.M. for picnicking. The fee is $10 per carload, humans and canines included. Canine music lovers must wear their leashes. For more information, call (978) 456-3924.

LEOMINSTER

PARKS, BEACHES, AND RECREATION AREAS

•Leominster State Forest 🐾🐾🐾 See **15** on page 190.
Our dogs love this place because they find a new place to sniff each time we visit. With over 4,200 acres, five ponds, and miles and miles of trails, we could keep going for years before it would become boring. This forest also has moose, and our dogs were intrigued by the novel smells—moose just aren't usually hanging out on the Boston Common.

Development is focused in two areas: the headquarters complex and the Crow Hill Pond swimming area. The less developed—and crowded—areas are farther along State Route 31. In fact, you can park by Rocky Pond (how could we resist a pond named for Rocky?) and hike back to the developed areas, thus avoiding having to pay to park.

Dogs must be leashed, and hunting is permitted here from October through February.

From U.S. Route 2, take Exit 28 to State Route 31 south for two miles into the park. There are several parking areas on State Route 31. The first lot at the developed swimming beach is a fee lot; the others are free. Open 8 A.M. to sunset. (978) 874-2303.

PLACES TO STAY

Motel 6: This is the place where they leave the light on. Rates range from $40 to $60 per night. Commercial Street, Leominster, MA 01453; (978) 537-8161, (800) 4-MOTEL6; www.motel6.com.

Inn on the Hill: This 100-room hotel offers comfortable, spacious rooms at affordable rates. Nothing fancy, but, for your pet, there's room at the inn. Rates range from $40 to $60, with an additional $10 pet fee. 450 North Main Street, Leominster, MA 01453; (978) 537-1661.

FESTIVALS

Johnny Appleseed Weekend: Yes, George, there really was a Johnny Appleseed. And every year Leominster honors native son John Chapman, a.k.a. Johnny Appleseed, by throwing him a birthday party. Chapman was the missionary who planted apple trees everywhere he went, ergo his nickname. Now they hold a parade down Main Street and a weekend full of activities every September. (978) 534-7500.

MONSON

PARKS, BEACHES, AND RECREATION AREAS

• **Conant Brook Dam** 🐾🐾🐾 🐕 See **16** on page 190.
This out-of-the-way dam project on Monson Reservoir is another great park from the U.S. Army Corps of Engineers. With five ponds, several streams, a wetland, and miles of hiking trails for your leash-free dog, you won't get tired of visiting this quiet scenic spot in southern Massachusetts.

There are four parking access areas into the park, and you can discover your favorite trail from any of them. The main parking area is at the dam off Wales Road. Walk across the dam to intersect with the trails that lead to the reservoir or to the northern section of the park.

Or, for the best trail access, park off East Hill Road. From there you'll walk along two streams on your way to Duck Pond or Squire Pond in the far southern section.

We suggest picking up a map at the East Brimfield Dam office (24 Riverview Avenue, Sturbridge) or consulting the map board at the dam trailhead.

From State Route 20, take State Route 32 south for four miles. Turn left onto Wales Road for 1.5 miles, then left onto Moore's Cross (follow dam sign) to the end and the dam. Open dawn to dusk. (508) 347-3705.

NEW SALEM

PARKS, BEACHES, AND RECREATION AREAS

• **Bear's Den** 🐾🐾 🐕 🐕 See **17** on page 190.
This is a small but very scenic six-acre reservation owned by the Trustees of Reservations. The heart of the park is the gorge that lies at the base of the 70-

foot-high granite cliffs towering above the Swift River. The beautiful waterfall (best seen in the spring) and the gentle pool at its base will make you feel like you are in a wilderness setting.

Named for a settler who killed a black bear here, legend has it that this place was visited by the great Wampanoag leader, King Phillip, and other tribal chiefs who used it as a hideaway from the settlers during their wars against the colonists in 1675. We like to think it looks much the same as it did over 300 years ago. The hike is short but well worth the trip. Dogs are allowed off leash, but the rocks are slippery so be sure you leash overly zealous pups.

From State Route 122, take U.S. Route 202 south for half a mile. Turn right onto Elm Street for one mile, then make a left onto Neilson Road for a half mile. The entrance and roadside parking are on the right. Open sunrise to sunset. (978) 921-1944.

NORTHFIELD

PARKS, BEACHES, AND RECREATION AREAS

• **Northfield Mountain Recreation and Environmental Center**
  🐾🐾🐾🐾 See **18** on page 190.

You wouldn't think an electric company could be a dog's best friend. But you'd be wrong. With 25 miles of well-manicured trails and a "user-friendly" layout, this lovely park, managed by the Northeast Utilities Company, is a terrific place to visit—and many people do. Don't expect solitude here; on weekends this is a very popular recreation area, but fortunately it is big enough for everyone and is used year-round for hiking, mountain biking, and cross-country skiing. The trail system features both narrow, rugged footpaths and grassy forest carriage roads.

One of our favorite trails is the Rose Ledge Trail which leads to the gentle summit of North Mountain and to the reservoir. This trail traverses all the park has to offer—brooks, cliffs, granite rock formations, and lovely maple forests—with stunning views along the route. If you go all the way to the summit (a fairly moderate trek) and back, you'll hike over 4.5 miles. A trail map is available at the trailhead to guide you. Dogs must be on leash.

From U.S. Route 2, take State Route 63 north for 5.5 miles to the entrance on the right. Open 9 A.M. to 5 P.M. (413) 659-3714.

PELHAM

PARKS, BEACHES, AND RECREATION AREAS

• **Buffum Falls** 🐾🐾🐾 See **19** on page 190.

This lovely park is an out-of-the-way treasure. Two brooks, the Buffum and Amethyst, meet to form the small falls here, and you can follow a horseshoe trail that leads along both branches. The path is mostly flat and easy to follow; any dog, large or small, will enjoy this woodland walk. The entire loop is about one mile and will take you about a half hour to walk. The trail starts at the house off North Valley Road. Dogs must be leashed.

From State Route 202, take Amherst Road west for three miles. Turn right onto North Valley Road for half mile to the turnoff on your left. Open sunrise to sunset. (413) 662-3135.

PETERSHAM

PARKS, BEACHES, AND RECREATION AREAS

• North Common Meadow 🐾🐾🐾 🐕 See **20** on page 190.

Another one of the Trustees of Reservations properties, this meadow habitat is a short stroll from downtown Petersham. Of course, downtown is a relative term—Boston it ain't. This little town has a general store marking the center of the business district. The 24-acre meadow is just that—a big, open, grassy field more suitable for a stroll than a hike. Trails meander around the grassy area and some lead to the old farm pond. Dogs can swim here, but they had better bring their duck boots. Dogs are not required to be on leash on reservation land, but make sure they are under good voice control this close to a road.

From State Route 122, take State Route 32 north for a half mile. The meadow is on your left. Open sunrise to sunset. (508) 840-4446.

• Federated Women's Club State Forest 🐾🐾🐾 See **21** on page 190.

After hearing the name of this place, George and Inu thought we were going to have tea before our hike. But this is not a tea-and-cookies kind of place. With well over 1,200 acres of rugged woodlands, it's a great place to get a sweat going and put a little mud on your boots.

We think every visit should include a hike to the Gorge, a magnificent rocky chute. Trail markers are more erratic than the boulders here, however, so finding the gorge could be an all-afternoon adventure.

This forest is named for the fundraising group that helped preserve this woodland, and we are thankful to them. In fact, in lieu of the tea, we always have a biscuit in their honor after our walk.

Dogs must be leashed.

The park is located off of State Route 122 near the New Salem town line on State Forest Road. Open sunrise to sunset or until 8 P.M., whichever comes first. (978) 939-8962.

• Harvard Forest and Fischer Museum 🐾🐾🐾 See **22** on page 190.

This place is a forest with a degree. Owned by Harvard University, these two forests and a farm, totaling over 3,000 acres, are living exhibits for the Fisher Museum of Forestry.

The museum and first set of woods are off State Route 32. From here, there are a few trails to choose from, including a self-guided natural history trail, which gives visitors an idea of how the natural landscape of New England has changed. Another 4.5-mile trail leads to Prospect Hill offering a wide-angle view of the entire area.

A trail map, available at the museum, is recommended. Dogs are permitted on leash.

From U.S. Route 2 in Athol, take State Route 32 south for three miles. The museum is on the left. Open 8 A.M. to sunset. (978) 724-3302.

PHILLIPSTON

PARKS, BEACHES, AND RECREATION AREAS

• **Eliot Laurel Reservation** 🐾🐾🐾 🐕 See **23** on page 190.
This stretch of meadow and wooded splendor is another one of the properties owned by the Trustees of Reservations. The open meadow is surrounded by woodland, with short trails traversing though the trees. The paths follow old stone walls through a forest heavily laden with mountain laurel, which makes it a truly lovely walk.

From State Route 32 in Petersham, take State Route 101 east for four miles. On the left is a small pull-off area for the reservation. Open sunrise to sunset. (508) 840-4446.

PRINCETON

PARKS, BEACHES, AND RECREATION AREAS

• **Wachusett Mountain State Reservation** 🐾🐾🐾 See **24** on page 190.
Wachusett Mountain, at 2,006 feet, is the highest point in eastern Massachusetts and probably the only place where you can view both the Berkshire Hills and the Boston skyline at the same time. You can also see Mount Monadnock in New Hampshire on a clear day.

The park, a popular ski resort in winter and a birder's paradise during the autumn migration, also has 17 miles of hiking trails, including the Midstate Trail which passes through here. Some of the trails run though woodland, while others follow old mountain roads.

At one time, there were a number of summer resorts here. The resorts may be history, but the roads remain. Up Summit Road and its companion, Down Summit Road, allow you to drive to the parking area near the summit, but what's the fun in that? Our adventurous crew hit the Pine Hill Trail, which also took us to the top, but on our own steam.

Dogs are required to be leashed here, and the neighboring Audubon Wildlife Sanctuary does not permit dogs.

From State Route 140 in Westminster, take Mile Hill Road south into Princeton and the park. You can hike through here 24 hours a day, but the gate is open from 8 A.M. to sunset. (978) 464-2987.

• **Redemption Rock** 🐾🐾🐾 🐕 See **25** on page 190.
The lore that surrounds this place has to do with Mary White Rowlandson and her children, sort of the Patty Hearsts of their time. They were kidnapped by Indians in 1676 and redeemed at a meeting at the flat rock in this park. Then Mary wrote a best-seller about her adventures as a prisoner of the Indians. The inscribed rock is still here; the Midstate Trail passes close by and offers the chance to continue your hike to Crow Hill Ledges, three miles away.

Enjoy being redeemed from the tyranny of leashes, as the Trustees permit dogs off leash on their lands.

From U.S. Route 2 in Westminster, take State Route 140 south for three miles. The parking area is on the right, just south of the Princeton/Westminster line.

To get to the Midstate Trail, walk north past Redemption Rock and cross State Route 140 to the trailhead. Open sunrise to sunset. (978) 840-4446.

ROYALSTON

PARKS, BEACHES, AND RECREATION AREAS

• **Birch Hill Dam and Wildlife Management Area** 🐾🐾🐾 See **26** on page 190.

Birch Hill Dam was built by the U.S. Army Corps of Engineers, and, as a result of their hard work, we get a spectacular river trail to hike. The wildflower fields and floodplain habitat make interesting viewing on the walk. At the dam, there are 100 acres with trails, as well as the main path, which can be driven (when the gate is open) or hiked. The wildlife management area contains 30 miles of multiuse trails, and, if that is not enough for you, some folks choose to hike the perimeter boundary which is marked with red and white blazes.

Dogs must be on leash.

From State Route 68 near Templeton, take River Street north for a half mile. Turn left onto Neale Road. The entrance is on your right. Open sunrise to sunset. (978) 249-4467

• **Doanes Falls** 🐾🐾🐾🐾 🐕 See **27** on page 190.

Doanes Falls is where the Lawrence Brook drops 200 feet into the valley of the Tully River. It's a killer view—and a killer river. A big sign at the parking area lists the number of swimmers who have lost their lives risking a dip in the falls. The Trustees of Reservations manage this property, and, although dogs are allowed off leash, keep an eye out for curious canines who wander too close to the edge.

A two-mile trail leads from the parking area to the picnic area. It's all downhill from here, so that makes it uphill on the way back; we confess it wasn't just the dogs who were panting by the time we got back to the car. You can continue on to Spirit Falls, which is also accessible from Jacobs Hill Reservation (see below).

From State Route 68, take Athol Road south for two miles to the intersection with Doane Hill Road and the reservation and parking area. Open sunrise to sunset, with ranger patrols from Memorial Day through Labor Day only. (978) 840-4446.

• **Jacobs Hill Reservation** 🐾🐾🐾🐾 🐕 See **28** on page 190.

This place is easy to miss, but try not to. With a wild, unspoiled natural beauty that we city dwellers long for, it's a spot to soothe the savage beast in all of us. If you see another hiker, you've come at rush hour. The Trustees of Reservations manage this land, making it not only beautiful—but also leash free. The trails are not well marked, or well visited, so be careful not to get in over your head here. The destination of choice is the top of Spirit Falls, accessible via the yellow-blazed trail.

From Royalston Center at Athol Road, take State Route 68 north for a half mile. The small, dirt parking area is on the left marked by a sign. Open sunrise to sunset. (978) 840-4446.

• **Royalston Falls** 🐾🐾🐾 🐕 See **29** on page 190.
Yet another of the Trustees of Reservations lands here in Royalston, this one is perhaps the most difficult to access, making it one of the least visited. That is a shame, because the woods, Falls Brook, and a waterfall offer some of the most serene wilderness in the state. A yellow-blazed trail running across the brook above the falls is part of the 20-mile Tully Trail (see Tully Lake/Tully Dam, page 192).

As with much of the Trustee's land, dogs are permitted off leash.

From State Route 68, take State Route 32 (Athol Richmond Road) north for 1.5 miles. Park at the Newton Cemetery. Open sunrise to sunset. (978) 840-4446.

PLACES TO STAY
Tully Lake Campground: See page 192.

SOUTHBOROUGH
PLACES TO STAY
Red Roof Inn: This comfortable motel offers clean, modern rooms ranging from $48 to $80 per night. Small pets only. 367 Turnpike Road, Southborough, MA; (800) THE-ROOF, (508) 481-3904; www.redroof.com.

STURBRIDGE
PARKS, BEACHES, AND RECREATION AREAS

• **East Brimfield Dam Project/Streeter Recreation Area** 🐾🐾🐾 See **30** on page 190.
For a great swimming and hiking area, you and your dog will love this beautiful park. The sandy beach at Streeter Recreation Area is one of the few places you can swim in the summer with your dog. Although dogs are not allowed within the roped-off bathing area, you can take your leashed dog down the beach to a grassy area along the lakeshore. The water is clean and clear, and our dogs didn't mind a bit being away from the sunbathers.

If you're looking for some exercise, head over to the East Brimfield Dam. A half-mile nature trail leads from the dam into a wooded area; self-guided interpretive maps are available at the trailhead. Another grassy bank also leads down to the lake where you and your water dog can spend some more time swimming.

There is a $2 day-use fee at Streeter Recreation Area. Dogs must be on leash.

To get to the dam from State Route 148, take U.S. Route 20 west for a half mile. Turn left onto Riverview Avenue to the end and the dam parking area. The recreation area is one block farther west on U.S. Route 20 off Old Streeter Road. The beach is open 10 A.M. to 6 P.M.; the trails and dam are open dawn to dusk. (508) 347-3705.

• **Tantiusques Reservation** 🐾🐾🐾 🐕 See **31** on page 190.
This 55-acre tract of land contains a graphite mine that John Winthrop (famous for being a Boston founding father) purchased from the Indians in

1655. The mining remnants are still visible today. The trail runs the perimeter of the property and takes visitors past the open-pit mine and the horizontal mining shaft. You can walk into the mine shaft, if you dare, although only Inu was brave enough.

From Interstate 84, take Exit 1 to Mashapaug Road south for 1.5 miles. Turn right onto Leadmine Road for a mile. The reservation is on the left, with parking for a few cars. Open dawn to dusk. (978) 840-4446.

•Wells State Park 🐾🐾 See 32 on page 190.

Although there are over 10 miles of quality trails in this central Massachusetts state forest, our intrepid canines have only two destinations in mind when they visit Wells State Park. These popular destinations are Walker Pond and Carpenter's Rocks. The pond is big, cool, clear, and refreshing after a good hike. Some good access points are off the Mountain Road Trail (at the end of Mountain Road) in the southern end of the park.

Carpenter's Rocks are a cliff formation in the center of the 1,400-acre pine forest that afford you some fine views. A number of different climbing approaches are available to the top of the rocky overlook; the shortest is a 1.5-mile round-trip. Trail maps are available from the ranger station.

The 60 campsites here do permit dogs and are open from May through October. Camping fees are $7 per night; reservations are needed. Call (877) 422-6762.

A $2 donation for parking is requested. Dogs are required to be on leash and are not permitted at the pond beach.

From State Route 20, take State Route 49 north for a half mile. The park entrance is on the left. Follow the entrance road for a half mile to parking and the ranger station. Open dawn to dusk. (508) 347-9257.

•Westville Lake 🐾🐾 See 33 on page 190.

This recreation area surrounds the Westville Dam on the Quinebaug River. Some of the land has been developed into picnic areas, and some is left untouched. Bird-watchers flock here to observe annual migrations. A hiking trail starts near the parking area and runs through the woods near the lake.

While birds fly free, dogs must be leashed.

From State Route 20, take State Route 131 east to Hobbs Brook Recreation Area on the left. Or continue for two miles and make a right onto Wallace Road for a mile to the parking area. Open 8 A.M. to sunset. (508) 764-6424.

RESTAURANTS

Bob's Homemade: Bob makes everything here—the ice cream, the toppings, the chili for the chili dogs—everything. It's hard to believe this tiny place does it all, but we didn't argue. We just ate. And ate some more. A few picnic tables are available near the take-away window, or you can sneak through the gate in the fence and enter the adjacent ball field for a picnic. George prefers the cherry dipped cone, and it seems he is not alone, judging by the number served during our last visit. 392 Main Street, (508) 347-3860.

Hebert Candies and Ice Cream: This is mecca for those with a sweet tooth. Referred to as Candy Mansion, this place put roadside candy shops on the map. A make-your-own sundae bar, with gobs of topping choices, is also popular. Step out to the big lawn outside for sharing the wealth. River Road, (800) 642-7702.

PLACES TO STAY

Best Western: This full-service pet-friendly hotel offers 54 modern and spacious rooms. Dogs under 200 pounds are welcome as long as their owners are well behaved. Rates range from $63 to $95 per night. State Route 20, Sturbridge, MA 01566; (800) 528-1234, (508) 347-9121.

Days Inn: This lovely wooded property, just a dog's nose away from Old Sturbridge Village, welcomes travelers with pets. Rates start at $40 for a room, and go as high as $150 for a suite. 66–68 Old State Route 15, Haynes Street, Sturbridge, MA 01566; (508) 347-3391; (800) 544-8313; www.daysinn.com.

Publick House Historic Resort: Dogs are welcome in the "country lodge"— read "motor inn"—at the Publick House. There are some 60 acres to explore, and you are right in the middle of town here. Rates range from $65 to $140 per night. On the Common, Sturbridge, MA 01566; (508) 347-3313, (800) PUB-LICK.

Wells State Park camping: See page 206.

DIVERSIONS

Old Sturbridge Village: This museum is really a re-created early 19th-century village, giving visitors a chance to see, hear, smell, and experience what it was like to live in New England way back when. The 200-acre town has costumed villagers who act as if it were 1830. Stroll the Freeman Farm or the Mill Neighborhood with your pooch in tow. And, although we are pretty sure that leashes are not historically correct for the 1830s, dogs still must bring them along.

Open every day except Mondays. The two-day admission fee is $16.50. (508) 347-5383.

Pet Rock: Hebert Candies holds an annual rock festival—for the animals! Dogs are welcome on the lawn of Hebert's Candy Mansion on State Route 20 for this all-day event. Co-sponsored by local breed rescue programs, we couldn't pass up an opportunity to go to a concert with our pooches alongside. George had his heart set on Three Dog Night but contented himself with the contests, music, food, and lots of good tail-wagging fun. For more information, call (508) 755-8004.

SUTTON

PARKS, BEACHES, AND RECREATION AREAS

• **Purgatory Chasm State Park** 🐾🐾🐾 See 🔢 on page 190.
With names like Purgatory Chasm, the Corn Crib, the Coffin, the Pulpit, Lover's Leap, and Fat Man's Misery, this is a fantastic place for you and your pet to explore. Purgatory Chasm is a quarter-mile-long swath through granite. In places, the walls are 70 feet high. And, for those of you trying to visualize a Fat Man's Misery, it's a tall, narrow chasm cut into the surrounding boulders, forming a thin passageway for hikers to traverse.

Dogs must be on leash in all state parks.

From State Route 146, take Purgatory Road west for a half mile into the park. Open sunrise to sunset. (508) 234-3733.

RESTAURANTS

West End Creamery: This old-time ice-cream parlor may be on Purgatory Road, but one taste of any of their 30 flavors and you'll think you're in heaven. The outdoor deck is a great place to kick back and enjoy. 481 Purgatory Road; (508) 234-2022.

TEMPLETON

PARKS, BEACHES, AND RECREATION AREAS

• **Otter River State Forest** 🐾🐾🐾 See **35** on page 190.

These 12,788 acres are dedicated to Joseph L. Peabody, a conservation officer who spent 38 years in the service of forest conservation in Massachusetts. Included in this thickly wooded forest are multiple hiking trails and a developed section designated as Lake Dennison Recreation Area. Lake Dennison is accessible via a two-plus-mile hiking trail though the forest, or, for more feeble folk, a car. The dense forest includes some diverse scenery for hikers, plus it abuts the Birch Hill Wildlife Management Area, adding miles and miles to your hiking options.

Dogs should be on leash.

From U.S. Route 2, take Exit 20 to Baldwinville Road north. Turn right onto State Route 202 for one mile. The park is on the left. Open 8 A.M. to sunset. (978) 939-8962.

TOWNSEND

PARKS, BEACHES, AND RECREATION AREAS

• **Pearl Hill State Park** 🐾🐾 See **36** on page 190.

The majority of the trails here are old fire roads, but George's paws-down favorite is the 1.5-mile trail that runs along the edge of the brook. It's scenic, it's cool, and it's perfect for a dip. This 1,000-acre parcel is one of a string of state lands, loosely connected by trails in some places, and separated by a few miles in other places. Willard Brook State Forest (see Ashby) is nearby and is accessible via the trail system. Dogs are allowed on leash throughout the park, but they are forbidden on the beach.

Camping is permitted in the park at the 51 primitive campsites. Rates range from $5 to $10 per night, depending on state of residency and shower preference. Call for reservations. (877) 422-6762.

From State Route 119, take New Fitchburg Road south for 1.5 miles into the park. Open 8 A.M. to sunset. (978) 597-8802.

PLACES TO STAY

Pearl Hill State Park camping: See above.

UPTON

PARKS, BEACHES, AND RECREATION AREAS

• **Upton State Forest** 🐾🐾🐾 See **37** on page 190.

This is one of the prettiest spots to get out into the woods in this part of Massachusetts. At 2,600 acres, the woods are large, with many trails and unpaved roads running through the forest.

From the parking area, the main choices are to head north to the windy Rabbit Run Trail, or east toward the town of Hopkinton, where your options are far more numerous. To reach the woods trails to the east, continue on the unpaved Loop Road a short distance, and you will find the Swamp Trail, the Hawk Trail, and the Mammoth Rock Trail, to name just a few.

Dogs must be leashed.

From U.S. Route 495, take exit 21B to West Main/Hopkinton Road west for 3.5 miles. Turn right onto Westborough Forest Road for two miles. The forest access road is on the right. Open sunrise to sunset. (508) 278-6486.

UXBRIDGE

PARKS, BEACHES, AND RECREATION AREAS

• **Blackstone River and Canal Heritage State Park** 🐾🐾🐾 👣 See **38** on page 190.

The Blackstone River and Canal Heritage State Park is part of the Blackstone River Valley National Heritage Corridor, created in 1986 by the National Park Service to oversee the preservation of this birthplace of the American Industrial Revolution.

The main section and entrance to this state park is at River Bend Farm. The farm, which was founded in 1720 and was once the largest dairy farm in New England, now houses a visitor center. The towpath, which runs along the canal bank, is widely considered to be the most scenic section of the historic canal. About a mile down the canal is the Stanley Woolen Mill and the falls that once powered the mill.

Another option is King Philip's Trail, which runs from River Bend Farm north to Lookout Rock and King Philip's Cave. The trail is about 1.5 miles long, and the view of the valley is stunning.

Horses and bikes are permitted on the trails, so keep alert. Dogs must be leashed and are not permitted in the buildings.

From State Route 122, take Hartford Avenue east for a mile. Turn right onto Oak Street into the park. Open 8 A.M. to sunset. (508) 278-7604.

• **West Hill Dam/West Hill Park** 🐾🐾 See **39** on page 190.

Located within the Blackstone River Valley National Heritage Corridor on the quiet border of Uxbridge and Northbridge is the West Hill Dam and its surrounding recreation area, West Hill Park. The West River winds through 557 aces of white pine and a red oak forest, providing shelter for all kinds of wildlife. Two miles of trails are available to explore here, but keep an eye out for coyote—they aren't just big dogs.

Dogs must be leashed.

From State Route 122, take Hartford Avenue east for two miles. Turn left onto Access Road into the park. Open Memorial Day through Labor Day, 8 A.M. to sunset. (508) 278-2511.

RESTAURANTS

The Hay Wagon: Drive past this place on "Cruising Monday," and you'll be stuck in the slow procession of gawkers who gather to look over the antique and restored cars that fill the lot on Monday evenings. Unable to convince any Corvette owners to take Inu and George for a ride, we sat down at the outside tables for dinner, which included seafood and grilled food and some of the best homemade ice cream found in these parts. On Friday nights they cook up a tasty New England Clam Chowder. This family-owned restaurant has indoor seating as well, but dogs need to stay outside. 321 North Main Street (State Route 122); (508) 278-3782.

Tracey's Country Kitchen: This little café has a menu choice for everyone. Ice cream, sandwiches, cheeseburgers, salads, grilled chicken, hot dogs, and even breakfast go down the easy country way. 614 Main Street; (508) 278-5150.

DIVERSIONS

Black Dogs on Blackstone: In the summer, the Blackstone Valley Paddle Club holds regular Tuesday-night paddles, each week exploring a different part of the Blackstone Valley River and Canal. You can bring your own equipment, or the club has a limited number of canoes available. Dogs are welcome, but both you and your dog need to wear life jackets. (401) 762-0250.

Singing in the rain or shine: Enjoy the summer concert series at the Canal in Heritage State Park. On Sunday afternoons in the summer, concerts are held at the River Bend Farm. For more information on the concerts, call (508) 278-7604.

WARWICK

PARKS, BEACHES, AND RECREATION AREAS

• **Mount Grace State Forest** 🐾 🐾 🐾 See **40** on page 190.

At 1,458 acres, this is a large state forest and with a myriad of trails you can wander to give a dog a workout. Mount Grace, the towering 1,625-foot peak (and second highest peak east of the Connecticut River), is the main attraction.

The name derives from the captive baby, Grace, who died here in 1676 during King Phillip's War. The Wompanoag Indians captured a group of colonists, including Mary White Rowlandson (see page 203) and her baby Grace, and began a march to Canada. Grace wasn't able to make the journey and was buried by her mother at the foot of the mountain. Mary eventually was able to negotiate her freedom for 20 English pounds.

Today this is a quiet corner of Massachusetts, and you'll often find you have the trail to yourself. Take the 2.8-mile round-trip to the summit, and, although not an easy hike—the grade moves steadily uphill most of the way—you'll agree it is worth the effort when you see the views on top.

Dogs must be on leash.

The park is located off State Route 78 just north of the town center. Open sunrise to sunset. (508) 544-3939.

WENDELL

PARKS, BEACHES, AND RECREATION AREAS

•Wendell State Forest 🐾🐾🐾 See **41** on page 190.

This large 7,566-acre forest is remote and mainly undeveloped with the exception of the swimming area around Ruggles Pond. Although your dog is not allowed on the beach in the summer, you can walk the 1.5-mile loop trail around the pond. Other pond access points are available where your dog can swim to her heart's content.

For a longer hike, start at the Metacomet-Monadnock Trail, marked by white blazes, which is accessed at the end of the parking area near some picnic tables. The trail is easy to follow and runs along several brooks, eventually leading to a series of small waterfalls. If you're really ambitious, you can continue on the trail uphill to an overlook about two miles away.

Dogs must be on leashes.

From U.S. Route 2, take Wendell Depot Road south for five miles. Turn right onto Montague Road for 3.5 miles, then make a right onto the park access road. Open sunrise to sunset. (413) 659-3797.

WESTMINSTER

PLACES TO STAY

Westminster Village Inn: The motel-style cottages here at the Village Inn are a perfect home away from home in these parts. The Midstate Trail crosses the back of the property, offering a great chance to just wake up and hit the trails. Rates range from $99 to $139, plus a $25 cleaning fee per visit. 9 Village Inn Road, Westminster, MA 01473; (978) 874-5351.

WORCESTER

PARKS, BEACHES, AND RECREATION AREAS

•Green Hill Park 🐾 See **42** on page 190.

This local park is considered quite lovely by its neighbors, but we can't call it a must-see for out of towners. It boasts quite a view from its hilltop perch, though, so, if you are in Worcester anyway, head on up to take a look around from the top of Millstone Hill. Your dog won't think it's much, but you might. Dogs have to be leashed in the park.

From Interstate 290, take Exit 20 to State Route 70 (Lincoln Street) south for one mile. Turn left onto Green Hill Parkway and into the park. Open 5 A.M. to 10 P.M. (508) 753-2920.

•Hadwen Park 🐾🐾 See **43** on page 190.

This elegant shady park made us envy the residents of the surrounding neighborhood—everyone's neighborhood park should be this lush, wooded, and serene. The old woods road is the best way in and out, and the lovely stone gates look like they belong to a country estate. The city ordinance requires that dogs be on leash. The park abuts a large cemetery, so the place is deadly quiet.

From Interstate 290, take Exit 1 to State Route 12. Follow State Route 12 until it turns sharply right; at that point, turn left onto Webster Street for a half mile. Turn right onto Knox street until the road ends. You'll see stone gates where the woods road starts. Park on Knox Street. Open 6 A.M. to 10 P.M. (508) 753-2920.

•Quinsigamond State Park 🐾🐾 See 44 on page 190.

This park along the river in Worcester offers one of the only large stretches of green within the city. In addition to the park's main entrance, there are two other entrances called Regatta Point and Lake Park. The best choice for exercising your pooch is the Lake Park section. A flat, paved walking path runs along the river. Regatta Point is known as the rowing capital of Worcester, but, unless your dog is a good coxswain, this section won't hold much interest.

For the main entrance, take State Route 9 west from the Shrewsbury town line. Take Lake Avenue south for one mile into the park. For Lake Park, take Lake Avenue one mile and turn right onto Hamilton Avenue. The parking area is on the left. For Regatta Point, make a right from State Route 9 onto Lake Avenue. A fee is charged for parking at the main and Regatta Point entrances. Open 10 A.M. to 8 P.M. For the state park, call (508) 755-6880.

RESTAURANTS

Common Grounds: This place just across the street from the Common is a gourmet coffee shop with a menu of sandwiches and delectable goodies to go. They are famous in these parts for something called frozen slush, a part-ice, part-magic elixir that cools us down on hot days. 40 Franklin Street; (508) 756-8292.

Regatta Point Deli and Sandwich Shoppe: This place honors the rowing tradition of its nearby neighbor, the Quinsigamond State Park. This real Italian deli serves up hot grinders, sandwiches, pastas, baked goods, and their signature Regatta Club sandwich, which is still only $3. 28 Lake Avenue; (508) 756-6916.

Wholly Cannoli: This old-fashioned Italian bakery is run by old-fashioned Italians—what else would you expect? The pastries are to die for, including the namesake cannoli. It's a place where everyone takes out, so the line moves quickly. 140 Shrewbury Street; (508) 753-0224.

FESTIVALS

Salisbury Street Sampler: In mid-September, Salisbury Street holds a one-day festival to highlight its contribution to the history of the city of Worcester, and it's quite a party. There are walking tours, music, exhibits, and food. Lots of food. In fact, we were stuffed from the "sampling" we did on Salisbury Street. The fair takes place on the street, which is blocked off from noon to 4 P.M. (508) 363-1131.

8
THE CAPE AND THE ISLANDS

THE CAPE

Since the 17th century, when the Pilgrims first landed on the tip of Province-town, the Massachusetts Cape has been a destination for city-weary travelers. With miles of unspoiled beaches and town after town of quaint seaside Americana, it's no wonder the Cape is such a summer mecca for New Englanders. Of course, paradise comes at a price, and for years the price was paid by your pup. "No room at the inn" was a common refrain forcing canine companions to be left home alone. The good news is that more and more hotels welcome our four-footed friends. It's true that most of the beaches don't allow dogs from May 15 to September 15, but we've found a few exceptions to that rule. Now dogs lucky enough to live here and pups who are just passing through all have some places to sniff and kick up their heels.

Cape Cod Baseball League: Baseball, hot dogs, and your dog—you can't get any more American than that! From mid-June to mid-August, you and your dog can catch a game at any of the 10 ballparks on the cape. You'll see some of the best amateur/collegiate ballplayers in the country and get a real taste

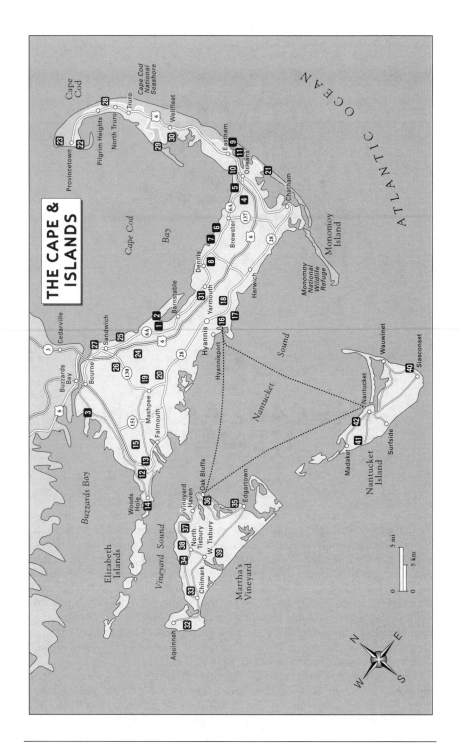

THE CAPE & ISLANDS

of old Americana. Admission is usually free, but they do pass the hat to cover the cost of the bats and balls.

For schedules and locations, check with each town's visitor center, look in the sports section of the *Cape Cod Times,* or contact the Cape Cod Baseball League at Box 164, South Harwich, MA 02661; (508) 432-1774.

Cape Cod National Seashore: Spanning 40 miles, the Cape Cod National Seashore encompasses most of the endless beaches, sand dunes, salt marshes, and seaside forests between Chatham and Provincetown. This is where the Pilgrims first landed, and the rich history of the seashore also includes the whaling industry, picturesque lighthouses, and tales from the sea.

Dogs are welcome year-round, but they must be leashed at all times and are not permitted on swimming beaches or on biking and hiking trails. But they can walk on all on all fire access roads and beaches that are not part of a life-guard zone or a posted nesting area.

For information or a park map, stop by the Province Lands Visitor Center in Provincetown or the Salt Pond Visitor Center in Eastham, or contact the Cape Cod National Seashore Headquarters at 99 Marconi Site Road, Wellfleet, MA 02667; (508) 349-3785.

Cape Cod Rail Trail: This fantastic 25-mile-long bike path replaced the Old Colony Railroad line. It runs from Dennis to Wellfleet through the towns of Harwich, Brewster, Orleans, and Eastham, taking cyclists, in-line skaters, joggers, walkers, and leashed dogs into some of the most scenic country on Cape Cod.

Parking is available at Nickerson State Park in Brewster, at the western terminus in Dennis, at the Cape Cod National Seashore Salt Pond Visitor Center in Eastham, and at the eastern terminus in Wellfleet.

Plans are underway to extend the bike path over the entire length of the cape. Open from dawn to dusk. For more information, contact Nickerson State Park at (508) 896-3491.

BARNSTABLE (HYANNIS)

Dogs who obey their owner's voice commands may go leash free in Barnstable's conservation areas. In the summer, dogs are not allowed on any town beaches.

PARKS, BEACHES, AND RECREATION AREAS

• Crocker Neck Conservation Area 😺 🐾 🐕 See ❶ on page 214.

Driving down the long dirt road to this 52-acre, out-of-the-way park in the village of Cotuit is a bit of a trek. But, if you persevere, your reward will be a wonderful walk—short, yet private and scenic. Take the main path from the parking area down a woodland trail that leads, after about a quarter mile, to the beach on Poponesset Bay, where you can sunbathe on the small sandy beach while your dog swims to her heart's delight. This whole peninsula is hard to reach, so most of the summer crowds don't congregate here, which makes it so much better for you and your dog—even in the height of the season.

From Falmouth Road/State Route 28, take Main Street south. Turn right on School Street, then left onto Crocker Neck Road and continue onto Santuit

Road. The park entrance is on the left. Parking is available. Open from sunrise to sunset. (508) 790-6245.

• Long Pond Conservation Area 🐾🐾🐾 🐕 See 🄋 on page 214.

Take several large meadows (or overgrown fields, as the conservation commission calls them), add lots of woodland trails and a large, clean pond where you and your dog can swim, and you've got the recipe for a darn good doggy day. You'll find all these things in this 37-acre conservation area in the village of Marstons Mills.

Follow the trail directly across the meadow from the parking area, and you'll soon enter a woodland. If you continue straight ahead, you'll come out on the first observation deck overlooking the pond. Here you can sit, dry off after a swim (be sure to bring your bathing suit on a hot summer's day), or just enjoy the view. Your leash-free dog, however, will probably be looking down from the deck, wishing to be elbow deep in water. The entire walk takes about an hour, depending on how long you linger at the pond.

From State Route 28, take Santuit-Newtown Road north onto Newtown Road. The park and a parking lot are on the left, just past Lady Slipper Lane. Open from sunrise to sunset. (508) 790-6245.

RESTAURANTS

The Barnstable Tavern and Grille: When the weather is good, you can eat on the patio at this upscale restaurant. Dogs are allowed at the outdoor tables and those on the outer patio as long as other patrons don't mind. The food is the traditional fare: steak, fish, and poultry. Bone appétit! 3176 Main Street/State Route 6A; (508) 362-2355.

Box Lunch of Cape Cod: We forgive this fabulous sandwich shop for not having a branch in Sandwich, because luckily there are plenty of locations throughout Cape Cod. The specialty is the Rollwich—a sandwich rolled up in softer-than-usual pita bread. You can eat it on the trail, on your bike, in the park, wherever—and it won't spill down your shirt and end up in the dog's mouth. Delivery is available. 357 Main Street/State Route 6A; (508) 790-5855.

Sea Street Café: In the summer you and your dog are welcome to sit at the outdoor tables at this easygoing family restaurant in Hyannisport. It's right across the street from several dog-friendly hotels (see below) and just up the street from the beach. You'll find the café to be a home away from home if you stay for the weekend. The standard family cuisine includes pasta, soups, salads, and homemade pies. 167 Sea Street; (508) 775-8790.

PLACES TO STAY

Glo-Min by the Sea: Located right in the heart of Hyannisport, this small complex of one- and two-bedroom cottages is within easy access of shops, restaurants, and parks. You and your dog will have plenty of privacy in the cute, clean cottages. The owners have dogs, though, so be sure your dog gets along with other canines if you decide to stay here. The owners ask that canine guests be over two years old—or at least out of that chewing, destructive-puppy phase. Reservations are required. Room rates range from $65 to $75. Cottages rent on a weekly basis only and range from $650 to $795. 182 Sea Street, Hyannis, MA 02601; (508) 775-1423.

Harbor Village: A real Cape Cod getaway, this top-of-the-line cottage village offers access to a private beach where your dog can romp with you. The one- to four-bedroom houses have full amenities and cove views. And, although it's close to town, guests enjoy plenty of privacy. A two-night stay is required in the off-season, and weekly stays are required in the high season. Weekend rates range from $105 to $165 a night; weekly rates range from $795 to $1,400. Marstons Avenue, P.O. Box 635, Hyannisport, MA 02647; (508) 775-7581.

Sea Breeze by the Beach: From the moment you drive up to this beautiful Victorian inn, you will be delighted. It rests at the end of Sea Street on a bluff overlooking the harbor in Hyannisport. Dogs aren't allowed in the main inn, but you can rent a new one- or two-bedroom cottage with your pal. Rates range from $795 to $995 a week, with a weekly minimum in season; call for off-season rates. 397 Sea Street, P.O. Box 553, Hyannisport, MA 02647; (508) 775-4269.

BOURNE

PARKS, BEACHES, AND RECREATION AREAS

• **Four Ponds Conservation Area** 🐾🐾🐾 See ❸ on page 214.
Prepare to be delighted at this charming park. A large map is posted at the main trailhead leading you to the four ponds in the 133-acre conservation area. We're happy to report that your dog will have great fun swimming in any of these water holes. If you want to extend your hike, back trails lead into the Bourne Town Forest. Dogs must be leashed.

From the State Route 28/28A rotary, take State Route 28A onto Lake Drive Extension, then onto Old County Road. Turn right onto County Road, and then turn right on Barlows Landing Road. The park and a parking area are on the right. Open from 6 A.M. to 9 P.M. (508) 759-0625.

NATURE HIKES AND URBAN WALKS
Cape Cod Canal Bike Path: A great place for dog walks with excellent views, the bike path runs on the U.S. Army Corps of Engineers canal access roads, which are closed to regular auto traffic. Both sides along the canal are open to cyclists and pedestrians and are much wider than regular bike paths. Dogs should be on leash.

Parking for the Cape Cod–side path is available at the Buzzards Bay Railroad Bridge, under the Bourne Bridge, and at the Sandwich Marina area. For the mainland path, park at the Buzzards Bay Railroad Bridge, under the Bourne Bridge, at Bourne Scenic Park, under the Sagamore Bridge, or at Scusset Beach. For information, call (508) 759-4431.

PLACES TO STAY
Yankee Thrift Motel: The rooms at this conveniently located motel right off the rotary over the Bourne Bridge are clean and spacious. Management welcomes your dog but asks that you not leave her unattended. Rates range from $50 to $80. 114 Trowbridge Road, Bourne, MA 02532; (508) 759-3883.

BREWSTER

PARKS, BEACHES, AND RECREATION AREAS

• **Nickerson State Park** 🐾 🐾 🐾 🐾 See **4** on page 214.
This exceptional state park is located on over 1,700 acres in East Brewster. Although much of the land is devoted to prime camping areas and bike paths, you and your dog will enjoy exploring two long and wonderful trails here. Both begin from the parking lot at the end of Flax Pond Road.

Our favorite hike is around Cliff Pond. The trail leads along the shoreline on one path and slightly above the pond on the other. Follow either path the whole way around for a three-mile hike that will take about 1.5 hours. You are welcome to swim, but the shoreline can get very busy on hot summer days.

Canine campers take note: This is one of the most popular camping destinations on Cape Cod, and the 420 campsites fill early in the season. It's no wonder why: All sites are in a wooded setting along one of the eight sparkling ponds, and trailer hookups, dump stations, showers, and picnic facilities are available. The fee is $6. We advise you to use the state park reservation system to book a site in advance; some sites are first come, first served, but they don't stay empty long.

Dogs must not be left unattended at the campground. They are not permitted at formal beach areas and must be leashed throughout the park at all times.

From State Route 6, take Exit 12 to State Route 6A west. The park and numerous parking areas are on the left. Open from 8 A.M. to 8 P.M. (508) 896-3491. For camping information, write to 3488 Main Street, Brewster, MA 02631; (508) 896-4615. For reservations call (877) 422-6762.

• **Spruce Hill Conservation Area** 🐾 🐾 🐾 🐕 See **5** on page 214.
A single-lane nature trail begins at the Museum of Brewster Historical Society in East Brewster and leads through a shady grove of pine and cedar trees before spilling out onto a beautiful beach. This is one of the few beaches you and your dog can use year-round, and doggone, is that a lucky break. This hidden treasure is nestled on the Cape Cod Bay and, with a view of the Plymouth coast in one direction and the tip of Provincetown in the other, you'll be in one of the most scenic spots around. The beach extends about half a mile before reaching private property, but your dog won't mind if you have to walk up and down several times to get enough exercise. Dogs need to be leashed in the summer.

From State Route 6, take Exit 12 to State Route 6A west. The park and a parking lot are on the right at the Museum of Brewster Historical Society. Open from 6 A.M. to 10 P.M. (508) 896-3701, extension 35.

• **Wing Island Conservation Area** 🐾 🐾 🐾 See **6** on page 214.
Although our pooches have never been big on art, they make an exception for the Brewster museums. That's because surrounding the Cape Cod Museum of Natural History is 150-acre Wing Island, which offers a nature trail that few parks can shake a stick at.

Walk behind the museum to find the northern John Wing Trail. A map at the parking area will show you exactly where the trail starts. Several miles of oceanfront await dogs who want to run, walk, and play. The ground is hilly and dunelike, and you are asked to avoid the dunes in the posted erosion areas. But once past the hills, you'll be on an open white-sand beach where you can roam in either direction, stopped only by the bay and the private property at the perimeters.

The second half of the conservation area is on the south side of State Route 6A and is accessed by the South Trail. Although this trail is the more beautiful and interesting of the two, it doesn't have the beach. In the winter you may choose to keep to the low trail, while in the summer you'll probably head for the surf. Dogs must be on leash everywhere to protect the fragile environment.

From State Route 6, take Exit 12 to State Route 6A west. The park and a parking area are found on the left and the right at the Cape Cod Museum of Natural History in West Brewster. Open from 6 A.M. to 10 P.M. (508) 896-3701, extension 35.

RESTAURANTS

Box Lunch of Cape Cod: Order the house specialty, the Rollwich—a sandwich rolled up in soft pita bread. They also deliver. Underpass Road in Brewster Village; (508) 896-6682.

Brewster Coffee Shop: If you're having a hard time keeping pace with your trail-happy hound, you'd better know where you can get a good cup of coffee without all the fluff. Brewster Coffee Shop serves it straight up so you can keep up. Plenty of other breakfast items are available to go. 2149 Main Street/State Route 6A; (508) 896-8224.

PLACES TO STAY

High Brewster: Located on over three acres, this elegant inn overlooks a beautiful pond in West Brewster. Stay here and you'll feel as if you're in a true getaway. This quiet, restful spot provides enough privacy, yet it's close to town and any amenities you may need. Although dogs are not allowed in the main inn, they can stay at any of the four cottages on the property. You should make reservations early because High Brewster is in high demand. Rates range from $165 to $220; a weekly stay may be required in the high season. Dogs must pay a flat fee of $25 for up to three days or $50 for a weekly stay. 964 Setucket Road, Brewster, MA 02631; (508) 896-3636.

Nickerson State Park camping: See page 218.

FESTIVALS

Christmas Prelude: In Brewster, the tree-lighting ceremony on the town common and the Christmas carolers are sure to fill you and your dog with the spirit of the season. Festivities begin the first weekend in December. For information, call (508) 255-7045.

CHATHAM

NATURE HIKES AND URBAN WALKS

Main Street Walking Tour: Because all Chatham beaches are off-limits to pooches, dogs have to be content with the action downtown. And there's plenty of that on Chatham's Main Street, which is lined with restaurants, cafés, antique stores, art galleries, and shops offering the latest in fashion—all with that Cape Cod appeal. The 10-block stretch gets busy on weekends and summer evenings. Dogs come from all over the Cape to socialize and revel in the many fond pats on the head. For more information, call the Chatham Chamber of Commerce at (508) 945-5199.

RESTAURANTS

Chatham Cookie Manor and Bob's Best Sandwiches: Have your cookie and eat it, too! The outdoor tables and the sandwiches are two great reasons to stop at this shop in the heart of town. You'll have a dog's-eye view of the passing parade of people. 499 Main Street; (508) 945-1152.

Chatham Village Café: Stroll up and down Main Street, and you'll be certain to work up an appetite. Fortunately this village café has a wide selection of specialty breads, pastries, and sandwiches. Enjoy your meal at the picnic tables out front. They even have parking—a Main Street rarity. 400 Main Street; (508) 945-2525.

PLACES TO STAY

Morgan Waterfront Houses: These three dog-friendly houses sit right on Pleasant Bay overlooking the North Beach sandbar and Atlantic Ocean beyond. In addition to your own private beach (that connects to miles of coastline), each rental has a full kitchen and hot tub. If that isn't enough, two other houses in town are also available for weekly rental: the 1800 House (built in 1792) and the Barn Loft (the original Chatham schoolhouse). Both are quaintly rustic but loaded with modern amenities. All welcome you and your four-footed friend. Open seasonally between May and November. Rates range from $900 to $2,800 a week. 444 Old Harbor Road, Chatham, MA 02633; (508) 945-1870.

DENNIS

PARKS, BEACHES, AND RECREATION AREAS

• **Crow's Pasture Conservation Area** 🐾🐾🐾 🐕 🦴 See **7** on page 214.

Although it's called Crow's Pasture, we don't think any crows have been cawing on this particular beach lately. Gulls, maybe, but you'll find lots of other ocean life on the miles of beaches and sandbars here. This is one of the most unusual locations on the cape and one of our personal favorites—where our dogs can run leash free most of the year.

At low tide you can walk a half mile out on the flat, wide sandbars. At high tide the dunes and beaches run several miles in each direction on quiet Cape Cod Bay. If you do have an all-terrain vehicle, you can drive across the access routes (stay off the dunes, please) and out to find your own private spot on the bay. If you're on foot, you can camp out for the day at the nearest sand drift or take a long walk in either direction. This is one of those great secret beaches that allows dogs in the summer, and you'll meet up with many happy canines who've been liberated from the summer beach ban. The area is managed by the Dennis Conservation Commission, which asks that dogs be leashed on the beach in the summer only.

From State Route 6A in East Dennis, take South Street north. When South Street becomes a dirt road, stay to the right at all forks in the road. The park is at the road's end, and there is room on the shoulder for parking. Off-road vehicles can continue to the beach. Open from 6 A.M. to 9 P.M. (508) 394-8300.

• **Flax Pond Conservation Area** 🐾🐾 🐕 See **8** on page 214.
Nestled on the Yarmouth border, this park offers a short walk around the edge of a quiet pond and through some thick, green woods. But the pond itself—a popular swimming area for people and dogs—is what makes the place worth a visit. The water is clear and clean with plenty of room around the shoreline for your dog to run free. The pond is under the management of the Dennis Conservation Commission, which says that dogs need only be leashed in the lifeguarded portion of the beach.

From State Route 6, take Exit 9 to State Route 134 north. Turn left on Setucket Road. The park and a parking area are on the right, just past Alexander Drive. Open from 6 A.M. to 9 P.M. (508) 394-8300.

RESTAURANTS

Box Lunch of Cape Cod: The specialty of this shop is the Rollwich, a sandwich rolled up in softer-than-usual pita bread. Get one to eat on the trail, on your bike, or in the park, without worrying that it will spill down your shirt and wind up a doggy snack. Delivery is available. Patriot Square; (508) 394-2202.

Captain Frosty's: After your dog spends the day at the beach helping you find seashells, you might want to head to Captain Frosty's to give her a taste of some real seafood. The clams, seafood rolls, and ice cream are local favorites, and the outdoor seating makes it easy to bring dogs. 219 State Route 6A; (508) 385-8548.

Lickety Split: Everyone on Cape Cod plays up the ice-cream angle, but don't let the name of this restaurant fool you. Yes, there are more flavors of ice cream than you'll care to count, but you can also get full seafood dinners, sandwiches, burgers, and all the trimmings. The setting is 1950s-diner style, complete with convenient outdoor seating. State Route 134 at the corner of State Route 6A; (508) 385-8707.

PLACES TO STAY

Lamplighter Motor Lodge and Cottages: You'll enjoy easy access to anywhere you want to go on the Cape from this motel on State Route 28. Dogs are welcome to bed down in the spacious rooms—with prior approval. Motel rates are about $67. Cottages are $425 to $550 per week in season. 329 Main Street, Dennisport, MA 02639; (508) 398-8469.

Marine Lodge Cottages: A pleasant surprise, this cluster of charming cottages is tucked away on a side street only a few blocks from the water. The one-to four-bedroom cottages are comfortable and well maintained, offering privacy as well as patio furniture in case you want to sit on the porch and meet your neighbors. The owners have done a great job of landscaping the complex, and the gorgeous flowers that bloom throughout summer will make you feel like you're staying in a home away from home (although we don't have flowers like this). Weekly rentals in season range from $550 to $1,075; it's closed from October to May. 15 North Street, Dennisport, MA 02639; (508) 398-2963.

EASTHAM

PARKS, BEACHES, AND RECREATION AREAS

• **Cape Cod National Seashore: Nauset Light and Coast Guard Beaches** 🐾🐾🐾 See **9** on page 214.

Our dogs are always up for a day at the beach, and these two beaches on the Atlantic Ocean are among their top destinations. The seemingly endless sandy shores are excellent spots to hunt for shells and other stinky sea stuff (which we leave for the dogs). A good place for exploring is south of Coast Guard Beach, where the seashore becomes a peninsula with the Atlantic on one side and Nauset Marsh on the other. You can walk on the peninsula for 1.5 miles to the southern point. Dogs have to be on leash and cannot enter bird-nesting areas or lifeguard zones.

From State Route 6, take Nauset Road east. Turn left on Cable Road and then right on Ocean View Drive. Both beaches are off this road, and plenty of parking is available. Open 24 hours; the parking area is open from 6 A.M. to 11 P.M. (508) 349-3785.

• **Rock Harbor Beach** 🐾🐾🐾 🐕 See **10** on page 214.

Dogs from all over Eastham flock to this beach. It's the only one in town that allows canines in the summer, thanks to the many dog lovers who petitioned to open up one beach to their four-legged friends.

It isn't large and there are no sunbathing areas, but your dog won't care. The tall grass helps keep the beach cool and provides more sniffing spots for curious pooches. And there are plenty of sandy patches along the simple paths. You'll meet up with many potential canine companions here, and we salute the dog owners of Eastham for their persistence in getting this leash-free beach opened up to landlocked pups.

From State Route 6 at the Eastham rotary, take Rock Harbor Road west. Continue left on Rock Harbor Road into Orleans. Turn right on Bridge Road and head back into Eastham. Turn left on Dyer Prince Road. The beach and a parking area are at the road's end on the right. Open from 6 A.M. to 9 P.M. (508) 240-5972.

• **Wiley Park** 🐾🐾🐾 See **11** on page 214.

When you are this far out on the cape, it's surprising to find a park that isn't right on the ocean. Wiley Park not only gives you a break from the sandy beaches, but the tall pitch pines provide plenty of shade for a calming, woodsy walk. There are even a couple of ponds for cooling off.

Approximately two miles of trails run between Great Pond, Bridge Pond, and Bridge Pond Creek. The most popular hiking route is the scenic trail that heads south from the parking area and passes between Great Pond and Bridge Pond.

The Eastham Conservation Commission requires dogs to be on leash and prohibits them from the playground and the beach at Great Pond.

From State Route 6, take Samoset Road west. Turn right on Herring Brook Road. The park and a parking lot are on the right. Open from 6 A.M. to 9 P.M. (508) 240-5972.

RESTAURANTS

Box Lunch of Cape Cod: Although this fabulous sandwich shop does not have a location in Sandwich, there are plenty of branches throughout the Cape. Try the house specialty: the Rollwich, a sandwich rolled up in pita bread. They'll even deliver. State Route 6; (508) 255-0799.

PLACES TO STAY

Blue Dolphin Inn: This motel is convenient to all beaches and parks on the end of the Cape. Unfortunately they only allow dogs in the off-season, namely from September to November and April to May. Rates range from $54 to $59, with a $10 fee for your dog per night. State Route 6, Eastham, MA 02642; (508) 255-1159.

Town Crier Motel: The views at this pleasant motel right on the main thoroughfare aren't spectacular, but the place is within easy distance of just about everything on the Cape. Availability is limited, so make your reservations in advance. Rates range from $69 to $95; dogs are $10 extra per night. P.O. Box 3620, State Route 6, Eastham, MA 02642; (508) 255-4000 or (800) 932-1434.

FALMOUTH

PARKS, BEACHES, AND RECREATION AREAS

• **Beebe Woods Conservation Area** 🐾🐾🐾🐾 See **12** on page 214.
There are almost 400 acres of prime woodland at this popular doggy hangout—once part of the old Beebe homestead. You'll pass historic Highfield—the summer residence built in 1878—on your way to the trail. In fact, the current parking area was once the graveyard for the family pets.

We suggest parking at the conservatory and consulting the map at the trailhead. If you take the long trail to Ice House Pond, the entire trip will take about 45 minutes. Head toward the Punch Bowl, a deep, clear swimming hole, and the loop will take another 45 minutes. To reach this scenic water hole, you'll hike uphill, then descend and emerge from the woods. For a shorter, 30-minute loop, head toward Ice House Pond and loop back when you reach the cutoff for the pond.

Dogs must be leashed

From State Route 28 near downtown Falmouth, take Highfield Drive west into the park and the Cape Cod Conservatory parking area. The trail starts behind the building. To get to the north entrance from State Route 28, take Ter Heun Drive west. The park and a parking area are on the left. Open from 6 A.M. to 11 P.M. (508) 548-7611.

• **Goodwill Park/Long Pond Watershed** 🐾🐾🐾 See **13** on page 214.
You will probably use this lovely, well-maintained park more in the off-season than in the summer months. That's because in July and August the beach along Grew's Pond is off-limits to dogs, and the park gets extremely crowded. The rest of the year, however, you and your leashed pooch will probably have the beach to yourselves. Best of all, there are five-plus miles of trails through the woods and along Long Pond (no beach access or swimming allowed in the public water supply) for you to enjoy.

The park entrance is off State Route 28 in West Falmouth, just north of Rogers Road. Two parking lots are available. Open from 8 A.M. to 8 P.M. (508) 548-7611.

• The Knob 🐾🐾🐾🐾 🐾 See **14** on page 214.

Have you given up trying to find a beach that allows dogs during the summer? Well, we almost did, and George was beginning to think his hair would never get those natural blond streaks. That was until we visited the Knob, a beautiful peninsula on Buzzards Bay in Woods Hole. George was surprised to find himself on a beach with no icicles dangling from his beard. The landscape is picturesque and amazingly varied for such a small area.

From the park entrance, follow the trail to your left along the shoreline of the tiny harbor. Here the water is calm, and the sand is soft and flat. The thin beach wraps around the peninsula and out to the bay, where the waves get a little stronger and the shore becomes rockier. You and your wet, sandy friend will find plenty of small inlets to call your own. At the tip of the peninsula is the Knob, a rocky strip of land that towers over Buzzards Bay. Relax on the bench there, take in the view, and dream of the million dollars you would need to win in the lottery in order to have a home here.

Dogs are required to be on leash here.

From State Route 28, take Locust Street south onto Woods Hole Road. Turn right on Quissett Harbor Road. The park is at the road's end. Parking is available on the shoulder. Open from 6 A.M. to 11 P.M. (508) 548-7611.

• Spectacle Pond Reservation 🐾🐾🐾 See **15** on page 214.

It's every dog for himself. The paths here are poorly marked, but, confusing trails notwithstanding, this park is definitely worth the trip. Just remember: If you head for the water, you won't get off the beaten track.

Several turnouts are located on either side of the access road. South of the road (to your left) are the many trails that lead to Spectacle Pond. To the north lie the trails that lead inland toward Deer Pond. And, if you drive to the fork in the road, the trails that go straight ahead lead to Mare's Pond. All of these hikes will satisfy your thirst for water and a woodland walk, and since we've never run into any other hikers at this reservation, you and your pal are almost guaranteed a solitary, scenic experience. Dogs need to be leashed.

From State Route 28, take Sandwich Road north. Turn left on Pinecrest Beach Drive. The park and turnouts where you can leave your car are on the left. Open from 6 A.M. to 11 P.M. (508) 548-7611.

NATURE HIKES AND URBAN WALKS

North Falmouth Historic Houses: Pick up a map at the Falmouth Visitor Center and take a self-guided walking tour along Old Main Road. Most of the houses date from the late 18th to the mid-19th century. The oldest site is the Mahagansett Indian Burying Ground (circa 1600), which overlooks Cedar Lake. The walk is only a few blocks long and will take you and your leashed dog about 30 minutes to complete. 20 Academy Lane; (508) 548-8500.

Shining Sea Bikeway: Covering a distance of 1.6 miles, this paved bicycle path follows what was once an ancient Wampanoag Indian trail and the Old Colony Railroad roadbed. The path, which is closed to auto traffic, goes from downtown Falmouth to Woods Hole, passing through scenic forests and marshes. It's also the only bike path on Cape Cod that runs along the seashore. In all, this is a great place to walk your dog, especially if you are on your way to catch a ferry to Martha's Vineyard or Nantucket.

Plans are underway to expand the bikeway to West Falmouth. Dogs need to be on leash, and everyone must stay to the right.

The path begins in downtown Falmouth at the intersection of Woods Hole Road and Mill Street; fee parking is available at the Steamship Authority off-site parking lot. The path ends at the ferry terminals in Woods Hole. (508) 548-8500.

RESTAURANTS

Box Lunch of Cape Cod: The specialty is the Rollwich, a sandwich rolled up in pita bread. You can eat it on the trail or in the park, and it won't spill on the ground to be gobbled up by your hungry dog. They even deliver. 781 Main Street; (508) 457-ROLS.

McMenamy's Fried Seafood: Order one of the many great seafood dinners and take it outside to eat on the patio. Your faithful companion can sit under the table and make sure you don't leave any scraps for the next dog. 70 Davis Straits/State Route 28; (508) 540-2115.

The Village Café: You'll be in the heart of Falmouth at this simple outdoor café. Fortunately the food will be easy on yours (heart, that is). There are plenty of low-calorie, fat-free foods to satisfy the most stringent of tastes. But those of you who've really worked up an appetite on the trail need not worry because there are also many gooey sandwiches to choose from. 188 Main Street; (508) 540-5234.

PLACES TO STAY

Falmouth Inn: Book a room at this dog-friendly inn in the center of Falmouth and you'll be glad you did. Dogs are not subject to size restrictions or extra charges, and the rooms are clean and spacious. Rates range from $60 to $130. 824 Main Street, Falmouth, MA 02540; (508) 540-2500 or (800) 255-4157.

Mariner Motel: You and your dog will feel right at home at this small motel within walking distance of historic Falmouth. One dog per room, please. Rates range from $69 to $99 in season, $42 to $69 during the off-season; dogs are $5 extra per night. 555 Main Street, Falmouth, MA 02540; (508) 548-1331 or (800) 233-2939.

Holiday Inn: All the sights and cafés in historic Falmouth are within walking distance of this conference-style resort hotel located just off Main Street. Trails behind the hotel lead to Morse Pond, where you and your dog can begin the day with a refreshing dip. You mustn't leave your four-legged friend unattended in the room. Rates are $189 in season, $69 to $89 during the off-season. 291 Jones Road, Falmouth, MA 02540; (508) 540-2000.

DIVERSIONS

A Star is Born: The Animal Rescue League sponsors a six-week pet education summer camp for children (sorry, dogs: no animals allowed in this part of the program). But at the end of the session (the last weekend in July), kids of all ages are invited to bring their pets along for the Animal Friends Pet Talent

Show. You can participate whether or not you've attended camp. The show is held at the Animal Friends Summer Camp at 96 Megansett Road. For more information, call the Animal Rescue League at (781) 461-8015, extension 23.

HARWICH

The town leash law states that dogs are to be leashed on beaches and in all public areas. Well-behaved dogs are allowed off leash only in conservation areas.

PARKS, BEACHES, AND RECREATION AREAS

• **Bell's Neck/Herring Run Conservation Area** 🐾🐾🐾🐾 🐕 See **16** on page 214.

Our favorite park in West Harwich covers more than 243 acres and offers a variety of terrain to keep the most demanding dog happy and tuckered out after a good off-leash run.

The best way to access the property is from Bell's Neck Road, a dirt road that divides the property and the reservoirs. You can park on any of the shoulder turnouts along the road. The best trails begin beyond the reservoirs, so try to park at the far end of the woods.

None of the trails here are marked, nor is there a sign identifying this area as conservation land, so it's up to you to discover which routes you like best. There are countless opportunities for exploration, and we know you'll have a great time finding the portion of the park that's right for you. Whether it's marsh, pond, bog, forest, or river, this place has it all.

From State Route 6, take Exit 10 to Pleasant Lake Avenue/State Route 124 south. Turn right on Main Street and proceed onto Great Western Road. Turn left on Bell's Neck Road (a dirt road) and continue into the park. Numerous parking areas are available off this road. Open from 6 A.M. to 11 P.M. (508) 430-7506.

• **Merkel Beach Conservation Area** 🐾🐾 🐕 See **17** on page 214.
With its sandy shore and tall beach grass, this seaside conservation area in Harwichport is a good doggy destination—if you can get to it. There's no place to park, so you either have to live here or be willing to walk a ways. But since it's one of the few beaches you can actually take your dog to in the summer, you might be willing to make that extra effort. Dogs must be leashed on the beach in the summer, but they're free to run off leash elsewhere.

From Main Street/State Route 28, take Snow Inn Road south. The beach is on the right at the road's end. No parking is available. Open from 6 A.M. to 11 P.M. (508) 430-7506.

• **Thompson's Field Conservation Area** 🐾🐾🐾 🐕 See **18** on page 214.
The 93 acres of rolling meadows and pines at Thompson's Field make this a popular place for leash-free dog walks in South Harwich. Your hike begins on wide trails in open fields, where you will have to dodge the pheasants and quail that rocket into flight out of the dry grass. The entire walk encompasses about a mile.

From Main Street/State Route 28, take Chatham Road north. The park and a parking lot are on the right. Open from 6 A.M. to 11 P.M. (508) 430-7506.

RESTAURANTS

Olde Towne Pizza: Every now and then, Inu hungers for his puppy days in the hills of Italy when mama would make meatball after meatball for him. Since he can't always get back to the Old Country, he heads for Olde Towne, where he can order all the pizza and pasta he wants. The place is open for breakfast, too, and outdoor seating is available. 703 Main Street; (508) 430-1904.

Schoolhouse Ice Cream & Yogurt: Okay, after all these years of hiking we finally have to tell the truth: we only do it for the ice cream. And the Schoolhouse ice-cream parlor in Harwichport is one of our favorites. Painted cow tables are available outside for you and your dairy-loving dog. Mooove on over! 749 Main Street/State Route 28; (508) 432-7355.

The Stewed Tomato: They say they named this deli for one of the unique, tasty dishes served here, but it could just as well have been in honor of the many tourists who come in after a day at the beach. Either way, tourists and locals know that the Stewed Tomato is the place to go for great takeout. They offer plenty of breakfast and lunch options, too, including muffins, eggs, soups, salads, and sandwiches. Order the home fries with cheese (wow!) and head to one of the picnic tables to devour them with your pooch. 707 Main Street; (508) 432-2214.

Sundae School: This is one school where you won't want to skip class. The staff here are the ice-cream professors when it comes to making malts, shakes, and, of course, great sundaes. Inu gives them an A+ for the creamiest vanilla on the Cape. There is plenty of outdoor seating. 606 Main Street/State Route 28; (508) 430-2444.

Thompson's Clam Bar: For some of the best fish-and-chips on the Cape, stop at this busy restaurant in the heart of town. Shaded tables are available on the outdoor patio, and the menu offers a large selection of items. Best of all, you won't shell out too many clams to enjoy these clams! 594 Main Street/State Route 28; (508) 430-1239.

PLACES TO STAY

Barnaby Inn: The owners of this lovely Victorian inn in the heart of town allow well-behaved dogs to join their people in one of the four rooms. A generous continental breakfast is served in your room each morning. This special hideaway provides the perfect retreat for both of you. Rates are $95. 36 Main Street, P.O. Box 625, West Harwich, MA 02671; (508) 432-6789.

Bayberry Motel: You'll love these charming cottages as soon as you drive up. Set just far enough away from the busy part of town, the Bayberry is like a home away from home. Each cottage offers plenty of privacy, and there's a fenced-in pool for socializing with your neighbors. Adirondack chairs are set up on the communal lawns so you can relax and enjoy those warm summer nights. In-season rates are $75 per night, $525 per week; call for off-season rates. 27 Old County Road, Harwich, MA 02661; (508) 432-2937.

FESTIVALS

Cranberry Harvest Fest: The cranberry bake-off, live music, fireworks, and arts-and-crafts fair should be enough to lure anyone to this festival, but we come for the Harwich Police Canine Demonstration. (Inu enjoys it, although he does get a little misty-eyed. He knows he could have gone pro if it hadn't been for that old college football injury.) The Cranberry Harvest Pet Show, sponsored by the Animal Rescue League, is open to children ages six to 12 and pets of all ages—so bring your four-legged wonder down for a little show-off session. Held from the second weekend through the third weekend in September. The canine demo takes place at the Harwich Little League field. For festival information, call (508) 430-2811. For details on the talent show, call (781) 461-8015, extension 23.

MASHPEE

PARKS, BEACHES, AND RECREATION AREAS

• **Lowell Holly Reservation** 😺 😺 😺 😺 🐕 See **19** on page 214.
A rare find, this 135-acre park managed by the Trustees of Reservations is located on the Conaumet Neck Peninsula. Not only are there two large and beautiful ponds for you and your dog to swim in, but you'll find plenty of unspoiled forest to explore. The natural foliage—including pine, cedar, red maple, and, yes, holly trees—makes for a particularly beautiful woodland experience. And even though your dog might not care two sniffs for the flowering trees, there are plenty of other sights and smells to keep her happy here. Dogs are required to be on leash.

From State Route 130, take South Sandwich Road north. The park is on the left on the Sandwich border. Free parking is available off Sandwich Road; a $6-per-day lot is located off the park access road and is open from 8 A.M. to 5 P.M. between Memorial Day and Columbus Day. Open from sunrise to sunset. (617) 740-7233.

• **Mashpee River Reservation/Mashpee River Woodlands** 😺 😺 😺 😺 🐕 See **20** on page 214.
With more than 500 acres of pristine river shoreline and woodlands, these two adjoining conservation lands (one a leash-free area) are the best doggy destinations on Cape Cod. If you want the incredible combination of solitude, excellent bird-watching, and dog friendliness, you'll find it here. The parks, managed by the Mashpee Conservation Commission and the Trustees of Reservations, are popular with canoeists, anglers, and hikers. Well-marked trails have been established on both sides of the Mashpee River, and there are two large parking areas. A large map is posted at each trailhead, and you can obtain other hiking maps at the town hall. Dogs are allowed off leash in the Mashpee River Woodlands, but they must wear their leashes when they cross into the Mashpee River Reservation.

From the Mashpee rotary, take State Route 28 heading south. Turn right on Quinaquisset Avenue. The southern parking lot is located on Mashpee Neck Road, which runs south from Quinaquisset Avenue. The park and a parking area are on the right. Open from 5 A.M. to 9 P.M. Mashpee Conservation Commission, (508) 539-1414; the Trustees of Reservations, (617) 740-7233.

RESTAURANTS

The Inside Scoop: Outside of this friendly little scoopery there are lots of tables where you can give your dog a few licks of homemade ice cream and sit in the sunshine with your neighbors. Oh, the ice cream is pretty darn good, too. Mashpee Commons; (508) 539-0090.

Picnic Box: You'll love this popular deli/diner—if you can fight your way through the early morning crowds to order breakfast or lunch. On the way to your favorite park, pick up a full breakfast or muffins to go. The easy call-ahead policy ensures that you won't have to wait. Dogs are welcome at the tables outside. Mashpee Rotary on State Route 28; (508) 539-0303.

Ultimate Edibles: The fare at this eatery next door to the Inside Scoop includes sandwiches and dinners. You can take your meal outside to one of the many tables. We're partial to the veggie burger, but the dogs think the real thing is a lot better. Mashpee Commons; (508) 477-2233.

ORLEANS

PARKS, BEACHES, AND RECREATION AREAS

• Cape Cod National Seashore: Orleans (Nauset) Beach 😺😺😺
See 21 on page 214.

During the summer when the cape is busy, many of the parks can get a bit crowded. That's when you and your dog need to head to Nauset Beach, which is nine miles long and covers the entire elbow of the Cape Cod arm. If you can't find elbowroom here, you're one big dog.

The barrier beach is exposed to the cold waters of the Atlantic Ocean on one side and the marshes of Pleasant Bay on the other. It's the place to go if you want to play beachcomber for an entire day. Just be sure to bring plenty of drinking water.

Dogs should be on leash on this property. You are asked to avoid all nesting areas.

From State Route 28, take Main Street east. Turn left on Beach Road and continue to its end. The beach is open 24 hours; the parking area is open from 6 A.M. to 11 P.M. (508) 349-3785.

RESTAURANTS

Box Lunch of Cape Cod: We forgive this fabulous sandwich shop for not having a branch in Sandwich, because there are plenty of locations throughout Cape Cod. The specialty is the Rollwich—a sandwich rolled up in softer-than-usual pita bread. You can eat it on the trail, on your bike, in the park, wherever, and it won't spill down your shirt and end up in the dog's mouth. Delivery is available. 217 Main Street; (508) 240-FAST.

Sundae School: This is one school where you won't want to skip class. The staff here are the ice-cream professors when it comes to making malts, shakes, and, of course, great sundaes. Inu gives them an A+ for the creamiest vanilla on the Cape. There is plenty of outdoor seating. 210 Main Street; (508) 255-5473.

PLACES TO STAY

Orleans Holiday Motel: Located in the heart of town, this comfy motel offers rooms with minor efficiencies (a sink, hot plate, and a small refrigerator). Dogs are welcome in certain rooms year-round by approval of the management. Dogs are not allowed in the common areas, but there is a landscaped area in the back where dogs can take a quick walk. Continental breakfast is included. Rates range from $49 to $105; pets are $10 more per night. 46–48 Cranberry Highway/State Route 6A, P.O. Box 386, Orleans, MA 02653; (508) 255-1514 or (800) 451-1833.

Skaket Beach Motel: Dogs are allowed at this spacious motel in the off-season (anytime except July and August). It is conveniently located near many walking areas and all the towns on the eastern side of the Cape. Rates are $43 to $99 in the off-season. 203 Cranberry Highway/State Route 6A, Orleans, MA 02653; (508) 255-1020 or (800) 835-0298.

DIVERSIONS

Pups in the Park: When JoAnna first heard about Pups in the Park, an outdoor concert given by the Cape Cod Symphony, she spent hours coaching George on how to hit the high notes so he would be ready for the big show. Inu and Chris were invited to attend George's debut performance. Fortunately for the audience, it turned out to be the Pops in the Park, but JoAnna didn't get over her "faux paw" for days. The event is held the last Saturday in August at Eldredge Park on State Route 28. And, yes, dogs are allowed, but only in the audience. For tickets and more information, call (508) 240-2484.

PROVINCETOWN

PARKS, BEACHES, AND RECREATION AREAS

• **Cape Cod National Seashore: Dike Trail and Long Point**
🐾🐾🐾 🖐 See **22** on page 214.

Folks and their salty dogs can have an adventure on the high seas in this portion of the national seashore. Here a three-quarter-mile-long dike—a series of well-placed stone blocks designed to control the flow of water around Provincetown Harbor—crosses the western end of the harbor from Provincetown out to Long Point. You can walk the entire length of the trail on top of it. Just be careful of high tides and slippery rocks.

Once across the dike, you'll be on Long Point, the fingertip of the Cape Cod arm. This part-time peninsula, part-time island—depending on the tide—is a beautiful, isolated seaside wilderness spanning over two miles. You and your dog can spend an entire day exploring the endless shores of this distant land.

Dogs must be on leash. On Long Point they are permitted only on the beaches, not the trails or dune areas.

The dike begins at the intersection of Commercial Street and Province Lands Road, just south of the State Route 6 and 6A terminus. The beach is open 24 hours; the parking area is open from 6 A.M. to 11 P.M. (508) 349-3785.

• **Cape Cod National Seashore: Race Point Beach and Herring Cove Beach** 🐾🐾🐾 See **23** on page 214.

At the very end of the Cape Cod peninsula at Race Point, you'll find these two large beaches. Race Point Beach is on the north end of the tip, and Herring Cove Beach is around the corner on the west end. Both offer beautiful white sand, spectacular views, wildlife, plenty of washed-up crab shells, and other exotic sea stuff for dogs to check out. The surf at Race Point is strong because this is where the waters of the Atlantic Ocean and Cape Cod Bay meet. So watch out for those big waves when your pooch is romping at the water's edge. Dogs must be leashed at all times.

Both beaches are near the State Route 6 and 6A terminus. Herring Cove Beach is just north of it on Province Lands Road. To get to Race Point Beach, take Province Lands Road north and then turn left on Race Point Road. Large parking areas are available at both beaches. The beaches are open 24 hours; the parking lots are open from 6 A.M. to 11 P.M. (508) 349-3785.

RESTAURANTS

Box Lunch of Cape Cod: The specialty is the Rollwich, a sandwich rolled up in soft pita bread. Delivery is available. 353 Commercial Street; (508) 487-6026.

Bubala's by the Bay: Dine alfresco while your dog laps up water from a Bubala Bowl. That's right, your dog can take home his very own bowl from this Fido-friendly restaurant. The atmosphere is unbeatable and the food is great—from the appetizers of nachos and steamed dumplings to the fish and poultry entrées. Best of all, well-behaved dogs get to eat at the feet of their best friends. 183 Commercial Street; (508) 487-0773.

Olde Aquarium Mall Food Court: Order your favorite food and take it outside to enjoy the best harbor view in town while you dine. We're not talking about fast-food fare, but rather small cafés that serve food to go. At the end of the mall is a picnic area with tables overlooking Provincetown Harbor. On a clear day you can look back toward Cape Cod Bay and see the mainland. Your pal will look forward to the crumbs that fall under the table. Note: The staff at Tailwaggers, a specialty pet store at the front of the mall, sets out a bowl of water for thirsty canines. 205 Commercial Street; (508) 487-2313.

PLACES TO STAY

Bayshore House: Yes, this spectacular complex on the harbor is pricey, but it gets our vote as the best place to stay in Provincetown. Many of the suites and cottages have waterfront views and total privacy. Decks and fireplaces are available in many others. A small private beach and patio area are provided for the exclusive use of guests. You'll be in the town center, within easy walking distance of everything you could need. Off-season rates range from $72 to $142; weekly rates, available in season only, are $695 to $1,295. 493 Commercial Street, Provincetown, MA 02657; (508) 487-9133.

Holiday Inn: Across the street is a public beach (where dogs, alas, are not allowed to set paw in the summer), and many of the clean and spacious rooms here have harbor views. The hotel is located just outside the main part of town, so guests enjoy the solitude of being away from the hubbub yet within walking distance of all the amenities. Room rates range from $79 to $149. State Route 6A at Snail Road, P.O. Box 392, Provincetown, MA 02657; (508) 487-1711.

White Wind Inn: Dogs weighing less than 35 pounds may stay at this elegant bed-and-breakfast, a charming alternative to some of the larger establishments in town. All the rooms in the restored Victorian inn in the heart of P'Town have private baths. Continental breakfast is included. A $75 deposit is required for folks with dogs. Rates range from $80 to $165. 174 Commercial Street, Provincetown, MA 02657; (508) 487-1526.

SANDWICH

PARKS, BEACHES, AND RECREATION AREAS

• Maple Swamp Conservation Area 🐾🐾🐾 🐕 See **24** on page 214.

The largest conservation area in Sandwich covers more than 500 acres and has plenty of trails for leash-free dogs to explore. The highlights are the two scenic outlooks along the main trail: on a clear day, you can see all the way to Provincetown on one side and across to Vineyard Sound on the other.

Winter and fall are the best times to visit this conservation area. The bugs can be fierce in the wet and hot seasons, and there are no ponds where your dog can cool down. But at any time of the year, the forest is lovely and the main access trails are well maintained.

From State Route 6, take Exit 4 to Chase Road south and immediately turn right on Service Road. The park and a parking area are on the left. Open from a half hour before sunrise to a half hour after sunset. (508) 888-4200.

• Murkwood Conservation Area 🐾🐾🐾 🐕 See **25** on page 214.

You'd think a place called Murkwood would be perched on a pinnacle with a crumbling witch's castle and a sky filled with thunder and lightning. Alas, if that's what you're looking for, you'll be disappointed because these woods are anything but murky. Located on a peninsula on Scorton Creek, Murkwood extends into marshlands and a lovely old pine forest, where you'll have a view of the river, the town beach, and a magnificent osprey nest. The Sandwich Conservation Commission maintains this 79-acre conservation area.

The park is on the north side of State Route 6A in East Sandwich, just east of Old County Road. Parking is available at the fire station. Open from a half hour before sunrise to a half hour after sunset. (508) 888-4200.

• Ryder Conservation Area 🐾🐾🐾 🐕 See **26** on page 214.

This large, leash-free conservation property encompasses 243 acres and abuts neighboring Lowell Holly Reservation (see page 228). There are two main parking areas with a series of trails, both set on the northern shores of Wakeby Pond. In the summer we recommend parking at the area off Cotuit Road because the trails at the main parking area off Sandwich Road lead to a heavily used public beach where your dog is banned from Memorial Day to Labor Day. If you start at the other area, you'll wind up at a section of the pond where dogs are welcome to swim.

From State Route 6, take Exit 2 to State Route 130 (Forestdale Road) south. Turn left on Cotuit Road. The park and a parking area are on the right, just past Boardley Road. Open from 8 A.M. to 8 P.M. (508) 888-4200.

• Scusset Beach State Reservation 🐾🐾🐾 See **27** on page 214.

When your dog has been banned from the beach, it seems as if finding a little patch of sand for the two of you is a tough thing indeed. But that's not a problem in Sandwich because dogs are welcome at Scusset Beach, on leash anyway.

The state beach is on the Cape Cod Bay, and the south side rests on the Cape Cod Canal. With its calm waters, the bayside beach is a good place to relax in the sun and cool off with a brief dog paddle. Afterward you and your pal can head over to the canal to watch boats taking the shortcut through the cape or hit the bike path for a good walk.

On weekends there's a $2 day-use fee per person. From the Sagamore Bridge rotary in Bourne, take Meeting House Road east into Scusset Beach Road. The park and a parking area are at the road's end. Open from 8 A.M. to 8 P.M. (508) 888-0859.

NATURE HIKES AND URBAN WALKS

Historic Sandwich Walking Tour: Sandwich is the oldest community on Cape Cod, and its rich history is reflected in this tour. Your walk will take you through the historic district and along Shawme Pond, where you'll visit the Dexter Grist Mill, a working mill built in 1640. Other sights include the Christopher Wren Church, constructed in 1847 by a Cambridge architect using actual Wren designs, and the Hoxie House, built in 1675. Pick up a map at the town hall on the corner of Main and Water Streets. (508) 888-5144.

RESTAURANTS

Carousel Candies & Fancies: The staff at this little shop in historic Sandwich will make a picnic lunch for you to take on the trail. Outside tables are available for those who wish to nosh here. Of course, if all you want is ice cream or candy, there's plenty of that. The peanut-butter fudge is especially good, but not for dogs! 132 State Route 6A; (508) 888-7000.

Sweet Tomatoes: Get the best pizza in town right here. The staff will make a deep-crust pie to suit your taste, and you can either take it with you or eat it at one of the tables that are placed outdoors in good weather. 148 State Route 6A; (508) 888-5979.

PLACES TO STAY

Sandwich Lodge & Publick House: Among the luxury amenities of this clean and spacious motel are corporate facilities, a spa, and a pool. It's located just outside historic Sandwich, yet close to town and all the parks. Dogs are allowed in the front rooms only, so when you make reservations be sure to specify that your canine will be accompanying you. Rates range from $54 to $125 and there's a $15 carge per stay for Fido. 64 State Route 6A, Sandwich, MA 02563; (508) 888-2275 or (800) 282-5353.

Wingscorton Farm Inn: Your dog will long remember the time you treated her to a stay at this special bed-and-breakfast inn. Located on a working farm, the place is charming, rustic, and enormously appealing. You will love the peace and quiet, and your dog will enjoy curling up on one of the big woven rugs that's provided in each room and cottage. To complete this picture of doggy heaven, nearby there's a private beach where your dog is welcome to explore—even in the summer. Full breakfast is included. Room rates range from $125 to $175 a night; cottage rates are $900 a week. There's a $10 fee per night for Spot. 11 Wing Boulevard, East Sandwich, MA 02537; (508) 888-0534.

TRURO

PARKS, BEACHES, AND RECREATION AREAS

• **Cape Cod National Seashore: Head of the Meadows Beaches**
🐾🐾🐾 See **28** on page 214.

One of the more popular stretches of the national seashore, this Atlantic Ocean beach is known for its soft sand, brilliant sunshine, and windswept sand dunes. Dogs just love being near the ocean and smelling the sea air, and yours will get her fill of both here. The undertow is strong, so be careful. At low tide, keep a sailor's eye out for some of the ancient shipwrecks just off-shore.

Dogs must be on leash.

From State Route 6, take Head of the Meadows Road east. The beach and a parking area are at the road's end. The beach is open 24 hours; the parking area is open from 6 A.M. to 11 P.M. (508) 349-3785.

RESTAURANTS

Jams, Inc.: Truro doesn't have much of a main street. In fact, this two-store complex, which includes the post office, is it. Luckily, this combination deli/gourmet eatery/bakery/grocery store will take care of most of your retail needs. You'll find the best coffee and scones around, fantastic pizzas, desserts, and snacks to die for, and just about any other foods you could desire. The staff will make box lunches for you to take to the beach, and there are picnic tables and a park across the street if you want to eat outside with your dog. Main Street at Truro Center; (508) 349-1616.

PLACES TO STAY

Outer Reach: Located on the windy cliffs overlooking the Atlantic Ocean, this is one of the first dog-friendly lodgings on the Cape. The large motel complex has many rooms and efficiencies, and it's within easy driving distance of nearby Provincetown. You and your dog will be greeted warmly upon check-in, and then given a handy map to guide you to the fire roads that lead down to the national seashore, which is just a few minutes' walk away. Rates range from $64 to $136. State Route 6, North Truro, MA 02652; (508) 487-9090 or (800) WHALE-VU.

WELLFLEET

PARKS, BEACHES, AND RECREATION AREAS

• **Cape Cod National Seashore: Duck Harbor Beach and Great Island** 🐾🐾🐾 See **29** on page 214.

While most visitors are basking on the beaches just off State Route 6 on the Atlantic Ocean side of the cape, dogs in the know head out to the shores of Great Island and Griffin Island on Cape Cod Bay. These beautiful beaches rest at the base of sandy cliffs that drop down from pitch pine forests.

If you're feeling energetic, you'll want to hike out to the Great Island penin-sula of Jeremy Point. It's four miles down the shoreline, and the peninsula is submerged except at the lowest tides, so bring water, a watch, and plenty of caution. The setting is wonderful, and the sunsets spectacular, but you don't want to be caught when the tide comes in. Dogs should be leashed at all times.

From State Route 6, take Commercial Street west into Kendrick Avenue and Chequessett Neck Road. Turn right on Griffin Island Road and proceed to the beach and a parking lot at the road's end. The beach is open 24 hours a day; the parking area is open from 6 A.M. to 11 P.M. (508) 349-3785.

• Uncle Tim's Bridge 🐾🐾 See **30** on page 214.

The fun part of this park is the wooden bridge over the estuary of Pine Point. Once across you'll discover a set of short, charming trails that lead on and over the hummock in the middle of the salty marsh. They eventually wind up at the scenic cove waters of Shirt Tail Point. The whole trail should take only half an hour for you and your leashed dog to walk, but the setting is unusual and rustic, accessorized by a couple of worn-out boats that haven't seen the high seas in quite some time. Watch out for dead fish; if you don't, your dog certainly will.

From State Route 6, take Commercial Street west. The park and a two-car parking area are on the left, just past Long Pond Road. Open from 7 A.M. to midnight. (508) 349-0301.

RESTAURANTS

Box Lunch of Cape Cod: The specialty is the Rollwich, a sandwich rolled up in a very soft pita bread. You can eat it on the trail, on your bike, in the park, wherever, without spilling most of it (sorry, dogs). They deliver, too. 50 Briar Lane; (508) 349-2178.

PLACES TO STAY

Brown's Landing: Dogs are welcome in most of these cottages nestled in a small wood on Indian Neck overlooking a quiet meadow marsh. Weekly rates are $495 to $625; it's closed from October through April. Located at the end of Indian Neck Road. P.O. Box 1017, Wellfleet, MA 02667; (508) 349-6923.

Friendship Cottage: You can really get away from it all at this private, quiet complex of cottages on the windy shores of Wellfleet. Right across the street is the town beach, where you may walk your dog. The cottages are just five minutes from town and another five minutes from the national seashore. Weekly rates are $500; it's closed from October through April. 530 Chequessett Neck Road, Wellfleet, MA 02667; (508) 349-3390.

DIVERSIONS

Dog days at the movies: The last of the big spenders—that's George and Inu. Anytime either of them has a hot date, they ask for the keys to the car and head off to the Wellfleet Drive-in. They get in for free and don't have to spring for dinner because they receive complimentary biscuits on the way in.

Family-oriented films are screened at this old-fashioned drive-in (the only one on the Cape) from May to September, depending on the weather. Admission for adults is $6; kids ages five to 11 are $3.50; children under five and pooches of all ages watch for free. Dogs are also welcome to browse at the flea market (yikes, fleas!) that's held here on Wednesday, Thursday, Saturday, and Sunday from

April to November; it features an average of 200 booths. Located on State Route 6 between Aspinet and West Roads; (508) 349-2520 or (800) 696-3532.

YARMOUTH

PARKS, BEACHES, AND RECREATION AREAS

• **Dennis Pond Conservation Area** 🐾🐾🐾 See **31** on page 214.
Good things come in small packages. Take the mile-long trail along Dennis Pond and you and your leashed dog will get a taste of everything a great park has to offer: water, trees, bushes, a pine-needle-covered path, and plenty of shade on a warm summer's day. When the rest of the world is at the beach, head for this fresh pond in Yarmouthport to cool off.

Dogs and nonresident parking are not permitted at the Dennis Pond public beach off Summer Street.

From Main Street (Cranberry Highway and State Route 6A), take Willow Street south. The park and a parking lot are on the left. Open from a half hour before sunrise to a half hour after sunset. (508) 394-3508.

NATURE HIKES AND URBAN WALKS

Historical Society of Old Yarmouth Trail: This mile-long nature hike passes through the beautiful woods of Yarmouth, which are preserved by the local historical society. The trail runs from the gatehouse behind the post office to Miller Pond and back again. Take the path around Miller Pond and you'll add another half mile to your walk (although it's not part of the nature trail). You can pick up a map in the post box next to the gatehouse at the trailhead; it details each of the 18 markers you'll encounter on the walk. A donation of $.50 per adult and $.25 per child is requested. Dogs must be on leash. For more information, contact the Historical Society of Old Yarmouth. Strawberry Lane; (508) 362-3021.

RESTAURANTS

Pizzas by Evan: Of course, you're number one in your dog's heart, but coming in a close second (and gaining, depending on when your pooch last ate) is pizza. The great pizza at this local pizzeria makes this a favorite spot when we are visiting the Cape. Plenty of seating is available out on the front porch. 554 State Route 6A; (508) 362-7977.

PLACES TO STAY

Brentwood Motor Inn: Dogs are allowed at these pleasant townhouses located close to town and all the amenities. Each unit is equipped with full efficiencies. Weekly rates range from $400 to $550; closed in the off-season. 961 Main Street, South Yarmouth, MA 02664; (508) 398-8812.

Colonial House Inn: If you're looking for a taste of Old Cape Cod complete with canopy beds, antique furnishings, and lovely gardens, this is the place for you. Located in historic Yarmouthport, this inn has all the modern conveniences combined with old-world charm. Best of all, your pet is welcome in all rooms. Rooms range from $50 to $100 per night. 277 Main Street (Route 6A), Yarmouthport, MA 02675; (800) 999-3416; www.bestinns.net.

Motel 6: All Motel 6 locations allow dogs, as long as you don't leave your pet unattended. Rates are $56 per night. 1314 State Route 28, South Yarmouth, MA 02664; (508) 394-4000; www.motel6.com.

The Village Inn: Offering old-fashioned hospitality, this quaint bed-and-breakfast inn is located in the Captain's Mile, the town's historic section. Your dog is welcome throughout the year but only in certain rooms, so make your reservations well in advance. A full breakfast is served to guests each morning. Rates range from $50 to $95. Main Street/State Route 6A, Yarmouthport, MA 02675; (508) 362-3182.

Yarmouth Shores: These seven cottages are perched right on the bay, with a private beach where you and your dog can play. All the units are charming and have a small patio in front. Rates start at $190 a week. 29 Lewis Bay Boulevard, West Yarmouth, MA 02673; (508) 775-1944.

MARTHA'S VINEYARD

Martha's Vineyard—named for a sea captain's daughter and the abundance of wild grapes on its hills—is located just eight miles across Nantucket Sound from the mainland. From Memorial Day to October 1—when the population swells from its winter average of 12,000 to an overwhelming 96,000—the beaches of Martha's Vineyard can get very busy. Happily, leashed dogs are allowed to romp on these sands before 9 A.M. and after 5 P.M. In the winter, dogs are free to visit the beach at any hour as long as they obey their owners' voice commands.

Martha's Vineyard boasts 100 square miles of rolling hills, white sand beaches, and quiet harbors. The first inhabitants were the Wampanoag Indians, and their ancient burial grounds and stone walls are still in evidence throughout the island. European settlers arrived in 1642, and visitors have been coming from the mainland ever since.

In most of the conservation regions featured here, dogs who are under voice control can go leash free. But, remember, this is a small island, and the more popular it becomes, the more rules get implemented. To help prevent everyone from losing the off-leash freedom we enjoy today, we suggest you follow these simple guidelines: Keep your dog leashed in town, pick up after her at all times, don't let her drink the sea water, and avoid crowded swimming areas when there are children playing.

Last, but certainly not least, we strongly urge you to have your dog inoculated for Lyme disease if you're planning even a weekend trip here. Deer ticks, carriers of this deadly disease, are a huge problem on the Vineyard, and we can't emphasize enough how important it is to both check your dogs for ticks after every woodland walk and take all necessary precautions in protecting your dog before you arrive.

Island-bound hound: One highlight of any island visit is a trip across Nantucket Sound. Ferries are the principal means of transportation between Cape Cod and Martha's Vineyard. Our canine pals are more than welcome on all the ferries at no extra charge, but they do have to be on leash. The Steamship Authority runs year-round from Woods Hole and Hyannis to Vineyard

Haven and Oak Bluff. All you and your dog need to do is show up and hop aboard, but, if you want to bring your car across in the summer, you must make reservations months in advance.

The following companies provide ferry service between Cape Cod and the Islands:

Hy-Line Ferries, Ocean Street Dock, Hyannis, MA 02601; (508) 778-2600.

Island Queen Ferries, 297 Billingham Avenue, Falmouth, MA 02540; (508) 548-4800.

Steamship Authority, Reservation Bureau, 509 Falmouth Road, Suite 1C, Mashpee, MA 02649; (508) 447-8600.

Martha's Vineyard Bicycle Path: A wonderful system of bike trails exists on the island. One path circles the center of the island and the state forest. Another follows the inland route between Vineyard Haven and Edgartown. Yet another takes the shore route from Oak Bluffs to Edgartown. More than 20 miles of paths in all are available for cyclists, in-line skaters, and walkers (including pooches, of course). Dogs are required to be leashed, and everyone who uses the trails must stay to the right. For information, contact the Martha's Vineyard Commission at (508) 693-3453.

Martha's Vineyard Land Bank Commission: The goal of this organization is to purchase and preserve land for the purposes of conservation, hiking, birding, farming, and hunting. Since 1986, more than 1,000 acres have been set aside for protection. Most of these lands—except for those deemed environmentally sensitive—are open to the public, and that includes dogs. Funding is generated from an islandwide public surcharge of 2 percent on most real estate transactions. For more information, contact the commission at P.O. Box 2057, Edgartown, MA 02539; (508) 627-7141.

Sheriff's Meadow Foundation: This privately owned conservation organization has been preserving natural areas on Martha's Vineyard since 1959. The goal is twofold: to protect wildlife and to set aside lands for humans to enjoy. More than 2,000 acres are managed by the foundation, and many of these places are open to the public. Picnicking and camping are prohibited on all the properties.

To receive information, make a donation of money or land, or find out what you can do to protect our open spaces, contact the Sheriff's Meadow Foundation at Lambert's Cove Road, RFD Box 319X, Vineyard Haven, MA 02568; (508) 693-5207.

AQUINNAH (FORMERLY GAY HEAD)

PARKS, BEACHES, AND RECREATION AREAS

• **Moshup Beach** 🐾🐾🐾 See **32** on page 214.

For a great seaside walk under the cliffs at the western tip of the island, begin on the sandy shores of Moshup Beach, where the surf is big and the views are endless. This is a great spot, but it gets even better as you and your leashed dog make your way down the beach heading west. The beach curves around a bend, and then cliffs rise up out of the sand behind it. These are the Gay Head Clay Cliffs, a National Historic Monument. The beach area is managed by the town of Aquinnah and the Martha's Vineyard Land Bank Commission.

The park is on the south side of Moshup Trail off State Road. Parking is available for $15 a day at the intersection of Moshup Trail and State Road. Open from dawn to dusk. (508) 627-7141.

CHILMARK

PARKS, BEACHES, AND RECREATION AREAS

• Peaked Hill Reservation 🐾 🐾 🐕 See **33** on page 214.

The best features of this reservation managed by the Martha's Vineyard Land Bank Commission are the two viewing points. Peaked Hill, at 311 feet above sea level, is the highest point on the island. Radar Hill (308 feet) is an old World War II lookout spot. From both hills you can see most of the island and the surrounding waters. On a clear evening, you can even watch the sun go down over Gay Head Clay Cliffs.

From Middle Road take Tabor House Road north for half a mile. Turn left on the dirt road across from the Chilmark landfill. Proceed, taking the right lane at each fork, to the park and a parking area at the road's end. Open from dawn to dusk. (508) 627-7141.

• Waskosim's Rock Reservation 🐾 🐾 🐾 See **34** on page 214.

The reservation is named for the gigantic boulder perched precariously along the trail on the western end. Apparently, it once marked the border between Wampanoag lands and those claimed by British settlers in the 17th century. You can still see the stone walls that the British constructed to further delineate the boundary.

Managed by the Martha's Vineyard Land Bank Commission, the 165-acre park has a lot to offer canine visitors. Trails are well marked, and you can pick up one of those great laminated maps at the trailhead—just return it when you're finished. The yellow trail is the most direct route to the view from Waskosim's Rock. The red trail branches off of it, following a more indirect loop around the yellow trail. This woodland walk is about 1.5 miles long.

The park entrance and a parking lot are located on the south side of North Road between Tea Lane and the West Tisbury town line. An auxiliary parking area is available on Tea Lane. Open from dawn to dusk. (508) 727-7141.

RESTAURANTS

Chilmark Store: The town's general store has everything you need before or after a long day on the trail, and then some. You can pick up snacks, drinks, and sandwiches for a picnic in the park. There's also a full Italian deli and Primo's Pizza if you want something spicier. Your dog may dine with you on the spacious and homey front porch. 7 State Road, at Beetlebung Corner; (508) 645-3655.

EDGARTOWN

PARKS, BEACHES, AND RECREATION AREAS

• Sheriff's Meadow Sanctuary 🐾 🐾 🐕 See **35** on page 214.

Offering charm and a convenient location, this 17-acre parcel of land was the first property acquired by the Sheriff's Meadow Foundation. It provides a sanctuary from the bustle of Edgartown, which surrounds it. If you live in town or are just staying here, you'll probably start and end your day with a walk at this park.

From Main Street, take Pease's Point Way north and veer onto Planting Field Way. The park is on your right. Park on the side of the road. Open from dawn to dusk. (508) 693-5207.

NATURE HIKES AND URBAN WALKS

Walking Tour of Edgartown: This seaside community is known for its elegant, white-shingled homes with classic black shutters. Sea captains owned many of these houses, which can be identified by their widow's walks and the commemorative plaques. Wander with your dog on the tree-lined streets or pick up a map at the visitor center on the corner of Pease's Point Way and Church Street. Be sure to include the shops on Main Street in your stroll. (508) 627-6180.

RESTAURANTS

Among the Flowers Café: Your dog is welcome to join you at this quaint café tucked down a lane just past Main Street. Breakfast and lunch are served (and dinner, too, in the summer). Order your food to go or find a table outdoors and let the staff serve you in style. If your dog doesn't have the patience to sit still for table service, you can leash her to a nearby bench while you eat. It's closed from October to April. Mayhew Lane; (508) 627-3233.

Edgartown Delicatessen: Head to this busy deli in the heart of town to get a sandwich or breakfast to go. The place is famous for its huge sandwiches and very extensive menu. You can sit in the small park right next door and let your dog entertain the crowds while you eat. 52 Main Street; (508) 627-4789.

Morning Glories Bakery: A stop here takes you back to the days when farm stands and country bakeries were common sights. We love the muffins, cider, and apples. Sit at one of the many picnic tables or find a cool place under a tree in the yard—the perfect country setting on a lovely day. Located east of Manuel F. Corellus State Forest on Edgartown–West Tisbury Road; (508) 627-9003.

PLACES TO STAY

Martha's Vineyard Vacation Homes at Lindsay Woods: One mile from the harbor in beautiful Edgartown, this complex of four single-family homes makes for a wonderful week on the island with your dog. You'll be close to everything, yet not in the thick of it. Weekly rates in the summer range from $850 to $1,800; call for winter weekend rates. There's a $100 pet fee per week. The homes are on Hamblin Way. For information, contact 10 Windwood Drive, Fairfield, CT 06432; (203) 365-0356 (fax) or (800) 544-2044.

The Victorian Inn: You'll feel as if you're in another era when you stay at this wonderful inn, one of the most special lodgings on the island. Elegant and tastefully decorated, the rooms are spacious and have been completely restored. Dogs are only allowed from November 1 to April 30. If you'll be visiting in the off-season, this is the place to be. Off-season rates range from $100 to $195. There's an additional charge of $20 per night for your dog. 24 South Water Street, Edgartown, MA 02539; (508) 627-4784.

OAK BLUFFS

PARKS, BEACHES, AND RECREATION AREAS

•**Ocean Park** 🐾 🐾 See **36** on page 214.
For a convenient romping ground with a great ocean view, you can't do better than this local park. Right in the heart of Oak Bluffs and across the street from the Steamship Authority, the spacious park is the site of many summertime activities. There's not much here, except an open grassy area, but it's fine for a quick walk with your leashed friend.

The park is near Oak Bluffs Harbor at the intersection of Lake, Ocean, and Seaview Avenues. Open 24 hours a day. (508) 693-5511.

NATURE HIKES AND URBAN WALKS

Walking Tour of Oak Bluffs: Walk through Oak Bluffs for a taste of old New England with a little bit of Oz. The colorful gingerbread cottages will dazzle you with their craftsmanship and architectural details. Others are noteworthy for their outlandish gaudiness. No matter which style you prefer, you'll enjoy strolling with your leashed dog through this town where, from the 1850s through the 1950s, Methodists retreated for old-time religious revivals. Pick up a map at the visitor center on the corner of Oak Bluffs and Lake Avenues. (508) 693-5511.

RESTAURANTS

Coop De Ville: Just sitting on the dock of the bay with George and Inu is a great way to eat a meal. And we can at Coop De Ville, where there's plenty of seafood and fine harbor views. Sit outdoors with your dog for a shared lunch or dinner or order food to go. Dockside Marketplace; (508) 693-3420.

Mad Martha's: At this famous ice-cream and sandwich place right in the heart of town, there are shaded tables where you and your dog can sit on the waterfront. Pick up a grinder to eat on the trail. Dockside Marketplace; (508) 693-9151.

Old Stone Bakery: You won't need a keen canine sniffer to pick up the wonderful aromas emanating from the Old Stone Bakery. Keep a tight grip on that leash and you'll be at the doorstep in no time. No dog or human can resist the tempting pastries, cookies, and fresh breads. Plenty of seating is available out front on the pedestrian walkway. Park Avenue; (508) 693-3688.

PLACES TO STAY

Island Inn: This 51-room motel, located between Oak Bluffs and Edgartown, allows well-behaved dogs in the off-season after Labor Day and before Memorial Day. Rooms range from $75 to $155. Beach Road, Oak Bluffs, MA 02557; (508) 693-2002.

Martha's Vineyard Surfside Motel: The most dog-friendly lodging on the island, this hotel is located right in the heart of town, next to the ferries, a park, and the main walking thoroughfare. The rooms are large, and some have water views. Rates range from $50 to $125. Dogs cost an additional $10 per night, and you must leave a $50 deposit. P.O. Box 2507, Oak Bluffs Avenue, Oak Bluffs, MA 02557; (508) 693-2500 or (800) 537-3007.

TISBURY

PARKS, BEACHES, AND RECREATION AREAS

• **Ripley's Field Preserve** 🐾 🐾 🐕 See **37** on page 214.
If you're looking for a secluded and peaceful hike, you can find it in this quiet forest and meadow. The main trail heads through a typical Martha's Vineyard wood, then loops around for about a mile before ending up back at the trailhead. Along the way you'll come to the centerpiece of the park: a large wildflower meadow where you can picnic, bird-watch, or just throw around a ball or Frisbee with your dog.

From State Road, take Lambert's Cove Road north. Turn left on John Hoft Road. The park and a parking area are on the left. Open from dawn to dusk. (508) 627-7141.

• **Tisbury Meadow Preserve** 🐾 🐾 🐕 See **38** on page 214.
This 84-acre preserve, managed by the Martha's Vineyard Land Bank Commission, offers a little something for everyone.

Follow the short yellow loop through an open meadow at the outskirts of the woodland trail (about a 20-minute walk). For a longer walk through an oak forest, you can get on the red trail, a well-marked route that meanders through a dense woodland. You can take the shorter loop on the yellow crossover or continue on to the green trail, which runs along Holmes Hole Road, an 18th-century cart path that once connected the interior of the island to the harbor. This walk takes a full hour and brings you back to the trailhead.

The park is located on the south side of State Road, just west of Lambert's Cove Road. Parking is available. Open from dawn to dusk. (508) 627-7141.

NATURE HIKES AND URBAN WALKS

Walking Tour of Vineyard Haven: The many shops and stores along Main Street in Vineyard Haven reflect the fact that the village has always been the island's main port. Highlights of a historic stroll with your dog include the Seaman's Bethel, now a maritime museum, at 15 Beach Street; the Old 1829 Schoolhouse on Main Street; and the homes along Williams Street. It's safe to tie your dog outside if you want to venture into any of the buildings. For more information and a map, stop by the Chamber of Commerce on the corner of State Road and Main Street. (508) 696-4200.

RESTAURANTS

The Black Dog Bakeries: Once upon a time, before the Vineyard was so popular, the Black Dog was the only tavern open for locals year-round. Folks would come to play chess, read, or just socialize in the cold, gray winter months. Today it's a famous retail store and mail-order house hawking everything from T-shirts to baby clothes to dog bowls—all emblazoned with the signature black dog with one white paw. Dog lovers can stock up on leashes, collars, and even some homemade gourmet dog biscuits to slip into the backpacks of their own black, brown, blonde, or spotted pooches.

The tasty baked goods and sandwiches are perfect for taking on the trail. You can still stop by the tavern or the bakery for a bite to eat, but you'll have to sit on the benches outside. The newer State Road branch offers a full café menu and doesn't get as crowded; leashed dogs are allowed at the outdoor tables there. Water Street; (508) 693-4786. A second location is at 162 State Road; (508) 696-8190.

Sandwich Haven: This off-the-beaten-track sandwich shack is a Vineyard Haven staple. Freshly squeezed juices, healthy shakes, Middle Eastern fare, and specialty pita sandwiches round out the menu. You'll have to put up with the local color, but we think that makes everything taste better. Benches are available nearby. Off Main Street by the Bowl and Board; (508) 696-8383.

PLACES TO STAY

Mayhew Cottages: Well-behaved pets may check into the housekeeping units of this private estate located just outside of town. It's a secluded getaway on four lovely acres, but you can pop into town easily. Rates are $800 to $975 per week in the summer. Dogs pay an additional $50 per week. Weekend rates in the off-season are $125 per night. P.O. Box 1644, Vineyard Haven, MA 02568; (508) 693-2809.

WEST TISBURY

PARKS, BEACHES, AND RECREATION AREAS

• **Sepiessa Point Reservation** 🐾 🐾 🐾 🐕 See **39** on page 214.
One of the best hikes on the island can be had at this 165-acre preserve, managed by the Martha's Vineyard Land Bank Commission. The park is on a peninsula surrounded by Tisbury Great Pond. Trails lead along both sides of this U-shaped pond, but the one to take is the wooded path along Tiah's Cove on your right. From most of this wide, well-used 2.5-mile trail, you can see the water and the various shorebirds there, including ducks, cormorants, and ospreys. Your dog might also find a few squirrels and chipmunks to chase. The trail ends at Sepiessa Point and a broad sandy beach that your dog will simply love. Best of all, from October through April, leashes are not required.

From the intersection of Old County Road and Edgartown–West Tisbury Road, take Edgartown–West Tisbury Road east. Turn right on New Lane and continue onto Tiah's Cove Road. The park and a parking area are on the right. Open from dawn to dusk. (508) 627-7141.

NANTUCKET ISLAND

A wonderful place to live, vacation, or just spend the day, Nantucket Island offers isolated, pristine beaches, quaint cobblestoned streets, and extremely friendly locals. The Wampanoag Indians called it Nantaticut, or "faraway island," and the rustic island is far enough from the mainland to provide peace and tranquillity. There isn't even a traffic light. In fact, the only connection to the hectic, time-driven world of everyday life is the ferry schedule.

Only 14 miles across, you can see the surrounding sea from almost any point. Unlike Martha's Vineyard, the terrain is flat with little dense forestland thanks to the early sheep farmers. In 1723, the first whalers settled here, and, by the end of the 18th century, Nantucket was the world's largest whaling seaport. Although that era is long gone, walk through town and you'll see many historic buildings and landmarks from this past life. Best of all, most of Nantucket's beaches are open to all. And thanks to the Nantucket Conservation Foundation, almost a third of the island is maintained as public conservation land.

Nantucket Bike Trail: Twenty-four miles of bike paths service the island of Nantucket, and they're all extremely popular with cyclists, in-line skaters, and walkers. Most are at least separated from the road by a grassy divide, if not more, and all are well paved. Four trails run along Cliff, Madaket, Milestone, and Surfside Roads. For more information, contact the Nantucket Commission at (508) 228-7237.

Nantucket Conservation Foundation: This conservation organization owns and preserves 8,272 acres—more than 27 percent of Nantucket Island. The principal goal is to protect public lands that have natural and historical significance and to promote conservation research and education.

Almost all of these places are open to the public—and dogs—for passive recreation. Some properties or sections of properties may be closed to protect environmentally sensitive areas. Each has its own requirements for keeping dogs restrained, and we've noted them in the following listings.

To become a member, make a donation, or get more information (including a property map), contact the Nantucket Conservation Foundation at P.O. Box 13, Nantucket, MA 02554; (508) 228-2884.

PARKS, BEACHES, AND RECREATION AREAS

• **Coskata-Coatue Wildlife Refuge/The Haulover/The Coatue Properties** 🐾 🐾 🐾 🐾 See **40** on page 214.

The vast beaches of the Great Point Peninsula, which forms the entire northeast corner of Nantucket and Nantucket Harbor, make a wonderful destination for dogs who love to walk. Isolated and pristine, the 17 miles of beachfront are spectacular to behold, offering expansive beauty and abundant wildlife, including gulls, terns, piping plovers, and common eiders.

Be prepared for an all-day affair. Getting out to one of the points is a real haul. If you have an off-road vehicle, you can drive out to Great Point via the 1.5-mile access road. The only entrance, it passes through private property from the park's gate to the beaches. Otherwise, you'll have to leave your car at the parking lot and walk all the way. Be sure to bring sufficient water for your four-footed friend. Dogs must be on leash.

Admission to the reservation costs $20 per vehicle. From Milestone Road, take Polpis Road north. Turn left on Wauwinet Road and proceed to the entrance at the road's end. If on foot, you can park at the entrance for free. Open from 8 A.M. to 5 P.M. The Trustees of Reservations, (508) 693-7662; Nantucket Conservation Foundation, (508) 228-2884.

• Sanford Farm/Ram Pasture/The Woods 🐾🐾🐾🐾 🐕 🦴 See **41** on page 214.

This is the place for Nantucket dogs, as any local canine will tell you. Although the entire island is pooch friendly, this is where dog lovers go when they want to give their four-legged friends an extra-special off-leash treat. The windswept marsh and meadow set on over 630 acres make for a unique hike. There are six-plus miles of trails to explore, and they'll leave you wanting to return again and again. In addition, the Nantucket Conservation Foundation has placed information markers all along the way pointing out unusual foliage and wildlife habitats. It's one of the most impressively managed parks we know of, with trail maps, easy-to-read signposts, and wide-open trails.

From Main Street, take Madaket Road west. The park and a parking lot are on the left, just past Mill Brook Road. A second parking area is located off Barrett Farm Road, a rough, dirt road. Open from dawn to dusk. (508) 228-2884.

• Tupancy Links Property 🐾🐾🐾 See **42** on page 214.

The rolling grassy fields of Tupancy Links make this a great place for your dog to walk and for you to take in some fantastic views of Nantucket and the sea. It's also the favored hangout for all the local island dogs. At 5 P.M. on any given day, dogs appear from every direction to meet and greet and swap "tails" of the day. The 73-acre property is on the island's northern plateau above Nantucket Sound, and a trail loops for a mile around the perimeter of the pasture. Steep cliffs on the far end of the park are off-limits to everyone; we learned this the hard way.

On our first visit here we foolishly ignored the cliff warnings. Usually our dogs stick close to us on the trails, but, if we're anywhere near water, they will run to it, especially George. He sprints to the beach, then sits near the shoreline with paws and tail tucked in tight around him, patiently looking back down the trail for us to appear.

However, George's first-to-the-beach routine creates a problem at Tupency Links, where the beach sits at the bottom of a hundred-foot cliff. As you walk along the rolling, grassy hills, you would never expect that such a drop exists until you're right over the edge.

Nearing the beach, George dashed for the water as usual, then disappeared over the rise. It wasn't until we saw the sign warning us of the dangers of the cliffs that, fearing the worst, we raced to the edge and peered over. And there he was. Crouched on the beach in that familiar position, looking up as if to say, "gee, what took you guys so long?"

We looked at each other, wondering how he got down there alive and, more importantly, how he was going to get back up. After shouting for him to come, he sprang to his feet and charged straight up the cliff, digging in hard as he neared the top. But he just didn't have the momentum. So after a few heart-stopping moments (for us), he turned and headed back down. Again he stood on the beach looking up at us. Again we called for him to come. Finally, with an aggressive snort and determined expression, he gave it everything he had. Sand flew out from under his paws as he attacked the cliff with his legs churning like a machine. We cheered him on louder and louder, and then—he was up! He flipped his tail and gave a head butt to Inu. Whew! Guess there's a leash law at this park for a reason.

From Madaket Road, take Cliff Road north. The park and a parking lot are on the left. Open from dawn to dusk. (508) 228-2884.

NATURE HIKES AND URBAN WALKS

Historic Nantucket Walking Tour: Highlights of this self-guided walking tour through Nantucket include the Whaling Museum, the island's oldest house (built in 1686), the birthplace of Benjamin Franklin's mother, the old gaol (1805), and other fascinating sites from the whaling days of early Nantucket. Dogs must be leashed. For a map and directions, stop by the visitor center at the entrance to the Steamship Authority. Steamship Wharf; (508) 228-1700.

RESTAURANTS

Claudette's: Selling gourmet sandwiches and specialty foods, this shop in tiny S'conset is open sporadically. But, if you time it right, you'll be treated to great sandwiches and bakery items that are out of this world. Pick up a box lunch for the trail or sit outside at one of the open-air tables when the weather is pleasant. Post Office Square, at the rotary in Siasconset; (508) 257-6622.

Espresso Café: You can get more than just java at this café in the heart of town. For a light breakfast, grab a cup of coffee and a scone. Folks with heartier appetites can get eggs, bacon, pancakes, and the like to go. Plenty of benches are available up and down Main Street if you want to take your food outside to share with your dog. Or pick up the White Bag Special (a sandwich, chips, and a cookie) to eat on the trail. 40 Main Street; (508) 228-6930.

Provisions: At this appropriately named place, you can stock up on enough food to keep you going for an entire expedition—and probably have a few scraps left over to toss to your pup. The Turkey Terrific and the Wharf Rat Club are just two of the giant sandwiches served on your choice of specialty breads. Don't forget to buy some cookies, too, just in case you get lost in the wilderness. There are plenty of places around the harbor to sit with your dog. 3 Harbor Square, Straight Wharf; (508) 228-3258.

The Rotary Restaurant: If you are going out for a spin, take a turn into the Rotary for a filling breakfast, lunch, or dinner. The menu includes pancakes, eggs, seafood, chicken, and burgers. Dogs are welcome at the outdoor tables. Milestone Rotary; (508) 228-9505.

The Tap Room: Your dog may join you for a wonderful meal or drink on the patio of this restaurant at the famous Jared Coffin House (see page 247). On busy nights, you may have to leash her along the railings on the outer edge of the patio, but, in the afternoon or during the week, she is welcome to sit at your feet and hope you drop something. The menu includes salads, burgers, sandwiches, and desserts. 29 Broad Street; (508) 228-2400.

Yogurt Plus: This yogurt shop is just the place for health-conscious folks who want to enjoy a cool and refreshing pick-me-up. Best of all, the staff loves dogs. On any given night, canines may outnumber human customers, so get in line and tell yours to bark for her own doggy sundae. 6 Oak Street; (508) 228-6616.

PLACES TO STAY

Jared Coffin House: Dogs are allowed to stay in the lap of luxury at this elegant, upscale inn. Each room of the historic landmark is unique, and the service is impeccable. But watch out: after staying here, your dog will demand extravagance whenever he's on the road—and this place is hard to match. Rates range from $160 to $210. Dogs are $15 extra per stay. 29 Broad Street, P.O. Box 1580, Nantucket, MA 02554-1580; (508) 228-2400 or (800) 248-2405.

The Nantucket Inn: Don't let the airport location fool you—this inn rolls out the red carpet for you and your pet. The spacious rooms are luxuriously appointed, and you'll be close to everything Nantucket has to offer. Rates are $190 in season; call for off-season rates. There's a $25 pet fee per stay. 27 Macy's Lane, Nantucket, MA 02554; (508) 228-6900.

Danforth Inn: When Beth and Rocky visit Nantucket, they always head straight here. A charming, antique-filled hideaway, this four-room bed-and-breakfast is just a short walk up Main Street from the ferry dock. Beth loves the New England hospitality offered by proprietor Lynn Danforth, and Rocky loves the big backyard where he can romp or rest under the spreading shade trees. Breakfast is included. Rates range from $75 in the off-season to $150 in season. 121 Main Street, Nantucket, MA 02554; (508) 228-0136.

Safe Harbor House: This charming five-room bed-and-breakfast, located right in town, provides an elegant old-world visit to the Island. Each room is lovingly decorated, and the owners are happy to accommodate you and your dog by request. Rooms range from $160 to $190. 2 Harbor View Way, Nantucket, MA 02554; (508) 228-3222.

FESTIVALS

Daffodil Festival: On the last full weekend in April Nantucket awakens from the long winter to celebrate spring with this flowery festival. Events are held throughout the island, but the festivities revolve around Main Street. Your dog can check out the parade of antique and classic cars, tailgate picnic, window-decorating contest, and, of course, the flower show. For a schedule and information, call (508) 228-1700.

Harbor View Music Festival: Each year from July through Labor Day, your dog can join you in town for the free outdoor concerts held every Thursday at 6:15 P.M. Each week features a different style of music—from oldies and folk to classical and jazz. Children's Beach Bandstand; (508) 228-7213.

DIVERSIONS

A Nose for Shopping: When you're in the market for treats for the dog in your life, stop by Cold Noses, a nifty little shop in the heart of Nantucket. We're not talking about the run-of-the-mill pet supplies. This store stocks gourmet biscuits made especially for cold noses (and growling stomachs). Well-behaved dogs are welcome to come inside and peruse the other specialty items, such as personalized collars, food bowls, books, treats, and other goods your pampered pooch will love. Tell them George and Inu sent you! On Straight Wharf; (508) 228-5477.

Be an Island Dog: If you are vacationing on Nantucket or are lucky enough to live there, Island Dogs offers a treat that can't be beat. Whether you're going boating, fishing, museum perusing, or any other activity where you might have to leave your dog behind, don't despair. Island Dogs will entertain your pet while you're out. Leave your pet for an hour, an afternoon, a day, or overnight in the comfort of owner Leslee Walkup's home. She offers pick up and delivery to and from your hotel or home and will design a schedule to fit your vacation needs. Her doggy field trips are so much fun that you may want to tag along! Rates range from $15 an hour to $50 for a 24-hour period. Call for reservations before you arrive on Nantucket. Spots for Spot fill up fast. (508) 325-5728; www.islanddogs.com.

9
GREATER BOSTON

Whether you're a city dog or a country dog, the counties in this chapter will satisfy even the pickiest of tastes. Covering much of Eastern Massachusetts and the horseshoe around its capital, Boston, the parks waiting for you and your canine companion are truly remarkable. Even better, there are more leash-free parks than you can shake a stick at. Whether your idea of a Boston tea party is to go wild in the woods of Wayland, Weston, or Wellesley; frolic on the pristine beaches of the North Shore; retrace the tracks of the Minutemen; or tiptoe through the tulips of the downtown Public Garden, you'll find just the right spot here.

Bay Circuit Trail: Linking parks and reservations between Plum Island on the North Shore and Kingston Bay on the South Shore, this trail will eventually connect more than 30 towns across 200 miles. For information, contact Bay Circuit Alliance, 3 Railroad Street, Andover, MA 01810; (978) 470-1982.

Metropolitan District Commission: Managing the Metropolitan Parks System, the MDC administers recreation areas in 34 towns and cities in the Greater Boston area, including many parks in this chapter. For information, contact 20 Somerset Street, Boston MA 02108; (617) 727-9547.

Essex County Greenbelt Association: For the past 27 years, the Essex County Greenbelt Association's efforts have led to the preservation of more than 4,000 acres in the Essex County region. Dogs are allowed leash free on all of its properties. For information, contact Cox Reservation, 82 Eastern Avenue, Essex, MA 01929; (978) 768-7241.

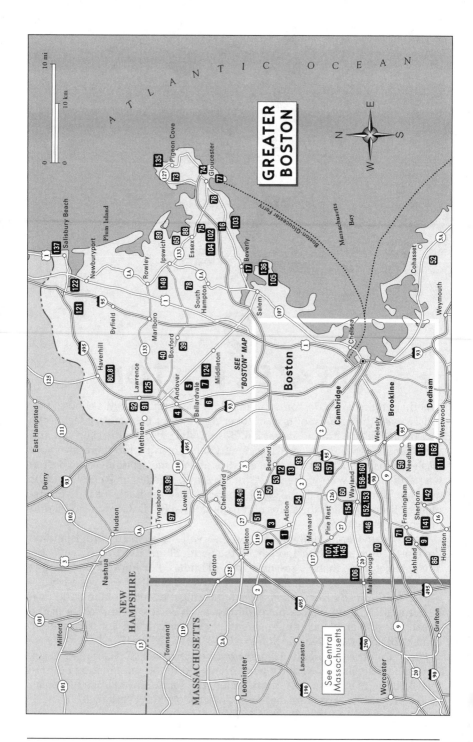

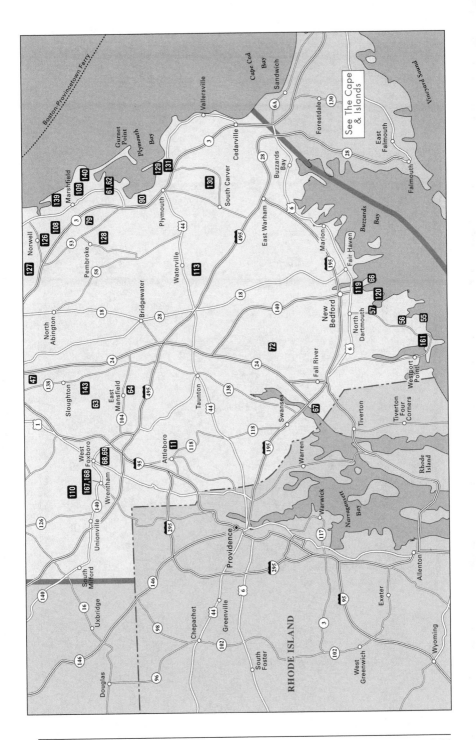

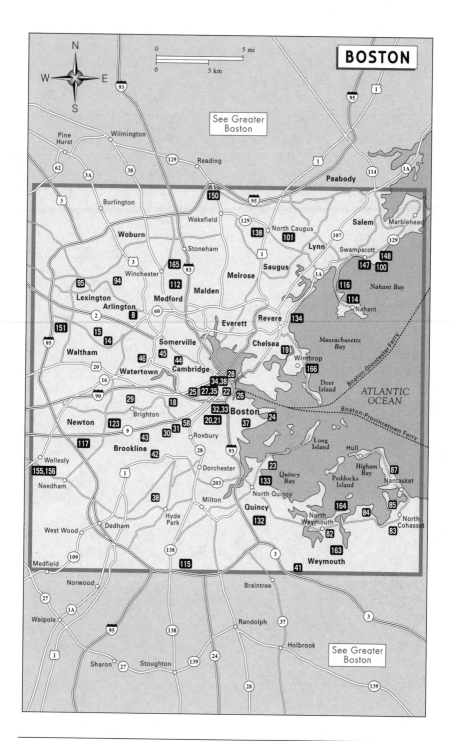

BOSTON

N W E S

0   5 mi
0   5 km

See Greater Boston

Pine Hurst
Wilmington
Reading
Peabody
Salem
Marblehead
Burlington
Wakefield
North Caugus
Lynn
Swampscott
Woburn
Stoneham
Melrose
Saugus
Winchester
Malden
Everett
Revere
Nahant Bay
Nahant
Lexington
Arlington
Medford
Somerville
Chelsea
Massachusetts Bay
Winthrop
Deer Island
Waltham
Cambridge
ATLANTIC OCEAN
Watertown
Boston
Newton
Brighton
Roxbury
Long Island
Hull
Higham Bay
Nantasket
Brookline
Dorchester
Quincy Bay
Peddocks Island
North Cohasset
Wellesly
Needham
Milton
North Quincy
North Weymouth
Quincy
West Wood
Dedham
Hyde Park
Medfield
Norwood
Weymouth
Walpole
Braintree
Randolph
Holbrook
Sharon
Stoughton

See Greater Boston

Boston-Gloucester Ferry
Boston-Provincetown Ferry

ACTON

We tip our hats to the people of Acton for securing so many beautiful areas for the enjoyment of the public, canine as well as human. The leash laws are flexible: to run freely, your dog must obey voice commands, and as a courtesy you should carry a leash to use in case other walkers are uncomfortable around untethered dogs.

PARKS, BEACHES, AND RECREATION AREAS

• Arboretum Conservation Land 🐾🐾🐾 🐕 🦴 See ❶ on page 250.

The winding trails and pathways of the 53-acre arboretum allow you and your dog to stroll from garden to garden along stone walls, through a variety of woods, and over boardwalks and bridges that traverse streams and bogs. Best of all, if your dog is well behaved enough to obey your commands, she can go leash free and sniff out trees and flowers without dragging you everywhere. The rich, diverse environment attracts hikers and wildlife, so you will likely encounter butterflies, songbirds, squirrels, and a few creatures in Reebok sneakers as you walk.

From State Route 2, take Main Street/State Route 27 north. Turn right on Taylor Road and continue to the arboretum. Parking is available. Open from sunrise to sunset. (978) 264-9631.

• Nagog Hill Conservation Area 🐾🐾🐾 🐕 See ❷ on page 250.

This is bird-watching territory, so be sure to bring binoculars if you want to observe herons, hawks, phoebes, cardinals, and numerous other species. Whether or not your furry friend is a bird dog, she can feel as free as a bird here, because as long as she obeys your commands, a leash is not required. In all, the 158-acre park is a good place to spend an hour or an afternoon with your dog.

Parking for approximately 10 cars is available at the trailhead. Across Nagog Hill Road is Grassy Pond Conservation Area, another spot you may want to visit in the same afternoon.

From State Route 2, take Main Street/State Route 27 north. Turn left on Nagog Hill Road and proceed to the parking lot on the right. Open from sunrise to sunset. (978) 264-9631.

• Nashoba Brook Conservation Area/Spring Hill Conservation Area 🐾🐾🐾 🐕 See ❸ on page 250.

Nothing but a stone wall divides these twin conservation areas, which together offer lucky dogs more than 300 acres of leash-free romping territory. The wall is more of a demarcation point than a barrier, so easy movement between the two areas is possible.

Inu and George recommend that you start at the Nashoba Brook trailhead and hike for about 1.5 miles toward Spring Hill. Park at the Wheeler Road entrance; picnic tables are available there, and you can chart your course using the well-placed map at the trailhead. If you enter on the Spring Hill side, you will find another map to help you chart your course through the area. The Spring Hill Trail covers almost three miles as it traces a large circle through a young forest of cedar, birch, and pine trees and around Red Swamp.

Well-placed walkways have been built around and over the mucky ground in the swamp, but it might be wise to avoid this area unless your dog will not wander from the trails and bridges. There is simply too much mud and mush begging to be wallowed in.

To reach the main trailheads of Nashoba Brook from State Route 2, take Main Street/State Route 27 north and cross Great Road/State Route 2A. Turn right onto Wheeler Lane and continue to the entrance and a parking area at the road's end. To get to the main trailheads of Spring Hill from State Route 2, take Wetherbee Street north. Turn left on Great Road/State Routes 2A and 119, and then make a quick right on Pope Road. Head left on Spring Hill Road and park at the end of the cul-de-sac. Open from sunrise to sunset. (978) 264-9631.

RESTAURANTS

Temptations: Formerly Phillips Coffee Emporium, this café/bakery still offers a hospitable stop before or after your hike. Grab a cup of coffee, fresh pastry, or a sandwich and beverage and take it outside to one of the benches in front to enjoy your refreshments in the afternoon sunshine. Temptations is located in the heart of town near the intersection of Massachusetts Avenue and Central Street. 5 Spruce Street; (978) 263-2233.

ANDOVER

PARKS, BEACHES, AND RECREATION AREAS

All of the parks listed in Andover are managed by the Andover Village Improvement Society (AVIS), a nonprofit, private organization. We've featured the parks that offer the best recreational options for you and your dog. You can obtain maps of all of the group's trails and reservations for $4 from the conservation office at Andover Town Hall or by writing to the group at P.O. Box 5097, Andover, MA 01810.

• **Baker's Meadow/Indian Ridge/West Parish Meadow Reservations** 🐾🐾🐾 See **4** on page 250.
Running across three great reservations, Reservation Road is aptly named. In reality, all of the reserves share the same 120-acre parcel of land, divided down the middle by the road. For a terrific three-mile hike with your leashed dog, follow the main trail through all three areas.

The entire loop through all three reservations is clearly marked by splotches of white paint; stick with the paint and you won't get lost. The esker trails lead you in a three-mile arc back to the parking lot, so it's up to your dog to choose which way to go.

The Andover Village Improvement Society manages the reservations. Dogs must be on leash.

From the town center at the intersection of Central, Elm, and Main Streets, take Central Street south. Turn right on Red Spring Road. The park is on the left; parking is available at the Andover High School auxiliary parking lot. Open from sunrise to sunset. (978) 623-8311.

• **Charles Ward Reservation** 🐾🐾🐾 See **5** on page 250.
So what will it be, the high road or the low road? Your experience at this lovely

640-acre park will depend entirely on which path you choose. No matter which route you follow, however, you and your leashed dog should enjoy a hike here. Begin at the parking area at the base of Holt Hill, and you'll have several choices.

The low road is a mile-long woodsy stroll. The route winds through a fascinating black spruce bog and out to Pine Hole Pond. Your dog can swim here, but because of limited access she'll have to dive in.

The high-road alternative is to cross Prospect Road, heading up the hill from the parking area to the Holt Hill Trailhead. At 420 feet, Holt Hill is the highest point in Essex County. On a clear day you can't see forever, but you can catch a glimpse of the Boston skyline and the Great Blue Hill in the Blue Hills Reservation. The story goes that on June 17, 1775, the town of Andover gathered here to watch the burning of Charlestown by the British. You'll also find the remains of the "solstice stones" put here by the widow of Charles Ward in 1940. Fascinated by Stonehenge after a visit to Britain, Mrs. Ward built her own miniature version of it in this meadow.

From Interstate 93 in Wilmington, take Exit 41 to Ballardvale Street/State Route 125 north into Andover and the Andover Bypass. Turn right on Prospect Road. The park is on the right, as is the parking lot. Open from sunrise to sunset. (978) 356-4351.

•The Goldsmith Woodlands 🐾🐾🐾🐾 See 6 on page 250.
Here's a personal favorite of ours and another example of the excellent stewardship of the Andover Village Improvement Society. This lovely, 170-acre woodland offers well-marked, easy-to-follow trails and a perfect swimming spot. It's along the peninsula at the end of the main trail and is named, appropriately enough, Journey's End.

On your way in, stick to the main trail, which is marked Zack's Way. You won't go wrong if you "follow the yellow brick road." Or, in this case, the yellow paint–splotched trees. Many smaller paths peel off the main trail into the woods, leading to picnic areas and vista points overlooking Foster's Pond. The best of these include Scout's Hollow and Bessy's Point (named for Bess Goldsmith, who, along with her husband, Clarence, originally donated this land for public use). Dogs can swim here, but the water is a little marshy; our advice is to continue to Journey's End and let your water dog take a dip there.

Dogs must be on leash.

From the town center at the intersection of Elm Street and Main Street/State Route 28, take Main Street south. The park is on the right, just past Gould Road. Parking is in a small lot across the street from the entrance. Open from sunrise to sunset. (978) 623-8311.

•Harold Parker State Forest 🐾🐾🐾🐾 See 7 on page 250.
With more than 3,500 acres and 25 miles of hiking trails, this terrific state forest offers enough sniffs and smells to satisfy the pickiest of pooches. Numerous ponds for swimming invite a dip, and thick and varied woods beg to be explored. Straddling Andover and North Andover (see also North Andover, Harold Parker State Forest, on page 328), the forest here is a blend of old and young groves, with ancient pines growing alongside relatively young, hundred-year-old trees.

Harold Parker State Forest has countless other forest trails for you and your dog to explore. We strongly recommend that you pick up a free trail map at the forest headquarters on Salem Street before setting out. The area is popular in summer so you might want to plan your visits to avoid the weekend. At other times you may find you have this special park all to yourselves.

You'll find a great campground here. Open from May to October, it has more than 130 campsites where you can pitch a pup tent with your pup, or just park your trailer for the night. Dogs cannot be left unattended and must be on leash when outside your tent or trailer. There are no RV hookups. Rates are $6 per night, and reservations are recommended. Call (877) 422-6762 or write to 1951 Turnpike Road, North Andover, MA 01845.

From Interstate 93 in Wilmington, take Exit 41 to Ballardvale Street/State Route 125 north into Andover and the Andover Bypass. Turn right on Harold Parker Road and continue into the park. Parking is available at most of the trailheads. Open from a half hour before sunrise to a half hour after sunset. (978) 686-3391.

RESTAURANTS

John's Village Deli: This busy little place serves only breakfast and lunch. You can get sandwiches, muffins, and bacon and eggs, among other selections. Plenty of picnic tables are available out back. And across the road is Duck Pond, where there are more tables to enjoy your meal while watching Daffy, Donald, and their ilk. The deli's just a stone's throw from Reservation Road, which runs through a wonderful trio of parks (see page 254). Pick up a picnic lunch and enjoy your day. 22 Andover Street; (978) 470-1492.

PLACES TO STAY

Andover Inn: Set on the grounds of the renowned Phillips Academy, this charming, historic bed-and-breakfast welcomes pooches and their human companions. Furnished with antique mahogany, it always seems to have a roaring fire blazing in the entryway when we arrive. The rooms are all decorated differently, and you'll enjoy wandering the grounds of the historic prep school when school is not in session. Breakfast is included. Rates range from $95 to $110. Chapel Avenue, Andover, MA 01810; (978) 475-5903; www.andoverinn.com.

Marriott Hotel: Dogs are welcome at this conveniently located hotel, but please let the management know that you will be bringing your pet before you arrive. Rooms range from $129 to $159. There is no extra charge for Rover. 123 Old River Road, Andover, MA 01810; (978) 475-5903; www.marriott.com.

Harold Parker State Forest camping: See pages 255–256.

ARLINGTON

PARKS, BEACHES, AND RECREATION AREAS

• **Menotomy Rocks Park** 🐾🐾🐾 See 8 on page 252.

This wonderful neighborhood park is a pint-sized, one square quarter mile all the way around. Hills Pond, in the center, is circled by a dirt path, three grassy fields, and a ring of woods that separates the park from the surrounding houses. The area takes its name from south Arlington's small rises or hummocks, of which Menotomy Rocks make up the highest point.

On a typical visit, the six of us receive a tail-wagging, dog-frisking welcome from local pooches already on the scene. Inu and George usually say hello and then quickly join the water dogs for a swim, while Rocky looks for biscuits. Except for the occasional duck, the pond is clear and uncluttered. A neighborhood group, the Friends of Menotomy Rocks Park, sponsors community events here and handles the upkeep of the place. The town leash law applies.

From State Route 60, take Gray Street west. Turn left on Jason Street. The entrance is at the intersection of Jason Street and Brantwood and Hillsdale Roads. No parking is allowed near the gate, but you can leave your car nearby on the neighborhood streets. Open from dawn to 9 P.M. (781) 641-5492.

RESTAURANTS

Au Bon Pain: Next door to Starbucks, this café serves sandwiches and coffee. You and your dog will find ample room to sit outdoors. 319 Broadway; (781) 641-4037.

Starbucks: This coffeehouse is one of the few places in Arlington Center with outdoor seating. Within close walking distance to the Minuteman Bike Trail, it's popular with the local dog community. Look for it on the corner of Massachusetts Avenue and Medford Street. 327 Massachusetts Avenue; (781) 641-2893.

ASHLAND

PARKS, BEACHES, AND RECREATION AREAS

• Ashland State Park 🐾 🐾 See 🯄 on page 250.

Dogs who desire little more than fresh air and scenic beauty will enjoy a trip to 47-acre Ashland State Park. Here the sparkling waters of Ashland Reservoir reflect the surrounding thick green pine trees. A single trail, carpeted in pine needles, follows the shoreline and crosses over the dam that created the reservoir. Alas, water dogs will get a tempting glimpse of the swimming area, where they are not permitted. Dogs are required to be leashed at all times. Park entrance costs $2 per carload.

From Interstate 495 in Hopkinton, take Exit 21 and head east on West Main Street to East Main Street/State Route 135. Continue into Ashland and to West Union Street. Turn right on State Park Road and proceed into the park. Parking is available. Open from 9 A.M. to 6 P.M. or as otherwise posted. (508) 435-4303.

• Ashland Town Forest/Cowassock Woods 🐾 🐾 See 🯅 on page 250.

In the language of the Magunkook, "Cowassock" means "the place of pines," and tree-loving pooches will be thrilled to find that this spot lives up to its name: the combined forest—Ashland Town Forest and Cowassock Woods—is dotted with pines, as well as an assortment of other hardwoods. Six-plus miles of trails traverse the 575-acre parcel of land, and a walk through the hilly terrain will be an enjoyable venture for any leashed dog who wants to exercise his sniffer as well as his legs.

From the town center at Main Street and Union Street/State Route 135, take Main Street north. Turn left on Pleasant Street and then right on Winter Street.

You'll find Ashland Town Forest and parking on the left. Open from dawn to dusk. Ashland Town Forest, (508) 881-0101; Cowassock Woods, (508) 443-6300.

RESTAURANTS

John Stone's Inn: Known for its fine food, this 1832 inn is one of the fancier restaurants featured in this book. With old-style gas lamps and a romantic atmosphere, it's a bit too refined for Inu and George (especially after a day on the trail), although smaller pups might love it. Dogs are welcome on the enclosed patio, but, if you want to dine with your pooch, she'll have to make an undignified entrance: while you can walk through the inn, dogs must crawl under the fence to reach the patio. The hassle is soon forgotten with the first bite of any of the delicious full-course meals, including traditional preparations of fish, meat, and poultry. 179 Main Street; (508) 881-1778.

ATTLEBORO

PARKS, BEACHES, AND RECREATION AREAS

• **Larson Woodland Reservation** 🐾🐾🐾 🐕 See **11** on page 251.

This conservation property on Mechanics Pond and the Ten Mile River has a tall, dark forest and a great, if short, trail system that winds through the many nooks and crannies of this important and scenic waterway. Hiking along, you will find remnants of the dam and canals that channeled the power of the river to the mills that once populated this area. You will also find that the pond attracts much wildlife.

The Attleboro Land Trust allows dogs off leash under voice control.

From Interstate 95, take Exit 3 to U.S. Route 123 east for two miles. Turn left onto Riverbank Road for a half mile. The park and roadside pullouts are on the left. Open dawn to dusk. (508) 226-7184.

BEDFORD

PARKS, BEACHES, AND RECREATION AREAS

• **Fawn Lake Conservation Area** 🐾🐾🐾 🐕 See **12** on page 250.

For years the magical waters of Fawn Lake have lured visitors to these shores. The Pawtucket Indians, early American farmers, spring-water bottlers, and resort mavens all believed the lake and nearby springs had a medicinal power that could restore and maintain one's health. In the 1800s, a health spa named Bedford Springs drew people here with promises of the water's curative properties. While we don't recommend that you drink the water, we do think that a short walk around the pond could do wonders for both you and your dog.

Dogs are allowed leash free at Fawn Lake if under voice control. The park is managed by the Bedford Conservation Commission.

From the town center at the intersection of Concord Road/State Route 62, Great Road, and Carlisle Road/State Routes 4 and 225, take Carlisle Road west. Turn right on North Road/State Route 4, then right again on Sweetwater Avenue. The park and a parking lot are at the road's end. Open from a half hour before sunrise to a half hour after sunset. (781) 275-6211.

•Wilderness Park Conservation Area 🐾🐾🐾 🐕 See **13** on page 250.

This 74-acre park isn't exactly a wilderness, but you and your leash-free dog will certainly enjoy visiting the lovely little forest. The 1.5-mile trail starts across from Middlesex Community College, where you'll find a huge parking area. Walk across the street and head down the dirt trail. Marked with blue paint, it serves as the main trail. There's also a paved bike trail leading off to the right, but that only leads alongside the road, so we recommend heading for the forest for a lovely woodland walk.

From the town center at the intersection of Concord Road/State Route 62, Great Road, and Carlisle Road/State Routes 4 and 225, take Great Road east. Turn left on Spring Road and continue past the Veteran's Administration hospital. The park is on the right; park in the Middlesex Community College auxiliary parking lot on the left. Open from a half hour before sunrise to a half hour after sunset. (781) 275-6211.

RESTAURANTS

Bedford Farms Kitchen: A local spot in the town center, this place is good for a quick sandwich or some refreshing ice cream after a run in the park. If you want a meal, go for the Smokey Joe sandwich with smoked turkey, bacon, barbecue sauce, and Swiss cheese. During the summer you can order from the outdoor windows and, if it's not too crowded, sit on the bench out front. 18 North Road; (781) 275-3040.

PLACES TO STAY

Stouffer Renaissance Bedford Hotel: Small pets are welcome at this hotel, but we suggest you call and tell the management what kind of dog you have, because "small" seems to be on a sliding scale. Nearby you'll find Bedford, Carlisle, and Concord parks, as well as easy access to State Route 128 and Interstate 95. A $50 deposit is required for dogs. Rates range from $89 to $159. 44 Middlesex Turnpike, Bedford, MA 01730; (781) 275-5500; www.renaissancehotels.com.

BELMONT

PARKS, BEACHES, AND RECREATION AREAS

•Beaver Brook Reservation 🐾🐾 See **14** on page 252.

John Winthrop, Boston's founder and the first governor of the Massachusetts Bay Colony, discovered many a beaver here and named the spot after the lot of 'em. The 59 acres were set aside in 1893, the year Charles Eliot and Sylvester Baxter began the Metropolitan District Commission, so Beaver Brook became the first reservation in the MDC park system. Trapelo Street/State Route 60 divides the park into two sections, Mill Pond and Waverly Oaks.

From the main parking area you'll see a small, mucky pond aptly named Duck Pond. Bagels, day-old rolls, and scraps of Wonder Bread fly in all directions, flung by enthusiastic duck feeders. If you can get by this flurry of activity, beyond the pond you'll discover some short but good trails that you can hike in the dry season. Use the path to the pond's left to saunter around the rocks, waterfalls, and greenery of Beaver Brook and Waverly Oaks. Head right and you'll discover Mill Pond. We don't recommend swimming at either pond as it can get pretty ducky.

Across the street at Waverly Oaks, you'll find a spacious field in the center, a bike path that circles it, and picnic areas. Dogs must be on leash.

The ponds are on Mill Street one-tenth of a mile north of the intersection of Mill Street, Trapelo Road, and Waverly Oaks Road/State Route 60. There is a small parking lot off Mill Street. Both sections are open from dawn to dusk. (617) 484-6357.

•Rock Meadow Reservation 🐾🐾🐾 See **15** on page 252.

Once farmland and fruit orchards owned by McLean Hospital, today Rock Meadow offers hikers a sea of rolling hills covered with grass and woodlands. Three miles of trails wind among the meadows here. For a longer hike, follow one of the trails deeper into the woods across McLean Brook in the western part of the park. George, full of energy, always wants to explore every inch of the place. Inu, social butterfly that he is, usually sets his sights on greeting the other dog walkers we meet along the way. The town of Belmont and the Metropolitan District Commission manage the park. Dogs must be on leash, primarily because of the many nesting birds here.

You can enter the park from the southwestern corner of the Mill Street and Concord Avenue intersection. The main entrance is off Mill Street, just north of Beaver Brook Reservation. The parking lot here can hold 15 to 20 cars. The other entrance, along Concord Avenue, is really just a turnout. It's a mile west of Highland Farm Wildlife Sanctuary. Open from dawn to dusk. (617) 489-8255.

FESTIVALS

Town Day: Held in Belmont Center, this annual street fair is a great excuse for Belmont residents to invite themselves and the rest of the world to a big block party. Traffic is closed on Leonard Street for the day as local merchants share their wares, food, and fun. The Belmont Animal Hospital always has a booth for dog lovers, and you and your pooch will enjoy wandering through this quaint little town on a spring day. The festival runs from 8 A.M. to 4 P.M. on the third Saturday in May. For more information, call (617) 489-4930.

BEVERLY

PARKS, BEACHES, AND RECREATION AREAS

•Beverly Conservation Area 🐾🐾🐾 🐕 See **16** on page 250.

Mountain bikers love this place, and it's no mystery why. The many rolling hills and rocky passageways give the most avid hiker or biker a thorough workout. Nestled in a countrified residential area on more than 150 acres, the park still offers plenty of privacy for you and your off-leash dog. The cart roads are fairly easy to follow, but foot trails here can be confusing. No matter how lost you get, though, you'll find your way back with a little exploring. In the meantime, you'll also discover some delightful country. Some trails lead through leaf-covered glades; others shoot straight up rocky hillsides. In the wet season some of the low-lying trails can get swampy, so bring a pair of sturdy boots. A jaunt around the entire reservation should take you well over an hour.

From State Route 128 in Wenham, take Exit 17 to Grapevine Road. Continue onto Hart Road in Beverly. Turn right on Greenwood Avenue. The park is at the road's end; street parking is available on the corner of Greenwood Avenue and Webster Avenue. Open from dawn to dusk. (978) 768-7241.

• **Lynch Park** 🐾🐾🐾 See **17** on page 250.
This may be the most scenic spot in Beverly. Here's the good news: It's got access to three white-sand beaches; a tree-lined, shady park area with picnic facilities; a walled-in grassy lawn on Woodbury Point at its southeastern end; and a great view of the North Shore Islands offshore.

Okay, now that you're ready to jump in the car, we have to break the bad news: No dogs are allowed from Memorial Day through Labor Day. On our first visit we reenacted that telephone commercial where the excited dog bounds out of the car and runs right past the big "No Dogs Allowed" sign. (Or, in our case, George lifted his leg on the sign. Who says that dogs can't read?) Dogs must be on leash at all times.

From State Route 128, take Exit 18 to Essex Street/State Route 22 south. Turn left on Dane Street at the Beverly Common and then left again on Hale Street/State Routes 62 and 127. Turn right on Obear Street. The park is on the right. Open from 7 A.M. to 10 P.M. (978) 921-6067.

RESTAURANTS

Taste Buds: This nifty little gourmet food shop is a real dog-friendly zone. The canine clientele waits impatiently outside while human friends get the goods inside: specialty sandwiches on homemade bread, muffins, gourmet coffees, and desserts.

We knew we liked this store when we noticed they had homemade dog biscuits for sale, right next to the fresh-baked chocolate-chip and oatmeal cookies, all for $.25. Then we turned to the ice-cream case. Alongside the Dove Bars, we found—are you ready?—Frosty Paws, frozen treats for your dog. Yes, we definitely came to the right place.

Owner Jane Pelligrini will make you a box lunch to take to the park, and you can put together your own picnic for your dog. Only a block from Lynch Park (see above) on State Route 127, this is definitely worth a stop. 151 Hale Street; (978) 922-0151.

BOSTON

Historically and culturally rich, Boston is a big little city or a little big city, depending on whether you put the emphasis on its population or acreage. Each neighborhood is different from the next. Unlike most dogs, who really couldn't care less whether they're labeled a poodle, a retriever, or a mutt, Boston natives take their cultural heritage very seriously, and their neighborhoods reflect their ethnic and civic pride. Explore these areas and their parks in the spirit of multiculturalism, and you'll find each place you visit different from the last. Dogs and their owners will discover that all Boston parks have one thing in common: leash laws.

The Emerald Necklace: In 1893, Boston parks founder Charles Eliot joined forces with landscape architect Frederick Law Olmstead to create the first planned park system in the United States. Their first project was the famous Emerald Necklace. This series of beautiful parks encompasses the Arnold Arboretum, Back Bay Fens, Boston Common, Commonwealth Avenue Mall, Franklin Park, Jamaica Pond, Olmsted Park, Riverway, and what many consider to be the crowning jewel of the necklace, the Public Garden. Extending from downtown Boston out to Jamaica Plain, it forms a chain of greenery amid Boston's man-made structures. As in all Boston parks, dogs must be on leash. The parks are open every day from 6 A.M. to 11:30 P.M. For more information, contact the Boston Parks and Recreation Department at (617) 635-4505.

Riding the T: We expect that you'll be traveling to most of these locations by car, and our directions reflect this assumption, but many parks can be reached by mass transportation. Most conveniently, you may take your pup on the Massachusetts Bay Transportation Authority (MBTA) subway system. We've taken our dogs on the "T" many times, and it's a terrific way to get around.

There are some restrictions: Your dog must be leashed at all times. If your pooch is small enough to fit in a lap carrier, you may bring her along for the ride at any time. Otherwise, during weekdays your dog may not ride from 7 A.M. to 9 A.M. or from 4 P.M. to 7 P.M. During off-peak weekday hours and throughout the weekend, however, Fido is free to ride the rails.

For more information, contact the Massachusetts Bay Transportation Authority at (617) 222-3200.

PARKS, BEACHES, AND RECREATION AREAS

• The Back Bay Fens 🐾🐾 See **18** on page 252.

While Fido can't escort you into venerable Fenway Park to catch the Red Sox in action, both of you can play ball in this large park beyond the bleachers. The Fens runs more than two miles along Hemenway Avenue, all the way from the ballpark, past the Museum of Fine Arts, to the Isabella Gardner Museum. You'll get in a good walk or run here, roll in the grass, or just kick up your heels. Bridges and benches await you, and your happy dog will find plenty of room to romp on leash.

Parking can be tough here. You'll find some metered parking along Park Avenue, Hemenway Avenue, and Boylston Avenue, but most spots are residential. Open from 6 A.M. to 11:30 P.M., but not recommended after dark. (617) 635-4505.

• Belle Isle Marsh Reservation 🐾🐾🐾 See **19** on page 252.

If you're looking for something a little different, but not too far out of the way, hop on the T and visit Boston's last remaining saltwater wetlands. The 152 acres of Belle Isle Marsh are part of the Metropolitan District Commission park system and provide a unique environment for a short walk with your leashed pup.

The well-maintained, mile-long crushed-stone path loops through tall reeds and open grassy expanses where the marsh has been mowed. Along the way, you'll find a short boardwalk and observation tower offering excellent views of the Boston skyline and Belle Isle Inlet. Although you might not think it possible given the color of the water here, there is an abundance of wildlife that thrives in this mixture of saltwater and grass. Look for crabs, herons, and blackbirds.

Take State Route 1A to Bennington Street/State Route 145 east 1.5 miles. The park is on the right. Open 9 A.M. to dusk. (617) 727-5330.

• Blackstone Square/Franklin Square 🐾🐾 See **20** on page 252.

Established in 1849 and separated by Washington Street, these twin parks are among the top places to go for South Enders. Each is a city block long, and fences protect your dog from the busy traffic on Washington Street.

As with any twins, similarities abound. Both squares are spacious and well maintained. Both feature large central fountains with clean, free-flowing water in which dogs are welcome to take a cooling dip. And both require that pooches be on leash, even when they're splashing in the drink.

The parks are located between Shawmut Street, St. George Street, Brookline Avenue, and Newton Avenue. Open from 6 A.M. to 11:30 P.M. (617) 635-4505.

• The Boston Common 🐾🐾🐾 See **21** on page 252.

Created in 1640 as an ordinary cow pasture, the Common lays claim to being the oldest public space in the country. If you live in Boston, this park is the most common spot to take your leashed dog on a daily basis. Located along historic Beacon Hill and the State House, the Common has been a gathering place for people and their animals for more than 300 years. Although it's small for a city park and often shows the wear and tear of continual use, it has managed to preserve the warmth of a small-town square.

On any morning from 6:30 A.M. to 8:30 A.M. you'll find a group of dogs playing and chasing each other on the open grassy areas adjacent to the Public Garden. Walk by again in the evening between 5 P.M. and 7 P.M. and you'll think they've been there all day. A Mutt Mitt dispenser is provided near the entrance of the park at Spruce and Beacon Streets.

The Metropolitan District Commission and the Boston Parks and Recreation Department jointly manage the Common. As in all Boston parks, your dog must be on leash at all times. And as tempting as it is during hot summer days, dogs are not allowed in the children's swimming pool, known as the Frog Pond.

The Boston Common is between Charles Street, Beacon Street, Park Street, and Tremont Street. Open from 6 A.M. to 11:30 P.M. (617) 634-4505.

• Bunker Hill Monument 🐾 🐾 See **22** on page 252.

On June 17, 1775, British and Colonial troops fought the first major battle of the Revolutionary War on Bunker Hill. Today the monument commemorating the event is the local dog hangout of choice in Charlestown. Only two city blocks square, it's not a big park, but it's the only centrally located green space in the area. A cast-iron fence surrounds the acre-square knoll, protecting your dog from the traffic speeding by. Since there's a strict leash law here, you shouldn't have to worry about Muttley making a beeline for historic Warren Tavern for a few beers with Paul Revere.

The monument is between Hill Street, Concord Street, Lexington Street, and Tremont Street. Open 24 hours. (617) 242-5669.

• Castle Island Recreation Area 🐾🐾🐾🐾 🐕 See **23** on page 252.

The entire Castle Island Recreation Area runs just under three miles along Day Boulevard from Fort Independence to Carson Beach. This park has it all: sand, sea, grass, fresh air, birds, squirrels, room to romp, and a beautiful view of the harbor. It's quite a find, and well worth the trip if you haven't had the pleasure of visiting before. Come in winter, spring, or fall, and you'll have the place mostly to yourself.

Our favorite area is along the fortified walls of Fort Independence, extending from Pleasure Bay out to the harbor and back around. Here's its history: Built in 1634, the stronghold was originally dubbed Castle William by the British, after King William III. During the Revolutionary War, it served as a British garrison until 1776. It kept its name until 1799, when President John Adams rededicated it as Fort Independence. Of course, your pup won't care a lick about the history lesson with all the sweet and salty sea air to inhale as you hike.

You can park in a lot at the end of Day Boulevard near the fort; street parking is also allowed as indicated. Dogs must be on leash.

Getting here can be a little tricky. If you're driving from downtown, take the Southeast Expressway to the JFK Library exit (#15) and follow signs to Day Boulevard. Or in South Boston, take Dorchester Avenue to East Broadway and continue to the beach. Open from dawn to dusk. (617) 727-5250.

• Charlesgate Dog Run 🐾🐾 🐕 See **24** on page 252.

Boston's first official dog run, opened in September 1998, is a step in the right direction. This small 55-by-80-foot rectangle nestled between busy Massachusetts Avenue and Storrow Drive serves as a place for dogs off leash but, unfortunately, it's too small to give dogs much exercise. Managed by the Back Bay Neighborhood Association, the park has a bench, two trees, some grass, and a good view of the Charles River. The entrance is located off the western side of the Massachusetts Avenue Bridge. Open from 6 A.M. to 11:30 P.M. (617) 727-5114, extension 538.

• Charles River Reservation See **25** on page 252.

The Charles River Reservation encompasses many sections across four neighborhoods. For the sake of convenience, we've divided it into segments, using the bridges along the river as boundaries. Dogs must be on leash. Managed by the Metropolitan District Commission, all sections of the reservation are open from 6 A.M. to 11:30 P.M. (617) 727-9547.

Christian Herter Park Section 🐾🐾🐾

This roomy spot in Brighton is a fine alternative to the often crowded Esplanade downtown and the busy stretches along Harvard University. The Publick Theatre unfurls its plays here, and you'll find canoe rentals, ample parking, long walkways (popular with runners, joggers, and in-line skaters), and easy swimming access to the Charles River.

This section runs from the Eliot Street Bridge to the Arsenal Street Bridge, along Soldier's Field Road.

The Esplanade 🐾🐾🐾🐾 🐾

Bike, jog, picnic, in-line skate, stroll, swim. No matter what activity you and your canine pal like, you'll find no roomier or more scenic spot in the city to enjoy it.

Nestled along the Charles River and stretching from the Museum of Science to Massachusetts Avenue, the Esplanade spans much of old-town Boston. From Back Bay, access is via the Dartmouth Street, Hereford Street, or Massachusetts Avenue Bridges. From Beacon Hill, you can reach the park by crossing Storrow Drive at the Charles Street Bridge or the Arthur Fiedler Bridge at Arlington Street.

The expanse between the Fiedler Bridge (named for Arthur Fiedler, the longtime conductor of the Boston Pops) and the Hereford Street Bridge is the best area for exercising your dog. A statue of Arthur Fiedler graces the grassy knoll beside the Hatch Shell amphitheater here. Generous swaths of grass, well separated from busy bike paths, provide plenty of room for stretching your legs. Most Back Bay dog owners use this space, and both you and your pooch can meet up with neighborhood regulars for a friendly hello. The two-mile loop from one end to the other takes about 40 minutes, give or take a few breaks for socializing.

If you venture along the walkway next to Storrow Drive, you'll find the Lotta Crabtree Dog Fountain, donated to the city in 1937 by, of course, Lotta Crabtree, a New York actress who retired to Boston at the turn of the century. Never married, she lived and traveled with her huskies throughout her career. The memorial (a statue of one of her beloved dogs) features a drinking fountain for thirsty canines.

Keep your dog on leash, as in all MDC parks.

On Sundays parking is allowed on Storrow Drive, between the Longfellow Bridge and the Esplanade's western end.

Western Avenue Bridge to Larz Anderson Bridge Section 🐾🐾

This is the only walk-worthy stretch of the reservation in Allston. Other segments constitute little more than thin stretches of paved path along Storrow Drive. But in this part you'll discover two wide, green lawns divided by the path along the river's edge. The John Weeks Jr. Bridge bisects the open areas. Looping gracefully over the river, this elegant stone footbridge is one of the loveliest sites along the Charles. It will take you over to Cambridge and Memorial Drive if you choose, or just provide a pleasant view over the water. You and your leashed dog can sun or play on the grassy areas, but expect to rub shoulders with lots of other folks on spring and summer days.

• Christopher Columbus Waterfront Park 🐾🐾 See 26 on page 252.

North End dog lovers bring their four-legged friends here to hang out and socialize. A lovely park along the water with some grassy areas, the main attraction is its lively canine social scene. Enclosed and geometrically designed gardens give the park a secret-hideaway feel. Dogs must be on leash.

The park is located off Commercial Avenue, between Commercial Wharf and Long Wharf. Open 24 hours. (617) 635-4505.

• **Commonwealth Avenue Mall** 😊 😊 🐾 See **27** on page 252.
Unarguably one of the most elegant streets in Boston, this famous boulevard park extends for seven blocks down the center of Commonwealth Avenue, from Arlington Street near the Public Garden to Hereford Street. Bordered by Victorian brownstones and lined with gas lamps, a stroll along this mall will have you believing you've gone back in time—to an age when dogs were born with silver bowls in their mouths and chased horse-drawn carriages down the avenue. Each block has a large green space divided by a wide walkway with shady elm trees, wrought-iron benches, and statues commemorating notables from Boston's past. It's a great place to walk your leashed dog, and it's well maintained, but cars speed by on both sides, so Fido must be a little street-wise. No fence prevents dogs from running out into the street.

The mall is open for strolling 24 hours a day. It's well lit and amply populated in the evening hours. (617) 635-4505.

• **Copp's Hill Burying Ground** 😊 😊 See **28** on page 252.
Now, let's not get into the morality of this. We won't discuss whether or not dogs should be allowed in cemeteries. But if you don't find the locale too creepy, Copp's Hill is a pretty good one to visit. The greenest area in the North End, it's completely fenced in from the city streets. It also has a great view of the North End Playground (see below), Boston Harbor, and Bunker Hill. Everyone else visits in the daylight hours, but local dogs think this is the place to go in the early morning and evening. One day we visited at 6:30 A.M. with a handful of cemetery canines. George and a new friend, Jonesy, a Jack Russell terrier, played the doggy version of hide-and-seek between the terraces and gravestones. The odd thing was that when the light of day appeared, Jonesy just disappeared. We looked and looked, but the only trace we found of him was his leash resting on the tombstone of Jones Y. Russell, a Boston merchant who died in 1829. Hmm. . . we wonder. . .

The cemetery is near the North End Playground, just across Commercial Street. It is between Hull Street, Salem Street, and Charter Street on the Freedom Trail. If you're going to visit both areas, be sure to use the Copp's Hill Terrace walkway. Open from 8 A.M. to dusk. (617) 536-4100.

• **Gallagher Memorial Park** 😊 😊 See **29** on page 252.
Water dogs will thank their lucky stars that this neighborhood park encircles Chandler Pond in Brighton, where swimming is allowed. And the water is fairly clean (by canine standards). For a pleasant, half-mile morning or afternoon stroll with your leashed dog, you can walk around three-quarters of the pond, but stay off the north side, which is private property. Street parking is allowed along Lake Shore Road, except on Boston College game days.

From Commonwealth Avenue, take Lake Street heading north. Turn right on Lake Shore Road and continue to the park. Open from 6 A.M. to 11:30 P.M. (617) 635-4505.

• **Jamaica Pond** 😊 😊 😊 See **30** on page 252.
Directly next to Olmsted Park in Jamaica Plain is its twin, Jamaica Pond, which was established a year after Olmsted Park (see next entry). The two

have similar terrain, but Jamaica Pond is on a larger piece of land. At the park's southern tip near Parkman Boulevard, a shore section offers easy access to the clear, deep water, where your dog can take a dip. Trails and walkways around the pond provide great strolls. Picnic facilities and benches are spread throughout the park, and plenty of sparse woods surrounding the main walkway offer sniffing opportunities.

Dogs must be on leash. Parking is scarce, but you can leave your car along Perkins Street if you're lucky enough to find a spot.

From State Route 9, take the Jamaicaway south. Turn right on Perkins Street. Open from dawn to 11:30 P.M. (617) 635-4505.

• Olmsted Park 🐾🐾 See **31** on page 252.

Established in 1891 as a link in Boston's Emerald Necklace, this park in Jamaica Plain provides a quiet respite from the furious pace of the Jamaicaway zipping by just feet away. Named for Frederick Law Olmsted, the primary landscape architect for the Boston park system (and New York's famous Central Park, as well), it offers a woodsy, meandering, mile-long stroll around Leverett Pond.

As in all Boston parks, dogs must be on leash.

From State Route 9, turn south on the Jamaicaway or Pond Street; you can enter the park from either side. Open from dawn to 11:30 P.M. (617) 635-4505.

• Peters Park Dog Run 🐾🐾🐾 🐕 See **32** on page 252.

Go dog, go! Big dogs, little dogs, black dogs, white dogs—all are happy campers in this latest addition to the soon-to-be-growing list (we hope!) of dog runs in the city. The run itself is an ample area with a few amenities, namely, a bench, a tree or two, and some trash cans. But the dogs don't seem to mind. We suggest you bring your own water in the summer months, as the grass is long gone and it can get pretty dry and dusty. The park at large is managed by the Boston Parks and Recreation Department; dogs must be leashed everywhere except the run and are not allowed on the ball fields or playgrounds.

The park is located between Washington Street and Shawmut Avenue near East Berkeley Street. Open 6 A.M. to 11:30 P.M. (617) 635-4000.

• Pope John Paul II Park See **33** on page 252

This latest project from the Metropolitan District Commission looks like a good one. As of this printing we have had to rely on an artist's rendering of the planned 65-acre park along the Neponset River, but the blueprints include restored salt marshes, open meadows, walking trails, bike paths, and sports fields. Entrances will be off Hallet Street and Gallivan Boulevard near the intersection of the Southeast Expressway and the Neponset Bridge. The park will open to the public in summer 2001. Dogs need to bring their leashes in all MDC parks. For more information, call the Metropolitan District Commission at (617) 727-9547.

• The Public Garden 🐾🐾 🦴 See **34** on page 252.

Walk across Charles Street from the Boston Common and you'll find yourself in the Public Garden. This beautiful and elegant park is the jewel of the Emerald Necklace, which makes up the Boston city parks. Set aside in 1867, this park, with its graceful willows, duck pond, famous Swan Boats, and lush green grass (all chronicled magically in the children's classic, *Make Way For Ducklings*) is arguably the most gorgeous park in the city of Boston. And, as in all city parks, your dog must admire it on a leash.

This is not a park for frolicking, but it's a great place to sit and watch the world pass by. If your dog can enjoy sitting quietly beside you, enjoy by all means! But if he needs a lot of exercise or is overly rambunctious and wants to chase every squirrel in sight, then this is probably not the park for you.

A Mutt Mitt dispenser is located at the Charles Street and Beacon Street entrances.

The Public Garden is between Arlington, Beacon, Charles, and Boylston Streets. Open from 6 A.M. to 11:30 P.M. (617) 635-4505.

• Southwest Corridor 🐾 🐾 See **35** on page 252.

No matter what the weather, this lengthy greenbelt along the border of Back Bay and the South End promises an enjoyable, protected stroll. (The corridor also stretches through Jamaica Plain, Roslindale, Hyde Park, and beyond, but we can only recommend the South End section for a visit.) A long sidewalk runs through the middle, bordered by grass and gardens on both sides. The many garden beds are cared for by local residents; in spring the blooms make a walk here really special.

The park is between Huntington Avenue and Columbus Avenue, extending from Yarmouth Avenue to Massachusetts Avenue. The main entrance is just across from the Back Bay T Station. Open from 6 A.M. to 10 P.M. (617) 727-0057.

• Stony Brook Reservation 🐾 🐾 🐾 See **36** on page 252.

Although it's only a stone's throw from Boston, this preserve has a true countryside feel. There are 464 acres of woods to sniff and explore, and 10 miles of easy-to-find trails to hike. Stony Brook is a well-kept secret, and you'll probably find yourself on a solitary walk. But the park is well maintained, so the silence will be welcome rather than eerie.

Dogs who like to swim should head to Turtle Pond in the reservation's western portion. The pond is just off the trail, about a quarter of a mile from the parking lot at Enneking Parkway. Dogs must be on leash.

The park is bordered by the Enneking Parkway, Turtle Pond Parkway, and Washington Street. Open from 6:30 A.M. until 11 P.M. (617) 361-6161.

• Thomas Park 🐾 🐾 🐾 See **37** on page 252.

This park, the recipient of a major face-lift in 1997, is part of the Boston National Historic Park system, an organization dedicated to preserving and commemorating important American Revolution sites in the city. On March 4, 1776, General John Thomas and his men placed an American artillery on this hill that finally forced the British to evacuate Boston on March 17, 1776. Dorchester Heights gave General Thomas a commanding view of the city and harbor, and you and your dog will experience the same exhilaration when you visit here. This isn't a big park, but it is the most popular hangout for dogs in South Boston, so you'll find plenty of canine companionship here. Dogs must be on leash.

At Sixth Avenue and G Street. Open from 6 A.M. to 11:30 P.M. (617) 635-4505.

• Titus Sparrow Park 🐾 🐾 See **38** on page 252.

This 1.5-acre park, part of the Southwest Corridor, is another popular gathering place for South End dog owners. It features a modest-sized hilly and grassy area where your leashed dog can romp with other canines. The small but well-maintained park is centrally located for most South End residents. The park is on West Newton Avenue, off Columbus Avenue. Open from 6 A.M. to 11:30 P.M. (617) 727-0057.

NATURE HIKES AND URBAN WALKS

Black Heritage Trail: Bone up on your history and take a walk, too! This historic tour through Beacon Hill commemorates the many contributions African-Americans have made to the growth of Beacon Hill, Boston, and the United States.

The tour's highlight is the celebrated Saint-Gaudens bas-relief memorial to Robert Gould Shaw and his 54th Regiment, whose story was depicted in the movie *Glory*. The route also includes the African Meeting House—the oldest black church in America—and the many majestic homes of Beacon Hill.

Obtain maps and brochures for self-guided walks, and additional information about ranger-led tours, at the Boston National Historic Visitor Center at 15 State Street. The visitor center is open daily from 9 A.M. to 5 P.M. (617) 742-5415.

RESTAURANTS

Angelo's Ristorante: This pleasant combination Italian restaurant and open-air café allows you and your pet a spot to rest after a day of sight-seeing or shopping. Located directly across from Copley Square and the old Trinity Church landmark, you can whittle away the hours while sipping a cappuccino or eating a hearty meal. Dogs are allowed on the patio only. 575 Boylston Street; (617) 536-4045.

Back Bay Brewing Company: Drop by fer a pint 'o ale, mate! This new addition to the burgeoning microbrewery business in Boston is a welcome one, for they allow dogs on their ample outside seating area. The food is a hodgepodge of basic pub fare, but the beers are exceptional. Try a "beer sampler" which gives you a taste of all six beers in five-ounce glasses. 755 Boylston Street; (617)424-8300.

Café Esplanade: Alongside the Hatch Shell on the Esplanade, this outdoor restaurant overlooks a peaceful estuary. It also offers a wide variety of soups, sandwiches, and unusual beverages, and a great patio for you and your dog to enjoy them on. At the back of the café is a dog bowl filled with fresh water. Open seasonally from April through October and on special-event weekends. On Storrow Drive at the Hatch Shell; (617) 722-8252.

Emack & Bolio's: All of this ice-cream shop's branches are dog friendly. If you ask, they'll serve a "doggy sundae," consisting of a good-sized sample of their famous vanilla bean in a cup. Try George's favorite, Raspberry Truffle. Inu is partial to Grasshopper Pie, and Rocky'll just eat anything. 290 Newbury Street; (617) 247-8772.

Hazel's Country Kitchen: After an invigorating walk along the Southwest Corridor (see page 268), be sure to end up at the eastern terminus of Copley Plaza for the good cooking served up at this neighborhood restaurant. You may sit outside at the outdoor tables or order to go and sit along the many benches along the corridor. We enjoyed a great brunch of potato pancakes, steak and eggs, and pan-seared trout, just to name a few of the many yummy offerings here. 130 Dartmouth Street; (617) 262-4393.

Joe's American Bar & Grill: This North End hangout overlooks the harbor and Christopher Columbus Park. A great place to stop after walking your dog, you and your pup are welcome along the outer perimeter of the patio. Offering a varied menu of Mexican, American, and Asian cuisines, there's something here for everyone. 100 Atlantic Avenue; (617) 367-8700.

Lilly's: This full-service continental restaurant welcomes canine patrons on the outside patio perimeter only, but those are really the best tables for people watching, anyway. The restaurant offers delicious salads and meat and fish entrées. Expect a long wait on warm summer days. 101 Faneuil Hall Marketplace; (617) 720-5580.

Marketplace Café: Seafood's the specialty at this spacious outdoor café. Dogs are allowed on the patio area as long as they're leashed, stay on the outer edge, and other patrons don't complain. We've never had a problem, but a good rule is to ask politely and expect them to say yes. 300 Faneuil Hall Marketplace; (617) 227-9660.

Milano: This Italian restaurant has a very large outdoor space and allows leashed dogs. On the corner of Newbury and Berkeley Streets, it's a great place to dog watch. A block down from the Ritz Carlton and near the expensive designer boutiques, this restaurant offers a respite from an oh-so-tough day shopping for Louis Vuitton doggy bags. 47 Newbury Street; (617) 267-6150.

Starbucks: Seattle's entry into the Boston coffee sweepstakes has two Newbury Street venues with outdoor seating. The largest, between Exeter and Dartmouth Streets, has a spacious patio where you and your dog can waste the day watching the beautiful people roam by. The second spot, at the west end of the street, is a little more crowded and draws the tattooed-and-pierced crowd. If that's your scene, you'll enjoy the local color (and the hair). It's conveniently located beside the Newbury Pet Center, if you need a few supplies. The roomier Starbucks is at 165 Newbury Street; (617) 536-5282. The second store is at 350 Newbury Street; (617) 859-5751.

Stephanie's On Newbury: Hip dogs and those who just want to be hip hang out at this outdoor café and pick up some new tail wagging moves while dining on a delicious selection of continental cuisine. 190 Newbury Street; (617) 236-0990.

To Go Bakery: A charming little neighborhood café, To Go has quite a few chairs outside on a sunny street where you can sip your espresso and munch on a freshly baked muffin. It's a hopping hangout for South End dog owners, with a very dog-friendly atmosphere. 314 Shawmut Avenue at Union Park; (617) 482-1015.

Travis Restaurant: Really a diner in fancy surroundings, this is one of the best places in Boston to get an old-fashioned breakfast; or, in the words of a great philosopher, good food, cheap. Best of all, you get outdoor tables on the most fashionable street in Boston. Your dog will love licking the scraps of your hash browns, and you'll enjoy having change in your pocket after a good meal. Open for breakfast and lunch only. 135 Newbury Street; (617) 267-6388.

PLACES TO STAY

Boston Harbor Hotel: Wander out the front door of this harborfront establishment, and you and your dog can stroll out to Christopher Columbus Waterfront Park (see page 265). A fabulous but pricey four-star hotel, it will accommodate its guests' four-footed friends. No size restrictions apply, but, if your dog is very large, we suggest you let the management know ahead of time. Rates range from $200 to $400. 70 Rowes Wharf, Boston, MA 02110; (617) 439-7000; www.bhh.com.

The Colonnade Hotel: This Back Bay hotel really rolls out the red carpet for Rover. There are no size restrictions or extra fees, but they do ask that you let them know your pet will be accompanying you. They will also provide extra dog bowls, leashes, and biscuits if you forget to bring them along. Rates range from $160 to $280 per night. 120 Huntington Avenue, Boston, MA 02116; (617) 424-7000; www.colannadehotel.com.

The Copley Plaza: This very ornate, elegant old hotel in Back Bay is now a member of the Fairmont chain, but you can expect the same fabulous service, and they still allow patrons to bring their well-behaved dogs. The rates are steep, but the unique rooms are gussied up in French and English Colonial style. Rates are $180 to $270 per night. On Copley Square at 138 St. James Avenue, Boston, MA 02116; (617) 267-5300.

Eliot Suite Hotel: This comfortable suite-style hotel is located in the heart of Back Bay, just a block from trendy Newbury Street and within easy walking distance of the Esplanade and Storrow Drive dog run. All suites have a kitchen area and living room. Dogs are welcome as long as they are not left unattended in the room; there are no size restrictions or extra fees for Fido. Rooms range from a pricey $225 to $375 per night. 370 Commonwealth Avenue, Boston, MA 02116; (617) 267-1607.

Four Seasons Hotel: Boston's only five-diamond hotel goes out of its way for dogs—and well it should for the rates it charges! When you check in, your pet receives a welcome package that includes pet menus, feeding bowl, dog bones, and a treat. Now that's doggone hospitable. Rates range from $195 to $2,200. 200 Boyslton Street, Boston, MA 02116; (617) 338-4400 or (800) 332-3442; www.fshr.com.

Hilton Back Bay: "Wherever you go, there you are" when you stay at this conveniently located hotel. Located right off Boylston Avenue, you'll be close to all the hot spots. There are great city views from the top floors and rooms big enough to feel right at home. Best of all, they like dogs! Please let the management know you will be traveling with your pet prior to arrival. Rooms range from $179 to $325. 40 Dalton Street, Boston, MA 02115; (800) 445-8667 or (617) 236-1100; www.hilton.com.

Howard Johnson Kenmore: Set in Kenmore Square, this hotel is only a subway stop away from either downtown Boston or Brookline. The Esplanade is also within easy walking distance. Pets of all sizes are welcome. Rates range from $80 to $155. 575 Commonwealth Avenue, Boston, MA 02215; (617) 267-3100; www.hojo.com.

Logan Airport Ramada Hotel: Whether you and your dog are heading into or out of town, this airport location is perfect for those times when you and your pup are too pooped to go any farther. No extra charge or size restrictions for Fido. Rates range from $129 to $249.75. Service Road, Boston, MA 02128; (671) 569-9300; www.ramada.com.

Sheraton at the Prudential Center: You'll find this hotel, located between Back Bay and the South End, a good city bet. The management asks you to notify them well in advance that you'll be accompanied by your dog. Rates range from $109 to $339. 39 Dalton Street, Boston, MA 02199; (617) 236-2000; www.sheraton.com.

Swissôtel Boston: Set near all the major city parks and walking tours, this beautiful European hotel is happy to accommodate your pet with all its old-world charm. Only small dogs are allowed, however. Rates range from $225 to $290. 1 Avenue de Lafayette, Boston, MA 02111; (617) 451-2600; www. swissotel.com.

The Westin at Copley Place: This deluxe hotel in the Copley Place shopping mall provides easy access to shopping and many nearby parks. Dogs under 25 pounds are allowed; please tell the management that you'll be traveling with your dog when you make your reservation. Your pal, of course, must be leashed at all times and isn't allowed in the mall. Rates range from $194 to $250. 10 Huntington Avenue, Boston, MA 02116; (617) 262-9600; www.westin.com.

FESTIVALS

Boston Pops Fourth of July Concert: No one makes a bigger deal out of Independence Day than Bostonians. The annual Boston Pops Fourth of July Concert and fireworks demonstration attracts more than 250,000 people, so get there early if you want a good spot. The seats around the Hatch Shell (for the Pops concert) are usually gone the day before, but, if you bring your blanket, Frisbee, picnic basket, and plenty of water, you won't mind staking out your territory along the banks of the Charles sometime during the day. The concert starts at 8 P.M. and is piped in all along the Esplanade (see page 265) for the 245,000 folks who can't get close to the live action. Fireworks begin at 9:30 P.M. (617) 266-1492.

North End Saints' Feasts: From late July through the end of September each year, the North End celebrates its Catholic patron saints by holding feasts and street festivals in their honor. The locations and saints honored vary, but not the fun. The biggest event is the Fisherman's Feast in mid-July. Some events feature fireworks, so stay away if your dog is skittish. (617) 391-7715.

DIVERSIONS

Bark around the clock: If your dog is nothin' but a hound dog, or at least howls like one, check out the free Friday night concerts in Copley Square. Every Friday evening from June through August, you can enjoy a live concert featuring folk, light rock, or jazz bands. Shows generally run from 5 to 7 P.M. Check your local listings for times and bands. (617) 787-0929.

Be a pinup pup: Is your dog worried that her wish list of chew toys won't make it to the North Pole in time for Christmas? Well, she can give Santa the list in person at the Massachusetts Society for the Prevention of Cruelty to Animals' Annual Santa Photo Days. The small fee for the photo benefits the

MSPCA's animal-protection and humane-education programs. Call the MSPCA for exact dates and time in December. 350 Huntington Avenue; (617) 522-7400.

Bless your pooch: The first week of May is National Be Kind to Animals Week. The Boston Animal Rescue League holds open houses all week, and on the first Sunday in May, a priest is on hand to administer a blessing upon you and your dog. This annual event is now held as part of That Doggone Walk at Castle Island. We don't know about you, but we could always use a little divine intervention! (781) 461-8015, extension 26.

Clang, clang, clang goes the trolley: Take your dog on a city tour of Boston. City View Trolley Tours offers a trip through Beantown that covers the Freedom Trail, Boston Tea Party ship, Quincy Market, the North End, Beacon Hill, Back Bay, Bunker Hill, and the New England Aquarium, among other sites. You can order tickets by phone at (617) 363-7899, or purchase them in person at the Boston Common Visitor Information kiosk at the Park Street Station or by the Long Wharf Marriott Hotel near the New England Aquarium. An all-day ticket includes unlimited reboarding. The full tour is narrated by a guide and takes one hour. All dogs must be leashed and be able to sit at your feet or on your lap. Hours of operation are daily from 9 A.M. City View, P.O. Box 267, Boston, MA 02132; (617) 363-7899.

Doggy Day Care: If you're visiting Boston and your trip includes an itinerary that doesn't always include your dog, Beacon Hill Pet Sitters is available to take your dog on afternoon field trips, walks in the park, or an all-day pet excursion. Call in advance of your arrival and let them know what your needs are, and they'll devise a schedule for you and your pet that will allow all of you to have a vacation worth remembering. They will pick up and deliver to your hotel or home. Rates range from $12 an hour to an overnight fee of $45. (617) 422-1PET (1738).

Do the reel thing: Grab a bucket of popcorn and a bag of squeaky toys and head for the Hatch Shell on the Esplanade (see page 265). On summer Friday nights at 8 P.M., the amphitheater becomes an outdoor movie theater. The flicks are family oriented and free for everyone, including the family dog. Inu prefers classic romances; George always hopes for action films. But both agree that Hollywood's animal films set standards they can never live up to—two paws down. Check local listings to see what's playing. The movie series runs from the first Friday in July to the last Friday in August. (617) 727-1300, extension 555.

Explore Beantown by foot: A nifty organization called Boston by Foot offers several walking tours through selected areas of the city. They encourage you to bring your dog along, on leash, and take special care to make sure your four-footed friend is comfortable. Choose between Freedom Trail tours, walks around historic Beacon Hill, an unusual walk along the Waterfront, or their popular Boston Underground tour which features the many engineering feats in Boston's history. There's even a Boston by Little Feet tour especially for children. Dogs are welcome on all tours. (617) 367-2345; www.bostonbyfoot.com.

Make tracks, do tricks: What dog doesn't love going for a walk? And dog owners love it, too, especially when the walk counts for something besides a breath of fresh air and a good sniff. On the third Sunday in September, the

Massachusetts Society for the Prevention of Cruelty to Animals (MSPCA) hosts its annual Walk for the Animals, a fund-raiser for its animal shelters. Take the 1.7-mile stroll around Jamaica Pond and then participate in Mutts 'n' Fluff 'n' Stuff, an amateur dog show. If your pooch boasts a hidden talent beyond the usual "roll over" or "shake" tricks, sign her up! Stupid pet tricks are encouraged. The event is held at Jamaica Pond (see pages 266–267), just off the Jamaicaway. Call the MSPCA for details at (617) 522-7400.

Pass the Milk Bone, matey: Hungry pups and their owners should check out the Boston Harbor Lunch Cruises. Rides take only 45 minutes; bring along your lunch and your dog. The cruises to nowhere provide a little boating pleasure and some fresh air for the both of you. They run twice a day, at noon and 1 P.M., from Monday through Friday in July and August. (617) 227-4321.

Say cheese with Santa: Pose your pooch with Santa for a memorable holiday snapshot. Pet photos with St. Nick are an annual event at Boston's Animal Rescue League. Get your dog's picture taken with the Jolly One on the first Saturday in December. The flashbulbs are popping from 10 A.M. to 2 P.M. at 10 Chandler Street; (781) 461-8015, extension 26.

Screen on the Green: Every June, HBO sponsors a film festival on the Boston Common. The classic movies are run on a giant screen near the Charles Street entrance and are free to the public. Bring the Milk Bones, the popcorn, and a pillow for old movies under the stars. Our dogs like *Homeward Bound*, although *My Dog Skip* gets a paws up, too. Every Monday night in June at 8:30 P.M. No phone contact; www.screenonthegreen.com.

Scrub a dub, three dogs in a tub: The annual Boston Common Dog Wash, held on the last Sunday in August, raises money for the Tufts University School of Veterinarian Medicine. Visit the Frog Pond in the Boston Common (see page 263) between 11 A.M. and 4:30 P.M. and, for a mere $5, get your dog scrubbed, rubbed, and smelling oh so good. Also, take home a goody sack filled with yummies from area pet stores. Local dog organizations sponsor booths. For more information, call the Tufts University School of Veterinarian Medicine at (508) 839-7910.

Strike up the band: From mid-June to early August, the Boston Pops performs free concerts every Thursday evening at 8:30 P.M. at the Hatch Shell on the Esplanade (see page 265). Bring a snack or dinner, plus chewies for your dog, and enjoy the classical music at a classical price. Check the local listings for dates and programs. (617) 266-1492.

Strut with your mutt: The Mutt Strut, an annual October event sponsored by Youth Sports, Art, and Recreation (SPARC), is a fun run or walk for dogs and their human companions. Participants can choose between a one-mile walk or a two-mile run. In addition, dogs can test their athleticism on an agility course. A grand old time is guaranteed, and the $15 entry fee supports after-school programs for city youth. Held at Christian Herter Park (see page 264), it starts at the registration booth at the children's playground. For the exact date and additional details, call (617) 561-1120.

Take a paws: Join the legion of two- and four-footed friends for this 2.5-mile walk around Castle Island the first weekend of May. That Doggone Walk, a fund-raising event for the Animal Rescue League, got off to a great start in 1998 and is now an annual event. You are encouraged to walk with your pets or in memory of pets that have departed. The event starts at 9 A.M. and goes on all day with various activities that include the Blessing of the Animals— administered by a nondenominational minister—pet education, pet vendors, and good food for all! (781) 461-8015, extension 26.

Tip a canoe, and Fido, too: Your dog may never want to set paw on dry land again after a day of canoeing the Charles River. From May to October, you can rent a canoe at the boathouse in Christian Herter Park (see page 264). The river bend around Allston-Brighton is especially popular with paddlers because of its many hidden coves and smooth-flowing water. Daily and hourly rentals are available. Turn into the Christian Herter Park parking area and follow signs to the Charles River Canoe and Kayak Center. In the Charles River Reservation, off Soldier's Field Road; (617) 965-5110.

BOXFORD

PARKS, BEACHES, AND RECREATION AREAS

• **Bald Hill Reservation, Eastern Section** 🐾 🐾 🐾 🐾 ◀● See **39** on page 250.

If you and your dog didn't get enough of the Waltons, then you're sure to enjoy a hike up Bald Hill. Only here it's the Russells: James, Rebecca, Perkins, and Peabody. The Russell family occupied Bald Hill from the mid-1700s to the mid-1800s, and many signs of the old farm remain: the foundations for the barns and homes, open fields and orchards, and even the family graveyard.

The main trail up the mountain is a country lane named Bald Hill Road. It winds past beautiful tall forests, scenic ponds, and marshes. Along the way, the intersections are coded to make it easier to find your way. To reach the hilltop, you'll just need to stay with the road until Intersection 12, where you turn right to complete the ascent. Up top the views are limited, but, if you follow the trail to the south, you'll reach an open meadow which is a great place for a picnic or some ball throwing. Dogs must be on leash.

From Interstate 95, take Exit 51 to Endicott Road west. Turn right on Middleton Road and continue to the park and parking lot on the right. Open from sunrise to sunset. (978) 369-3350.

• **Wildcat Conservation Area** 🐾 🐾 🐾 See **40** on page 250.

Wetlands and woodlands and wildcats, oh my! These comprise the highlights of Wildcat Conservation Area. Well, maybe just the wetlands and woodlands, but you never know what's out there. We'd like to think that there are still a few wildcats in the woods. When one shows up, we'll be ready.

Whether or not you encounter any wild beasts, your canine pal will love sharing the main trail here with you. It roams for 2.5 miles through rich forest, passing many ponds and streams. Along the way be on the lookout for the Ledge Trail, which veers off to the left and climbs for a higher route. The return loop is known as the Wolf-Pit Trail, where, we are told, you may pass an old wolf pit. The entire route makes a wonderful hike through marshes, stone walls, and ridges.

The Boxford Conservation Commission manages the park and requires dogs to be on leash.

From Interstate 95, take Exit 53 to Killam Hill Road west. Turn left on Kelsey Road, then turn right on Ipswich Road. Take a left onto Herrick Road. The park and a parking lot are on the right. Open from dawn to dusk. (978) 352-2538.

RESTAURANTS

Benson's Homemade Ice Cream: Of course there's no such thing as bad ice cream, but Benson's has some of the best around. Outdoor seating is available for all. 181 Washington Street/State Route 3; (978) 352-2911.

BRAINTREE

PARKS, BEACHES, AND RECREATION AREAS

• **Pond Meadow Park** 🐾🐾 See **41** on page 252.
Part of the Weymouth Braintree Regional Recreation Conservation Area (Whew, what a mouthful!), this park covers much of the southeastern corner of Braintree. An assortment of trails crisscross its 320 acres, looping around Pond Meadow. The pond lies at the park's center; on any given day, its serene beauty attracts plenty of wildlife, visitors, and at least two thirsty dogs we know. It's a perfect spot for a summertime doggy dip. Dogs must be leashed.

From State Route 3, take Exit 17 onto Union Street toward Weymouth. Turn right on Middle Street and then left on Liberty Street. The park and a parking lot are on the right. Open from sunrise to sunset. (781) 843-7147.

PLACES TO STAY

Days Inn: Well-behaved dogs are welcome here as long as you don't leave them unattended. Just notify the front desk at check-in that you're letting sleeping dogs lie. Rates range from $79 to $129. 190 Wood Road, Braintree, MA 02184; (781) 848-1260 or (800) DAYS-INN.

Motel 6: All Motel 6 locations allow dogs as long as you don't leave your pet unattended. This well-situated inn is just south of downtown Boston and on the way to South Shore parks and beaches. One dog is welcome per room. Rates are $62 to $83. 125 Union Street, Braintree, MA 02184; (781) 848-7890.

BROOKLINE

PARKS, BEACHES, AND RECREATION AREAS

• **Larz Anderson Memorial Park** 🐾🐾🐾 See **42** on page 252.
Donated to Brookline in the 1960s by philanthropist Larz Anderson, this is one of the best parks in the city. Don't take our word for it—visit any day and the happy dogs playing on the hill will tell you so themselves. Of course, happiness has a small price: your pup must be on leash and you have to clean up after him. Dog owners here are very militant about infractions of the pooper-scooper law. If you blow it, you'll have to answer to a lot of angry folks.

From State Route 9, take Lee Street south; follow Lee Street until it turns into Clyde Street and then turn left on Newton Street. Take an immediate left on Goddard Street and turn right into the parking area, or follow Newton Street one block and turn left into the Museum of Transportation. Open from dawn to dusk. (617) 730-2069.

• **Reservoir Park** 🐾 🐾 See **43** on page 252.
There's more reservoir than park here, but a quick run or walk along the water's perimeter makes a pleasant outing. Bikes are not allowed here, so, if you like to jog with your dog, this is prime real estate.

Dogs must be on leash here, and parking is scarce. Nonresidents must park on Dudley Street.

From State Route 9, take Warren Street south. Turn left on Walnut Street and then left again on Dudley Street. Open from 5 A.M. to 11 P.M. (617) 730-2069.

PLACES TO STAY

The Bertram Inn: Built in 1907, this stately manor home in Coolidge Corner is within easy walking distance of shopping and restaurants. Each of the 14 rooms is carefully decorated (two have fireplaces). Continental breakfast is served in the dining room each morning. In-season rates for rooms with a shared bath run from $69 to $94; rooms with a private bath are $94 to $219. Dogs stay free, but they must promise to wipe their muddy paws on the welcome mat before entering. Not a bad idea for humans, either. 92 Sewall Avenue, Brookline, MA 02146; (617) 566-2234 or (800) 295-3822.

DIVERSIONS

Book 'em, Fido: Normally we wouldn't include a retail store that allows dogs, but we have to make an exception for Brookline Booksmith & Soundsmith. Not only are four-footed patrons welcome inside the shop, but regulars know that all they have to do is sit politely by the front counter and they'll be rewarded with a dog biscuit. No purchase necessary! Of course, once you're in the store you'll have a hard time leaving without getting the latest pet book, always prominently displayed for their best customers. Want more proof that the place has gone to the dogs? Every few months the store's newsletter features a new Dog of Distinction, which includes a Miss America–style Q&A with the lucky pooch. In August the store's windows have a Dog Days display with all the great, soon-to-be-dog-eared books you and your pooch will enjoy. 279 Harvard Street; (617) 566-6660.

CAMBRIDGE

This eclectic college town proudly wears the title of Athens of America. Famous Harvard University and the Massachusetts Institute of Technology (MIT) reside here, and their influences are felt far and wide. And countless reminders of the past remain, from George Washington's headquarters during the American Revolution to the lecture halls where Timothy Leary first urged students to "tune in, turn on, and drop out" in the psychedelic '60s.

PARKS, BEACHES, AND RECREATION AREAS

• **Charles River Reservation** 🐾 🐾 See **44** on page 252.
For a 1.5-mile stroll, walk on the bike path along Memorial Drive from the elegant 19th-century Harvard Boathouse at Anderson Bridge and Harvard

Square to the ball fields at Magazine Beach. You'll share the path with in-line skaters, joggers, and cyclists. The route cuts through grassy areas where you and your dog can play or just soak up the sun. Separating Anderson Bridge and Western Avenue is the elegant John Weeks Jr. Bridge, a stone footbridge that provides access to the other side of the river.

Magazine Beach has an exaggerated name—at best you'll find a few rocky clearings close to the water—but the green space is perfect for sunbathing. The ball field here is off-limits when games are in progress, but on weekend mornings local Cambridge dogs and their owners gather here for some old-fashioned wagging and walking.

Except for the parking area at Magazine Beach, which can hold 40 cars, parking is scarce. To reach the Magazine Beach lot, from the Massachusetts Turnpike/Interstate 90 take the Cambridge/Allston exit on Cambridge Street. Cross the Charles River into Cambridge and River Street. Turn right immediately on Memorial Drive. The park and a lot are on the right. To get to the Harvard Boathouse and Harvard Square, drive 1.5 miles past the lot. Limited street parking is available along Memorial Drive. The following portion of the reservation runs along Memorial Drive on the Cambridge side of the Charles River. Below, we have divided it into sections. All are open 24 hours a day. (617) 635-4505.

• Danehy Park 🐾 🐾 🐕 See 45 on page 252.

Location counts, and this pleasant little park doesn't have the greatest one, but once you get here it's well laid out and—yippee!—it's got an off-leash dog run, which has a little pond (well, really a puddle), grass, gravel, and fences on three sides. Okay, it's not very big, only about 600 square feet, but it's popular on weekend mornings, when 15 to 20 pooches make the most of it. With three main lots, parking is easy, and maps at each entrance of the park make finding your way around a snap. Dogs must be leashed when not in the dog run.

Enter on New Street for quick access to the dog run. The other parking lots are on Sherman Street and Field Street.

From State Route 2, follow the Fresh Pond rotary to Concord Street and turn right on New Street. It looks like you are entering the back of Fresh Pond Mall, which you are, but the road also leads to the park. Or take Rindge Street off State Route 2 and turn right on Sherman Street. Open from 8 A.M. to 11 P.M. (617) 349-4376.

• Fresh Pond Park 🐾 🐾 🐾 🐾 🐕 See 46 on page 252.

If you live in Cambridge, this is a fabulous place to go. If you don't live here, it's still pretty terrific, but only if you have wings, because there's no place to park. We suspect Cambridge residents want to keep this little piece of doggy heaven to themselves—the parking lot is for residents only, and you're not supposed to park on nearby streets. (They do ticket occasionally.)

No matter how you get here, Fresh Pond is bound to be popular with your four-legged friend, since dogs can romp here off leash as long as they're under voice control and their owners pick up after them. Six Mutt Mitts dispensers are spread throughout the park, so you've got no excuse not to pick up after your dog. Don't blow it!

From State Route 2 and the Fresh Pond rotary, follow the Fresh Pond Parkway east toward Boston. The parking area is located on the right, just before you reach Huron Avenue across from Huron Road. It's not marked, so keep a lookout or you might drive right past it. Open from dawn to dusk. (617) 349-4793.

NATURE HIKES AND URBAN HIKES

Old Cambridge Walking Tour: Harvard Yard, Harvard Square, Cambridge Common, Tory Row, and the historical district of classic homes from the American Revolution are among the highlights of this self-guided two-mile walk. Free tour maps and brochures are available at the Cambridge Discovery Information Booth in Harvard Square or from the Cambridge Historical Society. For additional information on the walk, call (617) 497-1630.

RESTAURANTS

Au Bon Pain: This restaurant in the heart of Harvard Square has ample room for you, chess players, and your dog. (Categories are not mutually exclusive, of course.) Directly across from Harvard Yard and right off the Red Line T Station, the outdoor area gets more than enough activity to delight people watchers and dog watchers alike. You and your pup can nosh on a croissant as local chess pros match wits at the table beside you. With fresh lemonade in the summer and hot cider in the winter, it makes a great beverage stop after a walk along the river and shopping in the Harvard Square shops. 1360 Massachusetts Avenue; (617) 497-9797.

Carberry's Bakery & Coffee House: With more than 15 varieties of fresh bread baked on the premises, this delightful Central Square establishment is the best place to "loaf" around. We're partial to the rosemary French bread, but the cheese bread is pretty tasty, too. The coffee drinks and light menu are also terrific. In addition to outdoor tables, it's got a small parking lot—a big plus in parking-starved Cambridge—so you can enjoy this great little spot with Spot, stress free. 74–76 Prospect Street; (617) 576-3530.

Kendall Square Cafés: The restaurants in this little, lively outdoor enclave between Broadway and Hampshire Streets change regularly, so we only list the sure things. If you wander over here, you may find other delicious options that we haven't named. Eat your take-out food on outdoor benches along the street.

Sammy's Manhattan Deli Co.: Eat your corned beef at an outdoor table or take your sandwich to one of the many benches in the square. The cuisine is simple deli fare, reasonably priced. 1 Kendall Square; (617) 252-0044.

Sazarac Grove Bar & Grill: Students and twenty-somethings frequent this casual restaurant and bar. The fare is college continental: burgers, salads, pizza. The food isn't expensive, there are plenty of outdoor tables, and the regular clientele will probably lavish your pet with attention. 1 Kendall Square; (617) 577-7850.

PLACES TO STAY

The Charles Hotel: This pricey but outstanding hotel will put you right where the action is. Located in Harvard Square, the hotel is close to just about everything. There is no size restriction, but management requests you not leave your dog in the room unattended. A refundable $100 deposit is required.

Rates range from $199 to $389. 1 Bennett Street, Cambridge, MA 02138; (617) 864-1200 or (800) 882-1818.

Howard Johnson Cambridge: Right along the Charles River and close to walking areas and Harvard Square, this 205-room hotel allows your pet to stay with you. Notify the staff at check-in that you have a dog with you. Rates range from $89 to $250. No extra charge for your pet. 777 Memorial Drive, Cambridge, MA 02139; (617) 492-7777.

FESTIVALS

Cambridge River Festival: On the first weekend of September, Cambridge closes down Memorial Drive and turns it into the site of the annual River Festival. Musicians, dancers, artisans of all kinds, and international food booths abound, as the city holds this big block party. You and your dog are invited to the festivities, and it's worth checking out at least once in a lifetime. For details, call (617) 349-4332.

Head of the Charles Regatta: It wouldn't be October in New England without a trip to the largest single-day collegiate rowing event in the country. Rowers come from all over the world to participate. The race runs along the Charles River, and people line up early for a ringside seat. Our dogs love all the commotion, not to mention the tasty morsels dropped on the ground. The regatta is held every year, rain or shine, on the third Sunday in October from 8 A.M. to 4:30 P.M. (617) 864-8415.

Oktoberfest: A traditional German festival, this lively street fair takes over Harvard Square on the second Sunday in October. You'll enjoy the food, entertainment, and craft booths, and your dog will enjoy the food, the food, and the food. Did we mention the food? (617) 491-3434.

DIVERSIONS

Get jazzed with your pup: On Thursday evenings from the end of July through the end of August, listen to jazz in the open-air square next to the Charles Hotel during the Charles Square Summer Music Series. Beginning at 8 P.M., the casual concerts feature an array of local and name musicians. You and your dog will enjoy the music and the ambience—unless, of course, your pup insists on howling along with the saxophone. (617) 536-5352.

CANTON

PARKS, BEACHES, AND RECREATION AREAS

• **Blue Hills Reservation, Ponkapoag Pond Section** 🐾🐾🐾🐾 See **47** on page 251.

Many visitors use State Route 128 to reach the Blue Hills Reservation, and who can blame them—it runs right through the middle of the park. But the highway, also known as Interstate 93, can feel a lot like Mr. Toad's Wild Ride, with cars jockeying frantically for position. Most drivers are so busy navigating the traffic that they don't even notice the lovely, peaceful wilderness surrounding them.

If you're one of the lucky drivers taking the Ponkapoag Trail exit (yes, the trailhead has its own exit), get ready for a wonderful transformation.

The sunshine sparkles off the ripples on Ponkapoag Pond. In the eastern corner of the lake, marsh grasses sway in the cool breeze, and across the water the many colors dapple the Blue Hills in the fall. The Great Blue Hill itself towers over all this beauty in silent repose. (For details on the hill, see Milton, Blue Hills Reservation, Great Blue Hill Section on page 321.)

The Blue Hills attract many visitors year-round, but most of the crowds who come to climb the Great Blue Hill miss the Ponkapoag Pond section. In fact, our dogs often have the pond to themselves.

Dogs are welcome on leash in the Metropolitan District Commission park. Free trail maps are available at the park headquarters in Milton, and for $1 you can get a large color map.

From State Route 128/Interstate 93, take Exit 3 to Ponkapoag Trail south. The northern parking lot and trailhead are right at the highway exit. To reach the other park access points from State Route 128, take Exit 2A to State Route 138 south/Washington Street. The park is open from dawn to dusk, but the southern parking lot is only open from 9 A.M. to 4:30 P.M. (781) 698-1802.

CARLISLE

Here's good news for Carlisle dogs and their out-of-town visitors: If you love to roam leash free and are responsive to the sound of your owner's voice, the town of Carlisle doesn't require you to wear a leash! You know the deal with this privilege. Abuse it and we may lose it. Now let's be careful out there.

PARKS, BEACHES, AND RECREATION AREAS

• The Cranberry Bog 🐾🐾🐾 🐕 See **48** on page 250.

It looks like a cranberry bog, smells like a cranberry bog, and it's even called "The Cranberry Bog." But, unlike most bogs, this one you'll want to visit. In 1986, the towns of Carlisle and Chelmsford bought this private wetland, and now you and your leash-free dog are free to use it. The cities still lease out the bog to private farmers who harvest the berries, but, if you stick to the park's path through the area, you'll have your run of this terrific spot.

The entire round-trip walk takes about 45 minutes, and the unusual terrain makes it worthwhile. We've seen deer on every visit, and, if you're lucky, you might catch a glimpse of the beavers and muskrats that are rumored to reside in the ponds. As for the cranberries, in the fall months you can buy them at Great Brook Farm Ice Cream (see page 282), which you'll find just up the road.

From the town center at the intersection of Lowell Street and Westford Street/State Route 225, take Lowell Street north. Turn left on Curve Street. The park and a parking area are on the right. Open from dawn to dusk. (978) 369-0336.

• Great Brook Farm State Park 🐾🐾🐾🐾 🐕 🐾 See **49** on page 250.

With more than 900 acres and nine miles of trails, this is one of those great parks that you'll want to visit again and again. Our readers have told us this is one of their favorite parks in the entire book. In fact, most of the locals can't imagine making the effort to go anywhere else when they have Great Brook

Farm in their own backyard. It has a large meadow, pine and woodland forest, esker trail, swamp, and a lovely pond, not to mention a working farm and ice-cream stand. You'll probably discover your favorite trail and stick with it, but there are many combinations that you can put together to keep you and your dog entertained on every visit.

If it's your first visit, we recommend the Pine Point Loop. To reach the trail, drive North Road a quarter mile past Great Brook Farm to the Canoe Launch parking area. Follow the blue arrow to the Pine Point Loop; the trail starts at the fork. You can set out straight ahead or veer to the right. Either way, the trail will loop around and bring you back to the same spot.

The park offers many other worthwhile trails. Pick up a free map at the regional headquarters on Lowell Road or check out alternative routes on the posted map at the main parking area by the farm. Your dog may be off leash everywhere but Great Brook Farm itself.

From the town center at the intersection of Lowell Street and Westford Street/State Route 225, take Lowell Street north. Turn right on Curve Street, which leads into the park. The parking area is on the left. Open from sunrise to sunset. (978) 369-6312.

• Greenough Land 🐾🐾🐾 🐕 See **50** on page 250.
The trail at this wonderful 242-acre park twists and turns through a pine forest before delivering you and your leash-free dog to Greenough Pond at its center. It offers a decent hike, and the park has plenty of additional trails for those who want to explore the area further.

From the town center at the intersection of Lowell Street and Bedford Road/State Route 225, take Bedford Road east. Turn left on East Street, then left again on Maple Street. The park and a parking area are on the right. Open from dawn to dusk. (978) 369-0336.

• Towle Field 🐾🐾🐾 🐕 See **51** on page 250.
Although it covers only 112 acres, this terrific park feels a lot bigger because it encompasses so many different types of terrain. The trails weave their way through forest and field, over hills and rocks, crossing water at many spots where your off-leash dog can stop for a drink or a refreshing splash. There seems to be a wonderful surprise around every bend.

From the town center at the intersection of Lowell Street and Westford Street/State Route 225, take Westford Street west. The park and a parking lot are on the left, just past Salvation Lane. Open from dawn to dusk. (978) 369-0336.

RESTAURANTS

Great Brook Farm Ice Cream: Located within Great Brook Farm State Park (see pages 281–282), this ice-cream store could be your well-deserved reward after a long day of hiking on the trails. Park your automobile at the main parking area and go up the hill to the farm. There are plenty of signs to guide you; on a hot summer's day, just follow the crowds! Dogs must be leashed here because you're on a working farm, and you won't be welcome if Fido decides to run around and upset the barnyard animals. 247 North Road; (978) 371-7083.

Kimball Farm: I scream, you scream, and your dogs will even scream for this great little outdoor ice-cream and sandwich stand. The menu's gigantic, and plenty of benches and picnic tables are around the shop where you and your dog can enjoy lunch or a treat. It's open seasonally from April to October. 343 Bedford Road/State Route 225, just past Church Street; (978) 369-1910.

COHASSET

Hooray for Cohasset! The town has a flexible leash law. That means your well-behaved dog may walk around leash free as long as she is under voice control and accompanied by her owner.

PARKS, BEACHES, AND RECREATION AREAS

• **Whitney and Thayer Woods** 🐾🐾🐾🐾 🐕 See **52** on page 250. South Shore dogs know a good thing when they sniff it. And they'll find an abundance of exceptional sniffing spots on the 800 acres of beautiful woods and marshlands here. They'll also discover 12 miles of cart paths and trails to romp on leash free. That's right, dogs are allowed off leash as long as they obey their owners' voice commands, and their human pals pick up after them.

Enormous, glacially formed boulders dot the park, making fine rest stops or destinations. Trail maps indicate the locations of Bigelow Boulder and Ode's Den, both of which are worth visiting. Ode takes its name from the hermit who made a home among the rocks in a gorgeous hollow. You'll find it well worth the short hike.

Whitney and Thayer Woods is adjacent to Wompatuck State Park, making it easy to expand your hike by connecting to the numerous trails in the state park.

Maps are available for $1.25 at the Mobil Mart across State Route 3A. They're invaluable because the trail system can be confusing.

From State Route 3, take Exit 14 to Pond Street/State Route 228 north into Hingham. Turn right on Chief Justice Cushing Highway/State Route 3A and head east into Cohasset. The park is on the right at Sohier Street. A parking lot is available. Open from sunrise to sunset. (781) 821-2977.

• **Wompatuck State Park—See Hingham, Wompatuck State Park on pages 303–304.**

RESTAURANTS

French Memories Bakery: Pick up a cup of joe and a to-die-for cinnamon roll before you hit the trails on a sleepy Saturday morning. If the smell of the fabulous baked goods doesn't wake you up, the coffee will. 60 South Main Street; (781) 383-2216.

Really Great Pizza: We like a place that just comes out and says who they are. And whether you want pizzas or wraps, this place is as good as its name. So is the Really Great Patio where you can sit with your dog. This sunny spot is the place to see and be seen in the heart of this lovely resort town. 35 South Main Street; (781) 383-0464.

CONCORD

The first skirmish between the British and the Colonists took place in this famous New England town, which dates back to the late 1600s. The Old North Bridge, still standing, is the site of the "shot heard 'round the world" on April

19, 1775. You can visit many other historical points of interest, from Nathaniel Hawthorne's house to the home where Louisa May Alcott penned *Little Women*. You'll even discover old stone markers on the trails of some of the many leash-free parks here.

PARKS, BEACHES, AND RECREATION AREAS

• Estabrook Woods/Punkatasset Conservation Land
🐾 🐾 🐾 🐾 🐕 🐾 See **53** on page 250.

Has your furry ruffian been ruffhousing it too much lately? Is it time to hit some trails guaranteed to wear her out? If so, the ponds, pastures, and paths in this popular 800-acre spot may be just the thing for your pup. Dogs are permitted to explore these woods leash free, and you will have one happy, exhausted hiking companion on your hands at the day's end. Enter from Monument Street and you're in the Punkatasset Conservation Land section, managed by the Natural Resource Commission in Concord. Once you leave the pond area, you're in the vast Estabrook Woods, which is overseen by Harvard University.

The Native Americans who once lived in this area were the source of the name Punkatasset, which means "broad-topped hill," and, yes, there is one. The hill is among the highest vantage points in Concord and affords an excellent view of the surrounding countryside.

It shouldn't take your dog long to find Hutchins Pond, especially on a summer day. This great spot—one of the best pooch-friendly swimming holes featured in this book—will cool off both of you in hot weather. If you veer right at the trailhead, you'll soon come upon a wide beach area that's ideal for doggies who yearn to dive into the water. The last time we were there, Inu and George were so enthralled by their refreshing dip that we couldn't get them back on dry land.

This is one of the best-loved and most-trodden recreational hiking areas in the Boston area, and you will meet up with many dogs, hikers, mountain bikers, and other folk. It is also one of the hardest places to find unless you know where you're going. There are no signs, markers, or trail maps to guide you. Luckily, once you're here, even though there will always be others enjoying the spectacular park with you, you'll find there's enough space to get away from the crowds.

From the Concord town square, take Monument Street north until you pass the Old North Bridge. The park is on the left, about three-quarters of a mile past the Concord River. Park in one of the small turnouts along Monument Street. Open from sunrise to sunset. (978) 371-6265.

• Hapgood Wright Town Forest 🐾 🐾 🐾 🐕 See **54** on page 250.

In a startling new discovery, *The Dog Lover's Companion to New England* announces that Henry David Thoreau's cabin was not on the shores of Walden Pond. The writer actually spent two years in solitude at nearby Fairyland Pond, located in what is known today as Hapgood Wright Town Forest. Thoreau feared that his paradise would be overrun with visitors and subject to too many leash laws once his book *Fairyland* was published. His agent worried that the book's title might not have enough punch, so at the last minute he replaced all references to Fairyland Pond with Walden Pond.

The plan worked. Today, Walden Pond gets the crowds, and dogs have been banned from the pond and the surrounding Walden Woods. Yet half a mile away, in peace and solitude, fortunate dogs and nature lovers can enjoy the beauty and serenity of Fairyland Pond and the town forest that inspired Thoreau to write *Fairyland*, uh, *Walden*.

Leg pulling aside, a forest of majestic pines shelters Fairyland Pond, which is just large enough for a hot dog to take a refreshing dip on a summer day. In any season the hilly terrain is ideal for a short hike. Trails encircle the pond and crisscross the woods in various directions, and a few well-placed benches are situated along the way for pooches to sit a spell with their owners and contemplate the joys of few crowds and a leash-free walk.

From State Route 2 at the intersection with State Route 126, take Walden Street north. The park is on the right, across from the Concord-Carlisle High School. A paved parking lot is provided. Open from a half hour before sunrise to a half hour after sunset. (978) 371-6265.

NATURE HIKES AND URBAN WALKS

Historic Concord Walking Tour: Pick up a map at the North Bridge Visitor Center and treat yourself and your dog to a stroll through town and a lesson in American history. Sites along the way include the Old Manse (Nathaniel Hawthorne's home), the Ralph Waldo Emerson House, the Main Street Burial Ground, the Orchard House (Louisa May Alcott's home), and countless sites from the Revolutionary War. Dogs aren't allowed to participate in any of the museum tours, but you're free to leave your pooch outside while you enter any of the houses. (The houses are small, so she won't be waiting long.) For information, call (978) 369-3120.

Minuteman National Historical Park: You and your dog can reenact the "shot heard 'round the world" (the first time Colonists fired upon British forces) and the historic confrontation on the North Bridge. Take a self-guided tour on which you'll learn all about the battle or just stroll the grounds of the park along this scenic stretch of the Concord River. Dogs must be leashed, which might curb their firing power but not their fun. (978) 369-6993.

RESTAURANTS

Back Alley Café: Formerly called Key West Coffee and Teas, this cute shop makes a good stop for sandwiches on six-grain bread, salads topped with sprouts, finger pastries, and gourmet coffee. If your dog doesn't mind waiting outside, you can sit at one of the tiny tables with the cool coffee-crowd scensters. But, if your furry friend is all the company you need, there's a wobbly bench outside, just right for relaxing on a sunny day. 12 Walden Street; (978) 369-6636.

Sally Ann Food Shop: All sorts of hidden delights await at this gourmet food shop. If you crave it, they've probably got it: fresh breads, muffins, sweets. There are no outdoor tables, but it's a great place to pick up something tasty to eat on the trail, or, most likely, on the way to the trail. Before you head out to Estabrook Woods (see page 284) or Fairyland Pond (see pages 284–285), we suggest stopping here for a loaf of fresh bread, some juice or gourmet coffee, and the famous fruit salad. 73 Main Street; (978) 369-4558.

PLACES TO STAY

Best Western Concord: Well-behaved canines are allowed to stay with their well-behaved owners. The inn is conveniently located near the historic sites in Concord, not to mention the many great parks. Rates range from $89 to $125. 740 Elm Street, Concord, MA 01742; (978) 369-6100.

DIVERSIONS

All paws on deck: Canoeing the beautiful Sudbury River is more enjoyable when your favorite first mate comes along to keep you company. (No chewing the oars!) Take a leisurely paddle along the slow-moving river and get a different view of Concord and the shoreline. When you move into the quiet coves, you may see a heron or even a muskrat sunning itself in the shallows. Canoes can be rented by the hour or the day from South Bridge Boathouse, 496 Main Street; (978) 369-9438.

DANVERS

PLACES TO STAY

Motel 6: All Motel 6 locations allow dogs as long as they are not left unattended. Located near the intersection of Interstate 95 and U.S. Route 1, you'll find this a convenient stopover. Rates are $56 per night. 65 Newbury Street, Danvers, MA 01923; (978) 774-8045; www.motel6.com.

Residence Inn: A cross between a hotel and a motel, this inn has spacious rooms with small efficiencies included. The kitchen really comes in handy when you have your pooch along. Right off State Route 128, it's a great one-night stopover on your way to North Shore parks and beaches. A $100 refundable deposit is required. Rates range from $129 to $159, plus $7 for the dog. 51 Newbury Street, Danvers, MA 01876; (978) 777-7171.

DARTMOUTH

PARKS, BEACHES, AND RECREATION AREAS

• **Demarest Lloyd State Park** 🐾 🐾 🐾 See 55 page 251.

For people, this 1,800-foot sandy saltwater beach and the marshes lining the mouth of the Slocum River are a little-known coastal paradise with rolling hills of beach grass and shaded, grassy picnic areas. For dogs, it's a slightly different story. They are only permitted on leash at the picnic sites; they are not allowed on the beach or at the marsh.

The 222-acre park is open year-round to foot traffic (with parking at the gate) and open for full access with a parking lot and posted rangers and lifeguards from April 15 to Labor Day. There is a $2 picnicking fee charged in season.

From Interstate 195, take exit 12 to Faunce Corner Road south onto Chase Road for 4.5 miles. Turn right onto Russells Mills Road for 1.3 miles. Turn left onto Horseneck Road for 2.5 miles. Continue straight onto Barney's Joy Road for 1.5 miles. The park is on the left. Open sunrise to a half hour after sunset. (508) 636-3298.

- **Lloyd Center for Environmental Studies** 🐾 🐾 🐾 See **56** on page 251.

Just as the name says, this property is home to an environmental research and visitor center, as well as some pretty good hiking trails along the Slocums River. The three loop trails are all about a mile long and allow visitors to explore three different types of environments—a swamp with vernal pools, an old growth oak and hickory forest, and a kettle pond on the way to the river wetlands.

Dogs must be on leash.

From Rock O'Dundee Road, take Potomska Road south for two miles. The center is on the right. Parking is available. Open from dawn to dusk. (508) 990-0505.

- **Town Beach** 🐾 🐾 🐾 See **57** on page 251.

Imagine your own private, sandy beach on a picturesque, sparkling bay with a few sailboats added in from a quaint harbor village to give the intriguing scene a dash of color. Looks nice, doesn't it? Well, guess what? There is such a place. Granted, Town Beach, a Dartmouth Conservation Commission property, is only five acres, but Apponagansett Bay has plenty of water, and the views of the harbor and village of Padanaram are endless.

Dogs must be on leash.

From Elm Street in Padanaram Village, take Bridge Street west for a half mile. Turn left onto Smith Neck Road. The park and pullouts for parking are on the immediate left. Open dawn to dusk. (508) 999-0722.

RESTAURANTS

Cicily's Café: You'll have get it to go, but you're sure to enjoy any of the coffees, espressos, salads, sandwiches, soups, pastries, and breads. You had better like it because there isn't anything else in Padanaram Village. 6 Bridge Street; (508) 994-1162.

DEDHAM

PARKS, BEACHES, AND RECREATION AREAS

- **Wilson Mountain Reservation** 🐾 🐾 🐾 See **58** on page 252.

This 207-acre park is the largest remaining open space in Dedham. Purchased by the Metropolitan District Commission in 1995, the park offers scenic views of the distant Boston skyline and the Blue Hills.

There are two hiking trails: the longer two-mile loop covers a good portion of the park's perimeter, winding through a hilly terrain of granite outcroppings and hemlock forests. The shorter three-quarter-mile loop doesn't fool around. It takes you right where every hiker wants to go—to the top of Mount Wilson. Note that the trail here is steep and slippery in some places but negotiable for all but the tiniest of dogs.

From Interstate 95/State Route 128, take Exit 17 to Needham Avenue/State Route 135, then east onto Common Street for a quarter mile. The park and parking lot are on the right. Maps are displayed in the parking lot. Open dawn to dusk. (617) 698-1802.

FESTIVALS

Petoberfest at Pine Ridge Animal Center: Every October head on over to the Animal Rescue League in Dedham for their yearly fur-, er, fund-raising fair. This family event features games, crafts, a petting zoo, animal awareness education, food, and tons of fun for you and your pet. Take part in a pet talent show and a training session with local animal experts, plus enjoy lots of mingling with other dog folk. Call for exact date and details. 55 Anna's Place; (781) 326-0729 or (781) 461-8015.

DIVERSIONS

Bless your pooch: This annual event has now become part of That Doggone Walk (see pages 274–275) at Castle Island. In the 10-minute service, an Episcopal priest will bless your dog and lead a prayer for animals. The free event is nondenominational and all are welcome. It's held on the first Sunday in May. For more information, call (781) 326-0729.

Teach your children: Each June the Pine Ridge Animal Shelter sponsors a one-day obedience training course specifically for children and their pets. Kids are taught how to care for their animals responsibly. The course festivities conclude with a pet show featuring the most talented, best behaved, and cutest pets, and whatever other categories they can dream up. It's a great day for children and even better for their dogs. Call for more details and the exact date. (781) 326-0729.

DOVER

PARKS, BEACHES, AND RECREATION AREAS

• **Elm Bank Reservation** 🐾🐾🐾🐾 🐕 🖙 See **59** on page 250.
Here's a well-kept secret to tell your canine friends: the wonderful Elm Bank Reservation is a leash-free romping ground with plenty of trails and wildlife. Once a privately owned estate, it was passed from owner to owner until the state assumed ownership in the 1970s. And for years the land was slated for the auction block. Fortunately, the Metropolitan District Commission took over management of the 182-acre parcel in 1991. There are activities to suit every taste, and George thinks your pooch will enjoy it as much as he did.

The reservation is on an oblong peninsula surrounded by the Charles River on three sides, and numerous trails have been established. Dogs who obey voice commands are allowed off leash everywhere except the playing fields near the parking areas. From the Old Mansion (the original manor house, which is still standing, although it looks somewhat less stellar than in its heyday), take the loop path leading along the Charles for a great 45-minute walk.

The entrance is across the Charles River in Wellesley. From the intersection of State Routes 16 and 135 in Wellesley, follow Washington Street/State Route 16 west. The park is just past Pond Street on the left. Open from 5 A.M. to 9 P.M. (617) 727-4138.

- **Hale Reservation—See Westwood, Hale Reservation on pages 348–349.**

- **Woodlands** 🐾🐾🐾🐾 🐕 🦴 See **60** on page 250.

With 10 miles of hiking trails, four ponds, and a view of the Boston skyline from Noanet Peak, this place has it all. There is no better choice in the area for a special outing. The trails are so diverse and immense your only problem will be deciding which one to take and whether you can get back to the trailhead without completely wearing out your dog.

Local dog owners know that these are 695 pooch-friendly acres. On weekends a park ranger is often on hand to give directions, and we suggest you pick up a map when the information kiosk is open. It will help you untangle your way through the lush woods to all the best spots in this wonderful reservation.

After a few visits here, you'll discover your favorite stomping grounds, but none of the trails is as confusing as the new sign posted at the entrance to the parking lot which says "No Dogs!" This means no dogs are allowed in Caryl Park, which encompasses the parking lot at the entrance to Noanet Woodlands. Apparently, in a bizarre act of city planning, this means that although your dog can enter Noanet Woodlands, he cannot set foot in the parking lot that leads to the woods. This shouldn't be a problem on weekdays, but, on weekends when the parking lot gets full, you may choose to explore alternative entrances on Walpole and Powissett Streets. Both areas can accommodate up to four cars.

From State Route 128 in Dedham, take Exit 17 to State Route 135 west and proceed into Needham. Turn left on South Street just past the Charles River. Turn left on Chestnut Street and head into Dover; then make a right on Dedham Street just past the Charles River. The park is on the left, adjacent to Caryl Park. Open from sunrise to sunset. (781) 821-2977.

RESTAURANTS

Dover Store: Take a step back to yesteryear at this pharmacy with an old-style soda fountain. You can ask the soda jerk for a glass of pop or a root-beer float (for medicinal purposes, of course). Then take your treat outside to one of the benches or small tables. The fresh air will do you and your dog good. 60 Centre Street; (508) 785-0166.

FESTIVALS

Summer Solstice Celebration Reception: Hounds can herald the beginning of summer at this annual event held each June on the Sunday closest to the summer solstice. Festivities include guided hiking and bird-watching excursions through Elm Bank Reservation (see page 288), and there's a farmer's market and booths where you can get gardening tips and watch demonstrations. Leashed pooches are welcome to participate in all of the activities (bird-watching excluded), and they will have a wonderful time in the great outdoors. The celebration takes place at the reservation from 10 A.M. to 4 P.M. There's a nominal entry fee on this day only. (617) 536-9280.

DUXBURY

PARKS, BEACHES, AND RECREATION AREAS

• Bay Farm Field—See Kingston, Bay Farm Field on page 308.

• **Duxbury Beach** 🐾🐾🐾🐾 ◀● See **61** on page 251.

If you've ever wanted to know what it feels like to own a deserted island, try a visit to Duxbury Beach. If you're not a billionaire (and there are so few of us these days), it may be as close as you'll come to enjoying your very own private stretch of paradise.

Duxbury Beach is a remarkable geological formation in Cape Cod Bay. A peninsula that's more than four miles long, the beach is only a quarter mile wide at most points. Park in the lots on either side of the Powder Point Bridge—you can park and walk across or not, as traffic and weather dictate—and head to the right along the beach. In high season you'll need to keep your leashed dog close by you as you both navigate through the beachgoers near the parking area; continue another 500 yards and you'll have an undisturbed walk of approximately 3.5 miles each way.

From the Southeast Expressway/State Route 3, take Exit 11 to Congress Street/State Route 14 east. Follow State Route 14 onto West Street. Continue straight into St. George Street, which becomes Powder Point Avenue. Park in either lot before or after Powder Point Bridge. Open from 8 A.M. to 8 P.M. (781) 934-1104.

• **North Hill Marsh Wildlife Sanctuary/Round Pond** 🐾🐾🐾 See **62** on page 251.

Welcome to a wilderness playground for the big dogs. That's right, this is roll-and-tumble country, with just enough mud to send your leashed canine home filthy and happy.

The dense woods that surround North Hill Marsh, Round Pond, nearby Island Creek Pond, and Pine Lake are loaded with great trails, adventure, and plenty of swamps and bogs. That's why the area is so popular with mountain bikers, hikers wearing brand-new hiking boots, and dogs who have just had a bath. But we know how to change that in a hurry.

From the Southeast Expressway/State Route 3, take Exit 11 to Congress Street/State Route 14 east. Take an immediate right on Lincoln Street. After Lincoln Street becomes Mayflower Street, stay on Mayflower Street past East Street. Parking for Round Pond is on the right; parking for North Hill Marsh is on the left. Open from sunrise to sunset. (781) 934-1104.

RESTAURANTS

French Memories Bakery: After a morning wading through cranberry bogs and playing in the surf on Duxbury Beach (see above), you and your canine companion have enough grime and sand on you to earn the names Grunge Dog and Sandy Pants. It's time for a touch of class. And that's where the French come in. This quiet, outdoor café is the perfect place to relax in an atmosphere of sunny gentility while enjoying gourmet coffee and French pastries. The bakery prepares some delicious sandwiches, too. 459 Washington Street; (781) 934-9020.

EASTON

PARKS, BEACHES, AND RECREATION AREAS

• **Borderland State Park** 🐾🐾🐾 See **63** on page 251.

With 1,772 acres of open fields, deep woods, and more ponds than you can shake a stick at, this spacious park will have your pooch feeling doggone happy.

The land was once part of the Ames family estate, and many remnants of that past life are visible today. You and your leashed dog can wander by the family mansion, the farmhouses, and the white horse fences that surround the fields and dirt roads. There are six ponds and plenty of trails around them. (Swimming is not permitted; this goes for man and beast.)

All of the park's trails are easy to follow, and there are plenty of directional signs. Maps are available at the Ames Mansion.

The park is located on the Easton/Sharon border near the Mansfield town line, hence the name. From State Route 24 in West Bridgewater, take Exit 17 to Belmont Street/State Route 123 and proceed into Easton. Turn right on Washington Street/State Route 138, then left on Main Street, which becomes Lincoln Street. At the intersection of Bay Road, the main (west) entrance lies across the road. For the east entrance, take a left on Bay Road and then a right on Rockland Street. Turn right on Massapoag Avenue and the entrance is on the right. Open from dawn to the posted closing time, between 4 P.M. and 6 P.M. (508) 238-6566.

• **Wheaton Farm Conservation Area** 🐾🐾🐾 🐕 See **64** on page 251.

Somebody sure was thinking straight when they set aside this land in southern Easton. Ward Pond, Fuller Hammond Pond, the surrounding woodlands, and the cranberry bogs are all protected by the Easton Conservation Commission. It's easy to see why. We still reminisce about our first visit on a sunny afternoon early one winter. A thin layer of ice was clinging to the pond's edge, leaving plenty of room on the water for a handful of ducks. The trails and many pine trees had a light dusting of white from the season's first snowfall. The sun had melted the snowflakes from the boulders and rocks in the woods. As the day wore on, the melting continued, and the water droplets in the sunshine made the entire forest sparkle like a crystal fairyland. We can't wait to see it in the spring!

From State Route 24 in West Bridgewater, take Exit 16 to West Center Street/State Route 106 and proceed to Foundry Street and Easton. Turn left on Bay Road. The entrance gate is on the right, but the sign will be on the left. Park at the end of the access road. Open from sunrise to sunset. (508) 230-3349.

DIVERSIONS

Calling all canines: Join the puparazzi at Borderland State Park (see above) to participate in the Walk for the Animals, one of the most fulfilling pet events of the year. Not only do you and your dog get to walk through one of the primo parks in the area and enjoy a day of canine entertainment, you'll also be doing good deeds for dogs not as lucky as yours: all donations go to local animal shelters. There are agility events and obedience contests, and doggy bags for you and your pooch. Sponsored by the Neponset Valley Humane Society, this special event is held in May at Borderland State Park. (781) 341-2675.

ESSEX

PARKS, BEACHES, AND RECREATION AREAS

• **James N. and Mary F. Stavros Reservation** 😺 😺 See **65** on page 250.
The Stavros family donated this 73-acre park to the Trustees of Reservations. A prime spot of real estate, the views will be the reason to come back here again and again. As you make your way up the easy, grassy grade to the top of White Hill, you'll pass groves of red cedar and devil's walking stick. The path is just over a quarter mile long, but you climb high enough to enjoy spectacular vistas of Hog Island, Crane's Beach, and the salt marshes of the Essex and Castle Neck Rivers. We love the panoramic view, but energetic dogs may need a bit more stimulation. Dogs must be on leash.

The park is off John Wise Avenue/State Route 133 on Island Road; park at the small pullout. James and Mary once owned the adjacent Cape Ann Golf Course as well. Open from dawn to dusk. (978) 921-1944.

• **Wilderness Conservation Area—See Manchester-By-The-Sea, Wilderness Conservation Area on page 315.**

RESTAURANTS

Woodman's of Essex: Enjoy a feast of fried clams and lobster rolls while sitting at one of the 10 tables under the big tent out back. It's a beautiful setting for lunch or dinner because of the well-maintained lawn and the breathtaking views of the Essex River. There's also plenty of space to take an after-dinner stroll along the river with your dog. 125 Main Street/State Route 133; (978) 768-6451 or (800) 649-1773.

FESTIVALS

Christmas on the Corner: Although Inu is generally quite dignified, he just couldn't hold back. He saw Santa, hopped onto his lap, and pulled out a list about a mile long. We didn't get a close look at it, but the word "biscuit" appeared more times than once. While Inu and Santa reviewed the list, the rest of us watched the tree-lighting ceremony and even joined in some caroling. The street festival is held on the second Friday in December, along Main Street. (978) 283-1601.

FAIRHAVEN

PARKS, BEACHES, AND RECREATION AREAS

• **Phoenix Bike Trail** 😺 😺 See **66** on page 251.
This paved town bike path runs the length of Fairhaven, east to west, for 3.3 miles following an old railroad line. The popular path parallels South Street beginning at Main Street and ending at the Mattapoisett town line.

From U.S. Route 6, take Main Street south for a half mile. The path is on the left. Street parking is available. Open dawn to dusk. (508) 979-4085.

NATURE HIKES AND URBAN WALKS

Manjiro Trail: The Manjiro Trail tours the 19th-century historic buildings that were important in the life of Manjiro, an adopted son of an American whaling captain and the first Japanese citizen to live in America.

As a 14-year-old, Manjiro and the other members of a Japanese fishing party where shipwrecked and rescued by Captain Whitfield in 1841. While the other Japanese sailors where dropped off in Hawaii (Japan's ports were closed to foreigners at the time), Manjiro decided to stay on board and come to New Bedford, the captain's home port. Ten years later, he left to join the California gold rush and eventually returned to Japan where he had a role in opening up Japan's borders to the outside world.

The tour includes the captain's home and the town's school house and government buildings. Trail maps and brochures are available at the Fairhaven Visitor Center at 27 Center Street; (508) 979-4085.

PLACES TO STAY

The Huttleston Motel: This small no-frills motel allows well-behaved dogs on approval. Dogs cannot be left unattended. Rates range from $45 to $60; a $30 refundable deposit is required. 128 Huttleston Avenue, Fairhaven, MA 02719; (508) 997-7655.

FALL RIVER

PARKS, BEACHES, AND RECREATION AREAS

• **Fall River Heritage State Park** 😾 😾 🐾 See **67** on page 251.

This state park is better known as Battleship Cove and the home of the battleship USS *Massachusetts*. Since dogs are not permitted aboard the battleship, the destroyer *Kennedy*, the HMS *Bounty*, or the submarine *Lionfish*, the park's boardwalk is a good place from which to observe the impressive fleet. Views of the towering Braga Bridge, the Taunton River, and Mount Hope Bay are also on parade. The park is only 8.5 acres, so there aren't many grassy areas to romp through, but it's open and airy with some good water breezes.

Dogs need to be leashed in all state parks.

From Interstate 195, take exit 5 to State Routes 79 and 138 north for a tenth of a mile. Take the Davol Street exit, turn left at the light and then another left onto Davol Street. The park and parking are on the left. Open sunrise to sunset. (508) 675-5759.

• **Fall River State Forest—See Freetown, Fall River State Forest on pages 295–296**

FESTIVALS

Fall River Celebrates America: This annual, weekend-long, waterfront party features a parade of ships, fireworks, speed-boat races, concerts, and fairs—it's the highlight of the year for Fall River. It all takes place in August at Battleship

Cove and Fall River Heritage State Park. For more information and dates, call (508) 676-8226 or visit www.fallrivercelebrates.com.

FOXBOROUGH

PARKS, BEACHES, AND RECREATION AREAS

• F. Gilbert Hills State Forest 🐾🐾🐾🐾 See **68** on page 251.

This excellent 975-acre forest offers more than 10 miles of trails for your leashed dog to explore. You should discover your own favorite route, but for first-time visitors we recommend beginning at the beginning. And that happens to be the main entrance off Mill Street, where park headquarters is located. You can pick up a map, which will definitely come in handy, or study the detailed map at the trailhead to decide where to go.

Our pick is the Acorn Trail, a loop of about 2.5 miles. Just look for the blue sign with an acorn painted on it. Stick to this path and you'll avoid the mountain bike and bridle trails, although they do intersect at points. Dogs must be leashed, as in all state forests.

From Interstate 95, take Exit 7 to Commercial Street/State Route 140 north. Turn left on South Street, then right on Mill Street. The state forest and a parking area are on both sides of the road. Two smaller park access points are in Wrentham. The first is on State Route 1, just south of the state police headquarters. The other is on Thurston Street off State Route 1. The park is open from dawn to dusk; park headquarters and the parking area are open weekdays from 8 A.M. to 6 P.M. and weekends from 10 A.M. to 6 P.M. (508) 543-5850.

• Harold B. Clark Town Forest 🐾🐾🐾 See **69** on page 251.

Forests are not usually high on our list of doggy destinations, but this 300-acre forest is a wonderful exception. There is only one major trail, and it encircles Upper Dam Pond, built over a century ago to serve a mill that once operated here. The walk is easy yet scenic, and your leashed dog will love sniffing the woods along the pond before plunging into the cool, clean water.

Dogs must be on leash.

From State Route 1, take Main Street/State Route 140 heading south. Turn right on Lakeview Road and then right again on Forest Road. The forest and a parking area are located at the end of the cul-de-sac. A second access point is off Lakeview Road. Open from dawn to dusk. (508) 543-1251.

FRAMINGTON

PARKS, BEACHES, AND RECREATION AREAS

• Callahan State Park, South Section 🐾🐾🐾🐾 🐾 See **70** on page 250.

If your dog has never set paw in this beautiful state park, she's in for a major treat. Our dogs think these 423 acres are among the loveliest of the pooch-friendly parks in the Boston area. When you drive up to the parking area off Millwood Street, you'll be greeted by an expansive, scenic meadow. Spreading out across several acres, it is divided only by long trails that lead into the woods beyond.

Set off across the meadow and you'll soon reach two clean brooks that cut through the property. Just past the second brook, you'll encounter another meadow and, nestled there like a jewel, Eagle Pond, which looks more like an alpine pond than the typical New England swimming hole. The woods just beyond have a series of trails that are easy to follow.

As in all state parks, dogs are required to wear their leashes.

From Worcester Road/State Route 9, take Pleasant Street/State Route 30 west. Turn right on Belknap Road and then left on Millwood Street. The park and a parking area are on the left. Open from a half hour before sunrise to a half hour after sunset. (508) 653-9641.

•Farm Pond Park 🐾🐾 See **71** on page 250.

You always knew your dog was worthy of sainthood, and here she can walk on water—with the assistance of a land dam that splits Farm Pond, that is. This 43-acre park runs along the western edge of the pond, which is managed by the Metropolitan District Commission. A small wooded area is next to Dudley Road, but, when you and your leashed dog emerge from the trees, you can walk on a dry, flat, grassy area along the pond. She will probably love swimming here, and you'll love not having to haul her out of muddy water for a change.

From Waverley Street/State Route 135, take Fountain Street west. Head right on Dudley Road. The park and a parking area are on the right. Open from 8 A.M. to 8 P.M. (508) 620-4834.

PLACES TO STAY

Motel 6: All Motel 6s permit one small pooch per room. Rates for a double room are $56. 1668 Worcester Road, Framingham, MA 01701; (508) 620-0500.

Red Roof Inn: Dogs who weigh under 50 pounds are allowed to stay in this clean, fairly new motel with good-sized rooms. The Massachusetts Turnpike is far enough away that the traffic noise shouldn't disturb you. Rates are about $70 to $89. 650 Cochituate Road, Framingham, MA 01701; (508) 872-4499 or (800) THE-ROOF.

FREETOWN

PARKS, BEACHES, AND RECREATION AREAS

•Fall River State Forest 🐾🐾🐾🐾 See **72** on page 251.

Any park that is home to sled-dog races has got to be a good place for dog walking, and this state forest definitely qualifies. Fifty miles of footpaths and forest roads attract snowmobilers, mountain bikers, motorcyclers, horseback riders, cross-country skiers, hikers, hunters, and mushers (we don't think we left anyone out). It really is something to see these dogs working and having so much fun racing down the trail.

Good places to explore are Doctor's Mill Pond and The Ledge, an old quarry on the eastern end of the park. Another place of interest is Profile Rock. This 50-foot rocky outcropping gets it's name from the Wampanoags who

---

believe the face seen in the rock is that of Massasoit, a former great chief of the tribe. Note that the Wampanoag Nation considers Profile Rock sacred ground and that the tribe's Watuppa Reservation is within the park's 5,441 acres. Maps are available at the ranger station.

Dogs must be on leash. Note that hunting is permitted here from October through February and that dog sleds, bicycles, and horses have the right-of-way.

From U.S. Route 24, take Exit 9 to State Route 79 north for one mile. Turn right onto Slab Bridge Road for one mile. The park entrance is on the right. Open a half hour before sunrise to a half hour after sunset. (508) 644-5052.

GLOUCESTER

In the 1800s Gloucester stood as America's largest fishing port, and in the 1700s it was among the major Eastern hubs of the whaling industry. Even though its historic schooners are long gone, the town still retains the flavor of a rustic, weathered fishing village.

PARKS, BEACHES, AND RECREATION AREAS

• **Dogtown Commons** 🐾 🐾 🐾 🐾 🐕 ◀🐾 See **73** on page 250.

Could there really be such a place? The answer is yes. Well, at least there once was. In the early 1700s, Dogtown was primarily a farming community. However, after the American Revolution, the population declined sharply. Many local men did not return from the war, and those who did moved on to the coastal regions of Cape Ann. Left behind were the widows, the poor, and the abandoned family dogs. Eventually all the people left, and the area literally went to the dogs.

If you're just looking for a good place to hike, the 3,000 acres of forests, reservoirs, and marshes in Dogtown are perfect. The thick oak and pine woods are beautiful, especially in autumn. And, although the wild dogs are long gone, George insists he can summon their spirits out of the woods with one howl.

Dogs are not allowed to swim in the Goose Cove or Babson Reservoirs, but they can run free under voice command in the rest of Dogtown.

To get to the Dogtown Road parking area from State Route 128, take Exit 11 to State Route 127/Washington Street north. Turn right on Reynard Street and then left on Cherry Street. Turn right on Dogtown Road. (The street sign says "Historic Dogtown.") Park at the gate at the end of the pavement. Open from dawn to dusk. (978) 281-9720.

• **Good Harbor Beach** 🐾 🐾 🐾 🐕 See **74** on page 250.

Join the after-five dog crowd here. That's doggy happy hour on this beautiful beach. During summer—from Memorial Day through Labor Day—no dogs are allowed from 9 A.M. to 5 P.M.; after 5 P.M., however, Good Harbor should be called Great Harbor because your pooch can play here off leash. The wide-open area offers plenty of room to run, and our dogs just love to romp through the moist sand.

From State Route 128, take Exit 9 (the last exit) to the intersection of Bass Avenue and East Main Street. Turn left on Bass Avenue/State Route 127A, then left on Thatcher Road/State Route 127A. The beach and a parking lot are on the right. Open from dawn to dusk. (978) 281-9720.

• **Hardy Mountain Park** 🐾🐾🐾 🐕 See **75** on page 250.
If you've been searching high and higher for a decent place to take your Bernese mountain dog, then you should visit Hardy Mountain Park. The rocky terrain and dense woods of Hardy Mountain provide the perfect place for the lofty adventures that all dogs enjoy. And, as long as your canine companion is under voice control, he's allowed to enjoy it all off leash.

The park is tucked away in the western corner of Cape Ann along State Route 128. The park entrance feels like a secret passageway that opens up onto a room full of gold and silver—only here the treasure is a mountain of trails and woods. And to a dog's eyes that's worth far more than the loot.

Hardy Mountain lies on private land, and it's only due to the goodwill of the owners that hikers and dogs have access to the park. People are allowed to use a narrow brook trail to cross the property.

From State Route 128, take Exit 14 to Essex Avenue/State Route 133 west. Head to mile marker 38, next to the storage company. Leave your car at the small roadside pullout and walk into the park. Open from sunrise to sunset. (978) 281-9720.

• **Ravenswood Park** 🐾🐾🐾 See **76** on page 250.
Occupying 500 acres, this protected woodland makes a fine outing for hikers, both the two- and four-legged kind. As a Trustees of Reservations holding, it requires that dogs wear a leash. Still it's well worth a peek. It offers seven miles of trails, three miles of carriage roads, and an outstanding vista point on Ledge Hill overlooking the Atlantic Ocean. During the spring and summer, you and your dog will enjoy the well-maintained hiking trails and quiet forest shade; in the winter the carriage roads are perfect for cross-country skiing and snowshoeing.

From State Route 128, take Exit 14 to Essex Avenue/State Route 133 east. Turn right on Western Avenue/State Route 127 south. The park is on the right. Keep a close eye out for the park sign; it isn't well placed. Open from 8 A.M. to sunset. (978) 921-1944.

• **Wingaersheek Beach** 🐾🐾🐾🐾 🐕 See **77** on page 250.
Now this is a New England beach! This mile-long beach is absolutely beautiful, overlooking the Annisquam Lighthouse across the inlet. You get your choice of white sandy beaches nestled alongside grassy dunes, wooded hillsides surrounding the bay, or the open sea and large weathered rock formations splashed by the surf. You don't even have to worry about your leash after October; you'll have the place to yourselves. During the summer months, however, dogs are only allowed before 9 A.M. and after 5 P.M. and must be on leash.

From State Route 128, take Exit 13 to Concord Street north. Turn right on Atlantic Street. The beach and a parking lot are at the road's end. Open from dawn to dusk. (978) 281-9720.

NATURE HIKES AND URBAN WALKS

Gloucester Maritime Trails: Gloucester is the oldest working harbor in America and one of the world's major fishing ports. Its harbor is also a popular setting for local artists. The city has four self-guided, quarter- to half-mile walking tours that highlight the picturesque seaport. The trails focus on Stage Fort Park, Gloucester Harbor and the waterfront, Main Street and downtown, and the Rocky Neck artist's colony. All of the walks are short, close together, and marked by signs and a painted red line on the sidewalk. Free maps are available at the Gloucester Visitors Welcome Center in Stage Fort Park. (978) 283-1601 or (800) 321-0133.

RESTAURANTS

Boulevard Ocean View Restaurant: What a great place to take a break from dog walking and the usual New England cuisine. The American and Portuguese menu is not as bizarre as it sounds, and the small, umbrella-covered outdoor deck will allow you and your dog to enjoy the chow and the view. 25 Western Avenue; (978) 281-2949.

Harbor Point Ice Cream: Even though this treat shop doesn't have outdoor seating, it serves some good ice cream. And since Pavilion Beach is right across the street, you can pick up your favorite flavor and enjoy a pleasant harbor view from one of the beachside benches. 29 Western Avenue; (978) 283-1789.

PLACES TO STAY

Camp Annisquam: Located on the marshy fields of the North Shore wetlands, this campground is scenic but not deluxe. If you're looking for casual camping and a place to stay with your dog, this is a fine choice. It has a recreation room, a pool, fishing, and electrical hookups. If you don't want to sleep in your tent or RV, you could rent one of the rustic cabins. Camping rates are $16 a night, and cabins go for $425 per week. (We said they were rustic, not cheap.) It's along State Route 133, a mile past Exit 14. (978) 283-2992.

Cape Ann Motor Inn: Nestled on the edge of Long Beach on the border of Rockport and Gloucester, this clean, well-maintained inn can't be beat for location. Not only do the proprietors welcome dogs, they're proud to be the first motel on Cape Ann to do so. The 31 rooms are new and spacious, all with balconies overlooking the beach and ocean. There are no size restrictions, but a one-night's room deposit is required for your pet. Rates range from $68 to $148 (the honeymoon suite is more expensive). This is a great find for you and your pet. 33 Rockport Road, Gloucester, MA 01930; (978) 281-2900 or (800) 464-VIEW.

Ocean View Inn: Another great beachside getaway, this 5.5-acre resort boasts a manor house surrounded by balconied oceanfront rooms. There are 72 rooms in all. The original manor has an elegant restaurant and quaint rooms, some with fireplaces; the bungalows are less showy but offer more room. There are two pools and a somewhat rocky beach across the road from the inn. The proprietors try to welcome all dogs, but they suggest you call first, as they decide on a dog-to-dog basis. Pets may not be welcome in the manor house. Rates range from $69 to $180. 171 Atlantic Road, Gloucester, MA 01930; (978) 283-6200 or (800) 315-7557; www.oceanviewinnandresort.com.

Manor Inn: This little motel and its adjoining Victorian guest manor overlook the Annisquam River. It's within walking distance of amenities, but you'll have to drive into town. Dogs are welcome, but only in the motel. Rates range from $49 to $95. There is a $5-per-night fee for Fido. 141 Essex Avenue, Gloucester, MA 01930; (978) 283-0614.

FESTIVALS

Gloucester Waterfront Festival: An annual arts-and-crafts event, this festival shows off many of Gloucester's fine artisans. Although dogs aren't the focus, it's still a terrific outing in town. The festival is held the third weekend in August. (978) 283-1601.

DIVERSIONS

Be a Cape crusader: Pack some doggy Dramamine and take your pet on the high seas to Cape Cod. This boat trip leaves Gloucester for a 2.5-hour cruise across Massachusetts Bay, and dogs are allowed at the captain's discretion. We've never had a problem hopping aboard, so, if your dog is well behaved, you should be fine. You'll have four hours to explore Provincetown before the return trip departs back to Cape Ann. The round-trip excursion costs $45 for each adult; dogs travel for free. Call the Gloucester to Provincetown Boat Express for details. (800) 877-5110.

HAMILTON

PARKS, BEACHES, AND RECREATION AREAS

• **Appleton Farms Grass Rides** 🐾 🐾 🐾 ◄● See **78** on page 250.
How many times have you driven past a private farm with rolling hills and hay bales and had to tell your excited pooch that he couldn't get out and run? Probably so many times that you're still in therapy to get rid of the guilt. Another way to feel better is to visit the Trustees of Reservations' 228-acre Appleton Farms Grass Rides. (Yes, the name's confusing. A "ride" is a path made for horseback riding through the woods. Today, the paths are open to people and dogs, but not to horses because of the delicate nature of the soil.)

First tilled by Thomas Appleton in 1638, Appleton Farms just may be the oldest working farm in the United States. Be sure to stay on the trail as you pass right through the middle of corn and wild grass fields. The four-mile route leads from the farm into glorious woodlands, which are crisscrossed with a maze of old grass-covered carriage paths.

All of the trails eventually lead to the circular clearing in the park's center, known as Roundpoint. Here you'll discover a granite pinnacle that was salvaged from Gore Hall before the former Harvard College Library was torn down. The school bestowed the monument on Francis Appleton, who once served as the library's chairman.

Dogs must be on leash here.

You can find Appleton in northern Hamilton. From State Route 1A in Wenham, take Arbor Street north for 3.5 miles. Arbor Street becomes Highland Street in Hamilton. Turn right on Cutler Street. A parking lot is on the immediate right. The trailhead is across Cutler Street on the right. Open from dawn to dusk. (978) 921-1944.

RESTAURANTS

The Junction: Have you noticed that we have a nose for ice cream? Well, we've got another hot spot for Spot (and you). This little roadside creamery has plenty of parking and benches lining the surrounding woods, offering a great setting to sit awhile and enjoy a cone after a day's outing. The trees provide plenty of shade for weary human travelers and doggy explorers alike. 600 Essex Street; (978) 468-2163.

HANOVER

PARKS, BEACHES, AND RECREATION AREAS

• Indian Head River Greenway 🐾 🐾 🐾 See **79** on page 251.

The Wampanoag tribe once inhabited this land, and one of its riverside trails still remains for you to explore. It's a pretty two- to three-mile hike covering about 20 acres, and you can walk along either side of river. Our dogs like to wade in the shallow areas along the trail as we take the more boring land route. Do, however, watch out for the shallow rapids as the water speeds up around the river's boulders.

In the Luddams Ford section, you can find two open meadows for picnicking and playing; shady trees for meditating or napping beneath; a clean stream for swimming, fishing, or fetching; and plenty of parking off Water Street. Luddams Ford is also the entrance to the Wampanoag Passage hiking trail, so after some ball throwing and a picnic lunch, head upstream for a stroll.

From State Route 3, take Exit 13 to Washington Street/State Route 53 south. Washington Street eventually becomes Columbia Avenue/State Route 53. Turn right on Broadway. Turn left on Elm Street. The park entrance and a parking lot are on the right, just before the bridge over the Indian Head River. Open from dawn to dusk. Hanover Conservation Commission, (781) 826-8505; Wildlands Trust of Southeastern Massachusetts, (781) 934-9018.

HAVERHILL

PARKS, BEACHES, AND RECREATION AREAS

• Meadow Brook Conservation Area 🐾 🐾 🐾 See **80** on page 250.

We love this place in any season. It has enough trails to keep you and your leashed dog busy visit after visit. The forest's 248 acres surround Millvale Reservoir; although you can't swim in this glorious pond, you can take a dip in East Meadow Brook, which runs into the reservoir.

There are two main parking areas. The lot on Millvale Road, on the southwestern side of the dam, provides the most varied trails into the forest's interior. Here you can wander the main trail along the reservoir or explore the many esker trails and peninsulas that lead out over the water. The forest is dense and quiet, creating a beautifully hushed atmosphere for your walk.

If swimming is a priority, we suggest you park on the other side of the water, at the end of Thompson Road. The trail here leads by East Meadow Brook, where your dog can dip his paws. The brook slows down at a small dam here before running into the northeastern end of the reservoir. You can pick up an ever-valuable map at the town hall.

From Interstate 495, take Exit 52 to Amesbury Road/State Route 110 west. Turn left on Kenoza Street. Turn left on Centre Street and then left again on Middle Road. The park begins at the intersection of Middle and Millvale Roads. Parking is available on both roads. Open from a half hour before sunrise to a half hour after sunset. (978) 374-2334.

•**Winnekenni Park** 🐾 🐾 🐾 🐾 See **81** on page 251.

> *Lake of the Pickerel! Let no more*
> *The echoes answer back "Great Pond,"*
> *But sweet Kenoza, from thy shore*
> *And watching hill beyond.*

In 1859, John Greenleaf Whittier wrote those words on the occasion of the renaming of Great Pond. Apparently there were so many Great Ponds in Massachusetts that the towns were going to have to assign them numbers. This one was dubbed Kenoza, which means "Lake of the Pickerel" in one Native American language. One of the most beautiful areas around, this park circles the lake in a picturesque setting. A simple trail system leads around Kenoza, but you can't swim in the public's water supply, so you might want to hike the higher trail to Lake Saltonstall.

To reach Lake Saltonstall, drive past the main entrance (and the lakeside trail system) to the top of Castle Road. The large stone castle, built in 1875, served as the former summer residence of Dr. James Nichols, a local physician and fertilizer experimenter at a nearby local farm called Winnekenni. Park at the picnic area here and follow the path that leads behind the castle and away from Kenoza Lake. The short hike to the clear lake takes about 20 minutes, and you'll be rewarded by a pleasant swim at various points along the shore. Dogs and nonresidents aren't permitted at the public beach on the lake's west end.

From Interstate 495, take Exit 52 to Amesbury Road/State Route 110 west into Kenoza Street and then into Kenoza Avenue. The park and parking are on the right. Open from 8 A.M. to 8 P.M. (978) 521-1686.

NATURE HIKES AND URBAN WALKS

The Buttonwoods Trail, Hannah Dustin Trail, and Washington Street Historic District Trail are part of the Merrimack River Trail. For more information on the trail and on the Merrimack River Watershed Council which manages it, see below.

Buttonwoods Trail: Two and a half miles long, this trail in the eastern part of town follows the north shore of the Merrimack River. It runs from the Washington Street Historic District Trail in downtown Haverhill to Riverside Park near the Groveland border. The river route follows Riverside Avenue. Among the historic sites along the way is First Landing Park, where colonists first arrived in Haverhill.

Parking is available at Riverside Park and in downtown Haverhill. For more information, call the Haverhill Trails Office, (978) 374-2334, or the Merrimack River Watershed Council, (978) 681-5777.

Hannah Dustin Trail: This 2.25-mile trail follows the northern shoreline of the Merrimack River from the Methuen town line to the Haverhill historic district. The route runs through a tract of thin woods that slopes down to the river's edge. Along the way you get spectacular views over the broad, majestic river and a number of benches to rest your weary bones.

The trail was named for Hannah Dustin, who was abducted by Native Americans in 1698. She was held upriver in what is now Concord, New Hampshire, before escaping and finding her way back to Haverhill by canoe. The monument along the trail marks the spot where she supposedly landed on her return.

The main parking areas are off Merrimack Street/State Route 110, Western Avenue, and Bank Road. For more information, call the Haverhill Trails Office, (978) 374-2334, or the Merrimack River Watershed Council, (978) 681-5777.

Washington Street Historic District Trail: A two-mile trek, it ventures along city streets and sidewalks through the heart of historic Haverhill on Merrimack Street from Julian Street to the Basiliere Bridge. In the late 1800s, Haverhill was a booming town that thrived with the flourishing shoe industry. Many downtown buildings once operated as shoe factories; they have since been converted to shops and restaurants.

The trail connects Haverhill's two river paths, the Buttonwoods Trail in the east and the Hannah Dustin Trail in the west. Plenty of parking is available downtown. For more information, call the Haverhill Trails Office, (978) 374-2334, or the Merrimack River Watershed Council, (978) 681-5777.

RESTAURANTS

Bagel Shop: With yogurt, muffins, 10 flavors of coffee, gourmet sandwiches, salads, and practically anything else you can think of ordering, this café is much more than a bagel shop. There are several umbrella-shaded tables outside on a grassy area, so your dog is welcome to sit by your side. It's just minutes away from North Andover's Weir Hill Reservation (see pages 328–329) if you want to pack a picnic. 1181 Boston Road/State Route 125; (978) 372-7600.

HINGHAM

PARKS, BEACHES, AND RECREATION AREAS

• Bare-Cove Park 🐾 🐾 🐾 See 82 on page 252.

We started bringing our dogs here because we hoped to instill in them a sense of strict military discipline. Since a military base once occupied Bare-Cove, we thought the place might have an inspirational effect on them. Maybe if we visited often enough, we reasoned, our dogs would begin to obey our every command and march beside us in unison.

Well, as you probably guessed, we're not there yet. But the Rescue Dogs of New England train here, so we aren't the only ones who thought this would make a good disciplinary setting.

During most evenings and weekends, this park is a popular place for local dogs and their owners to meet and mingle. If you like socializing, you probably won't venture much farther than the front entrance. But if you want a lovely walk, Bare-Cove has three miles of hiking trails and paved roads along the Weymouth Back River. Your leashed dog will love roaming through the surrounding woods and fields, and, if you're traveling with a water dog, there are numerous access points that lead into the drink.

From the Southeast Expressway/Interstate 93/State Routes 1 and 3 in Quincy, take Exit 12 to State Route 3A south. Continue on State Route 3A through Weymouth into Hingham. Take the first right after the Hingham town line on Beal Street. Travel a quarter mile. The parking lot is on the right. Open from dawn to dusk. (781) 741-1464.

•Foundry Pond Conservation Area 🐾 🐾 🐾 See 83 on page 252.

Quaint, lovely Foundry Pond is the centerpiece of this 32-acre leash-free park on the Weir River. Thick woods blanket the pond banks, and scattered lily pads and majestic swans add just the right amount of color. It's a popular place for strolling along the water's edge or even putting in a canoe.

In spring when many birds and animals are raising their young, a walk in the woods at Foundry Pond can bring another kind of adventure altogether. Most wildlife avoid confrontations by fleeing at the sound of an approaching human or canine. When their young are not yet ready to travel, however, they're prepared to take on all comers, including you and your dog, as we discovered here.

From the intersection of Chief Justice Cushing Highway/State Route 3A and East Street/State Route 228, take Chief Justice Cushing Highway east to Kilby Street. Turn right on Foundry Pond Lane, just past Rockfall Road. Open from a half hour before sunrise to a half hour after sunset. (781) 741-1464.

•Wompatuck State Park 🐾 🐾 🐾 🐾 See 84 on page 252.

With 3,500 acres and miles of trails, this state park offers plenty of uncharted territory for you and your leashed dog to explore. Get a map at the park's visitor center-you'll need it to find your way through the seemingly endless woodlands of maple, oak, and pine.

Don't let the pavement and concrete here scare you off. The roads and odd-shaped buildings are only remnants of the park's past as a military base. What these structures were once used for is anyone's guess. It seems almost criminal to have ever allowed such ugly buildings to be built in the first place. Fortunately, Mother Nature is reclaiming the area as her own, just as squirrels and chipmunks are claiming the buildings as their stomping grounds.

Wompatuck has all the accoutrements and rules you'd expect at a state park: rest rooms, camping, interpretive programs, and, yes, a pesky leash requirement. The campground offers 400 tent and trailer sites in a wonderful wooded area. You can book a campsite up to six months in advance by calling the Massachusetts State Camping Reservation Center at (877) 422-6762. A minimum stay of two nights is required; you must reserve at least three nights on holiday weekends. It's open for camping from April 15 to October 15. Showers, electrical hookups, and dump stations are available. Dogs must be on leash when outside of your tent or trailer and cannot be left unattended. Campsites are $7 per night.

The Wompatuck State Park borders extend into Norwell, Cohasset, and Scituate, but Hingham provides the main access. The park's eastern portion, in Cohasset, borders Whitney and Thayer Woods (see page 283) and makes a great place for extended hikes.

From State Route 3 in Rockland, take Exit 14 to State Route 228 north/Main Street and Hingham. Turn right on Free Street. Take a left on Lazell Street. Turn right on Union Street. Parking is available throughout the park. The visitor center is a quarter mile into the park on the right. Open from dawn to dusk. (781) 749-7160.

•World's End Reservation 🐾 🐾 🐾 🐾 ◀● See **85** on page 252.
Every time we visit here, we find ourselves wishing that the world were actually flat. That way there would be more ends of the world to visit—and they would all be equally impressive. Two islands connected by a sandbar, 250-acre World's End overlooks Hingham Harbor, Weir River, and Boston Harbor Islands. The grass-covered hills on this Trustees of Reservations property are connected by four miles of well-laid-out, shaded carriage roads and three miles of trails. You and your dog can hike through a variety of terrain, including meadows, woods, and seashore.

World's End is a major stop for migratory birds, such as plovers, ducks, herons, egrets, and finches. It's also an extremely popular park with people, so arrive early to get one of the few parking spaces. Dogs, alas, must be on leash here. A bit of history and a cautionary word: World's End has always had a leash law, but for a long time the rule was not strictly enforced. This fact and the area's beauty attracted many dog walkers. Most were responsible; others were not, which caused an end to leash-free Nirvana at the World's End. There are some people who would like to ban dogs entirely from the park. That hasn't happened yet, but you know how easily it could. Please—pick up after your dog!

The day-use fee is $4. From the Southeast Expressway/Interstate 93/State Routes 1 and 3, in Dorchester, take Exit 12 to State Route 3A south. Continue on State Route 3A through Quincy and Weymouth into Hingham. At the Hingham Harbor traffic circle, leave State Route 3A via Summer Street. Turn left on Martin's Lane. Parking is at the road's end. Open from 8 A.M. to 8 P.M. in summer, and 8 A.M. to 5 P.M. in winter. (781) 749-8956.

PLACES TO STAY
Wompatuck State Park camping: See pages 303–304.

DIVERSIONS
Standish Humane Society Annual Benefit Walk: Take a walk on the Wompatuck side. Or in Wompatuck State Park, that is. Every September the Standish Humane Society sponsors a three-mile Benefit Walk for Animals which raises money for local spay and neuter programs. Featuring a festive day of prizes, exhibits, canine contests, and dog demonstrations, you and every other dog lover will find this walk in the woods one you won't want to miss. Registration is from 10 A.M. to 2 P.M. For details, call (781) 834-4663.

HOPKINTON

PARKS, BEACHES, AND RECREATION AREAS

• Hopkinton State Park 🐾🐾🐾 See 86 on page 250.

The average dog could get a good workout on the trails in this 1,450-acre park. But for some dogs—at least those who have an inexhaustible supply of energy—these trails are not enough. If that's the case with your canine, you'll want to head here on Patriot's Day for the annual Boston Marathon, which covers 26.2 miles from Hopkinton to Boston. (Actually, in order to qualify you must run on two legs and wear elasticized shorts, so maybe this isn't such a good idea.)

For normal dogs, the paths within the confines of the park and around Hopkinton Reservoir are just fine. Pick up a trail map at the main entrance or at park headquarters.

From Interstate 495, take Exit 21 to West Main Street heading east. Turn left on Cedar Street/State Route 85 north. The southern part of the park, park headquarters, and parking are on the left. Open from 8 A.M. to 9 P.M., unless otherwise posted. (508) 435-4303.

RESTAURANTS

Golden Spoon: Lumberjacks, truckers, railroad workers, and dog walkers have one thing in common: they all need a big, hearty breakfast before they can get out and do the job. Sit at the picnic table outside with your pal Joe and enjoy a cup of joe, flapjacks, and taters. There's no need to ask for extra butter. Don't forget your flannel shirt. 85 West Main Street; (508) 435-6922.

HULL

PARKS, BEACHES, AND RECREATION AREAS

• Nantasket Beach 🐾🐾🐾 See 87 on page 252.

Our dogs just love the beach; Nantasket is high on their list of favorites, and with good reason. During low tide the grainy beach is wide and easy to run or walk. And it's 3.5 miles long, which means we won't be going back to the car for at least an hour! Plenty of parking is available off Nantasket Avenue. Leashed dogs are welcome on the beach from October 1 through April 30.

From Chief Justice Cushing Highway/State Route 3A in Hingham, take East Street/State Route 228 east. Turn left on Hull Street/State Route 228 into Nantasket Avenue/State Route 228 and Hull. The beach and a parking lot are located on the right. Open from dawn to dusk. (781) 727-8856.

RESTAURANTS

Weinberg's Bakery: Coffee, bagels, pastries, the morning paper, and glorious sunshine. After a good workout on the beach, we like to head to Weinberg's for a break. Even when the weather is cooler, the small sidewalk tables really soak up the morning sun. 519 Nantasket Avenue; (781) 925-9879.

IPSWICH

PARKS, BEACHES, AND RECREATION AREAS

• **Greenwood Farms** 🐾🐾🐾 See **88** on page 250.

So you and your canine companion have been getting out there, visiting quite a few parks with all sorts of terrain, everything from beach to woods. Maybe you've even run with the big dogs at some of the city parks. You're feeling pretty confident. Yup, you and your pup can handle just about any trail that comes down the pike.

Well, good for you. But *The Dog Lover's Companion to New England* has a little challenge for you. Greenwood Farms just might have enough of a twist to give the two of you a little trail test.

The 120-acre park, managed by the Trustees of Reservations, starts out nice and easy. Open fields of cut grass lead you from the parking lot to the historic homes of the Paine family, who established the estate in the 1600s, and the Dodge family, who restored and donated the property. It's a quick walk up the gradual slope. From here you'll enjoy fine views of the tidal basin of the Ipswich River.

Just beyond the houses, however, you leave the high ground of the estate and enter the salt marshes to the left. And this is where the challenge begins.

How many of the marsh islands can your elite expedition team visit? You'll find five tiny islands on the estate, each a solid plot of land with trees and shrubs. Many marsh birds, such as blue herons and northern harriers, use them for feeding areas. Separating the islands are soft, grassy wetlands and Greenwood Creek. The marshy trail runs from island to island (reaching at least three of them). It gives you bridges to cross the two branches of the creek, but during high tide you'll have to navigate the flooded banks all by yourselves.

We made it to three of the islands, risking life and limb (not to mention a big laundry bill) in the process. It was worth it, though, just for the chance to experience the scenic beauty of the Ipswich River. We offer two helpful tips: Wear boots, and check your charts for low tide. It's a rough-and-ready trip. But if you're both rough and ready yourselves, we say, "Go for it!"

From State Route 1A and State Route 133 in central Ipswich, take County Road north. Turn right on East Street and then turn left on Jeffrey Neck Road. Go half a mile to the park on the right. Look for a small gravel parking lot; the Trustees of Reservations sign is hard to see. Open from dawn to dusk. (978) 921-1944.

• **Richard T. Crane Jr. Memorial Reservation** 🐾🐾🐾 🐾 See **89** on page 250.

In 1916 Richard Crane, a Chicago millionaire, bought this 800-acre parcel of Atlantic coast and built a 17th century–style, 59-room mansion known as the Great House. Now a historical landmark—*The Witches of Eastwick* was filmed here—the land has been managed by the Trustees of Reservations since Crane's death. Aside from being one of Massachusetts's most beautiful beaches, the wetland provides a home to thousands of coastal birds and animals. Because of the delicacy of the wetland preserve, you're not allowed to tramp through the protected areas. From October to May, however, leashed dogs are welcome on one of New England's most popular and well-known shore points, Crane Beach, a four-mile-long barrier beach that acts as a kind of seawall to the Essex and Ipswich River estuaries.

From State Route 128 in Beverly, take Exit 20N to State Route 1A north and the Ipswich town center. Turn right on Argilla Road. The beach gate is at the road's end. There is a $2.50 parking fee. Open from dawn to dusk. (978) 356-4351.

RESTAURANTS

Bruni's: We mention this gourmet grocery store because it has easy, self-serve sandwiches, bakery goods, soups, salad bar, and deli items. The food's delicious, outdoor seating is available, and there's a yogurt shop right next door just in case you aren't full enough after feasting on Bruni's many delicacies. Fast, easy, and dog friendly, this is our kind of place. Pick up something on your way in or out of town. 24 Essex Road; (978) 356-4877.

White Cap Restaurant: What else is there to eat in Ipswich besides Ipswich clams? This is the place to get them. Eat your clams and other baked, broiled, or fried seafood on the outdoor picnic tables. There's a big backyard for your faithful friend. Water is on the house (and under the deck). 141 High Street/State Route 133; (978) 356-5276.

White Farms Ice Cream Sandwich Shop: This is the place, or at least George thinks so. Doggy dishes of soft vanilla with a big biscuit are $.25 or free with another purchase. So of course we had to get something. JoAnna went with the popular Oinker Sandwich—ham, three kinds of cheese, tomatoes, onions, and a special mustard sauce. And then on to the ice cream! Outdoor seating is available. 1326 High Street; (978) 356-2633.

PLACES TO STAY

Whittier Motel: Just outside of town, this 20-room motel is still close to walking trails and a small park across the street. It has a coffee shop that serves breakfast, and the rooms are clean, if a bit dated. But they allow you to bring your dog, so it's okay in our book, and the price is right. Rates range from $62 to $89; it's $10 extra per night for your dog. There's no size restriction, but the management requests that you not leave your dog unattended in the room. 98 County Road/State Route 1A, Ipswich, MA 01938; (978) 356-5205.

DIVERSIONS

Pick an apple a day: In summer and fall try apple picking on one of the most scenic farms on the North Shore. Goodale Orchards, just up the road from Crane Beach, is the perfect place to pluck a basket of apples. If you want your dog to help, put a doggy knapsack on her and fill the pouch along with your own. Call for seasonal conditions. 123 Argilla Road; (978) 356-5366.

Take a three-hour tour, a three-hour tour: There's no telling when you'll want to return from your canoeing adventure on the Ipswich River. Its beauty and serenity will captivate you and your dog all day long. Renting a canoe is a perfect way to explore this quiet, winding river. Make sure your pooch is of the calm variety, or you'll play tippy-canoe all day. A canoe costs $28 per day; reservations are recommended for weekends. Visit Foote Brothers Canoe Rentals at Willowdale Dam, 230 Topsfield Road, or call (978) 356-9771.

KINGSTON

PARKS, BEACHES, AND RECREATION AREAS

• **Bay Farm Field** 🐾🐾🐾 See **90** on page 251.

Perched on quiet Kingston Bay, this beautiful spot is a great place for a picnic. If you park in the small lot on Loring Street and head across the open field on the Orange Loop, you'll reach a grove of oak trees and rocks overlooking the calm water. What could be better on a warm spring or summer day? The trail is only three-quarters of a mile long, so you won't work up a sweat or hunger pangs, but, if you bring your appetite with you, along with a picnic basket, it should provide a fun diversion on a lazy afternoon.

Trails are well marked and easily accessed; a map at the parking area will give you an overview. Of the routes, only the Blue Loop was somewhat disappointing. It meandered aimlessly through some shrubs and then back to the main trail. Even so, this short amble didn't elicit any complaints from our dogs. After lunch they just wanted to go back to roam until dinnertime.

From State Route 3, take Exit 10 to State Route 3A into Duxbury. Turn right on Parks Street. Turn left on Loring Street. The parking area is on the left by the open field. Open from sunrise to sunset. (781) 585-0537.

RESTAURANTS

Persy's Place: This place has claimed bragging rights as the best breakfast joint on the South Shore, and you won't get any arguments from us. Dogs are allowed on the outdoor patio on request (and as long as other patrons don't complain), or you can order your food to go and eat it on the bench outside. The menu is extensive and so are the weekend crowds. Don't be surprised if you have to wait for a table. One note: It's only open for breakfast and lunch, so don't work up an appetite on the trail and then show up at 4 P.M. for an early dinner, as we once did. If you do, you'll be out of luck. On State Route 3A, near Exit 9 by the Independence Mall; (781) 585-5464.

PLACES TO STAY

Inn at Plymouth Bay: Previously a Howard Johnson, this inn has been attractively updated by the new management. It's right next to State Route 3, so it can get a little noisy on the road side of the motel, but it also provides easy access to most of the South Shore towns. The rooms are clean and reasonably priced at $69 to $114. The management asks that you do not leave your dog unattended in the room. Let the front desk clerk know on check-in that you have a dog with you. 149 Main Street, Kingston, MA 02364; (781) 585-3831 or (800) 941-0075.

LAWRENCE

PARKS, BEACHES, AND RECREATION AREAS

• **Lawrence Heritage State Park** 🐾🐾 See **91** on page 250.

This park commemorates Lawrence's part in the Industrial Revolution. The Merrimack River and the canals here are lined with mills that once made this city the textile capital of the world. It also commemorates the unionist's Bread and Roses Strike of 1912, paving the way for worker's rights.

Dogs are not permitted in any of the buildings, but a walk along the canal, the river, and the numerous mills will give you an idea of what it's all about.

Dogs must be leashed in all state parks.

From Interstate 495, take exit 45 to Marston Street. Turn left onto Canal Street for three blocks then right onto Jackson Street. The visitors center is on the right. The center is open 9 A.M. to 4 P.M. and the canal paths are open 24 hours a day. (978) 794-1655.

• Lawrence Riverfront State Park 🐾🐾 See 92 on page 250.
This small state park (47 acres) is on the southern shoreline of the Merrimack River. Although mostly picnic areas, tennis and basketball courts, playgrounds, and a boat launch, there are some woods, a short paved path, and access to the Merrimack.

Dogs must be leashed in all state parks.

From Interstate 495, take exit 41 to State Route 28 north for two miles. Turn left onto Shattuck Street, which becomes Rowe Street which then becomes Wolcott Avenue for a total of four blocks. The park is on the right. Open dawn to dusk. (978) 794-1655.

LEXINGTON

What school kid hasn't heard of Lexington, the Minutemen, and the events that occurred here on April 19, 1775? Well, this is the place to see where the history of our country began. Remarkably well preserved from the days of the Revolutionary War, this area feels like a 200-year-old time capsule. White colonial buildings with black-and-green shutters dot the streets, and you and your dog will love sniffing out all of the notable spots in this beautiful town.

Lexington has a "flexible" leash law, meaning that in city parks you may forgo the leash if your dog is truly under voice control.

PARKS, BEACHES, AND RECREATION AREAS

• Minuteman National Historical Park, Battle Road Section 🐾🐾 🦴 See 93 on page 250.
Ever hear of the "shot heard 'round the world"? Well, this entire park is dedicated to that shot and the events of April 19, 1775. On that day the British took Battle Road through Lexington and Lincoln to reach the patriots' arms supply in Concord, and the Minutemen bravely defeated them here upon their return. You and your leashed dog are welcome to walk the quarter-mile-long, restored portion of Battle Road. As you do, try to imagine that you're British redcoats marching on the road, as the local militia waits in ambush behind every stone wall and tree you pass.

Other historic trails are at Fiske Hill and Hartwell Farm. Both offer roughly one-mile-long hikes in a preserved country setting. Dogs are not allowed in the park's visitor center.

From State Route 128, take Exit 30B to Marrett Street/State Route 2A west. Follow the signs to the national park and a parking area. Open from 9 A.M. to 5 P.M. (978) 369-6993.

• **Whipple Hill Conservation Area** 🐾🐾 See **94** on page 252.

At an elevation of 374 feet, Whipple Hill earns its place as Lexington's highest point. Although it falls short of being the tallest peak in the Commonwealth, the views are still breathtaking. This park encompasses the hill, along with more than 150 acres in Lexington's southeastern corner.

From State Route 2, take Exit 56 to Watertown Street north/State Routes 4 and 225. Turn right on Maple Street/State Route 2A and head straight onto Winchester Drive at the Lowell Street intersection. A parking lot is on the right, just past Russell Drive. Open from dawn to dusk. (781) 862-0500.

• **Willard's Woods Conservation Area** 🐾🐾🐾 🐕 🦴 See **95** on page 252.

In Willard's Woods's 100 acres, you'll find a picturesque setting of pine forests, open meadows, wetlands, and a few orchards that were once part of a farm. It's also a popular place for dog walking. You and your leash-free dog will love hiking through the woods on cushioned paths of pine needles or through the fields along trails lined with old stone walls.

The Lexington Conservation Commission protects and maintains these woods. As you explore the area, you will see signs that the forest is reclaiming pastures that once were cleared for farming. Young trees and thickets now blur the line between wild woods and cultivated fields. The flexible leash law applies here, as in the rest of Lexington, so your dog may go off leash if she obeys your commands.

From State Route 128, take Exit 32 to Middlesex Turnpike south, which becomes Lowell Street. Turn right on Adams Street and then right again on North Street. Turn left on Willard's Woods Road and continue a quarter mile to the park. A parking lot is at the end of the dirt road. Open from dawn to dusk. (781) 862-0500.

RESTAURANTS

A. E. Sops Bagels: It does sell the old standbys: cinnamon raisin and sesame seed. For a bit of flare, try the mocha chip and Dutch apple bagels. The outside seating consists of two small tables tucked away from the main sidewalk. It's a decent spot for a cup of joe and a spell of people watching. 1666 Massachusetts Avenue; (781) 674-2990.

Bertucci's: May we have more rolls, please? Bertucci's Italian menu is a hit all over New England, but the brick-oven rolls are what bring us back. That and the sidewalk seating area in the heart of Lexington. With George and Inu under the table, those rolls go even faster. 1777 Massachusetts Avenue; (781) 860-9000.

Wilson's Farm: Fall doesn't officially start until you make a trip to Wilson's and have your caramel nut candy apple. Savor it while overlooking the farm from one of the available benches. Your dog will be sitting happily right at your feet. (It's amazing how well she'll behave here.) Wilson's isn't a restaurant, but a food shop selling plenty of fruits and vegetables, jams and preserves, pies and breads, and flowers and seasonal decorations. 10 Pleasant Street, between State Routes 4 and 225; (781) 862-3900.

PLACES TO STAY

Battle Green Motor Inn: Don't let the name fool you. This quaint little spot is really more like a bed-and-breakfast than a motor inn, even though you can park your car in a lot under the facilities. Set in the heart of historic Lexington, you'll enjoy the easy walking distance to the Lexington Visitor Center, Battle Green, and Minuteman Bike Trail. Small dogs are preferred, but management will consider larger dogs on request. Rates range from $65 to $95. 1720 Massachusetts Avenue, Lexington, MA 02173; (781) 862-6100.

LINCOLN

Lincoln's civic leaders are lax on leashes. If your dog is obedient enough to follow your voice commands at all times, he can shed the dreaded leash. Otherwise you must tether up when you go for walks in this town.

PARKS, BEACHES, AND RECREATION AREAS

• **Mount Misery Conservation Land** 🐾🐾🐾 🐕 See 🔟 on page 250.

Misery loves company, and you'll surely get it when you visit this park. Mount Misery is the most popular dog-walking spot in Lincoln. Fortunately, you'll only feel miserable trying to figure out why they gave this place such an inappropriate name. It's as scenic as nearby Walden Woods, but, unlike that bucolic haven, dogs are allowed here. Because of this, the trails tend to get crowded on sunny weekend afternoons, a growing concern to the Lincoln Conservation Commission and many hikers.

The Mount Misery area covers 227 acres of conservation land, consisting mostly of pine forests. Atop Mount Misery itself and from some of the higher ridges you can look down on the Sudbury River, and access a number of minor connecting trails to other conservation areas in Lincoln. Dogs must be under voice control at all times.

From State Route 2 in Concord, head south on Walden Street/State Route 126, which becomes Lincoln-Concord Road. Turn right on South Great Road/State Route 117. The park is on the right. There are three parking lots. The first is the main lot, where most of the trails start. The other two, located on the western border of the park along the Sudbury River, also have trailheads and access to the canoe launch. Open from sunrise to sunset. (781) 259-2612.

FESTIVALS

Art in the Park Festival: Set on 35 acres that were once part of the DeCordova family estate, the unusual DeCordova Museum celebrates contemporary Massachusetts artists. During its annual outdoor art show, which is held the first Sunday in June, you can stroll around the sculpture garden on the beautiful grassy lawn and check out the many booths selling crafts and international foods. Your well-behaved dog is welcome to join you at the festival, on what is typically a lovely day. Musicians, magicians, and interactive art stations are all part of the fun. The festivities last from 11 A.M. to 5 P.M. Entrance to the museum is usually free, but there is a small admission fee for the festival. 51 Sandy Pond Road; (781) 259-8355.

LOWELL

PARKS, BEACHES, AND RECREATION AREAS

• **Lowell-Dracut-Tyngsboro State Forest** 🐾🐾🐾 See **97** on page 250.
This state forest of 1,150 acres is a popular place for hiking and horseback riding. Six miles of hiking trails and endless forest roads wind through a diverse forest, wetlands, ponds, and the remains of granite quarries. The granite was used in some of the nearby canals and factories.

Dogs must be leashed in all state parks. Hunting is permitted in the state forest between October and February.

From State Route 113, take Old Ferry Road north for a quarter mile. Turn left onto Varnum Avenue for a half mile then right onto Trotting Park Road to the end and the park gate. Parking is available. Open 5 A.M. to 11 P.M. (978) 453-0592.

• **Lowell Heritage State Park** 🐾🐾 See **98** on page 250.
This state heritage park works in conjunction with the Lowell National Historical Park to preserve the accomplishments of the American Industrial Revolution in Lowell. The highlight of the park is the two-mile grassy stretch of park land along the Merrimack River near the Pawtucket Dam. With plenty of access points for everyone along the easy flowing water, it is a popular spot for swimming and boating. A bike path also runs the length of the park.

Dogs must be leashed in all state parks, and they are not permitted on the designated beach area.

The park is located on State Route 113 between Mammoth Road and Wood Street. Parking is available. Open 5 A.M. to 11 P.M. (978) 453-0592.

• **Lowell National Historical Park** 🐾🐾 See **99** on page 250.
This national park commemorates the American Industrial Revolution and the progress of workers in America. The park includes textile mills, worker housing, 5.6 miles of canals, and 19th-century commercial buildings along the Merrimack River.

Dogs are not permitted in any of the buildings or on the canal trolley tour, but the park does have two great walks that are sure to please you and your pooch. The first is a mile-long loop through the historic downtown area which includes the canals and many of the textile mills. The second walk is the mile-long paved path along the Merrimack River starting at the bridge near the Visitor Center. Maps are available at the Visitor Center.

Dogs must be leashed in all national parks.

The park is located in downtown Lowell at the corner of Market and Shattuck Streets. Street parking is available. The Visitor Center is open 9 A.M. to 5 P.M., and the canal paths and city streets are open 24 hours a day. (978) 970-5000.

DIVERSIONS

Fido Goes Folk: The Lowell Folk Festival is the largest free folk festival in the United States. With six outdoor stages of traditional music and dance, street parades, dance parties, ethnic foods, and craft demonstrations, it's a folksy good time for all. The three-day festival takes place annually the last weekend in July at the Lowell National Historical Park. For more information on performers and dates, call (978) 970-5032.

LYNN

PARKS, BEACHES, AND RECREATION AREAS

• **King's Beach/Lynn Beach** 🐾🐾 See **100** on page 252.

Two, two, two beaches in one! These connecting beaches make up the entire eastern oceanfront of Lynn. Together, with adjacent Long Beach and Nahant Beach, there are 2.5 miles of waterfront for you and your dog to enjoy. King's and Lynn Beaches, however, are rugged cliffs with a sharp drop into the sea leading to the flat, sandy beaches found on the Nahant peninsula. So, go for a dip, if it's not too cold, at the Nahant Beach and then dry your pup off with a walk along the cliffs at the Lynn section.

Dogs are required to be on leash in all Metropolitan District Commission parks.

From State Route 1A, take the Lynnway to Lynn Shore Drive. Street parking is available on Lynn Shore Drive. Hours are dawn to 11 P.M. in the summer and dawn to dusk in the winter. (781) 662-8370.

• **Lynn Woods Reservation** 🐾🐾🐾🐾 🐕 See **101** on page 252.

It's easy to find open spaces and woods when you're far from Boston, but there's something special about finding that great escape close to the city limits. Lynn Woods is a great example. Lynn ranks as the 10th most populated city in greater Boston, but right in its backyard is Lynn Woods, a spacious, 1,800-acre forest wonderland dotted with ponds. The reservation makes up about a quarter of Lynn and has been preserved for over 300 years.

There are two major access points to the reservation. To the east is the Great Woods Road entrance and in the south is the Penny Brook Road entrance. The dirt roads were long ago closed to vehicle traffic, but there is plenty of parking at both gates.

From Great Woods Road, the eastern arm of Walden Pond (no, not that other pond immortalized by Thoreau) is easily accessible, reaching almost to the parking lot. A half mile down the road is a picnic area along the water. Walden Pond and its tree-lined shore is a wonderfully serene setting for just about any activity. We've spent many an afternoon here picnicking, while the dogs swim in the sparkling lake.

For hiking, there are plenty of other forest routes and trails to follow. Branching off Great Woods Road, before the picnic area, is Burrill and Loop Roads. Both will lead you to buena vistas that not only look out over Lynn Woods, but Boston and New Hampshire as well. On Burrill Hill is Stone Tower, an abandoned observation tower. At 285 feet, Burrill Hill is the highest point in Lynn.

You can reach the Great Woods entrance from State Route 128 by taking exit 44 to Lynnfield Street (State Route 129). Travel for three miles and make a right onto Great Wood Road.

To get to the Penny Brook entrance from State Route 1, take the Walnut

Street, Lynn exit and go two miles. Make a right onto Penny Brook Road. The park hours are dawn to dusk. (781) 593-7773.

RESTAURANTS

Superior Roast Beef: Before heading into the Lynn Woods, pick up some last minute subs here. Try and guess which is their specialty. (Hint: it's a "superior" meat!) On the corner of Lynnfield Street (State Route 129) and Great Woods Road; (781) 599-3223.

PLACES TO STAY

Diamond District Bed-and-Breakfast Inn: Built in the 19th century, this tiny, charming bed-and-breakfast is located only one-half block off Lynn Beach and is within easy access to the heart of town. There are eight rooms, all different; rates vary due to season from $69 to $125. Dogs are welcome, but please let the innkeeper know you wish to bring your pal when making reservations. 742 Ocean Street, Lynn, MA 01902; (781) 599-5122 or (800) 666-3076.

MALDEN

PLACES TO STAY

New England Motor Court: What this 21-room motel lacks in charm, it makes up for in convenience. Rates range from $45 to $65. 551 Broadway, Malden, MA 02148; (781) 321-0505 or (800) 334-1043.

MANCHESTER-BY-THE-SEA

PARKS, BEACHES, AND RECREATION AREAS

• **Agassiz Rock** 🐾🐾🐾 See **102** on page 250.
Short and sweet describes the trail up Beaverdam Hill. It's short, because the 1.5-mile loop quickly lets you and your leashed canine pal escape into the wilderness. It's sweet, because the trail is covered with pine needles, which give off a fresh scent as you hike.

This 101-acre Trustees of Reservations area is named for Louis Agassiz, a Harvard professor who studied glacial movement here. Agassiz first noted that the two giant boulders on the hilltop here were placed there by the glaciers that once moved across New England. The boulders are glacial erratics, a designation that refers to the random way they've settled. Little Agassiz is easily climbable and has great views over the reservation. The second, Big Agassiz, lies on the back loop and rises 30 feet out of the marsh. Because of the surrounding swamp, it's not possible to climb it.

From State Route 128, take Exit 15 to School Street north for about a half mile. The parking area is on the right; it's little more than a pullout off the road. Open from sunrise to sunset. (978) 921-1944.

• **Singing Beach** 🐾🐾 🐾 See **103** on page 250.
As scenic spots go, they don't get any better than Singing Beach. No, this beach doesn't get its name from anything dramatic like sirens singing on the rock, luring sailors to their destruction. In fact, when we asked how it came to

be named Singing Beach, we were told that when the wind blows, the movement of the sands creates a kind of "song."

Set at the end of Beach Street through Manchester Center, this big, open, sandy beach overlooks the Northern Harbor Islands. It'll seem like a dream to you, but not necessarily to your dog. As with all the prime beaches on the North Shore, your dog can't visit from May 1 through October 31. After that, your canine pal must be on leash.

From State Route 128, take Exit 15 to School Street south. Turn right on Union Street/State Route 127. Turn right again on Sea Street and then left on Beach Street. The beach and a parking lot are at the road's end. Open from dawn to dusk. (978) 526-2040.

•Wilderness Conservation Area 🐾 🐾 🐾 🐾 See **104** on page 250.
This spectacular reservation is in Essex, Hamilton, and Manchester-By-The-Sea. And even though it is composed mainly of swamps and rocky outcroppings, it seems everyone wants a piece of it. That includes developers. Fortunately for all of us, the Manchester Conservation Trust, Essex County Greenbelt Association, Trustees of Reservations, and the three town conservation commissions have been successful in protecting most of the more than 400 acres. The battle to conserve natural resources continues (and sometimes the good guys win).

This is a wonderful place for you and your dog to explore. A wide variety of terrain is available: open ponds, thick swamps, dense forests, rocky summits, and even a few flat, dry areas.

We recommend the newly protected Gordon Woods off of Pine Street on the Hamilton-Manchester border. Heron Pond and the Sawmill Swamp, off of School Street on Essex-Manchester line, is also worth a visit. The park also encompasses Agassiz Rock (see page 314). For membership and a good map, write to the Manchester Conservation Trust, P.O. Box 1486, Manchester, MA 01944.

The main parking area is on School Street. From State Route 128, take Exit 15 to School Street for a half mile. The parking area is on the left. For the Pine Street parking area, take Exit 16 from State Route 128 to Pine Street north. Small pullouts are on the left as the pavement ends. Other parking areas are at Warren-Weld Woodland in Essex and Agassiz Rock in Manchester. Open sunrise to sunset. (978) 526-4211.

RESTAURANTS

Scoops: This drive-up ice-cream and yogurt shop is a good excuse to stop for a sniff and a sundae. Open seasonally from April through November, it offers a great selection of homemade ice cream, frozen yogurt, soft serve, and sundaes. You'll find plenty of parking, picnic benches, and surrounding woods. Just past Pride's Crossing on State Route 127A; (978) 281-9720.

MARBLEHEAD

A major harbor since colonial days, this town served as a center of both the whaling industry in the 18th century and of the merchant trade in the 19th century. Today the homes of wealthy merchants and leaders of American independence are yours to explore, and the area's harbor views and natural beauty ensure that you and your dog will love every single minute of your visit.

PARKS, BEACHES, AND RECREATION AREAS

• **Devereux Beach** 🐾🐾🐾 See **105** on page 250.

Who needs a boogie board when you can bodysurf like Rocky? He's still, like, planning to catch the awesome waves at Maui, dude, but, until then, Devereux Beach is the place to be.

This small beach on the Marblehead Causeway is a great spot to ride the waves or just relax along the shore. It's only about a half mile long and, thanks to a profusion of seaweed, doesn't attract big summer crowds. That means there will be more dogs here than people—which makes it way cool in our book.

Here's our dilemma in telling you about this place: it's got a big "No Dogs" sign. But we've been coming to this beach for years (before we could read, obviously) and are always joined by other local dogs. So what's the scoop?

Parks Supervisor Tom Hammond assured us that we can, indeed, use this beach anytime from October 1 to May 1. The "No Dogs" sign pertains to summer months only. But canines must be on leash at all times, and you must pick up after your dog. Although this is still the official policy, there are plenty of folks in Marblehead who want to ban dogs altogether. The main reason? People don't pick up after 'em. So, please, if you use this beach, bring along a shovel and use it for more than building sand castles.

From State Route 1A, take State Route 114 east to Pleasant Street. Turn right on Ocean Harbor Avenue. The beach entrance is on the right at the start of the Marblehead Causeway. Open from dawn to dusk. (781) 631-3350.

NATURE HIKES AND URBAN WALKS

Marblehead Historic District Walking Tour: Explore Marblehead's rich maritime history on either a one- or two-mile tour through downtown and along the harbor. In its early years, Marblehead served as one of the principal ports of the New World, and the walk leads you to the 18th-century homes of its many artisans and craftspeople. It also passes landmarks of the American Revolution. The stroll ends at Marblehead's picturesque harbor, where you can grab a bite to eat or shop till you drop. Pick up a map at the Chamber of Commerce (52 Pleasant Street) or at the Visitor Center on the corner of Pleasant and Essex Streets. (781) 631-2868.

RESTAURANTS

Flynnies at the Beach: After a dunk and a splash at Devereux Beach (see above), stroll to this café and get a quick lunch to go. You can choose between seafood rolls or plates and something from the grill. They prefer to keep the outdoor patio for two-legged customers, but you're welcome to eat at any of the nearby public picnic tables along the beach. It's open from April 1 to October 1. Devereux Beach; (781) 639-3035.

The Landing: Dogs aren't allowed inside or on the porch at this restaurant for fine seafood, but that's okay. Just ask for the corner table on the patio, along the railing, and your dog can sit right next to you. From here both of you can count the sails of the many sailboats in the harbor. And as for the meal, you may be willing to pass him a piece of your roasted Marblehead scrod, but it's doubtful you'll want to share the garlic mashed potatoes. 81 Front Street; (781) 631-1878.

Scoops 'n Sprinkles: We really didn't want ice cream. No sir, that's the last thing we ever want on a sultry summer day. But they had a water dish for the dogs on the sidewalk, so what could we do? George recommends a cup of Maine Black Bear. That's raspberry ice cream with chocolate chips. 142 Washington Street; (781) 639-8028.

Truffles: A perfect spot if you just need a little something sweet or a lunch to go. Take a break on the quiet bench out front and watch the world go by. 114 Washington Street; (781) 639-1104.

PLACES TO STAY

Seagull Inn: Who couldn't love a place called Seagull Inn? Fortunately the name isn't even the best thing about it. This quaint bed-and-breakfast inn, right in the heart of town, affords a harbor or ocean view from every window. There are four rooms to choose from and all have small kitchen facilities; but we think the best thing about them is that all allow dogs. Rooms range from $100 to $200 per night. 106 Harbor Avenue, Marblehead, MA 01945; (781) 631-1893.

MARLBOROUGH

PARKS, BEACHES, AND RECREATION AREAS

•**Callahan State Park, North Section** 🐾🐾🐾 See **106** on page 250.
Although not as scenic as its southern counterpart, this 369-acre portion of the park is still worth checking out. The best parts are the trails around pretty Beebe Pond, which is accessible via two roads.

A high road heads north from the main parking area and follows the Backpacker Trail. On this meandering 1.5-mile trek to the pond, you'll walk north through a pine forest. You can loop around the pond and head back on the shorter Pine Tree Trail, or follow the Backpacker Trail into Callahan's southern section (see pages 294–295). Here you can hike up Gibb Mountain, the highest point in the park at 480 feet.

From Boston Post Road/State Route 20, take Farm Road south. Turn left on Broadmeadow Street. The park and a parking lot are on the left. Parking is also available at pullouts off Parmenter Road. Open from a half hour before sunrise to a half hour after sunset. (508) 653-9641.

•**Ghiloni Park, Concord Recreation Area/Marlborough State Forest** 🐾🐾🐾 See **107** on page 250.
To show your nature-loving companion a prime example of a planned recreation area that preserves the natural resources of the surrounding area, head to this beautiful park. The recreation area offers plenty of parking, rest rooms, a ball field, and the spacious, open Ghiloni Park, around which are breathtaking woods and well-manicured, paved trails. You and your leashed friend

can wander through the woods, play Frisbee on the grass, and explore everywhere except the ball field. To escape the activity, head across the access road into Marlborough State Forest. Although more rustic, these trails are equally pleasing to the eye, taking happy pooches through quiet woods with small gurgling streams. All in all, the park is a doggy delight and earns the town of Marlborough a tail-wagging salute for designing a big city park with all the amenities, yet preserving the innate beauty of the forest for those who desire a more natural retreat.

From Interstate 495, take Exit 24 to State Route 20 east. Go left on Concord Road. The park and parking are on the left. Open from 7 A.M. to 10 P.M. (508) 624-6925.

MARSHFIELD

PARKS, BEACHES, AND RECREATION AREAS

• **Corn Hill Woodland Conservation Land** 🐾🐾🐾 See 🔢108🔢 on page 251.

It's modest and it's swampy, but we like this tranquil little spot. Situated on 132 acres of woodland separated by marshy streams, it offers you and your leashed dog a leisurely hike along well-marked trails through white pine forest.

From State Route 3, take Exit 12 to State Route 139/Church Street/Plain Street east. Take an immediate left on Union Street. Turn left on Corn Hill Lane. The park is on the right. Park at the trailhead off Corn Hill Lane. Open from dawn to dusk. (781) 834-5573.

• **Webster Wilderness Conservation Land** 🐾🐾🐾 See 🔢109🔢 on page 251.

Deep in the jungle of the Webster Wilderness, the trail narrows to just a thin pass through the thick brush. The rich, green canopy of branches and vines blocks out the hot sun. As your imagination begins to run wild, you think you catch a glimpse of spider monkeys swinging through the trees and crocodiles along the shorelines. The sounds of tropical birds fill the air as you track the panting wild creature racing before you. No, wait. That's no exotic animal. That's your dog.

The terrain in the Webster Wilderness is truly junglelike. The Sapsucker and Teal Trails, both one mile long, work their way through the thick, marshy oak, pine, and elm woodland and dense ivy and vine undergrowth along Wharf Creek. Somehow the paths stay dry, even though they skirt dangerously close to the water's edge. When the trails border the water, you get spectacular views of the creek and surrounding ponds. When they turn back toward the trees, the paths lead over land bridges to other corners of the park. It's easy to get disoriented, so be sure to keep track of your route. Remember: It's almost a jungle out there. Dogs must be on leash.

From the town center at the intersection of Ocean Street/State Route 139 and Moraine Street/State Route 3A, take Ocean Street east. Turn right on Webster Street. The park is on the left, just past Schofield Road. A parking lot is available. Open from dawn to dusk. (781) 834-5573.

MEDFIELD

PARKS, BEACHES, AND RECREATION AREAS

• Noon Hill Reservation 🐾🐾🐾 **See 110 on page 251.**
Our pups renamed this large, wooded reservation High Noon Hill and declared it "not big enough for all of us." Whenever we come here, they battle it out among the trees and rocky outcroppings to see who is king of the hill and who has to get out of Dodge.

From the top of Noon Hill, at an elevation of 369 feet, there are fine views through the trees of the nearby Charles River and Stop River Valleys. The main trail, an old forest road, leads from the parking lot through the woods and nears the top of the rise before continuing into the surrounding woodland.

Because the main objective of every visit is to conquer the hill, you'll want to follow the dirt road upward. The road circles around the back of Noon Hill before splitting. Take the left branch, or the high road, to the top. You and your leashed dog can make a loop by taking one of the foot trails down the north side of the hill. They all lead eventually to the forest road. The entire journey is close to two miles.

From the town center at the intersection of State Routes 27 and 109, take Main Street/State Route 109 heading west. Turn left on Causeway Street, then left again on Noon Hill Road. The reservation and a parking area are on the right. Noon Hill Reservation is open from 9 A.M. to 6 P.M. (508) 921-1944.

• Rocky Woods Reservation 🐾🐾🐾🐾 🐕 🦴 **See 111 on page 250.**
Normally Inu and George are cool, calm, and collected canines. But they lose it whenever they hear the words "Rock. . . ." Whew, close call. They lose it whenever they hear R-O-C-K-Y-W-O-O-D-S. You see, this park, managed by the Trustees of Reservations, is one of their favorite places, and they do a wild dance of anticipation at the thought of bounding down the hilly trails and exploring the rocky formations and refreshing ponds in gleeful, leash-free abandon. And because we visit so often, Rocky thinks every park is named after him and that the two words are synonymous.

Nearly 500 acres of woods, rocky bluffs, and numerous ponds await, all accessible via trails and cart paths. The dogs love the twisting, winding routes that lead up and over ridges, around giant boulders, and along pools, brooks, and waterfalls. There are plenty of hiking options to choose from and many places to explore. Ask the park ranger for a trail map or just follow other hikers.

Dogs must be leashed in the parking area, around Chickering Pond, and near all park buildings. However, they can ditch the leash on the trails if they remain under strict voice control at all times. Due to construction, during summer 2001 the park is off-limits to dogs.

Entrance fees are $2.50 per person on weekends for non-TTOR members. From the town center at the intersection of State Routes 27 and 109, take Main Street/State Route 109 east. Turn left on Hartford Street. The park is on the left. On weekdays, park in the smaller pullouts along the access road. On weekends and holidays, follow the access road to the large parking area at the road's end. Rocky Woods Reservation is open from 9 A.M. to 6 P.M. (the gate closes at 5 P.M.). (508) 359-6333 or (781) 821-2977, extension 114.

RESTAURANTS
Casabella Pizza: Inu insisted we list at least one pizza parlor. After all, pizza is his favorite food. Actually he's also happy munching on a sub or calzone as long as it has plenty of cheese. Order whatever cheesy dish your dog prefers and head next door to the gazebo and town green to enjoy it. 454 Main Street; (508) 359-4040.

MEDFORD
PARKS, BEACHES, AND RECREATION AREAS

• **Middlesex Fells Reservation, Western Section** 🐾🐾🐾🐾 See **112** on page 252.

It's hard to believe that you could get so lost in the woods so close to Boston. Of course, the first time we visited this didn't happen to us, but it does happen to many of the visitors to the Middlesex Fells Reservation. Eventually, we, er, they, find the highway that runs through the middle of the park and find the way out. But with 2,060 acres and 50 miles of trails and carriage paths, things can get confusing.

The park is so big that it's spread across five towns: Malden, Medford, Melrose, Stoneham, and Winchester. The Northwest Expressway/Interstate 93 divides it down the middle, creating eastern and western sections. Before you head out on a hike, pick up a trail map from park headquarters in Stoneham. The map costs $4, is expertly made, and definitely comes in handy on the trail. Dogs must be on leash.

To reach the park headquarters from the Northwest Expressway, take Exit 33 to the Roosevelt Circle rotary. Follow the Fellsway West/State Route 28 north. Turn right on Elm Street and then head left on Woodland Road at Molyneaux Circle. The park office is on your right, just past Ravine Road, at the intersection with Pond Street. Open from dawn to dusk. (781) 322-2851.

MIDDLEBOROUGH
PARKS, BEACHES, AND RECREATION AREAS

• **Pratt Farm Conservation Area** 🐾🐾🐾 See **113** on page 251.

Whether your dog loves roaming woodsy trails, romping in meadows, or swimming in a sparkling pond, Pratt Farm is a doggone good place. An assortment of trails loop around the ponds and hillsides, so you can pick and choose the distance you and your dog want to go.

In the center of the 160 acres are Upper Mill Pond and Lower Mill Pond. Despite the power lines that pass over them, you and your dog will still like this section. Around the pond are the remnants of some of the mills that were built on the waterway. The park's main trail, about 1.5 miles long, goes directly to the ponds and loops between them. The Middleborough Conservation Commission requires dogs to be on leash.

From Interstate 495, take Exit 4 to State Route 105/South Main Street north. Follow State Route 105 until it becomes East Main Street. The park is on the right. Parking is available. Open from sunrise to sunset. (508) 946-2406.

PLACES TO STAY

Days Inn: Your dog is welcome here with a $3 charge per night. Rates range from $60 to $95. 30 East Clark Street, Middleborough, MA 02346; (508) 946-4400; www.daysinn-middleboro.com.

MILTON

PARKS, BEACHES, AND RECREATION AREAS

• **Blue Hills Reservation, Great Blue Hill Section** 🐾 🐾 🐾 🐾 ✦
See **114** on page 252.

A vast wilderness covering almost 6,000 acres across five towns, the Blue Hills Reservation is the single largest conservation area within 35 miles of Boston. The trail system here encompasses 125 miles, and the views from the hilltops are doggone spectacular. For details on the park's other sections, see Canton, Blue Hills Reservation, Ponkapoag Pond Section on pages 280–281.

If this is your first visit to the Blue Hills, then it's a must that you and your leashed dog make the climb to the top of Great Blue Hill. At 635 feet, it's one of the highest points on the Atlantic coast; you should be able to see your house from the observation tower. The two principal trails to the summit are the Great Blue Hill Trail and the Skyline Trail.

If your feet and your pup's want a somewhat flatter route, try the easy path around Houghton's Pond. It's only about a half-mile walk, and the clean lake is good for a refreshing swim. Or you can explore one of the many other trails in the park; you'll find enough to keep you busy for countless return visits.

From State Route 128/Interstate 93, take Exit 3 to Blue Hills River Road. Turn right on Hillside Street. A parking lot is on the right at Houghton's Pond. You can also park on Hillside Street, a quarter mile beyond the pond, at the reservation's headquarters. Obtain a free trail map here or buy a large, colorful park map for $1. Open from dawn to dusk. (617) 698-1802.

RESTAURANTS

Newcomb Farms Restaurant: One of our favorite things about hiking is starting off with a hearty meal. So before we hit the trail in the nearby Blue Hills, we stop at Newcomb Farms. There is no place to sit with your dog, but takeout is just fine and the food's great. It has a full breakfast menu, served anytime, and a lunch and dinner menu of charburgers, roll-ups, and hot and cold sandwiches. 1139 Randolph Avenue and State Route 28; (617) 698-9547.

DIVERSIONS

Head for them there hills: What a wonderful world it can be. Not only is the Blue Hills Reservation a great place for you and your dog to explore, but twice a year (in spring and fall) rangers sponsor a free, one- to two-hour hike called Canine Capers, just for dog walkers. The hike starts with information about how to keep your dog happy and healthy while out on the trail, and then a ranger guides everyone on a special hike. It's a terrific way to explore out-of-the-way spots on the reservation, and for once you won't feel like you're in the minority. You'll just be one of the pack. Dates and hikes are subject to change; call for details. (617) 698-1802.

NAHANT

PARKS, BEACHES, AND RECREATION AREAS

• Lodge Memorial Park/Marine Science Center on East Point
🐾 🐾 🐾 🐾 (residents) 🐾 (nonresidents) See **115** on page 252.

Nahant, occupying the entire Nahant Peninsula in Massachusetts Bay, is a lovely, quiet New England coastal town, and that's the way residents want to keep it. That means they don't need the likes of you and your big-footed dog coming around, messing things up. At least that's the less-than-warm message we got.

The tip of the peninsula, East Point, is home to Northeastern University's Marine Science Center and Lodge Memorial Park. Although the park is open to visitors and leashed dogs, the small parking area only welcomes residents, and street parking is prohibited. This is true for most of Nahant, and the fine is steep, $35, as we painfully discovered. If you're a nonresident skip to the next park. If you happen to be a resident or know someone who is, you're in luck.

The high cliffs of beautiful East Point signal the beginning of the rocky coastline for which northern New England is famous. From here, three miles into the bay, you get great views of seabirds, the coast, lighthouses, and passing ships. Explore some of the short, unmarked trails along the cliffs, or just grab a seat on the benches or rocks and take in the refreshing sea breezes.

From State Route 1A in Lynn, take the Lynnway east. At the rotary, take Nahant Road across the Causeway into Nahant. Follow the road to the end of the peninsula and the park. Open from dawn to dusk. (781) 595-5597.

• Long Beach/Nahant Beach 🐾 🐾 See **116** on page 252.

The Metropolitan District Commission doesn't allow dogs on the beach from May 1 through September 30, but the two of you can enjoy strolling along the sands during the off-season. The only exception to this rule is "Doggy Beach," a small strip of beach next to the old Fireman's House on the right side as you cross the Causeway, where dogs are welcome all year-round. Due to local outcry, the city has made this single exception to the no-dogs moratorium. Mutt Mitts are conveniently located at the entrance to the sandy beach for cleanup. You know the drill.

You'll have no trouble finding parking—there's space for more than 1,300 cars here. At one time there were plans to have a water ferry for North Shore commuters dock here. Although the ferry never materialized, the parking lot did. At least you won't be wondering where you're going to "paahk the caah." Dogs must be on leash.

From State Route 1A in Lynn, take the Lynnway east. At the rotary, take Nahant Road across the Causeway into Nahant; extensive beach parking is on the left. Open from dawn to dusk. (781) 662-5230.

NEEDHAM
PARKS, BEACHES, AND RECREATION AREAS

• **Hemlock Gorge** 🐾🐾 ◀🐾 See **117** on page 252.

"Raaahky. . . Raaahky." At Hemlock Gorge, calling your dog is easier than in any other park. That's because no other park has Echo Bridge. This National Historic Landmark, built by Boston Water Works in 1877, supports the Boston aqueduct over the Charles River, and, doggone, is it impressive! The bridge itself is an elegant granite structure surrounded by—you guessed it—a forest of hemlocks. But to really appreciate its span, you need to listen to it. The name Echo Bridge comes from the reverberations under its huge arch. Call your dog and she won't have any excuse to ignore you as her name echoes over and over across the glimmering water and beyond. Dogs must be leashed here, and you'll want to be sure to follow this advice as the railings are short and the walkway is pitched to both sides.

From Interstate 95, take Exit 20 to State Route 9 east into Newton. Turn right onto Chestnut Street, right onto Elliott Street, and back into Needham. The park and a parking lot are on the right immediately after crossing the Charles River. Open dawn to dusk. (617) 698-1802.

• **Ridge Hill Reservation** 🐾🐾🐾 See **118** on page 250.

Although it's only 220 acres, this manicured park offers enough goodies to entertain even the most finicky of dogs. Does your pup long to explore rolling meadows, thick woods, wetlands, and eskers? Does your pup know what an esker is? Well, it's a high ridge formed from deposits left by a river or stream flowing under a glacier. And if both of you want to see two of 'em, head on over to Ridge Hill.

The entrance and short park road open onto a grand meadow speckled with pine trees. This field alone is a fine place for you and your dog to romp and play. Most of the trails lead from various points in the grassy clearing.

Park headquarters are at the road's end. Facilities include a rest room and warming room after winter activities, but they're a bit run down. Dogs must be on leash.

From State Route 128/Interstate 95 in Dedham, take Exit 17 to Needham Street/State Route 135 north and Needham. Turn left on South Street and then right on Charles River Street. The park and a small parking lot are on the right. Open from dawn to dusk. (781) 449-4923.

NEW BEDFORD

"There she blows! There she blows! A hump like a snow-hill! It is Moby Dick!"
—*Moby Dick* by Herman Melville

All it takes is one walk through the historic harbor district of New Bedford, once known as the "Whaling Capital of the World," and you, too, will have the same Ahabian enthusiasm for the sea and all that swims in it or floats on it. Granted, New Bedford is no longer the metropolis it once was. The discovery of petroleum long ago started the decline of this seaport, but its rich sailing history and still-bustling fishing trade will captivate even the wobbli-est of land lovers.

PARKS, BEACHES, AND RECREATION AREAS

• Buttonwood Park 🐾🐾 See **119** on page 251.

You may think you are the number-one human in your dog's eyes, but, to be truthful, we all run a distant second to Fredrick Law Olmsted. During the 19th century, Olmsted created and designed many of the major parks and gardens in North America, including Washington's U.S. Capitol Grounds, New York's Central Park, Boston's Emerald Necklace, and New Bedford's Buttonwood Park. Without him, a walk in the park would be a far less pleasant experience for man or beast.

Of course, the 100 acres of Buttonwood Park do not compare to Central Park or the Public Garden, but it is easy to see Olmsted's attention to detail in the park's ponds and gardens and in his design for park usability with ball fields and bike paths.

The park is located at Brownell and Hawthorn Streets and Rockdale Avenue. Street and lot parking are available. Open 6 A.M. to 11 P.M. (508) 991-6178.

• Fort Taber Park 🐾🐾🐾 See **120** on page 251.

Fort Taber Park is just reopening to the public after undergoing a face-lift. The park, at the tip of Clark's Point between Clark Cove and the New Bedford Harbor, is home to Fort Taber (closed to the public) and plenty of rocky coast-line that both you and your pooch will enjoy. The park also has plenty of lawn areas and picnic sites.

The Joseph D. Savlinier Memorial Bike Path can also be accessed from here. This seaside, paved bike path runs around Clark's Point for 2.5 miles. It's an airy, open route that offers plenty of water access points and great views of Clark Cove and the New Bedford Harbor.

Dogs must be leashed.

The park is located at the southern bend of Rodney French Boulevard. There is limited parking for nonresidents. Open 6 A.M. to 11 P.M. (508) 991-6175.

NATURE WALKS AND URBAN HIKES

Wharf Rat: Two steps into either one of the two dock walks, and your dog will be intrigued enough by the scenic harbor and historic boats to turn into a wharf rat. And why not? The numerous types of boats, interpretive plaques about the town's whaling history, and the day-to-day workings of an active harbor make this a great place to explore time and again.

Dock Walk 1 circles Piers 3 and 4 and offers great views of the harbor. Dock Walk 2 covers the State Pier and Waterfront Park and more of the history of New Bedford.

For more information, maps, and brochures, visit the Waterfront Visitors Center at Pier 3 (on MacArthur Drive) or call (800) 508-5353.

A Whale of a Walk: In 1996, Congress recognized the historical signifi-cance of this 13-block area on the waterfront and established the New Bed-ford Whaling National Historical Park. Although dogs are not permitted in any of the buildings, you will both enjoy walking the "Nautical Mile" along the cobblestone streets. Explore the historic structures from the outside, such as the Seamen's Bethel immortalized in *Moby Dick*.

For more information and maps, contact the Bristol County Visitor Bureau at (508) 997-1250, or visit the Historic District Visitor Center at 33 Williams Street; (508) 996-4095.

Underground Hound: New Bedford's history is not just about whaling. The city was an important stop and final destination for the Underground Railroad. New Bedford, with a liberal attitude, rich economy, and a diverse population from all over the world, was a safe haven for people escaping slavery in the mid-1800s. You and your pup can follow the Black Heritage Trail past the stately mansions of Union Street and the historical points of the Underground Railroad.

For more information and maps, contact the New Bedford Historical Society at (508) 979-8828, or visit the Historic District Visitor Center at 33 Williams Street; (508) 996-4095.

RESTAURANTS

Clark's Point Creamery: Located near Fort Rodman and the Savlinier Bikepath, this is a convenient spot for lunch and snacks. The menu includes ice cream, fish and chips, and lobster rolls. They have outdoor seating, but George likes to get it to go and head over to the seaside parks. 26 Brock Avenue; (508) 990-0065.

Jungle Java: Jungle Java is the right place to go if you need a good cup of coffee, some tasty pastries, or a hearty helping of soup and a sandwich. Stay awhile and you'll be getting directions, a history lesson on the whaling industry, or the latest news on New Bedford's revitalization plan. Enjoy your meal and conversations at the café table along the cobblestone street. 24 North Water Street; (508) 991-5900.

DIVERSIONS

An Apple and a Biscuit a Day...: If the fish weren't biting on your fishing trip, you can still come home with the day's catch by stopping at the New Bedford Farmer's Market. You and your pet can haul in a net full of fresh fruits, vegetables, flowers, breads, and other bakery items. The market takes place Saturdays from 9 A.M. to 1 P.M. from mid-June through October at the Brooklawn Park on Ashley Boulevard (State Route 18). (781) 893-8222.

Canine Castaway: If you feel that Nantucket, Martha's Vineyard, and Block Island are all overrun with tourists, then take a trip out to Cuttyhunk, the westernmost island in the Elizabeth Island chain. It's 14 miles out from New Bedford and accessible to the public via a one-hour ferry cruise on the *Alert II*. Once on the scenic island, you'll find great beaches and dunes mixed in with a healthy dose of fresh salt air.

The *Alert II* departs from Fisherman's Wharf/Pier 3; parking is available for day-trippers. There are limited services on Cuttyhunk, and dogs must be leashed. Same-day round-trip fares are $17. For more information and departure dates and times, call (508) 992-1432.

NEWBURYPORT

PARKS, BEACHES, AND RECREATION AREAS

• Maudslay State Park 🐾🐾🐾 See **121** on page 250.

Flower fans, take note: This 476-acre state park along the Merrimack River is a garden paradise. In May and June, blooming azaleas and rhododendrons entice many hikers. In the winter, the mountain laurels attract nesting eagles. And all year long the charming gardens and ambling carriage trails draw numerous visitors. This park is a popular place for horseback riding in the summer and cross-country skiing and snowshoeing in the winter. Leashed dogs are welcome to enjoy the numerous and varied meadows, ponds, old-growth forests, and cliffs of the former Moseley family estate.

Maps are available in the parking lot and at the ranger station.

From Interstate 95, take Exit 57 to Storey Avenue/State Route 113 east. Turn left on Ferry Road. Ferry Road becomes Pine Hill Road just after crossing over Interstate 95. Pine Hill Road becomes Curzan's Mill Road upon entering the park. Parking is on the right. Open from dawn to dusk. (978) 465-7223.

• Moseley Woods Park 🐾🐾 See **122** on page 250.

Talk about a contrast! This park overlooks the peaceful flow of the majestic Merrimack River on one side and the frantic racing of interstate traffic on the other. Just look the right way and you'll be okay. Moseley Woods sits right between the Chain Bridge and the Whittner Memorial Bridge, which is the crossing for Interstate 95. Keep your eyes on the water and not the road, and you'll do just fine here. The views of the river and nearby Deer Island from the park's cliffs are especially impressive.

Stepping back from the river's edge, the park offers a forest of tall, shady pines with sheltered picnic areas, a small playground, and a few short trails through the woods. The main trail is a segment of the Merrimack River Trail system, which is still being completed through the towns along the river. It's an easy, half-mile loop through a lovely area. The only drawback is the inescapable highway drone in the background. Your dog must be on leash.

From Interstate 95, take Exit 57 to Storey Avenue/State Route 113 east. Turn left on Moseley Avenue. The park gate is on the right at the intersection of Merrimac and Spofford Streets. Open from dawn to dusk. (978) 465-4407.

RESTAURANTS

Coffee Aroma: You get two benches in front of this quaint breakfast nook. It's perfect for a quick stop for a cup of joe and a nibble before or after a run on the trails. 15 Water Street; there is no phone.

PLACES TO STAY

Essex Street Inn: Built at the end of the 19th century, this little inn is set in the heart of town near Newburyport's main thoroughfare. Dogs are welcome on approval, which means you should let the management know Fido will be joining you in advance; there may be a size consideration. Rates range from $75 to $195. 7 Essex Street, Newburyport, MA 01950; (978) 465-3148.

Windsor House: This inn has five rooms done in English colonial style, some with privates baths. Dogs are allowed on approval. Tell the staff your dog's size and needs when you make your reservation, and they'll try to accommodate you both. Rates are $110 to $135, including a full breakfast and afternoon tea. 38 Federal Street, Newburyport, MA 01950; (508) 462-3778; www.virtualcities.com

NEWTON

PARKS, BEACHES, AND RECREATION AREAS

As of press time, no decision had been made regarding adding a dog park in Newton, but this has been a hot topic recently. We suggest checking with the Parks and Recreation Department for the latest update, as this situation could change at any time. (617) 552-7120.

• Hammond Pond Reservation 🐾 🐾 See 123 on page 252.

Part of the Metropolitan District Commission system, this reservation borders the Webster Conservation Area and the Mall at Chestnut Hill. Hammond Pond itself is in the park's eastern corner, near the parking lot. Your dog can take a dip here, but she'll rub elbows with the anglers and geese who frequent the shore. From the pond, short and easy-to-follow trails head west and north into some densely wooded, rocky areas.

The drawback to the reservation is Hammond Pond Parkway, which tears right through the middle of the park. A four-lane road, it can be hard to cross, especially on a shopper's Saturday. This is a shame because the park's western portion has the better trails. To access this area, try taking advantage of some of the mall parking lots on the western side of Hammond Pond Parkway. Dogs must be on leash.

From State Route 9, take Hammond Pond Parkway heading north. The parking lot is immediately on the right. Open from dawn to dusk. (617) 698-1802.

• Hemlock Gorge—See Needham, Hemlock Gorge on page 323.

RESTAURANTS

Bruegger's Bagel Bakery: The best Vermont import since Ben & Jerry's, this bagel, sandwich, salad, and dessert spot will satisfy any craving. Nosh at an outside table or on the small grassy area across the street. 739 Beacon Street; (617) 630-9715.

Sabra: Eat in or take out a delicious meal from this Middle Eastern restaurant to share with your dog. The stuffed grape leaves are terrific. Enjoy the outdoor seating in the hub of Newton Centre. 57 Langley Road; (617) 964-9275.

Starbucks: Apparently, no town is complete without one. One of the more spacious locations, this coffeehouse is in the old Newton train station, now a T stop. Sit at a shaded outdoor table by the tracks or grab your coffee and muffin to go. 70 Union Street; (617) 332-7086.

Tutto Italiano of Newton: This Italian specialty shop makes *molto bene* sandwiches and pastas. Order your selection to go and sit across the way in the Centre Green. Our dogs love the authentic pizza, and we do, too. 1300 Centre Street; (617) 969-1591.

PLACES TO STAY

Sheraton Newton Hotel: With 272 rooms to choose from, there should always be room at this inn. Luckily, they also take dogs. Right off the Massachusetts Turnpike at Exit 17, you are near local shopping with easy access to many area universities and parks. Dogs under 25 pounds are preferred. Rooms range from $119 to $230. 320 Washington Street, Newton, MA 02458; (617) 969-3010; www.sheraton.com.

DIVERSIONS

Tip a canoe and your puppy, too: If your pooch dreams of high-seas adventures, she's bound to enjoy a refreshing day canoeing the Charles River. Rent a canoe, and your crew can coast along some of the more peaceful parts of the upper Charles River in Newton, Weston, and Waltham. Daily and hourly rates are available. Contact the Charles River Canoe and Kayak Center, 2401 Commonwealth Avenue; (617) 965-5110.

NORTH ANDOVER

PARKS, BEACHES, AND RECREATION AREAS

• Harold Parker State Forest 🐾🐾🐾🐾 See 124 on page 250.

Shared with the town of Andover, the bulk of this wonderful 3,500-acre state forest lies in North Andover. We recommend that you pick up a trail map at park headquarters to find all the great places for you to explore here. One of our favorite spots, Stearns Pond, is only a short hike through the woods from the headquarters parking area. A beautiful alpine pond, it makes a great swimming spot for both of you and offers lovely views across the water. You can make a loop around the water on unpaved Pond Road. There is beach access here, which can get pretty crowded on a summer day, but you should have it to yourself the rest of the year and in the morning or evening in summer. Dogs must be on leash.

From the intersection of the Andover Bypass/State Route 125 and Turnpike Street/State Route 114, take Turnpike Street south. Turn right on Harold Parker Road and proceed into the park. To reach park headquarters, continue on Harold Parker Road and turn left on Middleton Street. Headquarters is on the left. Open from a half hour before sunrise to a half hour after sunset. (978) 686-3391.

• Weir Hill Reservation 🐾🐾🐾🐾 🐾 See 125 on page 250.

You're in for a treat when you make the trip to Weir Hill Reservation. We suggest you consult the map at the trailhead and then head through the meadow and uphill to the trail that starts behind the meadow to the right. At first the trail goes straight up, so get ready for a workout. Although rather steep initially, it soon levels off, and it's a short hike to the lower summit of Weir Hill, where the path opens onto a lovely open meadow surrounded by woods. The view of the Merrimack Valley from up here is quite spectacular. This is where our dogs' tails really start to wag, because they know that once they trot down the hill from the meadow, they'll be at Stephens Pond. If you're looking for a good hike that will give you a solid workout, we guarantee that you'll return to this park again and again.

From the intersection of Andover Street/State Route 125 and Turnpike Street/State Route 114, take Andover Street heading north. Stay with Andover Street when it turns to the right off State Route 125. Turn left on Stephens Street. The park is located on the right. Plenty of parking is available on the shoulder of the road. Another entrance and additional parking are located off Pleasant Street. Open from dawn to dusk. (978) 356-4351.

RESTAURANTS

Bay State Chowda Company: Grab a great cup o' chowda or just about anything else you can imagine at this terrific café. Right in the heart of town, it has outdoor seating where your well-behaved dog will feel welcome. The food is delicious; eat it here or take it on a picnic. 109 Main Street; (978) 685-9610.

NORWELL

PARKS, BEACHES, AND RECREATION AREAS

• Albert F. Norris Reservation 🐾🐾🐾 See **126** on page 251.

In the 1700s, this area along the North River hummed with industrial activity. The rich woods, the brooks and ponds, the salt marshes, and the river itself made an ideal locale for mills and shipbuilding. Today the 101 acres of Albert F. Norris Reservation are still filled with activity. The ponds and marshes attract a variety of waterfowl. The forests provide an excellent habitat for numerous species of wildlife, and the easy trails and cool breezes coming off the North River make the area a favorite of hikers and leashed dogs alike.

From State Route 3, take Exit 13 to Washington Street/State Route 53 north. Turn right on Main Street/State Route 123 east. Turn right again on West Street and drive to the Dover Street intersection. A parking lot is at the intersection, off Dover Street. Open from sunrise to sunset. (781) 821-2977.

• Jacobs Pond 🐾🐾🐾 🐕 See **127** on page 251.

This conservation land has all the things your dog will love, including the privilege of sniffing out the good stuff while off leash. The town of Norwell keeps this lovely park well maintained, and the many trails help you and your dog get away from it all.

From State Route 3, in Hanover, take Exit 13 to State Route 53/Washington Street north into Norwell. Turn right on Main Street/State Route 123 east. Take a quick left on Jacobs Lane. The park and a parking lot are on the left. Open from dawn to dusk. (781) 659-8022.

• Wompatuck State Park—See Hingham, Wompatuck State Park on pages 303–304.

PEMBROKE

PARKS, BEACHES, AND RECREATION AREAS

• Hobomock Trails 🐾🐾🐾 See **128** on page 251.

Hidden away behind the elementary school, the wonderful trails here run along Herring Brook and lead to Glover Mill Pond and a lovely woodland. Rather curiously, all routes are marked in white. Every intersection we came to directed us to follow either the white trail or—the white trail. After a while, you just have to give up and go whichever way you choose. As the caterpillar said to Alice, "If you go somewhere, you'll surely end up there." So trust us, you'll never be far from somewhere worth going when you're on the white trail.

From the town center at the intersection of Oldham Street and Center Street/State Route 14, take Center Street west. Follow Center Street onto State Route 36 south. Turn left on Hobomock Street, then left again on Learning Lane. The park and street parking are at the road's end. Open from dawn to dusk. (781) 293-7211.

- **Indian Head River Greenway—See Hanover, Indian Head River Greenway on page 300.**

PLYMOUTH

If New England has a mecca for visitors, this just might be it. Even the Pilgrims, the first British tourists in the new England, grasped this simple truth when they landed here in 1620. History abounds, and you can find fascinating traces of life in the early days of the Massachusetts Bay Colony.

PARKS, BEACHES, AND RECREATION AREAS

- **Morton Park** 🐾 🐾 See **129** on page 251.

The town of Plymouth first established this cozy recreation area in 1889. With a sparse pine forest, pond, and sandy beaches, this is the local watering hole for residents who don't want to venture too far for a splash. A snack bar, rest rooms, and boat rentals are available. All these facilities add up to thick crowds on summer days, so it might not be the best place for you and your leashed dog to get some exercise.

If you decide to check it out, we can tell you that Little Pond is ringed with three public beaches and some nearby trails, which lead up into the surrounding woods. Dogs must be on leash. The fee is $10 on weekends, $7 on weekdays. It's probably worth a trip in the off-season, but don't bother in summer. You and your dog will be greatly outnumbered by the beachgoers.

From State Route 3, take Exit 6 to Samoset Street east. Turn right on Westerly Road and then right again on Summer Street. Turn left on Morton Park Road. Open from dawn to 9 P.M. (508) 830-4095.

- **Myles Standish State Forest** 🐾 🐾 🐾 🐾 See **130** on page 251.

At 14,635 acres, Myles Standish State Forest is the largest park in Eastern Massachusetts. If your dog can't find the room that he needs here, he'll never find it. Not only do you get acres upon acres of woods, fields, and lakes, but you'll encounter more trails and paths than you could cover in a lifetime. The forest offers trails geared to all sorts of recreational uses: all-terrain vehicles, bicycling, horseback riding, skiing, snowmobiling, and even motorcycling. Dogs and hikers are allowed on all of them, but you should be alert, especially when on the nonhiking paths. In Myles Standish State Forest, folks take their sports seriously.

If you want to stay overnight, the forest's campground offers 475 campsites, all available on a first-come, first-served basis. You can secure a spot at the main headquarters on Cranberry Road. There are no hookups, but people with tents and trailers can stay for $6 per night or $7 per night with a shower. Dogs are allowed on leash. All trails are closed on Saturdays and holidays from mid-October to January 2 and for one week in the late fall during hunting season. Hunting is not permitted on Sundays. Free park maps and information are available at forest headquarters. Spread across the towns of Plymouth and Carver, two-thirds of the park's acreage is on the Plymouth side.

From State Route 3, take Exit 5 to Long Pond Road south. The park entrance, Alden Road, is on the right. Follow the signs to the forest headquarters.

From Interstate 495, take Exit 2 in Wareham to Tremont Street/State Route 58 and Carver. Turn right on Cranberry Road and continue into the park. The forest headquarters is on the left. Open from dawn to dusk. (508) 866-2526.

• **Plymouth Beach** 🐾🐾🐾 See **131** on page 251.
More than 3.5 miles long, this thin peninsula stretches into Plymouth Harbor and overlooks the town center. From downtown you can easily reach the sandy beach by car or foot. It's long and wide, and if you get past the main area near the snack bar and parking lot, chances are you'll have a long uninterrupted walk. The local canine elite flock here in the morning and on weekends for doggy socializing. You'll be more interested in the beautiful view than all the gossip and lore that the dogs are barking about. Dogs must be on leash here.

Ample parking is available, but you must pay $6 to park here between Memorial Day and Labor Day.

From State Route 3, take Exit 4 to Plimoth Plantation Highway. Turn left on Warren Avenue/State Route 3A. The beach and a parking lot are on the right. Open from 8 A.M. to 8 P.M. (508) 830-4050.

NATURE WALKS AND URBAN WALKS

Plymouth Historical Walk: Take a stroll along the lovely waterfront overlooking Plymouth Bay, and you'll end up at historic Plymouth Rock. George and Inu eagerly sniffed the area—they could tell something exciting was going on—but they couldn't figure out why the rest of the folks were crowding around the small rock. It looked like—well, a rock. So what if it signifies the European entrance into the New World? They wanted to move on and get to Plymouth Beach. But, for you, the significance will not be lost. The coastal walk will take you only about 10 minutes, but you can breathe in the fresh sea air and absorb a little history while you're at it. For more information, stop at the Plymouth Visitor Center at 130 Water Street. (508) 747-7525.

RESTAURANTS

Gas Grille Diner: Set on the Plymouth-Bourne town line, this little diner is open for breakfast and lunch only. You can eat on the outdoor patio or pack your lunch to go and enjoy it on the trail. The food's good, simple, and cheap—just how we like it. 2291 State Road; (508) 888-1777.

Gellar's Snack Bar: This nifty little roadside grill is one of the hottest spots in town. Always crowded, it welcomes locals, dogs, tourists, and probably even cats if they wanted to come. The outdoor seating's limited (only two tables), but you'll enjoy just hanging out and jawing with the rest of the crowd. And save room for dessert; the bubble-gum ice cream isn't just for kids. 506 State Road; (508) 224-2772.

Lobster Hut: Serving fresh and fried fish at reasonable prices, this outdoor restaurant on the tip of the waterfront wharf has outside tables where you can perch with your dog. Town Wharf Road; (508) 746-2270.

Souza's Seafood: Take your pick of the seafood at this fishery, located in the restaurant cluster on the town wharf. The outdoor seating gives you a good view of the harbor, and the food's mighty fine, too. Town Wharf Road; (508) 746-5354.

Wood's Seafood Market & Restaurant: Our favorite fish place on the waterfront, it's got plenty of picnic-style seating outside, where you can eat with Rover. Town Wharf Road; (508) 746-0261.

DIVERSIONS

Hop aboard for a day on the bay: You and your seaworthy dog can catch the approximately two-hour boat ride from Plymouth Harbor to Provincetown at the tip of Cape Cod. Leashed dogs are welcome on board the small cruise boat, but you must get permission from the captain. The trip leaves every day at 10 A.M. from mid-June through Labor Day. After four hours of roaming around scenic Provincetown, return to the boat for the trip back to Plymouth Bay. The ride costs $25 per adult, with no extra charge for your four-pawed matey. For reservations, call Captain John Boats at (508) 746-2670 or (800) 242-2469.

QUINCY

PARKS, BEACHES, AND RECREATION AREAS

• Faxon Park 🐾🐾 See 132 on page 252.

For those dog owners in walking distance of Faxon Park, this is the local doggy hangout. The park underwent a major face-lift in 1997, and, unfortunately for the pooches, the beautiful 10 acres of woods shrank down to about two. The rest became a new ball field and playground in the middle of the park. No dogs are allowed on the playing fields, and your pup must be leashed at all times.

From the intersection of Hancock Street and Washington Street in downtown Quincy, head south on Hancock Street, which becomes Quincy Street. Turn right on Faxon Park Road. Open from dawn to dusk. (617) 727-9547, extension 450.

• Wollaston Beach Reservation 🐾🐾 See 133 on page 252.

This Metropolitan District Commission park on Quincy Bay is divided into three sections: Wollaston Beach, Caddy Memorial Park, and Moswetuset Hummock (say that three times fast!). At any time of day, any day of the week, you can find plenty of people and dogs here enjoying the sea air. Most of them are taking advantage of the 2.5-mile walkway that runs between Wollaston Beach and Quincy Shore Drive. The rest are exploring the beach where, miraculously, your dog is allowed.

From the Southeast Expressway/Interstate 93/State Routes 1 and 3, take Exit 12 to State Route 3A south. Turn left on Quincy Shore Drive. Parking is available along the beach and in the parking lots at Caddy Memorial Park and Moswetuset Hummock. (617) 727-5293 or, in the summer, (617) 773-7954.

NATURE WALKS AND URBAN WALKS

Quincy Historic Walking Trail: Although most of the notable sights are indoors, and consequently closed to dogs, you can still get a sense of Quincy's rich history on this short, 1.25-mile walk through downtown. Points of interest focus on the homes of Quincy's famous families, the Adamses and Hancocks. For a free detailed map to help you on this self-guided tour, stop by the Adams National Historic Site Visitor Center at 135 Adams Street. (617) 770-1175.

RESTAURANTS

Tony's Clam Shop: Here's another place for all the old salty dogs who have an appetite for fried clams and a view of Wollaston Beach. Enjoy them both from the outdoor picnic tables. 861 Quincy Shore Drive; (617) 773-5090.

RANDOLPH

PLACES TO STAY

Holiday Inn: Dogs are allowed in rooms on the first floor. When you make your reservation, let the management know your pooch will be staying with you. Rates range from $89 to $115. 1374 North Main Street, Randolph, MA 02368; (781) 961-1000.

REVERE

PARKS, BEACHES, AND RECREATION AREAS

• **Revere Beach** 🐾 🐾 See **134** on page 252.

A roomy paved path separates this narrow, three-mile-long beach from Revere Beach Boulevard. Even though dogs aren't allowed on the beach from May 1 through September 30, you and your canine companion can do some summertime people watching from one of the shaded pavilions along the paved walkway. The beach is managed by the Metropolitan District Commission, so dogs must be on leash.

From State Route 1A, take Beach Street to Revere Beach Boulevard. Parking is available right along the beach. Open from dawn to dusk. (781) 727-8856.

RESTAURANTS

Kelly's: A trip to Revere wouldn't be complete without a stop at Kelly's, which is world famous for its roast beef sandwiches and lobster rolls. Expect anything you order from one of the to-go windows to bring out your dog's "I'm-so-hungry" eyes. Across the street is Revere Beach (see previous entry), where you'll find plenty of seating along the beach pavilions. 410 Revere Beach Boulevard; (781) 233-5000.

ROCKLAND

PLACES TO STAY

Holiday Inn Express: Call in advance and let the folks here know your dog will be in tow. New and roomy, the place offers reasonable rates: $89 to $95 per night, including breakfast. It's right off State Route 3 at Exit 14. 909 Hingham Street, Rockland, MA 02370; (781) 871-5660.

Ramada Inn: When there's no room at the inn in some of the resort towns of Plymouth and Duxbury, try staying here. It's right off State Route 3 and accessible to all the South Shore stops. Standard room rates range from $65 to $105. Smoking rooms are used for guests with pets. 929 Hingham Street, Rockland, MA 02370; (781) 871-0545; www.ramada.com.

ROCKPORT

Samuel de Champlain first landed here in 1603 and named it Beauport for its stunning beauty. Today, the charming town has small shops, scenic harbors, and quaint B&Bs (sorry, no dogs allowed in most of them). You and your canine pal will love strolling the wharf at Bearskin Neck and dining alfresco over the water in the summer months.

PARKS, BEACHES, AND RECREATION AREAS

- **Dogtown Commons—See Gloucester, Dogtown Commons on page 296.**

- **Halibut Point State Park/Halibut Point Reservation** 🐾 🐾 ◀● See **135** on page 250.

If you like rocks, we've got rocks. And more rocks. Encompassing an old quarry and leading down to the edge of the Atlantic Ocean, this park offers a panoramic, almost primeval, view of the water from a vast field of glacially formed boulders. There isn't much of a beach, but if you like rocks. . .

Halibut Point, at the northernmost tip of Rockport, is small, only 68 acres, but big enough to be split between two park systems. The Massachusetts state park system and the Trustees of Reservations share administration duties.

There is a $2 parking fee between Memorial Day and Labor Day.

From State Route 128 in Gloucester, take Exit 11 to Washington Street/State Route 127 north and Rockport. Washington Street becomes Granite Street. Turn left on Gott Avenue. Parking is on the right. Open from sunrise to 8 P.M. (978) 546-2997 or (978) 921-1944.

RESTAURANTS

Lobster Pool: Here's where you'll find the best views in Rockport, and guess what? Your dog is invited along. Right at the water's edge in Folly Cove at the tip of Cape Ann, you can catch a great lobster or seafood dinner and take it outside to picnic along the ocean. Prices are moderate for seafood, so if you can accept eating on paper plates in a gorgeous but rustic setting, then we think this restaurant offers the best value in town. 329 Granite Street/State Route 127; (978) 546-7808.

Sundays: After lunch at the Lobster Pool, stop for ice cream at Sundays.

(Hey, it's only a few calories—and you'll be walking it off, right?) There are plenty of ice-cream stops in Rockport, but this cute shop on the wharf at Bearskin Neck has some terrific flavors. Chris had Muddy Sneakers, an appropriate choice considering the state of his own shoes. It's along the wharf on Bearskin Neck; there is no phone.

PLACES TO STAY

The Sandy Bay Motel: Located just outside town on the shore road to Gloucester, this clean and roomy motel is the only place in Rockport you can stay with your dog. You'll be a few short blocks from town and driving distance to all Cape Ann has to offer. Dogs are allowed in only one of their five buildings, so you must let them know you will be bringing your pet. Rates range from to $80 to $200, depending on the season. There is a $10-per-night charge for Rover. 173 Main Street, Rockport, MA 01966; (978) 546-7155.

SALEM

It's hard to resist calling this town bewitching. We're referring, of course, to the infamous Witch Trials of 1692, which shall forever be associated with Salem's name. However, Salem has managed to make a virtue of this dark moment in its history. Reminders of the witch hunt lure visitors to its Witch Museum, and, while in town, folks discover traces of its less notorious, more illustrious past as a maritime power.

PARKS, BEACHES, AND RECREATION AREAS

• **Salem Common** 😊 😊 See **136** on page 250.

A big, open, well-maintained park in the heart of town, Salem Common is a perfect spot for doggy socializing, ball throwing, or just a leisurely sniff. Protected from the traffic on Washington Square by a wrought-iron fence, this space offers plenty of room for you and your pooch to stretch your legs and meet the neighbors. Across the street from the Salem Witch Museum, it's in walking distance of many historical points of interest. If you live here, you probably use the park daily. If you're just passing through, we recommend it as a stop on your way in or out of town. Dogs must be on leash.

From the center of town at the intersection of State Routes 114 and 1A, follow Derby Street east. Turn left on Hawthorne Boulevard. The common is at the intersection of Washington Square. Open from dawn to dusk. (978) 744-0171, extension 21.

NATURE HIKES AND URBAN WALKS

Salem Heritage Trail: To take this 1.7-mile, self-guided walking tour of historic Salem, follow the painted red line along the city's sidewalks. Stroll past the House of the Seven Gables (immortalized in Nathaniel Hawthorne's novel of the same name), Pickering Wharf, and other notable wharves and maritime buildings. You'll also wander by the Salem Common (see above) and the many wickedly fascinating sites of the Salem Witch Trials. Dogs are not allowed inside any of the museums.

Pick up a free map at the National Park Service Visitor Center at 2 Liberty Street. (978) 744-0004.

RESTAURANTS

Derby Fish & Lobster: Whenever Inu and Chris meet for lunch in Salem, they do it here, right in the heart of town. The railed outdoor patio is a perfect place to hang out. A busy guy like Inu always arrives late, so Chris usually orders some chowder while he's waiting. Once Inu shows up, they order a full meal. The menu features grilled swordfish, seafood kabobs, bouillabaisse, and the best cornbread this side of the Mason-Dixon line. 215 Derby Street; (978) 745-2064.

PLACES TO STAY

Hawthorne Hotel: With 89 charming rooms, this beautiful and stately hotel in the heart of Salem is an upscale lodging where you and your pooch can bunk down in style. Right next to the Salem Common (see page 335), it's a stone's throw from the Salem Witch Museum, restaurants, and shopping. The management prefers smallish dogs; call ahead and discuss your dog's needs with them first. Rates range from $85 to $205. Dogs pay $15 per stay (whether it's one night or many). 18 West Washington Square, Salem, MA 01970; (978) 744-4080 or (800) SAY-STAY.

Salem Inn: A little gem of a bed-and-breakfast, this inn was built in 1834 by Captain Nathaniel West. It has 31 surprisingly spacious rooms, all with private baths. Continental breakfast will be served to you in the morning, but you'll have to bring the food for Fido. It's just a few blocks from the center of town on a rather busy thoroughfare, but for the charm and the price—from $109 to $189 a night—it's a good bet for an enjoyable weekend. 7 Summer Street, Salem, MA 01970; (978) 741-0680 or (800) 446-2995.

Stephen Daniels House: This historic bed-and-breakfast is within easy walking distance of all of Salem's haunts. It's small, only eight rooms, but very quaint and cheerful. You may bring your dog with you, but let them know you plan to do so when reserving your room. Small dogs are preferred, but large dogs won't be excluded necessarily. Rates range from $79 to $100. 1 Daniels Street, Salem, MA 01970; (978) 744-5709.

FESTIVALS

Salem Seaport Festival: On Memorial Day weekend each year, Salem launches its summer season with this annual fair held in the Salem Common (see page 335). You and your pup can mix and mingle with other folks while enjoying the food stands, arts and crafts, and entertainment. On every subsequent summer weekend, you'll find a festival—some big, some small—happening on the common. Most are suitable for your dog to attend. For specific information on each weekend's events, call the Chamber of Commerce at (978) 744-0004.

SALISBURY

PARKS, BEACHES, AND RECREATION AREAS

• **Salisbury Beach State Reservation** 😺😺😺 See **137** on page 250.
Salisbury Beach measures 520 acres, but its actual size can really vary, depending on the high or low tide. That's because the beach is about a quarter mile wide and five miles long, so when the tide's up, there isn't a lot of

sand. But at low tide, it's one of the best beaches we've found for taking a long, healthy run.

For folks who want to camp along the beach, the reservation has 483 camp-sites with electrical hookups. The campground is really a big parking lot for RVs and trailers. There are no tent sites or rest rooms, but it allows dogs. Call the Massachusettes State Camping Reservation Center at (877) 422-6762 to make sure you get a site. Dogs cannot be left unattended and must be on leash outside the RV or trailer. Rates are $7 per night for tent sites; $9 per night for RV hookups.

Dogs are only allowed on the beach during the off-season, from Patriot's Day to Columbus Day; they must be on leash at all times.

From Interstate 95, take Exit 58 to State Route 110/Elm Street east. Turn left on State Route 1 north. Take an immediate right on Beach Road/State Route 1A north. The park and a large parking lot are on the right. Open from sunrise to sunset. (978) 462-4481; www.ReserveAmerica.com.

PLACES TO STAY

• *Salisbury Beach State Reservation camping:* See pages 336–337.

SAUGUS

PARKS, BEACHES, AND RECREATION AREAS

• **Breakheart Reservation** 🐾🐾🐾 🐾 See **138** on page 252.
The first thing you'll notice about Breakheart Reservation is that a paved road loops through the middle of it. This need not break your heart. One-mile Pine Tops Road, a single-lane, one-way route, is closed to auto traffic most of the year. Bikers, walkers, runners, and stroller pushers who don't want to rough it on the hiking trails are the only traffic it sees.

The centerpieces of the reservation are Silver and Pearce Lakes. Surrounded by swaying pines, both clean, clear lakes sparkle in the sunshine. Pearce Lake has a public beach for swimming and a large parking lot. Dogs can swim in either lake, but they're not welcome on the beach. It's no great loss, however, as the Pearce Lake beach tends to get crowded. Silver Lake is smaller and more secluded—and a better bet for you and your dog.

Breakheart Reservation requires that visiting dogs be on a leash. The reservation's 640 acres are managed by the Metropolitan District Commission. Pick up a free trail map at the ranger station located at the main entrance.

From State Route 1, take the Lynn Fells Parkway west for a tenth of a mile. Turn right on Forest Street. Parking is available at the reservation entrance and during the summer at the two lakes. Open from 10 A.M. to 6 P.M., but the entrance gate closes at 5 P.M. (781) 233-0834.

NATURE HIKES AND URBAN WALKS

Saugus Iron Works National Historic Site: With your pooch by your side, you can tour Saugus's reconstructed ironworks and smelting furnaces and see for yourself why the town is considered the birthplace of the American iron and steel industry. Operated from 1646 to the 1670s, this was one of the first industrial sites in the New World. Most exhibits are outside, or inside the blast furnace barn and power mill; your leashed dog is more than welcome to view them with you. The site is open from 9 A.M. to 5 P.M. (4 P.M. from November to March), except on major holidays. Admission is free. 244 Central Street; (781) 233-0050.

SEEKONK

PLACES TO STAY

Motel 6: All Motel 6 locations allow dogs, as long as you don't leave them unattended. One dog is welcome per room. Rates are $59 a night. 821 Fall River Avenue, Seekonk, MA 02771; (508) 336-7800, (800) 4-MOTEL6.

Ramada Inn: Rates range from $80 to $120 plus a $10 nightly fee for your pet. 940 Fall River Avenue, Seekonk, MA 02771; (508) 336-7300.

SCITUATE

PARKS, BEACHES, AND RECREATION AREAS

• Humarock Beach 🐾🐾 See 139 on page 251.

We'd like to imagine that at one time this spot was called Bringarock Beach. Back then it was a white, sandy stretch of coast, but the name inspired people to actually haul stones and rocks here, and that's why the beach is now completely covered with them. The town of Scituate renamed the place so that folks would come down and hum a rock out into the sea, thus restoring the sandy shore. So far, it hasn't happened.

The beach runs about three miles, so you can get in a great workout here. There's only a small stretch of sand when the tide is low; otherwise, it's a rocky road. Unless your dog has figured out how to skip stones, the going can be tough on the paws. There are leash and pooper-scooper laws here, but dogs are welcome year-round, even in summer. Park at the lot on Marshfield Avenue, a block from the beach. Open from 6 A.M. to 10 P.M. (781) 545-8743.

• Scituate Driftway Recreation Fish and Wildlife Development 🐾🐾🐾 See 140 on page 251.

For such a simple, rustic place, this park has an awfully long name. But no matter the name, your dog won't be the first to blaze the trails here. There's an easy trail that loops about a mile along First Herring Brook. The river part of the trail can be a bit muddy, so, if you want to avoid wet feet, stick to the inland path that ventures through the sand dunes. Benches along the way make fine resting spots. This used to be a leash-free park, but recently the city revoked this privilege, and now dogs are required to be leashed. The reason? You guessed it. A poop problem. What can we say?

From the intersection of State Routes 3A and 123, take Country Way to New Driftway into Driftway. The park and a parking lot are on the right. Open from dawn to dusk. (781) 545-8721.

RESTAURANTS

Dribbles Ice Cream: In the heart of Scituate Harbor, this little creamery makes a good stop on a hot summer's day. Sit at an outdoor table or take your treat across the street to the benches overlooking the harbor. 4 Brook Street; (781) 544-3600.

Morning Glories Bakery: Dogs aren't allowed inside, but they're more than welcome to pop their noses out the car window as you pull up to the drive-in. This country bakery is a great morning stop for muffins and coffee to go on the way to Scituate Driftway Recreation Fish and Wildlife Development (see page 338). 52 Country Way; (781) 545-3400.

PLACES TO STAY

Clipper Ship Lodge: We would describe this 29-room motel's style as "corporate quaint." It's quaint because the rooms have pleasant floral wallpaper and mahogany furniture, but corporate because each one looks like the next. Still, it's right in the heart of town overlooking lovely Scituate Harbor, all rooms have great views, and dogs are welcome, so what are we complaining about? Room rates range from $72 to $159. There is an additional $10 charge for your dog per stay. 7 Beaver Dam Road, Scituate, MA 02066; (781) 545-5550 or (800) 368-3818.

SHERBORN

Fortunately for dogs, Sherborn has a flexible leash law: You may walk your dog unleashed in all parks and recreation areas if she is under voice control.

PARKS, BEACHES, AND RECREATION AREAS

• Barber Reservation 🐾🐾🐾 🐕 See **141** on page 250.
Your Yorkshire terrier may think of the English countryside when he lays eyes on this gentle 189-acre reservation. Beautiful meadows are surrounded by fruit trees and old stone walls. Once used for farming, the land is now a well-maintained open space that the public can enjoy. Your pup will love shedding his leash and kicking up his paws in the meadow grasses, while you might be drawn to the cooling shade of the nearby woods.

From the town center at the intersection of State Routes 16 and 27, take Washington Street/State Route 16 west. Turn right on Western Avenue. The park and parking are on the left. Open from dawn to dusk. (508) 921-1944.

• Rocky Narrows Reservation 🐾🐾🐾🐾 See **142** on page 250.
Boston may be only half an hour away by car, but this unique plot of land feels much more isolated than it is. Although the 157-acre reservation is accessible only by canoe, trails reach up and over the Charles River, providing a steep path down to the river and a great vantage point for watching the waters slide by. From the Forest Street entrance, take the pathway across the meadow on your left and follow it through the hemlock and pine forest for almost a mile until you reach the vista point overlooking the Charles River. There is actually a pretty steep drop here, suitable only for agile dogs. You can scramble down to the banks on a very narrow path if you choose, or enjoy the views from above. The trails wind about above the river, and the terrain is quite pretty: gently rolling open fields surrounded by pine, oak, and hemlock trees.

Canoeists can launch at the Bridge Street bridge and paddle to the reservation. Once there, be careful to note your location, as the trails can get somewhat confusing and are not very well marked. Dogs must be leashed throughout.

From the town center at the intersection of State Routes 16 and 27, take Main Street/State Route 27 south. Turn left on Goulding Street. The park entrance is at the Forest Street intersection, across the road. Open from 9 A.M. to sunset. (508) 921-1944.

RESTAURANTS

C & L Frosty: Your dog is more than welcome to join you at one of the picnic tables outside this nifty burger joint, which makes a great stop after a hot day on the trails. The extensive menu lists full dinners, sandwiches, and ice-cream sundaes. 27B North Main Street; (508) 655-7570.

SOMERSET

PLACES TO STAY

Quality Inn: Rates range from $90 to $100, and pets cannot be left unattended. 1878 Wilbur Avenue, Somerset, MA 02725; (508) 678-4545, (800) 228-5151.

STOUGHTON

PARKS, BEACHES, AND RECREATION AREAS

• **Bird Street Conservation Area** 🐾🐾🐾 🐾 🐾 See **143** on page 251.
This terrific park is definitely not just for the birds. When you drive to the end of Bird Street, your pup will soon learn that she's in for a "tweet." And you'll find lots to crow about, too. The 450-acre parcel of land can be explored via three main trails: the green and blue trails, which start at the Bird Street entrance, and the orange trail, just off the trailhead at the water tower. All are marked by colors blazed on tree trunks, so stick with the paint, and you'll be flying along the trails in no time.

Dogs must be leashed on all of the trails. Another drawback is that we occasionally run into those annoying dirt bikers, but they are restricted to the outer edge of the orange trail in the north end of the park by West Street.

From the town center at the intersection of Washington Street/State Route 138, Pearl Street, and Canton Street/State Route 27, take Washington Street south. Turn right on Plain Street, then left on Morton Street. Make a right on Bird Street and proceed to the end, where you'll find the park. Park on the street. Additional street parking is available at the end of Malcolm Road. To get there, take Marron Avenue south from Bird Street and turn right on Malcolm Road. Open from dawn to dusk. (781) 341-1300, extension 262.

SUDBURY

PARKS, BEACHES, AND RECREATION AREAS

• **Gray Reservation/Haynes Meadow Conservation Land**
🐾🐾🐾 🐕 See **144** on page 250.
This is one of George's favorite parks in Sudbury. The 35 acres of the Sudbury

Valley Trustees' Gray Reservation and the 37-acre parcel of Haynes Meadow offer a series of varied trails you and your leash-free dog will love. They'll take you through an old pine forest, along several brooks running through an open meadow, on an esker trail (a narrow ridge created by a glacier), and to a freshwater pond where you can take a dip.

From Boston Post Road/State Route 20, take Horse Pond Road north. Turn right on Peakham Road and then left on Blueberry Hill Lane. The park and a parking lot are at the road's end. Open from dawn to dusk. (978) 443-8891 or (978) 443-6300.

•Hop Brook Marsh Conservation Land 🐾🐾🐾 🐕 See **145** on page 250.

The big challenge of this 80-acre reservation is not the trail itself, but the fitness stations along the way. Your dog won't give two sniffs for the pull-up bars, the step course, the obstacle course, or the jungle gym—mainly because he'll be too preoccupied scampering about leash free. But you might wish to get in a little exercise of your own. It's a great alternative to sweating inside a gym, but don't feel threatened by the equipment if you just want to go for a gentle stroll through this pine forest.

From Boston Post Road/State Route 20, proceed north on Peakham Road. Turn left on Old Garrison Road and then right on Dutton Road. The park and a parking lot are on the left. Open from dawn to dusk. (978) 443-8891.

•Nobscot Conservation Land 🐾🐾🐾 🐕 See **146** on page 250.

A visit here will take you back to a time when life moved a tad slower and your best friend was your animal. Okay, so maybe people depended on their horses more than anything then, but now the dog is number one, and at this tranquil spot you can both make believe you're a part of old New England. A short distance from the historic Wayside Inn (see below), the entire 118-acre area looks much as it did in the 18th century. Trails will take you through an old apple orchard, over a dam built to supply running water to the Wayside Inn, and to the top of Nobscot Hill, the highest point in Sudbury. Your dog may not care about the view, but getting to the hilltop will be great fun for all.

From Boston Post Road/State Route 20, take Brimstone Lane south. The park and a parking lot are on the left. Open from dawn to dusk. (978) 443-8891.

NATURE HIKES AND URBAN WALKS

Longfellow's Wayside Inn: You and your dog can take a self-guided walking tour of the grounds of this wonderful old tavern, a must-see for Revolutionary War buffs. Immortalized by Henry Wadsworth Longfellow's famous poem "Wayside Inn," this tavern is the oldest operating inn in America. On this walk you'll see the Redstone School (a former student there was the inspiration for the nursery rhyme "Mary Had a Little Lamb"), the Martha and Mary Chapel, the Wayside Grist Mill, and of course the tavern itself, where revolutionaries met and planned the events of April 19, 1775. You and your dog will feel right at home exploring the well-marked trails through the rustic country grounds. Wayside Inn Road; (978) 443-1776 or (800) 339-1776.

SWAMPSCOTT

PARKS, BEACHES, AND RECREATION AREAS

• **Blaney Beach** 🐾🐾 🐕 See **147** on page 252.

This is a good news/bad news deal. Here's the bad news: dogs aren't even allowed to set paw on Blaney Beach from May 1 to October 1. The good news? The rest of the year dogs can romp leash free as long as they're under voice control and you're nearby to pick up after them.

From State Route 1A, take Eastern Avenue/State Route 129 east. After veering left, Eastern Avenue becomes Humphrey Street. Blaney Beach and the town pier are across from Greenwood Avenue. Park on Humphrey Street. Open from dawn to dusk. (781) 596-8871.

• **Phillips Beach** 🐾🐾 🐕 See **148** on page 252.

As at Blaney Beach (see previous entry), your dog is welcome off leash during the winter and spring, but he's not allowed here at all from May 1 to October 1. Also, as at Blaney, the surf is strong because half-mile-long Phillips Beach opens on the Atlantic Ocean. Inu loves to jump the waves as they come rolling in here. While your dog romps in the surf, watch him to make sure he doesn't get carried away (literally).

From State Route 1A, take Eastern Avenue/State Route 129 east. Where Eastern Avenue turns left into Humphrey Street, continue straight on Atlantic Avenue/State Route 129. Turn right on Ocean or Longley Avenues. Park on Ocean, Longley, or Shepard Avenues. Open from dawn to dusk. (781) 596-8871.

RESTAURANTS

Dale's Red Rock: This fine seafood restaurant along Nahant Bay has a take-out window and a couple of tables on the patio. The ocean views are reserved for the indoor seating, but we enjoy chowing down on the clams and watching the beach traffic idle by outside. 141 Humphrey Street; (781) 595-9339.

Newman's Bakery: Never mind the assortment of bagels and pastries for you, there are biscuits, water, and even an outdoor leash hook for your dog. And it's all right down the road from Phillip's Beach. 252 Humphrey Street; (781) 592-1550.

TOPSFIELD

PARKS, BEACHES, AND RECREATION AREAS

• **Bradley-Palmer State Park** 🐾🐾🐾 See **149** on page 250.

This nifty park has something to offer in any season. It features 721 acres of hilly terrain filled with open meadows, woodsy trails, and a serene, pretty section of the Ipswich River. Trails are great for hiking and jogging in summer. In winter folks can cross-country ski on the paths and snowshoe across the park's wide-open areas. And your leased canine companion can accompany you everywhere.

The park does come with some obstacles—to be specific, the 15-hands-high type of obstacle. You're in horse country when you enter Topsfield, and this park is heavily used by the towering, four-hoofed creatures. You must watch out on the trails, and for obvious reasons your dog must remain on leash to prevent either scaring the horses or getting hurt by them.

To reach the main entrance from State Route 1, take Ipswich Road east. Turn right on Asbury Street. The park entrance is on the left. Open from sunrise to sunset. (781) 887-5931.

RESTAURANTS

Busy B's: We don't know how busy they were "B"-ing, but this roadside eatery offers a wide range of burgers, fried fish, and box lunches in a scenic setting. The prices are moderate, the food is fine, and there's ample outdoor seating to accommodate you, your dog, and the rest of the world. A decent sniffing spot behind the restaurant will be a godsend if your dog has been traveling in the car for a while. Grab lunch on the way to or from your hiking destination. 41 Haverhill Road/State Route 97; (978) 887-8956.

WAKEFIELD

PARKS, BEACHES, AND RECREATION AREAS

• Lake Quannapowitt 🐾🐾 See **150** on page 252.
The three-mile loop around the lake makes a terrific weekend walk. You'll have to share the path with half the town, unfortunately, but that just means that it's a great community gathering place. Although it's popular with residents, the real local color is provided by the ducks and geese who angle for handouts on the lake. You'll love watching the windsurfers cut across the sparkling water, and your leashed dog will love taking a cool dip on a warm summer's day.

The lake is bordered by Main Street/State Route 129, Church Street, North Avenue, and Quannapowitt Parkway. From State Route 128, take Exit 39 to North Avenue south. The main parking area is at Veterans Field. Additional parking is along Main Street. Open from dawn to dusk. (781) 246-6345.

Diversions
Walk 9K with your K-9: Amble around Lake Quannapowitt and raise money for the worthy cause of the Muscular Dystrophy Association. You and your dog can join the throngs on a New England fall day. It's held on the last Sunday in September. For more details, contact the K-9 Walk for the Muscular Dystrophy Association, 20 Conant Street, Danvers, MA 01923; (978) 777-0333.

WALTHAM

PARKS, BEACHES, AND RECREATION AREAS

• Beaver Brook Reservation—See Belmont, Beaver Brook Reservation on pages 260–261.

• Prospect Hill Park 🐾🐾 See **151** on page 252.
The park is open year-round, but Prospect Hill Road, which runs through the middle, only allows vehicles from April to October. You and your leashed dog can always walk the 1.5-mile route—just be prepared for a hardy climb at the

start. Want to know how steep it is? Well, in winter, Prospect Hill offers a small downhill ski area. On top, however, the terrain levels out. The access gate to Prospect Hill Road is on the right at the park entrance.

From State Route 128, take Exit 27 to Totten Pond Road. The park entrance is on the right. Open from dawn to dusk. (781) 893-4040.

PLACES TO STAY

The Westin Hotel: Perched above State Route 128 but well away from the traffic noise, this hilltop hotel rolls out the red carpet for its four-footed guests. Rates range from $99 to $289. 70 Third Avenue, Waltham, MA 02154; (781) 290-5600; www.westin.com.

WAYLAND

Throughout Wayland, dogs can go off leash if they obey voice commands and remain in view of the person they're with at all times.

PARKS, BEACHES, AND RECREATION AREAS

• Castle Hill Conservation Area/Trout Brook Conservation Area
🐾🐾🐾 🐕 See **152** on page 250.

Set in an old pine forest, this park was one of the first conservation lands to be established in Wayland. The well-planned trails loop and meander through 60 stunning acres of woodland. Off the red trail, you'll see a deep kettle hole formed by an ancient glacier. You can't go too far because the trails simply loop around each other, but you can't get lost either. We like to take the trails up and down the hills and through the valleys until George and Inu are dog tired. Even though you're near homes here, there is something very peaceful about this forest. Take the yellow trail to return to the entrance. Dogs are allowed off leash.

From Boston Post Road/State Route 20, take Concord Road/State Route 126 north. Turn left on Sherman's Bridge Road and left again on Alpine Road. Parking is available on both sides of the road by the ball fields. Castle Hill is to the left of the ball fields. Trout Brook is at the intersection of Alpine and Sherman's Bridge Roads. Open from a half hour before sunrise to a half hour after sunset. Sudbury Valley Trustees, (978) 443-6300; Wayland Conservation Commission, (508) 358-3669.

• Greenways Conservation Area 🐾🐾🐾 🐕 See **153** on page 250.

The latest and greatest of Wayland's parks, 98-acre Greenways was acquired in November 1995. Plans for more trails are in the works, but it is still one of the best parks around.

The trailhead starts to the left of the old family homestead, directly beside and beyond the map board. You and your pooch will enter a narrow woodland before emerging at several lovely meadows. Cross through the middle of two meadows down to the Sudbury River. Picnic tables located along the trail are available on a first-come, first-served basis; the best site is at intersection G overlooking the river on one side and the expansive meadow on the other. Your leashless dog will love romping through the tall grass or going for a swim. You will love the peaceful, pastoral scene.

From Boston Post Road/State Route 20, take Cochituate Road/State Routes 27 and 126 south. The park is on the right, just past Windy Hill Lane. The new "temporary" parking area is across the street at Saint Ann's Church. Please park by the trailhead sign and away from the church facilities. Open from a half hour before sunrise to a half hour after sunset. Sudbury Valley Trustees, (978) 443-6300; Wayland Conservation Commission, (508) 358-3669.

• Upper Mill Brook and Lower Mill Brook Conservation Areas
🐾🐾🐾 🐕 See **154** on page 250.

Many paths and roads at this 200-acre conservation area await dogs with a yen to explore. You won't get to them all in one day, but the place is worth a return trip in any season. Managed in tandem by the Sudbury Valley Trustees and the Wayland Conservation Commission, the park provides something to suit most any doggy's tastes.

The trails are designated red, blue, and yellow, but they are randomly marked, so we suggest you rely on the intersection markers instead of the trail colors. It's also a good idea to get a map from the conservation office. Obedient dogs can go leash free.

From Boston Post Road/State Route 20, take Concord Road/State Route 126 north. The park is on the right, just past Claypit Hill Road behind the Peace Lutheran Church. Parking is permitted at the church, except on Sunday morning. Open from a half hour before sunrise to a half hour after sunset. Sudbury Valley Trustees, (978) 443-6300; Wayland Conservation Commission, (508) 358-3669.

RESTAURANTS

Caraway's: For all the makings of a great picnic, try this small deli, where you'll find everything from sandwiches, soups, and salads to baked goods, snacks, and frozen yogurt. Or just have a relaxing lunch on the outdoor patio. Either way, your hungry dog gets to sit by your side. 325 Boston Post Road/State Route 20; (508) 358-5025.

WELLESLEY

This graceful and wealthy suburb of Boston is home to Wellesley College and a very civilized leash law. Your dog is allowed to go leash free as long as she is under voice control.

PARKS, BEACHES, AND RECREATION AREAS

• Centennial Park 🐾🐾 🐕 See **155** on page 252.

Untamed and untrammeled—though we won't go so far as to call it wilderness—this lovely, uncluttered park in the middle of a residential area provides 35 acres of wide-open spaces where you and your dog can wander unfettered by leashes. There are no amenities, but we think that makes the outdoors experience that much better. At any given time of the day, you will probably meet up with other happy canine wanderers and their human companions.

From the parking area you can head off into the woods across the meadow to your right or climb the small hill directly ahead. There are no maps or special trails, so go in either direction as the whim or the whiff compels you. It will take you and your dog (who must be under voice control to go off leash) about an hour to explore the entire 40-acre park. Longfellow Pond is just up the road, and you may want to take in both places on the same day.

From State Route 128, take Exit 20 to State Route 9 west. Exit State Route 9, heading south on Cedar Street, and then veer into Hunnewell Street. Turn right on Oakland Street and proceed to the park, which is on the left. Parking is available. Open from 5 A.M. to 9 P.M. (781) 431-1019, extension 294.

- **Elm Bank Reservation—See Dover, Elm Bank Reservation on page 288.**
- **Lake Waban at Wellesley College** 🐾🐾🐾 🐕 🐾 See **156** on **page 252.**

A top weekend destination of dog lovers from throughout the Boston area, the attractive grounds of Wellesley College offer one of the best lakes around: Lake Waban. Follow the signs to the visitors parking area and head straight to the heart of campus to find this gem. You may hike along the shoreline here, but the north side of the lake is on private property, so please don't venture all the way around. College officials do not mind people with leash-free pooches using this beautiful space, but they ask that you limit your visits to weekends, holidays, and summer breaks—not when classes are in session. You will meet other dog owners here, and we think it will become one of your favorite spots, if it isn't already.

From State Route 128, take Exit 21 to Washington Street/State Route 16 west. Cross State Route 135 and the campus is on your right. Follow signs to the parking area. Open from 9 A.M. to 6 P.M. (781) 283-2376.

WESTON

PARKS, BEACHES, AND RECREATION AREAS

- **Cat Rock Park** 🐾🐾🐾 See **157** on page 250.

Your dog may have some reservations about visiting Cat Rock Park, but rest assured. Once here, he'll forget all about the name. In fact, this 65-acre park in the northeast corner of town is very popular with the canine set. Even our dogs have been converted.

The two highlights are Cat Rock Hill and Hobbs Pond. The hill towers over the park, providing grand views of Weston and Waltham to the east. The short climb to the top is strenuous, and you might want to attack it at the beginning of your walk when everyone has energy. You'll also find the town's water tank atop the hill. Head back down the hill and take any of the trails into the woods; they all lead to Hobbs Pond after about half a mile. The invigorating water is clean and cool, and the swimming hole is surrounded by woods. On the western shore there's a grassy field, a good place to dry off after a dip or to play and enjoy the sunshine.

From Interstate 95, take Exit 28 to Boston Post Road/State Route 20 west. Turn right on School Street, right on Church Street, left on North Avenue/State Route 117, and right on Drabbington Way. Parking is available at the road's end, and the trails begin behind the ball field. Open from dawn to dusk. (781) 893-7320.

• Doublet Hill/Elliston Woods Conservation Area 🐾🐾🐾 See **158** on page 250.

You and your leashed dog are sure to have a wonderfully diverse hiking experience at these two parks, which cover a total of 52 acres. Begin walking near the top of Doublet Hill, just to the left of the town's water tower. Doublet Hill is a rocky outcropping, but it's covered with plenty of shady trees and, in the spring and summer, wildflowers for eager noses to sniff. The climb to the hilltop is well worth the effort: you can sit and enjoy spectacular views of Boston and the Blue Hills after your mile-long walk. There are plenty of great spots on the hill for your dog to explore and for you to set out a picnic lunch.

From the Town Common in the town center, take School Street south into Ash Street. Turn left on Newton Street, then left on Doublet Hill Road. The park and a parking area are at the road's end. Open from dawn to dusk. (781) 893-7320.

• Sunset Corner Conservation Area 🐾🐾🐾 See **159** on page 250.

Whoever said the West Coast is the only place to see a sunset never made it to Sunset Corner. From high on the hillside there is an amazing view to the west of Mount Wachussett and, on a clear day, Mount Monadnock in New Hampshire. As evening begins, the sun fades out behind the peaks in a glorious array of colors.

Highland Street divides the 112-acre park into two sections. The upper portion, where you will find the viewpoint, has a number of wide forest roads that are popular with horseback riders and dog walkers alike. To get to the trails, follow the small stone stairway up the ridge. Just as it begins to plateau, take a moment to gaze out over the valley before continuing to the top of the rise.

From Interstate 95, take Exit 28 to Boston Post Road/State Route 20 west. Turn left on Highland Street. Look for the pullout on your right just after Love Lane. Open from dawn to dusk. (781) 893-7320.

• Weston Reservoir Conservation Area 🐾🐾🐾 See **160** on page 250.

Dogs agree: this is the place for walking in Weston and the most popular hangout in town. The reservoir itself is off-limits, separated by a fence from the rest of the park. But the wonderful country path that leads around the reservoir and through a thick pine forest has local dogs returning weekend after weekend (with their leashes, as required).

The dirt path can be a hound highway on weekend afternoons. Even though dogs cannot go for a dip in the public's water supply, four brooks flow by the path, offering well-placed rest stops along the way. Another good place to take a break is on the far north side at a large clearing overlooking the reservoir. You can't miss it: just look for the pack of happy dogs congregated there.

From Interstate 95, take Exit 28 to Boston Post Road/State Route 20 west. Turn left on Wellesley Street, then left on Ash Street. The park and a parking area are on the left and right sides of the road. Open from dawn to dusk. (781) 893-7320.

RESTAURANTS

Dairy Joy: The sight of the weekend crowds should tell you just how good the food is here, at one of our favorite places to eat. The full menu offers fish dinners, burgers, ice cream, frappés, the works. There are plenty of picnic tables where a dog can plop down to share the bounty, or you can stroll the grassy areas to escape the masses.

WESTPORT

PARKS, BEACHES, AND RECREATION AREAS

• **Horseneck Beach State Reservation** 🐾🐾🐾 See **161** on page 251.
This sandy barrier-island beach, located at the mouth of the Westport River, is a popular destination for humans, dogs, and an assortment of wildlife. The beach and its accompanying salt marsh is two miles long and totals about 537 acres looking out over the western end of Buzzards Bay.

Camping is also available. This oceanside state park has 100 sites for tents and RVs (no hookups) and a boat ramp. Dogs must be on leash and cannot be left unattended. Rates are $12 to $15 per night. Open Memorial Day weekend to Columbus Day weekend. For reservations, call (877) 422-6762.

Dogs must be leashed in all state parks.

From Interstate 195, take Exit 10 to State Route 88 south for nine miles into the park. Open sunrise to sunset. (508) 636-8816.

RESTAURANTS

Handy Hill Creamery: When everyone is hungry for something different, Handy Hill is the handy stop. The to-go menu includes ice cream, chowder, and clam cakes. Open Memorial Day to Labor Day. 55 Hixbridge Road (at State Route 88); (508) 636-0800.

PLACES TO STAY

• *Horseneck Beach State Reservation:* See above.

DIVERSIONS

Woof & Wine: Nothing is more relaxing than a picnic on a sunny afternoon. Add a bottle of wine, and you have something special. You and your dog are welcome to combine the two experiences on the grounds of the Westport Winery. Wine is available for sale, but you have to bring your own food. Dogs are not permitted in the buildings. Open daily from April to December, 12 P.M. to 5 P.M. 417 Hixbridge Road; (508) 636-3423.

WESTWOOD

PARKS, BEACHES, AND RECREATION AREAS

• **Hale Reservation** 🐾🐾🐾 See **162** on page 250.
A romp at this 1,200-acre reservation will be a highlight of any dog's trip to Westwood. With myriad trails, ponds, and meadows to sniff out, your pooch will want to return time after time. The good news is that there are over 10 miles of trails to explore. The not-so-good news is that dogs are not allowed around the ponds in the summer, when families buy memberships so they can use the ponds, and children come for the day to swim. No matter: the weather

is cooler in the winter, spring, and fall, and chances are good you'll have the place to yourselves then.

Free maps, which will help guide you on the marked and unmarked trails, are available at the front entrance. Dogs must be leashed.

From Interstate 95, take Exit 16 to High Street/State Route 109 west. Turn right on Dover Road. Turn right on Carby Street and proceed into the park. A number of parking lots are available off Carby Street. Open from 9 A.M. to dusk. (781) 326-1770.

RESTAURANTS

The Bubbling Brook: After one visit, it's impossible to cross another stream without wanting to return here for a piece of strawberry shortcake or just about any of the items listed on the extensive take-out menu. But don't take our word for it. Just follow the crowds that come from miles around. There are plenty of lunch and dinner specials to choose from and even an ice-cream parlor for dairy-loving dogs. Head out to the picnic tables on the grassy lawn to enjoy your meal. 1652 High Street/State Route 109; (781) 762-9860.

WEYMOUTH

PARKS, BEACHES, AND RECREATION AREAS

• **Great Esker Park** 🐾🐾🐾🐾 See **163** on page 252.

An amazingly varied, seemingly undiscovered world, Great Esker offers a wild adventure for you and your intrepid, leashed dog. Take your pick of terrain: hardwood forest high atop the Great Esker, marshy grassland in the low-lying country, or shoreline along the Weymouth Back River. Visit all three areas and marvel that so many different landscapes exist so close together.

From the Southeast Expressway/Interstate 93/State Routes 1 and 3, in Dorchester, take Exit 12 to State Route 3A south. Continue on State Route 3A through Quincy into Weymouth. Turn right on Green Street and then left on Julia Road. A parking lot is at the road's end. Open from dawn to dusk. (781) 337-3342.

• **Webb Memorial State Park** 🐾🐾🐾 🐾 See **164** on page 252.

Dogs aren't allowed to set paw on the Boston Harbor Islands, but they're welcome here on this majestic peninsula as long as they're wearing their leashes. The park juts out far enough into Hingham Bay to give your dog an island experience. Follow the crushed-stone paths over the rolling, grassy hills to the outermost points of the peninsula. Along the shore you'll find a mix of sand and pebble beaches. All have great views of Boston and the surrounding islands, including Grape and Slate Islands. Keep an eye out for harbor seals, which are being sighted more frequently in the harbor.

From the Southeast Expressway/Interstate 93/State Routes 1 and 3 in Dorchester, take Exit 12 to State Route 3A south. Continue on State Route 3A through Quincy into Weymouth. Turn left on Neck Street and continue on it as it becomes River Street. The park is on the left. A large parking lot is available. Open from dawn to dusk. (781) 740-1605.

RESTAURANTS

Mary Lou's News: For headline coffee, bagels, sandwiches, beverages, and more, take out the news at Mary Lou's. It's the top story in town for breakfast or lunch. Read all about it with your pup on the bench outside, or pack your meal for the trail. 768 Main Street; (781) 340-5146.

WINCHESTER

PARKS, BEACHES, AND RECREATION AREAS

• **Middlesex Fells Reservation, Western Section—See Medford, Middlesex Fells Reservation, Western Section on page 320.**

• **Mystic River Reservation, Mystic Lakes Section** 🐾🐾🐾 **See 165 on page 252.**

Although parkland covers much of the eastern shoreline of Upper and Lower Mystic Lakes, it's the Sandy Beach Peninsula that your dog will love the most. Safely tucked away from the busy traffic of the Mystic Valley Parkway, it offers plenty of room where she can kick up her canine heels and just be a dog.

Serious dog walkers like to use this area as a home base and journey down the trail that runs between Upper Mystic Lake and the Mystic Valley Parkway. You can follow it all the way into Medford and to Lower Mystic Lake. Although the path narrows in a few places, it's still a pleasant one-mile walk.

The Metropolitan District Commission manages the area and requires that dogs remain on leash. Another doggy downer is that canines are not permitted into the Sandy Beach swimming area. Oh well. Your pooch will have to content herself with the other pleasures this spot provides.

The park is located off the Mystic Valley Parkway, just south of Bacon Street and Lake View Terrace. A large parking lot is available at the park's northern end and small turnouts can be found at its southern end. Open from dawn to dusk. (781) 662-5230.

PLACES TO STAY

Ramada Inn: Within easy access of major routes into and out of Boston, this inn allows dogs. Rates range from $69 to $109. 15 Middlesex Canal Road, Woburn, MA 01801; (781) 935-8760.

Red Roof Inn: Although you won't find many parks nearby, this inn provides easy access to Boston and the North Shore. Rates range from $45 to $65. 19 Commerce Way, Woburn, MA 01801; (781) 935-7110.

WINTHROP

PARKS, BEACHES, AND RECREATION AREAS

• **Winthrop Beach See 166 on page 252.**

It's a bird! It's a plane! It's. . . both! Winthrop Beach isn't as noisy as nearby Yirrell Beach, and its shoreline is larger, but this is the first beach where we've encountered pigeons. And, yes, those other objects flying overhead are jumbo jets departing from Logan Airport. Our dogs don't seem to mind the planes or the pigeons, however. They just go on about their business of rolling in sea-weed and looking for stinky stuff. It's a dirty job, but they've got to do it. The gentle waves of Broad Sound should lure your pooch in for a dip.

Dogs aren't allowed here from May 1 through September 30; at all others times your pooch must be on a leash.

From State Route 1A, take State Route 145 to Winthrop Shore Drive. Park along the seawall. Open from dawn to dusk. (617) 536-1160.

WRENTHAM

PARKS, BEACHES, AND RECREATION AREAS

• **Birchwold Farm Conservation Area** 🐾🐾🐾 See **167** on page 251.
This is a prime destination for local dogs, and you'll soon learn why. The 80 acres of meadows, forest, and gentle hills are crisscrossed with many trails. Walk to your left or your right from the trailhead. Both paths lead over a small crest and tumble into an expansive meadow. Head across the field toward the fruit trees and explore the orchardlike terrain beyond. Or, if your leashed pooch is tired of sniffing trees, go to the left to find more open fields.

The paths are well trodden, so you won't have any trouble following them. Still, we suggest you look at the map in the open meadow just over the hill from the parking area for more details on the various hikes.

From the town center at the intersection of South Street/State Route 1A and East Street/State Route 140, take South Street south. Proceed straight onto West Street/State Route 121 and continue for three miles. The park and a large parking area are on the left. Open from dawn to dusk. (508) 384-5415.

• **F. Gilbert Hills State Forest—See Foxborough, F. Gilbert Hills State Forest on page 294.**

• **Joe's Rock Conservation Area** 🐾🐾🐾 See **168** on page 251.
Named for the towering rock at its center, this conservation area offers a lovely pond, uphill hiking trails, and one of the most beautiful views around from atop Joe's Rock. We recommend coming here just before sunset to sit with the special pooch in your life and watch the glorious display as the sun goes down over the pond. Birchwold Farms (see above) is across the street, and you might want to take in both places.

From the town center at the intersection of South Street/State Route 1A and East Street/State Route 140, take South Street south. Proceed straight onto West Street/State Route 121 and continue for three miles. The park and a parking area are on the right. Open from dawn to dusk. (508) 384-5415.

RESTAURANTS

Wampum Corner Drive-In: Plenty of outdoor tables are available for doggy diners at this local haunt that serves breakfast, lunch, and ice cream. Located just down the road from two conservation areas, Wampum is a good place to stop to gear up for a hike or relax after one. You can order eggs and coffee in the morning, burgers and fries in the afternoon. 121 South Street; (508) 384-7913.

VERMONT

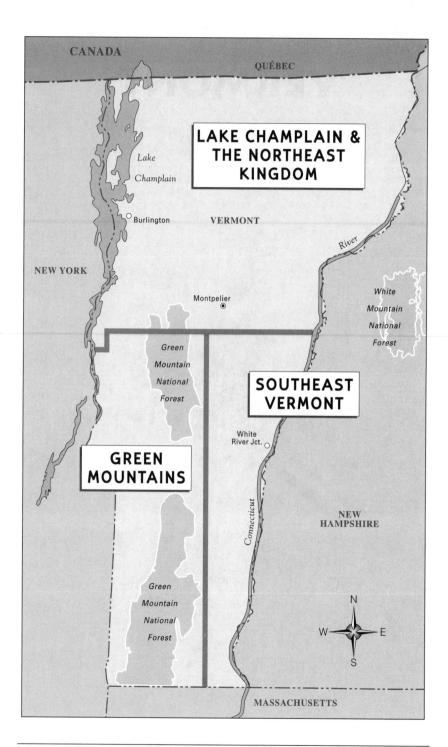

VERMONT

Vermont is among the most rural of all the 50 states, and the northern part of Vermont is the most rural part of the state, far, far away from the bright lights and big city. So undeveloped and undisturbed is much of Northern Vermont, you'll feel here as though you've traveled back in time.

Vermont has a rich history and played a large role in protecting the new American democracy. Prior to the Revolution, the Green Mountain Boys, led by Ethan Allen and Benedict Arnold (yes, that Benedict Arnold), led a revolt on Fort Ticonderoga, defeating the British in a protest against unfair taxation. In 1877, Vermont declared itself independent, and a constitution was drawn up outlawing slavery, private property, and wealth as requirements for voting rights. It remained independent for 14 years until it joined the Union in 1791 as the 14th state.

That spirit of independence remains today, and you will find that demonstrated in the parks and scenic byways throughout the state. Not as much parkland is available to dogs as in the other states, and the state parks can be downright inhospitable when it comes to our four-footed friends. But, fortunately, many quaint inns, private lands, and historical walks are available to keep you and your pup happy on a visit here.

State Parks and State Forests: If you plan to visit any state parks in Vermont, there are a few things you need to know about their rules and regulations. Dogs must be leashed. Occasionally, however, state park trails lead to forest trails, or the Long Trail, and your dog can be released there. Proof of rabies vaccination is required. This isn't just an idle rule. They really do check! A tag will do, and you're in. Dogs are not allowed in day-use-only areas, like picnic grounds and the swimming beaches. For information, contact (802) 241-3655.

Long Trail: If a little of Vermont's desire for autonomy has rubbed off on you, the 262-mile Long Trail awaits. Appropriately named, there are long miles of solitary splendor that run the entire length of the state from the Massachusetts border to Canada. With numerous side trails and 70 shelters, you can spend a day, a week, a month, or more on the trail. Some diehards commit to becoming "end-to-enders" by traversing the trail from one end to the other. Whatever your style, this is a beautiful backcountry trail, often described as a "footpath in the wilderness."

The trail was blazed by the Green Mountain Club (GMC), which still maintains and protects the trail today. In the southern portion of the state, the Long Trail doubles as the Appalachian Trail for 100 miles.

Dogs are permitted off leash on the trail under the tree line, but they must be leashed above the tree line. For the sake of the fragile arctic-alpine tundra found at higher elevations, both you and your dog need to stay on the trail at all times. Dogs should always be under voice control when not leashed.

For more information on the trail, contact the Green Mountain Club at (802) 244-7037, or visit their office at 4711 Waterbury Stowe Road, Waterbury Center, VT 05677.

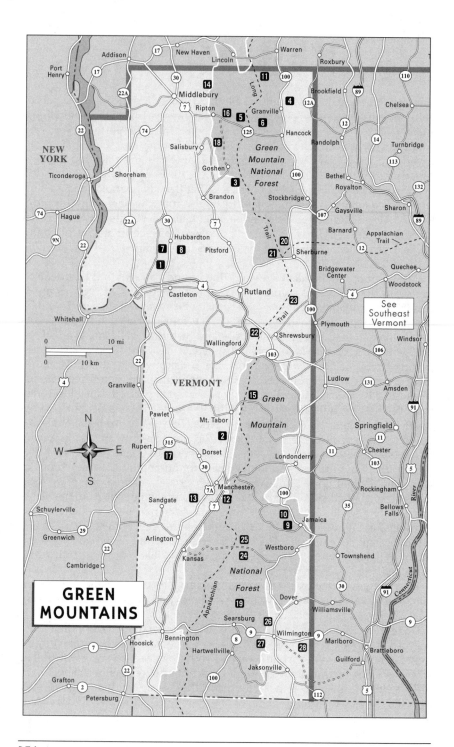

GREEN MOUNTAINS

10

GREEN MOUNTAINS

Vermont, or as it's affectionately known, the Green Mountain State, actually derives its name from the French words, *les verts monts,* or "green mountains." The origins of its name reveal how central this mountain range is to Vermont's identity. Covering 325,534 acres with over 500 miles of hiking trails, the Green Mountains simply dominate the heart of the state.

Green Mountains National Forest: Unlike the White Mountains in New Hampshire, which have long been a tourist mecca, the Green Mountain range has traditionally been a scenic but implacable presence. Virtually a wilderness until the late 18th century, but located dead center in the middle of Vermont, you can't avoid the Green Mountains even if you wanted to (and we can't imagine you would!). The majority of the state highways are forced to run north and south here with only a few steep, closed-in-winter, not–fully paved roads venturing east and west across the high peaks. And, yet, these rough roads are the most popular choices for hikers and outdoor adventurers. In simplest terms, if you are going to the Green Mountains, you are going to a great place; if you are going anywhere else, it's going to be a long drive around.

Dogs are required to be on leash here.

To cover this scenic wonder adequately we would have to devote an entire book to the many trails you will find here. Instead, we have highlighted some of the more popular, accessible, and dog-friendly hikes, but for more information we suggest you contact the National Forest District office at 231 North Main Street, Rutland, VT 05701; (802) 747-6700.

ARLINGTON

PLACES TO STAY

Cut Leaf Maple Motel: A stay at this popular inn on the western edge of the Green Mountains, if you can even get a reservation, includes breakfast on the indoor porch. There are eight comfortable rooms, all of which welcome dogs for a fee of $5. Rates range from $45 to $75. 3420 State Route 7A, Arlington, VT 05250; (802) 375-2725; www.virtualvermont.com/cutleafmaples.

Hill Farm Inn: This 17-room farmhouse and cottage complex allows dogs in the four simply furnished and charming cottages on the grounds. Your room rate includes a full breakfast each morning. Rooms range from $55 to $65. Dogs are an additional $5. Hill Farm Road, Arlington, VT 05250; (802) 375-2269 or (800) 882-2545; www.virtualcities.com.

Valhalla Motel: The rooms here are simple, but your friendly hosts, Bob and Claudette, will make sure you and your pet feel welcome. Your stay includes a country breakfast and six acres of lawns, which make the motel popular with a number of dog groups. Room rates are from $35 to $70; pets cannot be left unattended. State Route 7A, Arlington, VT 05250; (802) 375-2212, (800) 258-2212; www.virtualcities.com/vt/g/vtg9602.htm.

BENNINGTON

NATURE HIKES AND URBAN WALKS

Bennington Battle Monument State Historic Site: The 306-foot-high monument commemorates the 1777 Battle of Bennington, considered the turning point of the American Revolutionary War. It was near here that patriots from New Hampshire and Massachusetts and the Green Mountain Boys of Vermont defeated the British as they attempted to seize supplies from the Continental storehouse.

Although dogs are not permitted to climb the 412 steps of the monument, there are also five acres of grassy grounds, fresh breezes, and mountainous views.

From U.S. Route 7, take State Route 9 west for one mile. Turn right onto Monument Avenue. Parking is available. Open dawn to dusk. (802) 447-0550.

RESTAURANTS

Mexican Connection Café: Who says all there is to eat in Vermont are dairy products and tree sap? Not true! Enjoy a sandwich or Mexican dish on the outdoor patio and you'll see. Well, okay, they have ice cream too. 604 Main Street (State Route 9); (802) 447-9770.

Vern's Fish Fry: You'll get the usual fish sandwiches, burgers, and shakes here, but the friendly Vermont hospitality makes it worth the trip. Vern provides outdoor seating and a dish of water for your dog. 100 Depot Street; (802) 447-3474.

PLACES TO STAY

Apple Valley Inn and Café: This cozy 20-room motel/inn offers comfortable modern rooms in the heart of town. An on-site restaurant, pool, and simple amenities are available. Rates range from $35 to $75. State Route 7 South, Bennington, VT 05201; (802) 442-6588.

Bennington Motor Inn: The Bennington Motor Inn, three blocks from downtown, offers all the modern amenities with a country-inn atmosphere. There are 16 rooms, and rates range from $60 to $90 with an additional charge of $10 for pets per night. 143 West Main Street, Bennington, VT 05201; (802) 442-5479, (800) 359-9900; www.coolcruisers.net/benningtonmotorinn.htm.

Fife 'n' Drum Motel: This 18-room motel is open from the end of April to January and comes with a heated pool, three-acre lawn, and picnic area. There are also four efficiency units. Only small and medium-sized dogs are permitted with advanced notice, and pets can't be left unattended. Room rates are $49 to $85 plus an additional $5 pet charge per night. 693 U.S. Route 7 South, Bennington, VT 05201-9390; (802) 442-4074; www.sover.net/~toberua.

Knotty Pine Motel: This standard roadside motel has air-conditioning and a swimming pool. There are 17 rooms and two with efficiencies. Pets may not be left unattended. Rates range from $44 to $84. 130 Northside Drive, Bennington, VT 05201; (802) 442-5487; www.bennington.com/knottypine.

DIVERSIONS

Casey Canine: Casey Junior's comin' down the line, and your dog is too! All (and we mean all) aboard the Vermont Valley Flyer, a 15-mile scenic train ride from the North Bennington Depot to Manchester following the Battenkill River. Small dogs are welcome on the one-hour, round-trip excursion on the 1930s diesel train. Adult fare is $14. The train runs June through September. For schedule and information, call (802) 463-3069.

BRANDON

PLACES TO STAY

Brandon Motor Lodge: This standard roadside motel has 18 rooms and makes for a great base camp when exploring the Green Mountains. Rates range from $45 to $75 plus a $5 fee per pet per night. U.S. Route 7, Brandon, VT 05733; (800) 675-7614, (802) 247-9594.

Hivue Bed-and-Breakfast Tree Farm: Dogs stay in style at the Hivue, as they are welcome only in the suites at the inn. There are hiking trails just a tennis ball's throw from the back door. Suites start at $155 per night. 753 East Hill Road, Brandon, VT 05733; (802) 247-3042, (800) 880-3042.

Moffett House Bed-and-Breakfast: Dogs are happily accepted at the Moffett House. This Victorian home is filled with antiques, and provides seven guest rooms—three with private baths. Rates range from $70 to $125 depending on the room and the season. 69 Park Street, Brandon, VT 05733; (802) 247-3843, (800) 394-7239.

The Gingerbread House Bed-and-Breakfast: This lovely antique filled home has one suite for guests and welcomes well-mannered dogs, for a small surcharge of $10 per pet. Room rates start at $60. 232 State Route 73 East, Brandon, VT 05733; (802) 247-3380.

CASTLETON

PARKS, BEACHES, AND RECREATION AREAS

• **Bomoseen State Park/Bomoseen State Forest** 🐾🐾🐾 See ❶ on page 356.

You get two parks for the price of one in this scenic area located at the tip of Lake Bomoseen. Bomoseen State Park, a 365-acre property, actually lies within the larger 2,940-acre Bomoseen State Forest, making for some impressive acreage. With miles of steeply wooded trails, remote ponds, and wetlands along smaller 202-acre Glen Lake, your pup will be in water-world heaven.

The park lies in the Taconics Range, once known as the slate-producing region of Vermont, and several old quarries are located within the park. Several slate buildings and foundations also remain here, and you can review this mountain history on the mile-long self-guided Slate History Trail along Lake Bomoseen. Brochures are available at the ranger station.

Several trails provide great hiking opportunities through the woods. There is the challenging, occasionally steep, five-mile Glen Lake Trail which leads to Half Moon State Park (see Hubbardton), taking you past some old farming remains and forests of oak and hickory. For the less agile pup, the 1.5-mile Bomoseen Hiking Loop provides a moderately easy walk through the wildlife preserve.

Dogs must be leashed in the parks and kept out of day-use areas. Proof of rabies vaccination is required. There is a $2 entrance fee.

From U.S. Route 4A, take West Shore Road north for four miles to the park. Open dawn to dusk, mid-May to Columbus Day. (802) 265-4242.

NATURE HIKES AND URBAN WALKS

Delaware and Hudson Rail Trail: This flat, grassy trail runs for 10 miles along an old rail bed from Castleton to Poultney, making it an easy walk for you and your pup. Access the trail along North Road near the junction of State Routes 4A and 30. (802) 241-3655.

DORSET

PARKS, BEACHES, AND RECREATION AREAS

• **Emerald Lake State Park** 🐾🐾 See ❷ on page 356.

Although Vermont's state parks don't exactly roll out the red carpet for dogs, they are permitted on the short trails in this particular park. Luckily, the paths lead to a few of the more remote spots on the lake. Dogs must be on leash are not permitted in any of the day-use areas. There is a $2 entrance fee.

The park is located off U.S. Route 7. Open dawn to dusk from mid-May to Columbus Day. (802) 362-1655.

GOSHEN

PARKS, BEACHES, AND RECREATION AREAS

• **Green Mountain National Forest—Mount Horrid** 🐾🐾🐾 🥾 **See 3 on page 356.**

We have no idea why this lovely place has such a "horrid" name. We can assure you, it's anything but. Unlike the wooded summit of Mount Horrid itself (which doesn't have views at all—maybe that's why it's called "Horrid"!), the view from the bald open rocks of the Great Cliff is stunning. This fairly steep 1.2-mile round-trip provides a quick return for little investment, but it is not for older dogs. Dogs on leash, please.

To reach the cliffs, take the Long Trail north from Brandon Gap (State Route 73) for six-tenths of a mile. Look for a short side trail on the right. If you continue north another six-tenths of a mile, you can complete the climb to 3,216-foot Mount Horrid and its wooded summit. Dogs must be on leash in the national forest.

From State Route 53 in Brandon, take State Route 73 east for five miles. Parking is available at the Long Trail trailhead. Open 24 hours a day. (802) 747-6700.

GRANVILLE

PARKS, BEACHES, AND RECREATION AREAS

• **Granville Reservation State Park** 🐾🐾🐾 🥾 **See 4 on page 356.**

The 1,171 acres at Granville Reservation State Park are a canyon of natural beauty. However, because of limited trail access into this wilderness, most of it must be viewed from your car. The sheer rock drops of the Granville Gulf create an impressive chasm to drive through, but at its base there is little room for more than the seven-mile stretch of State Route 100 and the river that runs alongside.

If a drive isn't enough for your leashed dog, you can hike a short quarter-mile boardwalk to Moss Glen Falls. At 30 feet high, it flows into the headwaters of the Mad and White Rivers and is one of the state's most popular falls.

Dogs must be on leash in all state parks.

The park is located on a seven-mile stretch of State Route 100 beginning just north of the center of Granville and running to the Warren town line. Open dawn to dusk. (802) 388-4362.

HANCOCK

PARKS, BEACHES, AND RECREATION AREAS

• **Green Mountain National Forest—Middlebury Gap** 🐾🐾🐾 **See 5 on page 356.**

This divide in the Green Mountains marks the difference between a raindrop ending up in the Connecticut River or in Lake Champlain. Perhaps this realization has given nearby Silent Cliff its name, as pooch after pooch sits quietly upon this rocky outcrop contemplating the significance of an inch or two in the life of a raindrop.

To reach this philosophical pinnacle, follow the Long Trail north four-tenths of a mile to the Silent Cliff Trail on your right. It's another easier half mile to the prominent cliffs and panoramic views of Middlebury Gap and much of the central Green Mountains.

Dogs must be on leash in the national forest.

From State Route 32 in Ripton, take State Route 125 east for 5.5 miles. Parking is available at the Long Trail trailhead. Open 24 hours a day. (802) 747-6700.

• Green Mountain National Forest—Texas Falls 😊 😊 🐾 See 6 on page 356.

Take this easy, one-mile loop trail from Texas Falls along a spectacular gorge carved out by the Texas Brook. You might say its all downhill from here, for the impressive falls are located at the trailhead and the loop begins after crossing a rustic bridge over the brook. Throughout the gorge are a series of falls, potholes, and other wild formations created by the endless forces of moving water. There is also a picnic area along the trail.

Dogs must be on leash.

From State Route 100, take State Route 125 west for three miles. Turn right onto a secondary forest road (look for the Texas Falls sign) for a half mile. Parking is on the left and the trailhead is on the right. Open 6 A.M. to 10 P.M. (802) 747-6700.

HUBBARDTON

PARKS, BEACHES, AND RECREATION AREAS

• Half Moon State Park 😊 😊 😊 See 7 on page 356.

Half Moon Pond is at the center of 50 acres of dense woods within Bomoseen State Forest and Half Moon State Park. The pond is sparkling clean, but your pooch is not permitted on the swimming beaches. The Crossover Trail, which leads from Half Moon State Park to Bomoseen and Glen Lake, runs five miles through lovely woodland.

For a shorter but equally scenic hike, take the Nature Trail starting near the entrance of the park.

Dogs must be leashed and are not permitted in day-use areas. There is a $2 entrance fee.

From State Route 30, take Town Road west for two miles. Turn left onto Moscow Road for 1.5 miles. Look for the wooden signs to the entrance. Open dawn to dusk mid-May to Columbus Day. (802) 273-2848.

• Hubbardton Battlefield State Historic Site 😊 😊 😊 See 8 on page 356.

On this grassy hill of 352 acres, the only Revolutionary War battle in Vermont laid the groundwork that finally led to the defeat of the British at Saratoga. In 1777, when British General Burgoyne captured Mount Independence and Ticonderoga, the American troops had to beat a hasty retreat, fleeing through Hubbardton. Here, some troops stayed behind to fight, hoping to give the main force time to escape. It worked, and, although the troops were defeated, they kept the British from advancing. This turned out to be a crucial turning point in the war.

George and Inu like to stage their own mock battle, chasing each other over the rolling hills and wide grassy lawns. Dogs are permitted on the battlefield, but they need to be leashed.

The Visitor Center is open late May through Veterans Day, Wednesday through Sunday, 9:30 A.M. to 5:00 P.M.

From U.S. Route 4, take East Hubbardton Road north seven miles. The battlefield is on your right. Open 24 hours a day. (802) 828-3051.

JAMAICA

PARKS, BEACHES, AND RECREATION AREAS

• Ball Mountain Dam and Lake Recreation Area 😺 😺 😺 😺 🐕 See 9 on page 356.

For almost 50 years, the Brattleboro Railroad ran through this 85-acre property along the West River until the tracks was destroyed by a flood in 1927. This devastation, in part, led to an overhaul of the flood-control system in the state.

Today, the Ball Mountain Dam, at 275 feet, is the tallest dam in the Green Mountain State and towers over a vast floodplain and recreation area of water, woods, and trails. What remains of the washed-out railroad bed is now the main connector between the Lake Recreation Area and adjacent Jamaica State Park. It's also a great place for a three-mile trek along the river. Maps are available at the park entrance.

Dogs need to be under voice control.

The park is off State Routes 30 and 100 just north of Jamaica State Park. Open 6 A.M. to 9:30 P.M. (802) 874-4881.

• Jamaica State Park 😺 😺 😺 See 10 on page 356.

Lovely Jamaica State Park, totaling over 756 acres, is located on the West River just below the Ball Mountain Dam. Two weekends a year, in late April and late September, the park is literally flooded with canoeists and kayakers when Ball Mountain Dam opens its floodgates. It's a wet and wild time whether you come to paddle or just to watch.

During the rest of the year, you'll want to explore the several trails that run through this park. In addition to the railroad bed that runs along the Ball Mountain Dam, you'll enjoy the one-mile route to Hamilton Falls along Cobb Brook.

Seasonal camping is available in the park at any one of the 43 tent or trailer sites. Rates range from $11 to $19.

Dogs must be leashed.

From State Routes 30 and 100, take Depot Street east for a half mile. Open dawn to dusk. Call (802) 874-4600 from the end of April to Columbus Day, and (802) 885-8891 off-season.

PLACES TO STAY

Jamaica State Park camping: See above.

LINCOLN

PARKS, BEACHES, AND RECREATION AREAS

• **Green Mountain National Forest—Lincoln Gap** 🐾🐾🐾🐾 See **11** on page 356.

Lincoln Gap is a popular hiking gateway into the Green Mountains. There are myriad trails you and your dog can explore, so don't let us curb your creativity.

To the north is a popular, if difficult, trail to Mount Abraham. At 4,006 feet, it is one of only five peaks in Vermont over 4,000 feet. At the treeless summit, you'll find unobstructed views in all directions. The strenuous, rocky hike has a one-way distance of 2.6 miles and an elevation gain of almost 1,600 feet. A shorter destination and good place to take a break is at two boulders called The Carpenters, 1.2 miles from the same trailhead.

To the south of Lincoln Gap is an easier walk to Eastwood's Rise, a rocky ledge, which appears to burst out of the woods for views all the way to the Adirondack Mountains in New York.

Dogs must be on leash in the national forest.

From State Route 100 in Warren, take Lincoln Gap Road west for 4.7 miles to Lincoln Gap. Parking is available at the Long Trail trailhead. Open 24 hours a day. (802) 747-6700.

MANCHESTER

PARKS, BEACHES, AND RECREATION AREAS

• **Green Mountain National Forest—Lye Brook Wilderness** 🐾🐾🐾 See **12** on page 356.

To reach two of the most scenic spots in the Green Mountains take a hike on these two moderate trails to Lye Brook Falls and Prospect Rock.

The Lye Brook Trail has a round-trip distance of 4.6 miles and gradually climbs 600 feet on an old logging road. The falls are some of the highest in Vermont and will be a refreshing reward for you and your dog after a good hike.

The Prospect Rock Trail has a round-trip distance of 3.6 miles and also follows an old logging road to this rocky outcropping, where the views overlooking the town of Manchester and the surrounding mountains are more than worth the effort getting there.

To get to Lye Brook Falls from U.S. Route 7, take Exit 4 to State Routes 11 and 30 west for 1.25 miles. Turn left onto Richville Road then left onto East Manchester Road. Pass under U.S. Route 7 and turn right onto Glenn Road and straight onto Lye Brook Road to the parking area.

To get to the Prospect Rock Trail from U.S. Route 7, take exit 4 to State Routes 11 and 30 east for half a mile. Turn right onto East Manchester Road and make an immediate left onto Rootville Road to the parking area at the end. Open 24 hours a day. (802) 747-6700.

• **Mount Equinox** 🐾🐾 See **13** on page 356.

You take the high road and I'll take the low road, and I'll get to Mount Equinox before you. Of course, that depends on whether or not one of us will be driving a car. There are two ways to get to the peak of scenic Mount Equinox. The first is on the Burr-Burton Trail, which is free, but strenuous. The second is the Mount Equinox Skyline Drive, which allows your dog to sit with his head out the window but costs $6 for the first adult and car plus $2 more per additional adult. (Dogs don't count.)

The summit, at 3,835 feet, is the highest point in the Taconic Range. It towers over the town of Manchester and offers panoramic views in all directions. Dogs are allowed on leash only.

Skyline Drive is located off State Route 7A at the Arlington-Manchester town line. To get to the Burr-Burton Trailhead from State Route 7A, take Seminary Avenue west to the Burr-Burton Seminary. The trail and parking are in the back parking lot.

Skyline Drive is open May 1 to November 1 from 8 A.M. to 10 P.M. The Burr-Burton Trail is open year-round. (802) 362-1114.

RESTAURANTS

Jerry D's Dairy Bar: The Mexican roll-ups are Rocky's favorite, but burgers and shakes are on the menu too. All can be enjoyed on the shaded outdoor patio. 6137 Route 7A; (802) 362-0199.

MIDDLEBURY

PARKS, BEACHES, AND RECREATION AREAS

• Green Mountain National Forest—Abbey Pond 🐾🐾🐾 See 14 on page 356.

We like this fairly easy four-mile round-trip to Abbey Pond; in fact, the hardest part is figuring out what to do with the wet dog on our return. Not only is Abbey Pond a great spot to swim, but the trail, which climbs 1,160 feet through a rich forest, follows a number of stream crossings and marshes along the way. So do what we do—bring a towel!

Dogs must be on leash.

From State Route 125, take State Route 116 north for 4.3 miles. Turn right onto Abbey Pond Road (a dirt road). The road splits immediately. Take the right fork for four-tenths of a mile to the end, where the trailhead is in front of you and roadside parking is available. Open 24 hours a day. (802) 747-6700.

RESTAURANTS

Angela's: Mangia! Mangia! And that is exactly what we do here with plates full of linguini, lasagna, and calzones. Dogs are welcome at the outdoor seating under the awning. 1062 U.S. Route 7 North; (802) 388-0002.

Baba's Market & Deli: Whether you're stocking up, filling up, or just looking to hang with the Middlebury College crowd, this deli has a full selection of sandwiches, burgers, and snacks for the hungry traveler. 6 College Street; (802) 388-6408.

Otter Creek Bakery: There was a time when Inu and Chris would hit the trail before the crack of dawn with just a leftover bagel to start the day, but, after their first tasty stop at Otter Creek, we're lucky if we can get either of them to budge before the last pastry disappears. 1 College Street; (802) 388-3371.

PLACES TO STAY

Fairhill Bed-and-Breakfast: This charming, mountainside 1820 farmhouse has three rooms on a quiet country lane with refreshing valley views. Rates are $75 to $95; pets are only allowed with prior approval. RD 3, Box 2300, Middlebury, VT 05753; (802) 388-3044.

The Middlebury Inn: This charming inn, built in 1827, comprises four separate but adjacent buildings all on Court Square. Dogs are permitted only in the contemporary wing. Rates range from $95 to $150. P.O. Box 798, Court Square, Middlebury, VT 05753; (802) 388-4961, (800) 842-4666; www.middlebury inn.com.

Sugar House Motel: This is a standard roadside motel with coffee in the morning and campfires at night. Rates range from $55 to $100 with an additional $8 per dog per night. Dogs cannot be left unattended and cannot be given a bath in the room. (Hey, we don't make these things up!) State Route 7, Middlebury, VT 05753; (802) 388-2770, (800) 784-2746.

DIVERSIONS

Musical Mutts: Join the fun at the week-long Middlebury Festival on the Green. This fun, free, and Fido-friendly performing arts festival features folk, jazz, and classical music, plus dance, storytelling, and children's programs. Held annually on the Green during the Fourth of July holiday, dogs are reminded that barking at the performers is considered a sin. Donations are gladly accepted.

For more information and schedules, call (802) 388-0216.

MOUNT TABOR

PARKS, BEACHES, AND RECREATION AREAS

• White Rocks National Recreation Area—Big Branch Wilderness
🐾🐾🐾🐾 See **15** on page 356.

At the northern end of the southern half of the Green Mountains National Forest (are you with us?) is the White Rocks National Recreation Area. These vast 36,000 acres feature breathtaking peaks, valleys, trails, and forests.

One of our favorite destinations is Baker Peak. It tops out at 2,840 feet and has some nice, open vistas, including views of the marble quarries on Dorset Peak to the west. One of the routes to the peak is via the Long Trail and includes crossing the Big Branch River on a suspension bridge.

We couldn't possibly describe all the trails you can find here, so we suggest you pick up a map at the National Forest district office in Manchester or Rutland.

Dogs must be on leash.

To get to the northern trailhead at Big Branch Picnic Area from U.S. Route 7 near Brooks Road in Danby, take Forest Road 10 east for 3.5 miles. Parking and picnic tables are available. Open 24 hours a day. (802) 747-6700.

RIPTON

PARKS, BEACHES, AND RECREATION AREAS

• **Green Mountain National Forest—Robert Frost Interpretive Trail** 🐾🐾🐾 🐾 See **16** on page 356.

Two roads diverged in a wood and I—I took the one less traveled by, and that has made all the difference.

There are many roads and paths to take, but, as long as they are somewhere in the Green Mountains, you don't have to worry about making the wrong choice.

This particular trail commemorates Robert Frost, a Vermont resident, four-time Pulitzer Prize winner, and one of America's favorite poets.

The scenic trail and boardwalk follows a one-mile level loop through forest and fields. Along the path you'll find signs about Frost and his work, patches of wild blueberries and huckleberries, and access to the South Branch of the Middlebury River.

From State Route 32, take State Route 125 east for two miles. A parking lot and the trailhead are on the south side of the road. Open 24 hours a day. (802) 747-6700.

RUPERT

PARKS, BEACHES, AND RECREATION AREAS

• **Merck Forest and Farmland Center** 🐾🐾🐾🐾 See **17** on page 356.
Merck Forest is a working farm, museum, educational forestry operation, and recreation center all rolled up into 3,100 wonderful acres. Wander through fields, woods, and pastures on 28 miles of trails. Maps are available and so are plenty of streams and great ponds for swimming.

The visitor center is open daily from 8 A.M. to 4:30 P.M.

Camping is also permitted; with 17 sites, you have your choice of cabins, lean-tos, and tents. Rates are $25. Dogs are permitted on leash.

From State Route 30 in Dorset, take State Route 315 west for 3.5 miles. The park is on the right. Open dawn to dusk. (802) 394-7836; www.merkforest.org.

PLACES TO STAY

Merck Forest and Farmland Center camping: See above.

RUTLAND

PLACES TO STAY

Econo Lodge: This clean, efficient motel has 67 rooms, with rates from $99 to $109. There is no additional pet charge at this location. Route 4, Box 7650, Rutland, VT 05701; (800) 424-4777; www.econolodge.com.

Highlander Motel: Pets stay for free here, and rates start at $60 per night, depending on the season. 203 North Main Street (U.S. Route 7), Rutland, VT 05701; (802) 773-6069, (800) 884-6069.

Holiday Inn: Located downtown, this Holiday Inn location has 150 rooms. Rates range from $100 to $200 plus a $10-per-pet, per-stay charge. 411 South Main Street, Rutland, VT 05701; (802) 775-1911, (800) 465-4329; www-holiday-inn.com.

Howard Johnson: This Hojo's location is in downtown Rutland and offers 96 rooms. Dogs cannot be left unattended. Rates range from $60 to $130. 378 South Main Street, Rutland, VT 05701; (800) I-GO-HOJO, (802) 775-4303; www.hojo.com.

DIVERSIONS

Dancing in the Streets: Every third Sunday in May, the dogs take to the streets. That's when the Rutland County Humane Society holds its annual fund-raiser, the Walk-a-thon. Take a 1.5 mile stroll with your pooch—free T-shirts for all walkers and bandanas for the dogs. All proceeds benefit the local animal shelters. Contact the Rutland County Humane Society for more details at (802) 483-6700.

SALISBURY

PARKS, BEACHES, AND RECREATION AREAS

• **Branbury State Park** 🐾🐾🐾 ◀● See **18** on page 356.

This 69-acre park on Lake Dunmore is located on a turn-of-the-century farm at the foothills of the Green Mountains. Today much of the farm is the park's campground.

Although dogs are not allowed at the lake's swimming area, you can access the lake from other points. Besides camping, you and your dog will also enjoy a one-mile walk to the Falls of Lana along the Sucker Brook. The popular cascading falls have a total drop of 100 feet.

Maps are available at the park ranger station. Camping is an option in season, and the rates range from $11 to $16 per site. Dogs must be on leash. There is a $2 entrance fee.

From U.S. Route 7, take State Route 53 south for four miles into the park. Open dawn to dusk, mid-May to Columbus Day. (802) 247-5925.

PLACES TO STAY

Branbury State Park camping: See above.

Salisbury Village Bed-and-Breakfast: You and your dog can join the three resident golden retrievers here at this converted 1815 four–guest room farmhouse. The inn has 15 acres of hiking trails, and well-behaved dogs are permitted in the lower guest room. Pet bed blankets are available on request. Rates are $65 a night with breakfast. West Shore Road, P.O. Box 214, Salisbury, VT 05769-0214; (802) 352-6006.

SEARSBURG/SOMERSET

PARKS, BEACHES, AND RECREATION AREAS

• **Searsburg and Somerset Reservoirs** 🐾🐾🐾 🐕 See **19** on page 356.

This area is so big that it covers three towns—Searsburg, Somerset, and Stratton—and you can hike all of it leash free. Most of the trails run north and south along the Deerfield River and the Somerset Reservoir. That's a distance of 10 miles as the crow flies, but the hiking trails total over 25 miles; some of the trails are overgrown and do not get much use.

To reach the southern trailhead near the Searsburg Dam, take a footbridge across the Deerfield River. The trails in the north are accessible by hiking south from Grout Pond (see Stratton—Green Mountain National Forest—Grout Pond).

From U.S. Route 8, take State Route 9 east for 1.5 miles. Turn left onto Somerset Road. You can park almost anywhere along the road. Open 6 A.M. to 9:30 P.M. (413) 424-7229.

SHAFTSBURY

PLACES TO STAY

Serenity Motel: You'll hit the brakes when you see the large "Pets Welcome" sign out front. And the 10 lovely, air-conditioned cottages will keep you coming back. Rates range from $50 to $80. 4379 Route 7A, Shaftbury, VT 05262; (802) 442-6490, (800) 644-6490.

SHERBURNE

PARKS, BEACHES, AND RECREATION AREAS

•Gifford Woods State Park/Gifford Woods Natural Area 🐾🐾🐾 See 20 on page 356.

This park is home to Gifford Woods Natural Area, a seven-acre stand of virgin hardwoods. It is perhaps Vermont's best known old-growth northern hardwood stand, with many grand individual trees of sugar maple, beech, yellow birch, basswood, white ash, and hemlock. It was designated a National Natural Landmark in 1980 and a State Fragile Area in 1982. No trails have been created in the stand in order to preserve its natural state. Needless to say, keep your dog on leash to prevent any damage to the undergrowth.

In the park, dogs must be leashed and have proof of rabies vaccination. There is a $2 entrance fee.

From the intersection of U.S. 4 and State Route 100, take State Route 100 north for a half mile. The park is on the left. Call (802) 775-5354 from mid-May to Columbus Day, (802) 886-2434 off-season.

•Green Mountain National Forest—Sherburne Pass 🐾🐾🐾 See 21 on page 356.

A drive up Sherburne Pass feels like going to the top of the world, but you can still go a little farther by making a short hike up to Deer Leap Mountain. Simply follow the Long Trail/Appalachian Trail north for less than a mile to the 2,782-foot-high peak. The steep start gets the dogs panting right away, but the path eventually levels out and all fatigue is forgotten when you reach the peak and its views of the pass and surrounding mountains.

From the intersection of U.S. Route 4 and State Route 100, take U.S. Route 4 west for three miles to the Long Trail/Appalachian Trail crossing. Parking is available. Open 24 hours a day. (802) 747-6700.

PLACES TO STAY

Cascades Lodge: Dogs are allowed here in the summer and fall. Two rooms are reserved for pets for an additional $10 per night or $25 per stay. Please, do not leave your pet unattended in the room. Rates range from $65 to $94. RR 1, Box 2848, Killington, VT 05751; (802) 422-3731, (800) 345-0113; www.cascadeslodge.com.

Cortina Inn: This 100-room, full-service hotel allows well-behaved dogs in the first-floor rooms. The rooms are spacious and charming, and some have fireplaces and refrigerators. Rates range from $89 to $179 per night. There's a nearby nature trail for morning walks. State Route 4, Burlington, VT 05751; (800) 451-6108, (802) 773-3333.

Econo Lodge: This 53-room Econo Lodge is practically slopeside to Killington Ski Resort. Dogs under 20 pounds are welcome for a fee of $10. Bigger dogs are welcome, but the pet fee may be higher. Rooms range from $69 to $139. 1961 Shelburne Road, Killington, VT 05751; (802) 985-3377 or (800) 55-ECONO; www.hotelchoice.com.

SHREWSBURY

PARKS, BEACHES, AND RECREATION AREAS

• **Appalachian Trail/Clarendon Gorge** 🐾🐾🐾 See **22** on page 356.
Just being on the Appalachian Trail is exciting enough for most dogs, but you haven't lived until you cross the suspension bridge over the Clarendon Gorge. With 100-foot sheer walls plunging straight down into the rocky Mill River, one look down and you'll be half way to the trail's southern terminus in Georgia.

From the intersection of U.S. Route 7 and State Route 103 in Clarendon, take State Route 103 east for two miles into Shrewsbury to the Long Trail/Appalachian Trail intersection. Parking is available. Open 24 hours a day. (802) 244-7037.

• **Coolidge State Forest—Shrewsbury Peak** 🐾🐾🐾 See **23** on page 356.
Shrewsbury Peak, at a height of 3,700 feet, is a popular hiking destination. A moderate 1.5-mile climb to the top, winding through a rich forest of spruce and fir trees, leads to rewarding views.

Dogs must be on leash.

From State Route 100 in Plymouth, take Old CCC Road (a dirt road) west for 3.5 miles in Shrewsbury. The trailhead and parking are on the right. Open 24 hours a day. Call (802) 672-3612 from mid-May to Columbus Day, (802) 886-2434 off-season.

STRATTON

PARKS, BEACHES, AND RECREATION AREAS

• **Green Mountain National Forest—Grout Pond** 🐾🐾🐾🐾 See **24** on page 356.
Grout Pond and the surrounding forest, bogs, streams, and fields are located

high in the Green Mountains. Yet despite this mountainous environment, there are over 10 miles of flat trails creating a series of easy hiking loops around the pond.

The shortest and most refreshing walk is a three-mile loop around the immediate perimeter of the pond. The trail switches back and forth between shoreline and woods. The longest loop runs 6.5 miles around the pond and is less traveled. You'll find solitude and some good bogs to traverse.

Dogs must be on a leash.

From State Route 100 in Wardsboro, take Stratton-Arlington Road west into Stratton and Kelley Stand Road for about 6.5 miles. Turn left onto Grout Pond Road for one mile to the pond, parking, and ranger station. Open 24 hours a day. (802) 747-6700.

•Green Mountain National Forest—Stratton Mountain 🐾🐾🐾 See **25** on page 356.

It was here on top of the highest peak in southern Vermont that the Long Trail was conceived by James Taylor in 1909.

This portion of the trail, from the parking lot to the summit at 3,936 feet, is difficult but doable for energetic dogs, with an elevation gain of 2,044 feet and a round-trip distance of 6.6 miles.

For a lowland hike, Stratton Pond is a great destination. The popular Stratton Pond Trail is 3.9 miles long, but it's an easy, flat route through some beautiful, high-country woodlands.

Dogs must be on leash.

From State Route 100 in Wardsboro, take Stratton-Arlington Road west into Stratton and Kelley Stand Road for over seven miles. The trailhead and a parking lot are on the right. Open 24 hours a day. (802) 747-6700.

WILMINGTON

PARKS, BEACHES, AND RECREATION AREAS

•Green Mountain National Forest—Haystack Mountain and Pond 🐾🐾🐾 See **26** on page 356.

Oh, it's another trail through a wonderful wilderness leading to some spectacular views and a nice pond. Ho hum. In the Green Mountains, just about every trail gets a high paw rating; they're a dime a dozen around here.

This trail, leading to Haystack Mountain and Pond, follows a gradually ascending forest road for the first eight-tenths of a mile and then turns (to the left at the road gate) onto a footpath. The footpath continues for a steep six-tenths of a mile to the summit of Haystack Mountain with a southerly view into Massachusetts.

If you continue for another 1.5 miles on the forest road (beyond the gate), there is a lovely mountain pond, perfect for swimming. Dogs must be on leash.

From State Route 100, take State Route 9 west for one mile. Turn right onto Haystack Road for just over a mile then left onto Chimney Hill Road. Turn right onto Binney Brook Road (bear left) for one mile and then right onto Upper Dam Road for two-tenths of a mile. The trailhead is on the right. Roadside parking is available. Open dawn to dusk. (802) 747-6700.

• Harriman Reservoir 🐾🐾🐾🐾 🐕 See **27** on page 356.

For a hike on 12 miles of flatness with about 300 billion gallons of water at arm's reach, follow this old railroad bed along Harriman Reservoir's wooded, western shoreline from Wilmington to Whitingham.

Of course, you don't have to trek the entire trail to find happiness because anywhere along the way is a great spot for you and a dog to kick back, enjoy the water, and just look at the surrounding high peaks.

The reservoir, also called Lake Whittingham, is the largest man-made lake in Vermont at 28 miles around. It was created in the 1920s with the damming of the Deerfield River in Whittingham.

To get to the dam entrance in Whittingham from State Route 100, take Dam Road north for 1.5 miles to the dam, picnic area, and parking. Walk across the 200-foot-high dam to get to the trailhead. Open 6 A.M. to 9:30 P.M. (413) 424-7229.

• Molly Stark State Park 🐾🐾 See **28** on page 356.

These popular 168 acres of woods and open lawns are named after the wife of Revolutionary War general, John Stark. Dogs must be on leash here and are not permitted in any of the day-use areas, which, unfortunately, means most of the developed sections of the park.

One place you *can* go is to the fire tower on Mount Olga. The Mount Olga Trail, which starts across the road from the ranger station, is a moderate 1.5-mile round-trip walk, and, at 2,145 feet high, the views are spectacular.

There is a $2 entrance fee.

From Interstate 91 in Brattleboro, take Exit 2 to State Route 9 (Molly Stark Trail) west for 15 miles. The park is on the left just over the Wilmington town line. Open dawn to dusk from mid-May to Columbus Day. (802) 464-5460.

RESTAURANTS

Vermont House Tavern & Restaurant: You can enjoy breakfast, lunch, or dinner on the front porch of this historic tavern. Dogs are happy to sit alongside and enjoy the activity in this classic Vermont town. Main Street (State Route 9); (802) 464-2280.

PLACES TO STAY

Inn at Quail Run: Located on 15 pristine wooded acres and connecting to miles of cross-country and hiking trails, you'll enjoy the 11 comfortable rooms here. Most rooms have gas fireplaces and antique or brass beds. Rates range from $115 to $150, including breakfast. Pets are an additional $15 with approval. 106 Smith Road, Wilmington, VT 05363; (802) 464-3362, (800) 343-7227; www.bbonline.com/vt/quailrun.

11

LAKE CHAMPLAIN AND THE NORTHEAST KINGDOM

In the northern part of Vermont, you'll find numerous historic sites, lots of charming small towns, mountain after mountain, working farms, and woods, woods, woods. And did we mention pristine lakes? Lake Champlain, at 125 miles long, is among the United States' largest lakes. Discovered in 1609 by French explorer Samuel de Champlain, both Vermont and New York share its borders, offering bountiful recreational and scenic splendors for people and their dogs. A ferry system crosses the lake at four different points (see below), and dogs are allowed to make the crossing with you.

East of Lake Champlain is a region called the Northeast Kingdom. This area, stretching from Wells River to the Canadian border, is perhaps the most unspoiled of all the unspoiled areas in the state. It has a quiet, restful, hasn't-been-altered-in-a-hundred-years air, with few modern influences. You won't find any tall buildings or big city atmosphere here. These three counties combined offer over 71,000 acres of state forest land and parks, over 37,000 acres of public lake surface, and 3,800 miles of rivers and streams. That's enough to make any dog feel like a king.

The state park and state forest systems provide a framework for accessing the open spaces here, but our dogs' aversion to leashes and our own aversion to primitive camping kept us looking for additional ways to get up close and personal with Vermont. We found some stellar choices. Be prepared to visit breathtaking views and stunning natural beauty.

Lake Champlain Ferries: Whether you just want to kick back with a relaxing cruise on the lake or take that elusive photo of Champ, the rumored resident

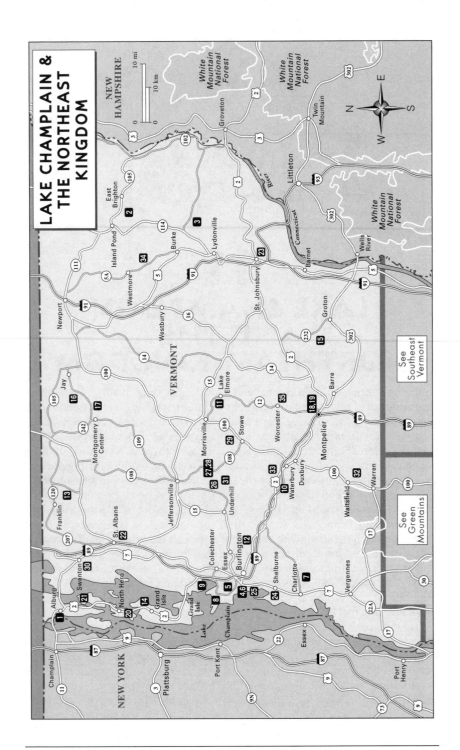

serpent, Lake Champlain Ferries welcomes you and your pet aboard. Dogs are welcome on leash with no extra change.

Burlington to Port Kent, New York, from mid-May to mid-October—one hour; adult ticket is under $4 each way.

Charlotte to Essex, New York, year-round—20 minutes; adult ticket is under $3 each way.

Grand Isle to Plattsburgh, New York, year-round—12 minutes; adult ticket is under $3 each way.

Shoreham to Ticonderoga, New York, year-round—6 minutes; adult ticket is $.50 each way.

For departure times and more information, call (802) 864-9804, or visit the website at www.ferries.com.

ALBURG

PARKS, BEACHES, AND RECREATION AREAS

• **Alburg Recreation Rail Trail** 🐾🐾 See ❶ on page 374.

We were sure we were in the wrong place, because the approach to the Rail Trail looks more like you are headed onto private property. But fear not. We aren't leading you astray. To reach the trail, look for the trailhead on your right directly after the asphalt turn-around. There is a fire hydrant (maybe your dog will spot it first) located at the start of the trail.

The trail is six miles long, following a converted railroad bed now filled with fine cinder. The only thing harder to find than the trailhead is a park ranger, so don't expect to see one. However, Vermont's state leash law still does apply.

From State Route 78, take U.S. Route 2 west for three miles. The entrance is across from the firehouse; a brown wood sign marks the entrance. Open dawn until dusk. (802) 796-3980.

RESTAURANTS

S. D. Burger Bus: The name says it all—it is a bus, and it serves amazing burgers. Oh, and it is bright blue—a can't-miss-it-for-a-mile blue. The bus cooks up burgers and other delectables, and you and your furry friend can dine together at the picnic tables in front. This bus is seasonal, so look for it in the warm weather next to the Alburg Elementary School. U.S. Route 2; No phone.

Alburg Country Store: We love Vermont country stores. They are always so charming, and this one serves ice cream, too. Beth took a scoop of Rocky's favorite (what else but Rocky Road?) to share with him at the benches outside. U.S. Route 2; (802) 796-3417.

PLACES TO STAY

Auberge Alburg: Well-behaved pets are welcome to share the palace with the owner's mixed breed, a half-golden, half-sneaky-neighbor's-dog. There is a wide range of accommodations here, from a suite in the renovated barn that overlooks Lake Champlain, to dormitory digs for seasonal cyclists. Rates range accordingly, from $45 to $75. The best part of all is the on-site restaurant, with porch, called Café Etc. You can bring your dog down to breakfast, provided you select porch seating. 54 Fells Main Road, Alburg, VT 05440; (802) 796-3169.

BARNET

PLACES TO STAY

The Inn at Maplemont Farm: Maplemont is a horse farm overlooking the Connecticut River, and if you are a lucky dog, you'll have a river view too. Rates start at $70 per night. This elegant inn welcomes pets, with advance notice, so be sure to call ahead. Max, the official greeter at the Inn, will meet your pooch at the door. 2742 U.S. Route 5 South, Barnet, VT 05821; (802) 633-4880 or (800) 230-1617.

BRIGHTON

PARKS, BEACHES, AND RECREATION AREAS

• **Brighton State Park** 🐾🐾🐾🐾 See 🄋 on page 374.

Brighton State Park sits on the west shore of Spectacle Pond and the south shore of Island Pond. This park is pretty wild, reflecting the character of the Northeast Kingdom itself. The town of Island Pond was once a railroad mecca and much bigger than it is today. Now, the area is rapidly returning to its wilderness roots.

A number of old logging trails wind through the park's 152 acres, but the best-marked trails are the nature trail and the hiking trail that abut the border of Spectacle Pond. The nature trail starts at the camping area, near the Nature Center, and runs to Campers Beach. The hiking trail breaks off from the nature trail about a quarter mile in and loops around through the woods. Both are easy trails.

This is a state park, so dogs are permitted on leash, but not on the beach. There is a day-use fee of $2.

From State Route 114, take State Route 105 east for two miles. Turn right onto Pleasant Street for three-quarters of a mile. The park is on the left. Open 10 A.M. to 8 P.M., mid-May to mid-October. (802) 723-4360.

BURKE

PARKS, BEACHES, AND RECREATION AREAS

• **Darling State Park** 🐾🐾 See 🄌 on page 374.

Instead of starting at the bottom and hiking up, you can reverse things here. Darling State Park is located at the summit of Burke Mountain, accessible by car via a toll road, or by foot via the same road for free. The park's 2,000 acres crisscross Burke Mountain, which rises 3,267 feet above sea level and provides some breathtaking views of the surrounding valleys. Much of the park is left untended by the State Parks Department, so expect this park to be less developed than others.

One of the most interesting trails begins as a small road to the right of the ski area parking lot located midway up the mountain. After less than a mile on that path, you will see the markings for the Red Trail on the left, which climbs to intersect the Blue Trail, which in turn leads to the summit ridge. The Profile

Trail leads to the summit tower and some very scenic vistas. Overall, you are looking at a 3.5-mile round-trip, and an elevation gain of over 1,200 feet. Dogs must be on leash. There is a day-use fee of $2.

From East Burke, take Mountain Road one mile to the Burke Mountain/ Sherburne Lodge parking lots, or continue all the way up the toll road to the top parking area. Open mid-May to mid-October, dawn until dusk. (802) 244-8711.

PLACES TO STAY

Old Cutter Inn: Cattle dogs will be sniffing the air here, as this inn started its life as a dairy farm, close to the foothills of Burke Mountain. Dogs are welcome to stay with their owners in the rooms in the detached carriage house. Rates range from $52 to $115. RR 1, Box 62, Pinkham Road, East Burke, VT 05832; (800) 295-1943.

The Village Inn of East Burke: Pets are permitted at this charming five-room inn in the center of East Burke. You can walk to town, and there is a big porch for you and your pooch to enjoy. The inn features a guest kitchen, where you can prepare your own meals. In nice weather, there's an outdoor kennel and dog run. Rates start at $60 per night, with no additional fee for pets. P.O. Box 186, Route 114, East Burke, VT 05832; (802) 626-3161.

RESTAURANTS

The River Garden Café: This yummy, healthy restaurant serves lunch and dinner and holds a few tables on the patio for you to dine al fresco with your canine companion. There is no wait service at those tables, but the super-dog-friendly staff will do everything they can to make your meal a pleasant one. The owners pride themselves on using the freshest ingredients—mostly from local Vermont suppliers—in very creative ways. 427 State Route 114; (802) 626-3514.

FESTIVALS

Berry Me in Burke: Every summer, Burke holds their annual Strawberry Festival. If your dog is a strawberry shortcake fan, get yourself over to Burke for some of the freshest you have ever tasted. Festivities include outdoor activities, music, and strawberries galore. The event is held on the lawn in front of the Burke Mountain clubhouse. For more information, call (802) 626-9696.

BURLINGTON

Burlington, the largest city in Vermont, has an independent spirit defined by three things: Lake Champlain, Ethan Allen, and the University of Vermont. Burlington is one of the largest ports on the massive lake, and much of the town's industry is founded on making, processing, and transporting goods across the lake and the Winooski River. Ethan Allen is not only a hero of the American Revolution and a founding father of Vermont, he's one of the original settlers of the city. He specifically established his Burlington homestead on the Winooski River, in what was then wilderness, to open up the frontier of northern Vermont. Today, that frontier is still being pushed and tested with a fascinating mix of Vermont tradition and new-age thinking from the state's biggest university. It's this mix that makes Burlington one of the most prosperous and livable cities in Vermont.

PARKS, BEACHES, AND RECREATION AREAS

• Battery Park 🐾 🐾 See ❹ on page 374.

This three-block city park, on the cliffs overlooking Lake Champlain and adjacent Waterfront Park, is a popular gathering place for local residents. The park offers great views, lawns, shady trees, picnic tables, and walkways. The high cliffs, which separate the park from the Waterfront Park on the lower flats, were used as a battery during the War of 1812.

Dogs must be leashed and are not permitted in the playground area.

This downtown park is located between Battery Street (State Route 127), North Street, and College Street. Limited street parking is available. Open 6 A.M. to 11 P.M. (802) 864-0123.

• Ethan Allen Homestead 🐾 🐾 🐾 See ❺ on page 374.

Ethan Allen's name is on just about everything in the Burlington area, but we'd like to think that he's most proud of lending his name to this park. First of all, it's his final and only remaining home, and secondly because it's a great place for a walk.

Originally from Connecticut, Allen was one of a number of settlers to obtain invalid land grants in the Green Mountains from the governor of New Hampshire. Once the settlers' land rights were questioned, it was Allen who led the fight to create an independent Vermont. Many of his and the state's independent philosophies were established on this homestead on the shores of the Winooski River, now preserved by the Winooski Valley Park District as a park and educational center.

The park has four miles of trails through forest, fields, and wetlands. The most impressive route is the Peninsula Loop. It's almost a mile long and covers the northern tip of the park along the river. There are plenty of access points. But not to be missed are the River and Homestead Loops and the Wetlands Walk.

The Homestead accesses the Burlington Recreational Path and numerous picnic spots.

Dogs must be on leash and are not permitted in any of the buildings. Maps and other information are available at the park's visitor center.

From State Route 127, take the Northern Avenue/Beaches exit. The park entrance is off of the exit. Parking is available. Open sunrise to sunset. For more information, contact the Winooski Valley Park District at (802) 863-5744 or the Ethan Allen Land Trust at (802) 865-4556.

• Waterfront Park and Promenade 🐾 🐾 🐾 See ❻ on page 374.

The landfill between the Burlington cliffs and Lake Champlain has come a long way since it was created back in the 1890s by the Vermont Central Railroad. Back then, this area was just a yard for loading and unloading trains and boats.

Today the groomed lawns and short, harborside walkways make it a popular destination for tourists and residents alike. There are plenty of benches and lake views to enjoy, but water access is limited because of the lake wall. Most dog walkers simply enjoy the lawns and cool breezes of the park or just pass through along the Recreational Path (see below). Dogs must be leashed.

The downtown park is located at the end of Lake Street just off Battery Street (State Route 127). Limited street parking is available. Open 6 A.M. to 11 P.M. (802) 864-0123.

NATURE HIKES AND URBAN WALKS

Burlington Recreational Path: This seven-mile-long, paved bikeway is located along a former railroad bed beside Lake Champlain. Running the entire length of the Burlington waterfront, north to south, it winds through a number of city parks.

The path is motor-vehicle free, but dogs do need to be on a leash.

You can find access points and parking at the Ethan Allen Homestead, Oakledge Park and Waterfront Park and Promenade. Open 6 A.M. to 11 P.M. (802) 864-0123.

RESTAURANTS

Church Street Marketplace Restaurants: For food, shopping, entertainment, and socializing, the place to be is the Church Street Marketplace. This pedestrian-only, bricked street is four blocks long (from Main Street to Pearl Street) right in the center of the city. The open-air marketplace teems with activity any day of the year but comes especially alive at lunch and on warm nights. It's a great place just to stroll with your dog or get something to eat. Your choices are endless, from appetizing food carts to a number of outdoor cafés, restaurants, and bars. We can't list them all, so here are a few we like best.

NECI Commons: If these guys can't cook up something tasty, who can? NECI stands for the New England Culinary Institute, and it's their chefs and chefs-to-be that prepare fantastic to-go menus for breakfast, lunch, and dinner. In the morning are great pastries and breads. At lunch are delicious sandwiches like the smoked salmon club; there is a full dinner line up, too. 25 Church Street; (802) 862-6324.

Smokejacks: Hey Jack! (and George and Inu and Rocky. . .) Hop on over to this busy restaurant for a brew or a burger or a salad, and enjoy the company of other Jacks (and Busters and Barneys and Beauregards). Dogs are allowed at the outdoor tables. 156 Church Street; (802) 658-1119.

Sweetwaters: You'll be in the thick of the pack here at this popular café. Choose from a delicious array of chicken, fish, and meat entrées while taking in the local street scene. Your faithful companion may join you at the outdoor seating. 120 Church Street; (802) 864-9800.

Uncommon Grounds: When the hustle and bustle of Church Street tires you out, head to Uncommon Grounds for a pick-me-up. Their tasty coffee, teas, and pastries will give you all the lift you need to keep going. There's outdoor seating, too. 42 Church Street; (802) 865-6227.

Cobblestone's Deli: For a quick sandwich that tastes anything but ordinary, stop at this great deli on Battery Street. Our dogs wait for the crumbs to fall, but there's always a big scramble for the extra turkey. Benches are available outside or take it to go. 152 Battery Street; (802) 865-3354.

PLACES TO STAY

Radisson Inn Burlington: The Radisson has plenty of room—256 newly renovated rooms—and plenty to do nearby. Located right in downtown, several parks are across the street and the popular shops and entertainment of Church Street are only a few blocks away. Rates range from $99 to $199. 60 Battery Street, Burlington, VT 05401; (802) 658-6500 or (800) 333-3333.

FESTIVALS

Caroling Canine: Any day of the year something is happening at the Church Street Marketplace, but things really heat up during the winter holidays. From November 26 through January 1, the Marketplace glows with 100,000 white lights, a 25-foot Christmas tree, caroling, holiday entertainment, and a joyous spirit sure to warm your heart. The season opens with a Musical Lighting Ceremony on November 26 and closes with First Night. For more information, call (802) 863-1648.

Frozen Fifi: Cold days and nights don't stop Burlington dogs. In fact, everyone comes out for the Winter Festival held annually the third weekend in February. This celebration of winter is held at Waterfront Park with a snow-sculpture competition, family activity exposition, snowshoe obstacle course, dogsled rides, and entertainment. The weekend highlight is the Penguin Plunge where about 800 hearty souls do a charity jump into Lake Champlain. For more information, call (802) 864-0123.

Cajun Canine: Where's the best place to celebrate Mardi Gras? No, it's not New Orleans but Burlington's own Church Street Marketplace. One of the most popular events in Vermont, the annual Mardi Gras Parade and Block Party is held annually in the beginning of March. Don't miss the floats as they parade up Church Street tossing out Louisiana moon pies, candy, and endless bead necklaces to the thousands that line the parade route. The parade, which starts at 4 P.M., is followed up with a rambunctious outdoor block party. For more information, call the festival's sponsor, The Magic Hat, at (802) 658-2739.

CHARLOTTE

PARKS, BEACHES, AND RECREATION AREAS

• **Pease Mountain Natural Area** 🐾🐾🐾 🐕 See **7** on page 374.
Pease Mountain was designated by the University of Vermont as a natural area, so do not be surprised to find students along the trail. The 180-acre natural area contains some beautiful vistas, and the summit hike is a not-too-taxing 1.5-mile trail. The month of May brings wildflowers to the meadow areas here, and wild turkeys—if you can spot one—are here year-round.

Dogs are permitted here off leash as long as they are under voice control.

From U.S. Route 7, take Church Hill Road east for a half mile. Turn right onto Hinesburg Road and park in the lots for Charlotte Central School. Open 24 hours. (802) 656-4055.

COLCHESTER

PARKS, BEACHES, AND RECREATION AREAS

• **Delta Park** 🐾🐾🐾🐾 See **8** on page 374.
This is simply one the best places to savor Lake Champlain, the Winooski

River, and the nearby Burlington skyline. The 55-acre park is literally a giant sandbar created where the Winooski River flows into Lake Champlain.

The designated trails are only a little more than half a mile in length but, with 2,700 feet of shoreline, they afford plenty of opportunity to wear out your dog.

You will also find two observation platforms along the trail. One provides views of the wetlands created by the sandbar and the other of the mouth of the Winooski River. The marshes and beaches are a great place for bird-watching or catching the sunset over the lake to the Adirondack Mountains beyond.

Dogs must be on leash.

From State Route 127, take Pointers Point Road north for 1.5 miles. Turn left onto Airport Road for three quarters of a mile, then left onto Windemere Way for a mile into the park. Parking is available. Open sunrise to sunset. (802) 863-5744.

• Mallett's Bay State Park 🐾🐾🐾 See 9 on page 374.

The state park system is considering upgrading this undeveloped park on the shores of Lake Champlain, but the dogs hope it remains just as it is.

As far as facilities go, not much is here—just a dirt parking area, and that's fine with our pack. They know that other facilities, like picnic areas, generally come with a big "No Dogs" sign. And as far as simply getting out into the great outdoors, this state park has much to offer. A wide, one-mile trail runs through a 200-acre hardwood forest that leads to a wonderful, sandy beach on tranquil Mallett's Bay. The shallow water is a little grassy or weedy in spots, but it's still a great place for swimming.

Dogs must be on leash in all state parks.

From Interstate 89, take Exit 17 to U.S. Route 2 north for one mile. Turn left onto Raymond Road for a half mile. On your left, near the road's end, is the park's unidentified parking area. Open dawn to dusk. (802) 879-5674.

PLACES TO STAY

Motel 6: All Motel 6 locations allow dogs, as long as you don't leave your pet unattended. This brand-new motel is located just off of Interstate 89 and only five miles from downtown Burlington. One dog is welcome per room. 74 South Park Drive, Colchester, VT 05446; (802) 654-6860 or (800) 4-MOTEL6 (800-466-8356); www.motel6.com.

DUXBURY

PARKS, BEACHES, AND RECREATION AREAS

• Camel's Hump State Park 🐾🐾🐾🐾 🐕 See 10 on page 374.

These 20,000 acres within six towns were purchased by Colonel Joseph Battell who sought to protect it from development. Today, the breathtaking views and many trails of Camel's Hump State Park are enjoyed by countless visitors.

If you are coming here—and you should make every effort to—be sure to get a map first. They are available at most of the trailheads, or you can contact the park service. With over 22 miles of trails, you'll need a good guide.

The 4,083-foot peak of Camel's Hump is considered one of the most impressive mountains in all of New England. Well above the tree line, the alpine summit has views beyond compare, and the arctic terrain is only found on two other Vermont peaks: Mounts Abraham and Mansfield. To reach the summit, take the Forestry Trail in the northeastern part of the park.

If you need a place to cool off after a jaunt through the woods, the Winooski River awaits. And so does your dog—what are you waiting for?

Dogs are required to be on leash above the tree line to protect the alpine vegetation, but they can be under voice control in the rest of the park.

From Interstate 89, take Exit 11 to U.S. Route 2 east for five miles. Turn right onto Cochran Road over an old bridge crossing the Winooski River. At two-tenths of a mile, turn left onto Duxbury Road. From here, the canoe launch parking area is at 2.3 miles and the Long Trail parking area is at 2.5 miles. Open 24 hours a day. (802) 879-6565.

ELMORE

PARKS, BEACHES, AND RECREATION AREAS

• Elmore State Park 🐾 🐾 🐾 🐾 See **11** on page 374.

Local dogs give this place a paws up, so we had to check it out. As usual, local dogs know all the best spots, and this is one of them. This park has a lake, a mountain, and some stunning views of both the Green and the White Mountains.

The trailhead for the 4.5-mile Elmore Mountain Trail starts near the park gate, heading up 1,470 feet in elevation to the summit of Elmore Mountain. Passing by an abandoned cabin and ending at the fire tower on top, 2,608-foot Elmore Mountain provides some stunning views in all directions.

Other trails lead to sparkling Elmore Lake (where dogs are banned from the beaches but can access the water along the shore) and the Balancing Rock, a precarious boulder on the mountain's edge.

Dogs are allowed on leash with proof of rabies vaccination. Dogs are not permitted in the day-use-only areas. The day-use fee is $2.

From State Route 100 in Morristown, take State Route 12 south for five miles to the park entrance on the right. Open 10 A.M. to sunset, mid-May to Columbus Day. (802) 888-2982.

ESSEX

PARKS, BEACHES, AND RECREATION AREAS

• Overlook Park and Woodside Natural Area 🐾 🐾 See **12** on page 374.

These two parks would be one, but the Central Vermont Railway needed a little room to pass through, hence the two halves, which are both managed by the Winooski Valley Park District. Most dogs and hikers like Woodside Natural Area for its mile-long trail along the Winooski River and through a scenic woodlands with two ponds. Overlook Park has a short nature trail but is really more of a picnic area.

Dogs must be on leash.

From State Route 2A, take State Route 15 (Pearl Street) west for 2.5 miles. Turn left onto the park access road across from Dalton Drive. Open sunrise to sunset. (802) 863-5744.

FERRISBURGH

NATURE HIKES AND URBAN WALKS

Rokeby Museum: Pay a visit to the family farm; the Robinsons will all be there. This family of Quaker pioneers, farmers, abolitionists, and artists lived here from the 1790s to 1961 when the farm became a museum. You and your dog are welcome to hike and explore the spacious grounds of woods, orchards, and exhibits. Dogs must be leashed and are not permitted in the buildings. The museum is located on U.S. Route 7. (802) 877-3406.

RESTAURANTS

The Starry Night Café: The inviting back porch of one of the oldest cider mills in Vermont is a perfect setting for breakfast pastries and coffee, lunch, or dinner. 5467 U.S. Route 7; (802) 877-3668, (877) 877-5556.

DIVERSIONS

An Apple a Day. . . : And then some if your dog is anything like ours in an apple orchard. You and your dog can pick and eat your fill of Macs and Grannies at Ferrimont Orchard located right on U.S. Route 7. The three-week apple season runs from mid-September to early October. For more information, call the Ferrisburg Apple Company at (802) 877-6962.

FRANKLIN

PARKS, BEACHES, AND RECREATION AREAS

• **Lake Carmi State Park** 🐾🐾🐾 See **13** on page 374.

George makes a break for the lake here, for this park allows dogs to swim at its boat launches. Lake Carmi, the fourth-largest lake completely within Vermont's borders, is 7.5 miles around, averages 20 feet in depth, and is popular with boaters and anglers. It is definitely the main attraction on any visit here, and there are plenty of spots to stop with Spot—with the exception of the recreational swimming area.

This 482-acre park also contains wetlands and some iffy hiking trails through pine, spruce, and hardwood forests. Stay clear of the peat bog unless you bring your mukluks!

You can camp with your pooch in Camping Area A, with 178 wooded tent sites with facilities and 35 lean-tos with easy access to the lake available. Rates are $12 to $15 per night. (802) 241-3655.

Dogs must be leashed, have proof of rabies vaccination, and avoid day-use areas. The day-use fee is $2.

From State Route 105, take State Route 236 (State Park Road) north for three miles. Turn left onto Marsh Farm Road into the park. Open Memorial Day to Labor Day, 10 A.M. to 8 P.M. (802) 933-8383.

Lake Carmi State Park camping: See page 383.

GRAND ISLE

PARKS, BEACHES, AND RECREATION AREAS

• **Grand Isle State Park** 🐾🐾 See **14** on page 374.

The sign leading into Grand Isle reads "Welcome to Grand Isle—The Beauty Spot of Vermont." That made our friend Heather, a native Vermonter, raise her eyebrows. Not that Grand Isle isn't beautiful—it's just that Vermont is full of beauty spots. The park started out as a private resort called Birchcliff, which was purchased by the state of Vermont in 1959. The original 54 acres have been expanded over time to the present 226 acres. The park boasts 4,150 feet of Lake Champlain shoreline, which helps makes Grand Isle the most popular state park for campers.

The park itself is mostly a campground for tent camping, but there are also trails for hiking. Just before getting to the official park entrance, a nature trail begins on State Park Road. This trail is grassy, easy to follow, and showcases the flora and fauna of Vermont. A fitness trail also winds through the entire park; your dog may not care about flat tummies, but she'll definitely like the flat, open trails! Stop by the Activity Center to see a schedule of daily events, including interpretive programs, games, and entertainment.

The full-facility campground features 155 tent sites and 35 lean-tos. Many have lakefront access, which may be your only chance to get to the water as all of the recreational beaches are off-limits to dogs. Rates range from $13 to $18 per night. Dogs must be leashed; the admission fee is $2

The park is located on the eastern shore of South Hero Island on State Park Road off of U.S. Route 2. Open 10 A.M. to sunset mid-May to Columbus Day. (802) 372-4300.

PLACES TO STAY

Grand Isle State Park campground: See above.

GROTON

PARKS, BEACHES, AND RECREATION AREAS

• **Groton State Forest** 🐾🐾🐾🐾 See **15** on page 374.

Groton State Forest, with its six state parks, is the second-largest piece of public land in Vermont. At 26,000 acres, the forest extends across the towns of Groton, Peacham, Marshfield, Orange, and Topsham. Within its boundaries, you'll find Big Deer State Park, New Discovery State Park, Ricker Pond State Park, Seyon Ranch State Park, Stillwater State Park, and Boulder Beach State Park—this is where you'll find day-use facilities, camping, and trails that lead to lakes, ponds, and mountains in this vast state forest.

From New Discovery State Park, we suggest taking the Big Deer Mountain Trail to (where else?) Deer Mountain. The 3.4-mile hike leads to great views of Peachum Pond and the White Mountains to the east.

You can also access the Owl's Head Summit from this park. The three-mile round-trip hike starts behind the forest's picnic pavilion, beginning with a set of steps. Stay on the main trail, and in no time you'll find yourself at the stone fire tower that marks the summit of Owl's Head. From here you will be rewarded with views of Kettle Pond and Big and Little Deer Mountains.

At Ricker Pond State Park, the camping sites on popular Lake Groton fill up quickly, and, although dogs are not allowed at the swimming beach, there are plenty of places to swim along its edges. Our favorite trail here is the Montpelier and Wells River Trail, which runs along the river on an old rail bed. This flat, open path runs seven miles to Ricker Mills and back. Along the way your pup will enjoy guilt-free swimming away from the crowded lake beach.

From Deer Mountain State Park, also located on Lake Groton, we recommend hiking the Osmore Pond Loop, which leads around the pond on a flat, if rocky, trail. Leading through marshes and a lovely hardwood forest, you can also join tails with the Deer Mountain Trail, which will take you to the summit for outstanding views.

The hiking-only trails are blue blazed, and multipurpose trails are marked with orange markers. Dogs must be leashed, and proof of rabies vaccination may be required if you enter the forest via a state park.

Camping is allowed at Ricker Pond, Big Deer, and New Discovery State Parks. The 110 popular sites along Lake Groton at Ricker Pond and Big Deer Campgrounds fill up quickly. If you're shut out along the water, try New Discovery Campground, which has 61 wooded sites and a great trail system. In all three campgrounds, flush toilets and hot showers are available; tent sites are $13 per night and lean-tos are $16. For reservations, call (802) 584-3820, (802) 584-3821, or (802) 584-3822.

Stillwater and Boulder Beach State Parks are day-use-only facilities, and dogs are not allowed.

From U.S. Route 302, take State Route 232 north for four miles into the state forest. The trailheads, state parks, and parking are all along State Route 232. The state parks are open mid-May through mid-October from 9 A.M. to 9 P.M.; the state forest is open year-round 24 hours a day. (802) 584-3823.

PLACES TO STAY

Big Deer State Park camping: See page 384.
New Discovery State Park camping: See page 384.
Ricker Pond State Park camping: See page 384.

JAY

PARKS, BEACHES, AND RECREATION AREAS

• **Jay State Forest** 🐾🐾🐾 🐕 See **16** on page 374.
Jay Peak and the surrounding 1,390 acres of forest are named for John Jay, the first Chief Justice of our fledgling country. Jay helped settle a land dispute between the state of Vermont and the state of New York, and the state gratefully acknowledged his contribution by naming this peak for him. Jay Peak marks the last and most northern peak of the Green Mountain chain.

The 3.5-mile-long trail to the 3,861 foot summit is part of the Long Trail and provides rather challenging hiking over rocks and steep inclines. Agile dogs will be fine here, and, if you think you're up to it, you'll be rewarded by views of the White Mountains, Green Mountains, and Owls Head in Quebec. Dogs may be off leash here but must stay on the trails.

The Long Trail is best accessed from the parking area on Vermont State Route 242, approximately seven miles from Montgomery Center. Open dawn until dusk. (802) 244-7037.

RESTAURANTS

Jay County Store: This quintessential country store in Jay makes a great pup-stop for groceries, sodas, and deli sandwiches. The green benches that line the porch invite you to sit awhile or picnic. 1077 State Route 242; (802) 988-4040.

MONTGOMERY CENTER
PARKS, BEACHES, AND RECREATION AREAS

• Hazens Notch 🐾🐾🐾🐾 See **17** on page 374.
Rocky joined his friends Hector and Beaudreaux in giving this park a four paws up. This park is home territory for them, and are they lucky dogs! Hazens Notch consists of a 500-acre conservation area, donated by Sharon and Rolf Anderson, joined with land from over 25 local landowners, creating over 30 miles of trails and nearly 1,500 acres of private land opened for public use. With so many great trails to choose from, it's hard to know where to start.

Beaudreaux's favorite trail is the Burnt Mountain Trail, easily accessible from the High Ponds Trailhead parking lot. The trail climbs to an elevation of approximately 2,700 feet, following a restored woods road through to Window Rock. You'll be rewarded with some excellent views there, and, if you're up to it, you can continue over ledges to a ridge that ends on an open rock summit with 360-degree views.

If a steep hike is too taxing for your hound, try the Beaver Ponds Trail, which connects to the Sugar House Trail. It's a more moderate two-mile hike, running past streams, marshy meadows, and beaver ponds.

Because this is private land, you must be extra respectful of the property. The Andersons were wary about allowing us to list this wonderful place for fear they would be overrun by thoughtless dog owners. Don't make us look bad!

You can pick up a trail map to help plan your visit at the parking areas or by contacting the Hazens Notch Conservation Lands. Dogs must be on leashes.

From State Routes 118 and 242, take State Route 58 east for a mile. The park is on the left. Open dawn to dusk. (802) 326-4789.

RESTAURANTS

Kilgore's General Store: This true Vermont general store has a wide porch with benches, just right for taking a break and watching the world go by. Thet also have a deli, bakery, and old-fashioned ice-cream counter, if you are planning an al fresco lunch at Hazen's Notch. Be forewarned: stuff closes early in

Vermont, so make your visit before 6 P.M. 91 Main Street, Montgomery Center, VT 05471; (802) 326-3058.

MONTPELIER

Montpelier holds the distinction, if it can be called that, of being the smallest of all the state capitals. It may be small, but do you remember the old adage about good things coming in small packages? Montpelier is charming, historic, and worth a visit—when not underwater. Built on a floodplain, it has experienced a number of major floods in its history. The Great Flood of November 1927, the last major flood, ended with water over 12 feet deep at the downtown intersection of State and Main. Building nearby watersheds has helped with this problem, but the city has flooded as recently as 1992, once again turning the streets into canals.

PARKS, BEACHES, AND RECREATION AREAS

• Hubbard Park 🐾🐾🐾🐾 🐕 See 18 on page 374.

Boy, oh boy, do our dogs love this place. This 200-acre park right in the middle of Montpelier feels like it's miles from civilization once you enter its hallowed arbors. You can leave the leash in the car for this park opts instead for a "Canine Code of Conduct." The code includes having updated rabies shots, not allowing your dog to charge or jump on others, and scooping the poop. Sounds reasonable to us.

The trails are well marked, and there are lots of choices. George's favorite path is the one that leads to the Tower. Built in 1920, it rises a few stories high and provides a nice view of downtown Montpelier for those willing to make the climb. Inu suggests you check out the pond near the park entrance for a quick dip—or a not-so-quick-dip. We could barely get him out of the pond once he got in.

From State Street, take Elm Street for a half mile then turn left onto Winter Street into the park. Open 9 A.M. to 9 P.M. (802) 223-5141.

• North Branch River Walk 🐾🐾🐾 See 19 on page 374.

The newest of Montpelier's hiking trails is also the hardest to find. It begins across a footbridge behind the Montpelier Recreation Field where a sign marks the start of the trail on the far side of the North Branch River. When the trail splits a quarter mile into your hike, we suggest taking the left fork which continues several miles into the woods and along the river. River otter can be spotted at times here, so keep your eyes open. This trail connects with Hubbard Park via a connector trail, which is closed in the winter.

Dogs must be leashed on the River Walk.

From State Street, take Elm Street (State Route 12) for 1.5 miles. Turn right into the Montpelier Recreation Field and Picnic Area. The trail begins across the wooden footbridge. Open 9 A.M. to 9 P.M. (802) 223-5141.

NATURE HIKES AND URBAN WALKS

Historic State Street Tour: Montpelier is home to many historic buildings, all of which make for interesting viewing from the street. Parading down State Street with your pooch is a great way to get a feel for Montpelier's history. Of particular note is No. 89, a Federal-style house built in 1810, which was likely one of the first on the street. Maps are available at the information booth on State Street. (802) 229-5711.

RESTAURANTS

Fiddleheads Restaurant and Bar: This is a capital spot for food whether you're a fiddlehead or a Fido. In the warm months, they have outdoor seating right on State Street, where you can leash your dog under your table. They'll even bring you a bowl of water. Fiddleheads serves a lunch menu of upscale salads and sandwiches, and turns downright elegant at night. 54 State Street; (802) 229-2244.

Capitol Grounds: This funky espresso bar gets our vote for a great place to grab a coffee and some bakery items any time of day. There are two outdoor tables where your dog is welcome to join you, and political hounds can order their coffee in one of four politically inspired sizes: Conservative (the smallest), Moderate, Liberal, or Radical (the largest). 45 State Street, Montpelier, VT; (802) 223-7800.

NORTH HERO

PARKS, BEACHES, AND RECREATION AREAS

• **Knight Point State Park** 🐾 🐾 🐾 See **20** on page 374.
This park is named after John Knight, who ran the first ferry to the Knight's Point Island in 1785. His house and the historic ferry landing are still intact, so be sure to check them out. An expansive lawn dominates the center of this 54-acre park, and a meandering trail loops up from the meadow and around the point, offering some great views of Lake Champlain. For water lovers, boat rentals are available here, including canoes and paddleboats.

You'll need to keep your pup on leash.

Located on U.S. Route 2 at the southern tip of North Hero Island. Open from the end of May to Labor Day, 10 A.M. to 8 P.M. (802) 372-8389.

• **North Hero State Park** 🐾 🐾 See **21** on page 374.
The Hero Islands are named for early Vermonters who served in the American Revolution. Almost one-third of this 399-acre park lies below 100-foot elevation, and Lake Champlain fluctuates seasonally, so much of the park is subject to seasonal flooding.

Pets are not allowed at the swimming beach but are welcome to swim at the boat launch area on Lake Champlain. There is a well-marked and maintained Nature Trail which can be accessed from Loop 3 in the camping area. The trail is wide and grassy and heads through meadows into the woods. George spent hours trying to herd the butterflies, to no avail.

Camping is available at the 117-site campground for $13 per night. Flush toilets and hot showers are available.

Dogs must be leashed. There is a $2 day-use fee.

From U.S. Route 2, take Lakeview Drive north for four miles to the northern tip of North Hero Island and the park. Open 8 A.M. to 10 P.M. mid-May to Labor Day. (802) 372-8727.

PLACES TO STAY

North Hero State Park camping: See page 388.

Shore Acres Inn and Restaurant: This inn is aptly named, with acres of open land plus shoreline access to Lake Champlain available for your pooch to romp. The rooms have views of the lake, with semiprivate decks on which to relax. Rates range from $78 to $140 per night. Pets are $10 the first night and $5 each additional night. RR 1, Box 3, Route 2, North Hero Island, VT 05474; (802) 372-8722.

NORTHFIELD

NATURE HIKES AND URBAN WALKS

Covered Canines: Vermont is renowned for its covered bridges, and in Northfield Falls you will find three of them within walking distance of each other. Walk along Cox Brook Road, which will take you through three covered bridges and over one dam. For a side trip you can also visit historic Slaughterhouse Bridge on Slaughterhouse Road; this is a good spot for your water dog to take a dip in Dog River. (Yes, there really is such a place!) Cox Brook Road is off State Route 12. (802) 828-3226.

RESTAURANTS

DeFelice's Sandwich Shop: Located right in the center of town, this is a great place to watch the world go by. Deli sandwiches and hot grill food is available for you to eat at the outdoor tables. Depot Square; (802) 485-4700.

Falls General Store and Dairy Bar: The take-out window is your ticket to a cool cone on a hot day. From the store, you can stroll over the adjacent covered bridges (see Nature Walks and Urban Hikes, above). Route 12 and Cox Brook Road; (802) 485-8044.

Red Kettle Restaurant: You can order inside and then sit outside at the covered tables in nice weather. This place has the standard burger-and-fries offerings, but the best choices are the homemade "comfort food" specialties of the house. The meatloaf gets us all drooling! 165 Route 12; (802) 485-4336.

FESTIVALS

Love's Labors Found: Northfield labors hard to put on one fine Labor Day Festival. Held on Depot Square, the festival boasts homemade pies, a parade, and a small carnival of activities. Most activities are outdoors, and your leashed pooch can help you celebrate. (802) 229-4619.

SAINT ALBANS

PARKS, BEACHES, AND RECREATION AREAS

• Taylor Park 🐾 🐾 See **22** on page 374.

Located on the corner of Fairfield and Main Streets, this five-acre park in the middle of town is ringed by very striking Victorian architecture, including a schoolhouse that dates back to 1860. Although it doesn't provide a huge place to let your dog romp and roll, it has lovely grassy lawns, a bandstand, picnic areas, and some paved paths that run throughout. Dogs must be on leash.

The park is at the intersection of Main Street (U.S. Route 7) and Fairfield Street. Open 6 A.M. to 10 P.M. (802) 885-3042.

NATURE HIKES AND URBAN WALKS

Saint Albans Historical Walk: In its heyday, Saint Albans was a prosperous railroad center, and many well-preserved Victorian buildings are still in evidence today. Pick up a map and information at the Chamber of Commerce at 2 North Main Street. (802) 524-2444.

FESTIVALS

I'm Dreaming of a Canine Christmas: Every December, Taylor Park is home to Christmas in the Park, a festival that makes you swear Charles Dickens is still alive. Festivites include sleigh rides, caroling, and general holiday merriment. Dogs are welcome at all outdoor activities. For more information, call (802) 524-2444.

Pumpkin Pups: Ever seen a jack-o'-lantern? Ever seen hundreds of them? If you'd like to, head over to the annual Pumpkin Lighting Festival at Taylor Park in late October. The town turns out with their carved pumpkins, and they all get lit at once. Dogs are permitted in the park and at the outdoor activities. For more information, call (802) 524-2444.

SAINT JOHNSBURY

PARKS, BEACHES, AND RECREATION AREAS

• **Dog Mountain** 🐾 🐾 🐾 🐾 🐕 See **23** on page 374.

Just north of town you will find this piece of dog heaven. Located on private land but open to canine visitors, Dog Mountain is the name given to this 150-acre property surrounding artist Stephen Huneck's art gallery and workshop. His commitment to dogs means you and your completely leash-free pooch can explore Dog Mountain's fields, woods, ponds, outdoor sculpture garden, and picnic areas. The nature walk provides some beautiful vistas.

You might run across a few of the artist's "dog models" and employees' dogs, as well. You can cap off your romp with a visit to the gallery, with its dog-themed art and furniture (see Diversions below).

Dogs are permitted off leash if under voice control.

From Interstate 93, take Exit 1 to U.S. Route 2 west for seven-tenths of a mile. Turn right onto Spaulding Road for a half mile. The park is on the left. Hours vary by season. (802) 748-2700 or (800) 449-2580.

DIVERSIONS

A Nose for Art: Monet had his water lilies, Degas had his ballet dancers, and Stephen Huneck has his Labrador retrievers. This renowned artist has a gallery and workshop filled with art and furniture inspired by dogs. You can visit the gallery with your canine companion or the 150 acres surrounding the farmhouse-turned-gallery (See Dog Mountain, above). Be sure to check out the artist's rendering of what's really inside your dog's brain. The gallery is open June through October, and by appointment in the off-season. Spaulding Road, St Johnsbury, VT 05819; (802) 748-2700, (800) 449-2580; www.huneck.com.

PLACES TO STAY

Fairbanks Motor Inn: This clean, modern motel offers morning coffee and doughnuts to its guests, canine included. The ground level rooms, with easy access to outside, are the designated "pet rooms," and the yard out back makes a great romping area. Rates range from $65 to $100, with an extra $5 for pets. 32 Western Ave, Saint Johnsbury, VT 05819; (802) 748-5666.

SHELBURNE

PARKS, BEACHES, AND RECREATION AREAS

• **Shelburne Bay Park** 🐾🐾 See **24** on page 374.

This 93-acre park was once part of Shelburne Farms, where dogs are not permitted. Boy, are we ever glad this land is now owned by the town of Shelburne, because it means that now you and your leashed pet can enjoy the stunning Lake Champlain views from Allen Hill.

There are two trails to choose from here, the Recreational Path and the Clarke Trail. The Clarke Trail is closer to the lakefront and views of the lake but can be quite muddy, so choose your visits well. The graveled Recreational Path runs a little over a mile through a variety of native fauna and hardwood trees; there are periodic connectors between the two for a longer hike.

Dogs are permitted on leash.

From U.S. Route 7 in Shelburne, take Bay Road west for 1.5 miles. The park is on the right. Open dawn until dusk. (802) 985-9551.

RESTAURANTS

Shelburne Bake Shop and Restaurant: You don't have to worry about crowds of tourists here, just the line of locals trying to get in the door. That just means the food, soups, sandwiches, burgers, ice cream, and a wild assortment of baked goods are fabulous. Get your goodies to go and enjoy them at their picnic area. 14 Falls Road; (802) 985-2830.

SOUTH BURLINGTON

PARKS, BEACHES, AND RECREATION AREAS

• **Red Rocks Park** 🐾🐾🐾 See **25** on page 374.

This heavily wooded bluff is located right on Lake Champlain. About 2.5 miles of good, crisscrossing hiking trails are available, and one day we might even explore them all. But try as we might, our walks in the woods get shorter and shorter as the dogs make a break for the lake earlier and earlier. Next time we'll go right for the beach and see if they make a run for the trees.

We can't blame them. There is plenty of beach—about two miles worth—on this partial peninsula, and you can walk most of it. Of course, the water is always refreshing with plenty of boat traffic to marvel at.

Dogs must be on leash and are not permitted at the designated swimming area.

From U.S. Route 7, take Queen City Park Road west for half a mile. The park entrance and road is on your right. Parking is available. Open dawn to 8 P.M. (802) 846-4108.

NATURE HIKES AND URBAN WALKS

South Burlington Recreation Path: This little-known, 3.5-mile bike path probably has some of the best views of Lake Champlain and the distant Adirondack Mountains of New York. The paved path runs from Red Rocks Park (see listing above) along the water and heads west for 2.5 miles through woods and farmland, gradually climbing the hills that line the Vermont side of the big lake. Parking is available at Red Rocks Park. Open dawn to 9 P.M. (802) 846-4108.

STOWE

Stowe Village is what most people picture when they think of Vermont—a classic white-steeple church at one end and 100-year-old buildings along Main Street—like a postcard come to life. Mount Mansfield, the highest point in Vermont, makes an imposing and scenic backdrop. No wonder this place is a must-see for tourists. Although most people come here for the skiing, it's also a great summer and fall destination. And with so many great hiking spots, your dog will want to "stow" away every time you visit.

PARKS, BEACHES, AND RECREATION AREAS

• Mount Mansfield State Forest 🐾🐾🐾🐾 See **26** on page 374.

Mount Mansfield is the highest point in Vermont, and it seems to keep getting higher. In 1998, it gained two feet when it was remeasured. It currently stands at 4,395 feet in elevation, and the state forest is comprised of some 37,242 acres. The summit is accessed primarily by an auto toll road, which ends at a Summit Station over 4,000 feet in elevation. From there you can hike to the summit via the half-mile Tundra Trail north to Drift Rock; another mile takes you to the summit of Mount Mansfield. Or, you can hike up the whole road, which is 4.5 miles long.

On foot, you can also select from one of nine hiking routes up the mountain. Our favorite is the Profanity Trail—named, no doubt, after the words that climbers use when ascending this steep trail.

Dogs must be leashed.

The toll road is open 10 A.M. to 5 P.M. from late May through October, weather permitting, at a cost of $12 per car. Foot traffic is free.

From State Route 100, take State Route 108 west six miles to the toll road. Open dawn until dusk. (802) 253-3000.

• Smugglers Notch State Park 🐾🐾🐾 See **27** on page 374.

Smugglers Notch is a narrow pass through the mountains and comes by its dishonest name honestly. This notch has a long-standing history of being used by smugglers of all types. As far back as 1807, when President Jefferson issued an embargo on trade with Canada, this notch was used to support illegal trade with the north. Later, Smugglers Notch was used as an escape route for fugitive slaves headed to Canada. And during Prohibition, liquor was smuggled into the country through the Notch. We felt free to continue the tradition and smuggled in lunch to take advantage of the picnic benches located near the start of the trail.

The park is only 25 acres, but it's 1,000 feet straight up to the Notch. At 2,162 feet in elevation, it is quite a climb. Some of the plants found here are endangered arctic-alpine species and are found nowhere else in Vermont, so be careful to stay on the path. The Notch is known for interesting rock formations, including one called The Hunter and His Dog. While it didn't fool our dogs for one minute, the rock does look surprisingly like a hunting dog. You can also access trails leading to Mount Mansfield State Forest from here, opening up over 37,000 additional acres for your hiking pleasure.

Dogs must be on leash.

From State Route 100, take State Route 108 west for 10 miles. Parking is on the right and the trail is on the left. The Notch is closed in the winter. Open dawn until dusk. (802) 253-4014.

• Sterling Falls Gorge Natural Area 🐾🐾🐾 🐕 See 28 on page 374.

This area is not very big, but it packs a lot of beauty into a small space. The trail that leads into the gorge is only a half mile long, but you will be rewarded with breathtaking views of waterfalls and cascades. The trail starts just over the bridge from the parking area.

This area is a public nonprofit trust and abuts other conservation land. Dogs are permitted leash free if under voice control.

From State Route 100 (north of Stowe center), take West Hill Road 1.2 miles west (it becomes a dirt road). At the T intersection, turn left. Continue for two miles to the parking area for the Catamount Ski Trail and the Sterling Falls Gorge. Open dawn until dusk. (802) 253-9035.

• Stowe Pinnacle 🐾🐾🐾 See 29 on page 374.

Ho, hum. Just another great park with a fabulous view. What else is new? The trail covers about three miles total, with an elevation gain of 1,500 feet, so it's a little bit of a climb but quite manageable. At the top, you will be able to take in the Waterbury Reservoir, as well as the Worcester Mountain Range.

Dogs are permitted if kept on leash.

From State Route 100, take School Street east for a half mile. Bear right onto Stowe Hollow Road onto Upper Hollow Road for 2.5 miles total. The small parking area is on the left. Open dawn until dusk. (802) 253-7321.

NATURE HIKES AND URBAN WALKS

Stowe Recreation Path: This 5.5-mile "rec path" runs through the heart of Stowe's downtown area and is a great place for a jaunt with your Jack Russell. This paved path opened in 1984 and runs along the banks of the West Branch River and into town. It's not a loop, so plan your trip accordingly because you won't end up where you started. But the few scenic miles take you through woods and meadows and over a number of old bridges. The path also doubles as a pedestrian alternative to Route 108, so there is easy access to Stowe's restaurants, shops, and inns. This means that you and your leashed dog might have to share the path with walkers, rollerbladers, and bicyclists. If the non-canine traffic is a bit overwhelming, try the Quiet Path; it's a mile-long walking-only loop along the Mayo River that diverges from the main path. (802) 253-7350.

RESTAURANTS

Gracie's Restaurant: It figures that a restaurant named for a dog would welcome dogs. A picture of Gracie, the owners' dog, hangs inside. The outdoor patio, open in warm weather, is where you can dine with Rover. You'll love the dog-themed menu and continental cuisine, so pop in for a bite. The restaurant is right in the heart of Stowe Village. Main Street behind the Carlson building; (802) 253-8741.

DIVERSIONS

Strutting with your Mutt: If people tell you how much you and your dog look alike, hightail it to Stowe in late August for the annual "Mutt Strut" to benefit the North Country Animal League. The dog-and-owner look-alike contest is a hoot, and you will also love the costume contests and other canine capers. Admission is free. It's held every year at the Mayo Farm Events Field in Stowe; for dates and information, call (802) 253-7321.

Expose Yourself to Art: Every summer, all summer long, Stowe hosts an outdoor art exhibit called "Exposed!" The art installations are strategically located throughout the town and along the Stowe Rec Path (see above), so walk the dog and get some culture at the same time! (802) 253-7321.

PLACES TO STAY

Burgundy Rose Motor Inn: This friendly 10-room motel allows dogs in selected rooms with no more than two dogs per room allowed. Standard double rooms and two efficiencies are available. Rates are $49 to $85, with a $5 pet fee. State Route 100, P.O. Box 488, Stowe, VT 05672; (802) 253-7768 or (800) 989-7768; www.burgundyrosemotorinn.com.

Mountain Road Resort: The Mountain Road Resort boasts 30 rooms and suites with acres of lawn where you can romp with your dog. Some suites have full efficiencies, while others have kitchenettes. Rates range $95 to $170. Dogs are an additional $25 per stay. 1007 Mountain Road, Stowe, VT 05672; (802) 253-4566; www.stowevtusa.com.

Commodore's Inn: George felt right at home at this 100-room hotel. All rooms are spacious, and some are equipped with kitchenettes. A three-acre pond is out back, and dogs are welcome to swim. Paddleboats are also available for rent. Rates range from $92 to $138. Pets are an additional $10. P.O. Box 970, Stowe, VT 05672; (800) 447-8693; www.stoweinfo.com.

Green Mountain Inn: Founded in 1833, this inn in the heart of Stowe generally houses its canine guests in the newer annex with separate outside entrances. Stepping out the door of your room, you'll find yourself in Stowe's shopping and dining center. Rates range from $113 to $250 per night. Main Street, Box 60, Stowe, VT 05672; (802) 253-7301 or (800) 253-7302; www.greenmountaininn.com.

Stowe Inn at Little River: Dogs are welcome in the carriage house across from the main inn. These rooms are motel style and include breakfast. Rates range from $65 to $210 per night. 123 Mountain Road, Stowe, VT 05672; (800) 227-1108 or (802) 253-4836; www.stoweinn.com.

The Riverside Inn: Stay motel style or at the lodge. Dogs are most often kept in the rooms with direct access to the great outdoors, but you can make a case for the lodge if your pooch is well trained. Rates range from $39 to $89, depending on the room and time of year. 1965 Mountain Road, Route 108, Stowe, VT 05672; (802) 253-4217.

Ten Acres Lodge: This antique-filled bed-and-breakfast features lovely cottages with two to three bedrooms, pine floors, and cozy comforters. Rates range from $125 to $300 per night. Dogs are welcome in two cottages. 14 Barrows Road, Stowe, VT 05672; (802) 327-7357.

Topnotch at Stowe Resort and Spa: This four-star resort will pamper you and your pooch. Dogs are permitted in the hotel proper but not the townhouses. An indoor pool and spa are available for you, and miles of hiking trails on the property will thrill your pet. Rates start at $200 and can go as high as $710 for a suite in season. 4000 Mountain Road, Stowe, VT 05672; (802) 253-8585 or (800) 451-8686.

SWANTON

PARKS, BEACHES, AND RECREATION AREAS

• **Missisquoi National Wildlife Refuge** 🐾🐾🐾 See **30** on page 374.
This wildlife refuge is 5,829 acres of wetlands and forest on the eastern shores of Lake Champlain. Named for an Indian word meaning "much waterfowl," this is a great place to see thousands of marsh and bay ducks and other water birds, but please note that this area is highly sensitive to the damage caused by visiting humans and dogs.

For a great birds-eye view, try the Maquam Creek Trail, a 2.7-mile trail through the wetlands that passes by beaver houses and other points of interest. You'll end up at Lookout Point after an easy, flat hike. You can connect to the Black Creek Trail for a different view on the way back.

Dogs must be on leash.

From U.S. Route 7, take State Route 78 west for two miles into the park. Open dawn to dusk. (802) 868-4781.

UNDERHILL

PARKS, BEACHES, AND RECREATION AREAS

• **Underhill State Park** 🐾🐾🐾 See **31** on page 374.
This 150-acre park is located within Mount Mansfield State Forest. From here you can hike one of the four trails to the summit of Mount Mansfield, the state's highest point at over 4,300 feet. Trail maps are available at the ranger station.

The three-mile Sunset Ridge Trail (that's six miles round-trip) is the most popular. Another choice for the summit climb is the Laura Cowles Trail, which goes to the summit via sets of stone steps. The Long Trail also passes through this area and heads to the summit, as well.

From State Route 15, take River Road east into the village of Underhill Center and Pleasant Valley Road. Turn right onto Mountain Road for four miles to the park. Open sunrise until sunset. (802) 899-3022.

VERGENNES
RESTAURANTS

Main Scoop: After a day on the trail, nothing is more rewarding than a cool, creamy something. For that, most people head to the Main Scoop. They offer a wide assortment of flavors, sizes, and specialties and outdoor seating, too. 61 Main Street; (802) 877-6201.

Luigi's Italian Specialties: No matter what you call it, Italian Specialties or Pizza and Subs, it's still Inu's favorite type of menu—one with lots of cheese. And with sidewalk tables, he can enjoy pasta while keeping up with all the Main Street action. 141 Main Street; (802) 877-6873.

PLACES TO STAY

Basin Harbor Club: This lovely 77-room lakeside inn is a place for special occasions. Of course, we think special is when you make it to Friday each week, so why wait? Each room is decorated with colonial antiques, handmade quilts, and luxurious furnishings. A spa, restaurant, health club, and walking paths are on-site, and we love those little chocolates that are part of the turndown service. Rates are steep, but you only live once: $140 to $400 per night. Small dogs only for an additional $8 per night. Basin Harbor Road, Vergennes, VT 05491; (802) 475-2311.

WAITSFIELD
PARKS, BEACHES, AND RECREATION AREAS

• Scrag Mountain Municipal Forest 🐾 🐾 See **32** on page 374.

This town forest and its single trail to the peak of Scrag Mountain is a popular outing for local Vermonters and visitors alike. The trail runs through a lovely woodland from the end of Palmer Hill Road to the summit at 2,923 feet. Up top, there are good views of the Mad River Valley and the Green Mountains. The hike is three miles round-trip with a strenuous climb on the first half.

The path is managed by the Mad River Valley Path Association, and they require dogs to be on leash.

From State Route 100, take East Road east for a half mile. Turn right onto Cross Road, a dirt road, onto Palmer Hill Road for a total of a mile. The parking area and trailhead are at the end of the road. Open dawn to dusk. (888) 445-3766.

NATURE HIKES AND URBAN WALKS

Mad River Greenway: This town footpath along the Mad River traces every bend and ripple in the river for three miles. Watch out when the river runs "mad." It does flood from time to time. The trail runs from Trembly Road to the Moretown border.

To add a little variety to your walk, circle back from Meadows Road on North Road, which runs parallel east of the footpath. This will give you the chance to cross the Pine Brook Bridge, a 48-foot-long covered bridge built in 1872. (888) 445-3766.

Waitsfield Historic Walking Tour: This short, self-guided, historic walking tour of stately Main and Bridge Streets will give you a real feel for what Vermont was like in the early 19th century. The two-block tour includes the home of General Waits, the town's founder, the first school house, and the Village Bridge over the Mad River. The 105-foot covered bridge was built in 1833 and is the second oldest Vermont bridge still in use. For more information and maps, contact the Central Vermont Chamber of Commerce at (802) 229-4619.

WARREN

RESTAURANTS

Warren Store: In all our travels through New England, we searched for the quintessential general store; the one with the ancient hardwood floors, cast-iron stove, and a series of fresh baked goods cooling in the window. . . you know, that one.

Luckily, the Warren Store is everything we hoped for and more. Why, just stepping onto the front porch takes you back to the 1800s, and going inside takes you back even farther. The refrigerators are real ice boxes made of beautiful wood and glass, and a cast-iron stove and ancient hardwood floors completed the picture.

And the food is all fresh baked. The country deli has delicious breads, bagels, muffins, and pastries to start your day and great sandwiches for the midday meal. They even have a nice wine selection.

Yes, we admit, if we actually did live in Warren and needed to shop for real supplies, we would probably be forced to drive into Montpelier. But we would first give it a real go of living on wine and bagels! Main Street; (802) 496-3864.

PLACES TO STAY

Golden Lion Riverside Inn: This cozy inn is located at the scenic base of Sugarbush Mountain. Pets are only permitted in a few rooms, but each room comes with the modern luxuries of a full-scale hotel and the warmth of a mountain inn. The rooms sleep two to four people. Rates range from $65 to $125. Box 20, State Route 100, Warren, VT 05674; (802) 496-3084.

Powderhound Inn: With a name like this, we had to take notice. Okay, so the name refers to powder skiers rather than canines, but there is more than enough room at this 100-year-old converted farmhouse for both skiers and hounds. In fact, we left with more dogs than we came with. Granted, the new additions were small stuffed dogs given to us courtesy of the owners, but it shows how welcome dogs are here. Our dogs enjoyed themselves in the spacious two-room condo with small kitchenette, and, while Inu made himself at home by drinking from the toilet, Rocky was busy making the acquaintance of the resident horses. The whole crew enjoyed Michael's, the superb hotel outdoor restaurant, and we caught George sneaking into the Doghouse Tavern for a pint with the locals. Dogs are an additional $5 per night and the hotel provides a small list of very reasonable "pet rules" at check-in. Rates range from $75 to $135. State Route 100, P.O. Box 369, Warren, VT 05674; (802) 496-5100, (800) 548-4022; www.powderhoundinn.com.

Sugarbush Village: There are 200 condos at this resort and some allow pets. All have kitchens and fireplaces and a health club is on-site. Rates range from $125 to $600. RR 1, Box #68-12, Warren, VT 05674; (802) 583-3000.

WATERBURY

PARKS, BEACHES, AND RECREATION AREAS

• Little River State Park 🐾🐾🐾 See 33 on page 374.

Little River State Park, opened in 1962, is encompassed in the "Ricker Block" section of Mount Mansfield State Forest. This area is named for Joseph Ricker, who founded the first farm in the area. It was farmed for 90 years, starting in 1816; in 1927 floods drove off the last of the area residents.

As you hike, you will find remnants of the past, making this forest a great place to explore. The Stevenson Brook Trail begins near the contact station and heads up through a hemlock grove. Once you hit Stevenson Brook, you can continue on or take a connecting trail to the Dalley Loop Trail. Be forewarned of the stream crossings—they can be difficult and muddy, especially in times of high water. Along the three-mile path you will pass the foundations of the original farmhouses. You will even pass the Ricker Cemetery, surrounded by white cedar trees, planted to honor those buried here. You can obtain information on the history of this area at the contact station.

Dogs are permitted on leash.

From State Route 100, take U.S. Route 2 west for 1.5 miles. Turn right onto Little River Road for 3.5 miles into the park. Open dawn to dusk, mid-May to Columbus Day. (802) 244-7103.

PLACES TO STAY

The Old Stagecoach Inn: This beautiful old inn was really once a stagecoach stop and is now listed on the National Register of Historic Places. There are eight bedrooms and three efficiency suites, ranging from $45 to $110 per night. Well-behaved dogs are welcome, and you might even find a canine friend or two in residence. 18 North Main Street, Waterbury, VT 05676; (800) 262-2206, (802) 244-5056.

RESTAURANTS

Ben & Jerry's Ice Cream Factory: This place is like a mecca, drawing ice-cream addicts from around the globe. It is well worth a visit, even if you are one of the two people on the planet who has never heard of this ice cream. Trust us, your dog will thank you. The factory is situated on a dairy farm, and you and your leashed pooch are welcome on the grounds. It is quite a place to visit, with a carnival-like atmosphere and lots of Ben & Jerry's ice cream to sample. The factory tour is off-limits to your pup, but food vendor booths and outdoor take-away windows abound. Tie-dye colored picnic tables are nearby where you can dine al fresco on a variety of foods, including Ben & Jerry's finest. Sit a spell in the Adirondack chairs, or check out the dairy cows responsible for the premium milk that creates this one-of-a-kind ice cream. U.S. Route 2, (802) 882-1240.

WESTMORE

PARKS, BEACHES, AND RECREATION AREAS

• **Willoughby State Forest** 🐾🐾🐾 See **34** on page 374.

Willoughby State Forest is 7,500 acres that will leave you breathless from both the elevation gain on the trails and the views you get from the top. Within the boundary of the state forest are a number of mountains, so your pooch has her pick of the litter.

Our dogs chose Mount Pisgah which lies on the east bank of Lake Willoughby. The sheer cliffs of this mountain are unique, and they have been designated a National Natural Landmark, ensuring that this mountain will be protected.

The summit trailhead starts across the street from the parking area; the 1.7-mile trail is moderately difficult. On the way up, you'll see a sign for the Pulpit Rock Trail, which will add another two miles to your round-trip. Keep a firm hold of your pup, as Pulpit Rock is actually a rock overhang far above the lake, and your water-loving canine might be tempted to take a really high dive.

Dogs are permitted on leash.

From U.S. Route 5, take State Route 5A north for 5.5 miles to the parking lot on the left. Open dawn to dusk. (802) 241-3650.

PLACES TO STAY

Willough Vale Inn and Restaurant on Lake Willoughby: This inn is beautiful, and the lakeside cottages have fireplaces and kitchenettes for that "home-away-from-home" feeling. We especially love the big wraparound porch where our dogs can watch the world go by. Rates start at $75. State Route 5A, Westmore, VT 05860; (802) 525-4123; www.willoughvale.com.

WORCESTER

PARKS, BEACHES, AND RECREATION AREAS

• **C. C. Putnam State Forest** 🐾🐾🐾 🐕 See **35** on page 374.

Well, here we go: 13,000 acres and not a leash in sight! This part of the C. C. Putnam State Forest is a favorite because of its leash-free attitudes. You can take the four-mile climb to the top of Hunger Mountain via the Waterbury Trail, where you'll have far-reaching views.

Within the forest, you will find Moss Glen Falls, considered one of Vermont's most unique natural features. The falls have a total drop of over 100 feet and are one of the highest and most scenic falls in the state. In the northern part of the forest, you will find Mount Worchester, a bit off the beaten path for most, but the 2.5-mile trail up the summit is fairly easy for pups.

From State Route 12, take Minister Brook Road 1.5 miles west. Turn right onto Hampshire Road for 2.5 miles into the park. Open sunrise to sunset. (802) 241-3350.

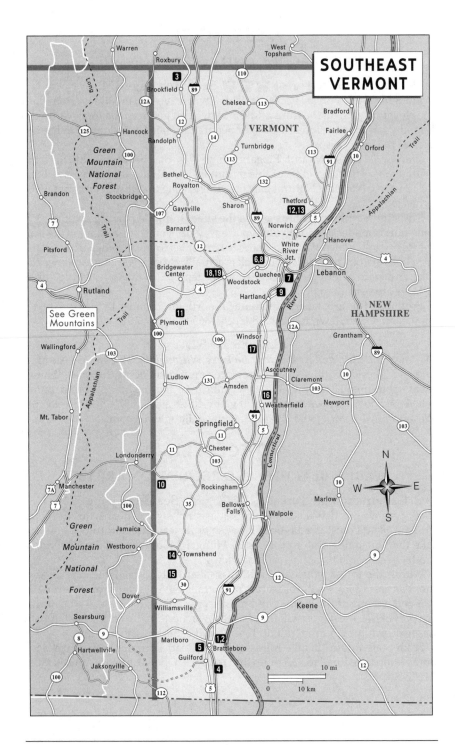

SOUTHEAST
VERMONT

VERMONT

NEW
HAMPSHIRE

See Green
Mountains

Green
Mountain
National
Forest

Green
Mountain
National
Forest

12
SOUTHEAST VERMONT

The southern portion of Vermont is nestled between the Green Mountains to the west and the Connecticut River to the east. With gentle, rolling hills and lush, open valleys, this area is often the place folks visualize when they think of Vermont. In the fall, Brattleboro teems with leaf peepers, a kind of tree frog. Blazing yellow and orange trees blend with soft green hills and blue skies. In the winter, Woodstock looks like a scene out of Currier and Ives. In the summer, you'll enjoy canoeing the rivers and swimming in the ponds at White River Junction. No matter when you visit, you'll delight in Vermont's natural splendor. And, better still, your pooch will enjoy experiencing it with you because in this neck of the woods dogs are rarely turned away.

ANDOVER

PLACES TO STAY

Inn At Highview: Resident top dog, Brenda the cocker spaniel, will be at the door to welcome you when you arrive. Dogs stay in style here, as the pet rooms are two-room suites with outside decks. The decks overlook the 72-acre property that beckons your dog for a leash-free romp. Rates start at $155 and

---

include breakfast. No additional pet fee is required. 753 East Hill Road, Andover, VT 05143; (802) 875-2724; www.innathighview.com.

BETHEL

PLACES TO STAY

Greenhurst Inn: This grand 1890s Victorian inn with turrets and wraparound porch has 13 rooms, half with private baths, and a view overlooking the White River. Pets need prior approval. Rates range from $35 to $100. Breakfast is included. River Street, Bethel, VT 05032; (802) 234-9474, (800) 510-2553.

BRATTLEBORO

"Oh, now and then you will hear grown-ups say,

'Can the Ethiopian change his skin or the Leopard his spots?' I don't think even grown-ups would keep saying such a silly thing if the Leopard and the Ethiopian hadn't done it once, do you? But they will never do it again, Best Beloved. They are quite contented as they are." From *How the Leopard Got His Spots* by Rudyard Kipling

Perhaps Brattelboro should change its spots or its name. Many towns are named for prominent founders or residents, but Brattleboro is named for a man who never lived or even visited the town. Brattleboro was chartered in 1753 and named after the land's title holder, William Brattle who lived in Boston. We think this is a bit odd. Rudyard Kipling lived here in the early 1890s while writing the *Jungle Book.* How about naming it after him?

PARKS, BEACHES, AND RECREATION AREAS

• The Common 🐾 🐾 See ❶ on page 400.

This centrally located green is the essence of New England—park benches, picnic tables, band shell, and packs of local pooches playing. It's not a big space, but a nice path circles the Common, and it does overlook a large meadow called Retreat Meadows, which is accessible a half mile farther north up State Route 30 (Lindon Street). The visitor center on the common is a first stop for most visitors. The war memorials are a reminder of the town't patriotic past. Dogs must be leashed.

At the corner of Putney and Lindon Streets and Park Place. Open 24 hours. (203) 254-4565.

• Living Memorial Park 🐾 🐾 🐾 See ❷ on page 400.

The picnic areas, playground, and ball fields hint at the family activity that takes place here. Keep going from the entrance, as the best dog sniffing spots are farther up the hill. At the top, you are rewarded with not just amazing views, but also with hillside open spaces for playing with your pooch. To get to this park, you have to drive through the 1879 Creamery Bridge, one of the still-standing covered bridges that Vermont is so famous for.

Brattleboro requires leashes in this park.

From U.S. Route 5, take State Route 9 west for four miles. Turn left onto Guilford Street. The park is on the right. Open dawn to dusk. (802) 254-6700.

NATURE HIKES AND URBAN WALKS

Common to Connecticut Canines: The walk from The Common to the Connecticut River Bridge down Main Street is a wonderful, two-block stroll in turn-of-the-20th-century Vermont. It's scenic, historic, and a good way to experience the city—and the view of the river from the bridge is photo worthy. If you are feeling adventurous, you can cross the bridge into New Hampshire and head on into Wantastiquet Mountain Natural Area (see page 468). Our dogs like to venture onto an island in the river accessible from the bridge. It's a refreshing spot where George and Inu can dip their paws into the water. Rocky, ever the worrier, stays on the shore and barks about swimming so soon after a meal. (203) 254-4565.

RESTAURANTS

Collected Works and the Café Beyond: This bookstore/coffeehouse combo is more than just a great place to browse for a dog book. They serve up tasty lunch, cookies, and coffee that customers and canine companions can enjoy at the outdoor tables in front of the bookstore. Inu recommends the peanut butter cookies. 29 High Street; (802) 258-4900.

Rays Diner: This traditional diner welcomes visitors on their way into Brattleboro. They have one outdoor table, and that's all we need! It's just the spot to grab some simple soup or even prime rib and lobster. 45 Canal Street; (802) 254-0090.

PLACES TO STAY

Colonial Motel: This quiet motel with 74 rooms and an Olympic-sized indoor pool is located right off Interstate 91 (Exit 3). Rates range from $46 to $90 plus a $10 fee per night for you dog. 889 Putney Road, Brattleboro, VT 05301; (802) 257-7733; www.colonialmotel.com.

Econo Lodge: This 42-room chain motel is conveniently located near downtown and the highways into the Green Mountains. Rates range from $50 to $105. 243 Canal Street, Brattleboro, VT 05301; (802) 254-2360, (800) 55-ECONO; www.econolodge.com.

Motel 6: All Motel 6 locations allow dogs, as long as you don't leave your pet unattended. Take Exit 3 from Interstate 91. 1254 Putney Road, Brattleboro, VT 05301; (802) 254-6007, (800) 4-MOTEL6; www.motel6.com.

FESTIVALS

Gallery Walk: From June to September on the first Friday of each month, the town of Brattleboro hosts an art exhibit called First Friday. Local artists display their work both outdoors and in the stores along Canal and High Streets. It makes this scenic stroll even more pleasant, and many of the stores are dog friendly. (802) 254-4565.

Patriotic Pup: Brattleboro celebrates Independence Day with a bang—actually lots of them, in the form of fireworks. The whole day is given over to a morning parade and an afternoon of games, food, and entertainment. The parade takes place downtown, but the afternoon celebration is at Living Memorial Park. Leashed patriotic dogs are welcome all day, just be careful of the fireworks. For information, call (802) 254-4565.

BRIDGEWATER

RESTAURANTS

Bridgewater Corners Country Store: This quaint country store is just what you had in mind when you thought of a roadside stop in Vermont. It has a big red barn, with a porch that beckons. If you and the pup need a pit stop, this is it in these parts. Snacks, deli items, and beverages are available. Located at the intersection of U.S. Route 4 and State Route 100A; (802) 672-3451.

PLACES TO STAY

The Corners Country Inn: This five-bedroom, country-style bed-and-breakfast is close to Killington and Woodstock. All rooms have private baths. Well-behaved pets are welcome with prior approval but cannot be left unattended. Rates range from $55 to $95. 318 Upper Road, Bridgewater, VT 05035; (802) 672-9968; www.cornersinn.com.

BROOKFIELD

PARKS, BEACHES, AND RECREATION AREAS

• **Allis State Park** 🐾🐾 See **3** on page 400.

This park is located on the summit of Bear Mountain and is a gift to the people of Vermont from Wallace Allis. The park has limited recreation facilities for dogs and two short loop trails around the wooded peak at 2,020 feet.

We listed it because the centrally located campground is a good place to stay if you want to explore the Green Mountains to the west and Montpelier to the north. The wooded campground, just off the summit, has 18 tent sites and eight lean-to sites and offers modern plumbing and hot showers. Rates range from $11 to $15.

Dogs must be leashed and are not permitted in the day-use areas. There is a $2 day-use fee.

From State Route 12, take State Route 65 east for 1.5 miles. The park is on the right. Open dawn to dusk, mid-May to mid-October. (802) 276-3175.

PLACES TO STAY

Allis State Park camping: See above.

CHESTER

NATURE HIKES AND URBAN WALKS

Chester's Bester: Pick up a map for a self-guided walk of historic Chester at the Chamber of Commerce information booth on the Chester Green. Numerous buildings are on the National Register of Historic Places in Chester, and you and your pooch will enjoy the stroll. Don't miss the Fullerton Inn, at the hub of the shopping district—it's a beauty. If you're feeling frisky, keep going to the north end of town to see the distinctive "Stone Village" houses. For information, call (802) 885-2779.

RESTAURANTS

Raspberries and Tyme: This yummy restaurant in the middle of town does takeout to a tee, offering tasty soups, salads, sandwiches, and burgers for lunch, and seafood and chicken specialties for dinner. There is no outdoor seating, but you can dine al fresco with your furry friend at the Chester Green. On the Green; (802) 875-4486.

PLACES TO STAY

Glen Finert Farm: This is one of the longest-standing bed-and-breakfasts in the area. Set high on a hill, the farmhouse contains three guest rooms with shared baths. Rates range from $50 to $60 per night with a $5 charge for Buster. Flam Stead Road, Chester, VT 05143; (802) 875-2160; www.chester-lodging.com.

FAIRLEE

PLACES TO STAY

Silver Maple Lodge and Cottages: The Silver Maple is one of the oldest continuously operating country inns in Vermont. The restored inn, a historic farmhouse dating back to the late 1700s, has been welcoming guests since the 1920s. Pets need prior permission and are only permitted to stay in the knotty pine cottages. Breakfast is in the dining room or on the wraparound porch. Cottage rates range from $79 to $89. 520 U.S. Route 5, South Fairlee, VT 05045; (802) 333-4326, (800) 666-1946; www.silvermaplelodge.com.

GUILFORD

PARKS, BEACHES, AND RECREATION AREAS

• Fort Dummer State Park 🐾🐾🐾 See 4 on page 400.

In 1724, Fort Dummer became the first permanent white settlement in Vermont. The site of the fort is near the park but under water now, thanks to the Vernon Dam built in 1908. A real example of progress over posterity, we think. Two short hiking trails wind through the 217 acres here. The paths lead through hardwood forests and overlook the site of the fort.

Dogs must be leashed and are not permitted in day-use areas.

From Interstate 91 in Brattleboro, take Exit 1 to U.S. Route 5 north for one-tenth of a mile. Turn right onto Fairground Road for a half mile then make a right onto Main Street for one mile into Guilford and Old Guilford Road. Open from 9 A.M. to 8 P.M., mid-May to Labor Day. (802) 254-2610.

• Sweet Pond State Park 🐾🐾🐾 See 5 on page 400.

We have nothing against development and friendly park rangers, mind you, but our favorite state parks are the remote, undeveloped ones you have all to your lonesome. Sweet Pond, a 120-acre state park, is just that. It has only one trail, a two-mile easy loop around scenic and inviting Sweet Pond and through wetlands and whispering pine forests. Solitude, sweet solitude!

As in all Vermont state parks, dogs must be on leash.

From U.S. Route 5, take Guilford Center Road west. Turn right onto Sweet Pond Road for 2.5 miles. The park is on the left. Open dawn to dusk. (802) 241-3655.

HARTFORD
(AND THE VILLAGES OF QUECHEE AND WHITE RIVER JUNCTION)

PARKS, BEACHES, AND RECREATION AREAS

• **Quechee Green** 🐾🐾 See **6** on page 400.

The green is adjacent to Lake Pinneo in the center of Quechee. The green runs behind the row of shops on Main Street, so you will have to drive behind them to find it. A large, flat, green lawn with a gazebo for sitting a spell, this is a nice stop after shopping in Quechee's unique shops. The lake is accessible here, but dogs must stay on leash.

Between Main Street and River Road. Open 24 hours. (802) 295-5036.

• **George Ratcliff Park** 🐾🐾 See **7** on page 400.

This small park may have your pooch chomping at the leash, but it has one redeeming quality: swimming access to the Connecticut River. If you have a sure-footed pooch, take the gravel trail to the water's edge. Your pup can head down the hill to the river's edge for a quick dip.

Dogs must be on leash.

Take South Main Street from the White River Junction town center. Turn left on Nutt Lane and cross the railroad tracks. Take the first right onto Latham Works Lane for the main parking lot. You can reach the back entrance by continuing on Nutt Lane. Open sunrise to sunset. (802)295-5036.

• **Quechee Gorge State Park** 🐾🐾🐾🐾 🐕 See **8** on page 400.

Known as "Vermont's Little Grand Canyon," this mile-long, 150-foot deep gorge is part of 611-acre Quechee Gorge State Park and attracts 500,000 visitors a year. Many of the visitors come just to cross the U.S. Route 4 bridge over the gorge. Your dog may appreciate the spectacular views from the span but will certainly have more fun on the trails into and around the canyon.

The main route starts at the bridge and Quechee Gift Shop (on U.S. Route 4). From here it drops down into the gorge and runs along the Ottauquechee River for the full length of the gorge. Along the way, you will find the remnants of mills and a dam from when the A. G. Dewey Company owned this property at the turn of the century. At the end of the gorge, you can loop back on the rim via a series of paths called the Wilderness Trails.

Other areas to head for in the park are Dewey Pond and the Falls Overlook.

The park's campground is located on what was once the mill workers' recreation area. Dogs are permitted at any of the 47 lean-to, tent, or trailer sites. Facilities include two bathrooms with hot showers. Site fees range from $12 to $16 per night.

The park is owned by the U.S. Army Corps of Engineers but managed by the State of Vermont Department of Forest and Parks. Dogs must be kept on leash in the improved areas but are permitted off leash on the trails.

From Interstate 89, take Exit 1 to U.S. Route 4 east for 2.5 miles into the park. Open 9 A.M. to 8 P.M. Call (802) 295-2990 from mid-May to Columbus Day, (802) 886-2434 off-season.

NATURE HIKES AND URBAN WALKS

Sugarbush Farm: Visit a real working maple and dairy farm and see how "sugaring" is done and how to make Vermont's famous cheese.

On the grounds, there is a "Maple Walk"—a 15-minute nature walk through one of the trails that the farm uses for sugaring in the winter. Signs explain the process along the route. Dogs are welcome on the farm, on the trail, and in the maple-sugar exhibit, but are not permitted in the cheese-making facility, for the obvious health code reasons. Sugarbush Farm Road; (802) 457-1757.

RESTAURANTS

Ott Dog Snack Bar: Just past the gorge on U.S. Route 4, the Snack Bar serves burgers, ice cream, and—what else?—hot dogs. The outdoor picnic tables allow you to share your lunch with your lucky dog. Open mid-May to late October. Quechee Gorge, U.S. Route 4; (802) 295-1088.

PLACES TO STAY

Best Western at the Junction: All doors open to the outside for easy "walkies" at this 110-room, full-service hotel. Rates range from $89 to $130; pets are an additional $10. 306 North Hartland Road, White River Junction, VT 05001; (802) 295-3015; www.bestwestern.com.

Pleasant View Hotel: This hotel takes dogs with approval, and the biggest knock-out factor is your dog's choice of sleeping location. The hotel really, really does not want dogs on the bed, so plan accordingly. Rates are $47 per night. 65 Woodstock Drive, White River Junction, VT 05001; (802) 295-3485.

Quechee Gorge State Park camping: See pages 406–407.

Quality Inn at Quechee: This 59-room motel is pretty standard as far as Quality Inns go, but it's right next to the Quechee Gorge, so you can't beat the location. Pets are permitted in selected rooms with prior permission. Rates range from $65 to $129. U.S. Route 4, Quechee, VT 05059; (802) 295-7600, (800) 295-7600.

Quechee Vacation Rentals: You can rent a condo with your canine in Quechee, condo capital of Vermont. Rates vary depending on the size of the unit and your length of stay. 26 Main Street, Quechee, VT 05059; (800) 262-3186, (802) 295-3186.

Ramada White River Junction: This hotel has set aside special "pet rooms." Rates range from $78 to $90. 8 Holiday Drive, White River Junction, VT 05059; (802) 295-3000, (888) 298-2054; www.ramada.com.

Sugar Pine Farm Bed-and-Breakfast: Pets are occasionally permitted here, depending on the pet and the time of year. Off-season is your best bet. If your pet is well behaved, you stand a good shot. In fact, this place once even let a very well-behaved wolf—who was part of the public relations school tour about reintroducing wolves to Vermont—stay here. Rates range from $75 to $95. U.S. Route 4, Quechee, VT 05059; (802) 295-1266; www.virtualcities.com.

DIVERSIONS

Casey Canine: Casey Junior's comin' down the line, and your dog is too! All (and we mean all) aboard the River Valley Rambler, a 10-mile scenic train ride from White River Junction's Union Depot to Norwich following the Connecticut River. Small dogs are welcome on the 45-minute, round-trip excursion on the 1930s diesel train. Adult fare is $8. June through September. For schedule and information, call (802) 463-3069.

HARTLAND

PARKS, BEACHES, AND RECREATION AREAS

• **North Hartland Lake Dam and Recreation Area** 🐾🐾🐾 🐕 See **9** on page 400.

The U.S. Army Corps of Engineers manages the North Hartland Dam, which controls the Ottacuquechee River and creates the North Hartland Lake. The recreation area surrounding the lake is 1,700 acres in size and offers endless hiking opportunities beginning with a short self-guided nature trail. Once done with that, you'll have endless lakeside marsh and woodlands to explore via undeveloped trails and forest roads.

Dogs are prohibited from the swimming beach and must be leashed in the other developed areas of the park. They can be leash free in the backcountry.

From U.S. Route 5, take Clay Hill Road west one mile. The dam's entrance on the left. Open 7:00 A.M. to 3:30 P.M. (802) 295-2855.

LONDONDERRY

PARKS, BEACHES, AND RECREATION AREAS

• **Lowell Lake State Park** 🐾🐾🐾 See **10** on page 400.

This rather undeveloped state park on Lowell Lake is a pleasant surprise for any dog. The remote lake is large, gorgeous, and surrounded by a thick pine forest, footpaths, and forest roads that are closed to vehicles. No matter which route you take you will find plenty of water access and some very nice picnic spots along the way.

Other hidden treasures include the small dam at the south end of the lake with its shady grass lawns and an almost forgotten historic cemetery where several Revolutionary War veterans—our Green Mountain Boys—are buried.

Dogs must be leashed.

From State Route 100, take State Route 11 east for three miles. Turn left onto Lowell Lake Road for seven-tenths of a mile to the end. Make a right onto Park Road into the park. Open 9 A.M. to 8 P.M. (802) 241-3655.

PLACES TO STAY

White Pine Lodge: This small inn offers five efficiency apartments, each equipped with a sitting area and full kitchen. Rates range from $55 to $125 with an additional $7 fee per pet per night. State Route 11, Londonderry, VT 05148; (802) 824-3909.

LUDLOW

RESTAURANTS

The Art of the Chicken: What they offer is chicken everything. From chicken-broccoli quiche to chicken wings and chicken salad to chicken-noodle soup, this place stands a cluck above. Take it out to the waiting picnic tables to share with your four-footed friend. (George prefers the tomato maple–glazed chicken.) Lamere Square, State Route 100; (802) 228-7180.

Scoops Ice Cream: Inu was a big hit on the porch of Scoops, using his golden good looks to gain many pats and a few ice-cream licks from the gathered crowd. Beth highly recommends the milk shakes, made with fresher-than-fresh Vermont dairy products. Lamere Square, State Route 100; (802) 228-2135.

Taco Tacos: All of Lamere Square beckons dog owners, but no place more so than Taco Taco. The comfortable outdoor picnic tables provide plenty of room for this traveling herd. The menu of burritos, tacos, and other Mexican favorites is as fresh as it gets. Lamere Square, State Route 100; (802) 228-7899.

PLACES TO STAY

Cavendish Pointe Hotel: This 70-room, full-service, and three-diamond-rated hotel is close to the major ski resorts of Okemo and Killington and the rest of the Green Mountains. The hotel has an indoor pool and a two-story fireplace in the relaxing lobby. Be sure to bring a biscuit for Sparky, the hotel's resident Jack Russell and official guest greeter. Rates range from $89 to $189. State Route 103, Ludlow, VT 05149; (802) 226-7688, (800) 438-7908; www.okemo-cavendishpointe.com.

Combes Family Inn: This inn started out as a farm in 1891 but now houses a comfortable, 11-room, family inn on 50 acres of rolling hills and meadows. Rates range from $55 to $104. 953 East Lake Road, Ludlow, VT 05149; (800) 822-8799; www.combesfamilyinn.com.

Timber Inn Motel: The Timber Inn has 16 rooms finished in knotty pine and cedar, but only one of the rooms is reserved for dogs and their owners. Guests will find room to stroll along the Black River. Rates range from $79 to $129. 112 State Route 103 South, Ludlow, VT 05149; (802) 228-8666; www.vermontlodging.com/timber.

PLYMOUTH

Plymouth Notch is only about 10 miles from the modern-day Vermont ski capital of Killington, yet it is a world apart. When you set paw in Plymouth, you feel like you have stepped into the 1920s. This town's greatest claim to fame is as the birthplace and family home of Calvin Coolidge, the 30th President of the United States. The town is perfectly preserved, and old "Silent Cal" himself would never believe how long he's been gone.

PARKS, BEACHES, AND RECREATION AREAS

• **Coolidge State Park/Coolidge State Forest** 🐾🐾🐾 See **11** on page 400.

Taken together, Coolidge State Forest and Coolidge State Park contain a total of 16,566 acres scattered throughout seven towns, including Plymouth and Shrewsbury.

The state forest is where your dog is going to find the room to roam and the trails to explore this mountainous and wooded area in central Vermont. One of the most popular hiking areas is in the Shrewsbury Peak Natural Area. This peak has an elevation of 3,700 feet, and the climb is quite scenic. The red spruce and balsam fir forests make it seem an unspoiled paradise. The trailheads to this area and for the Long Trail are in Shrewsbury off of Old CCC Road and Cold River.

Other areas to explore include Slack Hill and Pinney Hollow Brook off State Route 100A. Throughout the woods, you will find extensive stone walls and foundation remains from when the forest was farmland. Trail information is available at the campground.

The 500 acres of Coolidge State Park offer camping and picnic areas. The wooded campground, with 60 sites for tents, RVs, and lean-tos, offers flush toilets and metered hot showers. Rates range from $11 to $16 per night.

Dogs must be leashed and are not allowed in the day-use areas.

From State Route 100, take State Route 100A north for two miles. The park is on the right. The state park is open 10 A.M. to sunset, mid-May through October. State forest trails are open 24 hours a day, year-round. Call (802) 672-3612, mid-May through October, (802) 885-8891 off-season.

NATURE WALKS AND URBAN HIKES

President Calvin Coolidge State Historic Site: America's 30th president was born and raised in the small town of Plymouth, and much of his childhood home remains here for you to visit. The grounds of his homestead, birthplace, presidential swearing-in site, and grave are accessible to both canine and human visitors; the buildings are not open to dogs. The site is beautifully preserved, and the historic markers help guide your tour. The homestead is on State Route 100A; the grounds are open year-round. (802) 672-3773.

PLACES TO STAY

Coolidge State Park camping: See page 409.

PUTNEY

PLACES TO STAY

Putney Inn: This inn is centered around a 1790s farmhouse, offering 25 rooms in an adjoining building. All are dog friendly with private baths and Queen Anne–period replica furnishings. Dinners at the farmhouse are rated some of the finest in the area. Rates range from $88 to $138 with an additional $10 per pet per night. P.O. Box 181, Putney, VT 05346; (802) 387-5517, (800) 653-5517; www.putneyinn.com.

DIVERSIONS

Has the whole world gone to the dogs?: Established in 1990, Camp Gone to the Dogs is located on more than 500 acres, where you and your dog can hike, swim, and have an all-around fun time together. All activities are optional, so you can go from morning to night until you're dog tired or simply pick and choose a few favorite activities. For example, you can teach an old dog some new tricks at the tricks classes, put on the dog at the weekend costume parade, or leap tall obstacles at agility training. There are face-kissing, tail-wagging, and wienie-retrieving contests, and, for more sober-minded sorts, there are lectures on canine health and behavioral problems. The list is endless.

The cost of a one-week session in June and July ranges from $950 to $1,200 per person and includes all activities and meals. There are also special weekend camps throughout the year for about $450 per person. Reservations are recommended because the spots for 120 humans and 250 dogs fill up fast. For more information, call (802) 387-5673.

Pass the Sugar: Vermont magically creates maple syrup from maple sap, in a process called sugaring. The best place to learn about this is Harlow's Sugar House, on the Brody farm. Don Brody does the whole Vermont farm thing so well, Martha Stewart comes to him for advice. Dogs are welcome on the farm for pick-your-own in the summer and for sugaring in the winter. In fact, Brody, the resident golden, will keep your pup company on his visit. Our crew enjoyed the homemade biscuits sold here, too. (802) 387-5852.

ROCKINGHAM
(AND THE VILLAGE OF BELLOWS FALLS)

NATURE HIKES AND URBAN WALKS

Bellows Falls: Bellows Falls is an impressive site—one of the largest natural falls on the Connecticut River, although you may have to cross over into New Hampshire to get the full impact of the falls. Old mill and railroad buildings line the nearby streets, the remnants of an 1802 canal are visible, and, if you continue down to the river itself, you can see carvings made by Indian tribes who came to the falls to fish.

And did someone say fish? What about jumping fish? What about lots of jumping fish? The fish ladder on Bridge Street in Rockingham, adjacent to the falls, is alive with fish when the Atlantic salmon and the American shad heed the call of nature to head upstream and spawn. For information, call (802) 463-4280.

DIVERSIONS

Casey Canine: Casey Junior's comin' down the line and your dog is too! All (and we mean all) aboard the Green Mountain Flyer, a 26-mile scenic train ride from Bellows Falls to Chester following the Connecticut and Williams Rivers. Small dogs are welcome on the two-hour, round-trip excursion on the 1930s diesel train. Adult fare is $10. June through September. For schedule and information, call (802) 463-3069.

Dazed by the Days: Rockingham rocks the first weekend in August, as the town celebrates its history with a weekend full of events, dubbed "Old Rockingham Days." Many of the events take place outdoors, and several restaurants offer sidewalk dining, so it's a great time to take your dog to Rockingham. Be forewarned that fireworks are involved; if your dog is like George, be prepared to hightail it out of town before the loud noises begin. Call the Chamber of Commerce for a complete schedule at 802-875-2939.

SPRINGFIELD

NATURE HIKES AND URBAN WALKS

Eureka Schoolhouse State Historic Site: Rocky, an obedience school dropout, looked a little worried when he found out we were going to a school. Fear not, it's only the Eureka Schoolhouse, the oldest one-room schoolhouse in Vermont and one of the state's oldest buildings. The 1785 building turned out to be a delightful diversion for all of us. On the compact grounds is the restored Baltimore Covered Bridge, which was built in 1870, and the picnic areas have scenic views of the Black River. Open Memorial Day through Columbus Day, Wednesdays through Sundays. Located on State Route 11, just west of the U.S. Route 5. (802) 885-2779.

PLACES TO STAY

Holiday Inn Express: Pets are permitted in the smoking rooms only, and there are a few rules. Dogs must be quiet and are not to be left alone in room. The hotel does boast a "Pet Paws" plan that provides a gift for your dog on arrival. Rates range from $80 to $129. 818 Charlestown Road, Springfield, VT 05156; (802) 885-4516.

FESTIVALS

An Apple a Day: Every September, Springfield pays homage to the fruit that helps keep their town healthy. The Annual Vermont Apple Festival and Craft Show boasts an animal exhibit, an apple pie contest, hot air balloons, and fresh-pressed apple cider. Events are at numerous sites around the town. (802) 885-2779.

STOCKBRIDGE

PLACES TO STAY

White River Valley Camping: Every now and then, JoAnna and George like to get away from it all, but not too far away. That's why camping on the river at 21-acre White River Valley is so appealing to her. They can spend the day tubing or canoeing on the White River or hiking in the nearby Green Mountains, but they still have access to all the amenities that this full-service family facility offers, including a whirlpool. The 100-site campground has full hookups and a camp store, too. Sites are $20 with a $1 pet fee. Open May to mid-October. State Route 107, Gaysville, VT 05746; (802) 234-9115; www.sover.net/~river.

THETFORD

PARKS, BEACHES, AND RECREATION AREAS

• **Thetford Hill State Park** 😺 😺 See **12** on page 400.
This state park, like most of Vermont's state parks, is not very inviting for canines and is more of a campground than anything else. Dogs are not permitted in the day-use areas, so that only leaves the short hiking trails, some small waterfalls, and scenic vistas of the West River to keep your dog entertained here.

If you are camping, there are 16 sites for tents and RVs with flush toilets and metered showers. Rates range from $11 to $16. Dogs need to be on leash; there is a $2 entrance fee.

From Interstate 91, take Exit 14 to State Route 113 north for one mile. Turn left onto Academy Road for 1.5 miles. The park is on the right. Open dawn to dusk, mid-May to Labor Day. (802) 785-2266.

• **Union Village Dam and Recreation Area** 🐾🐾🐾 🐕 See **13** on page 400.

This is another U.S. Army Corps of Engineers dam project to control river flooding and, more importantly in our dogs' eyes, another area for leash-free hiking. The property is a 979-acre, six-mile gorge cut by the Ompompanoosuc River, and it offers numerous hiking opportunities. The highlights are the 2.5-mile-long forest road/bike path through the gorge. This flat, gravel route is the best way to explore the gorge. Another easy hike is the Demo Trail, an easy 1.3-mile-long interpretive trail that begins at the dam parking area.

Dogs need to be leashed in developed areas and under voice control on the trails.

From State Route 132, take Academy Road north for a quarter mile. Turn left into the dam access road. Parking is available. Open 6 A.M. to 9:30 P.M. (802) 649-1606.

PLACES TO STAY

Thetford Hill State Park camping: See page 412.

TOWNSHEND

PARKS, BEACHES, AND RECREATION AREAS

• **Townshend Lake Recreation Area** 🐾🐾🐾 🐕 See **14** on page 400.

Townshend Lake and the West River cover 95 acres, so there's more water here than your dog will know what to do with, plus one big dam! Two hiking trails, one on either side of the dam, give you a good chance to explore the lake and the surrounding countryside.

The Ledges Overlook Trail, on the west side, is a rugged 1.7-mile climb offering great views above the dam and lake. The West River Trail, on the east-side shoreline, is easier and considerably longer. It follows what remains of the old State Route 30 after it was washed away by a flood. The trail runs north following the river for three miles. and efforts are underway to connect the trail to Bald Mountain Dam and Lake Recreation Area.

Dogs must be leashed in developed areas and under voice control in other areas.

From State Route 35, take State Route 30 north for 2.5 miles. The park and dam are on your left. Open 8 A.M. to 8 P.M.; (802) 365-7703.

• **Townshend State Forest/Townshend State Park** 🐾🐾🐾 👞 See **15** on page 400.

Together these two parks total over 1,095 acres and, if you combine them with neighboring Townshend Lake Recreation Area (see above), you really have a vast and varied place to play. There is hiking, camping, historic sites, engineering marvels, lake and river swimming, and everyone's favorite, bridge jumping. The West River is the main and most inviting feature here. You'll find numerous access points along the river and Town Road to cool your paws.

The most crowded spot on the river, however, is at the Scott Covered Bridge. The bridge, built in 1870, is the longest covered bridge in Vermont. It's closed to vehicles, but you can walk across all 276 feet of it. The popular, if not crazy, thing to do is jump from the bridge into the river. We don't recommend it, but it sure is fun to watch.

For hiking, the main trail is the climb to the Bald Mountain summit at 1,680 feet. The Bald Mountain Trail is a moderate hike of 3.1 round-trip miles, beginning next to the ranger station in the state park and then running alongside Negro Brook.

The 41-acre Townshend State Park is primarily a camping area, with 34 tent, trailer, and lean-to wooded sites near the West River. Camping is available mid-May to Columbus Day and rates are $11 to $15. Dogs must be on leash.

From State Route 35, take State Route 30 south for 1.5 miles. Turn right onto Town Road for three miles. The parks are on your left. Open mid-May to Columbus Day; call (802) 365-7500 mid-May to Columbus Day, (802) 886-2434 off-season.

RESTAURANTS
Dam Diner: This place made us smile, and not just because of its cute name. The old-fashioned, good-hearted folks who work here serve up some tasty grub, including breakfast all day and ice cream, all within the shadow of the dam. Get it to go, and then sit at the picnic tables they provide for outdoor seating. State Route 30; (802) 874-4107.

PLACES TO STAY
Boardman House Bed-and-Breakfast: This country home on the village green has six rooms decorated in Shaker style, for simple, casual elegance. Rates range from $65 to $80; pets require advance notice. Box 112, Townshend, VT 05353; (802) 365-4086.

FESTIVALS
Annual Pumpkin Festival: The folks in Townshend really get Halloween rolling with the Annual Pumpkin Festival on the Townshend Common. Held in mid-October, festivities include contests for pumpkin decorating, costumes, scarecrow decorating, and crafts. Dogs on leash are welcome to join in the frightful fun. (802) 365-7793.

WEATHERSFIELD
PARKS, BEACHES, AND RECREATION AREAS
• **Wilgus State Park** 🐾🐾 See **16** on page 400.
This 89-acre park is one of the prettiest stretches on the Connecticut River, and it's perfect if you are planning on canoeing any of it. If you're not on the water, the best way to enjoy this beautiful area is from the Pinnacle summit at 600

feet; two half-mile trails lead to it. While they are not long, they are steep, but the view of the river is well worth it.

Leashes are required and there is a $2 entrance fee.

From Interstate 91, take Exit 8 to U.S. Route 5 south for 1.5 miles. The park is on the left. Open from 9 A.M. to 8 P.M., mid-May to Columbus Day. (802) 674-5422.

RESTAURANTS

Country Creemee Restaurant: This place serves up good grub cheap, and you can enjoy it outside with your pooch. They offer the traditional New England fried seafood offerings, as well as other standards like hamburgers and ice cream. Downers Four Corners, State Routes 106 and 131; (802) 263-5677.

WESTON

PLACES TO STAY

Darling Family Inn: This 1830 colonial inn has two small kitchenette cottages available for guests with pets. There are also 450 acres of mountaintop meadows available to your pet and breathtaking views for you. Cottage rates are $105. Pets may not be left unattended unless they are crated. 815 State Route 100, Weston, VT 05161; (802) 824-3223; home.att.net/~darlingfamilyinn.

WINDSOR

PARKS, BEACHES, AND RECREATION AREAS

• **Ascutney State Park** 🐾🐾 See **17** on page 400.

Most of Vermont can boast impressive mountain ranges, but here in Windsor County there is only one mountain. But when it's a mountain like Mount Ascutney, one is enough. Part of the 2,362 acres of Ascutney State Park, it dominates the eastern Vermont countryside at 3,150 feet and offers spectacular views in all directions.

An excellent way to the top is on the Brownsville Trail off State Route 44. It's a round-trip route of 6.4 miles with an elevation gain of 2,400 feet. If the hike is too much for you and your pet, you can drive the Summit Road to the top. And if the hike is not enough for your energetic team, Mount Ascutney is a popular place for hang gliding. Don't forget your goggles!

Dogs must be on leash.

From U.S. Route 5, take State Route 44A west for one mile. The park and Summit Road are on your left. For the Brownsville Trailhead, continue on State Route 44A onto State Route 44 west. The starting point and parking is on the left. Open dawn to dusk. Call (802) 674-2060 mid-May to Columbus Day, (802) 886-2434 off-season.

PLACES TO STAY

Burton Farm Lodge Bed-and-Breakfast: George always feels home on a farm, and this was no exception. The lodge has two units, with rates from $60 to $70 per night. 27 Cross Road, West Windsor, VT 05089; (802) 484-3300; www.bbon-line.com/vt/burtonfarm/.

WOODSTOCK

Woodstock has been a popular, year-round playground for the rich and famous for over a century. When local girl Mary Billings married Laurance S. Rockefeller, it was a fairy tale for the whole town. Together, the Rockefellers were responsible for much of the preservation of Woodstock, which became a popular hotspot for the New York well-to-do. It's still a place that looks like it's right out of central casting, a Vermont town that is almost too perfect in its quaint country charm. Dust off Spot's pedigree for a trip into Woodstock. Who knows what famous hot dog he'll meet!

PARKS, BEACHES, AND RECREATION AREAS

• Marsh-Billings-Rockefeller National Historical Park 🐾🐾🐾 See 18 on page 400.

Mary Billings Rockefeller and her husband, Laurance S. Rockefeller, donated the land and the residence that now comprise Vermont's first national park—the Marsh-Billings-Rockefeller National Historic Park, established in 1998. Thank Frederick Billings, Mary's grandfather and a railroad magnate, for the 20 miles of wide sloping carriage roads that traverse the park. Billings, who purchased the property in 1869 from the Marsh family, also helped to reforest Mount Tom, which abuts the property.

Both trails and carriage roads, open year-round, are on the property. If you hike to the top of Mount Tom, you'll find a 14-acre pond and some picture-worthy views of Woodstock. You can also connect to neighboring Mount Tom's trail system from here.

The park's two Visitor Centers have maps of the trails; one center is shared with Billings Farm, and the other is located at the Carriage Barn. To get there, walk up the carriage road toward the mansion, and on the left is the Carriage Barn Visitor Center.

Dogs must be leashed. They are not permitted at Billings Farm, except in the parking lots.

From U.S. Route 4, take State Route 12 north for a half mile. Bear right onto River Road. The park entrance is on the right. Open 10 A.M. to 5 P.M., mid-May through October. (802) 457-3368.

• Mount Tom Forest 🐾🐾🐾🐾 🐕 See 19 on page 400.

Mount Tom, at 1,250 feet, is a great way to get a bird's-eye view of Woodstock and some up-close wildlife viewing. In fact, there are white-tailed deer here that are thankful for Rocky's poor eyesight.

For hiking, most of the trails begin in the community green, Faulkner Park. The Faulkner Trail crisscrosses up Mount Tom to its peak; you can then either reverse your steps or take Precipice Trail back down. Faulkner Trail leads up from the asphalt path in Faulkner Park. The North Peak Trail is the longest of the trails. It crosses Mount Tom to North Peak at an elevation of 1,357 feet.

Dogs are permitted off leash on Mount Tom's hiking trails but must be leashed in Faulkner Park.

From State Route 106, take U.S. Route 4 a quarter mile west. Turn right onto Mountain Avenue. Faulkner Park is on the left. Open dawn to dusk. (802) 457-3555.

NATURE HIKES AND URBAN WALKS

Woodstock Walk: Downtown Woodstock is a lovely Vermont town, with many arts and antique stores to explore, many of which welcome your pet. Start your stroll at Woodstock Green. It's a tiny, diamond-shaped park in the center of this jewel of a town. Head up Main Street to Elm Street. This is the epicenter, and you'll find many diversions to explore. Don't miss Stephen Huneck's gallery devoted to his special brand of dog art; the dog statues were so realistic that George stopped for a sniff. Woodstock has a charmingly old-fashioned "Town Crier": it's a chalkboard at the intersection of Main and Elm Streets that posts the list of the town's activities for the week. Check it out before you make any plans in the area. Along Main and Elm are a couple of ice-cream parlors vying for your dog's wag of approval, all with outdoor seating. If you are so inclined, you can walk from the Village Green to Faulkner Park, which will take you over the Middle Bridge, a covered bridge that dates back to 1969. For bridge aficionados, the Middle Bridge was built by Milton Grafton, known as "the last of the covered bridge builders" in the Town Lattice style. (802) 457-3555.

DIVERSIONS

Here We Come A'Wassailing: In early December, Woodstock puts on its finery for a Christmas celebration unrivaled in Vermont. The festive weekend includes many outdoor events such as a parade of horse-drawn carriages around Woodstock Green, caroling, and lighting ceremonies. Wassail Weekend is a wonderful picture postcard of traditional holiday cheer. So, bundle up yourself and the dog, and make sure to teach your mutt some Christmas carols. (802) 457-3555.

RESTAURANTS

The Chocolate Cow: Chocolate cows, chocolate pumpkins, and chocolate pretzels—these folks seem to cover everything in chocolate. And quite deliciously so. This café also serves lunch and is known for miles around for its signature hot chocolate. The iron tables and chairs on the sidewalk provide a chance to dine al fresco with your pup. 24 Elm Street; (800) TRUFFLE.

Pane Salute Italian Bakery: From the aroma that wafts out the door of this bakery, you know it's going to be good. Try anything—it's all fantastic. The outdoor café seating is custom-made for you and your pooch to dine together. 61 Central Street; (802) 457-4882.

PLACES TO STAY

Applebutter Inn: This historic bed-and-breakfast inn is a restored 1830 Federal mansion, with six guest rooms. Small pets are permitted in two of the rooms with prior approval. Rates range from $125 to $165. Happy Valley Road, Woodstock, VT 05071; (802) 457-4158.

Braeside Motel: The Braeside has 12 rooms, and pets are permitted. Rates range from $50 to $90, including breakfast. U.S. Route 4, Woodstock, VT 05071; (802) 457-1366, (800) 303-1366; www.vermontel.com/braeside.

Kedron Valley Inn: The Kedron Inn sits next to the South Woodstock swimming pond, but, unfortunately, dogs are not permitted on the beach. The rooms are lovely, and a collection of antique quilts dominates the public spaces. Rates are $120 to $215. State Route 106, South Woodstock, VT 05071; (800) 836-1193, (802) 457-1473.

Three Church Street: This grand Georgian mansion near the center of town holds 11 rooms, some with shared baths. Dogs are welcome with approval, but cannot be left alone in the room. From here, you can walk to the Green, Mount Tom, and Mount Peg. Rates range from $75 to $105 per night. 3 Church Street, Woodstock, VT 05091; (802) 457-1925; www.pbpub.com/vermont/3church or www.scenesofvermont.com/3church/index.html.

The Winslow House: There are four rooms in this restored farmhouse, and each comes complete with a full country breakfast. Rates range from $68 to $95. 38 U.S. Route 4, West Woodstock, VT 05091; (802) 457-1820.

NEW HAMPSHIRE

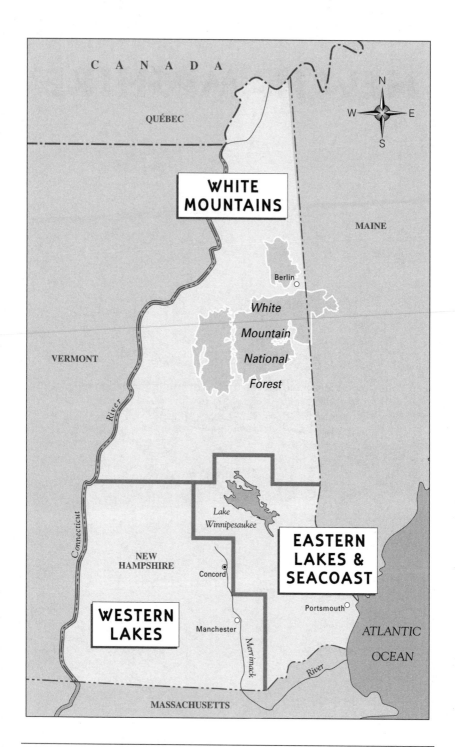

NEW HAMPSHIRE

Although New Hampshire is known more for its lakes, mountains, and recreation areas, this small state is also proud of its activism. As a fierce protector of the early American Revolution, and now as the first state to cast votes in the primary elections, New Hampshire has always lived up to its "live free or die" motto. Those words were first spoken by Revolutionary War hero General John Stark, and they represent more than a license plate slogan.

Of course, that's not to say New Hampshire doesn't also fiercely protect its lakes, mountains, and recreation areas. There are several organizations working to maintain these natural resources, and you and your dog will be thankful when you visit here. Between the private, state, and town lands, the Granite State is home to some of our favorite haunts.

Audubon Society of New Hampshire: Unlike most of the Audubon properties in the other New England states, New Hampshire actually allows dogs on many of their properties. Because many of these sanctuaries are in out-of-the-way places, the society understands dog owners may be the only ones who visit. If we list them here, you're in. If we omit certain properties, that means dogs are not allowed on these lands. But you should remember, because most of these lands are preserved for wildlife-watchers and birders, having your big-footed galoot of a dog bound down the trails disturbing everyone and thing in her path is not the best way to get invited back. So make sure you keep your dog on leash and on the trails. For trail information or questions, contact the Audubon Society of New Hampshire at 3 Silk Farm Road, Concord, New Hampshire 03301; (603) 224-9909.

Society for the Protection of New Hampshire Forests: The largest and oldest conservation organization in the state was founded in 1901 to protect New Hampshire forests from the onslaught of logging. Many of their properties were almost totally devastated by the ax in the early part of this century. The forests are now making a magnificent comeback thanks to the protective stewardship of this excellent organization. With almost a million acres throughout the state, dogs are allowed off leash on these properties, if under voice command. For more information or to become a member, contact the society at 54 Portsmouth Street, Concord, NH 03301; (603) 224-9945.

State Parks and Forests: Pets are allowed in many of the state parks in New Hampshire, but not all. As a general rule, most of the beaches and recreational swimming areas are off-limits to your pooch in the summer. Along the coast, they are banned all year. But at all other inland parks, your leashed pet is welcome. We have listed the parks that allow dogs in these chapters; if a park is not listed, you can be sure your pet is not allowed. In all state parks, dogs must be leashed.

Leashed dogs are allowed in all state forests, although, in general, these lands are not the best properties in the state. Used mostly for logging, hunting, or snowmobiling, the state forests have unmarked trails and no services. For more information contact the New Hampshire Division of Parks and Recreation, P.O. Box 1856, 172 Pembroke Road, Concord, NH 03302; (603) 271-3556.

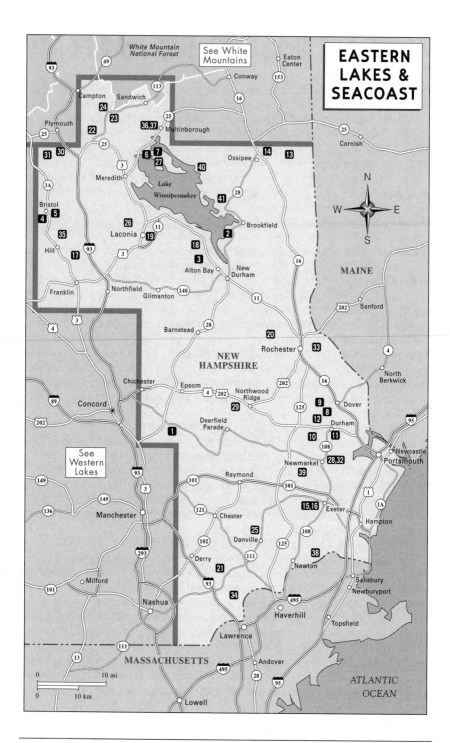

EASTERN
LAKES &
SEACOAST

See White
Mountains

White Mountain
National Forest

Conway

Eaton
Center

153

Campton

Sandwich

113

Plymouth

Multinborough

Cornish

Meredith

Ossipee

Lake
Winnipesaukee

Bristol

Laconia

Brookfield

Hill

New
Durham

Alton Bay

Franklin

Northfield

Gilmanton

MAINE

Barnstead

NEW
HAMPSHIRE

Rochester

Sanford

North
Berkwick

Chichester

Concord

Epsom

Northwood
Ridge

Dover

Deerfield
Parade

Durham

See
Western
Lakes

Newmarket

Newcastle
Portsmouth

Raymond

Manchester

Chester

Exeter

Hampton

Milford

Danville

Derry

Newton

Salisbury
Newburyport

Nashua

Haverhill

Topsfield

Lawrence

MASSACHUSETTS

Andover

ATLANTIC
OCEAN

0   10 mi

0   10 km

Lowell

13
EASTERN LAKES AND SEACOAST

The Eastern Lakes region in New Hampshire has been a visitor's paradise since James I of England granted a parcel of land between the Merrimack and Piscataqua rivers to John Mason in 1629. Mason's grant was described as containing "divers lakes, extending back to a great lake and a river." Those "divers lakes" still define the area today—Winnipesaukee, Squam, and Newfound being the largest of the 1,300 lakes scattered across the state.

Wealthy travelers of the 19th century built elegant summer places on many of the old farms around the lakes. Then the railroad came through, opening the area to ordinary folks as well. Summer hotels and boarding houses sprang up in Alton Bay, Weirs Beach, and Meredith, and the railroad companies ran steamboats on the lakes to transport summer people to the nearly 300 islands. Today you and your dog can ride these trains and stay in the same bed-and-breakfasts that were once residences for the rich.

East of the lakes, you'll find the tiny stretch of New Hampshire seacoast. Only 18 miles are claimed by the Granite State, and the good news is that over half of it is public land. The bad news, however, is that none of the beaches allows dogs. So, on second thought, maybe we're glad New Hampshire didn't get more of the coast.

But the historic towns that dot her landscape are rich in the early history of our nation. From Odiorne Point, site of the first European settlement, to colonial Portsmouth where Paul Revere first rode to warn of the British invasion, to New Castle and Exeter, sites of the Revolutionary War, there is much to discover and explore—except the beaches, of course!

Lakes Region Conservation Trust: The LRCT is a nifty little organization dedicated to protecting the lands around the Lake Winnipesaukee area.

Founded in 1979, it has since protected over 6,000 acres in the "Lakes Region." We list several of their dog-friendly properties in this chapter; dogs are allowed off leash on LRCT properties if under voice control.

LRCT is a private, nonprofit organization supported by member contributions. For more information or to become a member, contact them at P.O. Box 1097 Meredith, NH 03253; (603) 279-3246; www.lrct.org.

ALLENTOWN

PARKS, BEACHES, AND RECREATION AREAS

• **Bear Brook State Park** 🐾🐾🐾 See ❶ on page 422.

This 9,500-acre park offers a wide range of hiking experiences: ponds, streams, forest groves, and the occasional small hill. The good news is that you can hike the extensive trails with your dog; the bad news is that dogs are not allowed in any of the day-use picnic areas or beaches. Dogs on leash are allowed, however, in the Beaver Pond Campground. Go figure.

As you drive along Bear Brook Road, you'll see sign after sign saying "No Pets Allowed." However, if you walk to the trails away from the public areas, we promise you, you and your dog will be welcome. There are countless trails in this oft-used park, and Ranger Marty assures us he welcomes well-behaved pooches. We suggest you pick up a map at the park headquarters on Bear Brook Road or off Deerfield Road to guide you on your way.

Camping is available at the 97-site campground. The sites are primarily for tent use but there are few RV hookups. The facilities are clean and friendly, and easily accessible hiking trails are nearby. Reservations are required. (603) 271-3628.

Dogs on leash, please.

From State Route 3, take State Route 28 north 3.5 miles. Turn right onto Bear Brook Road into the park. Open dawn to dusk. (603) 485-9874.

PLACES TO STAY

Beaver Brook State Park camping: See above.

ALTON

PARKS, BEACHES, AND RECREATION AREAS

• **Knight's Pond Conservation Easement** 🐾🐾🐾 🐕 See ❷ on page 422.

Take this 2.5-mile loop around Knight's Pond for an isolated and quiet wilderness walk. Located just south of Wolfeborough, these 332 acres circle a beaver pond surrounded by extensive woodland. A well-maintained trail skirts the entire shoreline, crossing the pond's outlet over a wooden bridge and entering a shaded hemlock forest.

Dogs are allowed off leash if under voice control. The reservation is managed by the Lakes Region Conservation Trust.

From State Route 28 near the Wolfeboro border, take Rines Road two miles east. The conservation road and parking is on your left. Open dawn to dusk. (603) 279-3246.

• **Mount Major State Forest** 🐾 🐾 🐾 See **3** on page 422.

The main feature in this small state forest is Mount Major itself. (Why? Because it's there. . .) To climb to the 1,786-foot summit, you'll easily find the trailhead from the parking area off State Route 11. This popular three-mile trail can be a strenuous hike, and you shouldn't tackle it unless your dog will be up to the task. But, on the day we visited, there were more dogs on the trail than you could count. (We should also tell you that there were many doggie calling cards left along the trail—the surest way to get dogs banned here, so please pick up after your dog—even in the "wilderness.") Once you reach the top and see the view of Lake Winnipesaukee spread out before you, you won't care how long it took to get there.

Dogs must be on leash. From State Route 11A, take State Route 11 east for four miles. The trail and parking is on your right. Open sunrise to sunset. (603) 224-9945.

RESTAURANTS

Bay View Pavilion: This popular restaurant offers outdoor seating overlooking the tip of Lake Winnipesaukee in Alton Bay. Great continental cuisine and the view can't be beat. State Route 11; (603) 875-1255.

DIVERSIONS

Alton Summer Concert Series: Every Tuesday from June to August between 7 P.M. and 9 P.M., the place to be is at the Alton Bay Bandstand. You and your dog will be treated to everything from country western to Bach. (Sorry, George, no Snoop Doggy Dog!) For schedules, contact Alton Parks and Recreation Concert Series at (603) 875-0109.

PLACES TO STAY

Joy Cottages: This eight-cottage motel complex offers comfortable no-frills lodging. Rooms include kitchenettes and double beds. Rates range from $60 to $75 per night. Roberts Cover Road, Alton, NH 03810; (603) 569-4073.

ASHLAND

RESTAURANTS

Riverside Dairy Joy: This handy roadside eatery right across from Squam Lake makes a handy stop for those ice-cream runs after a hike. They have the usual seafood and burger menu, too. Feast on Mooseberry ice cream or a Bubble Gum frappé. George's favorite is Dinosaur Crunch. State Route 25; (603) 968-7147.

PLACES TO STAY

Black Horse Motor Court on Squam Lake: Right across U.S. Route 3 from Squam Lake, you can enjoy your own sandy beach when you stay at one of the cottages or motel efficiencies here. The staff is friendly, the rooms comfortable, and, best of all, your dog is welcome here. Rates range from $42 to

$92 per night or $280 to $685 per week depending on season and unit. Dogs are an additional $10 per night or $30 per week. RR 1, Box 46, Ashland, NH 03217; (603) 968-7116.

Yogi Bear's Jellystone Park: Leashed dogs are welcome at this camping "theme park." There are 43 cabins and cottages plus 228 camping sites available along the Pemigewasset River. Activities include outdoor movies, swimming, canoe rentals, and free hayrides. Rates range from $33 to $40 per night. Open May to October. RR 1, Box 396, State Route 132, Ashland, NH 03217; (503) 968-9000.

White Oak Motel and Lakefront Cottages: This lakefront resort with a private beach and full amenities is great for all members of your family. Dogs are welcome in the off-season—before July 8 and after September 5. Rates range from $49 to $125. RR 1, Box 238, Ashland, NH 03217; (603) 968-3673 or (888) 965-1850; www.lakesregionlodging.com.

BELMONT

RESTAURANTS

Jordan's Ice Creamery: For the best Blue Goo ice cream east of the Mississippi (and perhaps the one and only. . .), head here. There are plenty of tables outside to sit with your dog, and Jordan's sponsors a fund-raising event every August for the New Hampshire Humane Society (see below). That makes this more than just an ice-cream stop in our book. Entrances are off State Route 106 and North Main Street. (603) 267-1900.

DIVERSIONS

Dog Days of Summer: This annual fund-raiser is held from noon to 6 P.M. at Jordan's Ice Creamery in August. Get your free T-shirt and ice cream for participating in many fun events for dogs and humans. For more information, contact the New Hampshire Humane Society at (603) 524-8236.

BRISTOL

PARKS, BEACHES, AND RECREATION AREAS

• **Profile Falls State Natural Area** 🐾🐾🐾 🐕 See **4** on page 422.
Visit this dramatic waterfall where the Smith River tumbles down over huge slabs of granite. From the parking area off Profile Falls Road, the trail is easy to follow for a quarter-mile hike to the scenic falls. Just before you reach the falls there is a fork in the trail; keep to the left fork and the sound of distant water. The other path heads into the woods for a shady woodland walk.

Plans are in the works for the Heritage Trail to eventually connect this trail to the Franklin Falls Trail for an eight-mile hike along the Merrimack River. Dogs should be on leash and are not allowed to get too close to the rushing water.

From State Route 104, take State Route 3A south 1.5 miles. Turn left onto Profile Falls Road for a quarter mile, then right onto the Profile Falls access road for a quarter mile. Go through state barriers to the first parking area on your right. Open 8 A.M. to dusk. (603) 934-2116.

• **Slim Baker Conservation Area** 🐾🐾🐾🐾 🐕 See **5** on page 422.

This conservation area is a delightful place to hike with your dog. Located on and around Round Top—a breathtaking outcrop that overlooks the town of Bristol—there are several trails that run within these woods. The red trail loop leads to Inspiration Point and back. If you're short on time and want a worthwhile hike, check this one out. It's not a long hike, but it's a steep climb to the top, so you'll feel as if you've gotten a workout.

From State Route 104, take State Route 3A south a quarter mile. Fork to the right at the 1889 church onto High Street. Make an immediate right onto New Chester Road for a mile following signs to Slim Baker Lodge. At the end, the road turns to dirt and you'll see the parking area. Dogs allowed off leash under voice control. Open dawn to dusk. (603) 744-8478.

RESTAURANTS

Bristol Bakery and Ice Cream: There are benches outside this café/bakery, but you can also order your lunch to go and hike up to Inspiration Point for a great picnic spot. Stop for a scoop of ice cream, too. 8 Central Square; (603) 744-5510.

The Patio on Newfound Lake: For a full café menu served on an outdoor patio across from Newfound Lake, try this friendly restaurant. Breakfast, lunch, and dinner are available for you and your pup. Ice cream, too! State Route 3A; (603) 744-9599.

Shackett's Seafood Shack: For scrumptious seafood right across from Newfound Lake, try this popular eatery. Full dinners and lunches of fish and chips, clam rolls, and scallops are available to take out or to eat on one of the several picnic tables outside. West Shore Road; (603) 744-3663.

CENTER HARBOR

PARKS, BEACHES, AND RECREATION AREAS

• **Chamberlain-Reynolds Memorial Forest** 🐾🐾🐾 🐕 See **6** on page 422.

This fabulous little point on Squam Lake, named for two New Hampshire conservationists, is one of the few places you and your dog will feel like you're *On Golden Pond.* Fortunately, you won't care about going anywhere else once you come here.

Located on Dog Cove (how can you go wrong with a name like that?), the forest occupies 150 acres with almost two miles of hiking trails—most along the water. There are several wonderful beaches that George and Inu thoroughly checked out, and we're happy to report that you can swim in the cool, clean water and romp on extremely well-maintained trails.

Camping is available from Memorial Day to Labor Day, and reservations must be made through the Squam Lakes Association which maintains the area. Campsites are $36 a night, with the exception of the Great Swamp Campground (accessible only by canoe or boat) which is $100 per night. For reservations, call (603) 968-7336.

Dogs must be kept under voice control on the trails and on leash in the camping areas. Trail maps are available at the eastern entrance off College Road.

From U.S. Route 3, take State Route 258 east a quarter mile. Turn left onto College Road for a quarter mile. The park is on your right. Open dawn to dusk. (603) 253-4582.

• Proctor Sanctuary 🐾🐾🐾 See **7** on page 422.

This Audubon Sanctuary, located on 47 acres, makes for a leisurely afternoon walk, and the well-maintained trails make it easy to find your way around. From the trailhead, head down the footpath until you reach a stone wall. After a short distance, the trail divides. It doesn't really matter which way you go because both trails lead you back to your starting point. The lower portion of yellow-blazed Brookside Trail can be a bit muddy in the spring and during wet spells, so don't forget to pack a towel. A few picnic tables are available at the brook if you wish to bring lunch. Dogs must be on leash.

From State Route 25 in the middle of town, take State Route 25B north for one mile. Turn right onto Centre Harbor Neck Road for one mile. Look for ASNH trailhead sign on left. Park in the pulloff across from the sign. Open dawn to dusk. (603) 224-9909.

RESTAURANTS

Sam & Rosie's Café and Bakery: Outdoor seating is available at this local roadside café—not to mention the best breakfasts in the area. For blueberry pancakes, sandwiches, and bakery goods that will make Rover's mouth water, you'll love this place. State Route 25 at Lake Street; (603) 253-6608.

PLACES TO STAY

Chamberlain-Reynolds Memorial Forest camping: See pages 427–428.

Lake Shore Motel and Cottages: This comfortable 14-unit complex along the lake offers cottages, efficiencies, and motel rooms. Dogs are allowed in three of the units; only one dog per room, please. Rates range from $55 to $125. Open seasonally from May to October. RR 2, Box 16H, Center Harbor, NH 03226; (603) 253-6244, (941) 439-6625; www.lakesregionlodgingnh.com.

Meadows Lakeside Lodging: Here you'll find comfortable, no-frills beach-front lodging on Lake Winnipesaukee, featuring 35 rooms, some with kitchenettes, and a private beach. Best of all, the owners welcome your pets for an additional fee of only $7. Rooms range from $55 to $110. Box 204, State Route 25, Center Harbor, NH 03226; (603) 253-4347.

Watch Hill B&B: This historic home, overlooking the lake and the mountains, is a true getaway. A delicious country breakfast is served each morning, and you're only a short walk from the beach and town. Dogs are allowed on approval. Rates range from $69 to $85 per night. Box 1605, State Route 25, Center Harbor, NH 03226; (603) 253-4334.

DIVERSIONS

Paddle on the wild side: Rent a canoe or double kayak at Wild Meadows Canoes and Kayaks and explore the lakes region from the water. Instruction, guided tours, or rentals are available. Free shuttle service is included. Call for packages and prices. (603) 253-7536.

DERRY
NATURE HIKES AND URBAN WALKS

Robert Frost Farm Historical Site: Although the words "and miles to go before I sleep" may sound like something the authors of the *Dog Lover's Companion to New England* might say while researching this book, it was really Robert Frost who first wrote those words. And you can visit the farm where he lived and wrote from 1900 to 1911.

The farmhouse, typical of New Hampshire buildings of the late 1800s, is open to visitors. Although your dog can't come into the buildings, she can hike the nature trails and enjoy the same natural wonders that inspired Frost's poetry. The buildings are open Wednesday through Sunday from 10 A.M. to 5 P.M. in summer (mid-June through Labor Day). The grounds are open without charge from dawn to dusk year-round. State Route 28; (603) 432-3091.

RESTAURANTS

Clam Haven: This almost 50-year-old Derry institution is just a roadside eatery, but what good eating it is! For a heaping plate of the best seafood, burgers, or ice cream, stop by after a visit to the Robert Frost Farm. But don't be in a hurry. There's always a line outside. Picnic at the many tables outside or take your food to go. Junction of State Route 28 and the 28 Bypass; (603) 434-4679.

Jay's Paradise Café: This funky little coffeehouse in the heart of Derry Village makes for a good breakfast or lunch run. Invite your dog to sit at one of the outdoor tables with you while you both nosh on standard coffeehouse fare. George is still picking poppy seeds out of his teeth! 42 East Broadway (State Route 102); (603) 437-5567.

DOVER
PARKS, BEACHES, AND RECREATION AREAS

• Bellamy River Wildlife Sanctuary 🐾🐾🐾 See 🐾 on page 422.

Managed by the Audubon Society of New Hampshire, this scenic and out-of-the-way wildlife refuge is challenging to find but worth the trip. Several trails will take you through fields, marshes, and along the Bellamy River. With over 1,000 acres to explore, you and your dog should be happy as mud hens (and in low tide, probably just as muddy!).

From U.S. Route 4 (Portland Avenue), take State Route 108 (Central Avenue) south for one mile. Turn left onto Back River Road for under a mile, then turn right onto Bayview Road to the end. Bear left onto an unmarked gravel road to the parking area. Open dawn to dusk. (603) 224-9909.

• Garrison Hill and Tower 🐾🐾🐾 🐕 See 🐾 on page 422.

On a clear day you can see forever, and this may be the place to do it. In one direction, look toward the vast expanses of southwestern Maine; in the other direction you can see Mount Washington (it's a clear day, remember).

This is a short half-mile walk to the summit from the hospital on Old Rollinsford Road, but on a clear day. . . it'll be worth it. You'll meet up with plenty of other dogs here, as well. Dogs must be under voice control. From U.S. Route 4 (Portland Avenue), take State Route 108 (Central Avenue) north for one mile. Turn right onto Old Rollinsford Road to the end. Park at the gate and walk a quarter mile up the road to the trailhead. Open dawn to dusk. (603) 742-2887.

NATURE HIKES AND URBAN WALKS

Dover's Heritage Trails: Dover is the oldest continuous settlement in New Hampshire, established in 1623. You can learn more and have fun at the same time on any of the three self-guided walking tours, including the Cochecho River Walk. Maps are available at the information booth on Central Avenue. (603) 742-2218; www.dovernh.org.

PLACES TO STAY

Days Inn: This 63-room hotel is located near the heart of historic Dover. Offering full-service amenities, continental breakfast, and kitchenettes in some rooms, you and your dog will be comfortable here. Rooms range from $65 to $125 per night. 481 Pleasant Street, Dover, NH 03820; (603) 742-0400 or (800) DAYS-INN; www.daysinn.com.

DURHAM

This small college town has more wonderful parks in its tiny radius than many of the larger towns in this book. Best of all, there is dog-friendly culture at work here. People come from all over the seacoast area to walk their dogs, socialize, and connect with their community in these excellent parks. So when the rest of the New Hampshire seacoast is off-limits to dogs, we recommend that you and your pooch head for Durham.

PARKS, BEACHES, AND RECREATION AREAS

• **Adams Point Wildlife Management Area/Jackson Estuarine Research Laboratory** 🐾🐾🐾🐾 See **10** on page 422.

Adams Point offers double the pleasure and double the fun (good thing, considering how long the name is!). Originally the base camp for a Native American tribe from 600 to 850 a.d., it was bought by "Reformation" John Adams—cousin to the more famous presidential branch of the Adams Family—in the 1850s. Four generations of the Adams family tree lived here until it became state property in the 1930s.

As you drive along the access road, you'll pass through Adams Point Wildlife Management Area, offering many trails and access points into the lovely pine forest. At the end of the point is University of New Hampshire's Jackson Estuarine Lab, where you can park and wander through open fields on the self-guided Evelyn Browne Trail or just observe the bay from the dock.

Pick up an interpretive pamphlet at the end of the road where the trail begins. Dogs must be leashed.

From State Route 4, take State Route 108 south for one mile. Turn left onto Durham Point Road for four miles, then turn right at the gate marked "Jackson Estuarine Lab." Park along the road or at the end of the point. Gates are open 10 A.M. to 4 P.M. (603) 868-1095.

• College Woods 🐾🐾🐾🐾 🐕 See **11** on page 422.

This land, which is owned and managed by the University of New Hampshire, is crisscrossed with an endless array of paths, some of which run down to the Durham Reservoir. Dogs love this park for its maze of trails, and you'll meet up with plenty of other area dog lovers at all times of day.

In the early hours of the day or evening, you'll see plenty of wildlife; on our last visit a great horned owl watched us condescendingly from his perch high in an old tree. Trails begin behind the University of New Hampshire (UNH) athletic fields or off several turnouts along Mill Road.

From State Route 4, take State Route 155A east for a mile to the UNH campus. Turn right at the athletic fields and drive to the end of the parking area next to the woods. Or, continue past the campus a quarter mile and turn right onto Mill Road for a quarter mile. The first parking turnout is on your right and other turnouts are located farther along. Open 6 A.M. to 8 P.M. (603) 862-3951.

• Wagon Hill Farm 🐾🐾🐾🐾 🌊 See **12** on page 422.

Well, if you live in southeast New Hampshire or southern Maine, this is the place for dogs! Simply one of the best parks in this book, it not only makes for a scenic hike with woods, open meadows, and great shoreline access on the Great Bay, but, most importantly, this park has gone to the dogs. Practically everyone who comes here does so with their dogs, and you'll meet dog lovers from all over the area on these 140 acres.

You'll see the wagon wheel on the hill from the road as you drive up the long gravel road to the trail. Go across the open meadow toward the bay and, just before you enter the woods, you'll have the option of walking on the Lower Trail (which leads through a pine forest along the western side of the point) or the Upper Trail, which heads straight for a small beach through a meadow. Picnic tables are situated near the water, and on any given day you'll find other dogs and their owners fraternizing by the bay. All the trails are flat, wide, and well marked.

Until the summer of 2000 this park was leash free, but some local people complained that they didn't feel comfortable bringing their children here with dogs off leash. So the city has begun to patrol the area, although most of the dog owners we talked to didn't seem to realize the rules had changed. Although beautiful parks should be enjoyed by everyone, there are countless places to take children that don't allow dogs. For once, the leash-free privileges weren't lost because of poop infractions (there are plenty of garbage cans and mutt mitts distributed throughout the park). With so many beaches and other swimming areas off-limits to dogs in the summer, we are disappointed that the town of Durham didn't see fit to reward responsible dog owners with a park all their own. Oh well. We know we're preaching to the choir here. Dogs must be on leash.

From U.S. Route 16, take State Route 4 over the bridge for 1.5 miles. Turn left into the park entrance and up the hill to the parking area. Open 8 A.M. to dusk. (603) 868-5578.

RESTAURANTS

The Licker Store: At this cute little café, Moonlight in New Hampshire, the Great White, and Main Street aren't songs, sharks, or streets, but they are some of the best sandwiches you'll ever taste. Stop by this bakery/café for a take-out picnic or lunch at one of the outdoor tables. They serve coffee, breakfast, lunch, dinner, and ice cream. George likes the sundried-tomato foccacia bread, while Rocky is partial to the parmesan cheese bread. 44 Main Street, (603) 868-1863.

Three Chimney's Inn: This lovely inn opens its patio terrace during the summer months, and you and your dog are welcome to dine al fresco at this bistro-style café. Reservations are recommended for lunch and dinner, and please tell them you'll be bringing your dog. 17 New Market Road; (603) 868-7800.

EFFINGHAM

PARKS, BEACHES, AND RECREATION AREAS

• **Green Mountain State Forest** 🐾 🐾 🐕 See **13** on page 422.

The highlight of this small state forest is Green Mountain itself, and you can climb to its summit via three different trails.

The best and most scenic is also the newest addition: the southern Dearborn Trail. To reach the trailhead, enter on Hobbs Road where you will be entertained by a historical marker for "the first normal school in New Hampshire." Since the school is long gone, we can't vouch for the accuracy of this claim, but we could probably use a few more "normal" schools everywhere, so we hope it is true. (Actually, the Normal School was a teaching institution for prospective instructors.)

After following an old logging access road, the trail narrows and leads through various pine forests and open ledges before reaching the summit 1.5 miles away. If you wish to make a loop, descend to the fire warden's cabin on the Libby Road Trail, which will lead you back to Hobbs Road. Dogs must be on leash.

From State Route 25, take State Route 153 south for 3.5 miles. Turn right onto Hobbs Road for 1.5 miles. The trail starts on your right. Open dawn to dusk. (603) 271-3556.

• **Pine River State Forest** 🐾 🐾 🐾 See **14** on page 422.

One of the nicer state forests in New Hampshire, this one actually welcomes you with a sign (as opposed to the usual unmarked trails and logging roads that are indicative of most of the state's forests). There are plenty of turnouts and trails along Hutchins Pond Road, but we recommend the two trails that run on either side of Hutchins Pond. Dogs must be leashed

From State Route 25, take Green Mountain Road south for 5.5 miles, where it turns into Drake Road. Continue another half mile to the junction of Drake Road and Hutchins Pond Road. Park at the turnout on your left. The trails begin at the dam straight ahead.

Open dawn to dusk. (603) 271-3254.

EXETER

The charming 17th century village of Exeter is dominated by the renowned Phillips-Exeter Academy, founded in 1781 and school to various presidents, poets, and many a who's who in American business. Once the capitol of New

Hampshire during the Revolution, Exeter was also one of the four original towns of the Massachusetts Bay Colony until it declared itself independent in 1680. Its illustrious history is visibly noted on historical markers throughout town, and the preservation of this history has resulted in some wonderful, untouched parks that allow you and your dog to experience nature as it was 300 years ago.

PARKS, BEACHES AND RECREATION AREAS

• Academy Woods 🐾🐾🐾🐾 See **15** on page 422.

Take your pup back to school! Fast learners will be able to roam over three miles of fabulous hiking trails at the famed preparatory school, Phillips-Exeter Academy. That's right, behind the Academy, right in the heart of Exeter, are 300 acres of lovely pine woodlands that are open to the public.

For a three-mile loop, take the Red Trail which circumvents the entire property and leads along the Exeter River. For a shorter one-mile loop, take the Blue Trail. All trails are well marked and maintained.

A map board is located at the entrance off Drinkwater Road. Although you can enter the woods from behind the stadium on campus, school officials ask that you refrain from using that entrance as dogs are not allowed on the playing fields. Dogs must be leashed.

From State Route 108, take State Route 27 and 111 east for one mile. Turn right onto Drinkwater Road for one mile. The trailhead is on the right, and you can park at the turnout. Open dawn to dusk. (603) 772-2411.

• The Lagoons 🐾🐾🐾 See **16** on page 422.

This unique trail, running along the Squamscott River, is a scenic delight. You and your leashed dog can walk along the estuary on flat gravel paths, overlooking the idyllic Swansey Park (where dogs can't go), the gently flowing river, and the historic town of Exeter. The entire loop is about 1.5 miles and follows the river the entire trip. Dogs must be leashed.

From the center of town on State Routes 27 and 111, cross over the String Bridge and turn left onto Chestnut Street for one block to the end. Turn left on Jady Hill Road. Parking and the trail are on your right. Open dawn to dusk. (603) 772-2411.

RESTAURANTS

Me & Ollie's Bakery & Café: For the best fresh-baked bread around, stop at this wonderful little café and bakery right in the heart of town. You can order any of their self-proclaimed "honest food" which includes sandwiches with sun-dried tomato mayonnaise or olive tapenade and your choice of scrumptious breads; eat outside at one of the café tables or have a picnic along the river. 64 Water Street; (603) 772-4600.

PLACES TO STAY

Best Western Hearthside: Located on State Route 108 just outside of town, you'll still be close to the historical center of Exeter. This full-service hotel has 33 rooms, and pets are welcome for an additional $10 per night. Rooms range from $50 to $100. 137 Portsmouth Avenue, Exeter, NH 03833; (603) 772-3794 or (800) 528-1234; www.bestwestern.com.

FRANKLIN

PARKS, BEACHES, AND RECREATION AREAS

• **Franklin Falls Dam** 🐾🐾🐾🐾 🐕 **See 17 on page 422.**

This long, winding 3,897 acres runs along the Pemigewasset River through three towns: Franklin, Bristol, and Northfield. Hiking trails, ample river access, cross-country trails, and beautiful woods will keep you exploring for miles.

The newly constructed Heritage Trail (which will eventually run 230 miles through the entire state) runs through this park and will one day connect up with trails along the Merrimack, Pemigewasset, and Concord Rivers. Make sure you hike up to the bridge across the dam for a breathtaking view. This park is managed by the U.S. Army Corps of Engineers, and dogs are allowed off leash if under voice control. Maps are available at the ranger station off State Route 127.

From Interstate 93, take Exit 22 to State Route 127 south for three miles. The park entrance is on your right. Open 7 A.M. to 3:30 P.M. (603) 934-2116.

NATURE HIKES AND URBAN WALKS

Daniel Webster Historic Site: Visit the historic birthplace of statesman Daniel Webster and walk the ground he walked upon. Although he went on to an illustrious career as a congressman from New Hampshire; Secretary of State under Presidents Harrison, Tyler, and Fillmore; and finally U.S. senator from Massachusetts, this remarkable orator came from humble roots.

Take the half-mile, self-guided loop trail around the homestead and back to the parking area. Dogs must be leashed. Open May to October. There is no admission fee for the trail. The site is on North Road off State Route 127. (603) 271-3254.

RESTAURANTS

The Sunflower Café: This cute café serves healthy cuisine in a quaint setting. Fresh bread, homemade soups, and salads will satisfy the health-conscious folks; superb bakery items will sweeten the mix for those who, like JoAnna, think a chocolate-chip muffin is diet food. You and your dog are welcome to dine on the small tables outside. Located on Main Street (State Route 3); there is no phone.

PLACES TO STAY

D. K. Motel: This simple 10-room motel is located along State Routes 3A and 11. You won't be in luxury digs here, but they do allow dogs and you'll be close to the river. Rates range from $39 to $69. Pets are $5 extra. At State Routes 3A and 11, Franklin, NH 03235; (603) 934-3311.

GILFORD

PARKS, BEACHES, AND RECREATION AREAS

• **Gunstock Recreation Area** 🐾🐾🐾🐾 🐕 **See 18 on page 422.**

Most of the trails in this wonderful recreation area begin at the main Gunstock ski area parking lot. The best of the bunch is the Round Pond Trail/East Gilford Trail which leads three miles south to beautiful Round Pond. Along the way you'll cross several trails, giving you unlimited hiking options.

For a hike with a view, try the Overlook Trail, which also begins at the main parking lot and provides access to both Belknap and Gunstock Mountains. Although the hike to either summit is over three miles each way, you do reach a stunning overlook at about the one-mile mark, in case you want to cut your hike short. Maps are available at the main office.

Dogs are allowed off leash under voice control on the trails; they must be leashed in the camping area and in the main parking area.

Camping is available at the over 300 tent and RV sites plus a limited number of camping cabins. Proof of rabies vaccination is required for your pet. Camping fees are $22 to $29 per day. (603) 293-4341, extension 191;

From State Route 11 in Alton, take State Route 11A west for five miles into Gilford. The recreation area is on your left. Open dawn to dusk. (603) 293-4341, extension 191, (800) GUN-STOCK.

•Weeks Forest 🐾🐾🐾 🐕 See **19** on page 422.

This 86-acre new-growth forest has a two-mile loop trail through what was once a burgeoning farm in the 1850s. The trees have now begun to replace the open meadows and sheep pastures; the area has been preserved for hiking and tree management since 1988 when the Weeks family donated it in memory of their son, Robert.

This isn't a strenuous hike, but you'll get a fabulous view of the Belknap Mountains from the crest of one of the old fields on the western side. Dogs are allowed off leash if under voice control. This property is managed by the Society for the Protection of New Hampshire Forests.

From U.S. Route 3 in Laconia, take State Route 11A east for four miles into Gilford. The forest is on the left just east of Gilford Village, directly across from the Gilford Public Works facility. Open dawn to dusk. (603) 224-9945.

PLACES TO STAY
Gunstock Recreation Area camping: See page 434.

DIVERSIONS
A Walk in the Woods: Afraid to go into the woods alone? That's not a problem at the annual Walk for Kindness. You'll have plenty of company on the 1.5-mile walk through the woods of the Gunstock Recreation Area. Held on the second Saturday in May, there are dog demonstrations, an agility course, and talent shows that follow the walk. All funds raised go to the New Hampshire Humane Society. For more information, call (603) 524-8236.

FARMINGTON

PARKS, BEACHES, AND RECREATION AREAS

• Blue Job State Forest 🐾🐾🐾 See **20** on page 422.
The Blue Job Mountain Trail beats a hasty path to the summit of 1,357-foot Blue Mountain for an excellent view. It begins on First Crown Point Road through the right-hand gate, and, although only a half mile in length, gives you a lot for very little effort. Old boy Inu loves the wide flat paths, and you will love the panoramic scene on top. Dogs must be leashed.

From U.S. Route 16 in Rochester, take State Route 202A west for three miles. Turn right onto First Crown Point Road for 5.5 miles into Farmington to two gates close together on the right side of the road. The trail starts here. Open from dawn to dusk. (603) 271-3556.

HAMPSTEAD

PARKS, BEACHES, AND RECREATION AREAS

• **Hampstead Conservation Area** 🐾🐾🐾 🐕 See **21** on page 422.
For your choice of four leash-free trails, hightail it to this 150-acre conservation area, just outside the charming village of Hampstead. All the trails interconnect, and maps are posted at both trailheads to help you find your way. Our favorite trail is the Oak Trail which offers the soft, pine-needled woodland walk of the other three trails, but adds some open meadows for ball throwing. The best access point for this trail is off West Road.

From State Route 121, take West Road for a mile. The trailhead is on your left just past Governor's Island Road. Another entrance is located off Stage Road (State Route 121) just south of the town center across from the Hampstead Garage. Open dawn to dusk. There is no contact.

HAMPTON

PLACES TO STAY

Lamie's Inn and Tavern: This historic tavern offers 31 colonial-style rooms near the beach. Small pets are allowed with prior approval. Rates range from $60 to $105 per night. U.S. Route 1, Hampton, NH 03842; (603) 926-0330 or (800) 805-5050.

Stone Gable Inn: This comfortable inn has 63 modern rooms with full-service amenities for you and your pet. Dogs are allowed with prior approval. Rates range from $45 to $65 per night. 869 Lafayette Road, Hampton, NH 03842; (603) 926-6883 or (800) 737-6606.

HAMPTON FALLS

PLACES TO STAY

Hampton Falls Inn: This comfy inn offers 47 rooms and suites on nine acres. Some rooms have small fridges and microwaves, and all are spacious. Pets are allowed with prior approval. Rates range from $40 to $75. 11 Lafayette Road, Hampton Falls, NH 03844; (603) 926-9545, (800) 356-1729; www.hamptonfallsinn.

HOLDERNESS

PARKS, BEACHES, AND RECREATION AREAS

• **Cotton Mountain Trail** 🐾🐾🐾 🐕 See **22** on page 422.
For a short walk up Cotton Mountain with breathtaking views of Lake Winnipesaukee about 1,000 yards up the trail, take this moderate hike located off

State Route 113. A popular trail on weekends, you'll meet many other happy trail dogs along the way.

The sign is easy to see from the road, and a small turnout is alongside the trailhead. A map is clearly visible on the board as you enter.

Dogs must be under voice control.

From State Route 25, take State Route 113 north for two miles. The trail is on your left. Open dawn to dusk. (603) 279-3246.

• Rattlesnake Mountains 🐾🐾🐾 🐕 See **23** on page 422.

The Rattlesnake Mountains consist of 173 acres of protected, privately owned property in Holderness. One of the most popular trails is the Old Bridle Path up the western side, which offers the easiest ascent to impressive views of Squam Lake and beyond. A larger network of trails on the Rattlesnake Mountains provides a variety of options for a longer day of exploring.

To reach the eastern side, take the Ridge Trail, which connects to the Old Bridle Path at the summit. We suggest you call for a map of the area, as most of the paths aren't well marked at their intersections. Voice-controlled dogs are allowed off leash. The area is managed by the Lakes Region Conservation Trust.

From State Route 25, take State Route 113 north for almost seven miles. Turn right onto Pinehurst Road. The trail is at the end of the road by the gate. Or continue north on State Route 113 and park on the right just past Pinehurst Road. Open dawn to dusk. (603) 279-3246.

• Squam Mountains Trails 🐾🐾🐾🐾 🐕 See **24** on page 422.

All of the land in this low mountain region is privately owned, which means that, although your dog is allowed off leash, you should be careful not to disturb the peace or you might lose the privilege! It also means that the trails are not maintained by any particular group, but our favorite route, the Mount Percival–Mount Morgan Loop is oft used and, therefore, well marked. This trail can get very busy on summer weekends, but the views of Squam Lake and beyond warrant its popularity.

A good starting point is at the Mount Morgan trailhead off State Route 113, where parking is also available. The trail is a rather moderate, if occasionally steep, trek towards the summit of Mount Morgan where you can either go all the way to the top or veer off just below the summit onto the Crawford-Ridgepole Trail, which will take you to Mount Percival.

This route becomes more and more interesting, as you walk through several boulder caves and fabulous views of Squam Lake. The trail loops back just north of the Mount Morgan parking area—it's just a short hike back to your car.

From State Route 25, take State Route 113 north almost 7.5 miles. The parking area and trailhead are on your left about a half mile past Pinehurst Road. Open dawn to dusk. (603) 279-3246.

DIVERSIONS

On Golden Pond *meets* **The African Queen:** Mix movie classics on this boat tour of Squam Lake with Captain Pierre Havre and his canine first mate, Bogie. Instead of *The African Queen,* however, the movie being revisited is *On Golden Pond,* filmed on this very lake. You'll recognize the "Thayer" cottage and Church Island. The tour season runs from Memorial Day through mid-October, and the boat sails daily except Tuesdays at 10:30 A.M. and 1:30 P.M. The tour is $10 per person. Dogs must be leashed and get along with Bogie. (603) 279-4405.

PLACES TO STAY
Yankee Trail Motel: This cozy motel, located within easy access to beautiful Squam Lake, has 10 comfortable rooms. The owners have two dogs of their own, so they will happily welcome your well-behaved pet. There's even a nature trail on the property for early morning walks with your dog. A breakfast restaurant is on-site. Rates range from $60 to $75. Route 3, P.O. Box 15, Holderness, NH 03245; (603) 968-3535, (800) 972-1492; www.yankeetrail.com.

KINGSTON

PARKS, BEACHES, AND RECREATION AREAS

• **Kingston State Park** 🐾🐾 🐕 See **25** on page 422.
This tiny state park is off-limits to dogs from May to October, but you can walk your dog on the several trails along Great Pond in the off-season (November to May).

Dogs must be leashed.

From the junction of State Routes 107, 111, and 125, take Main Street south a half mile. The park will be on your right. Open dawn to dusk. (603) 642-5471.

RESTAURANTS
Memories Ice Cream at Red Hill Farm: Somehow you know you're in the right place when the black-and-white logo on the sign matches the actual black and white cows lazily munching on grass behind the ice-cream store. Located on a working farm, the ice cream comes directly from the barn to the customer, and, moo!, is it good! Plenty of picnic tables are outside for you and your dog to share a scoop. 95 Exeter Road (State Route 111); (603) 642-3737.

LACONIA
(INCLUDING THE VILLAGE OF WEIRS BEACH)
There aren't many parks that allow dogs in Laconia. All of the beaches ban dogs year-round, and the state forests allow dogs but have no formal trails. But there are plenty of other things to do in Laconia, so our advice if you are visiting or if you live here is to take your walk somewhere else.

RESTAURANTS
The Marketplace on the Boardwalk: There are three restaurants here, any one of which will satisfy all tastes. The Italian Garden is a full-service Italian restaurant with plenty of tables in their back garden that will serve you and your pup. For ice cream, try Scoops for a cone to go and a walk along the boardwalk. For hamburgers and other fast food to go or to eat at the outside tables, try Stage View. All can be reached at (603) 366-5800.

Tamarack's Restaurant & Drive-In: To sample some great seafood and a little bit of history, stop at Tamarack's, a Weir's Beach institution for 37 years. If you're lucky enough to find a free picnic table on a busy summer day, you and your dog will enjoy a great meal and a great place to people watch. This place is so popular, they claim to have served 834 lobster rolls in one day and to have made enough onion rings to reach the top of Mount Washington several times over. Open seasonally. State Route 3; (603) 366-4687.

PLACES TO STAY

Channel Inn & Cottages: Located right on Lake Winnipesaukee, you can enjoy 12 one- or two-bedroom waterfront cottages, all with kitchens. Close to town and all amenities, your well-behaved pets are welcome with approval. Rates range from $59 to $124. P.O. Box 5106, Weirs Beach, NH 03247; www.channelcottages.com.

Paugus Bay Campground: This 130-site campground features woods, bay views, and a sandy beach for swimming. Pets allowed on leash. Open mid-May to mid-October. Rates are $30 per night. 96 Hillard Road, Laconia, NH 03246; (603) 366-4757.

Sun Valley Cottages: This cottage facility isn't big on atmosphere, but it is pet friendly and close to everything. The 12 cottages in the woods, with knotty-pine interiors and homey furnishings, all have kitchens and some have fireplaces. Rates range from $48 to $80. 686 Endicott Street North, Laconia, NH 03246; (603) 366-4945; www.sunvally.com.

DIVERSIONS

Sit down, you're rockin' the boat!: Winnipesaukee Pier Boat Rentals rents motorboats by the day or half day. Well-behaved dogs are allowed to join you for a trip around the lake. At Winnipesaukee Pier; (603) 366-5188.

Ride the rails: Relive the nostalgic elegance of the past on the Winnipesaukee Scenic Railroad. Part of the old Concord-to-Lincoln line, the trains have been restored to their original prime when wealthy New Yorkers and Bostonians traveled to their summer mansions on Lake Winnipesaukee. Your dog is allowed to accompany you on leash for this historic ride—but not in the dining cars. All dogs ride in Leo's Party Caboose, directly behind the engine. So, party animals—all aboard! Trains depart from Weirs Beach at the pier every hour; admission is $ 7.50 for the one-hour ride. Open May to October. (603) 745-2135; www.hoborr.com.

Strike Up the Band!: The Riverside Concert Series is held at the Rotary Riverside Park every Thursday night from July through August from 6:30 to 8:30 P.M. Bring your dog and the whole family to this varied summer concert series. (603) 524-8813.

LOUDON

PLACES TO STAY

Lovejoy Farm Bed-and-Breakfast: This lovely country inn, converted from a 1790s farmhouse, has seven guest rooms and a carriage house, all with private baths. Two of the suites have fireplaces. You can enjoy hiking on the grounds or relaxing by the fire in this lovely setting. Full breakfast is served each morning. Pets are welcome on the bottom-floor rooms that open up onto the grounds. Rooms range from $87 to $97. 268 Lovejoy Road, Loudon, NH 03301; (603) 783-4007, (888) 783-4007; www.lovejoy-inn.com.

MEREDITH

PARKS, BEACHES, AND RECREATION AREAS

• **Waukewan Highlands Community Park** 🐾🐾🐾 See **26** on page 422.

Usually a community park conjures up visions of ball fields and "No Dogs" signs. But this wonderful woodland park is the best place in town to take your dog. Located off State Route 106, these 190 acres feature countless trails on soft pine needles through a serene forest—and nary a ball game in sight— except of course when George makes an impromptu grab for Inu's grubby tennis ball. Although a fairly new acquisition by the city of Meredith, the trails are well maintained, and plans are underway for an interpretive trail in the future.

Dogs must be leashed.

From U.S. Route 3, take State Route 106 south for one mile. The park and a parking area are on your right. Open dawn to dusk. (603) 279-4538.

RESTAURANTS

Boathouse Grille: Overlooking Lake Winnipesaukee at the Inn at Bay Point, you and your dog can dine in style on the spacious patio of this lovely restaurant. Enjoy fish, steak, or pasta from a variety of offerings. And don't forget the seasonal berry pie for dessert! State Route 25 at the Meredith Boardwalk; (603) 279-2253.

Flurries: For the famous mixed-in goodies and ice-cream concoction (known as a "flurrie"), fish-and-chips, and burgers, you can't do better than this cute little café. Just off the boardwalk in town, plenty of picnic tables overlooking the lake are avilable for you and your dog to enjoy your lunch or dinner. A water bowl outside welcomes you and your pet after a day of hiking. 41 State Route 25; (603) 279-5554.

Franky's Grilled Dogs & Ice Cream: Don't tell your dog the name of this place for she might get worried, but, if you're longing for a good old-fashioned hot dog, try this lakeview restaurant with plenty of excellent dockside seating for you and your own hot dog. State Route 25 at the Meredith Boardwalk; (603) 279-3445.

PLACES TO STAY

Clearwater Campground: This full-service campground offes both tent sites and camping cabins. Rates range from $32 to $36 per day for tent campers; $45 to $65 for the cabins. Dogs are allowed on leash. Open May to October. 26 Campground Road off State Route 104, Meredith, NH 03253; (603) 279-7761; www.ucampnh.com.

DIVERSIONS

Ride the rails: (See also Laconia, Diversions, page 439.) Trains depart every other hour on the Lake Winnipesaukee Railroad. Admission is $8.50 for the two-hour rides from Meredith Station. Open May to October. (603) 745-2135; www.hoborr.com.

MOULTONBOROUGH

PARKS, BEACHES, AND RECREATION AREAS

• **Red Hill Trail** 🐾🐾🐾 🐕 **See 27 on page 422.**

This hike to the fire tower on Red Hill offers a great walk through a hardwood forest, with rewarding views of the Sandwich Range and the Ossipees from the trail. The summit ridge features views of Lake Winnipesaukee, the Belknap Mountains, and Copple Crown. Dogs may leave their leashes in your pocket as long as they are under voice control. The property is owned and managed by the town of Moultonborough.

From State Route 25, take Old Red Hill Road, a rather bumpy dirt road, east for two miles. You'll see the small parking area and trailhead on your right just north of Sibley Road. (603) 253-4582.

RESTAURANTS

Artie's Place: This family restaurant allows dogs at the many outside tables. Order your food inside then bring it out picnic style. This roadside eatery gets busy in the summer months, so expect a wait, but the food is hearty and appetizing. They even have a walk-up ice cream window. State Route 25 at the State Route 109 intersection; (603) 476-2655.

Bad Moose Café: This Mexican grill offers the most unusual fare in Moultonborough. From a Crazy Moose Wango Tango BBQ disc (or pizza) to Howling Moose sticks (cheese-stuffed jalapeño peppers), you'll find plenty to satisfy the hungry dog in you. Plenty of outside tables will accommodate you and Fido. State Route 25; (603) 253-6226.

PLACES TO STAY

Kona Mansion Inn: This gorgeous Tudor-style mansion is located on 150 acres on Moutonborough Neck. The guest rooms and cottage efficiencies all have an old-time resort elegance. Dogs are allowed in the cottages only and must be on leash in all public areas. Cottages range from $450 to $550 per week. P.O. Box 68, Jacobs Road, Moultonborough Neck, NH 03226; (603) 253-4900.

Olde Orchard Inn: This 1790 Federal-style B&B is located on a working orchard. You and your four-footed friend will stay in style at this quiet nine-room inn—all equipped with private baths and fireplaces. Rates range from $95 to $125 per night. RR 1, Box 256, Moultonborough, NH 03254; (800) 598-5845; www.oldeorchardinn.com.

NEW MARKET

PARKS, BEACHES, AND RECREATION AREAS

• **Heron Point Sanctuary** 🐾🐾🐾 🐕 **See 28 on page 422.**

All we can say about this scenic conservation area is Woof! (translation: great park!) Although we drove in circles trying to find this place, its out-of-the-way charm is only accentuated by the fact that not many people know about it. (So let's just keep it among ourselves, shall we?). Located on 32 acres along the Lamprey River, it is truly a sanctuary of solitude for you and your unleashed pooch.

The trails are extremely well laid out, with several boardwalks and view-points built along the river for you to sit and relax. Of course, your dog will be urging you into the forest or along the water's edge, so you may not have much chance to figure out the latest mathematical theorem or work on a solution for global warming, but the opportunity is there if you wish. Managed by the town of Newmarket; dogs must be under voice control.

From State Route 152 in the town center, take State Route 108 north. Turn right onto Bay Street for a quarter mile then right onto an unmarked mobile home park access road for a tenth of a mile. Turn right onto Heron Point Road (dirt road) for a quarter mile to the park at the end. Open dawn to dusk. (603) 743-3262.

NORTHWOOD

PARKS, BEACHES, AND RECREATION AREAS

• **Northwood Meadows Natural Area and Pioneer State Park**
🐾 🐾 🐾 See **29** on page 422.
This nearly 700-acre park was rescued from the bulldozer just six years ago. Developers planned to build condominiums, but today, thanks to the efforts of 350 volunteers, this park is the newest addition to the state's properties. Walk the 1.5-mile loop trail around Meadow Pond and enjoy this special place. Part wooded, part open, part shoreline, the park attracts birds, nature lovers, dogs, and at least one moose (or so they say). Plans are in the works for more trails and an educational center in the future.

From the junction of State Routes 43 and 9/4/202, take State Routes 9/4/202 west three miles. The park entrance is on your left. Open dawn to dusk. (603) 271-3254.

PLACES TO STAY

Lake Shore Farm Resort: This 1926 farmhouse inn offers rustic but comfortable lodging. Some of the 32 rooms have fireplaces, and the grounds offer plenty of recreational options. There's a pond on-site and several acres to wander with your pet. Dogs are allowed in most rooms. Rates range from $110 to $150. 273 Jenness Pond Road, Northwood, NH 03224; (603) 942-5921.

PLYMOUTH

PARKS, BEACHES, AND RECREATION AREAS

• **Fox Park/Keniston Woods** 🐾 🐾 🐾 See **30** on page 422.
This local village park just outside of town is one of the better city parks we've found. You'll find picnic and swimming facilities and excellent walking trails through the surrounding Keniston Woods. Dogs aren't allowed in the day-use areas on summer weekends, but you can always get your exercise with a woodland walk. Dogs must be on leash.

From Interstate 93, take Exit 25 to Main Street (U.S. Route 3 and State Route 25) south. Turn left onto Warren Street for two blocks then right onto Langdon Street. The park is on your left. Open dawn to dusk. (603) 536-1397.

- **Green Acres Woodlands Conservation Easement—Sutherland Trail** 🐾🐾🐾 🐕 See **31** on page 422.

Within this conservation area lies Plymouth Mountain, with views of New-found Lake to the southwest and the White Mountains to the north. The four-mile Plymouth Mountain/Sutherland Trail is the most popular route to the summit. This moderate trail is well marked with white blazes and features several steep ascents. Dogs may be off leash if they're under voice control.

From U.S. Route 3 and State Route 25, take Texas Hill Road west for two miles. Turn right onto Cummings Hill Road, and then make a quick left at the "big rock" fork. There's a sign on the right for Plymouth Mountain. Drive past the house and park at the trailhead. Open 24 hours. (603) 536-1001.

NATURE HIKES AND URBAN WALKS

Plymouth Heritage Trail: Take this self-guided 5.5-mile loop of 14 historically significant sights in Plymouth, featuring a tour of Plymouth State College, the Historical Society, and various town markers commemorating important events in the town's history. You can pick up maps at the Plymouth Chamber of Commerce on Main Street. (603) 536-1001.

PLACES TO STAY

The Plymouth Hotel: There are 102 modern, comfortable rooms at this full-service hotel. An on-site restaurant is available for room service. Dogs are allowed in select rooms only, so please inform management you will be traveling with your pet at the time of your reservation. Rates range from $59 to $109. Main Street, Plymouth, NH 03264; (603) 536-3520, (800) 370-8666.

Pilgrim Inn & Cottages: This small inn features rooms and cottages with names like "The Birdcage" and "The Garden Cottage." All are cheerily decorated, and most have kitchenettes or refrigerators. Pets are allowed with advanced permission. Rates range from $45 to $95; cottages are $55 to $145. Continental breakfast is included. Route 3N, Plymouth, NH 03264; (603) 536-1319, (800) 216-1900; www.pilgriminn.com.

FESTIVALS

Village Fair: Join local artists and craftsmen at the Annual Whole Village Fair held the last Saturday in June from 10 A.M. to 2 P.M. Activities include musical entertainment, contests, food booths, clog dancing, face painting (or tail painting, if you prefer), and a whole village of fun! Admission is free. Call for exact dates and schedule. (603) 536-1001.

DIVERSIONS

Kenniston-Freeman Summer Concert Series: Join the town for a concert on the common every Wednesday evening from 7 to 8:30 P.M. from July through August. On the Common; (603) 536-1001.

PORTSMOUTH

PARKS, BEACHES, AND RECREATION AREAS

- **Urban Forestry Center** 🐾🐾🐾 See **32** on page 422.

This 180-acre urban forest was created to improve public awareness about the wilderness and the state's environmental practices. The park land was donated to the state in 1976 by John Elwyn Stone and is now used as an environmental learning center, tree farm, wildlife sanctuary, and public outdoor space. Numerous grass- and dirt-covered forest roads and a hiking trail traverse the varied property. The paths take you along the pristine salt marshes of Sagamore Creek and through forest management areas where you will find special sections dedicated to specific plant species such as red pines, spruce trees, and meadow grass. It's a great way to get to know your trees.

Dogs are required to be on leash and asked to respect wildlife.

From the Portsmouth Traffic Circle, take the U.S. Route 1 Bypass south for one mile onto U.S. Route 1. Continue for three-quarters of a mile then turn left onto Elwyn Road for a quarter mile. The park entrance is on the left. Open dawn to dusk. (603) 431-6774.

NATURE HIKES AND URBAN WALKS

Portsmouth Harbor Trail: Take this walking tour through the downtown district of Portsmouth, and you and your harbor hound can walk the trail in its entirety (in about 2.5 hours) or choose to do one of the three sections: Downtown/Waterfront, the South End, or Haymarket Square. All offer many interesting sites including the John Paul Jones House, Market Square, Morgan Tugboats, the Piscataqua River, Portsmouth Naval Shipyard, and Strawberry Banke—the oldest section of the city with a number of restored buildings from the 1600s and 1700s. Dogs can walk the 10-acre grounds for free.

Maps and guides are available for $2 from the Chamber of Commerce at 500 Market Street and the information kiosk at Market Square. Guided tours are also available during the summer. (603) 436-3988.

RESTAURANTS

Bagel Works: Whether it's a bagel, coffee, a specialty sandwich, or a tasty dessert, it all works for our dogs especially when they can sit at this sidewalk café and enjoy dog and people watching in the heart of Portsmouth. 9–11 Congress Street; (603) 431-4434.

Café Brioche: "Ooh la la" is what your pet will say when she sees the menu of specialty salads, sandwiches, soups, coffees, and treats. You can get everything to go or relax at one of the many outdoor tables in the heart of downtown Portsmouth. 14 Market Square; (603) 430-9225.

Me & Ollie's Bread: Inu loves to watch the hustle and bustle of Market Square almost as much as he loves food. At Me & Ollie's Bread, where they make some of the best bread in all of New England, he can enjoy both. This outdoor café also serves sandwiches, coffee, pastries, and ice cream. Try the Buttermilk Potato bread. Wow! 10 Pleasant Street; (603) 436-7777.

PLACES TO STAY

Anchorage Inn: This 95-room motel offers a choice of double rooms or suites—which have private whirlpools. Continental breakfast is included. Pets are allowed in most rooms. Rates range from $50 to $150 per night. 417 Woodbury Avenue, Portsmouth, NH 03801; (603) 431-8111 or (800) 370-8111.

Meadowbrook Inn: This roadside motel is conveniently located at the Portsmouth Traffic Circle, the crossroad of Interstate 95, U.S. Route 1, and

State Routes 4 and 16. The standard rooms are comfortable and clean. Rates range from $48 to $90. Portsmouth Traffic Circle, Portsmouth, NH 03801; (603) 436-2700, (800) 370-2727.

Residence Inn by Marriott: You probably won't stay at this 90-room suite-style hotel for only one night because, although they welcome your pet, there is a $250 nonrefundable deposit required for your pet no matter how long you stay. Most people who stay in these studios or one- or two-bedroom suites stay for up to a month. If you need a place for that long, this might be just the right spot for Spot. But for a night, well, that pet charge is a bit pricey. All rooms have full kitchens, and continental breakfast is served each morning. Rooms start at $179 a night, but go down in price the longer you stay. 2501 International Drive, Portsmouth, NH 03801; (603) 436-8880; www.marriott.com.

Wren's Nest Village Inn: Located on four acres, this lovely bed-and-breakfast inn offers 35 rooms or cottages each decorated country style. The cottages have porches and decks, and breakfast is served each morning. Pets are allowed in select rooms. Open all year, the rates range from $70 to $170; dogs are an additional $10 per night. 3548 Lafayette Road (State Route 1), Portsmouth, NH 03801; (603) 436-2481.

FESTIVALS

First Night: Being outside late at night on December 31 in New Hampshire may seem like a chilly proposition to some, but downtown Portsmouth really heats up with thousands of celebrants ringing in the New Year. Dogs are not permitted in any of the inside events, but they'll enjoy the many outdoor events and ringing in the new year with their best friend. (603) 431-5388.

DIVERSIONS

Market Square Day: Any day of the year Market Square is teeming with activity, but on Market Square Day it really steps on the gas. That's when Portsmouth turns all of downtown into a giant pedestrian mall. The street festival has over 300 vendors featuring arts and crafts, food, live music, and entertainment. The day is followed with a finale concert and fireworks on the shores of the Piscataqua River. It's held the second Saturday in June from 9 A.M. to 5 P.M. (603) 431-5388.

ROCHESTER

PARKS, BEACHES, AND RECREATION AREAS

• Hanson Pines Conservation Area 🐾 🐾 🐾 See **33** on page 422.

For an interesting variation on the usual city park, try this pine forest right in the center of town. Part forest, part riverfront park and including a new inter-city recreation trail, this conservation area is worth a visit. Located behind Spaulding High School in the center of town, it's easy to miss. But, if you're looking for a trail that leads to the Cocheco River, take the paved path next to the tennis courts, which leads directly to the river. For those who would like to combine a river dip with a longer hike, many intersecting woodland paths lead off this trail which will take you through a pine forest.

At the main trailhead, running parallel to Chestnut Hill Road, is a newly completed recreation trail over an old railroad bed. The trail is wide and flat, and will eventually run all the way to Sanbornville. Although not particularly scenic except at the beginning, this provides a long hiking corridor for the dog who needs a lot of exercise. You can literally walk for miles. Dogs must be on leash.

From State Route 125 (Wakefield Street), take High School Road a half mile west. Turn left onto Chestnut Hill Road. The park and parking is on the right. Open dawn to dusk. (603) 332-2130.

PLACES TO STAY

Anchorage Inn: This newly renovated motel offers 31 rooms and a free continental breakfast each morning. Some efficiency units with kitchenettes are also available. Most rooms have two double beds and a sitting area. Pets are welcome. Rates range from $49 to $65 per night. State Route 125, Rochester, NH 03867; (603) 332-3350 or (800) 370-8111.

RYE

PLACES TO STAY

Rosewood Inn at Rye: This 31-room motel welcomes you and your pet. Each of the rooms has two double beds plus kitchenettes and coffee makers. Rates range from $60 to $95, depending on the season. 150 Lafayette Road, Rye, NH 03870; (603) 964-9700.

DIVERSIONS

Seadogs, Strutt Your Stuff!: Every second Sunday in September, the New Hampshire Society for the Prevention of Cruelty to Animals sponsors the Seaside Stroll for the Animals. It's a full day of doggie activities at Wallis Sands State Park including a three-mile walk (less energetic dogs can turn back halfway for a 1.5-mile walk) on the shore road, the Perfect Pet Talent Show, the Doggie and Human Fashion Show, K-9 Rescue demonstrations, and plenty of sponsored goodie bags. A $12 donation is requestd or, if you like, you can collect pledges. Contact the NHSPCA for more information at (603) 772-2921.

SALEM

PARKS, BEACHES, AND RECREATION AREAS

• **Salem Town Forest** 🐾 🐾 See **34** on page 422.
This pleasant town forest has extremely well-maintained trails that cross over and along Spicket Brook. You'll find 48 acres of quiet woodland that weave in and around a residential area. You won't get a workout here, but, for a daily stroll, your dog will appreciate it. Managed by the Salem Conservation Commission; dogs must be leashed.

From State Route 28, take State Route 111 east for a half mile. The park and a small parking area will be on your left. Open sunrise to sunset. (603) 890-2000.

PLACES TO STAY

Holiday Inn: This 84-room full-service hotel is located right off Interstate 93 for easy access to all New Hampshire locations. All rooms have modern amenities, and continental breakfast is served each morning. Dogs are welcome with a $50 refundable deposit. Rooms range from $75 to $225 per night. 1 Keewaydin Drive, Salem, NH 03079; (603) 893-5511, (800) HOLIDAY; www.holiday-inn.com

Red Roof Inn: Located just off Interstate 93, this 108-room motel offers simple but modern accommodations. Small pets are welcome. Rooms range from $40 to $65 per night. 15 Red Roof Inn, Salem, NH 03079; (603) 898-6422 or (800) THE-ROOF; www.redroof.com.

SANBORNTON

PARKS, BEACHES, AND RECREATION AREAS

• Mike Burke Memorial Forest 🐾 🐾 🐕 See **35** on page 422.

The Mike Burke Memorial Forest was acquired by the New England Forestry Foundation in 1996 and dedicated to the memory of a New England Forestry consultant who died abruptly from leukemia in 1995. The 500-acre parcel is located between Hersey and Sanbornton Mountains.

The trail starts off Knox Mountain Road, and you'll soon pass a small pond on your right. Once you've satisfied your dog's desire to swim, continue past a stone wall into the forest. Here the trail forks; the left fork will take you up towards Hersey Mountain and the Knox Mountain Tree Farm, where you can also walk your dog on well-manicured trails; the right fork crisscrosses several old stone walls through a forest that was once 19th-century farmland. Maps are available from the New England Forestry Foundation. Dogs may be off leash if under voice control.

From Interstate 93, take Exit 22 to State Route 127 west for one mile. Make a right onto Prescott Road, then an immediate left onto Weeks Road for 1.5 miles. Turn left onto Knox Mountain Road for 2.5 miles until you see a parking area in a small turnaround on the left. Open dawn to dusk. (603) 588-2638.

SANDWICH

PARKS, BEACHES, AND RECREATION AREAS

• Eagle Cliff Conservation Area 🐾 🐾 🐾 🐕 See **36** on page 422.

This 102-acre property offers a rather steep woodsy hike to the top of Red Hill fire tower on the Eagle Cliff Trail. And, if you can find the trail, hearty dogs and hikers will be rewarded with panoramic views of Winnipesaukeeand Squam Lakes, and the Ossipee and Belknap Mountains.

The trailhead is located just off Bean Road in Sandwich and is almost impossible to see from the road. If you're directionally challenged like JoAnna and George (well, okay, not George—he found the trail in about two seconds once JoAnna finally located the right turnout), you might spend a good portion of your hiking time driving back and forth on Bean Road.

The fire tower can also be reached from the Teedie Trail less than a half mile south of the Eagle Cliff Trail at a parking area next to a privately owned tennis court. This trail is a more gradual climb to the top, but we found it to be a wetter and, therefore, muddier hike. You can hike up one trail and return on the other to form a loop. Dogs must be under voice control.

From State Route 25, take Bean Road north for four miles (just a quarter mile north of the Sandwich-Moultonborough town line). The turnout is on your right just past the red house. Going south on Bean Road from State Route 113, drive three miles and look for the "Turning and Entering" sign past Range Road. Park at the turnout along the lake; the trailhead is located in a small ditch opposite the sign. Open dawn to dusk. (603) 279-3246.

• **Five-Finger Point** 🐾🐾🐾 🐕 See **37** on page 422.

From the Rattlesnake Mountain trails in Holderness you can access Five-Finger Point, a small peninsula shaped vaguely like a hand, which allows you to walk close to the water, wade along the secluded beaches, and nibble on the wild blueberries of Squam Lake. Stay on the Pasture Trail from Pinehurst Road and you'll see signs to direct you to this wonderful little waterland spot. Dogs will love swimming here.

From State Route 113 in Holderness, take Pinehurst Road south into Sandwich for a mile to the gate. Park here; the trail to Five-Finger Point starts on your left. Open dawn to dusk. Managed by three different organizations: (603) 968-7336 Squam Lakes Association; (603) 279-1309 Squam Lakes Conservation Society; (603) 862-3951 University New Hampshire.

SOUTH HAMPTON

PARKS, BEACHES, AND RECREATION AREAS

• **Pow Wow River Conservation Area** 🐾🐾🐾🐾 🐕 See **38** on page 422.

For a walk on over 200 acres along Lake Gardner, hightail it to this fabulous conservation area which borders South Hampton, New Hampshire, and Amesbury, Massachusetts. Countless interconnecting trails weave through the area, all well mapped out at intersections and on the map board at the parking area off State Route 107A.

You can walk along the Stagecoach Trail Road to reach Lake Gardner or throw a ball through open meadows at the Community Gardens. Dogs are not allowed at the connecting Camp Kent Environmental Center, but, since you'll be romping leash free everywhere else at this park, we doubt if she'll mind.

From State Route 150 in Amesbury, Massachusetts, take State Route 107A north for a half mile. Signs for Battice Farm and the park entrance are on your left. Park in the farm lot and proceed to the trailhead. Open dawn to dusk. (978) 388-8100.

STRATHAM

PARKS, BEACHES, AND RECREATION AREAS

• **Stratham Hill Park** 🐾 🐾 🐕 See **39** on page 422.

This hilltop park surrounds the glacially formed Stratham Hill—commonly known as a drumlin. Millions of years ago, as the glacier made its slow journey southeast, it carved a half-mile-long swath in the earth that is now this small hill where we can enjoy the view.

This is not a long walk, but it's a historically interesting one. Not only will you find a plaque where Robert Lincoln (son of Abraham) declaimed the Declaration of Independence on July 4, 1860, while a student of nearby Philips-Exeter Academy, but on the top of the hill is an 1881 viewfinder identifying local points of interest—most of which no longer exist. The total loop is a mere mile, but this is a great walk for a clear, sunny afternoon. Dogs may be off leash on the trail.

From Interstate 95, take Exit 3 to State Route 33 west for five miles. The park is on your left just past the New Hampshire Technical College. The trail begins through the fenced-in gate. Open dawn to dusk. There is no contact.

RESTAURANTS

Hodgies Ice Cream: Look for the pink building with the friendly flowers and long lines of people outside, and you won't miss Hodgies, George's pick for the best blueberry ice cream around. Plenty of picnic tables and a grassy area are outside where you and your dog can enjoy a treat after hiking. Stratham Hill, 95 Portsmouth Avenue (State Route 108); (603) 775-0223.

DIVERSIONS

A Tree Grows in Stratham: Celebrate the holiday season at the New Hampshire Society for the Prevention of Cruelty to Animals' Annual Tree Lighting. Of course, there's the tree, but there's also caroling, shelter tours, Santa photos, arts and crafts, raffles, and a good time for one and all. The free event is held the first weekend in December. Contact the NHSPCA for more information. 104 Portsmouth Avenue; (603) 772-2921.

A year's supply of dog bones, my own hydrant, leash-free walking everyday. . .: Here's your dog's chance to personally deliver his Christmas list to Santa. Each year in November, Santa visits the New Hampshire Society for the Prevention of Cruelty to Animals for Pet Portrait Day. The pictures with Santa are professionally done, and the photo packages cost $25. Contact the NHSPCA for more information. 104 Portsmouth Avenue; (603) 772-2921.

TILTON

RESTAURANTS

Tilt'n Diner: This old-fashioned diner doesn't really tilt, but the food is so good it may rock your world. A grassy picnic area with tables is outside where you and your dog can eat your meal. Try a vanilla coke and Shepherd's Pie. Exit 20 off Interstate 93 (State Route 132); (603) 286-2204.

PLACES TO STAY

Country Lake Resort: This facility offers camping, motel rooms, and cottages. Something for everyone! Best of all, "everyone" includes your dog. This resort is right on the water with its own private beach, so you can be close to the town or away from it all. Open all year, rates range from $34 to $109 per night. Dogs are only allowed in certain rooms, so call in advance. There is $25 refundable security deposit, and proof of rabies vaccination and registration is required. Winnisquam Lake, 788 Laconia Road, Tilton, NH 03276; (603) 524-6897 or (888) 855-6897.

Tilton Manor B&B: This small Victorian bed-and-breakfast inn has four rooms and welcomes you and your pet. Located on three acres, you can walk your dog on the grounds on leash. Breakfast is included. Rooms range from $65 to $80 per night. 408 Chestnut Street, Tilton, NH 03276; (603) 286-3457.

DIVERSIONS

Tilton Island Concert Series: Come join the fun at the Savina Hartwell Memorial Park on Tilton Island. Located on a grassy knoll surrounded by a lovely stream, you can sit on the available chairs or bring your own for an evening of music on Sunday nights from June through August at 6:30 P.M. Call for schedules. (603) 934-6909.

TUFTONBORO

PARKS, BEACHES, AND RECREATION AREAS

• **Abenaki Fire Tower** 🐾 🐾 🐕 See **40** on page 422.

For a birds-eye view of the surrounding valley, take a short hike through a lovely shaded forest to this scenic overlook. Named for the Abenaki, who lived along the shores of what they called "beautiful water in a high place," you'll enjoy looking out over Lake Winnipesaukee as much as they did.

The trail is brief, but your dog won't mind spending extra time identifying all the dogs who came before him while you take in the view. Dogs must be under voice control.

From State Route 109A in Melvin Village, take State Route 109 south for a half mile. The tower is clearly signed on your left. Open 8 A.M. to 8 P.M. (603) 569-2200.

WOLFEBORO

PARKS, BEACHES, AND RECREATION AREAS

• **Bridge Falls Urban Trail** 🐾 🐾 🐾 See **41** on page 422.

This trail leads from the center of downtown along a back bay of Lake Winnipesaukee via an abandoned railroad bed. The city has done a great job of grooming the "Back Bay" (as locals call this trail), and it has become a much-used bike, jogging, and walking path just a beat away from the hustle and bustle of downtown.

The trail starts behind the old railroad depot on Railroad Avenue, and you can walk a pleasant two miles past the old Berry Excelsior Mill and over a land bridge on Crescent Lake. Stop at the many benches near the lake and have a picnic or a quiet moment with your dog. One morning George and JoAnna took a walk along this trail and, while George swam on one side of the land bridge, JoAnna enjoyed watching a muskrat make his way through the quiet pond on the other side. Dogs must be leashed because the trail does traverse private property.

From State Route 28 (South Main Street), take North Main Street (State Route 109) west for less than half a mile. Turn right onto Railroad Avenue and park at the railway depot. Open 6 A.M. to 11 P.M. (603) 569-2200.

RESTAURANTS

Bailey's: This renowned Wolfeboro institution is on the grounds of the Lake Motel (see below) and serves up some of the best meals around. Take a hot blueberry muffin with you as you're heading out onto the trails, or stop by for an ice-cream frappé at the end of the day. Meals are available to go or to eat outside. State Route 28; (603) 569-3662.

Maddies by the Bay: Located along Lake Winnipesaukee, this little seafood café has tables outside overlooking the lake or walk-up windows for picnickers. Either way you'll get a great meal of salads, fish-and-chips, or burgers. The location can't be beat. On the Wharf; (603) 569-8888.

Wolfe's Tavern at the Wolfeboro Inn: Sit on the terrace of this lovely pub and enjoy a great English meal. Well-behaved dogs who don't beg like Oliver Twist are allowed to dine here with their human pals. 20 Main Street (State Route 28); (603) 569-3016.

The Yum Yum Shop: For pastries and bakery goods that will tempt the most self-controlled soul, we recommend you check the calorie counter at the door and treat yourself to one of their delicious baked goods. Eat a freshly baked sticky bun or a "picnic pack" of fresh bread while you watch the world go by from one of the outdoor tables. Top it all off with a chocolate brownie, and you'll be ready to walk the dog again. 16 North Main Street (State Route 28); (603) 569-1919.

PLACES TO STAY

The Lake Motel: The Bailey family has operated this motel and the famous Bailey's restaurant next door for 50 years. They have 650 feet of pristine lake frontage for swimming, sunbathing, or boating. (Boats are available for rent.) The motel has 16 acres of lawns and woodland to explore and enjoy, plus you're within easy walking distance of the beautiful town of Wolfeboro. "Quiet, well-behaved pets who leave nothing behind" are welcome. Rates range from $80 to $108. Open seasonally from mid-May to October. State Route 28, Box 887-B, Wolfeboro, NH 03894; (603) 569-1100.

FESTIVALS

In the Paint: Join the fun at the On the Green Arts & Crafts Festival. With over 200 exhibitors from all over New England, live music, food, and raffles, you and your dog will love being in the paint at this annual event the first weekend in July. Held at the Brewster Academy Common, Main Street (State Route 28); (603) 528-4014.

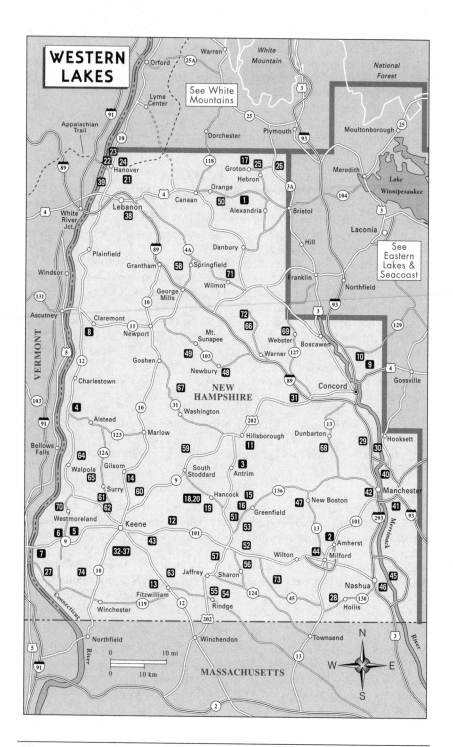

WESTERN LAKES

Warren

White Mountain

Orford

25A

National Forest

Lyme Center

See White Mountains

3

Moultonborough

25

Appalachian Trail

91

25

Dorchester

Plymouth

93

Meredith

104

Lake Winnipesaukee

23

22 24

Hanover

21

118

17 **25**

Groton Hebron

26

39

Orange

3A

Canaan

50 **1**

Alexandria

Bristol

Laconia

4

Lebanon

38

Danbury

Hill

See Eastern Lakes & Seacoast

Plainfield

89

4A

Grantham

58

Springfield

71

Franklin

Northfield

Windsor

131

George Mills

Wilmot

10

Ascutney

Claremont

11

Newport

8

Mt. Sunapee

72

66

69

Webster

Boscawen

129

Warner

127

10

9

4

5

12

Goshen

49

103

Newbury

48

89

31

Concord

Gossville

Charlestown

67

NEW HAMPSHIRE

31

4

Alstead

10

31

Washington

202

Dunbarton

13

29

Hooksett

103

123

Marlow

Hillsborough

11

68

91

Bellows Falls

64

12A

Gilsom

59

30

Walpole

65

14

South Stoddard

3

Antrim

40

42

Manchester

Surry

60

9

18,20

Hancock

15

136

47

New Boston

41

61

70

62

19

16

Greenfield

101

293

Westmoreland

51

13

6 **5**

Keene

12

53

2

Amherst

9

43

101

52

Wilton

44

Milford

7

32-37

57

Sharon

56

73

27

74

10

63

Jaffrey

45

28

Nashua

45

13

55 **54**

124

130

46

Fitzwilliam

Rindge

Hollis

Winchester

119

12

Northfield

202

Winchendon

Townsend

3

River

MASSACHUSETTS

5

91

2

VERMONT

Connecticut River

0   10 mi

0   10 km

N W E S

14
WESTERN LAKES

The western part of New Hampshire hearkens back to the New Hampshire of a hundred years ago. Each lovely village has its own white-spired church and tiny town hall and here, amid the soft rolling hills and distinctive mountains of the charming New England countryside, the pace of life feels perceptibly slower. Often referred to as the "Monadnock Region," this area is dominated by majestic Mount Monadnock, but since your dogs can't go to the reservation, you won't be hearing much about it in this book.

What you will be hearing about is all the other mountain peaks you can climb, lakes you can swim in, and restored B&Bs where you and your dog can relax. Long a haven for artists, writers, and other summer residents, the towns here have inspired a play (Thornton Wilder's *"Our Town"* was modeled after Peterborough) and spawned *Yankee Magazine* and the *Farmer's Almanac*. We hope a little of that inspiration will rub off on you and your canine pal as you explore the scenic Western Lakes.

The Cheshire Trail: This newly acquired rail trail follows an old Boston-Maine Railway route and is slowly being converted into a recreation trail. Currently the trail is completed between Fitzwilliam at the Massachusetts border, through Keene, following State Route 12 most of the way. You can access it through many parks along the way, but the best access is at Rockwood Pond in Fitzwilliam and Ashuelot River Park in Keene. Eventually the trail will run north to Walpole at the Vermont border. (603) 271-3556.

Dartmouth Outing Club: This wonderful organization, run by Dartmouth College for over a 100 years, manages a 75-mile stretch of the Appalachian

---

Trail from Vermont into the White Mountains. For a description of all their trails throughout New Hampshire and for information about lodging and equipment rentals, contact the DOC at P.O. Box 9, Hanover, NH 03755; (603) 646-2428.

Wapack Trail: Managed by the Friends of the Wapack, this 21-mile trail extends along the mountain ridges from the Pack Monadnocks in Greenfield, New Hampshire, to Watatic Mountain at the Massachusetts state line, taking its name from both ridges. When the trail opened in 1922, it was the first interstate footpath in the Northeast (the Appalachian Trail wasn't completed until 1937) and was a very popular hike in the 1930s and '40s. It fell into disrepair in the following decades, but work has now begun to restore the trail to its former glory. The southern end of the trail connects to Massachusetts's Midstate Trail. Contact the Friends of the Wapack at P.O. Box 115, West Peterborough, NH 03468.

ALEXANDRIA

PARKS, BEACHES, AND RECREATION AREAS

• **Welton Falls State Natural Area** 🐾🐾🐾 🐕 See ❶ on page 452.
For a beautiful waterfall walk, George recommends you head for the falls. This scenic picnic and hiking area is located near Mount Cardigan State Park (see page 482) and, when you and your pup are banned from the beaches of Newfound Lake, where better to cool your tails on a hot summer day? It is a little less than a mile walk to the falls from the parking area, and most of the path is near or over the Fowler River.

To reach this rather remote area, you will park at the head of a logging road off Fowler River Road. Walk up the road for a quarter mile where another older logging road intersects to the left. Follow that road to the river. Once you cross the river, you'll pick up a trail that runs along the water for another half mile; that trail will lead you to the falls and the "lunch rocks"—flat open rocks that make for a perfect picnic spot for you and Spot. Dogs must be under voice control.

From State Route 104 in Bristol, take State Route 3A north for three miles. Turn left onto West Shore Road for two miles. At the fork, keep left onto Fowler River Road (Cardigan Mountain Road) for 1.5 miles. Then keep right at the fork remaining on Fowler River Road for an additional six miles to the end of the road. Open dawn to dusk. (603) 744-2197.

RESTAURANTS

Frosty's Dairy Bar: For the best soft-serve ice cream around, get in line at this popular ice creamery. All of their homemade ice cream is low fat, and they can make just about any flavor combination you can dream up. Try the dreamsicle or peanut butter and bananas. 354 West Shore Road; (603) 744-5257.

PLACES TO STAY

Appalachian Mountain Club—Cardigan Lodge: Nestled at the base of Mount Cardigan, the lodge and camping area offers over 50 miles of hiking trails leading from the front door to several nearby peaks. The lodge is open daily to the public for accommodations and meals from the last weekend in June through Labor Day. Dogs are allowed at the campsites which are equipped with picnic tables, fire rings, water, and facilities. Rates are $12 per night. RFD #1 Box 712, Bristol, NH 03222; (603) 744-8011.

AMHERST

PARKS, BEACHES, AND RECREATION AREAS

• The Joe English Reservation 🐾🐾🐾 🐕 See ❷ on page 452.

This 370-acre reservation is the largest and best-known property in Amherst. Located on the lot of original Amherst settler Samuel Lamson in 1748, this land was a thriving sawmill in the 1800s, and you'll still see evidence of its history as you explore the woods.

The reservation is named for the Native American guide, Joe English, who helped the white settlers in their wars with other Native Americans. According to legend he was the grandson of Masconnomet, the Agawam chief who had converted to Christianity. Joe was known for his affinity for all things "English," hence his nickname. In 1697 he was captured along with a small group of settlers, and he convinced his captors to let him lead an "attack" on Deerfield, Massachusetts. Once there he warned the village folk, who turned their guns on the Native Americans. Furious at his betrayal, he became Enemy Number One with his own people for years as they pursued and finally killed him for his treachery. A hill in New Boston was named in his honor as the site of one of his more famous escapes.

At this reservation which also honors his memory, a variety of flat, open walking trails crisscross the entire woodland, all perfect for you and your dog. A popular hiking and cross-country skiing area in the winter, you'll meet up with plenty of other dog lovers on a visit here. Dogs must be under voice control; maps are available at both parking areas.

From State Route 13, take State Route 101 north for two miles. Turn left onto Horace Greeley Road for 1.5 miles, then turn left onto Chestnut Hill Road for one mile. The park is on the left. Another access point is at the northern end of Brook Road off of Horace Greeley Road. Open dawn to dusk. (603) 673-5339.

NATURE HIKES AND URBAN WALKS

B & M Trail: This old Boston-Maine railway trail runs two miles between Baboosic Lake Road and Walnut Hill Road offering a peek at the bygone days of rail travel in southern New Hampshire. Beginning on Baboosic Lake Road (adjacent to the Route 101 eastbound entrance ramp, and marked by a small sign), the trail crosses a small wooden footbridge and traverses a swamp and wetland area. While somewhat overgrown, the raised railroad bed provides dry footing and access to this wildlife habitat. Beyond the wetland, the flat, open trail widens and the terrain changes to a mixed coniferous forest. The trail ends off Walnut Hill Road near the intersection of Clark Island Road.

Off-street parking is available for several cars on Walnut Hill and Baboosic Lake Roads. Open dawn to dusk. (603) 673-5339.

ANTRIM

PARKS, BEACHES, AND RECREATION AREAS

• **McCabe Forest** 🐾🐾🐾 🐕‍🦺 See **3** on page 452.

In 1982 Dorothy McCabe deeded these 192 acres to the Society for the Protection of New Hampshire Forests, and they have used the gift wisely. Today it is one of five demonstration wildlife habitats in the state offering ways for rural homeowners to make their land more attractive to wildlife.

Walk the 1.5-mile loop with your dog and see the many "stations" along the way—each explaining how and why it makes the area a more vital habitat for animals. Your dog won't need any instruction. He'll know a good place when he sees it—especially because dogs can run leash free here if under voice control.

From State Route 31, take State Route 202 north for one block. Turn right onto Elm Street Extension Road. The park is on your immediate right. Open dawn to dusk. (603) 224-9945.

PLACES TO STAY

Maplehurst Inn: This bed-and-breakfast allows dogs on the weekdays in the first-floor room only. There are 13 comfortable rooms in a charming country-style setting. A continental breakfast is served each morning. Rates range from $75 to $90. 67 Main Street, Antrim, NH 03047; (603) 588-8000.

BENNINGTON

PLACES TO STAY

The Econo Lodge: This standard 31-room hotel is comfortable and clean. Ask for trail maps at the front desk for hiking with your dog. Pets are allowed in four of the rooms for an additional $25. Be sure and make your pet's reservation when you make your own. Rates range from $49 to $89 and include continental breakfast. 634 Francestown Road (State Route 47), Bennington, NH 03442 (603) 588-6735, (800) 55-ECONO; www.econolodge.com.

CHARLESTOWN

PARKS, BEACHES, AND RECREATION AREAS

• **Claybrook Nature Trail** 🐾🐾 See **4** on page 452.

This one-mile nature trail winds along scenic Clay Brook on an unmarked path. Begin your walk at an old dam off Old Gristmill Road; after you enter the forest you'll hear the rushing waters of Devil's Gulley where Clay Brook makes a dramatic 100-foot drop into the ravine. An old 1774 gristmill was once located here, and you'll see evidence of its activity. The trail continues to descend as the brook cascades gently downstream for the rest of your walk.

The hike ends where an old stone bridge used to connect the shore to the town. There are plans to build another bridge, thereby linking this trail with the Charlestown Historic District Walk (see below). Maintained by the Charlestown Conservation Commission, dogs must be on leash.

From State Route 11 (Old Springfield Road), take State Routes 11 and 12 (Main Street) north for a half mile. Turn right onto Fling Road (also called Old Gristmill Road) for a quarter mile. The parking area is on your right before you reach the three-way intersection. Open dawn to dusk. (603) 826-4400.

NATURE HIKES AND URBAN WALKS

Charlestown Historic District Walk: Wander along charming Main Street and visit over 60 historic structures dating back over 200 years. Charlestown was the site of Old Fort Number 4, the northernmost settlement along the Connecticut River and site of a three-day battle during the French-Indian War in 1747. The historical town has since been relocated a mile away, but Main Street still has markers where the original fort and settlement existed. Pick up a map at the information booth at 26 Railroad Street. (603) 826-4400.

CHESTERFIELD

PARKS, BEACHES, AND RECREATION AREAS

• **Chesterfield Gorge Natural Area** 🐾🐾 🦴 See **5** on page 452.
These 13 acres won't give your dog a long walk but, for sheer natural beauty, this area is well worth the visit. The one-mile loop trail heads down and through the gorge, a narrow rock ravine formed by erupting volcanoes and glacial movement. It isn't the Grand Canyon, but the cliffs and rock formations will thrill you nonetheless. Dogs used to be relegated to the trails marked "dog trail" and not allowed in the gorge. But, today, as long as your dog is leashed, she is allowed. But keep a tight rein, and, if you have an especially rambunctious dog, you might choose to stick to the trails marked for dogs.

From State Route 63, take State Route 9 east for five miles. The park entrance and parking are on your left. Open dawn to dusk. (603) 547-3373.

• **Friedsam Town Forest** 🐾🐾🐾 🐕 See **6** on page 452.
This 200-acre forest is managed by the Chesterfield Conservation Commission. The trails are well maintained and include several cross-country skiing trails in the winter. The Sargent Trail leads from the main parking area off Twin Brook Road to a smaller parking area on State Route 63. Park at either area to access the trail. Along the way you'll explore a beaver pond, a glacial pothole, the lovely Twin Brook, and some beautiful deciduous forests. Your leash-free dog will want to visit in all seasons, but fall is an especially gorgeous time to visit. Trail maps are available at the main parking area.

From State Route 9, take State Route 63 south for a half mile. Parking is on your right. A parking area is also located off Twin Brook Road. Open dawn to dusk. (603) 363-8071.

• **Madame Sherri Forest** 🐾🐾🐾🐾 🐕 See **7** on page 452.
We just love this conservation area. It has everything a dog could want. Great hiking trails, a wonderful swimming pond, plenty of woodland to sniff, and, best of all, leashless freedom. Whether you're exploring the area or just passing through, this forest is also conveniently located off Interstate 93 (but feels miles away).

The forest gets its name from Madame Sherri, an eccentric but wealthy Ziegfield Follies costume designer who, supposedly, made forays into nearby Keene dressed in her furs, jewels, and, well, nothing else. You can still see the remains of her "castle" where she threw wild parties in the 1920s. The once-magnificent house was destroyed by fire in 1962, so all that's left are the stone pools and arched stone foundation of her terrace. You can imagine Wordsworth waxing rhapsodic about this place; the ruins look like a miniature Tintern Abbey as they are slowly being reclaimed by the forest.

The Ann Stokes Loop Trail leads to Indian Pond, a clear, clean swimming pond with a grassy beach perfect for picnicking or relaxing. The entire two-mile forest loop is well worth exploring, but, if you're in a hurry to get to the pond, take the easier half-mile path straight there. The castle is located off a right spit trail at the trailhead.

From Indian Pond, you can access Miners Ledge in nearby Wantastiquet Natural Area or take a spit trail into Cook's Forest, a 53-acre parcel that has been newly acquired by the Chesterfield Conservation Commission.

Maps are available at the parking area, although the trails are well marked without a map. This 488-acre parcel is jointly managed by the Chesterfield Conservation Commission, the Nature Conservancy, and the Society for the Protection of New Hampshire Forests. Together, the total of the three areas make up over 1,000 acres of conservation forest. Dogs must be under voice control.

From Interstate 91, take Exit 3 to State Route 9 east for a quarter mile. Turn right onto Mountain Road and make an immediate left onto Gulf Road, a dirt road, for 2.5 miles. The parking area is on your right. Open dawn to dusk. (603) 224-9945.

PLACES TO STAY

Chesterfield Inn: This beautifully restored farmhouse offers 15 elegant rooms—all with private bath and eight with fireplaces. Walk the gorgeous gardens and look out over the Connecticut River Valley from this hillside perch. Pets are allowed in select rooms with prior approval. Rooms range from $150 to $250 per night. State Route 9, Box 155, Chesterfield, NH 03443; (603) 256-3211 or (800) 365-5515; www.chesterfieldinn.com.

CLAREMONT

PARKS, BEACHES, AND RECREATION AREAS

• Moody Park 🐾 🐾 🐾 See 🖥 on page 452.

Your leashed dog will love coming to this excellent urban park. Although it gets fairly crowded on weekends, during the week you'll have the woodland trails to yourselves.

One access road runs directly through the middle of the park; from there you can park at one of the many picnic turnouts and access the branching trails in either direction. Most splinter off and lead into the woods or connect to another trail that will lead you back to the main road. You can't get lost, but you will find a little respite from the sounds of the city beyond. Dogs must be leashed.

From State Route 103 (Main Street), take State Route 11 (Pleasant Street) south for 1.5 miles. Turn right onto Maple Avenue for one mile then left onto Moody Park Road into the park. Open 8 A.M. to 8:30 P.M. (603) 543-1296.

NATURE HIKES AND URBAN WALKS

Historic Walking Tour of Claremont: Take a walk through the past dating back to the late 1600s. A self-guided walking tour will take you by the sites of the glory days of this old mill town. Pick up a map at the Claremont Chamber of Commerce at Tremont Square. (603) 543-1296.

RESTAURANTS

Candy Works: This old-fashioned ice-cream parlor has tables outside where you and your dog can contentedly share an ice-cream cone or chocolate soda while watching the town go by. 26 Tremont Square; (603) 542-3338.

Shadrack's Rib Shack: For great ribs and barbecued chicken, stop at this tiny take-out restaurant. Order full dinners, mashed potatoes, and fresh cornbread for a meal that'll stick to your ribs. A small picnic table is available outside but mostly it's set up for take out. So order dem bones and take your meal down the road to Moody Park for a finger-lickin' picnic. 143 Pleasant Street (State Route 11); (603) 542-0011.

PLACES TO STAY

Claremont Motor Lodge: This 19-room motel was renovated in 1997 and offers clean and simple rooms. A free continental breakfast is served each morning, and Fido is welcome with no extra charge. Rates range from $59 to $79. Beauregard Street, Claremont, NH 03743; (603) 542-2540.

CONCORD

PARKS, BEACHES, AND RECREATION AREAS

• **Merrimack River Outdoor Education Area and Conservation Center** 🐾 🐾 🐾 🐕 See **9** on page 452.

This 75-acre site houses the headquarters of the Society for Protection of New Hampshire Forests in a solar-heated facility that's worth stopping for by itself. A view deck out back affords a spectacular view of the Merrimack River Valley, and a bookstore offers helpful trail maps and guidebooks of the area.

Follow the steep wooden stairs down the ravine to the path along the Merrimack River for a self-guided tour through tree farms amid the marshes and channels of the floodplain. The river flows fairly easily here so you can allow your dog to swim, but keep an eye out for the tricky currents.

The headquarters is located at 54 Portsmouth Street, but you can access the trails from the parking area just west of the center. Dogs are allowed off leash except around the center itself.

From Interstate 93, take Exit 14 to State Route 9 east for three miles. Turn left onto Portsmouth Road for 1.5 miles. The Center's driveway will be on your left. Open dawn to dusk. (603) 224-9945.

• **Oak Hill Conservation Area** 🐾 🐾 🐾 🐕 See **10** on page 452.

Managed by the Concord Conservation Trust, this 300-acre property has a network of interconnected trails that meander through open farming land, lovely woodlands, and a final climb to the summit of Oak Hill.

To start, take the Lower Trail from the northern trailhead and head toward the Swope Slope or Krupa Trails, which will eventually lead to the summit. None of the trails is lengthy or strenuous; the total distance to the summit is a little over 1.5 miles in each direction. But the trails are well marked and, with the exception of the power lines that run through one section, provide a scenic afternoon stroll through the quiet countryside.

Dogs are allowed off leash here.

From State Routes 383/4/202, take State Route 132 (Side Road) north for three miles. Fork right onto Shaker Road for three miles. The turnout and hidden sign are on your right. Open dawn to dusk. (603) 225-8500.

RESTAURANTS

Cafeino's: This popular coffeehouse offers Main Street seating outdoors during the summer months. Enjoy a bagel, foccacia sandwich, or a great cup of Green Mountain coffee while you watch the other dogs saunter by. 84 North Main Street; (603) 229-0020.

Eagle Square Deli and Catering Company: Your dog may join you during warm weather at one of the many outdoor tables at this upscale deli and eatery on popular Eagle Square. Dine on standard deli fare or full chicken or fish dinners. 5 Eagle Square; (603) 228-4795.

Yellow Submarine: We included this place because we liked the name and the food. A cute little roadside eatery just outside of town, you can dine al fresco on one of the picnic benches or take a quick meal on the road with you. Try the hot veggie sandwich with extra onions! 192 North State Street (State Route 3); (603) 228-4500.

PLACES TO STAY

Comfort Inn: Pets are welcome at this pleasant motel right downtown. Offering comfortable rooms and complimentary continental breakfast each morning, you and your dog will be close to everything in town. Rates range from $59 to $165. 71 Hall Street, Concord, NH 03301; (603) 226-4100, (800) 228-5150.

Holiday Inn: This newly renovated 122-room hotel allows pets on approval. A restaurant is on-site, and full amenities are found in each room. You can walk downtown in minutes. Rates range from $65 to $145. 172 North Main Street, Concord, NH 03301; (800) 465-4320.

FESTIVALS

Strike Up the Band!: Join the fun at the "Music in America" Concert Series. These free outdoor concerts in Eagle Square feature popular show tunes and great American standards. The festivities, sponsored by the Museum of New Hampshire, start at 7:00 P.M.

Call for dates and schedules. (603) 226-3189.

DIVERSIONS

These paws are made for walkin': Before winter sets in, bringing solitary dog walks in sub-zero temperatures, join the pack this autumn at the annual Walk for the Animals. At the New Hampshire Technical Institute, this one- to five-mile walk is held in mid-October with contests, a raffle, agility courses, and Fly-Ball demonstrations. "Paw"ticipants are asked to make a donation or collect pledges to raise money for the Concord Society for the Prevention of Cruelty to Animals. For more information, contact the Concord SPCA at (603) 753-6751.

"Canoo" on the Contoocook: Canoeing is a great way to enjoy this lovely river and visit the various parks that snuggle its edge. Rent a canoe at Contoocook River Canoe Company, and, if your dog has her sea legs, she's allowed to join you for the ride. River Road; (603) 753-9804.

CORNISH

NATURE HIKES AND URBAN WALKS

Saint-Gaudens National Historic Site: Your dog will become an art lover after a trip to this lovely former estate of one of America's foremost sculptors, Augustus Saint-Gaudens (1848–1907). The grounds are almost as beautiful as his magnificent sculptures. Two hiking trails, the quarter-mile Blow-Me-Up Brook Trail, which passes by Blow-Me-Down Pond on the return loop, and the two-mile Blow-Me-Down Natural Area Trail, covering over 80 acres, wander through lovely wooded ravines and forests. Dogs must be on leash at all times and are not permitted in the buildings. There is a $4 admission fee.

The site is located on State Route 12A in the village of Squag City. The grounds are open from 8:00 A.M. to dusk. (603) 675-2175.

DIVERSIONS

With a star to guide you: Take a relaxing canoe trip down the Connecticut River with a rental canoe from North Star Canoe Rentals. Free shuttle service is available for half-day, full-day, or multiday trips. (603) 542-5802.

DEERING

PARKS, BEACHES, AND RECREATION AREAS

• Deering Sanctuary 🐾🐾🐾 See **11** on page 452.

This lovely wildlife sanctuary is managed by the Audubon Society of New Hampshire. During the great forest logging of the late 1700s, this whole area was plowed under, and you can still see the remnants of stone walls peeking out from the lush undergrowth.

From the first parking area, take the yellow-blazed Old Orchard Trail which leads to. . . you're way ahead of me here. . . the old orchard. The ground cover in the spring and summer is a carpet of wildflowers, but the real centerpiece of the sanctuary is Black Fox Pond.

This artificial pond was created by the damming of Smith Brook. The pond area totals just over 36 acres, with an undeveloped shoreline, so, although your dog will probably find a place to plunge in, it can be a bit muddy around the edges. The woods road continues through the forest and back to the parking area.

Other trails in the sanctuary are the Smith Brook Trail and the red-blazed

Hemlock Woods Trail. A map is available at the mailbox by the parking area. Dogs must be on leash.

From U.S. Route 202 in Hillsborough, take State Route 149 south for one mile into Deering. Turn left onto Clement Hill Road for 1.5 miles. The park and parking area are on the right. Open dawn to dusk. (603) 224-9909.

DUBLIN

PARKS, BEACHES, AND RECREATION AREAS

• **Eliza Adams Gorge Walk** 🐾🐾🐾 🐕 🔵 See **12** on page 452.
Part of the Monadcock-Sunapee Greenway, this two-mile stretch is a scenic pleasure. Begin off State Route 101 at the Monadnock Wilderness Girl Scout Camp sign. You'll speed right by if you're not looking for it, and it's almost impossible to see if you're traveling east on State Route 101. But for those determined travelers, we assure you it's worth the trouble to find.

You'll start on a wide rocky road that climbs slightly before entering a birch woodland. Your dog will have plenty of room to navigate off leash as you make your way on this trail. Follow the white-blazed trail and signs marked "M-S Trail" to stay on the path. Eventually you'll come out on Eliza Adams Gorge, a spectacular falls that tumbles down into the Howe Reservoir.

From State Route 137, take State Route 101 for 5.5 miles. Look for the Girl Scout sign on your right. You'll see the Eliza Gorge sign up the trail 50 feet. Park on the roadside. Open dawn to dusk. (603) 224-9945.

RESTAURANTS

Dublin General Store: Stop by for a picnic lunch from the deli. This cheerful little store also has tables outside. State Route 101; (603) 563-8501.

FITZWILLIAM

PARKS, BEACHES, AND RECREATION AREAS

• **Rockwood Pond** 🐾🐾🐾 🐕 See **13** on page 452.
This lovely out-of-the-way pond offers excellent swimming for two- and four-footed friends. A long and lovely grassy shelf along the northern edge of the pond is perfect for sunning and beach access. Your water dog will love spending a day here. And when the other local lakes and parks are banning your pal in the summer, you'll be thrilled to have this lovely pond to yourself. You can also access the Cheshire Rail Trail from here if you desire a hike. Dogs are allowed off leash if under voice control.

From State Route 119, take State Route 12 north for 2.5 miles. Turn left onto Bowkerville Road, which turns into the dirt Rockville Pond Road a half mile west. Go another mile and the pond is on your left. Open sunrise to sunset. (603) 585-7270.

PLACES TO STAY

The Unique Yankee B&B Lodge: Located on the former Holbrook estate with 18 private mountain-view lakeside acres, the five B&B suites and two cottages—all with private baths and romantic in-room fireplaces—await you.

Two "English" cottages are also available with fireplaces and lake views. Well-behaved dogs are welcome in the cottages by prior arrangement. Rates range from $64 to $130 per night. P.O. Box 571, Fitzwilliam, NH 03447; (603) 242-6706; www.parpac.com/uniqueyankee.

FRANCESTOWN

PLACES TO STAY

The Inn at Crotched Mountain: You will love staying at this friendly B&B. There are 13 charming rooms at this country inn—eight are private, five share a bath—and all of them will accommodate your pet. Please call well in advance of your stay. Rooms are $100 per night, including a full breakfast, plus $5 per night for your dog. 534 Mountain Road, Francetown, NH, 03403; (603) 588-6840.

GILSUM

PARKS, BEACHES, AND RECREATION AREAS

• **Bears Den Natural Area** 🐾🐾🐾 🐕 See **14** on page 452.

For an interesting geological walk, you will enjoy a visit to this unusual park, named for the rocky outcroppings that once housed hibernating black bears. Only a single trail runs through the 60 acres, but along the way you'll see large "potholes" (rocky depressions in the earth) and glacial rock formations. The trail leads to the "grotto," a primeval bed of ferns and mossy trees nesting in the shadow of the rocky ledges. You will enjoy the unusual geology, and your dog will enjoy her leash-free freedom. The park once had state park designation but is no longer maintained by the state parks system, so there are no longer signs at the trailhead. But as the Cheshire Cat would say, "if you here, then you've arrived!"

From State Route 9, take State Route 10 north for five miles; a large unmarked clearing on your right marks the trail. From the north it is about a half mile south of the Surry Road intersection. Open sunrise to sunset. (603) 271-3556.

GREENFIELD

PARKS, BEACHES, AND RECREATION AREAS

• **Crotched Mountain—Greenfield Trail** 🐾🐾🐾 🐕 See **15** on page 452.

This 1.5-mile trail to the top of Crotched Mountain starts out on a flat gravel road to Lookout Rock, a wonderful vantage point to take in the valley below. At a stone wall it connects to the steeper Bennington Trail to the summit. (But make sure when you're returning that you follow the Greenfield Trail—George and JoAnna made the mistake of missing the cutoff and ending up at the Bennington Trailhead—many miles from where the car was!). This is a good hour-long hike that will satisfy a dog's need for exercise, but be sure to bring water as there are no water sources along the way. Dogs are allowed off leash if under voice control.

From State Route 136, take State Route 31 north for 1.5 miles. Turn right at a road leading to the Crotched Mountain Rehabilitation Center and follow the road uphill for 1.5 miles. The trailhead is one-tenth of a mile past Gilbert Varney Drive on the left. Open dawn to dusk. There is no contact.

• **Greenfield State Park** 🐾🐾🐾 See **16** on page 452.

Dogs are allowed on the trails of this 400-acre park from October to May only. In the summer months, the beach at Hogback Pond is crowded with swimmers, and dogs aren't welcome. Dogs are allowed, however, at the camping area, but, since you can't swim at the pond and can't go anywhere but the hot asphalt road between campsites, we suggest avoiding the park altogether unless you need someplace to stay the night.

If you do visit in the other seasons, we suggest the Hogback Pond Trail. The trail starts next to Campsite 247, down the "Dead End" road off the main entrance road. It is clearly marked as a hiking trail, so feel free to park on the side of the road here. Follow the blue blazes and keep to the left, which will lead you beside the pond. In all, the trail forms a 1.5-mile loop. The pond is a bit marshy, and your dog won't really be able to swim here, but he will enjoy this wonderful woodland walk on a cool spring or fall day. Dogs must be on leash on all state land.

From State Route 31, take State Route 136 west for a half mile. The park is on your right. Open dawn to dusk. (603) 547-3497.

GROTON

PARKS, BEACHES, AND RECREATION AREAS

• **Sculptured Rocks Natural Area** 🐾🐾🐾 See **17** on page 452.

This is an out-of-the-way spot, but it's well worth the drive. Ice-age potholes, worn and sculpted by the effects of water and friction, make a stunning centerpiece for this pleasant, shady area. A bridge spans the river and a woods road allows for walking, but most dogs never get past the water. So if you can't beat 'em, join 'em and jump in after your four-footed friend. Dogs must be on leash.

From State Route 3A in Hebron, take North Shore Road west for four miles. Turn right onto North Groton Road for 1.5 miles into Groton. Turn left onto Tale Nell Road (a dirt road) for three miles. The park is on your left. Open dawn to dusk. (603) 271-3254.

HANCOCK

PARKS, BEACHES, AND RECREATION AREAS

• **Harris Center for Conservation Education** 🐾🐾🐾🐾 See **18** on page 452.

Hike the popular three-mile Harriskat Trail to the top of Skatutakee Mountain at 2,002 feet. Along the way you'll pass brooks, streams, meadows, and views of picturesque white steeples in the towns below. Located on the 7,000 acres of the Harris Conservation Center, the trail moves gradually to the peak, so you'll have a little energy left when you actually get to the top.

The trail is located behind the Harris Center offices; you can pick up a trail map when the center is open—weekdays from 9:30 A.M. to 5 P.M.

From State Route 137, take State Route 123 north for 2.5 miles. Turn left onto Hunts Pond Road (unmarked, look for the Harris Center sign) for a half mile, then left onto Kings Highway, a dirt road, for a half mile to the end and the park (follow signs). Open dawn to dusk. (603) 525-3394.

• Juggernaut Pond Conservation Area—Thatcher Memorial Forest 🐾🐾🐾 🐕 See 19 on page 452.

For an off-the-beaten-path hike to crystal clear Juggernaut Pond, start at the trailhead of Thatcher Memorial Forest. Managed by the New England Forestry Foundation, this 92-acre park provides a wonderful woodland walk on well-maintained trails in a quiet forest.

Because Juggernaut Pond is a public water supply, no swimming is allowed, but you'll be able to cool off in the stream that runs through the property. Dogs are allowed off leash if under voice command.

From the town center, take State Route 137 south for a quarter mile. Turn right onto Old Dublin Road for 1.5 miles. The trailhead and turnoff will be on your left. Open dawn to dusk. (603) 588-2638; www.neforestry.org.

• McGreal Forest 🐾🐾🐾 🐕 See 20 on page 452.

Located on 26 acres, this small conservation land has been protected since 1968 by the Society for the Protection of New Hampshire Forests. Hike a one-mile loop trail to and around Hunt's Pond dam for a quick afternoon walk. Well-behaved dogs are allowed off leash.

From State Route 137, take State Route 123 north for 2.5 miles. Turn left onto Hunts Pond Road (unmarked, look for the Harris Center sign) for a half mile, then turn left onto Kings Highway, a dirt road, for a quarter mile. The park is on the right. Open dawn to dusk. (603) 224-9945; www.spnhf.org.

HANOVER

This scenic college town, home of Dartmouth College, takes advantage of its location in the hills bordering Vermont. First established in 1769 as place to educate "youth of the Indian tribes," Dartmouth lays claim to such illustrious alumni as Daniel Webster and Nelson Rockefeller. With the Dartmouth Outing Club overseeing the management of countless recreation lands, it's lucky for dogs that Hanover has a flexible leash law, meaning that dogs are allowed off leash if under voice control.

PARKS, BEACHES, AND RECREATION AREAS

• Dartmouth Outing Club Recreation Area 🐾🐾🐾 🐕 See 21 on page 452.

Take a one-mile hike on the Appalachian Trail from this entry point on Dartmouth College land. Enter the trail next to the cemetery following the white and orange blazes. (Dartmouth maintains this section of the trail and marks it with orange; the white marks are for the Appalachian Trail.) You'll cross Mink Brook, an apple and cherry orchard, and stellar woodlands. This is a great hike for dogs of all ages and sizes. (That description includes hikers, as well!) Dogs are allowed off leash if under voice command.

From King Road in the village of Etna, take Two Mile Road north for one mile to the town cemetery on the left. You'll see a sign and orange and white blazes where the trail starts. Park on the side of the road. Open dawn to dusk. (603) 646-2428.

• Mink Brook Natural Area 🐾🐾🐾 🐕 See **22** on page 452.

This open land along Mink Brook will provide you and your dog both water access and a pleasant hike along the water's edge. Not many people know about this remote spot, so, if you can find it, you'll probably enjoy a relatively solitary walk (or swim, if your dogs are anything like ours. We barely get to the end of the trail because the main attraction is always the brook.). The trail extends about a half mile to the junction with the Connecticut River. You'll return the same way you came. Dogs are allowed off leash if they're under voice control.

From Hanover center, take South Main Street (State Route 10) south for a half mile. Turn right on the small unnamed gravel road just before the power station and continue to a hard-to-see sign for the Mink Brook Natural Area. Park here and walk over the chain off the parking lot to the bank of Mink Brook. Open dawn to dusk. (603) 643-2134.

• Pine Park 🐾🐾🐾🐾 🐕 See **23** on page 452.

The 150-year-old pines in this beautiful 90-acre park have been protected since 1900 when a group of concerned citizens saved the park from logging at the hands of the Diamond Match Company. Later it was entrusted to the town of Hanover and Dartmouth College, and we are fortunate both organizations have been such good stewards. This is easily our favorite walk in Hanover, with all the things a dog could want: water; shade; trees; wide, flat walking paths; and leash-free freedom.

The trail tiptoes across Hanover Country Club land before traversing Girl Brook and leading down to a soft pine-needle covered path along the Connecticut River; you'll be surrounded by water and woods for your entire walk. The view along the river is spectacular and is frequently used by runners and cross-country skiers in the winter. An entire round-trip loop is about 1.5 miles long and ends up at Occom Pond just below the clubhouse where you parked.

A word of caution: Because you will walk on the golf course for about 100 feet, we urge caution and consideration. Make sure there are no loose balls flying overhead or a party of four yelling Fore! as you pass.

From town center, take North Main Street (State Route 10) north onto Rope Ferry Road for a quarter mile. Turn left into the Hanover Country Club and park at the far end above the clubhouse (you'll see a small trail sign there). Follow the wide path across the fairway for about 100 feet to a small trail sign on your right. Open dawn to dusk. (603) 646-2428.

• Storr's Pond Trail 🐾🐾🐾 See **24** on page 452.

Take a 1.5-mile loop around Storr's Pond in the winter, spring, or fall, because during the busy summer months, dogs aren't allowed. Fortunately, it is beautiful in any season, and, with the exception of a few joggers, you'll enjoy this beautiful forest walk without dodging the crowds that arrive in the summer.

The trail starts just beyond the brook which runs past the pool house. Follow this road past Area I and continue to your left until it returns to the tennis courts. The "No Trespassing" sign at the far end of the pond refers to the dock and dam. You are free to access the path here. Dogs must be on leash.

From town, take North Main Street (State Route 10) north for three miles. Turn right onto Reservoir Road to the end, then turn left into the Storrs Pond Recreation Area. Open sunrise to sunset. (603) 643-2134.

RESTAURANTS

Dirt Cowboy Café: For a great cup of coffee and a health-food menu of fresh breads, sandwiches, and soups, stop by this friendly little coffeehouse on Main Street. You may sit outside on benches or tables, or take your meal across the street to the Village Green. Either way, your dog will be watching eagerly for a few fallen crumbs as you eat. 7 Main Street; (603) 643-1323.

Hanover Inn Terrace Restaurant: Serving lunch and dinner, this comfortable dining patio located in the Hanover Inn will accommodate dogs on the outer tables of their open patio. Dine al fresco on an adventurous menu featuring spicy salmon tartare, roasted duckling, calamari, and portobello mushroom sandwiches. Main Street; (603) 643-4300.

Molly's Restaurant & Bar: Enjoy the outdoors at the Patio Café of this popular Hanover restaurant. Located down a brick walkway behind the regular restaurant, you may dine comfortably with your canine pal at this delicious café. Order from the traditional pub menu or the special café menu which changes daily. Main Street; (603) 643-2570.

Patrick Henry's: Eat on the side patio of this excellent restaurant in the heart of Hanover. Featuring a menu of ribs, quiche, pasta, and Hawaiian chicken, we feel certain every appetite will be satisfied here. Dogs are welcomed as long as they don't beg from other tables. 39 Main Street; (603) 643-2345.

PLACES TO STAY

Hanover Inn: Fortunately for the canine crowd, the only place in town that allows dogs is also the best place in town: the graceful Hanover Inn. This elegant hotel overlooks the Village Green and Dartmouth College in the center of town. Stay in tonied luxury at this 100-year-old inn. Well-behaved dogs are allowed in certain rooms with advance reservations. East Wheelock and Main Streets, P.O. Box 151, Hanover, NH 03755; (603) 643-4300, (800) 443-7024; www.hanoverinn.com.

DIVERSIONS

Winter wonderland: For the winter event of the season, grab your mittens and woolies and head over to Dartmouth College for the annual Winter Carnival. Featuring ice sculptures, food, entertainment, sled races, and countless other events all over town, this is THE place to be each February. Call for events and dates. (603) 643-3512.

HEBRON

PARKS, BEACHES, AND RECREATION AREAS

• **Hebron Marsh Wildlife Sanctuary** 🐾🐾🐾 See **25** on page 452.

A visit to this scenic area, maintained by the Audubon Society, is a treat and a privilege. Dogs are allowed on leash here, but this is an actively used bird-watching area, so we suggest you go here only if your dog is well behaved.

You may hike along the Beaver Trail—an open-cut trail that loops through a meadow along the forest—or the Heron Trail, which leads to the marshes along Newfound Lake. Both trails are a short half mile, but the views of the lake are lovely and the trails easy to walk. Picnic tables are located on the lake side of the park.

From Bristol, take State Route 3A north to North Shore Road. Turn left. Go almost two miles to signs for the parking area at Ash House on your left. The Heron Trail starts here; the Beaver Trail is across North Shore Road.

From State Route 3A, take North Shore Road east for three miles. The sanctuary is on your left. Open dawn to dusk. (603) 224-9909.

• **Plymouth Mountain Trail** 🐾🐾🐾 🐕 See **26** on page 452.

This trail is a popular and time-worn hike—and the easiest way to the top of Plymouth Mountain. On the way you'll have fabulous views of Newfound Lake, Franconia Notch, and the White Mountains. The hike is a moderate three miles each way; your dog must be under voice control.

From North Shore Road, take State Route 3A north for 500 feet. The trail and turnout are on your right. Open 24 hours. There is no contact.

RESTAURANTS

The Village Store: Stop by this convenience store for a burger or sandwich from their deli, and sit outdoors on the patio benches or take it just down the road to the Hebron Marsh Wildlife Sanctuary for a great picnic lunch. Junction of North Shore Road and West Shore Road; (603) 744-8765.

HINSDALE

PARKS, BEACHES, AND RECREATION AREAS

• **Wantastiquet Mountain Natural Area** 🐾🐾🐾 🐕 See **27** on page 452.

For a lovely afternoon's hike to the summit of Wantastiquet Mountain, take the Summit Trail to the top. This gradual, two-mile climb on an unpaved quarry road is more than a casual stroll, but it will also afford you and your dog a scenic woodland walk overlooking the quaint countryside of white-spired churches and cozy New England towns. Along the way colorful plant life will brighten your walk and rocky ledge "seats" will beckon for a little rest and contemplation of how to say "Wantastiquet" three times fast.

The road was built in 1890 and has a granite monument on top erected in 1806 in "loving memory of a friend." You can also access this park through the Madame Sherri Forest in Chesterfield (see pages 457–458) via the trails on Indian Pond. Voice-controlled dogs are allowed off leash.

From Main Street in Brattleboro, Vermont, take Bridge Street east for a quarter mile into New Hampshire. The park entrance is on the left. Open dawn to dusk. (603) 271-3556.

HOLLIS

PARKS, BEACHES, AND RECREATION AREAS

• **Beaver Brook Association Land** 🐾🐾🐾🐾 🐕 See **28** on page 452.

This is one of our favorite parks. A trip here is worth the drive from anywhere. Beaver Brook's 1,730-acre reservation includes more wonderful trails than you can explore in just one visit, and you'll find yourself returning again and again. Best of all, you can allow your dog to be off leash on most of the trails.

Our favorite trail (this week, anyway) is the Wildlife Pond Loop Trail located off State Route 130. A wonderful pond is a half mile up the trail where George, Inu, and Rocky can swim, and countless trails lead around the pond or off into the woods beyond for more exploring.

A note on the leash law. There are some conflicting signs saying dogs must be on leash and others that say they must be under control. The official scoop is this (and we got it from the dog's mouth): The association asks that you keep your dog on leash in the main parking areas, but once you're out on the trail, they can enjoy the park leash free.

Stop at the office at Maple Hill Farm for information and maps of the more than 30 miles of trails through woods, fields, and wetlands, although maps are posted at most of the trailheads, as well.

From State Route 130, take State Route 122 south for 1.75 miles. Turn right onto Ridge Road for 1.5 miles. The park is on the right. Open dawn to dusk. (603) 465-7787.

RESTAURANTS

Christopher's Subs and Pizza: Stop by this roadside eatery for a little trail food or a pizza to devour on one of the picnic tables outside. Either way, George likes the Steak Bomb Special—a steak sub with the works. 22 Ash Street (State Route 130); (603) 465-7200.

FESTIVALS

Summer Solstice Celebration: Held on the closest Saturday to June 21, this annual family celebration features live entertainment and a bring-your-own picnic around the Maple Hill Barn at the Beaver Brook Association headquarters on Ridge Road. (603) 465-7787.

HOOKSETT

PARKS, BEACHES, AND RECREATION AREAS

• **Hooksett Pinnacle** 🐾🐾🐾 🐕 See **29** on page 452.

Praised by Henry David Thoreau as a "scene of rare beauty and completeness, which the traveler should take pains to enjoy," this modest hill is noted more for its history than for its height. Although the scene Thoreau describes from the pinnacle in his *A Week on the Concord and Merrimack Rivers* has changed somewhat, some sights still remain the same as they were over a hundred years ago when the Merrimack Valley was a bustling farming community.

This short walk to the summit will only take you about 15 minutes, but the views spread out in all directions (including the less-than-attractive Interstate 93). Dogs under voice control may walk without leashes.

From Interstate 93, take Exit 11 to State Route 3A north for one mile. Turn left onto Pine Street and take your first left onto Ardon Road. To reach the trail, park at the turnaround at the end of Ardon road and follow the woods trail to the right. Open dawn to dusk. (603) 269-4073.

• **Lambert Park** 🐾🐾 See **30** on page 452.
This simple riverside park won't satisfy the dog who needs to get out and run, but it is a scenic and convenient stop in town. Located right on the Merrimack River, there is a small beach here where your water dog can take a swim. Dogs must be on leash.

From State Routes 3 and 28 in town, follow the fork onto Main Street north for a half mile. Turn right onto Veterans Drive for a half mile. The park is on your left. Open 6 A.M. to 11 P.M. (603) 269-4073.

HOPKINTON

PARKS, BEACHES, AND RECREATION AREAS

• **Hopkinton-Everett Lake Project—Elm Brook Park** 🐾🐾🐾 See **31** on page 452.
Elm Brook Park is an 8,000-acre U.S. Army Corps of Engineers flood-control project. Hopkinton Lake, created by the Hopkinton Dam, is located in the center and includes a swimming area with a broad, sandy beach. (Dogs are not allowed on the swimming beach in the summer, but you can still swim in the lake from other access points.)

A wooded nature trail and several other well-groomed and easily traversed trails loop through the park. From the nature trail, a side trail leads to a cleared area where an old cemetery used to be—it was moved because when the reservoir is full, this field is underwater. Not to be irreverent to the dead, but this area makes for a great ball-throwing field. The combination of wooded, open, and wetland habitats makes this a wonderful park for Spot.

From State Route 89, take Exit 6 to State Route 127 west. Go one mile to the entrance on your left. Open 8 A.M. to 4 P.M. (603) 746-4775 or (603) 746-3601.

JAFFREY

PARKS, BEACHES, AND RECREATION AREAS

• **Gap Mountain Reservation (see Troy, page 488)**

RESTAURANTS

Kimball Farm Ice Cream and Restaurant: This popular local stop is packed with visitors on weekends and during the lunch hour. And why not? The ice cream is the best around, and the restaurant has good simple food served on a boss's deadline. Plenty of tables are outside so you can share your lunch or scoop with your dog. Their sister location is in Carlisle, Massachusetts. State Route 24; (603) 532-5765.

KEENE

Keene has a flexible leash law which means dogs must be leashed in all commercial areas (like downtown) but may be off leash in the parks as long as they are under voice control.

PARKS, BEACHES, AND RECREATION AREAS

• Ashuelot River Park 🐾🐾🐾🐾 🐕 See **32** on page 452.

This excellent park in the center of town is a great example of community and city organizations getting together to create a sense of pride and ownership. Mutt Mitts dispensers are located throughout the park, provided by the Cheshire Kennel Club. MacMillan Company has built a beautiful suspension bridge over the Ashuelot River, and countless private donors have contributed money to make the park its beautiful best. Their names can be read on the many granite stones that line the gardens.

A single trail starts at West Street and runs through the park for almost two miles along the Ashuelot River. You'll find you have company; this is a popular place for joggers, walkers, and dog lovers. But even as busy as it gets, you'll still feel as if you've escaped your urban surroundings.

The hiking trail runs into the bike trail at State Route 9, so we suggest you turn around here and backtrack through the lovely woods and water. You can also access the Cheshire Rail Trail from here. Dogs must be under voice control, and Keene is serious about their pooper law, so please pick up after your pet!

From State Routes 9, 10, and 12 (Monadnock Highway), take West Street east for a half mile. Turn left into the park. Parking is in the shopping mall next to the park entrance. Open 6 A.M. to 10 P.M. (603) 352-0133.

• Beaver Brook Falls 🐾🐾 🐕 🐾 See **33** on page 452.

This short hike is more for you than your dog, although we feel certain your dog will enjoy it, too. Your hike follows the Old State Route 9 before the new bypass was built in 1978. Now the abandoned road is a half-mile walking trail that leads up a gorge to the scenic Beaver Brook Falls. Dogs may be off leash.

From the town rotary on State Route 12A (Main Street), take Washington Street north for 2.25 miles. Turn right onto Concord Street at the fork in the road. Take an immediate left onto the Washington Street Extension. Park at the end of the road by the gate. Open dawn to dusk. (603) 352-0133.

• Goose Pond Preserve 🐾🐾🐾🐾 🐕 See **34** on page 452.

This is one of the best parks we've visited, and we feel certain you and your dog will enjoy it, too. With 500 acres and scenic Goose Pond at its center, there is plenty here for a dog to love. Originally Goose Pond was created in 1868 as a water supply for Keene. Fortunately, the plan never materialized, and in the 1980s this beautiful preserve was designated as a nature park.

Many trails lead through the gorgeous woods to the pond, but the most easily accessible ones are from the main parking area off East Surry Road. A trail map is posted on the kiosk here, and the trails are well marked and easy to follow.

You'll love the wide, flat paths and will meet many other happy dogs along the trail. In fact, the only thing wrong with this park is that there are too few parking spots. Even during the week, the small parking area is full, and parking along East Surry Road is scarce. Even paradise has its imperfections. A small price to pay for a leash-free romp in the woods! Dogs must be under voice control.

From State Route 9 and 10 (Franklin Pierce Highway), take State Route 12A north for one mile. Turn right onto East Surry Road for a half mile to a small parking area on your right. Open dawn to dusk. (603) 352-0133.

•Otter Brook Lake 🐾🐾🐾 See **35** on page 452.
Another fine example of a U.S. Army Corps of Engineers Project park, this dam project is a good news/bad news story. The good news is that with 458 acres, there are many trails that lead in and among the woods for you and your dog to explore. The bad news is that the trails aren't marked, and your dog is not allowed at the main recreation area along the lake. You have to use the dam entrance off State Route 9.

The woods are lovely here, but, unless you know the area or are an experienced hiker, be careful not to stray too far from the beaten path. A walk on the dam, however, provides a panoramic view for those who aren't afraid of heights. Dogs must be on leash.

From State Route 12A, take State Routes 9 and 10 (Franklin Pierce Highway) east for two miles. Turn right on Sullivan Road to the dam. Gates are open 8 A.M. to 3 P.M. (603) 352-4130.

•Robin Hood Forest 🐾🐾🐾 🐕 See **36** on page 452.
Although we can't imagine Robin Hood hiding his Merry Men in this beautiful 130-acre woodland park, they probably would have loved to if given the chance! Given to the city of Keene in 1889 by George Wheelock, Keene's first park commissioner, this park is a delight. Woodland trails stretch back through the pine woods along the small reservoir and plentiful picnic areas are near the water. You need to keep your dog leashed around the recreation pool and picnic spots, but he is free to romp leash free in the woods.

Trail maps are available at City Hall for $.50, but you shouldn't have any trouble following the well-marked trails without a map. Dogs must be under voice control.

From the center rotary on Main Street (State Route 12A), take Roxbury Street east for a half mile. Turn left onto Dam Street and into the park. Open 6 A.M. to 10 P.M. (603) 352-2447.

•Wheelock Park 🐾🐾 🐕 See **37** on page 452.
Mainly a recreation area, some woodlands that surround the park offer a place to walk the dog. Also, the bike trail through the camping area in back connects you to Ashuelot River Park so you can access both parks from here. Dogs must be under voice control.

From State Routes 9, 10, and 12 (Monadnock Highway), take West Street for a half mile west. Turn right onto Park Street for a quarter mile. The park entrance is on your right. Open 6 A.M. to 10 P.M. (603) 357-9829.

RESTAURANTS

Brewbakers: This cozy café has the best smoothies around. Located right in the heart of town, you'll dine on healthy sandwiches, espresso, and café cuisine. Dine at the tables outside on Main Street. 97 Main Street; (603) 355-4844.

Kristin's Bakery Café: This cheerful little café offers salads, soups, and great bakery items at outdoor seating in the Colony Marketplace. George likes the banana muffins. 222 West Street; (603) 352-5700.

Stage Restaurant & Deli: Be your own star at this cozy deli/restaurant located on the town common. Plenty of shaded seats are available outside where your dog can join you for a meal. 30 Central Square; (603) 357-8389.

PLACES TO STAY

Best Western Sovereign Hotel: The only full-service hotel in Keene, the Best Western Sovereign features a restaurant and lounge along with free breakfast and an indoor pool. Each of the 131 rooms is spacious and includes all the amenities. Pets are made to feel very welcome. Rooms range from $90 to $170. 401 Winchester Street, Keene, NH 03431; (603) 357-3038, (800) 533-6364; www.bestwestern.com.

Days Inn: Pets are welcome at this 80-room motel. Complimentary continental breakfast is served in the lobby, and the rooms are clean and comfortable. Call ahead for reservations and be sure to mention your pet. Small pets are preferred. Rooms range from $75 to $90 per night. 175 Key Road, Keene, NH 03431; (603) 352-7616, (800) 325-2525; www.daysinn.com.

Wheelock Park: Thirty woodland camping sites are available here. The daily fee for residents of Keene is $8.50; nonresidents pay $13.50. Pets are allowed on leash. Wheelock Park, Keene, NH 03431; (603) 357-9832.

FESTIVALS

Howlin' Halloween: You and your pet will have a howling good time at the Keene Pumpkin Festival. From 10 A.M. to 10 P.M. on October 30, Main Street glows with originally carved jack-o'-lanterns. We always have a good time at this bring-out-the-town festival, even when George gets freaked out by the ghoulish heads or Inu tries to eat one. (603) 358-5344.

DIVERSIONS

Starry, starry night. . . : Bring your dog, a lawn chair, and a picnic dinner to Central Square for the Summer Concert Series every Wednesday night from 6 to 7:30 P.M. from July through August. For a schedule and information, call (603) 357-9829.

LEBANON

PARKS, BEACHES, AND RECREATION AREAS

•**Colburn Park** 🐾 See **38** on page 452.

Located in the center of town, this village common won't offer your dog much more than a quick walk and sniff around a grassy acre. But if you need a clean, green spot for Spot, this park will suffice. Dogs must be leashed.

The park is between Mascoma, Bank, and Parkhurst Streets. Open 8 A.M. to 11 P.M. (603) 448-5121.

• **Lebanon Picnic Area** 🐾 🐾 See **39** on page 452.

This roadside picnic area has a lovely view of the Connecticut River. A few unmarked trails lead up into the woods, but mostly you will enjoy this park as a lunch stop on your way elsewhere. There is water access, but the river can be deceptively swift, so watch your dog carefully. Dogs must be on leash.

From Interstate 89, take Exit 19 to State Routes 4 and 10 north for three miles. Keep on State Route 10 as it branches to the right (from U.S. Route 4), and the picnic area will be a mile ahead on your right. Open dawn to dusk. (603) 448-5121.

RESTAURANTS

Lebanon Health Food Store: This cheerful health-food store and café will pack you a great lunch to take on the road. Outside tables are available if you're worried about your sprouts wilting. For a break from the usual fish-and-chips and burgers, the dogs suggest you try a tuna sandwich on sprouted whole wheat with soy cheese. 90 Hanover Street; (603) 448-3700.

Sweet Tomatoes Trattoria: This excellent and popular Italian restaurant overlooks the town common and offers great outdoor seating for you and your pet. There were several dogs there in addition to our dogs the night we dined, and all seemed to be enjoying spending an evening out in the warm summer air. Enjoy the summer concerts at Colburn Park while you dine (see below). 1 Court Street; (603) 448-1711.

PLACES TO STAY

Airport Economy Inn: Okay, so it's the airport, but this isn't Logan Airport so we guarantee you'll be able to sleep at night. It isn't luxurious, but it makes for a comfortable stop on your way to Vermont or the White Mountains. Dogs are welcome with prior notice. Rates range from $45 to $75 per night. Airport Road, West Lebanon, NH 03784; (603) 298-8888, (800) 845-3557.

Days Inn: This former Holiday Inn Express now allows dogs in smoking rooms only. Rooms range from $99 to $129 per night. 135 State Route 120, Lebanon, NH 03766; (603) 448-5070 (800) 325-2525; www.daysinn.com.

The Fireside Inn: Formerly a Radisson Inn, this newly renovated hotel has 125 rooms and suites, and all allow your pet. Full service and modern amenities are available in each comfortable room. A buffet breakfast is included each morning in the on-site restaurant. Rooms range from $100 to $130 per night. 25 Airport Road, West Lebanon, NH 03784; (603) 298-5900 or (800) 333-3333; www.afiresideinn.com.

MANCHESTER

PARKS, BEACHES, AND RECREATION AREAS

• **Livingston Park** 🐾 🐾 See **40** on page 452.

Livingston Park surrounds Crystal Lake, and dogs are allowed along the trails around the lake, but not on the swimming beach. There are several wooded paths and fields for ball throwing, so your dog will still get a good workout on a visit here. Dogs must be on leash.

From Interstate 93, take Exit 9 to Hooksett Road (State Route 3 and 28) south for a half mile. The park is on your right. Open 8 A.M. to 8 P.M.(603) 624-6565.

• Lake Massabesic Recreation Area 🐾🐾🐾🐾 See **41** on page 452.

With over 50 miles of access roads surrounding this beautiful lake, you won't get tired of coming here again and again. Although the lake is the source of Manchester's water supply and is thus off-limits for swimming, you can hike the many fire roads and woodland trails surrounding the lake. Dogs must be on leash.

From U.S. Route 101, take Exit 1 to State Route 28 south for a quarter mile. Go through the rotary and take your second left into the recreation area. Open 8 A.M. to 8 P.M. (603) 624-6482.

• Rock Rimmon Park 🐾🐾 See **42** on page 452.

Rock Rimmon, the biggest park in Manchester at almost 140 acres, is a traditional urban park. This means that the picnic areas, ball fields, and recreation areas are all off-limits for your dog. But because of its size, some trails also lead up the "Rock"—a sizable hill with a terrific view of the city from the top of the ledge, which is easily reached by a gentle climb up the back. The park entrance is on Mason Street. Dogs must be leashed.

From Bridge and Amory Streets at the Merrimack River, take Coolidge Street north for three blocks. Turn left onto Mason Street for five blocks into the park. Open 8 A.M. to 8 P.M. (603) 624-6565.

NATURE HIKES AND URBAN WALKS

Amoskeag River Walk: Walk along the Merrimack River through the historic mill section of Manchester. The walkway is paved for an easy half-mile stroll in either direction, and the views of the river are fabulous. You'll be joined on a warm summer's night by many locals and their dogs. Parking is available on Commercial Avenue. (603) 624-6565.

RESTAURANTS

Fratello's Ristorante Italiano: Well-behaved dogs are allowed at this popular Manchester restaurant overlooking the Merrimack River. During the summer the outdoor patio is open, and, as long as your dog won't look longingly at the lasagna on the tables nearby, she is welcome to join you in dining al fresco. We should warn you—the food is great here and it gets very busy! Reservations are recommended. 155 Dow Street; (603) 624-2022.

Psaris Bistro: This elegant Mediterranean seafood restaurant has a few outside tables where you and your pet can dine. Located on Elm Street, you can catch the street scene in the heart of Manchester and enjoy a lovely meal at the same time. No credit cards are accepted, and the liquor policy is BYOB. 915 Elm Street; (603) 645-5998.

Stage Door Café: Enjoy a continental dining selection at this café that caters to the theatre crowd. Outdoor tables are available where your own stage-struck dog can join you for a meal. 100 Hanover Street; (603) 625-0810.

PLACES TO STAY

The Center of New Hampshire Holiday Inn: Pets are welcome at this 250-room hotel in the heart of town for an additional $25 per stay. Crates are recommended but not required. Rates range from $129 to $149 per night. 700 Elm Street, Manchester, NH 03103; (603) 625-1000; www.holiday-inn.com.

Comfort Inn: Conveniently located in the center of downtown, this 100-room hotel provides all the amenities, including continental breakfast. Dogs are allowed in certain rooms only, so please make advance reservations. Rates range from $64 to $200. 298 Queen City Avenue, Manchester, NH 03102; (603) 668-2600 or (800) 228-5150; www.comfortinn.com.

Econolodge: Pets are welcome at this 100-room motel for an additional $10 per night. A steep but refundable $100 deposit is also required. Room rates range from $60 to $90. 75 East Hancock Street, Manchester, NH 03102; (603) 624-0111; www.econolodge.com.

DIVERSIONS

Hanover Happenings: Join the celebration with outdoor presentations of live theatre, music, and dance. Visit this street fair every Saturday evening throughout the summer from 6 to 8 P.M. on Hanover Street between Chestnut and Elm. (603) 624-6600.

Is there a doctor in the house?: The American Red Cross holds monthly classes featuring pet CPR. You and your dog can attend a class that just might save your pet's life one day. Elm Street; (603) 624-4307.

Wag that tail, lift those paws!: Dogs need stimulation and fun just like people, and at The All Dog's Gym, your dog will get that and much more! This activity center features doggie day care, play groups, an agility course, games, and special members-only events. Membership is $35 per year ($60 for two dogs) which gives you discounts on classes and events, a quarterly newsletter, and other perks. 801 Perimeter Road; (603) 669-4644.

MARLBOROUGH

PARKS, BEACHES, AND RECREATION AREAS

• **Meetinghouse Pond Wildlife Sanctuary** 🐾🐾🐾 See **43** on page 452.

Meetinghouse Pond is a 45-acre sanctuary basking in the shadow of Mount Monadnock which soars in the distance. One-third of the forested shoreline has been protected for over 200 years as town land. Another third is held in a family trust. Because of this protection, the pond has always been an undisturbed haven for wildlife, and you'll see plenty of creatures on a visit here. Beavers, muskrats, geese, herons, and even bear make their homes here.

Park at the boat launch and take the main trail that leads into the woods and along the eastern shoreline; a small shoreline path runs along the pond. The swimming is easily accessible here, and your water dog will love the cool, fresh water.

Or, park at the small dam a quarter mile west of the boat launch and enjoy a picnic under the shady pine trees before following the shoreline path to the main trailhead. Maps are available at the boat-launch parking area. Managed by the Audubon Society of New Hampshire, dogs must be leashed.

From State Route 101, take State Route 124 south for 2.5 miles. Turn left onto Underwood Road and continue a half mile to the boat launch and pond on your right. Open dawn to dusk. (603) 224-9909.

PLACES TO STAY

Peep Willow Farm: This 20-acre horse farm is also a cozy country inn. With three comfortable rooms, one with a fireplace, you'll find this country get-away a welcome escape from city life. Leashed dogs are welcome as long as they don't disturb the farm animals. Rooms are $60 per night. Bixby Street, Marlborough, NH 03461; (603) 876-3807.

MERRIMACK

PLACES TO STAY

Residence Inn by Marriott: You can stay at this suite-style hotel by the night or the week, but given the hefty pet charge, we think it only makes sense if you stay a week. The efficiency suites range in size from studios to two-bedroom units, and pets are welcome for $5 per night with a nonrefundable $50 cleaning charge. Suites range from $103 to $165 per night, including continental breakfast. 246 Daniel Webster Highway, Merrimack, NH 03054; (603) 424-8100.

MILFORD

PARKS, BEACHES, AND RECREATION AREAS

• Emerson Park 🐾 🐾 See **44** on page 452.

This small but lovely park in the center of town offers a few flat white-gravel paths along the Souhegan River. Your dog won't work up a sweat, but, if you're looking for a little water access and a quiet walk under the pines, you'll enjoy this spot. Dogs must be leashed.

From State Route 101A, take Main Street (State Route 13) one block north (just past the Milford Oval). The park is on your left. Open dawn to dusk. (603) 672-1067.

RESTAURANTS

Riverhouse Café: Stop by this country café in the heart of Milford for some good old-fashioned cooking. Take your food to go and walk across the street to the Milford Oval for a picnic on one of the many benches. 123 Union Square at the Milford Oval; (603) 673-9867.

PLACES TO STAY

Ram in the Thicket: A name like this can be intimidating, but nothing could be further from the truth at this friendly bed-and-breakfast. This lovely Victorian mansion has nine rooms and two suites, all with private baths. You and your dog will feel spoiled after a stay here—there are some hiking trails on the grounds and continental breakfast is served on the large wrap-around porch each morning. Rates range from $70 to $85; dogs are $10 per day. 24 Maple Street, Milford, NH 03055; (603) 654-6440.

DIVERSIONS

Reel Magic: Watch a movie the old-fashioned way at the Milford Drive-in. Open seasonally between June and August, you won't have to leave your pup behind when you catch a first-run flick at this drive-in movie theatre. They even have double features! Movies start at dusk. $15 per car. State Route 101A; (603) 673-4090.

NASHUA

PARKS, BEACHES, AND RECREATION AREAS

• **Greeley Park** 🐾 🐾 🐾 See **45** on page 452.

This large urban park stretches on both sides of Concord Street and across to Manchester Street on Nashua's north end. Although the eastern side is mainly made up of ball fields and recreation areas where your dog can't go, the west side has an extensive wooded area where you can walk on the spongy pine needles and feel like you're miles away from the city. There's a big open field for ball throwing, too. Dogs must be leashed.

From Lowell Street (State Route 101A) downtown, take Concord Street north for 1.5 miles into the park on your left. Parking is available along the access road. Open 6 A.M. to 10 P.M. (603) 594-3346.

• **Mine Falls Park** 🐾 🐾 🐾 🐾 See **46** on page 452.

This is the place to go for local dog owners. Located in the very heart of the city, this park boasts over 325 acres of land along the recently rescued Nashua River. Always busy, you'll find hikers, joggers, and dogs enjoying the natural world in this beautiful city park. Your biggest problem may be finding a parking spot.

Several walking trails loop through the park between the river and an old canal, which used to power Nashua's mills. You'll find a surprising array of wildlife, especially birds, and an old mill pond, gatehouse, and dam. Managed by the Nashua Conservation Commission, dogs must be on leash.

From U.S. Route 3, take Exit 5 to West Hollis Street (State Route 111) east for less than a quarter mile. Turn left onto Simon Street for two blocks then left onto Whipple Street. The park and parking is at the end of street. Open 6 A.M. to 10 P.M. (603) 594-3411.

RESTAURANTS

Martha's Exchange Brewing Company: Dine along Main Street at this pub-style café. The menu includes standard pub fare of salads, burgers, meat, and seafood. 185 Main Street; (603) 883-8781.

San Francisco Kitchen: Real dogs eat quiche! Or at least they will at this excellent café. You can watch the world go by and eat California-style cuisine at the outdoor tables of this local eatery. 133 Main Street; (603) 886-8833.

PLACES TO STAY

Motel 6: All Motel 6 complexes allow one small pet per room, and dogs may not be left unattended. Please inform the management upon check-in of your pet as all rooms may not allow dogs. But they will leave the light on! Room rates are $52 to $58 per night. 2 Progress Avenue, Nashua, NH 03062; (603) 889-4151, (800) 4-MOTEL6; www.motel6.com.

Nashua Marriott: You can see this new hotel from Route 3, but once you get to it you won't feel close to the highway. There are 241 guest rooms and four suites with efficiencies. A hiking trail runs through the woods where you can take your dog for a walk. Pets are allowed on leash with advance reservations. Rates range from $79 to $159. 2200 Southwood Drive, Nashua, NH 03063; (603) 880-9100, (800) 228-9290.

Red Roof Inn: This comfortable motel surrounded by woods is just off Interstate 93. Pets are welcome with a prior reservation. Room rates are $53 to $85. 77 Spitbrook Road (State Route 3), Nashua, NH 03063; (603) 888-1893, (800) THE-ROOF.

Sheraton Nashua Hotel: This Tudor-style "castle" features luxury rooms and complete facilities. Small pets are welcome, but you must inform management of your pet when making your reservations. Rates range from $109 to $159 per night. 11 Tara Boulevard, Nashua, NH 03063; (603) 888-9970.

DIVERSIONS

Dog Walkathon: Is your dog a Canine Good Citizen? Take a test to find out at this one- to two-mile canine walk and fund-raiser for the Humane Society of New England. Featuring demonstration booths, training, games (like musical sits and hot-dog bobs), and other fun-filled activities for your pet, the annual event is usually held in May. For more information, call (603) 889-2275.

All I want for Christmas: Get your photo with Santa at this December fund-raiser sponsored by PetSmart at 213 Daniel Webster Highway. Local animal shelters provide volunteers and receive half the donations. For more information and exact date and time, call (603) 888-7599.

NEW BOSTON

PARKS, BEACHES, AND RECREATION AREAS

•**Woodland Associates Forest** 🐾🐾🐾 🐕 See **47** on page 452.

This 174-acre forest is close to the center of town and offers an enjoyable woodland walk along the southern branch of the Piscataquog River. Two trails lead into the property and are marked by gates on Old Coach Road. There are plenty of points along the way to stop and swim or picnic by the river.

Protected since 1988, this conservation land is managed by the Society for the Protection of New Hampshire Forests and, as in all their properties, dogs are allowed off leash if under voice control.

From State Route 13 in the center of town, take Old Coach Road west. You'll come to the first gate in a quarter mile; the second gate is farther down the road on the left. Open dawn to dusk. (603) 224-9945; www.spnhf.org.

NEWBURY

PARKS, BEACHES, AND RECREATION AREAS

• **The Hay Reservation at the John Hay Wildlife Refuge**
🐾🐾🐾 🐕 See **48** on page 452.

The Hay Reservation comprises 675 acres of the 1,300-acre John Hay National Wildlife Refuge, the former estate of John Hay, ambassador to Great Britain and personal secretary of Abraham Lincoln. The historic house and immediate grounds, known as "The Fells," are managed by the Friends of John Hay National Wildlife Refuge and, unfortunately, dogs are not allowed on the estate trails. Luckily, you can walk across State Route 103 and let your dog run leash free on the Hay Reservation.

The Society for the Protection of New Hampshire Forests conducts a conservation education program and manages the area designated as the Sunset Hill trails opposite The Fells. This is where you and your pup will head. Climb Sunset Hill, an easy, gentle ascent to the top of this 1,841-foot hill, for a wonderful view of Lake Sunapee and the surrounding landscape. Along the way you will follow well-marked trails through woods and glacial erratics, remnants of glacial activity in the area 12,000 years ago.

The refuge is located along one mile of undeveloped Lake Sunapee lakeshore and, although you may park on a turnout on Rollins Road, there is a large parking area at The Fells entrance off State Route 103. Dogs must be under voice control.

From Interstate 89, take Exit 12 to State Route 103A south for three miles. The reservation is on your left; parking is on your right. Open dawn to dusk. (603) 224-9945.

• **Mount Sunapee State Park** 🐾🐾🐾 See **49** on page 452.

This 2,893-acre park at the northern end of Lake Sunapee is best known for downhill skiing in winter and fishing in summer. But you can hike to the 2,743-foot summit for spectacular views of the surrounding mountains, lakes, and valleys.

Dogs are not allowed on the beach at Lake Sunapee, but one of the most popular trails is the two-mile Lake Solitude Trail which leads to a beautiful lake on the eastern side of Mount Sunapee. You and your dog will be rewarded with views and a welcomed swim in this mountain lake. The trail starts just past the concession stand in the main parking area. Follow the "All Trails" sign and take the Lake Solitude Trail marked by yellow blazes. Dogs must be on leash in all state parks. There is an admission fee of $2.50.

From Interstate 89, take Exit 9 to State Route 103 north. Go 13 miles to the entrance road on your left. Open 8 A.M. to 8 P.M. (603) 763-5561.

RESTAURANTS

Murphy's Grille: Located right next to the Best Western Lodge, this local watering hole has plenty of patio tables where you and your dog may dine. Delicious and hearty breakfasts or dinners featuring ribs, seafood, or Mexican dishes make choosing what to eat the hardest part. State Route 103; (603) 763-3113.

PLACES TO STAY

Best Western Sunapee Lake Lodge: This clean, friendly inn, built in 1995, has 55 rooms and suites (with kitchenettes) and is close to the Mt. Sunapee ski area and Lake Sunapee. Dogs are welcome with advance reservations. Rates range from $89 to $159. 1403 State Route 103, Mount Sunapee, NH 03255; (603) 763-2010, (800) 606-5253; www.sunapeelodge.com.

NEWPORT

NATURE HIKES AND URBAN WALKS:

Sugar River Covered Bridge Trail: For one of the most unusual trails in this book, walk along the Sugar River on an old carriage road that has been turned into a terrific hiking trail. Besides a beautiful walk on a flat, open floodplain along the river, you'll travel over two covered bridges, the Pier Bridge and Wright's Bridge, which are no longer accessible by car.

These historic monuments offer a unique look back to a quieter time, and you and your unleashed dog will love experiencing the New Hampshire of 100 years ago. Built in the 1850s, these old bridges have stood the test of time and nature. As a special bonus, the river access along the way is excellent; your dog will certainly enjoy the swim as much as you'll enjoy the bridges.

From the trailhead, it is 1.5 miles to the Pier Bridge; it is another half mile along the road to the Wright's Bridge trail.

The parking area is on the northern side of State Routes 11 and 103 just west of the Sugar River and Sugar River Drive. The trail runs under the road to the south. (603) 863-1510.

PLACES TO STAY

Northstar Campground: This comfortable 60-site family campground is open seasonally from mid-May to mid-October. And here the whole family can enjoy the fun since leashed dogs are allowed. Swimming, fishing, hiking, and full bathroom facilities are available in a quiet, safe environment. Rates are $20 to $30 per day depending on the size of your party. 43 Coon Brook Road, Newport, NH 03773; (603) 863-4001; www.northstarcampground.com.

DIVERSIONS

Farmer's Market: Every Friday from 3 to 6 P.M. join the festivities at the Newport Farmer's Market. Fresh produce, crafts, and homemade goodies are on display. You and your dog will enjoy the hustle and bustle of this weekly summer event held on the Newport Common. (603) 863-1510.

Newport Concerts on the Common: Every Sunday between the end of June and the end of August, the Newport Opera Association sponsors a concert on the Common, located at the Newport Rotary. Bring a picnic, a blanket, and join the fun from 6 to 8 P.M. (603) 863-1510.

ORANGE

PARKS, BEACHES, AND RECREATION AREAS

• **Mount Cardigan State Park** 🐾🐾🐾 See **50** on page 452.

This 5,000-acre state park includes most of Mount Cardigan, a 3,100-foot summit. Mount Cardigan is the highest peak in southern New Hampshire and offers some of the best views in the area from the steep-domed "Old Baldy" on top. Left bare by a fire in 1855, this flat and open granite outcropping makes a great place to picnic or contemplate with unobstructed views in all directions.

The best and easiest trail to the summit is the West Ridge Trail. Follow the orange blazes for 1.5 miles from the parking area over brooks, bridges, and to the open ledges at the top. The Holt Trail on the eastern side is a little more difficult and, unless your pup is part mountain goat, this may not be the best choice for your dog. Don't miss the delightful picnic area with beautiful pine trees and great rock formations on the western slope of the mountain. Dogs must be on leash.

From U.S. Route 4 in Caanan, take State Route 118 north for less than a half mile. Turn right onto Orange Road for four miles into Orange, following signs to the park entrance. There is a $2.50 admission fee. Open 8 A.M. to 8 P.M. from mid-May until mid-October. (603) 271-3254.

PETERBOROUGH

Don't let the sleepy Main Street fool you. The inspiration for Thornton Wilder's classic *Our Town,* this lovely New England town is as sophisticated as it is scenic. Home to the famed MacDowell Colony, a well-known artist and musician's retreat, Peterborough has been attracting creative folk to its boundaries for over a hundred years. Walk through the quaint streets and breathe in the rarified air.

PARKS, BEACHES, AND RECREATION AREAS

• **Edward MacDowell Lake Project** 🐾🐾🐾 See **51** on page 452.

Located on over 1,000 acres of land, this man-made lake is named after the composer Edward MacDowell, who also established the MacDowell Colony. The park features a trail which begins at the main parking area and loops around the lower branch of the lake. Along the way you'll walk beside the water's edge, through a beautiful pine forest which will shade you on hot summer days. The peace and quiet will only be interrupted by the sound of the water birds and your leashed dog panting at your side. This property is maintained by the U.S. Army Corps of Engineers.

From State Route 101 in West Peterborough, take Union Street northeast for two miles. Turn left onto Windy Row for two miles then left onto Spring Road for one mile, where you'll turn left into the main entrance. Parking is available. Open 7 A.M. to 3:30 P.M. (603) 924-3431.

• **Miller State Park** 🐾🐾🐾 See **52** on page 452.

Established in 1891, this scenic state park is New Hampshire's oldest, and, as you drive up to the entrance, you will feel as if you've stepped back in time. The facilities are modernized but the wooden structures and the old forest hearkens back to another era.

The main attraction in this quiet state park is the hike to the summit of Pack Monadnock with views that extend as far as Boston. The trail to the summit is well marked, and maps are available at the park entrance to guide you on your way. Most of the trail follows the Wapack Trail, which you can also access off State Route 101 just east of the park entrance; you'll see the granite marker.

There is a day-use fee of $2.50 per adult. Dogs are allowed on leash.

From U.S. Route 202, take State Route 101 east for 5.5 miles. The park is on the left just before the Temple Mountain Ski Area. Open April to November from 8 A.M. to 8 P.M. (603) 924-3672.

• Shieling State Forest 🐾🐾🐾 See **53** on page 452.

For a fairly small park, this 45-acre forest has over two miles of well-designed hiking trails. Named for the Scottish word meaning "shelter," this forest was once the sheltering home of Elizabeth Yates McGreal who donated her land to the state in 1980. You can hike through an old-growth forest and a wildflower garden, plus pass over Dunbar Brook and through giant glacial boulders.

The main trail, the Boulder Trail, takes you on a loop through the entire acreage. Dogs must be leashed on all state land.

From the intersection of U.S. Route 202 and State Routes 123 and 136, take Old Street Road south for a half mile. The entrance is well marked on your right. Open dawn to dusk. (603) 271-3457.

RESTAURANTS

Nonie's Restaurant and Bakery: For takeout, bakery items, or a great breakfast or lunch outside, head for Nonie's. Located right in the heart of Peterborough, they are famous for their fantastic breakfasts, but the sandwiches from the deli are pretty doggone great, too. 28 Grove Street; (603) 924-3451.

Peterborough Diner: This old-fashioned diner at Depot Square has outdoor picnic tables where you and your dog can your takeout meal. It features standard diner fare, but there's nothing standard about the taste. 10 Depot Square; (603) 924-3346.

Twelve Pines: This gourmet market and eatery has carry-out cuisine (a cut above "to go") or a café menu if you wish to dine on the tables on the veranda. Try one of their many fabulous sandwiches for a real treat. 11 School Street at Depot Square; (603) 924-6140.

RINDGE

• Annett State Park 🐾🐾 See **54** on page 452.

Stop at this state park and either picnic at the Wayside Park along Cathedral Road or explore the many trails that lead from the main entrance. Although there are 1,336 acres of woodland and a myriad of trails, there isn't a ranger station or map display at this park, so it may be a bit hard to know where you're heading. But if you're looking for easy woodland hiking, you can't go too far wrong here.

From the main picnic area, you can take a trail on the right of the main entrance road which will eventually lead to Hubbard Pond a mile to the south. For more direct access to the pond, take the dirt road to your left just south of the entrance on Cathedral Road. This leads directly to the pond, where your dog can take a swim. We have to warn you, however, that the surrounding area was a bit muddy and trashy, and there were swarms of bees everywhere the day we visited. It definitely took the buzz out of the place, if you know what we mean! Dogs must be on leash.

From State Route 202, take State Route 119 east for 1.5 miles. Turn left onto Cathedral Road for two miles. The park entrance is on your right. Open dawn to dusk. (603) 532-8862.

• **Betsy Fosket Sanctuary** 🐾🐾🐾 See **55** on page 452.
This wildlife sanctuary, managed by the Audubon Society of New Hampshire, is 35 acres of densely wooded land on the shores of Crowcroft Pond. Trails lead along the eastern shore of the pond and then back along an old woods road. The pond is fairly marshy, so this isn't a great swimming pond, but your dog can dip his feet into the brook that meanders through the property. To reach better water access, take the Pond View Trail, a short path that leads to the water. Dogs must be on leash.

From State Route 202, take State Route 119 east for 1.5 miles. Turn left onto Cathedral Road for a half mile then right into Cathedral Estates for a quarter mile. Make a right at Emerson Lane to the end. Park in the cul-de-sac. Open sunrise to sunset. (603) 224-9909.

RESTAURANTS

Marshall's Kitchen: This restaurant doesn't look like much. It's in a grocery store behind the BP gas station. But looks can be deceiving. They're open for breakfast, lunch, and dinner, the food is great, and they have a covered deck where you and your dog can dine. Full seafood, pasta, and chicken dinners are served, as well as hot and cold sandwiches and full breakfasts. Try the surf and turf with a sour cream and chives baked potato. On State Route 119 and Cathedral Road; (603) 899-6333.

PLACES TO STAY

Woodbound Inn: This charming inn and lakefront cabin resort is located on 200 acres along Lake Contoocook. All the rustic cabins have kitchens and fireplaces. An extensive trail system is right outside your door for hiking, biking, or cross-country skiing; they even have a private beach on the lake for guests only. Dogs are welcome in the cabins only. 62 Woodbound Road, Rindge, NH 03461; (603) 688-7770 or (800) 688-7770; www.woodbound.com.

SHARON

PARKS, BEACHES, AND RECREATION AREAS

• **Lincoln Davis, Morse, and Cabot Memorial Forests** 🐾🐾🐾 🐕
See **56** on page 452.
These three connected forests jointly offer over 966 acres for you and your dog

to explore. Trails connect from one property to the next covering two towns, although the main access is in Sharon. The Lincoln Davis property was the first parcel given to the New England Forestry Foundation in 1945, and the other two properties were added in 1964 and 1995, respectively.

Much of the Monadnock region, including these three forests, was devastated by the hurricane of 1938. Old-timers speak of this force of nature in a kind of hushed, "where were you when" tone. Today, the forests clearly show how resilient nature can be, as it is hard to imagine the devastation that swept through this area. The forests of 60-year-old trees house abundant wildlife, and you'll find the trails easy to follow. Stone walls mark old farmland boundaries, and an old blueberry pasture along the brook is just a short walk from the main parking area.

Maps are available from the New England Forestry Foundation. Dogs are allowed off leash if under voice control.

From State Route 123 in the center of town, take Mountain Road east for a half mile to the forests. Open dawn to dusk. (603) 588-2638; www.neforestry.org.

•Wales Preserve 🐾🐾🐾 🐕 See **57** on page 452.
Just south of Peterborough, these 48 acres are located on a plateau of rolling, wooded, hilly uplands that rise almost 1,200 feet above sea level. Through the center of the preserve flows the Gridley River, where you and your dog can cool off or listen to the gentle murmuring as it passes by. Dogs are allowed off leash.

From State Route 202 in Peterborough, take Sharon Road south for three miles. Turn right onto Spring Hill Road for a half mile. The preserve is on the right. Open dawn to dusk. (603) 224-9909.

SPRINGFIELD
PARKS, BEACHES, AND RECREATION AREAS

•Gardner Memorial Wayside Area—Gile State Forest 🐾🐾 See **58** on page 452.
Meet a friend here for a private picnic alongside a classic babbling brook. You'll see the remnants of the 18th-century mill, and, if the weather is warm, you and your dog might want to take a quick swim in the cool water.

For a longer hike, Giles State Forest is right next door. Take the trail that begins in the forest over the footbridge. From here it's a short half-mile walk to the Butterfield Pond. Unless you want your dog covered in pond scum, however, keep him from the swamp to your right. Dogs must be on leash.

From U.S. Route 4 in Andover, take State Route 4A west for eight miles. The park is on your right. Open dawn to dusk. (603) 271-3254.

STODDARD
PARKS, BEACHES, AND RECREATION AREAS

•Pierce Wildlife and Forest Reservation 🐾🐾🐾 🐕 See **59** on page 452.
This vast 3,500 acres, managed by the Society for the Protection of New Hamp-

shire Forests, wins the award for best trail name: the Trout-N-Bacon Trail (covering the distance between Trout Pond and Bacon Ledge, naturally!). The whole hike is just over four miles, but you'll be rewarded with a great view from Bacon Ledge and the lovely solitude of Trout Pond. Our dogs love swimming at the pond, but, for a shorter walk, follow the one-mile trail to Bacon Ledge and skip the rest. Dogs are allowed off leash if under voice control.

From State Route 9, take State Route 123 north almost two miles to Mill Village. Turn right on the bridge over Island Pond and then make an immediate left onto Shedd Hill Road for a half mile up a hill. At the top, park on the right at the SPNHF sign. Open dawn to dusk. (603) 224-9945.

SULLIVAN

PARKS, BEACHES, AND RECREATION AREAS

• **Piper Memorial Forest** 😊 😊 🐕 See **60** on page 452.
This 199-acre park was donated in 1993 in memory of Allison Nims Piper and occupies what was once farming land. Now the forest is reclaiming the site, and it is home to many small and even large mammals—including moose. The trail, once an old logging road, will lead you on a one-mile loop to the top of Boynton Mountain—the highest point in Sullivan at 1,761 feet. For maps and more information, call the Society for the Protection of New Hampshire Forests (see below). Dogs are allowed off leash if under voice control

From State Route 9, take State Route 10 north for six miles. Turn ight onto Gilsum Road for one mile. The forest is located on your right at Gilsum Road and Church Street. Open dawn to dusk. (603) 224-9945.

SUNAPEE

PARKS, BEACHES, AND RECREATION AREAS

• **Mount Sunapee State Park (See Newbury)**

PLACES TO STAY

Burkehaven Resort Motel: This comfortable motel offers 10 efficiency units with lake views. Rates range from $69 to $89 per night. 179 Burkehaven Hill Road, Sunapee, NH 03782; (603) 763-2788, (800) 567-2788.

Dexter's Inn and Tennis Club: This lovely inn has 17 guest rooms and a small cottage on what was once a private summer estate. The grounds are beautiful, and you can take your leashed dog for a walk on the gorgeous lawn or the woods around the property. Dogs are welcome in the cottage or annex for an additional $10 per night. Rooms range from $105 to $185. 258 Stagecoach Road, Box 703NH, Sunapee, NH 03782; (603) 763-5571, (800) 232-5571.

The Seven Hearths Inn: This charming 10-room bed-and-breakfast inn dates back to 1801. You won't be "ruffing" it here; the inn has all the modern amenities. Dogs are welcome in several rooms with prior approval, so be sure to make your reservation in advance. A full breakfast is served each morning. Rooms range from $120 to $150 plus an additional $5 fee for your pup. 26 Seven Hearths Lane, Sunapee, NH 03782; (603) 763-5657 or (800) 237-2464.

DIVERSIONS

Anchors a' weigh: Take a two hour cruise around beautiful Lake Sunapee on the MV *Sunapee* which circles the lake during the summer months. Leashed dogs are allowed on the general cruise, but not on the dining cruise. Admission is $12 per person. (603) 763-4030.

SURRY

PARKS, BEACHES, AND RECREATION AREAS

• **Indian Arrowhead Forest Preserve** 🐾🐾🐾 🦮 See **61** on page 452.

We can't promise any arrowheads in this 282-acre preserve, but if you're looking for a nice woodland walk, this is a good place to stop. This forest has excellent trails but terrible parking. But since we think the trails are more important than the car, we guess this means your dog gets the good end of the deal.

Located off State Route 12, you'll have to keep an eye out, or you'll drive right by. But once there, a wide, flat pine-covered trail leads back into a dense, quiet woodland. The main trail leads in a loop for a hike of two miles. Dogs may be leashless if under voice control. This property is managed by the Society for the Protection of New Hampshire Forests.

From State Routes 9/10, take State Route 12 north for four miles. Look for the sign on the right, across from a red wooden building. Park along the road. Open dawn to dusk. (603) 224-9945; www.spnhf.org.

• **Surry Mountain Lake Project** 🐾🐾🐾 🦮 See **62** on page 452.

Surry Lake takes up most of the 1,625 acres here, but, for a nifty little hike, take the Beaver Lodge Trail which leads to. . . what else? An active beaver pond with its own small dam to mimic the larger dam that creates Surrey Lake.

The trail starts beyond the picnic area in the southwest corner of the first parking area before you get to the main swimming beach (where dogs can't go during the summer months). It leads into an old grove of white pines and crosses back over the entrance road before leading down a ravine trail and across a footbridge to the pond. If you're quiet, you might see the beavers working, although the sounds of the busy beach are never far away. The hike is only a half-mile long, but it's enough to enjoy this beautiful area.

If you park off Dam Road, there are countless trails beyond the dam on the mountain ridges. None of the trails are marked, so you're on your own here, but the locals tell us that most lead to Lily Pond, a mountain lake nestled in the pocket of two mountains, 750 feet high with a depth of 80 feet in some places. We never found it, but maybe you will. Dogs are allowed off leash on the dam trails.

From State Routes 9/10, take State Route 12A north for four miles. The entrance is on your right. To reach the dam (where you can go in the summer), turn off Dam Road a mile south of the main entrance. The parking area and gate are straight ahead. The recreation area is open 8 A.M. to 5 P.M.; the dam gate is open 8 A.M. to 3 P.M. (603) 352-2447.

TEMPLE

PLACES TO STAY

The Auk's Nest: This charming 1770s cottage offers two guest rooms and a suite overlooking orchards and gardens. Located two miles outside of the town center, you can hike on the property or neighboring Heald Tract (see Wilton) which abuts the inn. A full breakfast is included each morning. Rooms are $65 per night. Your pet is an additional $5 per night. East Road, RD #1, Temple, NY 03084; (603) 878-3443.

TROY

PARKS, BEACHES, AND RECREATION AREAS

• Gap Mountain Reservation 🐾🐾🐾 🐕 See **63** on page 452.
You'll think you're an extra in the *Last of the Mohicans* when you wander the beautiful woods in this forest. Trails lead through and over stone walls—19th-century property boundaries being reclaimed by the forest—and the sun peeks through the dense woods of pine, maple, and cedar. Views of Mount Monadnock are evident at certain clearings, and the whole woodland experience is one of solitude and enjoyment.

Our dogs love visiting this reservation and compete to see who can run up and down the hills the fastest. Most of the property is in the town of Jaffrey, but the entrance is in Troy. Managed by the Society for the Protection of New Hampshire Forests, dogs may be off leash here.

From State Route 119 in Fitzwilliam, take State Route 12 north for four miles into Troy. Turn right onto Quarry Road for a mile to where the road makes a direct left turn. There is an old woods road that leads uphill, but no sign. Park here and walk up the hill for a quarter mile. Near the top of the hill, trail markers bear left through the woods and over a stone wall into the reservation. Open dawn to dusk. (603) 224-9945; www.spnhf.org.

RESTAURANTS

Gap Mountain Breads: The little town of Troy doesn't have many commercial establishments, but you don't need many when you have Gap Mountain Breads. Located on Central Square, the bakery serves pizza, pastries, and sandwiches—all on the best homemade bread you've ever tasted. Outdoor tables are available, or you can order a picnic basket to go. 31 Central Square; (603) 242-3284.

PLACES TO STAY

The Inn at East Hill Farm: Yes, this is a real farm where you can relax in the shadow of Mount Monadnock or roll up your sleeves and milk the cow while your dog rounds up the sheep. (Okay, just kidding about that last part!) This fabulous complex of cottages and inn rooms is a place the whole family will love—and that includes all four-footed members. All meals and activities are included in the daily or weekly rates. Hiking trails, boat rentals, children's activities, night hikes, and shady picnic spots where you can relax or swim are all waiting for you here. Dogs are allowed in the upper-floor inn rooms and many of the cottages.

Rates range from $74 daily per person to $518 weekly per person. Dogs are an additional $10 per day and must be leashed on the property. Monadnock Street, Troy, NH 03465; (603) 242-6495, (800) 242-6495; www.east-hill-farm.com.

WALPOLE

PARKS, BEACHES, AND RECREATION AREAS

• Mill Pond Trail Conservation Area 🐾🐾🐾 🐕 See 64 on page 452.

This generous parcel of land, donated to the city in 1977, follows a path along Mill Pond and through the surrounding woods. George and Inu love this trail for it gives them a chance to navigate their way along a hillside path with plenty of spots to jump into the water along the way. The pond is also a quiet place to watch wildlife. On our last visit we watched a weasel jump from rock to rock across the pond until he disappeared into the woods beyond.

Just past Mill Pond you'll reach a beaver dam; a quarter mile from there is a beaver causeway that you can walk across to reach the woods on the other side of the conservation area and a series of woodland trails. The trail will lead you back in a loop to the parking area for a little over a mile walk.

The park is managed by the Walpole Conservation Commission. Dogs may be off leash if under voice control.

From State Route 123, take State Route 12 south for two miles. Turn left onto South Street for a half mile then left onto Hubbard Street/Main Street for a mile. Turn right onto Bellows Falls Road for a half mile. The park and a small parking area will be on your right. Open dawn to dusk. (603) 756-3514.

• Warner Forest 🐾🐾🐾🐾 🐕 🐟 See 65 on page 452.

This hilly park leads you up over open fields and woods that offer fabulous views of Grand Monadnock and the Connecticut River Valley. From the parking area, follow a woodland trail a quarter mile where a left fork turns into the High Blue Trail owned by the Society for the Preservation of New Hampshire Forests. You'll enter a large hayfield which opens up onto glorious views of the valley below. Stay awhile enjoying the scenic splendor while your pup romps in the open field or chases a ball.

If you backtrack to the Society's sign, you might also wish to hike up the right fork which leads to another meadow and pond. The view here is equally great, extending out over the Connecticut River Valley, making this a good place to stop and have a picnic or let your dog refresh himself.

From State Route 12A in Keene, take Walpole Road north for six miles through Surry into Walpole and Old Wilbur Road. Turn right (a mile into town) onto Crehore Road for a quarter mile to a T intersection. Take a left at the T for a quarter mile then right onto Scovill Road, a dirt road, for a half mile to a junction with another unmarked road. In muddy season, park here and walk a quarter mile to the sign and trail. Open dawn to dusk. (603) 224-9945.

PLACES TO STAY

Alyson's Orchard Conference Center and Lodge: Located on a real, working 500-acre orchard, you can go fruit picking here and stay the night! The new conference center provides a unique experience: you get to observe a working farm up close and luxuriate in the simplicity of country living without the work. While you're there, you can hike the grounds or go fruit picking on your own. Well-behaved pets are welcome. P.O. Box 534. Wentworth Road, Walpole, NH 03608; (603) 759-9090 or (800) 856-0549; www.alysonsorchard.com.

WARNER

PARKS, BEACHES, AND RECREATION AREAS

• **Mount Kearsarge State Forest—Rollins State Park** 🐾🐾🐾 See **66** on page 452.

Mount Kearsarge State Forest encompasses two smaller state parks within its borders: Winslow State Park (see Wilmot) and Rollins State Park. The main attraction is Mount Kearsarge itself, a 2,930-foot peak with great views from its summit. The two trails leading from the south are both the shortest and the longest way to the summit.

The shortest hike to the top is on the Warner Trail, accessible via a carriage road at the gated parking area (open only during the summer months), only a half mile from the summit.

The Lincoln Trail, a much longer but more satisfying hiking experience, takes you along 4.5 miles of meadows, woods, and fabulous views all along the way to the summit. This trailhead can be reached from the entrance to Rollins State Park via Black Mountain. Since this route is much less traveled than the other paths to the summit, you can easily spend a day picnicking and hiking in relative solitude.

To cut your hike in half, you may wish to go to Black's Ledge, halfway to the summit, which also offers outstanding views to the south. Dogs must be on leash. There is a $4 admission fee in the summer months.

From Interstate 89, take Exit 9 to State Route 103 north. Go five miles to Kearsarge Gore Road. Follow signs to the park entrance. Open dawn to dusk. (603) 456-3808.

WASHINGTON

PARKS, BEACHES, AND RECREATION AREAS

• **Pillsbury State Park** 🐾🐾🐾 See **67** on page 452.

With more than 8,000 acres, this is a gem of a park with very few visitors. You'll find countless trails to explore, and, although we don't want to ruin a good thing by telling everyone about it, you're sure to find enough wide-open spaces here to tire out the most energetic pooch.

Our favorite trail is the two-mile Mad Road Trail which runs between May Pond and Mill Pond on its way to Bacon Pond. Canoes are available to rent if you wish to explore May Pond with your dog. Dogs must be on leash.

From State Route 10 in Goshen, take State Route 31 southeast for four miles into Washington. The park entrance will be on your left. Open dawn to dusk. (603) 863-2860.

PLACES TO STAY

Happy Days Campground: This 50-site full-service campground is located near Highland Lake. Open all year-round, the rates are $15 to $20 per night. 928 Valley Road, Washington, NH 03280; (603) 495-0150 or (888) 293-4556; www.campingnh.com.

WEARE

PARKS, BEACHES, AND RECREATION AREAS

• Everett Lake Dam 🐾🐾🐾 See **68** on page 452.

Just across the lake from Clough State Park (where dogs can't go) is Everett Dam and a wide-open dirt road that leads to a point jutting into the lake. While all those sunbathers are enjoying the lake on a busy beach in the state park, you can enjoy this quieter area with your dog.

Park your car at the parking area through the gate and walk across the dam. A road leads just past the dam into the woods and along the lake. It is a 1.5-mile hike to the point. Dogs must be on leash.

From State Route 114 in the village of Riverdale, take River Road north for three miles and turn right onto Clough Park Road. Go two miles to the dam, just past sign for Clough State Park. Open 7 A.M. to 3:30 P.M. (603) 228-2784.

DIVERSIONS

Strut Your Stuff: At the annual Mutt Strut, southern New Hampshire dogs come from miles around for the social event of the year. The one-mile, wooded walk takes place the third Saturday in September at the Center Woods School on State Route 114. The event also includes search-and-rescue teams and working dog demonstrations. Join the egg race or cake walk and compete against other dog/owner teams. All walkers are asked to give a donation or to raise funds through sponsorship. For more information, contact Weare Animal Guardians at (603) 529-5443.

WEBSTER

PARKS, BEACHES, AND RECREATION AREAS

• Blackwater Dam Project 🐾🐾🐾 See **69** on page 452.

Located on 3,600 acres of land, this pristine wilderness on the Blackwater River will be a treat for you and your dog. There are eight miles of hiking trails—the best one leads from the parking area and runs along the western section of lake. Along the way you'll view rapids, wildlife, and many scenic spots to have a picnic along the river. Dogs must be on leash.

From Interstate 89, take Exit 6 and follow State Routes 103/127 north for 12 miles. Turn left onto Warner Road and into the park. Open from 7 A.M. to 3:30 P.M. (603) 934-2116.

WESTMORELAND

PARKS, BEACHES, AND RECREATION AREAS

•Warwick Preserve 🐾🐾🐾 🐕 See **70** on page 452.

This beautiful woodland, owned by the Nature Conservancy, is located on 63 acres of land on Parrot Ridge. The well-maintained Brook Trail runs along the ridge and into a maple and pine forest. This off-the-beaten-track conservation area will offer you and your dog a peaceful, quiet walk. Dogs must be under voice control.

From State Route 12, take State Route 63 south for three miles. The small parking area will be on your left. The trail begins to the right of the parking area. Open dawn to dusk (603) 224-5853.

RESTAURANTS

Putter's Family Restaurant: This local roadside restaurant and ice-cream parlor offers standard seafood and burgers for lunch or dinner and ice cream for dessert. Picnic tables are available outside, and a driving range is right next door. You might even want to hit a bucket of balls while you wait for your fish-and-chips. On our visit, it was high noon and the local postman was hitting a bucket before getting back in his postal truck and, presumably, continuing his route. Neither rain nor snow can slow down the mail delivery, but I guess a driving range on a sunny day can. State Route 12; (603) 352-4431.

WILMOT

PARKS, BEACHES, AND RECREATION AREAS

•Bog Mountain Easement 🐾🐾🐾 🐕 See **71** on page 452.

There are two worthwhile trails in this conservation area and, best of all, both allow your dog off leash! Climb the Bog Mountain Trail to the top of this smallish mountain (1,787 feet), and you'll have a lovely moderate climb through untrammeled woods with excellent views to the south on the open ledges just below the summit.

The Klimpton Brook Trail runs along the brook for a lowland walk amongst wildflowers and meadows. Both trailheads begin a half mile up Stearns Hill Road from the parking area; you'll see signs for the Bog Mountain Trail on your right, and the Klimpton Trail begins on your left.

From U.S. Route 4, take State Route 4A west for four miles and turn right onto Stearns Hill Road. Go a half mile to the bridge over Klimpton Brook where you can park. Open dawn to dusk. No phone is available.

•Winslow State Park 🐾🐾🐾 See **72** on page 452.

You might be glad to know that you don't have to climb Mount Kearsarge on foot in order to get the view. Take the auto road partway up the northwest slope of Mount Kearsarge to an elevation of 1,820 feet. The road ends at a delightful picnic area with views of both the Green Mountains in Vermont and the White Mountains in New Hampshire.

For those hounds who would like a little exercise after lunch, you can continue to the top of 2,937-foot Mount Kearsarge on the mile-long trail from the picnic area. Dogs must be leashed. There is a $4 day-use fee.

From Interstate 89, take Exit 11 onto State Route 11 east. Go five miles and turn right onto Kearsarge Valley Road. Go one mile and take a left onto Kearsarge Mountain Road. Follow the signs to the park entrance. Open 9 A.M. to 8 P.M. (603) 526-6168.

WILTON

PARKS, BEACHES, AND RECREATION AREAS

• **Heald Tract** 😊😊😊 🐾 See **73** on page 452.

This 674-acre, wonderful woodland conservation area is a place that you and your dog will explore over and over. Three different trails systems lead around four small ponds and wetlands. Your dog will be muddy but happy and, best of all, she can romp leash free.

Heald Pond is a marshy home to herons and other waterfowl; Castor and Camp Ponds are lovely spots to swim and sun after you explore the unusual rock formations between the two watering holes. For the most comprehensive loop of the whole property, park off Heald Pond Road and take the Pond Trail to the Fiske Trail. Trails are marked by color. The tract is managed by the Society for the Protection of New Hampshire Forests.

From State Route 31, take King Brook Road north for one mile. Turn left onto Kimball Hill Road and make an immediate right onto Heald Road. Go half a mile; the park is on your right. The trail begins near the dam. Open dawn to dusk. (603) 224-9945; www.spnhf.org.

RESTAURANTS

The Dog House: This humble little roadside stand on State Route 101A was voted one of the "best reasons to visit New England" by *Yankee* magazine in 1998. Owned and operated for 21 years by the Egan family, we can say that it's still one of the best reasons. For a homemade hot dog that only costs a buck, you and Spot will agree this spot is the top dog. For the adventurous, try a buffalo burger. Picnic benches are all around. State Route 101A just east of the town center; no phone.

PLACES TO STAY

Stepping Stones Bed-and-Breakfast: This quiet little house and surrounding gardens will provide a haven for both dogs and owners. Up the hill from historic Wilton Center, this is a true retreat where you can take a walk in the gardens or explore the town. With three guest rooms, all with private baths, you'll feel like you're at home—only much, much better. Full breakfast is served each morning. This place is popular, so reservations are strongly suggested. Rates are $59 to $75. No credit cards are accepted. 6 Bennington Battle Trail, Wilton Center, NH 03086; (603) 654-9048.

WINCHESTER

PARKS, BEACHES, AND RECREATION AREAS

• **Pisgah State Park** 🐾 🐾 🐾 See **74** on page 452.

Pisgah State Park is New Hampshire's largest at 13,000 acres. The trail system is minimal, leading to a rather rustic hiking experience, but, if you like to be away from the crowds, this park delivers. From the parking area at the Old Winchester Road intersection, many short but scenic trails offer a wide array of hiking choices. Our favorite is the North Ponds Trail which provides access to both the Lily Pond Trail and North Pond. Both are clear, lovely ponds that are rarely visited; the trail is fairly well marked with green blazes. For a shorter hike, park up the road at the Fulham Pond gate. The pond is close to the parking area, however, and gets a few more visitors. Dogs must be leashed in all state parks.

From State Route 10 in town, take Elm Street west for a half mile; it will turn into Old Winchester Road. Go another mile following signs to Fulham Pond, and park at the Reservoir Road intersection. Gates are open 9 A.M. to 5 P.M.; trails are open dawn to dusk. (603) 239-8153.

RESTAURANTS

Ashuelot Valley Coffee and Tea Emporium: This one stop can please the whole crowd, offering coffee, sandwiches, salads, and even ice cream. This cute and funky place is located on State Route 10 right in the heart of town. Umbrella tables are available outside for you and your pooch. 13 Main Street; (603) 239-4773.

The Blue Bird Restaurant: This roadside restaurant just outside of town offers a full diner menu and a take-out ice-cream window. Covered tables are available outside. 320 Keene Road (State Route 10); (603) 239-6900.

DeMille's Café: This quaint café offers full dinner and lunch every day. The menu changes nightly, but offerings typically include an excellent choice of lamb, beef, chicken, and seafood dishes. Lunch offers a choice of salads and specialty sandwiches. There are only two small tables outside, but, since there are only eight tables inside, the ratio is about right. 30 Main Street; (603) 239-7444.

PLACES TO STAY

Crestwood Chapel and Pavilion: For a unique, one-of-a-kind weekend or event, stay at this mansion and guest cottage which only caters to one guest at a time. You can arrange a wedding, an anniversary, a grand ball, or a doggie birthday party—Crestwood will take care of it all. Best of all, you'll have the 200-acre retreat grounds to yourself. They'll even rent a horse-drawn sleigh to get you to the ski slopes in the winter. Dogs are welcome depending on the event. Rates are $225 per night plus any catering or special requests. 400 Scofield Mountain, Ashuelot, NH 03441; (603) 239-6393; www.crestwd.com.

Forest Lake Campground: This 150-site campground is located right on Forest Lake and offers full amenities plus swimming, boating, and canoe rentals. Your leashed dog is welcome here. Fees are $19 per person; reservations are required. 331 Keene Road (State Route 10), Winchester, NH 03470; (603) 239-4267.

15
WHITE MOUNTAINS

Originally home to the Native-American Penacook tribe, the White Mountains have been attracting hikers, nature lovers, and tourists to New Hampshire since the early 1800s. At the turn of the last century, a vast network of grand hotels sprang up and wealthy Americans arrived in droves for the pleasure of summering in New Hampshire. Now shopping outlets and water parks mingle with the same wilderness that Nathaniel Hawthorne and painter Thomas Cole extolled in their work. Truly one of the natural wonders on the Eastern seaboard, there are more trails, waterfalls, and mountains to climb here than we could possibly do justice to in this book.

The Great North Woods is the area beyond the White Mountains, and, although stunningly beautiful, we only touch upon this area briefly. Much of the Great North Woods can be described as wilderness. Throughout this area you'll see miles of woods interrupted by lakes, rivers, and ponds. The headwaters of the Connecticut River are near Pittsburg, and the Androscoggin River flows from Lake Umbagog near Errol. If you can, take a canoe trip from the Androscoggin out into the lake. You'll see loons and ospreys and, with a little luck, the bald eagles that nest here. But beyond that, there are few maintained trails and roads in this great northern wilderness, offering little for most dogs. The trails that do exist are used mainly by snowmobilers in the winter and hunters in the fall and spring.

Appalachian Trail: New Hampshire's portion of the Appalachian Trail extends for 170 miles through the White Mountain National Forest and is considered one of the most scenic sections of the 2,000-mile-long path.

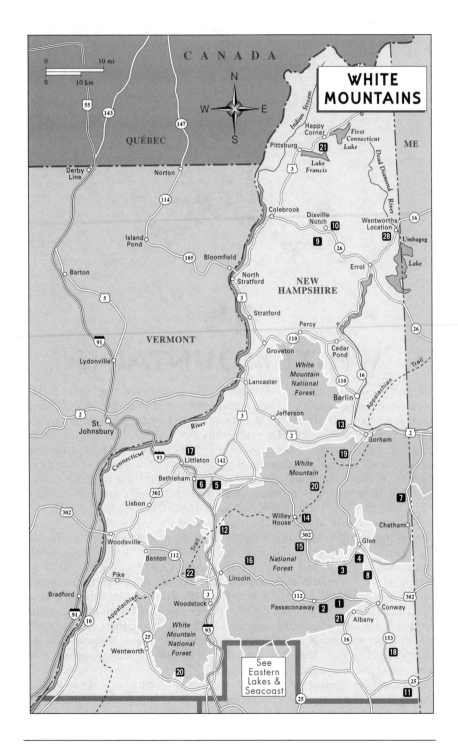

Dogs can be off leash on the trail, except in state parks. For the best maps, information, and additional suggestions on access points and day-hike possibilities, contact the Appalachian Mountain Club at Pinkham Notch State Park Visitor Center at (603) 466-2727.

White Mountain National Forest: Established in 1911 by the Weeks Act, which protected the area from the devastation wielded by overzealous lumber companies, the White Mountain National Forest (WMNF) covers over 770,000 acres in mid– and northern New Hampshire and is visited by over six million people a year.

The two scenic highways, the Franconia Notch Parkway and the Kancamagus Highway, named for the Penacook Chief Kancamagus, offer amazing scenery with countless trails for you and your dog to enjoy.

Dogs are allowed off leash on most of the trails in the White Mountains (exceptions noted) but must be under voice control at all times. Leashes are required in public day-use areas and in all state parks encompassed within the national forest.

Although we wish we could cover all the scenic trails here, it would take a book much larger than ours to do the area justice, so we encourage you to pick up trail maps and a guidebook to direct you to the many trails awaiting you in these mountains. We have highlighted special trails where we can, but please don't think they are the only paths you and your dog can roam.

Since 1997, all unattended vehicles parked on WMNF land have been required to display a parking pass. (The definition of unattended is a car that is left without an owner within eyesight. So you can stop to take a photograph but not to hike a trail.) The passes, which are $5 for a week and $20 for the year, are available from either the National Forest Ranger Stations or local area businesses (gas stations, convenience stores, etc.). Some trailheads lie just outside the park and are not subject to a fee, but, when in doubt, watch for signs posted at the parking areas notifying you of the permit requirement. The WMNF offices are currently located on North Main Street (P.O. Box 638), Laconia, NH 03247; (603) 528-8721.

ALBANY

PARKS, BEACHES, AND RECREATION AREAS

• White Mountain National Forest—Boulder Loop Trail
🐾🐾🐾 🐕 See ❶ on page 496.

For a three-mile loop over an authentic 1858 covered bridge and the Swift River and up to a wonderful scenic overlook, take this moderate hiking trail. Numbered stations along the way help you identify the many plant and tree species here. Maps of the interpretive trail are available at the trailhead or the Saco Ranger District Office on the Kancamagus Highway (State Route 112) near the State Route 16 junction. For a different hike, take the Deer Brook Trail which follows the Swift River on a flat, open path. The trail veers left from the covered bridge. Dogs are allowed off leash on the trails.

From U.S. Route 16, take the Kancamagus Highway west for six miles. Turn right into the Albany Covered Bridge parking area. The trail starts through the covered bridge. Open 24 hours. (603) 528-8721.

•White Mountain National Forest—Champney Falls Trail
🐾 🐾 🐾 🐾 🐕 See ❷ on page 496.

This popular hiking trail leads to scenic Champney Falls. It can get fairly busy on a summer day, but, if the water is high, the view and the falls are worth braving the crowds. Only a mile walk from the trailhead off the Kancamagus Highway, you and your pooch won't have to walk far for gratification. Dogs are allowed off leash, but you may want to leash them by the falls.

From U.S. Route 16, take the Kancamagus Highway west for 11.5 miles. The trail and parking area are on your left. Open 24 hours. (603) 528-8721.

PLACES TO STAY

Covered Bridge Campground: This lovely campground is nestled between granite boulders and the Swift River near the scenic Albany Covered Bridge. There are 48 campsites, 20 of which are along the river and must be reserved. Others are available on a first-come, first-served basis. Dogs are permitted on leash. Rates are $12 to $20 per night. Open May to October. State Route 112, Albany, NH 03818; (800) 280-2267.

BARTLETT
(INCLUDING THE VILLAGE OF GLEN)

PARKS, BEACHES, AND RECREATION AREAS

•Diana's Baths 🐾 🐾 🐾 🐾 🐕 🌊 See ❸ on page 496.

This wonderful trail, leading to a lovely cascading waterfall, is perfect for dogs. The gravel paths are flat and wide, with plenty of streams and rivers along the way to keep water dogs happy. An easy walk for dogs of all sizes and ages (people, too), it is only a half mile to the "baths"—a scenic waterfall along Lucy Brook with flat, open rocks for sunning or picnicking.

Swimming is allowed below the falls, and, when the water is high enough, there are ample pools in which to take a dip. The water, which runs over granite boulders, is so fresh and clean, early settlers called it "Diana's Baths" for the Roman goddess. Only a deity could choose a place this lovely. Today it is a popular place, so we suggest visiting on a weekday or in the off-season if you want it to yourself.

To double your hike, continue on the Red Ridge Trail, which follows the brook northward from the baths. As with all trails in the White Mountains, dogs are allowed off leash if under voice command.

From U.S. Route 16 in North Conway, take River Road west for one mile. Turn right onto West Side Road for 1.5 miles into Bartlett. The trailhead is on the left. Open 24 hours. (603) 528-8721.

•Saco River Conservation Easement—Thorne Pond 🐾 🐾 🐾 🐕
See ❹ on page 496.

When all the ponds are off-limits to dogs in the hot summer months, George, Inu, and Rocky head for this conservation area with an easy trail to the Saco River via quiet, privately owned Thorne Pond. The owners of Thorne Pond allow access as long as you are respectful of the property and don't fish.

We were greeted by an expectant gaggle of geese on our last visit, and they didn't seem to be threatened by the dogs swimming on their turf so we expect they are used to visitors. Once they discovered we weren't going to feed them, however, they turned away indignantly, most likely saying to themselves, "Tourists!"

From U.S. Route 16, take U.S. Route 302 west for four miles. The parking area is on your right just east of Attitash Ski Resort. Open dawn to dusk. (603) 374-2368.

RESTAURANTS

Cider Mill Company: Stop by this great little restaurant/general store for a cup of hot or cold cider (depending on the hourly weather conditions in New Hampshire!), coffee, or freshly baked breakfast goodies. You may sit at the outdoor tables or take your food to go. U.S. Route 302; (603) 447-2737.

Glen's Landing: For great seafood in a charming setting, you'll enjoy this restaurant in the village of Glen. Order your clam chowder to take out, or enjoy your fresh lobster at the shaded picnic tables outside. State Route 16; (603) 383-6072.

PLACES TO STAY

The Country Inn at Bartlett: This bed-and-breakfast inn and 16 cottages is a quiet and relaxing getaway from the rush-hour pace of North Conway, just a few miles down the road. Pets are permitted in the cottages only. All have fireplaces, kitchenettes, and a screened porch for enjoying warm summer nights. Rates range from $78 to $144. U.S. Route 302, P.O. Box 327, Bartlett, NH 03812; (603) 374-2353, (800) 292-2353; www.bartlettinn.com.

North Colony Motel: This no-frills motel is conveniently located near the center of town. The rooms aren't glamorous, but they make for a good stop on your way elsewhere. Rates are $49 to $89 per night. Box 1, Bartlett, NH 03812; (603) 374-6679.

The Villager Motel: Overlooking the Saco River, the facilities here include a main lodge and 37 motel-efficiency chalets. You're invited to take a walk on the 15-acre grounds along the river. Pets are permitted in the chalets for an additional $6 per night. Rates range from $65 to $145. Route 302, Barlett, NH 03812; (603) 374-2742, (800) 334-6988; www.villagermotel.com.

BETHLEHEM

PARKS, BEACHES, AND RECREATION AREAS

• **Bretzfelder Memorial Park** 🐾🐾🐾 🐕 See ⑤ on page 496.
This lovely 77-acre park was bequeathed to the Society for the Protection of New Hampshire Forests in 1979 as a memorial to Charles Bretzfelder, a New York lawyer who originally owned this property in the 1920s. Story has it that in the 19th century a single giant white pine sprouted up in the middle of what was once farmland, and Bretzfelder developed a special affinity for this brave soldier. Upon his death in 1943, he requested that his ashes be spread beneath the towering tree and that his family protect the tree for future generations.

Today the forest has four different intersecting trails for you and your leash-free dog to enjoy. To hike the entire property, look for the Ski Loop, a 1.5-mile loop from the parking area and back.

From Interstate 93 north, take Exit 40 to U.S. Route 302 east for 2.5 miles. Turn right onto Prospect Street for one mile. The park is on your left. Open dawn to dusk. (603) 444-6228 or (603) 224-9945.

• **The Rocks** 🐾🐾🐾🐾 🐾 See 🖥 on page 496.
The Rocks, an estate once owned by John Jacob Glessner, a Chicago business-man and one of the founders of International Harvester, is such a wonderful conservation area we hardly know where to start. Located on a hill overlook-ing the northern regions of New Hampshire, it is breathtakingly beautiful and a great place for dogs.

In 1882, Glessner and his wife decided to build a summer retreat and pur-chased land which came to be known as "The Rocks"—named for boulders left behind by Ice Age glaciers and now listed on the National Register of His-toric Places. In 1978, the 1,300-acre estate was donated to the Society for Pro-tection of New Hampshire Forests; today, to help sustain itself, The Rocks is also a working farm with 55,000 Christmas trees.

Approximately six miles of self-guided scenic and educational trails wind through the property, with maps to guide you located at the trailhead. Dogs are allowed off leash here, except on the Christmas Tree Trail during the holi-day season. They may still visit, but must be leashed from Thanksgiving through Christmas Eve.

From Interstate 93 north, take Exit 40 to U.S. Route 302 east for a half mile. The entrance road is on your left. Open dawn to dusk. (603) 444-6228 or (603) 224-9945.

RESTAURANTS

Lloyd Hills Restaurant: This family restaurant has outdoor seating for you and your pup. Offering a varied continental-cuisine menu, there's something here to satisfy every taste. Main Street (U.S. Route 302); (603) 869-2141.

Rosa Flamingo's: This festive restaurant offers a choice of Mexican, Amer-ican, or standard fare for the hungry traveler. You and your dog will be com-fortable on the outdoor patio. Main Street (U.S. Route 302); (603) 869-3111.

PLACES TO STAY

Beech Hill Campground and Cabins: Just a few miles from Bethlehem, there are 87 sites here for campers who like "ruffing it" in a comfortable environ-ment. A store, recreation facilities, and showers are available, plus a few cab-ins are available to rent. Sites start at $18 per night. Pets are allowed on leash. P.O. Box 129, Twin Mountain, NH 03595; (603) 846-5521.

Pinewood Motel: This comfortable 20-room complex offers rooms with kitch-enettes and some with fireplaces. Pets are allowed as long as they are not left unattended in the room. Rates range from $45 to $95 per night. 1214 Main Street, U.S. Route 302, Bethlehem, NH 03574; (603) 444-2075; www.quikpage.com.

Wayside Inn: This lovely motel overlooking the Ammonoosuc River and golf course allows pets in one room only—so make your reservations in advance. No exceptions are made on check-in. A restaurant is on-site, and the rooms are comfortable and modern. Rates range from $64 to $89; a one-night's refundable deposit is required for Rover. U.S. Route 302, P.O. Box 480, Bethlehem, NH 03574; (800) 448-9557; www.thewaysideinn.com.

DIVERSIONS

Rock Around the Christmas Tree: The Rocks Christmas Tree Farm sells Christmas trees every weekend from Thanksgiving to Christmas. Bring your dog along as you find the perfect holiday tree. You'll also enjoy festive carols and sleigh rides, too. (603) 444-6228.

CHATHAM

PARKS, BEACHES, AND RECREATION AREAS

• **Emerald Pool** 🐾🐾🐾🐾 🐕 See **7** on page 496.

Diamonds may not be a dog's best friend, but, when it comes to emeralds, nothing but the best will do. Fortunately the "best" is here in the White Mountains. This deep glacial hole, nestled beneath a waterfall on Charles Brook, is one of the best swimming holes you'll find.

The one-mile trail starts 50 yards north of the parking area off State Route 113 in North Chatham. Dogs may be off leash on the trails.

From U.S. Route 2 in Gilead, Maine, take State Route 113 south for eight miles into Chatham. The trailhead and parking area are on the right. Open dawn to dusk. (603) 528-8721.

CONWAY
(INCLUDING THE VILLAGE OF NORTH CONWAY)

North Conway is the central hub for activities in the Mount Washington Valley. There aren't many parks or hikes in this town, but there is plenty of everything else. Mostly known for its many shopping outlets (which, unless it's a Big Dog outlet, hold little interest for our dogs), we put our noses to the ground and came up with a few things besides shopping that you will all enjoy. For a hike, you can venture into neighboring Bartlett or Chatham.

PARKS, BEACHES, AND RECREATION AREAS

• **First Bridge Conservation Area/Hussey Field** 🐾🐾🐾 🐕 See **8** on page 496.

This is the doggy hangout for local dogs and their owners in North Conway. Although there aren't a lot of trails, this park has three things dogs like most: water, an open field for ball throwing, and other dogs. The two areas are on opposite sides of the Saco River; park at the First Bridge parking area, just before you go over the bridge.

From U.S. Route 16, take River Road west for a quarter mile. The parking area is on your right before you go over the bridge. Open 6 A.M. to 10 P.M. (603) 447-2639.

RESTAURANTS

Alpenglow Grill: This place isn't much on atmosphere, but their menu makes your mouth water (stop the drooling, Inu!). Dine on roasted corn chowder with basil, a portabello mushroom sandwich with melted smoked gouda cheese, or curried chicken over broccoli and orange couscous. Yum! Eat at one of their outdoor cafe tables with your dog drooling, uh, sitting by your side. Main Street (State Route 16); (603) 447-5524.

The Blueberry Muffin: For a quick breakfast or lunch stop, try this friendly little café next to the Yankee Clipper Motel. Outdoor tables under a shaded canopy are a perfect place for you and your dog to enjoy a hearty breakfast of ham and eggs. Main Street (State Route 16); (603) 356-5736.

Bobby-Sue's: For great ice cream after a long day on the trails, try this gourmet ice-cream shop. Homemade flavors like Raspberry Smear and Chocolate Moose taste great on a freshly made waffle cone. Main Street; (603) 447-6360.

Subway: Normally we don't include chain restaurants, but this one has great outdoor seating and is across from a scenic rest stop along the Saco River. Take your sandwich across the street and sit at one of the benches along the river. State Route 16; (603) 539-4442.

PLACES TO STAY

The Beach Camping Area: This place is appropriately named, and, if you're looking for a beach that allows dogs, this family campground will more than fill the bill. Of the 120 tent sites, one-third are located along the sandy shores of the Saco River, and the others have views or beach access. The camping fee is $18 a night, and reservations are recommended. 98 Eastern Slope Terrace, Box 1007, Conway, NH 03860; 603-447-2723.

Debbie Johnstone Realty: If you're looking to stay for a week or a long weekend, you might consider a vacation rental. Many of the units represented here allow dogs, and you'll have many home, condominium, and location options to choose from. Make sure you tell them you will be bringing your pooch along, as some units do not allow pets. P.O. Box 13, Intervale, NH, 03845; (603) 356-4871, (800) 372-5305; www.mutha.com/johnstone realty.

Mount Washington Valley Motor Lodge: This newly renovated motel, offering standard rooms in a modern setting, is right in the heart of town. Well-behaved pets are welcome on approval. Rates range from $49 to $89 per night. Dogs are an additional $10 per night. State Routes 16 and 302, North Conway, NH, 03845; (800) 634-2383 or (603) 356-5486; www.motorlodge.com.

North Conway Mountain Inn: This modern inn is quite a comfortable place to stay. The rooms are spacious with all the amenities and are conveniently located near the center of town. Dogs are welcome with no extra charge. Rates range from $59 to $129. P.O. Box 3175, Main Street, North Conway, NH 03860; (603) 356-2803 or (800) 319-4405.

Presidential Inn: This hotel has 14 tastefully decorated rooms, some with Jacuzzis. Every room has a VCR, and free movie "rentals" are available on-site. Conveniently located near town. Rooms range from $89 to $179; suites are $99 to $229. Dogs are an additional $10 per night. State Routes 16 and 302, North Conway, NH 03845; (603) 356-9744, (888) 568-3882; www.thepresidentialinn.com.

Stonehurst Manor: This fabulous resort is located on 33 acres overlooking the Mount Washington Valley. All rooms have fireplaces and are perfect in any season. Plenty of hiking trails are just outside your door. Best of all, pets are welcome in most rooms. Breakfast (for you) is included in the rate. Rates range from $106 to $186. A small refundable deposit is required for Fido. P.O. Box 1937, North Conway, NH 03860; (603) 356-3113, (800) 525-9100; www.stonehurstmanor.com.

Sunny Brook Cottages: This clean and cozy cluster of 10 cottages lies along Swift Brook, just off the main hub of town. Each has a fireplace and kitchen facilities. Well-behaved pets are welcome. Rates are $59 to $104. P.O. Box 1429, Conway, NH, 03860; (603) 447-3922; www.sunnybrookcottages.com.

Swiss Chalets Village Inn: This is a clean and friendly motel with spacious rooms in a lovely location. Accommodations range from an economy room to a two-bedroom suite. Rates range from $49 to $189 depending on the season. There is a $15-per-night fee for your dog. Route 16A, Intervale, NH 03845; (603) 356-2232, (800) 831-2727; www.swisschaletsvillage.com.

Tanglewood Motel & Cottages: This motel is off the beaten path in a wooded area by a stream. The rustic efficiency cottages sleep two to eight people. Motel rooms are also available. Rates range from $38 to $120. Pets are welcome. State Route 16, Conway, NH 03818; (603) 447-5932.

FESTIVALS

Ring in the New Year!: Celebrate New Year's Eve with the Mount Washington Valley First Night Celebration. Held throughout the valley, but mainly in North Conway's Schouler Park, the outdoor activities include a parade, fireworks, ice sculptures, live bands, and plenty of festive food. Dogs are allowed at all outdoor activities. To get an event schedule, call (603) 356-5701, extension 350.

DIVERSIONS

Bark Up!: This annual Bark in the Park event, sponsored by the Conway Area Humane Society, includes activities that both dogs and their humans can enjoy: a fund-raising dog walk, obstacle courses, canine demonstrations, crafts, food, and a flurry of furry fun. Area dog teams can compete in various categories, and the Barker's Bowl will be awarded to the team with the most points. All proceeds benefit this new organization whose facilities offer obedience training, animal rescue, doggie day care, and boarding kennels. The event is held from 9 A.M. to 3 P.M. in mid-September at Schouler Park. Call for exact date and details. (207) 935-7107.

Doggie Day Care: The new facilities at the Conway Area Humane Society offer short- and long-term care for your dog. Travelers through the area and take advantage of the one-hour or half-day doggie day care. Located on 25 acres, your pet will be pampered and played with while you are shopping or checking out the many activities in the Mount Washington Valley. This is not just a kennel, but a home away from home. (207) 935-4358.

Four Your Paws Only: To call this a pet store is to underestimate this friendly little pet gift and supply store. Normally we don't include stores, but this one is so much fun we made an exception. You'll find novelty gifts like signature dog bowls, monogrammed dog towels, doggie ice cream, and other gourmet "bakery" treats. This is where dogs in the know hang out every Saturday morning from 10 to 11 A.M.; if you stop by to mingle with the locals, they'll welcome you with a cool bowl of water and a gourmet dog biscuit for your furry pal. Main Street (State Route 16); (603) 356-7297; www.fouryourpawsonly.com.

Go West, young dog!: Go with Saco Bound Canoe Rentals. With advanced permission, you may take your dog boating along the westerly flowing Saco, where you'll observe beaver, muskrat, waterfowl, and the occasional moose. No disturbing the wildlife, please! Flat-water canoe or kayak rental is $25.50 per day; $3 more on weekends in July and August. Reservations are suggested for weekends. (603) 447-2177.

Strike up the Band: Join the locals and summer visitors at the gazebo at the North Conway Community Center for a free concert every Sunday from June through August. The hour-long concert starts at 6:30 P.M. Grab the kids, the dog, a lawn chair or blanket, and a picnic dinner and enjoy the night, the music, and the lovely setting. (603) 356-5701.

Take a journey back to the past on the Conway Scenic Railway!: This historic railway offers two tours—the Notch run and the Valley run. Leashed dogs are allowed on all Valley runs as long as they are on your lap or close by and the other passengers don't mind. (Only guide dogs are allowed on the mountain notch train.) Take a one- to two-hour saunter through the beautiful Mount Washington Valley between Bartlett and Conway and feel you've escaped to another century. Adults $10 to $19, children $7 to $14. The train operates seasonally from mid-April to mid-December. Reservations are suggested. (603) 356-8776; www.conwayscenic.com.

DIXVILLE

PARKS, BEACHES, AND RECREATION AREAS

• **The Balsams Wilderness** 🐾🐾🐾🐾 🐾 See **9** on page 496.
Well, the good news is that some of the best groomed trails in the Great Woods are found here in this 15,000-acre wilderness area. Owned by the Balsams Resort, one of the last grand hotels (located just north of here), they boast of over 40 kilometers of hiking on freshly groomed trails. You can obtain trail maps at the information booth on State Route 26 just across from the hotel entrance or at the hotel itself.

The better news is that you and your leashed dog don't have to be guests to hike the trails (and, unfortunately, you couldn't stay here even if you wanted, since they don't allow dogs). To reach the trailhead, take the road just southeast of the hotel entrance and park at the end of the road. Trails lead into the beautiful woods from there. There is no fee for hiking.

From U.S. Route 16 in Errol, take State Route 26 north for 13 miles. Trails and parking are on your left; the hotel entrance is on your right. Open from dawn to dusk. (800) 255-0600.

• **Dixville Notch State Park** 🐾🐾🐾🐾 See **10** on page 496.
Dixville Notch is the northernmost and smallest of the state's notches. And believe us when we tell you, it's just you, the trail, and the wilderness here. Enjoy waterfalls and a scenic gorge along the two mountain brooks within the 137 acres of parkland. The most popular hiking trail to Table Rock begins here. Called Table Rock because it's no wider than a table, this rock platform extends out from

the north side of Mount Gloriette. At 2,700 feet high, you and your leashed dog will have great views of the Balsams Wilderness Resort and Lake Gloriette.

Take the five-mile Dixville Notch Heritage Trail and you'll hit all the highlights of this beautiful area. Maps are available at the headquarters off State Route 26. Dogs must be on leash.

From U.S. Route 16 in Errol, take State Route 26 north for 12 miles to the park entrance. Open 24 hours. (603) 788-3155.

ERROL

PLACES TO STAY

Errol Motel: If you don't plan on camping out, this is your best bet for a place to stay in Errol. The motel has 12 rooms, including three efficiency units. Dogs on leashes are allowed, but you need to ask about other pets. Rates range from $39 to $49. On Main Street in Errol; (603) 482-3256.

Lake Umbagog Campground: This 59-site campground is a good launching spot if you're traveling to Lake Umbagog National Wildlife Refuge by canoe or boat. Located in the state park, dogs are allowed on leash. Rates are $18 to $22 per night. Reservations are recommended. (603) 482-7795.

FRANCONIA

PARKS, BEACHES, AND RECREATION AREAS

• **Franconia Notch State Park** 🐾🐾🐾🐾 See **11** on page 496.

This 6,440 acres is a wilderness playground in all seasons. There are so many hikes, activities, and natural wonders to choose from, you'll have to return again and again to discover them all (as many people do!). This is the home of the Old Man of the Mountain, Echo Lake, Profile Lake, and Lonesome Lake. The Cannon Mountain Ski area is in the park, as is the deep glacial pothole known as the Basin. The Appalachian Trail crosses the park just a mile north of the Flume, a spectacular, geological slide worn away by time and avalanches. Eight miles of the Franconia Notch Parkway wind through the park, and just about any turnout will yield a satisfying sight or trail.

One of the most popular trails is the Lonesome Lake Trail, a fairly moderate. 1.5-mile hike on an old bridle path leading to the lake and panoramic views of Franconia Ridge. The loop around the lake adds another half mile.

For the best waterfall walk, head for the Falling Waters Trail. Many of the waterfalls are on the lower end of the hike so you can reach them with little effort. For a full-day hike and spectacular views, continue up the trail to Franconia Ridge, a six-mile round-trip.

Dogs must be on leash; some trails restrict dogs, but signs will be posted. No dogs are allowed at the Lafayette Campground.

At the main visitors center located at the Flume, you can pick up maps and information about the entire park. Dogs are not allowed to walk to the Flume (mainly because it gets so crowded and there is only a narrow walkway), but there are "dog walks"—trails specifically designed for dogs—at both the Flume visitor center and at the Cannon Mountain Tram.

Located off Interstate 93. The park is open year-round; day-use areas are open from dawn to dusk. (603) 823-5563.

NATURE HIKES AND URBAN WALKS

Ridge Road: Poets are a dog's best friend, or they are now thanks to Robert Frost. For dogs (and people) are the lucky beneficiaries of Frost's good taste in dwellings. This home, listed in the National Register of Historic Places, is as scenic as his farm in Derry (see page 429) and both feature beautiful grounds that are open to the public in all seasons except winter. Walk the Poetry Trail or just wander the fields and enjoy the sight of the White Mountains in the distance. Ridge Road; (603) 823-5510.

RESTAURANTS

Dairy Bar Restaurant: Stop at this little roadside stand for some ice cream or lunch. Located right on State Route 116 in the heart of this quaint village, there are picnic tables outside for you and your dog to Sit! Stay! Relax. . . . State Route 116; (603) 823-5507.

PLACES TO STAY

Franconia Notch Vacations: If you're looking for a fully equipped house rental in the Franconia area, this friendly rental agency will be happy to help you find the perfect vacation spot with Spot. Most homes have two to five bedrooms, and some "pet units" are available. Please tell the agent you have a pet when making your reservation. Rates are $90 to $170 per night (with a two-night minimum) and $650 to $950 per week. Route 18, Franconia, NH 03580; (800) 247-5536.

Lovett's Inn By Lafayette Brook: Listed on the National Register of Historic Places, this 1784 inn has both a manor house and luxury cottages with fireplaces. You and your pet will be staying in style here. You can wander the 10 acres on the property or simply relax and enjoy your full breakfast and four-course dinner which is included in the room rate. Rates range from $130 to $195 per night. 1474 Profile Road (State Route 18), Franconia NH 03580; (603) 823-7761, (800) 356-3802; www.lovettsinn.com.

Westwind Vacation Cottages: Located just a couple of miles from the northern entrance to the Franconia Notch State Park, each of these eight cottages is unique, offering a variety of choices for you and your pet. Pets are allowed in five of the cottages for no extra charge. Rates range from $48 to $85 per night. 1614 Profile Road (State Route 18), Franconia, NH 03580; (603) 823-5532, (877)835-3455.

GORHAM

PARKS, BEACHES, AND RECREATION AREAS

• **Moose Brook State Park** 🐾🐾🐾 See **12** on page 496.
This state park covers 744 acres and offers walking trails, picnic areas, and a campground. With Mount Washington and the Presidential Range close by, you probably won't limit your activities to this park, but it makes for a convenient base camp for exploring the northern White Mountains. Dogs must be

on leash and are not allowed on the swimming beach.

From U.S. Route 16, take State Route 2 west for 1.5 miles. Turn right on Jimtown Road for a quarter mile. The park entrance is on your right. Open dawn to dusk. (603) 466-3860.

RESTAURANTS

Loaf Around: This little bakery and café has outdoor tables in the summer months. Take a sandwich to go or enjoy your fresh bakery item on the tables outside. 19 Exchange Street; (603) 466-2706.

The Lobster Pound: Stop by this seafood café right on State Route 2 in the heart of town. You can crack a lobster at one of the outdoor tables, although Inu figures it's easier just to order a lobster roll. Main Street; no phone contact.

PLACES TO STAY

Colonial Comfort Inn: This moderate hotel at the junction of State Routes 2 and 16N doesn't mess around. They tell us they are open 25/8 instead of the usual 24/7. So take advantage of the extra day and hour and get some sleep at this 15-room inn. Standard rooms have one bed and larger rooms have two double beds and a whirlpool tub. All rooms have a small refrigerator. Pets are welcome. Rates range $36 to $85. 370 Main Street, Gorham, NH 03581; (800) 470-4224; www.hikersparadise.com.

Gorham Motor Inn: This comfortable 39-room motel allows pets for an additional $6 per night. Room rates range from $38 to $96. 324 Main Street, Gorham, NH 03581; (603) 466-3381, (800) 445-0913; www.northernwhite-mountain.com/gmi.

Moose Brook State Park Campground: Pets are welcome at this state park, except at the swimming area. Fifty tent sites are available, and the facilities include showers. The fee is $14 per night. State Route 2, Gorham, NH, 03581; (603) 466-3860.

Royalty Inn: This large 90-room motel offers rooms with efficiencies and modern conveniences. Your pet is welcome for an additional $5. Rooms range from $59 to $90 per night. 130 Main Street, Gorham, NH 03581; (603) 466-3312 or (800) 43-RELAX; www.royaltyinn.com.

Town and Country Motor Inn: This 160-room motel is nestled in the valley surrounded by mountains. One of the nicest motel facilities around, the rooms are comfortable and there are trails on the grounds to walk your dog. Located right on the Gorham/Shelburne town line, both villages are easily accessible. Dogs are allowed with prior approval. Rates range from $49 to $90. State Route 2, P.O. Box 220, Gorham, NH 03581; (603) 466-3315, (800) 325-4386; www.townandcountryinn.com.

DIVERSIONS

Concerts on the Common: You and your dog will enjoy a wide variety of musical concerts every Tuesday evening from 6:30 to 8:30 P.M. during July and August on the Gorham Common on State Route 2. Call the Twin Mountain Chamber of Commerce for details and schedules. (603) 846-5058.

HART'S LOCATION

PARKS, BEACHES, AND RECREATION AREAS

• **Crawford Notch State Park** 🐾🐾🐾🐾 See **13** on page 496.

At this state park, you can hike along the six miles of trails that connect with the Appalachian Trail. The 5,950-acre park in the middle of the White Mountains features mountain streams, a self-guided nature trail, and plenty of hikes to scenic waterfalls. Dogs aren't allowed in the day-use or picnic areas, so you'll have to confine your visit to the trails.

The most unusual of these trails is the Webster Cliff Trail which traverses the magnificent cliffs that form Crawford Notch and lead north to the peaks of Mount Jackson and Webster. But don't let us curb you. Spend a day or a week and you still won't see it all.

Trail maps are available at the Willey House Visitors Center, named for a family killed in a massive avalanche in 1826. Dogs must be on leash.

The park is located off U.S. Route 302. Open 24 hours. (603) 374-2272.

PLACES TO STAY

Crawford Notch General Store and Campground: This is a great place to spend the night and stock up on supplies while in the White Mountains. This 75-site campground has a few more amenities than most of the campgrounds in this area, and the small general store makes the foraging for dinner a little easier. (They even have dog biscuits, which George says we never have enough of.) Leashed dogs are permitted, and reservations are recommended. Camping fee is $15 per night. Open seasonally from May to October. (603) 374-2779.

RESTAURANTS

As You Like It Bakery & Café: This convenient bakery, sandwich, and ice-cream shop overlooks a small lake in the center of town. You can sit on the veranda porch tables or walk across the street to the benches along the green. State Route 16B at the Jackson Falls Marketplace; (603) 383-6425.

Thompson House Eatery (or T.H.E.): For some "creative" country cooking, which includes Viva La Beef (a roast beef sandwich) and Seafood Francesca (pasta with scallops, shrimp, and garlic), stop by this great restaurant. Dogs may dine outdoors with you on "T.H.E." deck. There's also an ice-cream parlor for dessert or for takeout. U.S. Route 16 and State Route 16A junction; (603) 383-9341.

Wentworth Inn: Eat on the terrace of this elegant inn overlooking the golf course. Your dog may join you outside at one of the best restaurants in the Mount Washington Valley. Dine on seafood or lamb, but only if you're willing to withstand those longing looks from the dog at your feet. Save room for the tiramisu! State Route 16A; (603) 383-9700.

JACKSON

PLACES TO STAY

Dana Place Inn: Stay at this 100-year-old historic inn located on 300 acres by the Ellis River. Rooms and suites are available; full breakfast and afternoon tea are included in your nightly rate. Hike the grounds with your dog or cross-country ski in the winter. There's even a swimming hole on the river where you can cool off. Rates range from $90 to $160 per night. State Route 16, Box L, Jackson, NH 03846; (603) 383-6822, (800) 537-9276; www.danaplace.com.

Motel On The River: This simple motel offers rooms or adjoining house-keeping cottages. All units have kitchens and fireplaces. Dogs are welcome in the cottages. Rates range from $95 to $110 per night. Box N, Jackson, NH 03846; (603) 383-4241.

Village House: This cozy yellow inn is located in downtown Jackson. The inn rooms, decorated in colonial style, and individual cottages on this 100-year-old property are all dog friendly. The owners have two dogs of their own and make Yellow Dog Snow Gear (leashes and collars), so you know you and your dog will be welcome here! Rooms range from $65 to $130. P.O. Box 359, Jackson, NH 03846; (603) 383-6666, (800) 972-8343; www.yellowsnow.net.

Whitneys' Inn: This elegant 1840s New England farmhouse offers 29 comfortable rooms including a few cozy cottages with fireplaces. There is an on-site restaurant recommended by *Bon Appétit* magazine, and full breakfast is served each morning. The farm is located on the top of a hill next to a ski resort and is convenient to town and hiking areas. Pets are welcome in a few rooms, so make your reservations early. Rates range from $70 to $135 per night; dogs are an additional $25. P.O. Box 822, Jackson, NH 03846; (603) 383-8916, (800) 677-5737; www.whitneysinn.com.

JEFFERSON

PLACES TO STAY

Applebrook Bed-and-Breakfast: The views of Mount Washington, Marty's Marvelous Muffins, and fresh raspberries with breakfast bring guests back to this rambling Victorian farmhouse again and again. Room choices include bedrooms with private or shared baths or one multibed, dormitory-style room. The inn is open year-round. Well-behaved dogs are welcome, and the innkeepers will consider other pets, as well. Be sure to reserve in advance. Rates are $55 to $90 plus an extra charge of $6 per dog, half of which is donated to the Lancaster Humane Society. Route 115A, Jefferson, NH 03583; (603) 586-7713, (800) 545-6504; www.applebrook.com.

Josselyn's "Getaway" Log Cabins: These "real" log cabins come with fireplaces, kitchens, complete linen, and cook- and dinnerware. Cabins sleep four to 10 people. Dogs are welcome. Rates are $50 to $80. North Road, Jefferson, NH 03583; (603) 586-4507.

Little House Bed-and-Breakfast: This lovely bed-and-breakfast features three rooms in the main house and a barn loft that sleeps seven people with full kitchen and living quarters. Full breakfast is included at the inn. Rooms are $65 per night; the loft is $200 per night and $400 per weekend. Black Velvet Road, Box 123, Jefferson NH 03583; (603) 586-4373.

LINCOLN

PARKS, BEACHES, AND RECREATION AREAS

•White Mountain National Forest—Lincoln Woods
🐾🐾🐾🐾 🐕 🐟 See **14** on page 496.

We hate to bias anyone, but, for sheer variety of trails and scenic beauty, Inu and George confess that this is their favorite doggy haunt in the White Mountains. Once you enter this wonderful wilderness area, you won't need to go anywhere else.

Start at the Lincoln Woods parking area off the Kancamagus Highway (State Route 112), and you'll be on the Lincoln Woods Trail, an old logging road which conveniently runs along the Pemigewasset River. About 1.5 miles north, you can branch off onto the Osseo and Franconia Ridge Trails which lead you high into the White Mountains and up onto the spectacular Franconia Ridge. The ridge trail is steep and for experienced hikers, but, if you're game, the effort is worth it.

For a more moderate hike, stay on the Lincoln Woods Trail for another half mile and continue east on the Wilderness Trail for a flat, moderate hike through forests, streams, and marshes; or head north for Franconia Falls.

Please note that access is currently being limited to the falls so, if you plan to visit, permits are required and can be obtained from the Lincoln Woods Visitor Center at the main parking area. Maps and information are also available at the center. (During the winter the occasional cross-country trail may be closed to dogs, but this changes daily so please check on the trails before you come in the winter.)

Dogs are allowed off leash on the trails in all White Mountain forests. Please leash your pet in the picnic and parking areas.

From Interstate 93, take Exit 32 to the Kancamagus Highway east for 5.5 miles. The trailhead, visitor center, and parking are on the left. Open 24 hours. (603) 528-8721.

RESTAURANTS

Seven Seas Seafood Restaurant: Lahbstah, anyone? For a great Maine lobster, steamed clams, or any of a wide variety of seafood dishes, you can't go wrong at this friendly restaurant. Sit at one of the outdoor tables right here in the heart of Lincoln and satisfy your appetite after a long day at Lincoln Woods. Main Street (State Route 112), (603) 745-6536.

Sunny Day Diner: Just a skip away from the train station, this old-fashioned diner has a lengthy and excellent menu. Step back into the past when you eat at this 1950-style diner. Good food at good prices. Picnic tables are outside for you and your pup. U.S. Route 3; (603) 745-4833.

Whistle Stop Snack Bar: Located right next to the railroad station on U.S. Route 3, you can stop for a quick lunch or dinner here. Try a buffalo burger, hot dog, or a scoop of fresh strawberry ice cream. Tables are located along the station where you can see all the action. U.S. Route 3; (603) 7454-6115.

White Mountain Bagel Co.: Sit outside at this cheerful café right in the center of town. There are plenty of picnic tables where you and your pooch can nosh on chocolate chip bagels, a Turkey Roasted Red Pepper Special (that's a sandwich, of course!), or a cup of Green Mountain Coffee. 13 Main Street (State Route 112); (603) 745-4900.

PLACES TO STAY

Parker's Motel: This homey motel and cottage facility lies in the heart of the White Mountains. Dogs are welcome in the motel rooms only for an additional $5 a night. Rooms range from $62 to $89 per night. U.S. Route 3, Lincoln, NH 03251; (800) 766-6835; www.parkersmotel.com.

LITTLETON

PARKS, BEACHES, AND RECREATION AREAS

• **Dells Park Conservation Area** 🐾🐾🐾 See **15** on page 496.
This wonderful town park is a wooded getaway from the surrounding concrete. Take a two-mile loop trail that runs all around Dells Pond and through the surrounding woods; for a shorter walk, stick to the trails and boardwalks that center around the pond. Dogs must be leashed.

From Main Street (U.S. Route 302), take State Routes 18/135 west for one mile. Turn left into the park and parking area. Open dawn to dusk. (603) 444-6561.

NATURE HIKES AND URBAN WALKS

Littleton Historic Sites: Littleton was the home of many industrial millionaires and wealthy summer visitors in the 19th century, and you can retrace the past splendor on this interesting walking tour. Pick up a map at the Chamber of Commerce or the Village Bookstore, both on Main Street, and follow the paper trail to 12 unique historic and architectural sites. You'll enjoy the many modern sites on current Main Street, as well. (603) 444-6561.

RESTAURANTS

Bishops Homemade Ice Cream: Have a scoop of ice cream or a cup of frozen yogurt at this Littleton institution. Right in the heart of town, you and your dog won't have to walk far before you succumb to the lure of ice cream. 183 Cottage Street; (603) 444-6039.

Burrito Alley: For Tex-Mex cuisine hidden down a charming brick alley, try this little tucked-away café, just off Main Street. They serve a full menu of Mexican meals with a southwestern flavor; you can either dine at one of the café tables or order your meal to go in one of their microwavable take-out containers. 89 Main Street; (603) 444-2200.

Miller's Fare: For a great view overlooking the falls on the Ammonoosuc River, enjoy a light meal or cup of coffee at this coffee bar/brewery. They serve sandwiches, salads, and a full coffee bar menu. 16 Mill Street; (603) 444-2146.

Oasis Italian Restaurant & Brewery: This popular restaurant serves great Italian food for lunch or dinner. Best of all, they have a great patio where your dog may join you for a bite. Pasta, pizza, seafood, and veal are the specialties. Try a microbrew with dinner. 106 Main Street; (603) 444-6995.

PLACES TO STAY

Eastgate Motor Inn: This affordable and modern motel was rated an "unusually good value" by AAA, and we agree. George and JoAnna stayed here and found it one of the more comfortable and pet-friendly motels around. There is also a restaurant on the premises, and, although you can't eat there with your dog, you can order room service, which is a big plus after a long day hiking. Not all the rooms are available to dogs, and, because of the reasonable rates, it's a popular stop, so you should make advance reservations. Rooms are $40 to $70 per night. Cottage Street (U.S. Route 302), Littleton, NH 03561; (603) 444-3971; www.eastgatemotorinn.com.

Thayers Inn: This historic hotel (listed on the National Register of Historic Places), built in 1850, is located right on Main Street. It was the brainchild of Henry "Dad" Thayers, a local railroad magnate who wanted to open a hotel with all the "modern" conveniences. Throughout its history, it has been visited by such luminaries as Ulysses S. Grant, Bette Davis, and Presidents Franklin Pierce and Richard Nixon (not necessarily in that order). There are 31 elegantly decorated rooms, six family units, and two suites, all with private baths and free continental breakfast. Pets are welcome, but the management sets a limit of one dog per room, and dogs cannot be left unattended. Rates range from $49 to $109. 111 Main Street, Littleton, NH 03561; (603) 444-6469; www.thayersinn.com.

MADISON

PARKS, BEACHES, AND RECREATION AREAS

• **Hoyt Sanctuary** 🐾 🐾 🐾 See **16** on page 496.

This lovely wildlife sanctuary, donated to the Audubon Society of New Hampshire in 1989, was once the site of Camp Wampineauk for girls. Established by Ellen Hoyt in 1934, you can still see the granite bench placed here in her memory.

Today these 168 acres have several trails leading throughout a lovely woodland and on top of an esker trail overlooking Purity Lake. A lake is available for swimming or simply wandering along its shoreline. Wildlife flourishes here, and, if you're lucky, you will see many species quietly going about their daily routines. Dogs must be leashed.

From U.S. Route 25 in Effingham Falls, take State Route 153 north for 5.5 miles. Turn right onto Horseleg Hill Road (Cold Spring Road). The sanctuary and parking are immediately on your left. Open dawn to dusk. (603) 224-9909.

MOUNT WASHINGTON
(INCLUDES THE BOUNDARY TOWNS OF BEANS GRANT, BEANS PURCHASE, CHANDLERS PURCHASE, CRAWFORDS PURCHASE, CUTTS GRANT, GREENS GRANT, HADLEYS PURCHASE, LOW AND BURBANKS GRANT, PINKHAMS GRANT, SARGENTS PURCHASE, AND THOMPSON AND MESERVES PURCHASE)

South Dakota may have the faces of a few presidents on Mount Rushmore, but New Hampshire has a whole range of mountains named for some of our finest White House residents. These grand peaks, some of the highest on the Eastern seaboard, are made of a flinty granite and, although rugged and wild, they aren't really the best places to take your dog. The reason? The granite in the Presidential Range at higher elevations is extremely sharp, and, although dogs are allowed here, the rangers strongly recommend against it. There have been many "dog rescues" in recent years because dogs have cut their pads so badly they had to be carried out. As one ranger put it: "A dog will follow his master wherever he goes, but that may not always be a good thing." So be careful out there, and make sure you don't ask more of your pup than she can deliver.

PARKS, BEACHES, AND RECREATION AREAS

• Great Glen Trails 🐾🐾🐾🐾 🐕 See **17** on page 496.

Located right next to the Mount Washington Auto Route, we recommend you forgo the trip to the top of the mountain and just head straight to this fabulous recreation area instead. With 40 kilometers of well-groomed trails, this all-season recreation complex is the best place to hike with your dog in the Presidential Range. Because the trails stick to the valley, your dog won't be bothered by the sharp granite at higher elevations, and the trails provide perfect conditions for a dog to run off leash, swim, and chase his tail. Oh yes, and you'll enjoy it, too. Access to the trails is free but a donation is always appreciated. Dogs are allowed off leash on the trails, but please put on her leash at the center's parking area and outdoor store.

From State Route 2 in Gorham, take U.S. Route 16 south for eight miles. The parking area is on your right just north of the Mount Washington Auto Route. Open 8 A.M. to 5 P.M. (603) 466-2333.

• Mount Washington State Park 🐾🐾 See **18** on page 496.

This 52-acre park at the top of Mount Washington is the end of the trail whether you hike, drive, or ride the rails up the 6,288-foot mountain. You can't spend the night, but amenities include a post office, snack bar, and gift shop. This state park is surrounded by the White Mountain National Forest, and, although the view is amazing, we suggest you take your visit no farther than the parking area on top because of the rocky trail conditions. Also, weather conditions can be extreme on Mount Washington; you can get a snowstorm in the summer or a sudden temperature drop of 40-plus degrees. So pack for all kinds of weather on a trip here, and watch out for those rocks! Dogs on leash, please.

From State Route 2 in Gorham, take U.S. Route 16 south for eight miles. The auto route to park is on your right. Admission is $16 per car. Open 9 A.M. to 6 P.M. Memorial Day through Columbus Day. (603) 466-3860.

• **Pinkham Notch Scenic Area** 🐾🐾🐾 🐕 See **19** on page 496.
Although there are many trails that lead up to Mount Washington or throughout the Presidential Range from here, if you're hiking with your dog, we recommend the Lonesome Lake Trail, which is a fairly easy hike and sticks to lower elevations. The Zealand Falls Trail, which leads to the Whitewall Brook waterfall, is also a great choice.

Check out the full trail system at the Pinkham Notch Visitors Center off U.S. Route 16. Dogs are allowed off leash on the trails.

The scenic area is off U.S. Route 16 three miles south of Mount Washington State Park. Trails are open 24 hours; visitors center open 8 A.M. to 5 P.M. (603) 466-2727.

DIVERSIONS

Great Glen Outdoor Center: If you want to do more than hike, you can rent bikes, canoes, or snowshoes here and let your dog tag along. Access to the trails is free; bike rentals are $20 to $30 per day; cross-country skis are $16. (Note: although there are 40 kilometers of trails here, if you cross-country ski with your dog in the winter, you'll be limited to a five-kilometer special trail only; in the summer all trails are open to dogs under voice control.) U.S. Route 16 at Pinkham Notch. For more information, call (603) 466-2333.

PITTSBURG

Most of the land in this region is privately owned without any formal trail system, and it is mainly used by hunters and snowmobilers. Hence, there are plenty of places to stay, but very few reasons to go there unless you're a hunting dog. We've listed a few of these lodges because they are really quite wonderful and most have a trail system on their own property that you can explore as a guest.

Pittsburg does own an interesting bit of history, however. In 1832, as a piece of territory jointly claimed by both Canada and the United States, it became its own independent republic—the Republic of Indian Stream. As a republic, it had a constitution and was managing its own affairs until Canada decided to lay claim to it, bringing the U.S. in to seize it as part of New Hampshire.

PLACES TO STAY

The Glen: Once a private estate, this full-service sporting lodge offers three daily country-cooked meals in a cozy dining room complete with a fireplace. Dogs (and their human companions) may stay in some of the rooms in the main lodge or in the rustic log cottages along the lakeshore. Rates range from $125 to $150. 77 Glen Road, Pittsburg, NH 03592; (603) 538-6500, (800) 445-4536.

Tall Timber Lodge: Originally built as a hunting lodge in 1946, this beautiful resort on Back Lake has grown to include luxury cottages and rustic cabins of various sizes. Hiking trails are accessible on the grounds, and canoe and boat rentals are also available. Dogs are allowed in most of the cottages. Guests are expected to pick up after and control their pets while on the premises and are responsible for any damages that might occur. A $10-per-day pet fee is charged. Cottages range from $92 to $235 per night on the weekend and $615 to $1,200 weekly. Call for off-season rates. 231 Beach Road, Pittsburg, NH 03592; (800) 83-LODGE; www.talltimber.com.

FESTIVALS

Annual North Country Moose Festival: Join the towns of Pittsburg, Colebrook, and Canaan, Vermont, in celebrating their biggest event of the season. Each year during the last weekend in August the shy moose moves from the forests to center stage. Festivities feature "Moose Cruises," a mock Moose parade, local crafts exhibits, raffles, food, and entertainment. All events take place in the downtown areas of each town. Tickets are $16. Call for exact dates and schedule. (603) 237-8939; www.northcountrychamber.org.

RUMNEY

PARKS, BEACHES, AND RECREATION AREAS

• **Quincy Bog Natural Area** 🐾🐾🐾🐾 See **20** on page 496.
This wonderful conservation area is managed superbly by the Nature Conservancy and the Rumney Ecological Systems. The 44-acre park offers a rich woodland hike, and the area is both scenic and informational. Along the way you'll see the remains of a glacial pond surrounded by a sedge meadow, woodland forest, and excellent walking trails that cut through and over the bog.

Trail maps are available at the kiosk by the parking area. Dogs must be on leash because of the sensitive ecological area.

From State Route 3A, take State Route 25 west for four miles. Turn right on Main Street for one mile then right onto Quincy Road in the center of town for one mile. Signs for the park are on your left. Open dawn to dusk. (603) 786-9465.

RESTAURANTS

Steve's Restaurant: This seafood and chicken restaurant serves a wide variety of cuisines—from Mexican dishes to Italian food to lobster rolls. There are some outdoor tables alongside the restaurant where you and your dog can dine. Stinson Lake Road (Main Street); (603) 786-9835.

PLACES TO STAY

Philbrook Farm Inn: This family-owned farm, listed on the National Register of Historic Places, was built in 1861 and sprawls across 900 acres. Featuring a rambling old farmhouse and quaint cottages along the brook, dogs are allowed in the cottages only. There is plenty of hiking available on the property and gorgeous valley views. This is a true getaway you'll long remember. Rooms range from $120 to $150 per night. 881 North Road, Shelburne, NH 03581; (603) 466-3831.

SUGAR HILL

Although there aren't any parks or hikes in this tiny village, there are some wonderful places to stay while exploring neighboring Franconia Notch State Park.

PLACES TO STAY

Hilltop Inn: The six nonsmoking guest rooms all feature immaculate full private baths. During the summer and fall, pets may stay in a two-bedroom cottage that features a wraparound porch overlooking the surrounding hills and fields. Inn rooms are $35 to $75 per person, double occupancy. The cottage rate is $200 to $250 for up to four people. Main Street, Sugar Hill, NH 03585; (603) 823-5695; www.hilltopinn.com.

The Homestead Inn: This lovely inn, built in 1802, offers 18 charming rooms, most of which allow dogs with permission. Located overlooking a gorgeous valley and close to all nearby Franconia Notch hiking, you and your dog may not want to go anywhere else again. Full breakfast is included in the room rates, which range from $65 to $105. State Route 117, Sugar Hill, NH 03585; (603) 823-5564 or (800) 823-5564.

TAMWORTH

PARKS, BEACHES, AND RECREATION AREAS

• **Chocorua Lake Conservation Area** 🐾🐾🐾 See **21** on page 496.

Talk about an eye for an eye! According to legend, a white settler named Campbell accidentally killed the son of Native American Chocorua. Consequently, Chocorua took revenge and wiped out Campbell's family who, in turn, killed the chief at the top of the peak that bears his name.

Whether true or not, this unique rocky peak is one of the most photographed and traveled mountains in the area. Trails leading to the summit can be reached at the end of Scott Road (just north of Chocorua Lake). Or, for some leisurely fun, you and your dog are welcome to swim and sun at Chocorua Lake. There aren't many trails along the lake, but if you have a water dog or just want to beat the heat, this is a great place to do it.

Dogs must be leashed along the lake.

From State Route 113, take U.S. Route 16 north for 1.5 miles. The lake and turnouts are on your left. The hiking trails are at the end of Scott Road, a quarter mile north of the parking area, off U.S. Route 16. Open dawn to dusk. (603) 539-6201.

RESTAURANTS

Dam Ice Cream: And may we say this is the best dam ice cream we've tasted? Get your licks in at this scenic spot overlooking the waterfall on the Swift River. Picnic tables and grassy areas are perfect for your pup. And did we mention the dam ice cream? U.S. Route 16 at State Route 113; (603) 323-8745.

PLACES TO STAY

Chocorua Camping Village: This full-service family campground offers a swimming beach on Moore's Pond, boating, hiking, and children's activities.

Leashed pets are allowed in most areas. Tent camping and RV hookups are available. The camping fee is $20 per night. U.S. Route 16, P.O. Box 118, Tamworth, NH 03886; (888) 237-8642 or (603) 323-8536; www.chocoruacamping.com.

The Tamworth Inn: This lovely 165-year-old B&B offers 16 rooms and a suite, all with private baths. Located along the Swift River and across from the famous Barnstormers Summer Theatre, you and your small dog may stay in certain rooms with approval. Rates range from $99 to $150 per day with a $5 charge for Fido. Main Street at Tamworth Village, NH 03886; (800) 642-7352; www.tamworth.com.

WENTWORTH

PLACES TO STAY

Hilltop Acres Bed-and-Breakfast: This charming bed-and-breakfast inn has five beautiful rooms, all with private baths and some with fireplaces, plus a few fully equipped housekeeping cottages. Pets are welcome in the cottages only and cannot be left unattended. Breakfast is included. Rates range from $69 to $129. P.O. Box 32, Wentworth, NH 03282; (603) 764-5896.

WHITEFIELD

PLACES TO STAY

Spalding Inn: Built at the turn of the century, this family inn is located on over 200 acres overlooking the White Mountains. Accommodations include the inn's bed-and-breakfast rooms, family suites, and the carriage house. Several charming cottages with kitchens and fireplaces are also available. The cottages and luxury suites range from $99 to $1,000 per night, depending on the season and length of stay. Dogs are welcome in select cottages only. RR 1, Box 57, Mountain View Road, Whitefield, NH 03598; (800) 368-8439, (603) 837-2572; www.spaldinginn.com.

WOODSTOCK

PARKS, BEACHES, AND RECREATION AREAS

• **Lost River Reservation** 🐾🐾🐾 🐕 See **22** on page 496.

In 1911, the Society for the Protection of New Hampshire Forests began to purchase land to shelter New Hampshire forests from the devastation of the logging industry. Fortunately for us, they've done their job well, and this unique series of caves and potholes, formed from the underground flow of the Lost River, was one of their first acquisitions. Over the years, they've acquired 770 acres in the surrounding area, and the result is a great series of trails, ladders, and bridges from which to view these natural caves.

Unfortunately, dogs are not allowed in the gorge, but there are still plenty of trails for you to tackle in the surrounding reservation, including a self-guided Ecology Trail and nature garden. Or you can hike the Dilly Trail (not recommended for older dogs) or the Kinsman Notch Trail. Maps are available at the parking area to help you on your way. Dogs are allowed off leash on all trails but the Ecology Trail.

From Interstate 93, take Exit 32 onto State Route 112 east for seven miles. The reservation is on your right. Open May to October, dawn to dusk. (603) 224-9945; www.spnhf.org.

RESTAURANTS

Clement's Room Grille at the Woodstock Inn: For an elegant dinner at an elegant inn, try this terrace restaurant. Well-behaved dogs may join their human companions on the "petticoat patio" for a wonderful full breakfast or dinner of steak, fish, or lamb. Main Street (U.S. Route 3); (603) 745-3951.

Peg's Family Restaurant: This friendly diner right in the middle of all the action has outdoor tables in the summer where your dog may join you for a great breakfast or lunch. Open 5:30 A.M. to 2:30 P.M., this place is for the early dogs. Main Street, (603) 745-2740.

Sea to Thee Seafood Restaurant: This novel "Heat 'n' Eat" restaurant prepares full dinners to take home or on the road. For a dinner of lobster, swordfish, lasagna, shepherd's pie, and many other delectable choices, you can dine on excellent food at the picnic spot of your choice. Not your usual "take-out" joint, this place is perfect for folks traveling with their pet. Main Street (U.S. Route 3); (603) 745-3330.

PLACES TO STAY

Autumn Breeze Motor Lodge: This comfortable motor inn allows dogs in selected rooms. Guests with pets must first get prior permission. This policy is strictly enforced. Rates range from $40 to $79 per night. U.S. Route 3, Main Street, North Woodstock, NH 03262; (603) 745-8549, (800) 684-3543.

Lost River Campground: This 130-site campground welcomes leashed dogs and provides fairly extensive facilities while still offering an outdoors experience. Close to Lost River Gorge and the Beaver Brook Trail, you'll find this location central to anywhere you go in the White Mountains. Reservations are required for longer than a one-night's stay (overnights are on a first-come, first-served basis). Fees run from $20 to $30 per night. 951 Lost River Road, North Woodstock, NH 03262; (603) 745-8321; www.lostriver.com.

Lost River Cabins: This tiny cluster of cabins offers scenic solitude along the Lost River. All cabins have full kitchens and welcome your furry friend. Rates range from $70 to $85. (603) 745-2823.

DIVERSIONS

Woodstock water weekend: Take a kayaking trip with Outback Kayak on Main Street. Special tours or self-guided trips on the Lost River are offered. Half-day or full-day rentals are available. (603) 745-2002 or (800) KAYAKSS.

MAINE

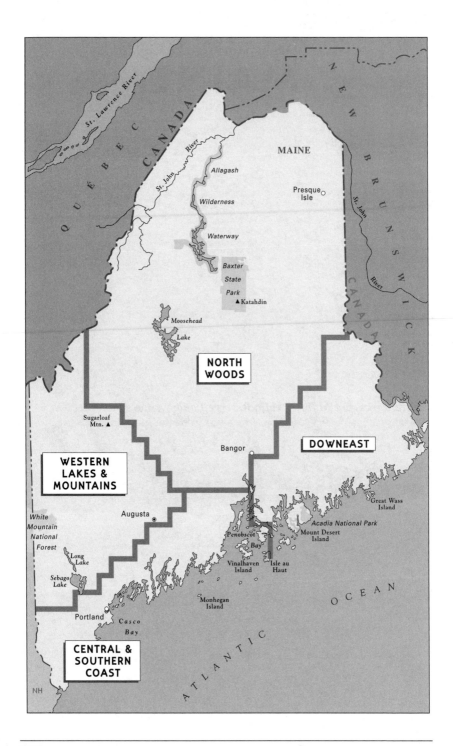

MAINE

Put all the other New England states together, and they still won't be as big as Maine. With 3,500 miles of coastline, acres of woodland wilderness, and thousands of off-shore islands, the Pine Tree State is bigger than any one dog can cover on one or a hundred visits.

"The Main," a term used by fishermen to distinguish the coast from the islands, was first explored by the Vikings in the 11th century. Six centuries later, the French established a colony here in "Acadia," where Acadia National Park now stands. For most of the next century, Maine was a battleground as the French and English struggled for dominance until it became part of the English Massachusetts Bay Colony in 1677 and, finally, a state in 1820. Today, the state's primary industries are fishing and lobstering. In fact, 85 percent of the nation's lobsters come from here.

Maine is a bucolic vacation spot. You and your dog will enjoy exploring such diverse areas as the Great North Woods, which is covered almost entirely by trees and mountains, interrupted here and there by a few lakes; the vast seacoast, dominated by glacially formed rocky coves and peninsulas; and the western lakes and rivers, where you won't find many formal parks, but you won't have any trouble finding a drop to drink. In all, the "main" reason to visit Maine is for the great outdoors and, fortunately for Fido, there is plenty of it!

State Parks and Maine Public Reserve Land: Maine's state park system covers just about every corner of the state from the mountains to the coast. These developed parklands typically have ranger programs, designated camping areas, entrance fees, and leash requirements for dogs.

The Maine Public Reserve Land system is similar to the State Forest programs in other states except, like everything else in Maine, much bigger. Totaling almost a half million acres, these multiuse wilderness properties provide recreational opportunities, hunting, timber, and protection for wildlife and nature.

Generally, dogs are permitted under voice control, and there are no fees for these remote and undeveloped lands. Note that hunting is permitted on many of these properties from October through February.

For more information, call the Maine Bureau of Parks and Recreation at (207) 287-3821. For state park camping reservations, call (207) 287-3824.

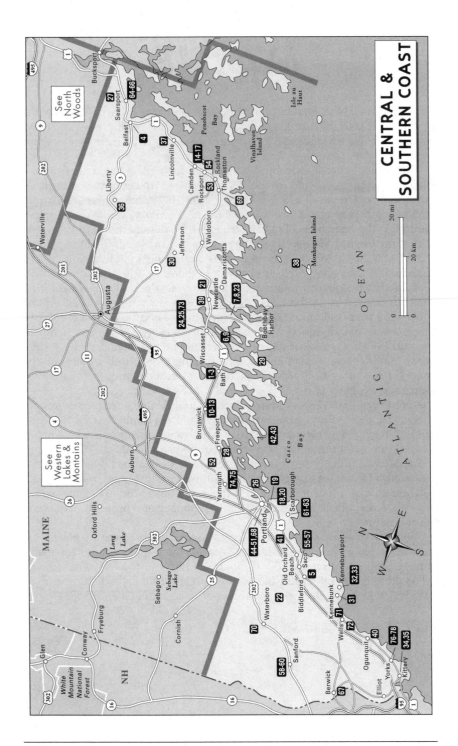

CENTRAL &
SOUTHERN COAST

16
CENTRAL AND SOUTHERN COAST

Think of Maine and the first thing that comes to mind is the spectacular rocky seacoast. The towns in this chapter capture that vision perfectly. From Portland to Boothbay Harbor, you'll find village after quaint village of rocky island coastline, elegant lighthouses dotting the landscape, lobster boats, and good old-fashioned Yankee charm.

This area has always been a popular summer tourist destination, and that remains true today. The wealthy resort towns of Kennebunkport, Ogunquit, and Old Orchard Beach still offer a vast selection of hotels and B&B's—many of which welcome dogs.

Finger peninsulas and islands abound here. There are about 365 islands off Portland alone, and, as you venture farther north, the scenery becomes even more rugged. And that's good news for dogs. In the south, you and your pooch have to compete with two-legged creatures for a little beach time. But as you head up the central coastal area, the beaches become more rocky and, therefore, more dog friendly. We'll tell you which beaches welcome your pup and which will make you wait for the off-season. But you can still enjoy the water with a trip out onto the sea. This is sailing and canoeing country, and we'll tell you where you can hop aboard a schooner or take a kayak trip under the stars. In all, a trip to Maine will be as advertised—a wilderness paradise with all the comforts of home.

Boothbay Region Land Trust: Since 1980 this conservation organization has managed six properties in Lincoln County, and all are wonderful places to take dogs. They rely on private donations to keep these parks in top shape. The trails are well maintained and allow dogs off leash. For trail maps, information, or to become a member of this nonprofit organization, write to P.O. Box 183, 1 Oak Street, Boothbay Harbor, ME 04538-0183; (207) 633-4818.

BATH

PARKS, BEACHES, AND RECREATION AREAS

• **Library Park** 😺😺 See **1** on page 522.

This small one-acre park isn't a must-see on anybody's list, but if you're staying in this historic town and need to let your dog sniff a little patch of green, this will suffice. Located in the center of town, there is one sidewalk that runs through the middle and a small pond on the eastern side. For literary dogs, the library occupies the western edge of the park. Dogs need to be leashed.

The park is located at Front and Summer Streets. Open 8 A.M. to 11 P.M. (207) 443-5141.

• **L. E. Temple Waterfront Park** 😺😺 See **2** on page 522.

This park offers a small gravel path that runs along the Kennebec River. There isn't any river access, and the current is rather swift here, but if you want a water view and a nice picnic spot, this is the best Bath has to offer. Dogs must be on leash.

Located on Commercial Street along the waterfront in the center of town. Open 8 A.M. to 11 P.M. (207) 443-5141.

• **Thorne Head Nature Area** 😺😺 🐕 See **3** on page 522.

We admit we had high hopes for this place, but currently it isn't what it may be in the future. Acquired by the Bath Conservation Commission in 1999, these 96 acres on Thorne Head Point have a series of undeveloped muddy roads that lead into a pine forest and along the water's edge. The town of Bath plans to clean up the park and develop a more cohesive trail system, so stay tuned. Dogs are allowed off leash.

From the center of town, follow High Street north two miles to the end. The park and parking area are at the end of the dirt road. Open dawn to dusk. (207) 443-9751.

NATURE HIKES AND URBAN WALKS

Historic Walking Tour: Take this daily tour of 19th-century homes and cemeteries in the Bath area. Guided tours begin at the Winter Street Church, or you can take your own self-guided tour down High Street. Markers are posted on each historical home and landmark. Dogs are allowed at all outdoor facilities. For more information, call (207) 442-8627.

RESTAURANTS

Kristina's Restaurant & Bakery: There aren't many outdoor seating areas in Bath, but fortunately you only need one. This café has a big porch outside where you and your dog may sit and eat scrumptious bakery items, lunch or dinner. 160 Centre Street; (207) 442-8577.

PLACES TO STAY

The Inn at Bath: This lovely Greek Revival bed-and-breakfast dates back to the early 1800s. Located within walking distance of all Bath historical sites, it has six elegant rooms, all with private baths, and one suite. Pets are allowed in select rooms, and a full breakfast is served each morning. Rates range from

$80 to $200. 969 Washington Street, Bath, ME 04530; (207) 443-4294; www. innatbath.com.

Holiday Inn of Bath: You'll be comfortable at this 141-room hotel just outside of downtown Bath, offering the convenience and modern amenities you'd expect from a chain hotel. Pets are welcome. Rooms range from $79 to $149. 139 Richardson Street, Bath, ME 04530; (207) 443-9741.

FESTIVALS

Bath Heritage Days: Come join the fun at this maritime festival that any seadog will enjoy. Three days of celebrating focuses around the Fourth of July holiday and Bath's illustrious maritime history. Events include a parade, fireworks, and free entertainment in Library Park. Call for details of specific events. (207) 443-9751.

BELFAST

PARKS, BEACHES, AND RECREATION AREAS

• **Belfast City Park** 🐾 🐾 See **4** on page 522.

This pleasant city park offers grassy picnic areas, a large grassy common for ball throwing, and a long stretch of rocky beach. Your dog can swim here since it doesn't compete with the local swimming pool steps away (where dogs can't go). The overlooking picnic tables make this a nice stop for lunch and a little exercise.

Dogs must be on leash.

From downtown on Main Street, take Northport Avenue (High Street) south for one mile. The park entrance is on the left. Open 8 A.M. to 8 P.M. (207) 338-1975.

RESTAURANTS

Bay Wrap: Eat in or take out a healthy portable "wrap"—a piece of flat bread wrapped around more choices of fillings than you can imagine. Try the Pesto Wrapture or the State of Confucious. Vegetarian choices are available, as well. 20 Beaver Street; (207) 338-9757.

PLACES TO STAY

Admiral's Ocean Inn: This cheerful 20-room inn offers comfortable rooms with simple amenities. Dogs are welcome with a $20 refundable deposit. Rooms range from $40 to $95, and continental breakfast is included. RR 1, Box 99A, Belfast, ME 04915; (207) 338-4260.

Belfast Bay Meadows Inn: This large Cape-style home is located on 17 acres and offers a private beach and hiking trails on the grounds. Each of the 20 rooms is tastefully decorated, and a full breakfast is included in your room rate. Dogs are welcome in the 14-room annex for an additional $15 per night. Rooms range from $85 to $170 per night. 90 Northport Avenue, Belfast, ME 04915; (207) 338-5715, (800) 335-2377; www.maineguide.com.

Belfast Motor Inn: This modern 60-room motel overlooking the bay is clean and comfortable and welcomes your pet for an additional $5 per night. Located on six acres, there is bay access and plenty of space to walk your leashed pet. Rooms range from $45 to $135 per night. RR 2, Box 21, Belfast, ME 04915; (207) 338-4260; belfastharborinn.com.

Wonderview Cottages: This quaint cluster of 20 cottages rests on a hill overlooking the bay. Each cottage offers fireplaces and efficiencies, and a private sandy beach is available to guests. Pets are welcome with a $25 refundable deposit. Cottages are available by the week for $400 to $900. RFD 1, Box 89 Route 1, Belfast, ME 04915; (207) 338-1455.

FESTIVALS

Belfast Bay Festival: This five-day festival takes place in mid-July at Belfast City Park and plays host to a whole assortment of entertaining events including the Saturday night fireworks, the town parade, and daily concerts. For more information, call (207) 338-5719.

Belfast Bear Fest: Bear with this unique festival which runs throughout the summer and features over 40 bears created by local Maine artists. The bears are located all over town; you can pick up an "overbearing" map at any local business to help you find all of these charming creations. For more information, call (207) 338-3879.

DIVERSIONS

Belfast Summer Nights: Come on downtown for free live street music on the wharf every Thursday night from 5:30 to 7:30 P.M. The fun runs from July through August. For more information and music schedules, call (207) 338-3879.

Fast Times in Belfast: These two-mile, personally guided walking tours of Belfast are packed with fun facts and architectural and historical information. The tours take place every Saturday at 10 A.M. from June to Labor Day, and every Wednesday through Friday at 10 A.M. and 1 P.M. from July to Labor Day. The cost is $10 per person. Meet in front of the post office on Main Street. (207) 338-6306.

BIDDEFORD

PARKS, BEACHES, AND RECREATION AREAS

• Clifford Park See 5 on page 522.

This small park is located right in town, but because it's hilly, wooded, and has some hiking trails, it feels like a wilderness experience without the traveling. The three short trails loop and crisscross so you can make some tracks even though you never get more than a quarter mile away from your car. The trail loops, a combined two miles in length, all begin at the same trailhead to the right of the ball field from the parking area.

Dog must be on leash and are not permitted at the ball fields or playgrounds.

From the intersection of State Route 9 (Alfred Street) and Pool Street, take Pool Street south for a quarter mile. The park and its parking lot are on the right. Open 8 A.M. to 8 P.M. (207) 282-1579.

BOOTHBAY

PARKS, BEACHES, AND RECREATION AREAS

• Linekin Preserve 🐾🐾🐾 🐕 See **6** on page 522.
This 95-acre parcel, located in East Boothbay on Linekin Neck, stretches from Route 96 to the Damariscotta River. The preserve offers over two miles of hiking trails and a small stretch of river frontage for a dip on those warm summer days. You'll find the trails well maintained and fairly isolated, and the leash-free freedom will make this park a definite escape for both you and your unleashed pooch.

From State Route 27 in Boothbay Harbor, take State Route 96 south for four miles into Boothbay. The park and a parking area are on the left. Open sunrise to sunset. (207) 633-4818.

• Marshall E. Saunders Memorial Park 🐾🐾🐾 🐕 See **7** on page 522.
The Marshall E. Saunders Memorial Park is a 22-acre park on the Damariscotta River located where Kelley Brook flows into Pleasant Cove. There is a one-mile loop trail that leads past the brook and down to the cove, the site of an old sawmill and brickyard. Along the way, you'll walk through a shady forest on flat, even trails, as the river breezes blow by. Dogs are allowed off leash here if under control.

From State Route 96 in Boothbay Harbor, take Back Narrows Road three miles north into Boothbay. At the intersection with Pleasant Cove Road, the park and parking is straight ahead. Open sunrise to sunset. (207) 633-4818.

• Ovens Mouth Preserve 🐾🐾🐾 🐕 See **8** on page 522.
Two, two, two parks in one! The Ovens Mouth Preserve is a unique 146-acre parcel of scenic shoreline bordered by swift tidal water, quiet coves, and salt marshes. Of the three Boothbay peninsulas at Ovens Mouth, the preserve includes the middle and eastern peninsulas. There are 1.5 miles of hiking trails on the east peninsula and three miles of hiking trails on the west peninsula.

You'll get a more strenuous hike on the west peninsula where eskers trails roll up and down. The eastern peninsula is flatter. Unfortunately the two peninsulas do not have a trail connecting them, so you'll have to make a choice between the two areas. Decisions, decisions. Dogs may leave their leashes behind if they are under voice control.

From State Route 27, take Adams Pond Road west. Turn right onto Dover Road for two miles. At the junction, bear right onto Dover Road Extension to the end for the east peninsula of the park. For the western peninsula, bear left at the junction onto Dover Cross Road for a tenth of a mile to the end. Parking is available. Open sunrise to sunset. (207) 633-4818.

• Porter Preserve 🐾🐾🐾 🐕 See **9** on page 522.
The Porter Preserve is a small 19-acre wooded shore property including a small offshore island—accessible only by canoe—and a beach where your dog can escape the heat on those hot summer days when all the other swimming beaches ban dogs. There are lovely southern views of the Sheepscot River and

a mile of trails. You won't get a workout here, but, if your dog likes water, come on down!. Dogs must be under voice control.

From State Route 27, take Corey Lane west a quarter mile. Turn right onto Barters Island Road for two miles, then left onto Kimballtown Road (on Barters Island) for a half mile. Turn left onto a dirt road at the fork to the park. Limited roadside parking is available. Open sunrise to sunset. (207) 633-4818.

PLACES TO STAY

Smuggler's Cove Motor Inn: The 60 rooms at this spacious modern motel complex are all on the water or have waterfront views of scenic Linekin Bay. There is even a private beach for guests (including your four-footed one). Continental breakfast is served each morning, and pets are welcome in most rooms. Rates range from $70 to $149. HC 65, Box 837, East Boothbay ME 04544; (207) 633-2800 or (800) 633-3008; smugglerscovemotel.com.

Water's Edge Motel and Cabins: Located on two acres of Ocean Point, this eight-cabin, 16-unit motel is a comfortable no-frills place to stay with your pet. A small beach is available, and there are walking trails through the surrounding woods. Rates range from $50 to $120 per night. Open seasonally. 545 Ocean Point Road, East Boothbay, ME 04544, (207) 633-2505.

BOOTHBAY HARBOR

This scenic and popular destination is one of the most dog-friendly towns around. You'll find water bowls all around town for your furry friend, and many of the local attractions and hotels welcome dogs. There aren't many parks here, but the conservation areas just outside of town make this a great place to vacation with your best friend.

NATURE HIKES AND URBAN WALKS

Mace Carter Memorial Footbridge: Take a scenic walk over Boothbay Harbor on this quaint footbridge. Connecting the east side of the harbor to the west, this is a fun short walk with water views all around. Access the walkway from Bridge Street. (207) 633-3112.

RESTAURANTS

Blue Moon Café: Sit on the deck overlooking the harbor at this quaint café. Open for breakfast and lunch, you can enjoy soups, salads, and great sandwiches with an equally great waterfront view. 54 Commercial Street; (207) 633-2349.

The Chowder House: Located right by the footbridge on "Granary Way," you can enjoy old-fashioned chowder, seafood, and other Maine recipes prepared in an open kitchen. Dine out on the waterfront deck with your pooch. 22 Granary Way; (207) 633-5761.

Christopher's Boathouse: This popular restaurant, featuring "new world cuisine," has great food and an even better waterfront deck where your dog may join you. Most dishes are prepared on an open-air wood grill creating a festive air of a local backyard barbecue party. 25 Union Street; (207) 633-6565.

Pattaya Thai: When you need a break from all the seafood around you, head to this exotic Thai restaurant. The food is exceptional, and you can order takeout or sit on the open-air deck across from the harbor. And for those of you who just can't get enough fish, there is a sushi bar, as well. 28 Union Street; (207) 633-0025.

Gray's Wharf: This is the place for casual seafood dishes served on the waterfront at Pier One. Enjoy a seafood kabob or a huge Maine lobster on the deck. Pier One; (207) 633-5629.

Greater Boothbay Ice Cream: Formerly known as Downeast Ice Cream, this ice-cream parlor in the center of town makes a wicked ice-cream soda. Yogurt, shakes, sundaes, and soft serve are available, with plenty of outdoor tables on Pier One where you and your dog can take a few lickings. Pier One; (207) 633-3016.

McSeagull's: Chicken, pasta, seafood, and beef dishes await you at this friendly harborside restaurant. Located on Pier One, you'll be in the middle of the action here. Dogs are allowed on the outdoor deck. Pier One; (207) 633-5900.

Quenchers: Quench your thirst at this multipurpose beverage bar. Scrumptious smoothies, dark coffee, amazing nectars, and ice-cream drinks await you. Sit outside at one of the tables or on the benches at Pier One. Slurps up! One Wharf Street; (207) 633-3464.

PLACES TO STAY

Harbor Motor Court: This 22-unit motel has one- and two-bedroom units with efficiencies. They offer clean, comfortable accommodations on several acres. Rates range from $39 to $75 per night. P.O. Box 326, State Route 27, Boothbay Harbor, ME 04538; (207) 633-5450; www.maineguide.com.

Harborside Resort: This lovely 35-room motel is one mile from downtown on a picturesque lakefront property. There are several rooms with efficiencies, and all rooms are pet friendly. Boats are available for rent, or you can canoe or swim in the freshwater lake—and the ocean is only a short walk away. Rooms range from $79 to $109 plus a small refundable deposit for your dog. P.O. Box 516, Boothbay Harbor, ME 04538; (207) 633-5381.

The Pines Motel: This 30-unit motel is on a secluded hillside pine grove overlooking the outer harbor. The rooms are spacious, clean, and comfortable. Pets are allowed in all rooms with prior approval. Rates range from $30 to $90. Open from May to October. Sunset Road, Box C, Boothbay Harbor, ME 04538; (207) 633-4555.

Spruce Point Inn: This fabulous resort, located at the entrance to the harbor, offers 72 rooms, many with efficiencies. Recently renovated, you'll stay in spacious quarters with all the modern conveniences. The views are excellent from most rooms and, although there is a shuttle to town, you may find yourself preferring to relax and stay "at home" at this home away from home. Rates range from $95 to $189 per night. Box 237, Atlantic Avenue, Boothbay Harbor, ME 04538; (207) 633-4152 or (800) 553-0289; www.sprucepointinn.com.

Welch House Inn: This elegant 16-room bed-and-breakfast has fabulous views from its hilltop perch on McKown Hill. Built in 1873, all rooms have private baths, and full breakfast is provided each morning. Plus it's only a quick walk to town. Pets are allowed in most rooms. Rates range from $60 to $145. 56 McKown Street, Boothbay Harbor, ME 04538; (207) 633-3431; www.welchhouse.com.

FESTIVALS

Fisherman's Festival: Join the festive boat parade celebrating the coming of the summer season. It's fish, fish, and more fish. Activities include, well, anything you can think of with fish. Held annually the first weekend in May. (207) 633-2353.

Windjammer Days Festival: Come on down to the harbor for this annual town celebration. Activities include concerts, fireworks, a downtown parade, and a harbor filled with majestic boats. Held annually on the third weekend in June. (207) 633-2353.

DIVERSIONS

Don't rock the boat!: Take a scenic one-hour harbor cruise or an all-day trip out to Monhegan Island on this charter boat. The island trip leaves at 9:30 each morning and returns to Boothbay Harbor at 4:15 P.M. Admission is $30 per person and $5 for your dog. The harbor cruise leaves every other hour. Adults are $9 and dogs are free. (207) 633-2284.

Paws 'n' Claws: Normally we don't include pet stores, but this one is an original. Pick up a blinking collar or pooch pack for your dog at Down East Paws and Claws, and, while you're at it, stop at their gourmet dog bakery. Water and free biscuits to all who enter. 5 Boothbay House Hill Road; (207) 633-0879.

Take a paddle on the wild side: At Tidal Transit Ocean Kayak & Bike Co., your dog may join you on one of the guided tours, or you can rent a kayak for your own exploration. Half-day or full-day rentals and tours are available. (207) 633-7140.

We're Jammin': Sail away on this 2-hour windjammer cruise which departs Fisherman's Wharf four times daily. The trip includes the outer islands and a visit to Seal Rocks. Dogs are allowed on leash. Admission is $20 per person. Dogs sail free. (207) 633-6598.

BRUNSWICK

PARKS, BEACHES, AND RECREATION AREAS

• Androscoggin River Bike Path 🐾🐾🐾 See **10** on page 522.

This winding bike path is three miles long and has been a real crowd pleaser for everyone in Brunswick and the adjacent town of Topsham since opening in 1999. There are also plenty of well-groomed grassy areas and river access points along the way allowing dogs the room to romp and roll to their heart's content.

There are, however, two sides to the bike path. One side has the beautiful Androscoggin River. On the other side is busy State Route 1. The bike path and the highway are safely separated by a fence, but there have been unconfirmed reports of walkers and bikers getting stiff necks from looking in only one direction.

Dogs need to be leashed.

To get to the western end from State Route 24 (Bath Road), take Federal Street north into Water Street. Parking and the start of the bike path are at the end of the road. The eastern terminus is off of Old Bath Road; a north entrance, in Topsham on Elm Street, crosses the State Route 196 bridge over the Androscoggin River. Open a half hour before sunrise to a half hour after sunset. (207) 725-6656.

•Bowdoin Pines 🐾🐾 See **11** on page 522.
If you and your dog can't swing a visit to the giant California redwoods, the next best thing is a trip to Bowdoin Pines. This small, but ancient, forest is a great place for a walk. The footpath is a mere half-mile loop, but your outing will take awhile as you marvel at the old-growth white pines, some of which are 90 feet tall, 10 feet around, and about 125 years old. Inu was so impressed with the trees, he almost dehydrated himself.

Parking is limited in this area, but you can park in the Pine Grove Cemetery (no walking your dog here) across the street. Dogs must be on leash.

From the intersection of State Routes 24 (Bath Road) and 123, take Bath Road east for one-tenth of a mile. The pines are on your left and the cemetery is on the right. Both are open dawn to dusk. (207) 725-6656.

•Brunswick Town Commons 🐾🐾🐾 See **12** on page 522.
The Brunswick Town Commons were established way back in 1719. And we're certain it was as popular then as it is now for dog walking. With three miles of trails through a rich pine forest and a heath of rhododendron and holly, this is one common that isn't common at all. Be sure to view the trail map display before heading out. Many of the looping trails branch off to open but private forests.

Dogs need to be leashed.

From State Route 24, take Harpswell Road (State Route 123) south for two miles. The park is on the right. Parking is available. Open dawn to dusk. (207) 725-6656.

•Park Row 🐾🐾 See **13** on page 522.
Park Row is a small strip of parkland on Maine Street running for three blocks under shady elms and well-manicured lawns connecting downtown and Bowdoin College.

Dogs need to be leashed.

The park is on Maine Street. Open 24 hours a day. (207) 725-6656.

NATURE HIKES AND URBAN WALKS
Androscoggin River Pedestrian Bridge: We give this shaky footbridge across the Androscoggin River a three-paw rating just for the pure adrenaline rush it gives those brave enough to cross it.

The 314-foot bridge, built in 1936, is one of only two suspension footbridges in the Pine Tree State; the other is in Waterville-Winslow (see pages 620–621). A crossing gives you a great view of the rocky river and the two towns it connects: Brunswick and Topsham.

You can help give the bridge a four-paw adrenaline rating by joining the few crazies who have actually jumped from the 30-foot-high bridge into the river. We don't recommend it, but apparently somewhere down there the water is 25 feet deep.

Dogs must be on leash.

The bridge is located on U.S. Route 1 and Cushing Street, just east of State Route 24. Roadside parking is available. Open 24 hours a day. (207) 287-2551.

RESTAURANTS

Brunswick Diner: This old-fashioned diner serves what you would expect a diner to serve. But they do it better than anyone, and the 1950s atmosphere makes it a fun stop for you and your dog. You can't eat inside, but there are picnic tables outside to enjoy your meal. 101 Pleasant Street (U.S. Route 1); (207) 721-1134.

Ernie's Drive-In: Pile everyone in, put it in reverse, and drive all the way back to the 1940s. That's how you get to Ernie's. In the '40s and '50s, drive-ins (and we mean real drive-ins with car service, not drive-up windows) were all the rage. But today few remain. Luckily, Ernie's hasn't changed a thing since opening in 1944. Simply park, put your headlights on, and wait for a waitress to come out and take your order. The menu is a classic, too, and will have Fido drooling all over your Edsel. Bath Road; (207) 729-9439.

Wild O.A.T.S. Bakery & Café: That's Original And Tasty Stuff in case you couldn't tell simply by taking in the appetizing aroma of freshly made soups, sandwiches, hot entrees, and bakery goods. Join the hip and well-fed college crowd at the outdoor patio on Maine Street. 149 Maine Street; (207) 725-6287.

PLACES TO STAY

The Atrium Travelodge Motel: This 186-room motel offers your standard motel amenities, but the rooms are spacious and comfortable. A restaurant is on-site so you can order room service. Rates range from $74 to $125. 21 Gurnet Road, Brunswick, ME 04011; (207) 729-5555.

Mainline Motel: This 52-room motel offers standard rooms and some suites with refrigerators. Pets are welcome in most rooms with an additional $5 fee. Room rates range from $69 to $129. 130 Pleasant Street, Brunswick, ME 04011; (207) 725-8761.

Viking Motor Inn: Stay at this friendly family-run motel in the heart of Brunswick. You can choose from standard motel rooms or efficiency units, which have kitchenettes, work areas, and all the modern amenities. Rates range from $69 to $95 per night. Weekly rates are available as well. 287 Bath Road, Brunswick, ME 04011; (207) 729-6661; www.vikingmotorinn.com.

DIVERSIONS

Music on the Mall: Make like a mall rat terrier and bring your dog along to the Brunswick Mall every Wednesday evening for a free outdoor concert during July and August. The fun begins at 7 P.M., but you can bring a picnic earlier and enjoy the festive night air. (207) 725-8797.

CAMDEN

PARKS, BEACHES, AND RECREATION AREAS

• **Camden Hills State Park** 🐾 🐾 🐾 See **14** on page 522.

Camden Hills State Park is one of the most popular destinations in Maine.

There are 5,474 acres of wooded, mountainous coastline, 30 miles of fantastic trails, plus camping and take-your-breath-away views. With the extensive trail system, you can design your own route or just let your dog lead the way.

Mount Battie, the main feature of the park, can be hiked or accessed via the auto route. And since the road allows every visitor to make it to the top, you don't want to be the only one staying behind. Take the steep, one-mile-long hiking trail to the summit, and you'll be rewarded by one of the more impressive views on the eastern seaboard.

Mount Megunicook, the highest mainland mountain (1,380 feet high) that slopes directly into the sea, is also found in this park, and we prefer climbing this peak instead of Mount Battie. The hike to the top is one mile in length, like the Mount Battie trail, and has equally amazing views along the way (although there are limited views from the wooded peak). On Mount Megunicook, though, you'll avoid all the Mount Battie crowds and the busy summit road.

Camping is available, but the 112 full-service sites fill up quickly. Pets must be leashed in the campground. Rates range from $16 to $20 per night. Call (800) 332-1501 for reservations in state and (207) 287-3824 from out of state.

Dogs need to be leashed in all state parks. There is a $2 day-use fee.

Trail maps are available at the park entrance.

From the intersection of U.S. Route 1 and State Route 52, take U.S. Route 1 north for two miles. The park entrance is on the left. Open 9 A.M. to sunset. Call (207) 236-3109 May 1 to October 15, (207) 236-0949 off-season.

• Merryspring Park 🐾🐾🐾 🐕 See **15** on page 522.

This lovely arboretum comprises 66 acres of woodland, gardens, and wetlands. Managed by Merryspring, Inc., a nonprofit organization, this park has been protected since 1972, and you won't find a more peaceful park for miles.

Several trails loop through cedar and white pine forests, meadows, and hills. A kiosk at the entrance offers several trail brochures as well as a brief history of this lovely place. Walk the self-guided nature trail or just wander and enjoy. Your dog will be way ahead of you either way. Dogs must be leashed near the entrance to the park but may be off leash on the trails if under control.

From U.S. Route 1 (Elm Street), take Conway Road north for a mile into the park. Parking is available. Open sunrise to sunset. (207) 236-2239.

• Ragged Mountain Trail and Recreation Area 🐾🐾 See **16** on page 522.

During the winter, Ragged Mountain and the Camden Snow Bowl are home to skiers and the U.S. National Toboggan Championship. During the summer, it's a great place to avoid the crowds on nearby Mount Battie and still enjoy spectacular ocean views from "where the mountains meet the sea."

The trail begins by following the ski lift but soon enters the woods and crosses some rocky ledges to the summit at 1,300 feet on a one-mile trek to the top. George doesn't mind hiking up along the ski lift, but he gets pretty disappointed about not being able to toboggan down.

At the base of the mountain is Hosmer Pond, a good place to cool off the piggies and pups.

From the intersection of U.S. Route 1 and State Route 52, take U.S. Route 1 south for half a mile. Turn right onto Hosmer Road for five miles. The Camden Snow Bowl is on the left. The trailhead is at the end of the parking area. Open sunrise to one hour after sunset, but the parking lot gate closes at 4:30 P.M. (207) 236-3438.

• **Village Green** 🐾 🐾 See **17** on page 522.
This small park overlooking Camden Harbor provides a lovely green space to picnic or watch the boats come in and out. There are benches and stone walls all along the walkways, and a waterfall cascades down a granite wall nearby. This isn't a large park, but your dog will enjoy the many spots to sniff and you will definitely enjoy the view. Dogs must be on leash.

Park is located at the harbor in the center of town at the intersection of U.S. Route 1 (Main Street) and State Route 52. Open 6 A.M. to 11 P.M. (207) 236-2239.

NATURE HIKES AND URBAN WALKS
Camden Historical Walking Tour: Take a walk through town on this tour, prepared by the Camden-Rockport Historical Society. Maps are available at the visitors center on the wharf. Audio-guided cassette tapes are available at the Village Shop on Elm Street for $12. (207) 236-2419.

RESTAURANTS
Bayview Lobster Restaurant: Overlooking the harbor, this excellent seafood restaurant has an outdoor patio where you and your dog can enjoy your meal. Their specialty is fresh Maine lobster, but our dogs prefer the surf and turf. Bayview Landing; (207 236-2005.

Cappy's Bakery: Cap off a great day in Camden by stopping at this little bakery and catering company for a boxed lunch to accompany you on the trails. Or, if you're feeling lazy, walk a block to the picnic area at the Village Green. The food is unusual with all the right touches. Definitely beats making a sandwich at home! 1 Main Street; (207) 236-2254.

PLACES TO STAY
Blue Harbor House: This quaint 10-room inn is located a short walk to town. Built in 1810, it features rooms with four-poster beds and elegant antiques. Dogs are welcome in the carriage house, so be sure you make your reservation early. Rates range from $99 to $160 per night. Breakfast is included. 67 Elm Street, Camden, ME 04843; (207) 236-3196; www.blueharborhouse.com.

Camden Hills State Park camping: See page 522.

Hardstone Inn: This elegant 1835 Victorian inn is located near town and offers tasteful, colorful rooms and suites in a luxurious setting. There are 10 romantic rooms available, all with private baths. A healthy continental breakfast is served each morning. Dogs are allowed in two suites for an additional $15 fee. Rooms range from $80 to $160 per night. 41 Elm Street, Camden, ME 04843; (207) 236-4259; www.midcoast.com/~hrtstone.

FESTIVALS
Christmas by the Sea: Get swept away by the spirit of the season when you see the sights on Elm Street during the holiday season. With a decorated

downtown and shops, a village green tree-lighting ceremony, and Santa arriving by lobster boat, you and your dog won't dare be Scrooges! Held the first full weekend in December. (207) 236-4404.

Windjammer Weekend: Set sail over the Labor Day weekend as Camden Harbor is awash in a sea of boat parades and fireworks. The annual event is the largest such gathering of the windjammer fleet in the state of Maine. (207) 236-4404.

DIVERSIONS

A two-hour cruise, a two-hour cruise: Take a two-hour trip on the schooner *Olad*, and we expect you'll return in a more timely fashion than Gilligan and his crew. This beautiful sailing ship leaves from Camden Harbor four times daily on a trip along the Maine coast. Dogs are welcomed aboard! Adults are $20, children $10, and dogs are free. Call (207) 236-2323 to reserve a spot for Spot.

Lord of the Dance: Take a half-day canoe trip with Riverdance Outfitters. They will arrange a specialized trip for you and your dog on the ocean, ponds, or lakes in the area. Included in the trip is a lunch from the Camden Deli and transportation to and from your destination. A sunset hiking tour is also available. Trips range from two to four hours, and the price ranges from $30 to $55. (207) 230-0033.

CAPE ELIZABETH

PARKS, BEACHES, AND RECREATION AREAS

• Crescent Beach State Park 🐾🐾 See 18 on page 522.

This is a popular beach on Seal Cove and, luckily, you and your dog are allowed here in the off-season. With a large sandy beach that has great views of Richmond Island, you'll enjoy those cool fall and spring days near the solitude of the sea. The 243 acres here also include some woods with a couple of short walking trails. But we have a hunch you won't get past the beach.

Dogs must be on leash and are not permitted on the beach from April 1 to October 1 during tern nesting season. There is a $2.50 entrance fee per adult.

The park is located off of Bowery Beach Road (State Route 77). Parking is available. Open dawn to dusk or 6:30 P.M. (whichever is later). (207) 799-5871.

> "Steadfast, serene, immovable, the same,
> Year after year, through all the silent night
> Burns on forevermore that quenchless flame,
> Shines on that inextinguishable light!"

• Fort Williams Park 🐾🐾🐾 ◀ See 19 on page 522.

Henry Wadsworth-Longfellow, the beloved Portland poet, took many walks down to the Portland Head Light to visit friends and marvel at the great beacon he loved, which is said to have inspired his poem, *The Lighthouse*. Luckily, the people of Maine recognize our fascination with lighthouses, and a strong effort is underway to preserve these aging lights. Unfortunately, "restoration" usually means fencing off the public from the light itself.

Amazingly, Maine's oldest lighthouse, the Portland Head Light, is also its most accessible. You and your seafaring dog can walk right up to its base. The 1791 light was commissioned by George Washington and still welcomes sailors into Portland Harbor today.

The light is located in Fort Williams Park, impressive in its own right. The high cliffs here in Cape Elizabeth have been the site of some kind of a fortification since 1872. Today, the open cliffs are used as a community recreation area with rolling lawns, ball fields, hiking trails, and bike paths. You'll find plenty of room to stretch your legs after a visit to the light. Or stretch your eyes. We're still counting, but it's said you can see 200 islands off the coast from here.

Dogs need to be on leash.

From State Route 77 in South Portland, take Cottage Road east into Shore Road and Cape Elizabeth. The park is on the left. Open sunrise to sunset. For Fort William Park, call (207) 799-7652, and for Portland Head Light, call (207) 799-2661.

• Two Lights State Park 🐾 🐾 See **20** on page 522.

This small state park is 40 acres of coastal, rocky shoreline. Mainly used as a picnic area, there are a few trails along the thin woods and rocky cliffs.

At the northern tip (at the end of Two Lights Road) is a small peninsula of solid rock, a short sandy beach, and the best vantage point for admiring Cape Elizabeth Light. The light is also called Two Lights because in 1829 there were two working towers. Today only one is operational.

Dogs must be on leash and are not permitted in the playground area. There is a $1 entrance fee per person.

From State Route 77, take Two Lights Road south for a mile. The park is on your right. Parking is available. Or take Two Lights Road to the end where there is another parking area. Open dawn to dusk or 6:30 P.M. (whichever is later). (207) 799-5871.

RESTAURANTS

The Cookie Jar Pastry Shop: There is no outdoor seating, but we doubt you'll mind once you taste their cookies. We have an "as many as you can carry" policy which extends to the delicious donuts and pastries, as well. It's doubtful the goodies would make it to the table anyway, even if they had one. 554 Shore Road; (207) 799-0671.

Two Lights Lobster Shack: You can't ask for a better setting for eating lobster. The Two Lights Lobster Shack has served great seafood on its rocky, seaside perch since the 1920s. A large patio ensures there's room for everyone, and the food is fantastic—full lobster dinners, shrimp, clams, chowders and stews, burgers and chicken, and homemade desserts. Open April to mid-October. 255 Two Lights Road; (207) 799-1677.

PLACES TO STAY

The Inn-By-The-Sea: This lovely inn is just a few quiet miles south of Portland, right on the seacoast of Cape Elizabeth. Beth and Rocky have stayed here often, and both agree it's a real find! There are 43 one- or two-bedroom suites, each featuring a kitchenette and ocean views. Rocky loves the dog-biscuit room service, pet menu, and dog-loving staff. Beth prefers the homemade cookies that are part of the nightly turn-down service. Walk to the ocean via a path over the wetlands for your own private beach getaway. Suites range from $130 to $449 per night with a two-night minimum required on weekends. 40 Bowery Beach Road, Route 77, Cape Elizabeth, ME 04107; (800) 888-4287, (207) 799-3134; www.innbythesea.com.

DAMARISCOTTA

PARKS, BEACHES, AND RECREATION AREAS

• **Salt Bay Farm Heritage Center** 🐾🐾🐾🐾 🐕 🦴 See **21** on page 522.

This is one of the best parks in this area, and we know your dog will love it as much as ours do. One of the Damariscotta River Association's most scenic protected areas, this 100-acre farm on the Great Salt Bay offers meadows, salt marshes, gorgeous woodlands, and excellent walking trails. With fresh-cut trails through open meadows and boardwalk bridges over muddy marshes, you and your pup will want to return again and again. A trail map is available at the trailhead kiosk.

Dogs must be leashed on the farmhouse side of the road and are allowed under voice control on the barn side, although there is a warning note on the map board stating that this off-leash policy is under review annually. So be respectful of this working farm and make sure your dog IS under control and that you pick up after him.

From U.S. Route 1, take Belvedere Road north for a three-quarters of a mile. The park is on both sides of the road. Open dawn to dusk. (207) 563-1393.

RESTAURANTS

Schooner's Landing: Dine on the open-air patio overlooking the Damariscotta River. This friendly restaurant offers a relaxed dining experience with a menu of baked or broiled seafood. Dogs get a water bowl on request. Main Street; (207) 563-7447.

PLACES TO STAY

Country Fair Motel: This 21-room motel isn't fancy, but it makes a comfortable roadside stop on your way up or down the seacoast. A continental breakfast is included. Rooms range from $50 to $75 per night plus an additional fee of $5 for your pet. State Route 1, RFD Box 36, Damariscotta, ME 04543; (207) 563-3769.

DAYTON

PARKS, BEACHES, AND RECREATION AREAS

• **Harris Farm** 🐾🐾🐾 See **22** on page 522.

There are 40 kilometers of trails at this wonderful 500-acre dairy and tree farm. A popular cross-country ski destination, you can also access the trails in other seasons. Wander over open meadows and through quiet forests on these specially groomed trails. There is a $12 fee to use the trails in winter; in the off-season the trails are free. Stop by for a pancake breakfast at the barn or free samples of maple syrup before you hit the trails. Now that'll get your blood sugar soaring! Dogs must be on leash.

From State Route 5, take State Route 35 south for a half mile. Turn left onto Buzzell Road; the visitors center is on your left. Open 7 A.M. to 4 P.M. (207) 499-2678.

EDGECOMB

PARKS, BEACHES, AND RECREATION AREAS

• Colby Wildlife Preserve 🐾🐾 🐕 See **23** on page 522.

This 12-acre park is nestled along Salt Marsh Cove on the Damariscotta River. The cove was once the site of an active saltworks, iceworks, a brickyard, ferry landing, sawmills, and gristmills. Now in its natural state, Salt Marsh Cove is environmentally important to the health of the Damariscotta River.

The trail starts on the old mill road. Follow the road a quarter mile to Salt Marsh Cove and wander a path along the water. The half-mile loop can get mucky during low tide, so be sure your dog brings her duck boots. (Or that you bring a big towel for use before she gets back in the car.) During high tide, you'll have a hard time keeping her from the cool, refreshing water.

From U.S. Route 1, take State Route 27 south for three miles. Turn left onto McKay Road for 1.5 miles, then make a left onto River Road for a mile. The park entrance is on the right. Open sunrise to sunset. (207) 633-4818.

• Fort Edgecomb State Historic Site 🐾🐾 See **24** on page 522.

The panoramic southern point of Davis Island in the Sheepscot River has been the home of Fort Edgecomb since 1808 when tensions with the British were mounting, eventually leading to the War of 1812.

You and your pet can enjoy the picnic area and water access while exploring the parade grounds, blockhouse, waterfront battery, and remaining earthworks.

Dogs need to be leashed and are not allowed in the blockhouse. There is a $1 day-use fee per person.

From U.S. Route 1, take Eddy Road south for a half mile. Turn left onto Fort Road to the park and parking. Open 9 A.M. to 5 P.M., Memorial Day to Labor Day. (207) 882-7777.

• Singing Meadows 🐾🐾🐾 🐕 See **25** on page 522.

Singing Meadows gets its name from the many "voices" of amphibians croaking on bass, birds on melody, and crickets, cicadas, and grasshoppers adding the string accompaniment. This 16-acre hardwood-rimmed field, once part of an old saltwater farm, is the only meadow the land trust owns, and it is a haven for a wide variety of wildlife, including white-tailed deer, fox, and moose.

The trail cuts through the open meadow and runs through a small wood at the far end. Your dog will love romping leash free through the high grass on the wide flat trail. The Boothbay Region Land Trust requires dogs to be under voice control.

From U.S. Route 1, take State Route 27 south for a mile. Turn right onto Eddy Road for a half mile, then left onto Cross Point Road for a quarter mile. The park and a parking area are on the right. Open sunrise to sunset. (207) 633-4818.

PLACES TO STAY

Sheepscot River Inn: This 40-room complex, formerly the Edgecomb Inn, offers rooms and cottages overlooking Wiscasset Harbor. A restaurant is on-site, and continental breakfast is served each morning. Dogs are welcome in the suites and cottages with prior approval. Rooms range from $65 to $119 per night. U.S. Route 1, 306 Eddy Road, Edgecomb, ME 04556; (800) 437-5503, (207) 882-6343; www.sheepscotriverinn.com.

ELIOT

PLACES TO STAY

The Farmstead Bed-and-Breakfast: Dogs cannot be left unattended, and they mean it. Apparently a few rule-breaking guests have found their dogs leashed up at the barn upon their return. Aside from that, they are extremely dog friendly. Rates range from $68 to $88. 379 Goodwin Road, Eliot, ME 03903; (207) 439-5033; www.farmstead.qpg.

FALMOUTH

PARKS, BEACHES, AND RECREATION AREAS

• Mackworth Island 🐾🐾🐾 See **26** on page 522.

Portland, and to a lesser extent Falmouth, is situated at the confluence of the Fore and Presumpscot Rivers and Casco Bay. This meeting of land and water results in numerous islands, coves, and waterways, and the Public Reserve Land of Mackworth Island offers a great opportunity to get out in the middle of it.

The center of the island is the home of the Baxter School for the Deaf and is off-limits to the public. But the outer perimeter is open to you and your dog for hiking. A trail follows the shoreline woods around the island for 1.75 miles offering bay-window views in all directions. The island can be accessed by car via the Martin Point Bridge.

Dogs must be on leash and are not permitted on the beach or near any of the buildings.

From U.S. Route 1 just north of the Martin Point Bridge over the Presumpscot River, take Andrews Avenue east for a half mile to the entrance. Parking is available. Open dawn to dusk or 6:30 P.M., whichever is later. (207) 778-4111.

FRANKFORT

PARKS, BEACHES, AND RECREATION AREAS

• Swan Lake State Park 🐾🐾 See **27** on page 522.

This 67-acre park on Swan Lake is one of the newest additions to the Maine park system. There aren't many trails here, but you won't care because there are plenty of picnic areas and a great beach. Luckily, dogs are welcome to cool off in the scenic lake year-round.

Dogs need to be leashed and are not permitted at the designated beach area (where the lifeguards are). There is a day-use fee of $2 per adult.

From State Route 141 in Swanville, take Frankfort Road east for 1.5 miles into Frankfort. The park is on the right. Open 9 A.M. to sunset. Call (207) 525-4404 Memorial Day to Labor Day, (207) 941-4014 off-season.

FREEPORT

PARKS, BEACHES, AND RECREATION AREAS

•**Wolfe's Neck Woods State Park** 🐾 🐾 🐾 See **28** on page 522.
This state park, at the end of Wolfe's Neck, is specially dedicated to nature appreciation. It offers five miles of interpretive trails through a diverse 233 acres. You and your leashed dog will traverse through woodlands, marshes, and along several beaches between Casco Bay and the Harraseeket River. One of the park's residents, the osprey, can be seen regularly from April to August while nesting on Goggins Island.

There is a day-use fee of $2 per adult.

From Flying Point Road, take Wolf Neck Road south for two miles into the park. Open from 9 A.M. to 6 P.M. Call (207) 865-4465 April through October, (207) 624-6075 off-season.

RESTAURANTS

Lobster Cooker: If shopping is your idea of a stupid pet trick, but you still want to experience the hustle and bustle of Freeport, then the Lobster Cooker is the place for you and your pet. You can dine on hearty chowder, clams, lobster, salads, and sandwiches, and enjoy it all on their cozy, red-bricked patio along Main Street. 39 Main Street; (207) 772-7647.

Mister Bagel: When you need a break from the frenzied shopping scene at the L.L. Bean Store or any one of the countless outlets on Main Street, head down to Mister Bagel. Tourists and locals grab the bargains on soups, salads, pizza, deli sandwiches, and, of course, bagels with all sorts of toppings. Outdoor seating is available. 2 Depot Road; (207) 865-3737.

PLACES TO STAY

Desert of Maine Campground: If you think you have a problem with your lawn, wait until you see the lack of grass at this place! The wooded campground is next to the Desert of Maine, a 40-acre sand pit and a horrible result of poor land management. Dogs need to be leashed and are only permitted at the 46 RV sites, which are $26 a night. Desert Road, Freeport, ME 04032; (207) 865-6962.

Freeport Inn: This lovely inn located on 25 acres of coastal property is close to everything in Freeport. There are 80 comfortable rooms, and most are available to you and your dog. You can hike on the property or rent a canoe for a trip along the river. Room rates range from $59 to $149. 335 U.S. Route 1, Freeport, ME 04032; (800) 998-2583, (207) 865-3106; www.freeportinn.com.

The Isaac Randall House: With six acres of land, a pond, and a country breakfast in the beam-ceilinged kitchen, this is a great place to spend a weekend in southern Maine. The inn, within walking distance of Freeport's shopping district, is a Federal-style farmhouse built in 1823 which was once a stop on the Underground Railroad. There are 11 rooms and some have working fireplaces. Pets are welcome in select rooms. Rates range from $65 to $135. 5 Independence Drive, Freeport, ME 04032; (207) 865-9295, (800) 865-9295.

3 Sisters: The truth is, only one of the sisters is here. A second sister is right next door, the owner of the Isaac Randall House (see above). And, well, the third had the nerve to go off to California. This cozy country inn is just as warm and inviting as its neighboring inn and just a little bit more modern. It's also on 1.5 acres within walking distance of downtown Freeport. A delicious breakfast is included. Rates range from $75 to $125. Open May to October. 3 Independence Drive, ME 04032; (207) 865-4405, (877) 865-4405.

FESTIVALS

Sparkle Weekend: Anytime is a good time to shop and enjoy Freeport's Main Street, but the first weekend in December is when things really get going. The outlet-crazed village, led by L.L. Bean, rings in the holidays with caroling, tree lightings, a parade of lights, and holiday window displays. Most of the celebration happens right on Main Street, so both you and your dog can partake in the festivities. For more information, call (207) 865-1212.

GEORGETOWN

PARKS, BEACHES, AND RECREATION AREAS

• Reid State Park 🐾 🐾 🐾 See 29 on page 522.

Located on the southeastern end of Georgetown Island, this is one of Maine's more popular beaches. Alas, dogs are not permitted on the sandy beach, but they can still get to the surf at other points along the mile and a half of oceanfront. Dogs are permitted on the rocky shoreline and where the grassy areas meet the sea. That's good enough for George and Inu, our designated sea dogs. The park's short, wooded hiking trails are also open to pets.

Dogs need to be leashed in all state parks. There is a day-use fee of $2.50 per adult.

From the southern end of State Route 127, take Seguinland Road south for a mile into the park. Open 9 A.M. to sunset. (207) 371-2303.

JEFFERSON

PARKS, BEACHES, AND RECREATION AREAS

• Damariscotta Lake State Park 🐾 🐾 See 30 on page 522.

This small state park is a 17-acre beachfront on the shores of Damariscotta Lake. The park also offers a picnic area. As usual, dogs are not permitted on the beach during the summer months except along the far right end. But hey! That's something considering how many beaches ban dogs altogether.

Dogs must be on leash. There is a day-use fee of $2 per adult.

The park is located in the center of town off of State Routes 32 and 126. Open 9 A.M. to sunset. Call (207) 549-7600 Memorial Day to Labor Day, (207) 941-4014 off-season.

KENNEBUNK

PARKS, BEACHES, AND RECREATION AREAS

• **Gooch's and Kennebunk Beaches** 🐾 🐾 🐾 See **31** on page 522.

These two flat and white sandy beaches are separated by a half-mile stretch of rocky shoreline, but they are connected by a sidewalk that runs along Beach Road. If you can get your dog off the beach, you can join the many walkers and joggers who exercise by going back and forth between the two beaches.

Dogs must be on leash.

From State Route 9, take Beach Avenue east for a mile. The beach is on the left. Limited street parking is available, and daily parking permits are required (available at the Chamber of Commerce at 117 Main Street). Open 6 A.M. to 11 P.M. (207) 967-0857.

NATURE HIKES AND URBAN WALKS

Historic Village Walk: The entire village of Kennebunk is listed on the National Register of Historic Places, and the Chamber of Commerce sponsors a walking tour through town and across the Kennebunk River. The highlights of the walk are the many historical and architecturally significant mansions that line Main and Dane Streets. Maps and information are available at 117 Main Street. (207) 967-0857.

PLACES TO STAY

Kennebuck Inn: This 29-room inn, built in the 18th century, offers elegant lodging in a convenient setting. Located right on the main route to the seacoast, you'll be close to everything. Some rooms have fireplaces and all have refrigerators. Pets are welcome with advance reservations. Rates range from $99 to $175. 45 Main Street, Kennebunk, ME 04043; (207) 985-3351.

The Lodge At Kennebunk Motor Inn: This 40-room, motel-style inn offers comfortable, modern rooms and suites. Most rooms have a small refrigerator and two double beds. Pets are welcome in most rooms. Rates range from $49 to $109. Route 35, Box 1580, Kennebunk, ME 04043; (207) 985-9010.

KENNEBUNKPORT

PARKS, BEACHES, AND RECREATION AREAS

• **Colony Beach** 🐾 🐾 See **32** on page 522.

Also known as Arundel Beach, Colony Beach is situated on the outer coast of Kennebunkport, and, although the beach is somewhat rocky, there are still plenty of sandy places for water dogs to enter the surf. You'll find the sunny views of the harbor and Kennebunk River worth the bumpy trail.

Dogs must be on leash and are not permitted from 8 A.M. to 6 P.M. from June 15 to September 15.

From State Route 9, take Ocean Avenue east a half mile. The beach and limited street parking is on the right. Open 6 A.M. to 10 P.M. (207) 967-0857.

• Goose Rocks Beach 🐾 🐾 🐾 See **33** on page 522.

This three-mile long beach is shaped like two crescent moons and is a beach-comber's delight. Rocks, driftwood, and shells wash up here from all over the world, and the jetsam is especially fun to sort through after a storm. The beach is wide, smooth, and sandy with beautiful coastal views of the Eastern Goose Rocks and Timber Island just offshore. The hard sand makes it perfect for ball throwing; you'll like it for the view of the shore and islands.

Dogs must be on leash and are not permitted from 8 A.M. to 6 P.M. from June 15 to September 15.

From State Route 9, take Dyke Road east for a half mile to the beach and limited street parking. Open 6 A.M. to 10 P.M. (207) 967-0857.

RESTAURANTS

Aunt Marie's: It seems that an afternoon scoop has become part of our daily summer routine. Luckily, Aunt Marie's has all our favorite ice-cream flavors. 10 Ocean Avenue; (207) 967-0711.

Dock Square Coffee House: Oh, you *thought* the Kennebunks would be relaxing, but with all the beach activities and downtown shopping and strolling, you may need a little pick-me-up from time to time. Dock Square serves it up hot, sweet, and creamed. 18 Dock Square (207) 967-4422.

Mermaids Café & Bakery: If you are heading to the beach or the woods, you had better pick up some sandwiches and treats at Mermaid's before you go. Union Square; (207) 967-5529.

PLACES TO STAY

Cabot Cove Cottages: Fall asleep listening to the waves lap against the shore. These charming wood-shingled cottages are tucked away in a tidal cove and offer privacy and solitude to the weary traveler. All the cottages are decorated in a casual beach style, and dogs are allowed for an additional $7. Rates range from $95 to $175 daily or $570 to $1,020 weekly. There may be a two-night minimum requirement during the high season. Open mid-May to mid-October. 7 South Main Street, P.O. Box 1082, Kennebunkport, ME 04046; (800) 962-5424; www.cabotcovecottages.com.

The Captain Jefferds Inn: This elegant 1804 home was originally built as a wedding present for Captain William Jeffers and his bride, Mary. Today it is an elegantly refurbished bed-and-breakfast decorated in a colonial style. The owners are very pet friendly and will greet you and your dog with a welcoming gift. They only ask that you not leave your dog unattended if you leave the grounds. Rates range from $135 to $285 including full breakfast. Dogs are $20 per night. P.O. Box 691, 5 Pearl Street, Kennebunkport, ME 04046; (800) 839-6844, (207) 967-2311; www.captainjefferdsinn.com.

Colony Hotel: Both you and your pet will be pampered at this 121-room 1914 Georgian-style hotel on the ocean and Kennebunk River. Originally a "grand hotel" in the resort heyday of Maine, the hotel features classic wrap-around porches and fabulous ocean views of the craggy coast beyond. The rooms are classically elegant and, boy, do they roll out the red carpet for your pet. Biscuits available on check-in! The hotel is open May to October. Rates range from $199 to $400 a night plus a $25 pet fee. P.O. Box 511 140 Ocean

Avenue, Kennebunkport, ME 04046; (800) 552-2363, (207) 967-3331; www. colonyhotel.com/maine.

Green Heron Inn: This lovely bed-and-breakfast is close to the ocean and the downtown shops. Guests with pets are assigned to three specific rooms or are welcome to stay in the cottage. Room rates are $80 to $105; the cottage rates are $115 to $165. Ocean Avenue, Kennebunkport, ME 04046; (207) 967-3315; www.greenheroninn.com.

Lodge at Turbat's Creek: Staying at this 26-room inn will make your visit to Kennebunkport a memorable one. Each spacious room has two double beds, a deck, and private bath. There are complimentary bikes available to ride on the many paths along the water. Breakfast is served each morning. Pets are welcome with a $50 refundable deposit. Rates range from $95 to $105. 7 Turbat's Creek Road, Kennebunkport, ME 04046; (207) 967-8700.

KITTERY

PARKS, BEACHES, AND RECREATION AREAS

• Fort Foster State Historic Site 🐾🐾 See **34** on page 522.

This fort, along with Fort McClary across Pepperell Cove (see next listing) and Forts Constitution and Stark on the New Hampshire side, protected Portsmouth Harbor and the Piscataqua River for 275 years. Although actual action was limited, they all served in the Revolutionary War, War of 1812, Civil War, Spanish-American War, and World War I. Today, only the Maine forts allow dogs.

You and your dog can explore the remains of Fort Foster and walk the short trails along the shore and in the surrounding woods. You'll also find a number of places to cool off in Pepperell Cove.

There is a $2 entrance fee plus a $2.50 fee per vehicle, if you drive in (you can park at the entrance gate and walk in for free). Dogs must be leashed.

From State Route 103, take Chauncey Creek Road a half mile. Turn right onto Pocohontas Road for 1.2 miles. Open 10 A.M. to 8 P.M., Memorial Day to Labor Day. (207) 439-3800.

• Fort McClary State Historic Site 🐾🐾 See **35** on page 522.

Here at Fort McClary you and your dog can walk the remains of this historic fort. With its great view of the harbor, you know this site was chosen for a reason. Dogs are welcome to explore the rifleman's house, block house, and massive granite walls.

Besides investigating the many nooks and crannies of the fort, you can cool off at the stone-covered beachfront and, across the road from the main entrance, enjoy the picnic area and a few short walking paths along the Spruce Creek.

Dogs must be on leash in all state parks. There is a $1 entrance fee.

From U.S. Route 1, take State Route 103 east for two miles. The fort is on the right and the picnic area is on the left. Open 9 A.M. to sunset. (207) 439-2845.

RESTAURANTS

Chauncey Creek Lobster Pier: For 40 years, this has been the place to eat lobster in southern Maine. Of course, the chowder, raw bar, and steamers aren't too shabby either! Best of all, you can try them all outdoors on the shady, enclosed deck on the banks of picturesque Chauncey Creek. Open Mother's Day to Columbus Day. Chauncey Creek Road (just off of State Route 103); (207) 439-1030.

PLACES TO STAY

Enchanted Nights Bed & Breakfast: This Victorian B&B will provide your pampered pet with the stay she so deserves. There are six rooms that sleep from two to five people, and all are decorated with fancy beddings and whimsical antiques. A full breakfast is included. Rates range from $50 to $140. 29 Wentworth Street, Kittery, ME 03904; (207) 439-1489; www.enchanted -nights-bandb.com.

LIBERTY

PARKS, BEACHES, AND RECREATION AREAS

• Lake Saint George State Park 🐾🐾 See **36** on page 522.

With 360 acres, hiking trails, and plenty of waterfront property on shining Lake Saint George, you will be on easy street when it comes to exercising your dog. The crystal clear lake is spring fed and offers your pool-party pup many opportunities for swimming.

The park is also a good access point to the numerous snowmobile trails that run through Waldo County. They also make for good hiking in the nonsnow seasons. And, if that's not enough, canoes are available for rent at $2.50 an hour or $10 a day.

Dogs need to be leashed. There is a day use fee of $2 per adult.

From State Route 220, take State Route 3 west for a mile. The park is on both sides. Parking is available. Open 9 A.M. to sunset. (207) 589-4255.

LINCOLNVILLE

PARKS, BEACHES, AND RECREATION AREAS

• Ducktrap Preserve 🐾🐾 See **37** on page 522.

This conservation property of wetlands and woodlands along the Ducktrap River is one of the newer acquisitions of the Coastal Mountains Land Trust. An official trail system has not yet been developed here, but the park does have some secondary paths that allow you to explore the Ducktrap before it flows out into Penobscot Bay. Your dog is welcome on leash.

From State Route 173, take State Route 52 north for two miles. At the river crossing, the park is on both sides and the parking area is on the left. Open dawn to dusk. (207) 236-7091.

RESTAURANTS

The Lobster Pound: This local restaurant has two locations on Lincolnville Beach. Your dog isn't allowed at the full-service restaurant, but fortunately you can still enjoy the same great meal at the take-out stand by the ferry. There are plenty of picnic tables overlooking the ocean. U.S. Route 1; (207) 789-5550.

PLACES TO STAY

Pine Grove Cottages: Located close to Camden and Maine's mid-seacoast, this pleasant seven-room cottage complex offers some efficiency rooms, fireplaces, and even a Jacuzzi. Pets are welcome for an additional $7 per night. Cottages range from $60 to $110 per night. State Route 1, Box 714, Lincolnville, ME 04849; (207) 236-2929 or (800) 530-5265.

DIVERSIONS

Row, row, row your boat: Rent a kayak or canoe and take a two-hour trip in the inlets and coves around Lincolnville. All-day tours are available, as well. (207) 236-8608.

MONHEGAN ISLAND (MONHEGAN PLANTATION)

Monhegan Island is 10 miles off the mainland coast, but it is a beautiful and tranquil world away. Although it's only one square mile in total, has no roads or vehicles, and has a year-round population of less than a hundred, the island is a haven for fishermen, artists, and naturalists alike.

If you go, you are going by boat. The simplest way is via the Monhegan Island Ferry from the village of Fort Clyde in Saint George. For more information, call the Monhegan-Thomaston Boat Line at (207) 372-8848.

PARKS, BEACHES, AND RECREATION AREAS

• Monhegan Island 🐾 🐾 🐾 🐾 See **38** on page 522.

It's hard to clearly identify a park on the island when 80 percent of it is uninhabited woods and rocky coastline—why almost the entire island is a park! And that includes about 17 miles of hiking trails on over 20 different routes.

The two primary hikes are the north and south loops. About two miles in length, they are the best way to explore Monhegan's diverse and rare coastal forests, like Cathedral Woods. You'll walk by The Headlands, some of the highest ocean cliffs in Maine, and Monhegan Light, an 1824 lighthouse.

To protect the fragile ecosystem, especially the island grass, dogs need to be leashed. Open 24 hours a day. (207) 596-0376.

PLACES TO STAY

The Island Inn: This lovely 35-room inn towers over the seascape on scenic Monhegan Island, offering comfortable rooms overlooking the harbor. The rooms have private or shared baths, and several suites are available, as well. Full breakfast is served and afternoon tea is offered each day. One dog per room is welcome for an additional $10 per day. Rooms range from $75 to $220. P.O. Box 128, Monhegan Island, ME 04852; (207) 596-0371; www.midcoast.com/~islandin.

NEWCASTLE

PARKS, BEACHES, AND RECREATION AREAS

• **Dodge Point Conservation Area** 🐾 🐾 🐾 🐾 🦮 See **39** on page 522.

This wonderful 500-acre preserve along the Damariscotta River offers three beaches, an old brickyard, a pond, an interpretive trail, and plenty of great walking trails. You and your dog will find countless reasons to dodge your old walking rut and start a new one here.

There are four main trails, varying from one to three miles each. Stroll along the river on the Shoreline Path or head for the woods on the Ravine Woods Trail. All trails intertwine so you can mix and match as desired, changing your hike each time you visit.

The Discovery Trail is a short self-guided interpretive trail that takes you through the rich history of the area. A map at the trailhead will help you find your way.

This park is jointly managed by the Maine Public Reserve Land and the Damariscotta River Association. Dogs must be under voice control.

From U.S. Route 1, take River Road south for two miles. The park entrance is on the left. Open dawn to dusk. (207) 563-1393.

OGUNQUIT

PARKS, BEACHES, AND RECREATION AREAS

• **Ogunquit Beach** 🐾 🐾 🐾 See **40** on page 522.

Ogunquit Beach is one of the best beaches on the Maine coast. This three-mile strip is a flat, sandy peninsula located where the Ogunquit River separates the beach from the mainland. On one side is the Atlantic Ocean; on the other is the river. Be sure to take a walk around the southern tip of the giant sandbar where the river meets the sea.

The beach is also one of the most popular and most restrictive. Dogs need to be on leash and are not permitted at all from May 15 to October 1. Even without the summer invite, Inu and George love the soft sand and room to roam here; if you visit in the first half of May or early October, you'll still find some sporadic warm weather, plenty of other beachcombers, and many shops and restaurants still open.

Beach parking is $8 a day.

From Main Street (U.S. Route 1), take Beach Street east for a quarter mile to the beach and the main parking area (hourly rates here). Another parking lot is at the end of Ocean Street (off U.S. Route 1) where there is a footbridge across the Ogunquit River to the beach. Open 6:00 A.M. to 10 P.M. (207) 646-3032.

NATURE HIKES AND URBAN WALKS

Marginal Way: Few Ogunquit visitors can resist the 1.25-mile cliff walk known as Marginal Way. The paved path runs from popular Perkin's Cove to downtown. Along the way are more than marginal views of the ocean and the surrounding shoreline including picturesque Ogunquit Beach. The path is well maintained with gardens many places to sit and enjoy the views.

Alas, as much as your dog may want to join in the fun, she's not permitted to do so during the summer season. Dogs are not allowed on the walk from May 15 to October 1 and need to be on leash at other times. Access and parking is at Perkin's Cove, just off the end of Shore Road, or in the center of town also off of Shore Road. For more information, call (207) 646-2939.

Perkins Cove: Whether you visit during the summer, when just about everything is off-limits to dogs, or in the off-season, the streets of the tiny fishing village of Perkins Cove make a good, dog-friendly destination. Along with the colorful fleet of lobster boats is a small community of shops, restaurants, and galleries where a dog can walk the streets and window shop to his heart's content. Be sure to venture across the pedestrian drawbridge over the Josias River. As boats approach, you may even be asked to raise the bridge. For more information, call (207) 646-2939.

RESTAURANTS

Bernard's Bakery: This local bakery has got the perfect "something sweet" when you really need a sugar rush to go. Conveniently located downtown at the northern end of Marginal Way, it's also a good stop in the morning for muffins and coffee. Shore Road; (207) 646-2698.

Charlie's Restaurant: Charlie's been serving Ogunquit beachgoers since 1932, and he'll be happy to serve you and your dog from the take-out window. Be sure to get some tasty fries with anything from the menu of sandwiches, lobster, burgers, and ice cream. 39 Beach Street; (207) 646-8280.

PLACES TO STAY

Studio East Motor Inn: This 25-room motel is clean, comfortable, and affordable for this neighborhood. There is a restaurant on-site, and pets are allowed with a $5 fee per night. Rooms range from $50 to $105. 45 Main Street, Ogunquit, ME 03907; (207) 646-7297.

Yellow Monkey Guest House: Whether you prefer the comfort of a cottage with a cozy fireplace or the convenience of an efficiency apartment, you'll find this 19th-century inn is dog friendly and conveniently close to the beach and downtown. Open seasonally from mid-April to mid-November; rates range from $90 to $125, plus an additional $5-per-night pet fee. 168 Main Street, Ogunquit, ME 03907; (207) 646-9056.

DIVERSIONS

Cruising Canines: The rocky seashore of Maine offers some of the most beautiful coastline on the eastern seaboard, and Finestkind Scenic Cruises offer a great way for you and your dog to view it from the sea. So set sail with your sea dog on any of the four boat cruises that leave from the docks at Perkin's Cove.

The Breakfast Cruise departs 9 A.M. to the Island Ledges. Coffee and muffins are served along with a good chance to see harbor seals. The evening Cocktail Cruises hug the coast north and south of Oqunquit. And continuously throughout the day are the Nubble Lighthouse Cruises and the Lobstering Trips, where you can experience lobstering firsthand. The excursions last from fifty minutes to 1.5 hours.

There is no extra charge for dogs, but they do have to be on leash and get final approval from the captain. Rates range from $8.50 to $20, and the season runs from May 1 to mid-October. For more information, call (207) 646-5227.

OLD ORCHARD BEACH

PARKS, BEACHES, AND RECREATION AREAS

• **Old Orchard Beach** 🐾 🐾 🐾 See **41** on page 522.

Old Orchard Beach has been a popular destination ever since 1867 when Thomas Rogers planted apple trees on the highlands above the beach. Back then, mariners used it as a landmark. Today, the seven-mile sandy beach is simply a great place to enjoy the seaside. With a beach this size you are sure to find plenty of room for your dog's favorite ocean activities, although we always have trouble getting the dogs past the amusement-park atmosphere that surrounds the beach.

Dogs need to be leashed and are not permitted on the beach from 10 A.M. to 3 P.M. from Memorial Day to Labor Day.

The beach is located along East Grand Avenue (State Route 9). Limited street parking is available. Open 6 A.M. to 11:30 P.M. (207) 934-2500.

PLACES TO STAY

Atlantic Breeze Motel: Guests must get prior approval, and pets left unattended must be crated. Some efficiencies are available. Rates range from $40 to $90 with a $50 deposit. 46 Saco Avenue, Old Orchard Beach, ME 04064; (207) 934-4208; mnet.work/atlanticbreeze.

Normandie Motor Inn: This motel overlooks a seven-mile strip of beach just steps away from all the excitement and activity of Old Orchard Beach. Rates range from $80 to $175 with a $25 fee for your pet. 1 York Street, Old Orchard Beach, ME 04064; (207) 934-2533; www.normandieinn.com.

Old Colonial Motel: Only dogs less than 50 pounds are allowed to stay at this motel right on the beach. Since our dogs heard the news, they've been trying to lose a few extra pounds to make the cut. Open seasonally from April 20 to November 7. Rates range from $115 to $175. 61 West Grand Avenue, Old Orchard Beach, ME 04064; (888) 225-5989, (207) 934-9863; www.oldcolonial-motel.com.

Sea View Motel: Now may be the time to put your dog on a diet because dogs are permitted in certain rooms here, but they cannot weigh more than 65 pounds. Rates range from $70 to $170 with a $100 refundable pet deposit. 65 West Grand Avenue, Old Orchard Beach, ME 04064; (207) 934-4180, (800) 541-8439; www.seaviewgetaway.com.

Waves Oceanfront Resort: This on-the-beach resort has 139 rooms and all have kitchenettes and private balconies. Guests with pets are assigned to specific buildings. Rates range from $69 to $125. 87 West Grand Avenue, Old Orchard Beach, ME 04046; (207) 934-4949; www.seenewengland.com/waves.

RESTAURANTS

Pic's Pizza: Pizza is one of the few meals that doesn't lose its appeal when mixed with blowing sand. Of course, our chow hounds are like Mikey—

they'll eat anything. Fortunately, Pic's serves some of the best pizza at the beach. There are picnic tables outside. 181 Saco Avenue; (207) 934-5567.

FESTIVALS

Caroling Coastal Canines: Help ring in the holidays beach style! Celebrate the Season by the Sea is a great way to get in the spirit of things with caroling, a tree-lighting ceremony, and a beach bonfire. It all happens the first weekend in December in Old Orchard Beach. (207) 934-2500.

DIVERSIONS

Canine Caruso: After a day at the beach, sit back and relax with the Concerts in the Square. They take place Mondays and Tuesdays at 7 P.M. from late June to Labor Day at the Town Square off Grand Avenue. For a list of performers, call (207) 934-2500.

Fired Up Fido: George doesn't care for fireworks at all, but Inu loves the weekly Thursday night display. To him it's just another party where he can work the crowd for pats and snacks. The fireworks go off every Thursday night from late June to Labor Day at 9:30 P.M. on the beach near the Pier. (207) 934-2500.

PHIPPSBURG

PARKS, BEACHES, AND RECREATION AREAS

• **Fort Baldwin and Fort Popham State Historic Sites** 😾 😾 See **42** on page 522.

Dogs are not allowed inside the enclosed fort areas, but at Fort Popham there are open grassy areas, a scenic picnic spot overlooking the water, and a small beach where your leashed dog can take a dip. For a longer hike, head over to Fort Baldwin just a half mile away. A one-mile trail leads through the woods behind the fort to the ranger station and back. This easy path offers a wide, open walk through some lovely pine woods.

From the intersection of State Routes 209 and 216, take State Route 209 south for 3.5 miles to the end. Fort Popham is on the right and Fort Baldwin is on the left. Open 9 A.M. to sunset. (207) 389-1335.

• **Popham Beach State Park** 😾 😾 See **43** on page 522.

This is a lovely state beach with a view of Seguin Island and beyond, but, unfortunately, dogs aren't allowed here during the summer months. So if you'd like to visit between October 1 and March 31, we know you'll still love the long stretch of beach, the solitude, and the sound of seagulls soaring overhead. But if you're looking for a little relief from the summer heat, you're outta luck here. We suggest you head down the road to Fort Popham where there is a small beach where your dog can swim.

Dogs must be on leash.

From the intersection of State Routes 209 and 216, take State Route 209 south for three miles. The park is on the left. Open 9 A.M. to sunset. (207) 389-1335.

PLACES TO STAY

Small Point B&B: This tiny, three-room bed-and-breakfast is located in a charming 19th-century farmhouse. Nestled on the edge of Cape Small in Phippsburg, you can fall asleep listening to the ocean outside your window. Dogs are welcome in one of the rooms with prior approval. Rates range from $50 to $85 per night including breakfast. State Route 216, Box 250, Sebasco Estates, ME 04565; (207) 389-1716.

Edgewater Farm: This eight-room bed-and-breakfast offers a quiet place for you and your dog to relax while visiting mid-coast Maine. There are six charming rooms and two suites available. Open from February to November, rooms range from $95 to $140. Breakfast is included. 71 Small Point Road, Phippsburg, ME 04562; (207) 389-1332.

PORTLAND

PARKS, BEACHES, AND RECREATION AREAS

• Baxter Woods 😺 😺 😺 🐕 See **44** on page 522.

This 30-acre nature preserve is an old-growth forest in the middle of Deering. The majestic trees are a gift from Governor Baxter in honor of his father, Mayor Baxter, an early advocate for Portland's parks. Some of the trees are over a hundred years old. Baxter Woods has an easy, half-mile loop trail that runs through the entire park.

An off-leash area is also available for dogs. You can't miss it—it's the only grassy clearing within the dense forest. Dogs need to be leashed in the rest of the park, which is managed by Portland Trails, a land conservation group.

From State Route 25 (Brighton Avenue), take State Route 9 (Stevens Avenue) north for three-quarters of a mile. The park and street parking are on your right at the New Street intersection. Open 5 A.M. to 10 P.M. (207) 775-2411.

• Capisic Pond Park 😺 😺 See **45** on page 522.

Filled with knee-high grass and wildflowers, six-foot-high berry bushes, and cattails that line Capisic Pond, this 18-acre nature preserve is an enjoyable place for a morning or afternoon stroll. A half-mile walking path of crushed stone runs through the meadow from the trailhead at Capisic Street to Brighton Avenue.

Dogs must be on leash.

From State Route 9 (Stevens Avenue), take Capisic Street west for a half mile. Turn right onto Macy Street. The trailhead and parking area are on the left. Open 5 A.M. to 10 P.M. (207) 775-2411.

• Eastern Promenade Trail/Back Cove Trail 😺 😺 😺 😺 See **46** on page 522.

If you happen to be visiting Portland on a Saturday or Sunday and the city appears deserted, it's because everyone and their dog are on the Eastern Promenade Trail. This bike path/walkway runs around the East End neighborhood along the harbor and then all around Back Cove through the neighborhoods of East Derring and Woodfords. This scenic recreation path, on a former railroad bed, is over 5.5 miles long and starts at the northern end of Commercial Street.

The Eastern Promenade Trail is best accessed from the northern end of Fore Street or from various points along Eastern Promenade Street. The Back Cove Trail runs parallel to Baxter Boulevard (U.S. Route 1). Street parking and a parking lot are available. Open 5 A.M. to 10 P.M. (207) 874-8793.

• Deering Oaks Park 🐾🐾🐾 See **47** on page 522.

This local park serves the city well. The 51 acres offer a variety of facilities including ball fields, playgrounds, short walking and bike paths, fountains, a band shell, and gardens.

For history buffs, the park is the site of a 1690 battle between Portland colonists and the French and Indians. For food lovers, the park hosts a farmer's market on Saturdays (summer to fall). And dog lovers will appreciate the paths in and around the oak trees at the far end of the playing fields.

Dog need to be on leash and are not permitted on the ball fields, playgrounds, or in the duck pond.

The park is located at the intersection of U.S. Route 1 and State Route 25. The main entrance and parking is off State Route 25. Open sunrise to sunset. (207) 874-8793.

• Lincoln Park 🐾🐾 See **48** on page 522.

This small, three-acre park in the heart of the city is simply a quiet little place to catch your breath. The bubbling fountain, benches, manicured lawns, and cast-iron fencing around the park make it a scenic place to take a break from the quick pace of Portland. Dogs on leash, please.

The park is located between Congress, Federal, and Pearl Streets. Street parking is available. Open 5 A.M. to 10 P.M. (207) 874-8793.

• Payson Park 🐾🐾 See **49** on page 522.

This is a 48-acre, all-purpose park off of Back Cove. Ball fields and playgrounds take up most of the space, but some open grassy areas are available for ball throwing. Take a scenic quarter-mile walk at Longfellow Arboretum or access the Back Cove Trail from here. Dogs need to be leashed and are not permitted on the ball fields.

From Interstate 295, take exit 9 to U.S. Route 1 (Baxter Boulevard) south for a half mile. The park and parking is on the right. Open 5 A.M. to 10 P.M. (207) 874-8793.

• Stroudwater River Trail 🐾🐾🐾 See **50** on page 522.

This riverside path is managed by Portland Trails, an urban conservation organization that promotes and protects green space within the city. The trail is 1.25 miles long and follows the beautiful Stroudwater River from Congress Street to Interstate 95. Plans are in the works to extend the path beyond Interstate 95.

Dogs need to be leashed.

From State Route 9 (Stevens Street), take Congress Street west for a mile to just past Westbrook Street and the Stroudwater River bridge. Turn right onto a gravel road to the trailhead and parking area. Open 5 A.M. to 10 P.M. (207) 775-2411.

•Western Promenade 🐾🐾🐾 See 51 on page 522.

Overlooking the Fore River and the rolling hills of South Portland, the Western Promenade matches the panoramic views of the Eastern Promenade. But because it's located in the stately West End on streets of elegant, upper-class homes, it has the ambience of a haughty poodle instead of a bulldog. While countless joggers are working up a sweat on the Eastern Promenade, the most strenuous activity on the Western Promenade is a casual stroll after Sunday brunch. (In truth, the views and mile-long bike path attract visitors from all classes and breeds.)

Open 5 A.M. to 10 P.M. (207) 775-2411.

NATURE HIKES AND URBAN WALKS

Portland Walking Tours: At the Portland Visitor Center (305 Commercial Street), you can get maps for three self-guided walking tours of historically important and architecturally significant districts of Portland. Most of Portland was destroyed by a fire in 1866 when a Fourth of July celebration got out of control. The city was rebuilt in a bricked-lined Victorian style, and much of this design is visible in the West End neighborhood around State and Congress Streets. Sites include Longfellow Square, the boyhood home of Henry Wadsworth-Longfellow, and the First Parish Church. Printed guides are a dollar each, and the tours are about a 1.5-hour walk.

For something simpler, be sure to take a walk on Commercial Street and Exchange Street in Old Port. These streets will give you a good taste of Portland, literally. Commercial Street runs along the harbor and the downtown district. Plenty of shops and restaurants will beckon, and the views of the harbor, islands, and boats are fantastic. For more information, contact the Portland Visitor Center at (207) 772-5800.

RESTAURANTS

Bakehouse Café: This popular bakery and café has a location, menu, and attitude to die for. The red-bricked, outdoor patio is right on Commercial Street and features a bakery serving breakfast, lunch, and dinner. Try a bowl of lobster stew or a grilled salmon salad followed with black beans and corn cakes or coconut curry grilled chicken. Your dog will fare equally well with leftover scraps furnished by a friendly staff. 205 Commercial Street; (207) 773-2217.

Beal's Old Fashioned Ice Cream: After a day of stepping out in the city, you'll need a place to cool off, and there's no better place than Beal's. The lines are long, but that's just because the ice cream is so good. Outdoor seating makes it easy to bring your friend along. 12 Moulton Street; (207) 828-1335.

Benny's Clam House: After you and the thousands of tourists have hit all of the sushi spots on Commercial Street, get a real taste of Portland at Benny's. The clientele are salty sea dogs and, of course, they know where to get the good stuff! Dine on the outdoor deck overlooking the docks, and you'll know why the fish dinners and haddock chowder are known all over the wharf. 199 West Commercial Street; (207) 774-2084.

Bill's Pizza: Location, location, location. Yes, the pizza is good and so are the subs, but the best thing about this place is the outdoor seating right on busy Commercial Street. 177 Commercial Street; (207) 774-6166.

Gritty McDuff's: Portland is known for its beer and brew pubs, and Gritty McDuff's is one of the reasons why. The atmosphere is lively and the food is excellent, but the beer is better. The menu includes standard pub fare. We like to visit in the fall for a pint of Halloween Ale. The outdoor seating, just off of Commercial Street, puts it all within your reach. 396 Fore Street; (207) 772-2739.

PLACES TO STAY

Andrews Lodging Bed & Breakfast: There are four rooms and two suites in this lovely Colonial-style bed-and-breakfast. Each room is elegantly furnished, and a full breakfast is included in your room's rate. Guests with pets must get prior approval and know that during peak season, the number of pets allowed may be limited. Room rates range from $99 to $165, plus a $10 fee per pet per night. 417 Auburn Street, Portland, ME 04103; (207) 797-9157; www.travelguides.com/bb/andrews_lodging.

Back Cove Inn: This bed-and-breakfast inn offers six private rooms, all with queen-sized beds and large shared baths. Your pet is welcome with prior approval and may stay on the first floor for easy access to the backyard. Rates range from $75 to $125. 575 Forest Avenue, Portland, ME 04102; (207) 772-2557; www.backcoveinn.com.

The Danforth: This elegant 1821 mansion overlooks the waterfront a few blocks from the downtown heart of the city. Featuring elegant rooms with four-poster beds and carved moldings, you'll feel you've stepped back to the time when Portland was lit by gas lamps, and carriages lined the streets below. Rooms range from $139 to $329. 163 Danforth Street, Portland, ME 04102; (800) 991-6557, (207) 879-8755; www.danforthmaine.com.

Doubletree Hotel: This full-service hotel offers modern conveniences in a central location. Rates range from $159 to $189. A $50 deposit is required, and pets are permitted only in the smoking rooms. 1230 Congress Street, Portland, ME 04102; (207) 774-5611, (800) 989-3856; www.doubletree.com.

Howard Johnson Hotel: This standard full-service hotel offers comfortable lodging for the traveler who is just passing through. Rates range from $99 to $129. A $50 deposit is required for your pet. 155 Riverside Street, Portland, ME 04102; (207)774-5861, (800)446-4656; www.hojoportland.com.

Inn at St. John: This 31-room inn is located in downtown Portland and offers simple lodging in the style of a men's club. Wood-lined walls and brass adorn the lobby. The rooms are small but comfortable. Small pets are welcome on approval. Rates range from $70 to $170. 939 Congress Street, Portland, ME 04102; (207) 773-6481, (800) 636-9127; www.innatstjohn.com.

Motel 6: All Motel 6 locations allow dogs, as long as you don't leave them unattended. One dog is welcome per room. Room rates are $59. 1 Riverside Street, Portland, ME 04103; (207) 775-0111, (800) 4-MOTEL6; www.motel6.com.

Radisson Eastland Hotel: Only small pets are permitted at this downtown location. Rates range from $105 to $137, plus a $25 deposit for your pet. 157 High Street, Portland, ME 04101; (207) 775-5411, (800) 333-3333.

FESTIVALS

Arf Art: You and your dog may not agree on the same pieces, but, with 100 artists, you should each be able to find something you like at the outdoor Old

Port Equinox Art Fair. The downtown event occurs annually in mid-September at Exchange and Fore Streets. For more information, call (207) 772-8766.

Ringing Rover: Ring in the new year with one of Maine's biggest celebrations, New Year's Portland. The citywide event, held annually on December 31, features numerous outdoor attractions including fireworks, music, ice sculptures, dance, and other live entertainment. For more information, call (800) 639-4212 or (207) 772-9012.

DIVERSIONS

Canine Caruso: In the summer Portland is alive with the sound of music. Free outdoor concerts are playing night and day throughout the city from June through August at the following locations:

The Deering Oaks Summer Concerts are Tuesdays at 7:30 P.M. at Deering Oaks Park.

The Sunset Folk Series concerts are Wednesdays at 7:45 P.M. at the Western Promenade.

The Summer Performance Series concerts are Monday to Friday at noon at various downtown parks and squares.

The Chandler's Band Concerts are Thursdays at 7:00 P.M. at Fort Allen Park.

For a complete list of performers, locations, dates, and times, call Parks and Recreation at (207) 874-8793 or the Downtown district at (207) 772-6826.

Island Bound Hound: The many islands off the coast of Maine are nicknamed the Calendar Islands because apparently there are roughly 365 of them. We certainly haven't been to all of them, but you and your dog can visit a few of them with Casco Bay Cruises. You'll find remote beaches and hiking trails on Long and Great Chebeague Islands, or stay onboard the vessel on the Moonlight Run.

Rates range from $10 to $15 per person (depending on your destination) with an additional $3 for your leashed pet. For more information and schedules, call (207) 774-7871; cascobaylines.com.

Walk with a Purpose: You and your dog can join the tens of thousands across America who walk to find a cure for diabetes. The American Diabetes Association sponsors America's Walk for Diabetes at over 300 sites in the United States held simultaneously the first weekend in October. The walk is five to six miles long, and walkers are asked to raise money through sponsors and donations. In Portland the walk begins and ends at the Southern Maine Technical College on Fort Street. (800) 254-9255.

POWNAL

PARKS, BEACHES, AND RECREATION AREAS

• Bradbury Mountain State Park 🐾 🐾 🐾 See **52** on page 522.

A must for any two- or four-legged visitor is the easy hike to the summit of Bradbury Mountain. You have your choice of the quarter-mile Summit Trail or the mile-long Northern Loop Trail. Along either route you will find many stone boundary walls from the days when this area was farmland.

Once at the rocky 485-foot summit, you'll have fine views of the park's 440 acres and even some of the islands just off the coast. Pick up a trail map at the park entrance for additional hiking trails throughout the park.

There is a day-use fee of $1.00 per adult. Dogs must be on leash.

From Pownal Center on Elmwood Road, take State Route 9 north for a quarter mile. The park entrance is on the left. Open from 9 A.M. to sunset. (207) 688-4712.

ROCKLAND

PARKS, BEACHES, AND RECREATION AREAS

• **Rockland Breakwater/Marie Reed Park** 😾 😾 😾 See 🔢 on page 522.

For a unique walk into Rockland Harbor, follow this rocky trail out to historic Rockland Breakwater Lighthouse. Completed in 1888, the breakwater took 18 years to build, and at each juncture a beacon was placed on the end so ships were warned of the rock wall extending into the harbor. Finally, in 1902, the permanent lighthouse took up its current residence at the end. The city of Rockland began managing the lighthouse in 1998, and, although it is still a working lighthouse, the city is currently restoring it to its historical elegance.

The breakwater begins at the end of Samoset Road at Marie Reed Park, where there are benches along the water and a small sandy beach for dog-dipping. The one-mile rock walkway has been smoothed over in recent years so you won't have to do a mountain-goat imitation to reach the lighthouse. Although we don't recommend it for small dogs or pooches with short legs, the average dog shouldn't have any trouble keeping up. Once at the lighthouse you'll have fabulous views of the coast, Penobscot Bay, and the surrounding islands. Dogs must be on leash.

From town, follow State Route 1 north to Waldo Avenue. Turn right and then another right onto Samoset Road. The park is at the end of the road. Open 8 A.M. to 8 P.M. (207) 596-0376.

NATURE HIKES AND URBAN WALKS

Rockland Harbor Trail: Follow the blue line for a four-mile urban walk along the waterfront of Rockland. Starting at Snow Marine Park on Mechanic Street, this footpath will lead you along the city streets connecting all the waterfront parks and historical sites from one end of the harbor to the next. The path culminates in the mile-long breakwater hike to Rockland Breakwater Lighthouse (see above). (207) 596-0376.

RESTAURANTS

Hole in the Wall Bagels: Grab a cup of joe and a fresh bagel at this little bagel bakery on Main Street. You can nosh at the outdoor tables or take your breakfast to go. Main Street; (207) 594-3600.

Kate's Seafood: Dine on fresh broiled fish or steamed clams at this local seafood restaurant. Dogs are allowed at the outdoor seating overlooking the bay. Open May to October. State Route 1; (207) 594-2626.

Salazar's: For take-out Mexican cuisine, take your hot tamale to Salazar's. Some tables are outside if you wish to eat on-site, but try taking their homemade burritos or tacos for a great picnic dinner or lunch. Ole! 2 Park Street; (207) 596-0955.

PLACES TO STAY

Navigator Motor Inn: This motor inn overlooks the Rockland Harbor and is conveniently located on U.S. Route 1 at the Maine State Ferry Terminal. Dogs are allowed in certain rooms with approval. Rates range from $45 to $99. 520 Main Street, Rockland, ME 04841; (207) 594-2131; www.navigatorinn.com.

Trade Winds Motor Inn: This lovely 142-room conference center overlooks Penobscot Bay and offers full-service facilities to you and your pet. Most rooms have a patio deck, and a small park overlooking the bay is nearby for morning walks. Rooms range from $49 to $129 per night. 2 Park View Drive, Rockland, ME 04841; (207) 596-6661; www.midcoast.com/~twmi/.

FESTIVALS

Summer Solstice Night: June 21 is the first day of summer, and this solstice celebration is a proper kickoff to the summer season. Held from 6 to 9 P.M., Main Street is closed to traffic for live music, entertainment, street dancing, food, and special events. For more information, call (207) 594-0751.

ROCKPORT

PARKS, BEACHES, AND RECREATION AREAS

• The Georges Highland Path 🐾🐾 See **54** on page 522.

The Georges Highland Path is managed by the land and water conservation group, the Georges River Land Trust. The trail is over 10 miles long and connects many of the important features of the Georges River watershed including Bald, Ragged, Spruce, and Pleasant Mountains and numerous ponds and streams in the towns of Camden, Hope, Rockport, and Warren.

Eventually the organization hopes to continue the trail all the way to the Thomaston Town Forest.

Dogs need to be leashed.

The best places to access the trail are off Mount Pleasant Road and off State Route 17 in western Rockport, at the Barnestown and Gillette Roads intersection in Camden, off Hope Street in Hope, and at the Camden town line. Open sunrise to sunset. (207) 594-5166.

RESTAURANTS

Sea Spirit: This traditional Maine café offers crab cakes and haddock jazzed up with quesadillas and portabella melts. Even the picnic area is covered with a festive big-top tent. U.S. Route 1; (207) 230-0897.

PLACES TO STAY

Oakland Seashore Cabins and Motel: This motel/cottage complex offers a private beach for guests (including the four-legged ones) and comfortable lodging in a no-frills setting. The 11 cottages have kitchenettes; the motel offers spacious rooms with modern amenities. Rates range from $37 to $110 for the rooms; $40 to $80 for the cottages. Open May to October. State Route 1, 112 Dearborn Lane, Rockport, ME 04856; (207) 594-8104.

Seven Mountains Motel: This no-frills motel offers 12 small rooms and fresh muffins each morning. Dogs are allowed with advance reservations. Rates range from $40 to $79 per night. 360 Commercial Street (State Route 1), Rockport, ME 04856; (207) 236-3276.

DIVERSIONS

Fur 'N' Foliage: October is always a great time to get out and enjoy the Maine foliage, but when you can do it to help support local animal shelters and with a street full of dogs, well, what could be better? The Fur 'N' Foliage Walk is about two miles long starting at the village green and follows the mansion-lined streets around Beauchamp Point and Aldermere Farm. The annual event happens on the first Sunday in October.

Walkers are asked to give a donation or find sponsors, and everyone gets a T-shirt, goodie bag, and a chance to win great prizes. For more information and exact date, contact the Knox County Humane Society at (207) 594-4897.

SACO

PARKS, BEACHES, AND RECREATION AREAS

• **Concord Trail and Sylvan Trail** 🐾🐾🐾 See **55** on page 522.
Although this series of looping trails can get a bit confusing, you don't have to worry about getting lost in these woods, because if you journey too far in the wrong direction, you come out either on U.S. Route 1 or the Maine Turnpike. Don't think a hike here is all highway driving, though. The park is a scenic woodland experience with about four miles of trails, two brooks, and a pine-tree farm.

The trails and property are managed by the Saco Bay Trails group. Dogs need to be leashed.

From U.S. Route 1, take Flag Pond Road west for a half mile. The park is on the right. Parking is available. Open sunrise to sunset. For more information, contact Saco Bay Trails, P.O. Box 7505, Ocean Park, ME 04063. There is no phone.

• **Ferry Beach State Park** 🐾🐾 See **56** on page 522.
Although dogs are not permitted on the beach, this rich and diverse area is still a good spot for a dog to stretch his legs. The 117 acres is made up of beach, swamps, dunes, and woodlands. Although most of the trails run to the beach, there are still a number of good paths that lead through the swamps and woods.

There is a day use fee of $2. Dogs are not permitted on the beaches and must be on a leash in all state parks.

The park is located on State Route 9 at Bay View Road. Open from 9 A.M. to sunset. Call (207) 283-0067 Memorial Day through September 30, (207) 624-6075 off-season.

• **Log Cabin Trail** 🐾🐾🐾 See **57** on page 522.
This trail, just over a mile in length, is a quick enjoyable outing past stone walls and through a young pine forest. Along the way you'll wander past a

pond teeming with wildlife and over a few marshy areas via a system of boardwalks. We like this short trail because it is quiet, scenic, and you usually have the trails to yourself. Dogs need to be leashed.

From U.S. Route 1, take Flag Pond Road west for two miles. Turn right onto Lincoln Road for a mile. The park is on the right. Parking is available. Open sunrise to sunset. For more information, contact Saco Bay Trails, P.O. Box 7505, Ocean Park, ME 04063. There is no phone.

PLACES TO STAY

Blue Haven Motor Court and Cottages: All rooms and cottages have kitchenettes and clean, comfortable furnishings. Rates range from $50 to $79 with an additional $5 fee for your dog. 1015 Portland Road, Saco, ME 04072; (207) 282-1476.

Crown 'N' Anchor Inn: There are six elegant rooms available in this 1760 farmhouse and 1827 manor house combining to give guests a historic and comfortable stay. Each room comes complete with Victorian furnishings and private bath, and a bountiful breakfast is included. The converted barn is now a library with over 4,000 books for your reading pleasure. Rates range from $65 to $120. 121 North Street, Saco, ME 04072; (207) 282-3829, (800) 561-8865.

Saco Motel: This 25-room motel complex is located in town and close to the beach. Rates range from $40 to $80; pets cannot be left unattended. 473 Main Street, Saco, ME 04072; (207) 284-6952; www.sacomotel.com.

Saco/Portland South KOA: This campground chain is located on a 30-acre wooded site just two miles from the beach. Dogs need to be leashed. Tent and RV rates range from $27 to $33. 814A Portland Road, Saco, ME 04072; (207) 282-0502, (800) KOA-1886.

FESTIVALS

Curb Your Culture: At the Saco Sidewalk Arts Festival on classic Main Street, you and your dog can discuss what's art and what's not. With hundreds of sculptures, etchings, paintings, prints, photographs, and performers, you'll have a wide range of crafts and culture to ooh, aah, and ugh at. This popular, free festival is held the last Saturday in June. For more information, call (207) 282-6169.

DIVERSIONS

See You at the Movies: The Saco Drive-in is the site of one of the most popular summer evening events in these parts, and our dogs don't want to miss any of the excitement, including the previews and popcorn. Gates open at 7:30 P.M. and shows start at dusk from June to September. $10 per car for two adults, $2.50 for each additional person. Dogs don't need to hide in the trunk! 969 Portland Road (U.S. Route 1); (207) 284-1016.

SAINT GEORGE

PLACES TO STAY

Craignair Inn: This modest inn-motel offers cottages and motel rooms near the water. There is also a seafood restaurant on-site, although there isn't any outdoor seating for your pup. The inn is open all year, and the rooms are clean and comfortable. Rates range from $60 to $120. 533 Clark Island Road, Spruce Head, ME 04859; (207) 594-7644; www.craignairinn.com.

SANFORD

PARKS, BEACHES, AND RECREATION AREAS

• Gowen Memorial Park 🐾🐾🐾 See **58** on page 522.

This beautiful town park is the southern terminus for the Mousam Way Trail and the chain of ponds on the Mousam River through the sister towns of Sanford and Springvale. The park is on North Pond, a popular place to take a dip or walk along the sidewalk that runs on the south side of the lake. The rest of the park offers open grassy fields and playgrounds. Dogs need to be leashed.

The park is located off of Main Street (State Route 109) in the center of town. Open sunrise to 9 P.M. (207) 324-9134.

• Holdsworth Park 🐾🐾🐾 See **59** on page 522.

This scenic town park is located along the dammed-up Mousam River and Mill Pond. It's also connected to the Mousam Way Trail, which offers a longer hike. But don't be surprised if you find your dog is content to stay in the park's big, open grassy fields, surrounding tall pines, and rocky hillsides.

Dogs need to be leashed.

The park is located off Main Street (State Route 109) in the center of town. Open sunrise to 9 P.M. (207) 324-9134.

• Mousam Way Trail 🐾🐾🐾 See **60** on page 522.

This trail runs along the Mousam River as it cuts through the towns of Sanford and Springvale, connecting a number of town parks. The route is about four miles long and runs from esker to esker, over foot bridges and auto bridges. Traverse the sidewalks and pine-covered paths as it continues back and forth between the forests, wetlands, and town streets. In addition to the river, you will find that North, Stump, and Mill Ponds are good water stops.

Dogs need to be leashed, and bug spray is recommended in warm months.

The trail is accessible from Gowen Memorial and Holdsworth Parks. Open sunrise to 9 P.M. (207) 324-9134.

RESTAURANTS

Shaw's Ridge Farm: With sunny outdoor seating in a farm setting and with delicious ice cream, Shaw's is a cool stop. If you are trying to be healthy, the farm is shared with Ridley Farm, which sells plenty of fresh fruits and vegetables. Ridley Road; (207) 324-2510.

SCARBOROUGH

PARKS, BEACHES, AND RECREATION AREAS

• Higgins Beach 🐾🐾🐾 See **61** on page 522.

News flash! This popular beach has sand! That's something of a rarity on the rocky Maine coast. And this beach is not completely free of the hard stuff, which makes it a fun place for dogs. The mixture of sand and huge boulders lying randomly on the beach makes a great playground for your pet. George likes to play hide-and-seek among the rocks while Rocky and Inu decide who has to be "It."

Dogs must be on leash. No dogs are permitted on the beach from 9 A.M. to 3 P.M. from April 1 to October 1.

You are on your own as far as parking goes during the summer. No street parking is permitted from April 1 to October 1.

From the intersection of State Routes 77 and 207, take State Route 77 north for a half mile. Turn right onto Ocean Avenue to the end. Open sunrise to sunset. (207) 772-2811.

• Scarborough Beach 🐾 🐾 See **62** on page 522.

A beach is a beach is a beach. Or at least that's how it seems when you're staring at the wide-open spaces where your dog can't go. Fortunately this 1.5-mile-long sandy beach is open to dogs in the off-season and is perfect for ball throwing and exploring the dunes and marshes.

Dogs must be on leash and are not permitted on the beach from April 1 to October 1.

From the intersection of State Routes 77 and 207, take State Route 207 south for one mile. The park and parking is on the left. Open dawn to dusk or 6:30 P.M. (whichever is later). (207) 883-2416.

• Scarborough Marsh Wildlife Management Area 🐾 🐾 🐾 See **63** on page 522.

This simple but invigorating hike follows a service road through the largest salt marsh in Maine. The thin dirt road runs for almost two miles between Pine Point and Black Point Roads. Experience the 3,000 marshy acres of tidal flats, tall grasses, numerous streams, and the Scarborough River.

Halfway across the marsh is a foot bridge and a lone tree that locals call the Wishing Tree. A tree is probably what most dogs on this path are wishing for, but we think this scenic area is already a wish come true.

Dogs must be on leash. Note that this area, managed by the state of Maine, permits hunting in season.

From the intersection of U.S. Route 1 and State Route 9, take State Route 9 (Pine Point Road) south for two miles, passing the Scarborough Marsh Nature Center. The park and parking are on the left. Open dawn to dusk. (207) 287-8000.

PLACES TO STAY

Pride Motel and Cottages: This simple motel complex offers comfortable lodging for the traveler heading up or down the coast. Rates range from $60 to $105. 677 U.S. Route 1, Scarborough, ME 04070; (207) 883-4816, (800) 424-3350; www.holidayjunction.com/usa/me/cme0004.html.

Residence Inn: This suite-style Marriott caters to long-term and relocating families. They welcome you and your pet for an additional $20 per night or $150 a month. The suites range from studios to two-bedroom units, and all include full kitchenettes. Rooms range from $99 to $150 a night. Call for monthly rates. 800 Roundwood Drive, Scarborough, ME 04070; (207) 883-0400; www.marriott.com.

SEARSPORT

PARKS, BEACHES, AND RECREATION AREAS

• **Moose Point State Park** 🐾🐾🐾 See **64** on page 522.
This 183-acre park offers a small rocky beach, trails, and a picnic area over-looking the ocean. Take the 1.5-mile hike to Moose Point just before sunset for a spectacular view over the coastal mountains in the west.

Admission is $1 per person, and dogs must be on leash.

The park is located off of U.S. Route 1, 1.5 miles south of the center of town. Open 9 A.M. to a half hour before sunset. Call (207) 548-2882 Memorial Day through October 1, (207) 941-4014 off-season.

• **Mosman Memorial Park** 🐾🐾🐾 See **65** on page 522.
This small oceanfront park offers a great swimming beach where dogs are actually allowed in the summer. On the bluff above there is a grassy open space for ball throwing and picnic tables for enjoying your lunch. Take the wooden stairway down to the beach and you and your dog can enjoy a sur-prisingly warm swim. Depending on the tide, you'll have a large or small beach area to kick up your heels.

Dogs must be on leash.

From U.S. Route 1 in the center of town, take Water Street south for a quarter mile. The park and parking is on the left. Open 6 A.M. to 11 P.M. (207) 548-2304.

• **Sears Island** 🐾🐾🐾 See **66** on page 522.
How about exploring an entire island to try and tire out your dog? It works for our Robinson Canines. Not only do they get to romp in the surf while play-ing their version of *Survivor*, but they also enjoy the five-mile hike around the perimeter of the island. The trail is a bit rough in places but generally follows the shoreline.

Dogs need to be leashed in all state parks.

From U.S. Route 1 (north of the center of town), take Island Road south for a mile across the causeway onto the island. Roadside parking is available at the gate. Open sunrise to sunset. (207) 941-4014.

RESTAURANTS

Cook's Crossing Ice-Cream Shop: Enjoy smoothies and a wide variety of hard and soft ice cream at their cute outdoor seating area. U.S. Route 1; (207) 548-2005.

Jordan's Restaurant: Enjoy outdoor dining at this family restaurant. Choose from the picnic tables at the take-out window or the patio attached to the full-service restaurant. Fish, burgers, ice cream, and pasta dinners will please all tastes and appetites. U.S. Route 1; (207) 548-2555.

SOUTH BERWICK

PARKS, BEACHES, AND RECREATION AREAS

• **Vaughan Woods State Park** 🐾🐾🐾 See **67** on page 522.
Vaughan Woods is 250 acres of an old-growth pine forest along the Salmon Falls River.

If you have never experienced an old-growth forest, this is a great opportunity to see why we should do everything we can to protect the few that remain. The tall pines, with their thick, high canopy, block most of the light and wind and prevent other plants from growing. So the giant forest is filled with a ghostly quiet. Even your footsteps are hushed on a forest floor covered with pine needles. And it's been that way for years. Even the trails are old. The River Run Trail along the Salmon Falls River was first used by Native Americans many years ago.

Another piece of history is Cow Cove, where the first cows landed in 1634. Located on the River Run Trail, this is one of the few places in the park where you can get down to the river. Most of the riverbank has a steep slope which gets you to the water quickly but makes for a tricky climb out (isn't that right, Inu?).

There is a $1 admission fee. Maps are available at the trailhead. Dogs are required to be on leash in all state parks.

From State Route 236, take Old South Road west for one mile. turn left onto Brattle Street for a quarter mile. The park is on the right. Open 9 A.M. to sunset. Call (207) 384-5160 Memorial Day through Labor Day, (207) 384-5160 off-season.

SOUTH PORTLAND

PARKS, BEACHES, AND RECREATION AREAS

• **Willard Beach** 🐾🐾 See 68 on page 522.
This small but sandy beach offers nice views and mild waves, but that's not why we come here. We're just happy to hear they allow dogs and there is no access fee. Now if only parking were available. Street parking is not permitted from April 1 to October 1. Dogs need to be on a leash.

From State Route 77, take Cottage Road east for 1.5 miles. Turn left onto Preble Street, then right onto Willard Street to the end. Open 8:30 A.M. to sunset. (207) 767-7669.

RESTAURANTS

Barbara's Kitchen and Café: Sure, we get excited when we find a great new park for the dogs, but when we're hungry, nothing compares to the joy of finding a wonderful restaurant. The menu here is mouth-watering delicious and the portions are huge. Just enough to satisfy your hunger and let you offer a few scraps to your hungry pal. The outdoor alley seating has limited views, to say the least, but you'll only be staring at the food anyway. Barbara also makes great box lunches. 388 Cottage Road; (207) 767-6313.

PLACES TO STAY

AmeriSuites: This 131-room corporate hotel is conveniently located off Interstate 95. Whether you're coming or going, this will be an easy stopover in comfortable digs. Rates range from $129 to $179, plus a $20 fee for your pet. 303 Sable Oaks Drive, South Portland, ME 04106; (207) 775-3900, (800) 833-1516; www.amerisuites.com.

Best Western Merry Manor Inn: There are 151 comfortable rooms at this full-service hotel and all welcome your pup. Each room is equipped with all the modern amenities, and the hotel is conveniently located off Interstate 95 near the Portland airport. Rates range from $119 to $139. Pets cannot be left unattended. 700 Main Street, South Portland, ME 04106; (207) 774-6151, (800) 528-1234; www.bestwestern.com/merrymanorinn.

Howard Johnson Hotel: This standard hotel offers clean, comfortable lodging at reasonable rates. Rooms range from $104 to $149. A $50 deposit is required for your pet. 675 Main Street, South Portland, ME 04106; (207)775-5343, (800) 446-4656; www.zyacorp.com.

Marriott Sable Oaks: Stay and pamper yourself at this modern corporate hotel which offers refrigerators, microwaves, and coffee makers in each room. An on-site restaurant, health club, and spa are also available. Rates range from $169 to $199, plus a $20 fee per pet per night. 200 Sable Oaks Drive, South Portland, ME 04106; (207) 871-8000, (800) 752-8810; www.marriotthotels.com/pwmap/.

SOUTHPORT

PLACES TO STAY

Lawnmeer Inn: This quiet, out-of-the-way spot on Southport Island is just a mile from Boothbay Harbor. With 32 rooms overlooking the ocean, this historic 1892 inn is a delightful place to stay. A large lawn and deck let you and your pet enjoy the ocean views. A private swimming cove is also accessible. Pets are allowed in certain rooms only, so advance reservations are required. Rates range from $75 to $195 per night. P.O. Box 505, West Boothbay Harbor, ME 04575; (207) 633-2544, (800) 633-7645; www.lawnmeerinn.com.

THOMASTON

PARKS, BEACHES, AND RECREATION AREAS

• **Thomaston Town Forest** 🐾 🐾 See 69 on page 522.

This forest offers six miles of hiking trails along the Oyster River. The trails form two loops—one is four miles long and the other is a two-mile trek—that run north from the trailhead. If you take the longer route, you will make it to Split Rock, a huge glacial erratic. Dogs need to be leashed; you know the drill.

From U.S. Route 1 in the center of town, take Booker Road north to the end and the Thomaston Pollution Control Plant where parking is available. Open sunrise to sunset. (207) 594-5166.

RESTAURANTS

Thomaston Café and Bakery: Our trail dogs seem to be able to go for days on a handful of dry biscuits and stagnant pond water, but Chris comes down with the shakes if there isn't a constant supply of coffee and a heaping pile of food at arm's length. Luckily, there are places like Thomaston Café and Bakery where he can stock up on healthy food prepared with a flair. Try their famous crab cakes, featured in *Gourmet* magazine. 154 Main Street; (207) 354-8589; www.thomastoncafe.com.

DIVERSION

Like a Rock: The Drew Griffith Memorial Canine Walk is dedicated to a K-9 police officer who was killed in the line of duty. The annual event is led by his former partner, Rock, a German shepherd. Walk from the State Police Barracks in Thomaston to the newly named Drew Griffin Bridge in Warren.

The annual fund-raiser takes place on the first Saturday in May, and the money goes to the local animal shelters. Walkers are asked to give a donation or find sponsors. Everyone gets a goodie bag and a chance to win prizes. For more information and exact date and time, contact the Knox County Humane Society at (207) 594-4897.

WATERBORO

PARKS, BEACHES, AND RECREATION AREAS

• Ossipee Hill 😷 😷 😷 🐕 See **70** on page 522.

Ossipee Hill is covered with woods but at the open summit you'll enjoy fine views of the Saco River Valley below and the distant White Mountains, including Mount Washington. This town-owned forest has a number of secondary footpaths that allow you and your pup to explore much of the area, even if many of trails seem to go nowhere.

The primary hiking route is on the fire road leading to the Ossipee Hill peak. The 1.5-mile climb is a gentle grade at first and then becomes steeper as you approach the summit. Once on top, we recommend enjoying the view and a picnic lunch.

Dogs need to be under voice control.

From Waterboro Center and State Route 5, take Ossipee Hill Road west. Make an immediate right onto McLucas Road (it becomes a rough dirt road) to the end and the trailhead. Open 24 hours a day. (207) 247-6199.

WELLS

PARKS, BEACHES, AND RECREATION AREAS

• Rachel Carson National Wildlife Reserve 😷 😷 See **71** on page 522.

If you do even a little driving around the southern coast of Maine, you will soon realize that the Rachel Carson National Wildlife Reserve is big. This national park protects thousands of acres of salt marshes, estuaries, and rivers from Portland to York. These wetlands are an important habitat for migrating waterfowl.

Although most of the reserve is inaccessible to hikers, one section, the Rachel Carson Interpretive Trail, is open to you and your dog. This mile-long, easy to follow path is a great way to experience this natural area. Along the way are boardwalks and lookout points from which sightings of great blue heron and snowy egrets wading in the Branch Brook or the Merriland River are common. Dogs must remain on leash and on the trail.

From the Maine Turnpike (Interstate 95), take exit 2 to State Route 9 and 109 east for 1.25 miles. Turn left onto U.S. Route 1 north to State Route 9 east for

1.5 miles. Make a right onto State Route 9 when the two highways fork and continue for a quarter mile. The park is on the right. Open dawn to dusk. (207) 646-9226.

• Wells Harbor Community Park 🐾🐾 See 72 on page 522.

This town park on the Webhannet River and Wells Harbor offers multiple choices for visiting dogs. A gazebo, picnic area, playground, boat launch, pier, and some woodland hiking trails are all available for exploration.

In the northern section is a short two-mile trail that runs through tall beach grass and marshy woodlands. A walk on the southern end of the park is a good way to explore the streams and tides of the Webhannet River. And if you head to the eastern end of the park by the boat launch and pier, you'll find a good place to let your dog swim.

Dogs need to be on leash.

From U.S. Route 1, take Harbor Road east for a half mile. The park and parking is on the right. Open sunrise to 9 P.M. (207) 646-2451.

RESTAURANTS

Big Daddy's Ice Cream: Bring your big appetite to Big Daddy, and he'll take care of you with all kinds of ice cream, yogurt, hot dogs, and burgers. Get your chow to go or enjoy eating with your chow at the picnic tables. U.S. Route 1; (207) 646-5454.

PLACES TO STAY

The Tidewood Motel and Cottages: The Tidewood complex, on three shady acres, is close to most of the southern Maine hot spots. You have your choice of one- or two-bedroom cottages with full kitchens, or motel rooms with patios. Open May to mid-November. Rates range from $49 to $89 for the motel and from $59 to $89 for the cottages. An additional $10 daily fee is charged for pets. 2062 Post Road (U.S. Route 1), Wells, ME 04090; (207) 646-5689.

WISCASSET

PARKS, BEACHES, AND RECREATION AREAS

• Sortwell Memorial Forest 🐾🐾 🐕 See 73 on page 522.

This 90-acre property of tall white pines, open meadows, and two brooks is owned by the New England Forestry Foundation, a private conservation group. The park has about two miles of hiking trails, many utilizing overgrown forest roads.

Dogs need to be under voice control.

From U.S. Route 1, take State Route 27 north for a half mile. Turn left onto Churchill Street, then right onto Old Dresden Road for a half mile. The property and a rough parking lot are on the right. Open dawn to dusk. (978) 448-8380.

NATURE HIKES AND URBAN WALKS

Wiscasset Historical Walking Tour: Take a guided tour through the historical past of this once-prosperous port. Dogs are allowed at all outdoor facilities but not on the interior tours of the sea captains' homes. By appointment only. (207) 443-5712.

RESTAURANTS

Red's Eats: This tiny burger stand is located right in town on U.S. Route 1 overlooking the Sheepscot River. Feast on haddock sandwiches, hot dogs, and even steaks! A few small tables are outside, but mainly this is a stand-and-eat establishment. We think you'll agree the food is worth rising for! U.S. Route 1 at the bridge; there is no phone.

Sarah's Café: Dine overlooking the Sheepscot River at this friendly café. Serving hearty breakfasts, light lunches, and full dinners, you and your dog are allowed out on the back water-view patio. Main Street; (207) 882-7504.

YARMOUTH

PARKS, BEACHES, AND RECREATION AREAS

• Pratt Brook Park 😾 😾 😾 🐕‍ See **74** on page 522.

This 200-acre park on Pratt Brook is managed jointly by the town and the Yarmouth Ski Club. Because it's used extensively for cross-country skiing, the park has quite a series of looping trails—about eight miles worth.

Dogs need to be under voice control and are not permitted on the cross-country ski trails in winter.

The park is located off of North Road, just south of Elm Street. Parking is available. Open dawn to 7:30 P.M. (207) 846-2406.

• Royal River Park 😾 😾 😾 🐕‍ See **75** on page 522.

This town park is a royal destination for the residents of Yarmouth and the surrounding communities. The winding Royal River carves its way through this park, but it's the mile-long bike path and acres of rolling, groomed fields that make this a princely spot for Spot.

On the river, which can move quickly, you'll find a few places to "put in" on a hot day. There are also some short falls, and the remains of old mills, bridge foundations, and dams line the shore. On hot summer days, our dogs offer an imperial salute for Royal River Park.

Dogs need to be under voice control.

From U.S. Route 1, take Main Street west for a half mile. Turn right onto Elm Street for a quarter mile. The park and a parking lot are on the right. Open dawn to 7:30 P.M. (207) 846-2406.

RESTAURANTS

Gillespie Farms: Gillespie Farms store is a great place to pick up a healthy snack. The fruits and vegetables are straight from the family farm in North Yarmouth. You can get a bag of delicious Macintosh apples to go or enjoy one at the picnic tables on the side. And, just in case you need a sugar fix, they also have homemade cookies and apple pie. 301 Main Street; (207) 829-5610.

PLACES TO STAY

Down-East Village Motel: This comfortable 32-room motel offers rooms with kitchens and many modern amenities. Located on the Royal River, you're just a short drive away from Freeport shopping and Portland restaurants. Rates are $99. Dogs are allowed in selected rooms. 705 U.S. Route 1, Yarmouth, ME 04096; (207) 846-5161, (800) 782-9338.

DIVERSIONS

Canine Caruso: After a day at the beach, sit back and relax with a picnic at the Summer Arts Series. This musical series takes place Wednesdays at 6 P.M. from late June to early August at Royal River Park. For a list of performers, call (207) 846-2406.

YORK

PARKS, BEACHES, AND RECREATION AREAS

• Long Beach 🐾🐾🐾 See **76** on page 522.

Along New England's rocky coastline, it is difficult to find a sandy beach and even harder to find a beach that allows dogs. This is why Chris and Inu come every spring and fall, year after year, to Long Beach. Dogs are not permitted during summer "rush hour," but, with a beach like this, we'll take what we can get.

Like the name says, it's a long beach, almost two miles in length, but, more importantly, the beach is smooth and flat, just the way Inu likes it.

When you aren't throwing the ball for your dog or bodysurfing in the waves, you can relax and enjoy the great views from the beach in either direction. Cape Neddick Light circles its beacon endlessly to the north and York Harbor lies to the south.

Dogs need to be on leash and are not permitted on the beach between 8 A.M. and 6 P.M. from May 1 to September 30.

The beach is located off of State Route 1A, 2.5 miles from U.S. Route 1 in either direction. Open 24 hours a day. (207) 363-1040.

• Mount Agamenticus 🐾🐾🐾 🐕 See **77** on page 522.

Mount Agamenticus, at 690 feet, is a monadnock, a lone peak in an otherwise rather flat landscape. And so, from the summit and the fire tower upon it, there are panoramic views of the southern Maine coast and New Hampshire's White Mountains. But you don't have to go to the top to enjoy an outing here. Surrounding the peak are numerous hiking trails, woods, streams, swamps, and ponds.

In total, there are over six miles of trails on the recreational peak, and you couldn't take the same route twice if you tried. Dogs are permitted under voice control.

From U.S. Route 1, take Mountain Road west for a total of 4.2 miles. Turn right onto Agamenticus Road (just before the pavement ends) and into a dirt parking area. There is another parking lot at the summit. Open dawn to dusk. (207) 363-1040.

• Sophier Park 🐾 🦴 See **78** on page 522.

Cape Neddick is home to Sophier Park and the Cape Neddick Lighthouse, nicknamed the Nubble Light. This rocky nubble, worn down by severe weather and churning seas, is a good example of how harsh the Maine coast can be. The 1879 lighthouse and great views illustrate, on the other hand, just how beautiful the Maine coast can be. And the parking lot during the summer demonstrates just what a zoo coastal Maine can be during high season. There are no trails here, and swimming is dangerous because of the rough surf and rocks. Yet it is one of the most popular destinations in Maine. Most visitors find a cozy place on the smooth rocks and enjoy the scene. Your dog probably won't give two sticks about the scenery, but she will enjoy all the great things to sniff.

There is no public access to the lighthouse. Dogs must be on leash.

From State Route 1A, take Nubble Road to the end. Open 5 A.M. to midnight. (207) 363-1040.

NATURE HIKES AND URBAN WALKS

Fisherman's Walk: The Fisherman's Walk is a one-mile, scenic path following the York River through York Harbor, the historic section of town. York has an on-going debate with neighboring Kittery about which town is the first one established in Maine. Whichever town is the oldest, it dates back to at least 1630.

The trail begins at Steadman's Woods, a tree-covered peninsula between the York River and the Barrell Mill Pond. The scenic pond, a popular swimming hole, was created by the completion of the Barrell Mill Pond Dam in 1726. It is an easy walk across the quarter-mile dam, but you'll need your sea legs to cross the Wiggley Bridge, a suspension footbridge over the dam's floodway. Along the way are helpful interpretive signs and great views of the harbor.

You can park at the intersection of State Route 103 and the York River. For more information, call (207) 363-7320.

RESTAURANTS

Brown's Ice Cream: There is something about the sea air that makes an ice-cream stop extra special. George agrees that Brown's Ice Cream, sea air or not, is good stuff. You can enjoy your tasty treat on one of the outdoor tables or, if you can resist eating it right away, take it to nearby Sophier Park and the Nubble Light. And if you want to be a real southern Mainer, you have to at least try the wild blueberry flavor. Nubble Road; (207) 363-1277.

Carla's Bakery & Café: If your idea of health food is a carrot muffin and low-fat chocolate chip cookies, you've come to the right place. If you'd rather have brownies and sticky buns, then so much the better. And if you're a hound who has never passed up a gourmet turkey sandwich with the works, then you'd better not waste any more time. The menu here includes all of the above and more. Chow hounds welcome! 241 York Street; (207) 363-4637.

Fox's Lobster House: Seafood, ice cream, outdoor seating, and a view of the Nubble Light. Does it sound tempting to you? Everyone else thinks it does, so don't be surprised at the crowds that will join you for lunch. Open May through October. Nubble Road; (207) 363-2643.

PLACES TO STAY

Country View Motel and Guesthouse: This guest house and motel complex offers an array of accommodation options for the vacationing traveler. The guesthouse features six charming rooms, all with private baths in a classic bed-and-breakfast setting. Just off the main house is a two-bedroom apartment, and in the motel facility there are cottages ranging from a studio apartment to a two-floor townhouse. Well-behaved dogs are allowed everywhere except the guest house. Rates range from $45 to $175, plus a $10 charge for each pet. No more than two pets are allowed per room. 1521 Route 1, Cape Neddick, ME 03902; (207) 363-7160, (800) 258-6598; www.countryviewmotel.com.

FESTIVALS

Light the Light: The holiday event of the season is the Lighting of the Nubble. The holiday lighting of the popular lighthouse takes place in late November at Sohier Park. Thousands of residents turn out for the festivities.

It's also the event of the summer season, for the Nubble is lit once again as part of the Christmas in July celebration. So if you missed it in November, don't miss it in July. Just tell your boss you're going to a Christmas lighting ceremony and you need the day off. Odds are, she's never heard that one before! The Seacoast Wind Ensemble accompanies both the lightings. For more information and exact dates and times, call (207) 363-1040.

17
DOWNEAST

The towns covered in this chapter run from Maine's charming mid-coast villages of Castine and Deer Isle all the way up to the Canadian border. The region is called "Downeast" for the trade winds that carry sailing ships eastward along the coast. The crown jewels in this elegant setting are Bar Harbor and Acadia National Park, the only national park listed in this book. Samuel de Champlain first arrived on these shores in 1604 and claimed "Acadia," as it was later known, for France. First as a fur-trading outpost, later as a fortification for the British during the Revolutionary War, the coves and islands in this region have been claimed by many, but owned by none.

You and your dog will love exploring the vast history here, found in the early European colonization and later in the industrial mill towns on rivers that run to the sea. There are beautiful forests, lovely meadows, and mountains surprisingly close to the ocean. Everywhere you go, you and your dog will delight in beautiful, wide-open spaces.

BAR HARBOR

In the late 19th and early 20th centuries, Bar Harbor was second only to Newport, Rhode Island, as a playground for the wealthy. Once trains became a predominant mode of transportation, rich New Yorkers and Bostonians arrived in droves to this beautiful paradise by the sea. Victorian summer mansions belonging to families like the Rockefellers, Astors, and Vanderbilts lined the streets of Bar Harbor. In fact, most of Acadia National Park is on land once owned by the Rockefellers. Unfortunately, most of these

---

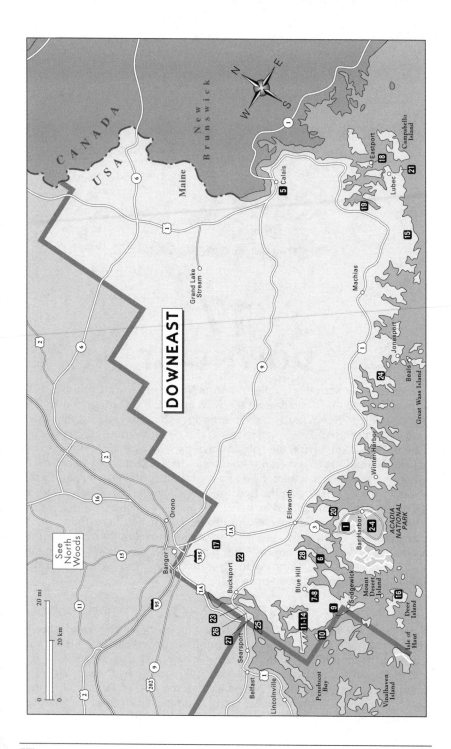

DOWNEAST

See North Woods

remarkable monuments to the Gilded Age have disappeared—destroyed in the devastating fire that swept through Bar Harbor in 1947.

Today Bar Harbor is still a popular tourist destination. Located at the gateway to Acadia National Park, you'll find more activities, restaurants, hotels, and dog-friendly fun than you can possibly do, see, or experience on one visit.

PARKS, BEACHES, AND RECREATION AREAS

• Acadia National Park 🐾🐾🐾🐾 See ❶ on page 572.
Acadia is the most visited national park in the country. With 200 miles of hiking and carriage trails and 34,000 acres, it is certainly not one of the largest parks in the United States, but once you visit you'll know why it's so popular. For a group of coastal islands, it has a remarkably varied terrain of rocky beaches, flat, open hiking areas, dense forests, and even mountains to climb.

At 1,531 feet, Mount Cadillac is a popular destination at sunset, affording 360-degree views from its open summit. The peak was named after Antoine de la Mothe Cadillac, a Frenchman who was given Mount Desert Island by Louis XIV in 1688 when France controlled New England or, as they called it, Acadia. Cadillac later moved on to found the city of Detroit. So drive your Cadillac up Mount Cadillac and enjoy the view. Or, even better, you can climb the peak from a seven-mile trail off State Route 3 opposite the entrance to Black Woods Campground. Follow the signs to Cadillac Mountain. Once you reach the top, plenty of flat rocks make perfect perches from which to enjoy the vista.

There are countless trails and destinations here, and we recommend stopping at the ranger station on your way into Acadia to pick up a park map. The trails, and especially the wide carriage paths (commissioned by the Rockefeller family before donating Acadia to the American people), are popular year-round with hikers, mountain bikers, and cross-country skiers.

The only places dogs are not allowed are on Sand Beach and any lake swimming area. But plenty of rocky beaches throughout the rest of the park are available for your dog to take a swim; Aunt Betty's Pond is the one exception to the "no lake swimming" rule. Day-use admission is $10. Open 24 hours a day. (207) 288-3338.

• Shore Path 🐾🐾 See ❷ on page 572.
This narrow crushed-stone path follows the scenic shoreline of Frenchman Bay from the piers at Waterfront Park to Cromwell Cove. Running a mile along the harbor, this popular walk offers great views of the ferries coming and going from Nova Scotia and all the activities in the water or at its edge.

Dogs need to be leashed.

The trail is best accessed from Waterfront Park on Main Street or from Wayman Lane. Open 24 hours a day. (207) 288-5103.

• Village Green 🐾🐾 See ❸ on page 572.
This small park is really just a green space in the center of town, but there are a few short paths that you and your dog can use to stretch your legs. Benches conveniently line the paths so you can sit and watch the swirl of people march by. Your dog won't be panting after a lap around this park, but, if you're staying in town and need a place to take a quick walk, this would be it.

Dogs must be on leash.

The park is located on Main and Park Streets. Open 6 A.M. to 11 P.M. (207) 288-5103.

•Waterfront Park 🐾🐾 **See ⑷ on page 572.**

Well, as a park for dogs, it's no match for nearby Acadia National Park, but the harbor views are unsurpassed and many pats are available from dog-starved tourists who sadly left their best friend at home. The grassy, hilltop harborside park is a little more that a city block in size.

Dogs need to be leashed.

The park is located between Main and West Streets and Newport Drive. Open 6 A.M. to 11 P.M. (207) 288-5103.

NATURE HIKES AND URBAN WALKS

Bar Harbor Walking Tour: Step into Bar Harbor's Victorian past on this one-hour guided walking tour through downtown Bar Harbor. Costumed guides will lead you through a "backstage" look at how the rich and famous lived 100 years ago. Sponsored by Coastal Kayaking Tours, call for reservations. (207) 288-9605.

RESTAURANTS

Bar Harbor Inn Terrace Restaurant: Dogs are allowed on the outdoor terrace at this elegant restaurant overlooking Frenchman's Bay. The menu is pricey but the food delicious. Dogs who don't chew with their mouths open are allowed! Reservations are recommended. 1 Newport Drive; (207) 288-3351.

CJ's Big Dipper: Stop by for a cool scoop at this friendly ice-cream parlor across the street from the Village Green. Outside tables outside and plenty of benches along Main Street allow you to share a cup of yogurt with the dog. 150 Main Street; (207) 288-2128.

Cottage Street Bakery and Deli: More than just a deli or a bakery, this full-service restaurant offers salads, soups, hot sandwiches, fabulous blueberry muffins, and full breakfasts on their outdoor shaded patio. You can even choose from an array of delicious boxed lunches to take on the trails. On a recent visit here our dogs worked the crowd for pats and treats at this friendly neighborhood eatery. 59 Cottage Street; (207) 288-3010.

Golden Anchor Pier Restaurant: Dine on seafood from the best seat in the house at this outdoor restaurant that juts into the harbor on the pier. Known for award-winning clam chowder, you can't beat the food or the location. Dogs are welcome on the outdoor pier patio. 55 West Street; (207) 288-2110.

Ocean Drive Dairy Bar: Stop by this roadside eatery on your way to Acadia National Park. Serving burgers, fish chowder, and ice-cream sundaes, it is right on the way into or out of the park. There are plenty of picnic tables outside. 444 Lower Main Street; (207) 288-5239.

Olde Flame BBQ Pit and Tap House: Dogs dig the huge helpings of dem bones at this rib joint. With plenty of outdoor seating and servings that will keep you filled for days, this is a great stop for dogs and humans with big appetites. Try the Brunswick Stew or Coastline Kabob. 131 Cottage Street; (207) 288-2800.

Parkside Restaurant: This excellent restaurant is our favorite place in Bar Harbor. With a great view of the busy street scene from the outdoor patio, you and your dog will be in the thick of the pack here. Better yet, they go all out to make dogs feel welcome. Dog biscuits, bacon treats, and a bowl of water are offered to your pal when you dine here. Oh, and the food for humans is pretty darn good, too! 185 Main Street; (207) 288-2700.

Village Green Café: Plenty of outdoor seating is available at this pleasant café just down the street from the Village Green. Breakfast, lunch, or dinner will satisfy all appetites. 189 Main Street; (207) 288-9450.

PLACES TO STAY

Atlantic Oakes by the Sea: This lovely ocean resort was once the estate of Sir Henry Oakes, one of the world's richest men in the early 20th century. He founded the Lake Shore Mines, the second largest strike in the Western Hemisphere. This estate reflected Sir "Harry's" extravagant lifestyle until he met an untimely death in 1942 when he was mysteriously and brutally stabbed while he slept. His son-in-law was tried for murder but was eventually acquitted.

We doubt your stay here will be as dramatic; quite the opposite, a stay at this inn will refresh and relax you. All 150 rooms have balconies, and some efficiency units are available. No dogs are allowed during July and August, but they are welcome the rest of the year. Rates range from $85 to $122 in the off-season. 119 Eden Street (State Route 3), P.O. Box 3, Bar Harbor, ME 04609; (207) 288-5801; www.barharbor.com.

Barcadia Campground: This oceanfront campground has ocean sites as well as forest camping. Full facilities, showers, a beach, and kayak rentals are available. Located just outside Acadia National Park, pets are allowed on leash. Open May to October. Rates range from $14 to $36. RR 1, Box 2165, Bar Harbor, ME 04609; (207) 288-2840; www.campbarcadia.com

Bar Harbor Inn: This fabulous resort hotel is located right on the waterfront in town. There are over 100 rooms—most with ocean views—on eight acres along the harbor. Pets are allowed in the first-floor rooms only, for an additional $15 per night. Rates range from $99 to $359. A generous continental breakfast is included. Open from April to December. 1 Newport Drive, Bar Harbor, ME 04609; (207) 288-3351; www.barharborinn.

Hanscom's Motel and Cottages: These 12 simple cottages are located three miles outside of town surrounded by an oak grove. This is no-frills lodging, but the units are clean and priced reasonably. Open May to October. Rates range from $42 to $84. RR 1, Box 1070, Bar Harbor, ME 04609; (207) 288-3744 or (207) 288-0039; www.hanscommotel.com.

Ledgelawn Inn: Stay at one of the area's last remaining summer mansions at this turn-of-the-century inn located just steps away from downtown in the historic corridor. Dogs are allowed in certain rooms. Breakfast is served each morning. Rates range from $55 to $225. 66 Mount Desert Street, Bar Harbor, ME 04609; (207) 288-4596; www.barharborvacations.com.

Primrose Inn: This lovely 1878 Victorian bed-and-breakfast is located in Bar Harbor's historic corridor and offers spacious rooms, afternoon tea, and a full breakfast each morning. Dogs may stay in the ground-floor apartment only for a nonrefundable $75 one-time fee. This means that if your dog is well behaved, the next time you stay here you will not have to pay the additional $75. The apartment rents by the week for $600 to $700. Be sure you make reservations in advance as it books early. 73 Mount Desert Street, Bar Harbor, ME 04609; (207) 288-4031.

Wonderview Motor Lodge: This fabulous motel facility is located on the old estate of Mary Rinehart, the famous mystery writer. And when they say "wonder" view, they mean it. The view from atop the hill is simply breathtaking. It is located less than a mile from the harbor, and the shuttle to town comes right to their door. We stayed here while exploring Bar Harbor and can tell you this is a far cry from a "motel." The rooms are quite large, the service exceptional, and well, there's that view of Bar Harbor and the islands beyond from your picture window. The rates are quite reasonable given the comfortable accommodations. Rooms range from $69 to $189. Each pet costs an additional $15 per night. Box 25, Bar Harbor, ME 04609; (207) 288-3358; www.wonderviewinn.com.

DIVERSIONS

Acadian Nature Cruises: Take a one- or two-hour nature cruise along the coast of Acadia National Park. Choose from a wildlife cruise in search of sea mammals, a sea tour of the mansions along the coast, or a lighthouse cruise. Leashed dogs are allowed on the outside deck. 1 West Street; (207) 288-3322.

And the bands played on: Join the fun on the Village Green every Monday and Thursday evening from June to August at 8 P.M. for the annual summer concert series. Bring a picnic and a blanket and be ready for a howling good time. For information, call (207) 288-5103.

Ding, ding, ding, goes the trolley: Take a trip back to Bar Harbor's historical past on Oli's Trolley. Offering one- to 2.5-hour tours, you and Rover will be entertained by tales of a bygone era. Dogs must be on leash and availability is at the driver's discretion. 1 West Street; (207) 288-9899 or (207) 288-5443.

Island Dogs: The Island Explorer is a free shuttle service which travels throughout Acadia National Park, Bar Harbor, and to select hotels. Leashed dogs are allowed. Schedules are posted throughout town or at the Visitor Center on State Route 3A. You may also purchase your park entry pass on board. For times and information, call (207) 288-4573.

Rub a dub, dub, three dogs in a tub: Rent a Boston Whaler or Mako power boat and explore the coast at your own pace. Harbor Boat Rentals offers weekly, daily, or hourly rentals. 1 West Street; (207) 288-3757, or after hours at (207) 244-0557.

Tip a canoe and Fido, too: Rent a canoe or kayak at National Park Canoe Rental and take your dog to Long Pond in Acadia National Park or on a sea kayaking nature tour along the coast. 39 Cottage Street; (207) 288-0342.

We're jammin': Take a two-hour sail on the *Margaret Todd,* one of the most beautiful schooners around. This 151-foot master schooner with the distinctive red sails leaves Bar Harbor three times daily for a trip along the coast. You and your dog should gather your sea legs and hop on board for a once-in-a-lifetime treat. Bar Harbor Inn Pier; (207) 288-4585 or (207) 546-2927.

FESTIVALS

Independence Day Festivities: From the annual Fourth of July parade to a free town band concert on the Village Green and fireworks over Frenchman's

Bay, Bar Harbor knows how to keep you busy on Independence Day. You and your dog can enjoy all of the outdoor activities. Call for times and events. (207) 288-5103.

BARING

PARKS, BEACHES, AND RECREATION AREAS

• **Moosehorn National Wildlife Refuge** 🐾🐾🐾🐾 See 5 on page 572.

It's easy to see why this park has national status and federal protection. Covering almost 25,000 acres of pristine forests, rolling hills, and glaciated rocky ledges, you'll also discover streams, bogs, and lakes here. In the southern half of the park, some pretty amazing tidal fluctuations have a 24-foot difference between high and low tides. Oh, and your dog might be interested in the 50 miles of trails that traverse through it all.

For a complete list of trails and hiking options, pick up a map at the park headquarters. Dogs must be leashed and remain on the trails at all times.

From Calais, take U.S. Route 1 north for four miles into Baring. Turn left onto Charlotte Road for two miles. The park headquarters is on the right via a gravel road. Open sunrise to sunset. (207) 454-7161.

BLUE HILL

PARKS, BEACHES, AND RECREATION AREAS

• **Blue Hills Falls** 🐾🐾 See 6 on page 572.

For an interesting natural site, visit this unique pair of reversing falls between Blue Hill Bay and Salt Pond. As the tide goes out, the waterfall rushes one way; as the tide come back in, it reverses itself. The gravitational pull is great so your dog won't want to swim right at the falls, but there are rocks and marshy areas you can walk along that offer your dog safer water access.

This is also a great picnic location. Choose your favorite spot from two locations along State Route 175.

Dogs must be on leash.

From State Route 15, take State Routes 172 and 175 south for two miles. Turn left onto State Route 175 for a half mile to the falls. Roadside parking is available. Open dawn to dusk. There is no contact.

• **Blue Hill Town Park** 🐾🐾 See 7 on page 572.

This small waterfront park will provide your sea dog with some ocean cavorting—at least when the tide is in. At low tide you might want to think twice about a visit here. Our dogs came back from their romp looking like creatures from the black lagoon.

Dogs must be on leash.

From the center of town on State Routes 15, 172, and 176, take State Route 176 east for a block and turn right onto Water Street. The park is at the end of the street. Open sunrise to sunset. (207) 374-2281.

• **Blue Hill Trail** 🐾🐾🐾 🐕 **See 8 on page 572.**

Blue Hill is 940 feet high and a little more than a mile hike if you've got a hankering for being top dog. Blue Hill is named for the blueberries that cover it, so, if you pick your season carefully, you might be able to snack along the way. The trail makes a steady climb through an open field at the trailhead, while leading along the side of the hill. Eventually the trail disappears into the trees but comes out at the fire tower on top for a great view of the coast. The trails are managed by the Blue Hill Heritage Trust, and dogs are allowed off leash if under control.

From the center of town on State Routes 15, 172, and 176, take State Route 15 north for a half mile. Turn right onto Mountain Road for a quarter mile. The trailhead and a roadside parking area are on the left. Open dawn to dusk. (207) 374-5118.

RESTAURANTS

The Fishnet Restaurant: As you arrive in Blue Hill, you'll be greeted by the delicious smell of fresh seafood and long lines waiting to eat at this busy roadside fish restaurant. If you weren't hungry before, you'll certainly be once you see the servings. Eat outside on the picnic tables or take your meal to go. Main Street, (207) 374-9970.

Jean Paul's Bistro: This charming French restaurant is open for lunch or dinner. Located in a white clapboard house right in town, you and your dog may dine on the garden patio terrace outside. Serving café-style lunches and continental cuisine for dinner, all we can say is bon appétit! Main Street; (207) 374-5852.

BROOKVILLE

NATURE HIKES AND URBAN WALKS

• **Bagaduce Falls** 🐾🐾 **See 9 on page 572.**

Your pooch won't get much exercise here, but the reversing falls of the Bagaduce River are a real head turner, at least twice a day. As the tides change the falls "reverse" themselves—falling one way with the low tide and flowing in the opposite direction with the high tide. A good viewing spot is from the bridge over the falls on State Route 175/176.

But our favorite place to view the falls and picturesque Bagaduce River is from Bagaduce Lunch on the Sedgwick side of the falls. The restaurant's peninsula picnic area is also a great little park.

The falls are located on State Routes 175 and 176 at the Brookville-Sedgwick border. Limited roadside parking is available. Open 24 hours a day. There is no contact.

• **Holbrook Island Sanctuary** 🐾🐾🐾🐾 **See 10 on page 572.**

This beautiful wildlife sanctuary offers 1,231 diverse acres to explore. There are beaches, mud flats, ponds, and pine forests to visit and ancient volcanoes to climb. Nine different trails stretch out for you and your leashed dog to traverse, and, rather than blaze new trails through the ecosystem, the sanctuary paths follow old carriage roads and animal trails.

From the parking areas along Lawrence Hill Road, you can access the trails that lead to an active beaver frontage or Goose Pond. Goose Falls, located where Goose Pond empties into the bay, is a short one-mile walk from the parking area at the dock.

The Back Shore Trail, accessed off Indian Bar Road, traverses through fields of an old estate down to the bay; the two-mile Iceworks Trail leads through a lovely woodland to Fresh Pond. There are countless combinations for you and your dog to enjoy, and we've discovered new trails on each visit. The sanctuary has a series of guided nature walks; dogs are allowed on certain excursions.

The park headquarters is located along Indian Bar Road overlooking Penobscot Bay. A scenic picnic area is available on this point for a snack before or after your hike.

We recommend that you pick up a trail map, available at the park headquarters or at most of the trailheads. Because this is a delicate area, dogs need to be leashed.

From State Route 176, take Cape Rosier Road west for 1.5 miles. Turn right onto Lawrence Hill Road into the park. Open 9 A.M. to sunset. (207) 326-4012.

RESTAURANTS

Bagaduce Lunch: This little roadside eatery has the grandstand seats to view the reversing waters at Bagaduce Falls. Pick up a burger or clam roll and sit at one their many picnic tables on the grassy point overlooking the harbor. State Route 175/176; (207) 326-4729.

PLACES TO STAY

Breezemere Farm Inn: This inn and cottage complex allows dogs in their five cottages or family-sized apartment (which is located in the old barn). Originally built in the mid-19th century, this secluded working farm offers simple but cozy lodging on 10 beautiful acres. You and your dog will enjoy the ocean views and the spruce forest trails located behind the farm. Pets are welcome, but because this is a working farm, dogs must be leashed. Rates range from $55 to $95 per night. Full breakfast is included. RR 1, Box 290, Brooksville, ME 04617; (207) 326-8628; www.bbonline.com/me/breezemere.

BUCKSPORT

NATURE HIKES AND URBAN WALKS

Waterfront Walk: Take a walk along the waterfront with views of the Penobscot River, Fort Knox, and the Waldo Hancock Suspension Bridge. Plans are in the works to extend the current half-mile walk, but for now the crushed-stone path is short but scenic. Picnic tables are situated along the way if you'd like to stop and enjoy a meal by the water. Dogs must be on leash. The walk and a parking lot is off Main Street (State Route 15). Open dawn to 9 P.M. (207) 469-6818.

RESTAURANTS

Dairyport: Stop by for a snack at this little ice-cream store on Main Street before you stroll along the waterfront. Homemade flavors include Mountain Blueberry and Fresh Vanilla. Open seasonally from May to September. Main Street; there is no contact.

PLACES TO STAY

Best Western—Jed Prouty Motel Inn: This motor inn is located right on the Penobscot River near U.S. Route 1. Be sure to request a waterfront room because the views of the river, Fort Knox, and the Waldo Hancock Suspension Bridge are spectacular. Dogs cannot be left unattended in the rooms. Rates range from $69 to $99. Main Street, P.O. Box 826, Bucksport, ME 04416; (207) 469-3113, (800) 528-1234.

CASTINE

A friend of ours grew up in this lovely seaside town and remembers never locking his door his entire childhood. When his family sold the house and moved to Boston, there was no key to give the future tenants from New York who still toss and turn at the thought of an unlocked door.

Idyllic is the word often used to describe this quiet but affluent town. Rumor has it that the set designer of the most recent revival of the musical *Carousel* on Broadway reportedly used Castine as his model for the picturesque New England town. We know you and your pup will enjoy the scenic beauty, fascinating history, and easy-going way of life here.

PARKS, BEACHES, AND RECREATION AREAS

• Dyce's Head Lighthouse 🐾🐾🐾 See 🏙 on page 572.

The centerpiece of this four-acre park is the beautiful Dyce's Lighthouse. Built in 1828, it's use was discontinued and it was replaced by a beacon on the rocks in the 1930's. Today you can visit this symbol of Maine's past or picnic by the bay on one of the several picnic tables along the water. From the open meadow surrounding the lighthouse, take the trail down to the Penobscot River for a cool dip in the fresh water. Dogs must be leashed.

From the southern intersection of State Routes 166 and 166A, take State Route 166 south for a quarter mile. Turn right onto Battle Avenue for a half mile to the end of the road and the park and lighthouse. Street parking is available. Open dawn to 9 P.M. (207) 326-4502.

• Hatch Natural Area and Fredrick D. Foote Family Natural Area 🐾🐾🐾 See 🏙 on page 572.

With a name as long as this, it's easy to see why these coastal woodlands are better known as Witherle Woods by the town folk. The park is an impressive 133 acres on Blockhouse Point and Penobscot Bay with three miles of hiking trails. The trails, once wide carriage paths built in the 1870s by George Witherle for public use, cover the entire property, including the rocky shoreline, offering hilltop views and spruce and fir forests.

The park is managed by the Maine Coastal Heritage Trust. Dogs need to be leashed.

From the southern intersection of State Routes 166 and 166A, take State Route 166 south for a quarter mile. Turn right onto Battle Avenue for a half mile to just before LaTour Street. The trailhead is on the right. Roadside parking is available. Open dawn to 9 P.M. (207) 729-7366.

• **Fort George** 🐾 🐾 See **13** on page 572.

This small park is located on the site of the old Fort George, built by the British in 1779. Little remains of the fort today except the grass-covered fortifications that outline where the fort once stood. Reportedly the site of Hancock County's first hanging, the ghost of the doomed drummer boy is said to be heard every August. Now the site is mainly a ball field, but you can walk your leashed dog on the trail that leads along the outer edge.

From the southern intersection of State Routes 166 and 166A, take State Route 166 south for a quarter mile. Turn right onto Battle Avenue for a quarter mile. The park entrance is on the right. Open dawn to 9 P.M. (207) 326-4502.

• **Wadsworth Cove Beach** 🐾 🐾 🐾 See **14** on page 572.

This lovely beach opens onto quiet Wadsworth Cove and provides a half mile of beachfront where you and your dog can walk, swim, or work on your tan. George likes to keep those natural highlights in his furry locks, so beach access in the sunny summer months is very important. And although it can get crowded in the summer, for most of the year you'll have this beachfront property to yourself.

Dogs must be on leash.

From the southern intersection of State Routes 166 and 166A, take State Route 166 south for a quarter mile. Turn right onto Wadsworth Cove Road for a quarter mile. The beach and parking area is on the right. Open Sunday to Thursday, 5 A.M. to 11 P.M. and Friday and Saturday 5 A.M. to 12 A.M. (207) 326-4502.

NATURE HIKES AND URBAN WALKS

Walking Tour of Castine: From its first days as a French trading post under Samuel de Champlain in 1604, to the British occupation during the Revolutionary War, Castine has always weathered its history well. This walking tour covers all the major historical points in town, leading from the various sea captain's mansions to remnants of the British occupation and beautiful Dyce's Lighthouse. Pick up a map at the Castine Historical Society at the town common or almost anywhere in town. (207) 326-4118.

PLACES TO STAY

Castine Harbor Lodge: This 16-room bed-and-breakfast has the distinction of being Castine's only waterfront lodging. Gaze upon the Maine seacoast from gracious wraparound porches or stay in the charming private "honeymoon" cottage by the water. The rooms are filled with antiques and other collectibles; a homemade continental breakfast is served each morning. You and your dog may never want to leave. Rooms range from $75 to $175 per night; the cottage is available weekly for $950. Dogs are allowed for an additional $10 per night. Perkins Street, Box 215, Castine, ME 04421; (207) 326-4335; castinemaine.com.

Pentagoet Inn: This stately and beautiful bed-and-breakfast was first built in 1894, and staying here will remind you what life must have been like a hundred years ago. Named for Castine's first trading outpost, this Victorian mansion has 16 elegant rooms, two of which are reserved for folks traveling with their dog. Rates range from $89 to $169 per night. Currently there is no extra charge for your dog, but the owners are considering charging a small fee in the future. Main Street, P.O. Box 4, Castine, ME 04421; (207) 326-8616, (800) 845-1701.

DIVERSIONS

Steam Ahead: Step back in time aboard the Steam Launch *Laurie Ellen* which claims to be the "only wood-fired, steam-powered, USCG inspected, passenger steam launch in the country!" In the 1800s, steamboats were seen up and down the Maine seacoast. Today this might be your only chance to hitch a ride on a replica of the real thing. The ship leaves from Dennett's Wharf and travels along the waterfront and through the many islands in Castine Harbor. Dogs are allowed on leash. So hop on board and take a unique trip on a steam blast from the past. $17.50 per person. Dennett's Wharf; (207) 326-9045.

Kayakers, ahoy!: Take an unusual guided kayak tour in the waters around Castine. This friendly operation offers half-day and full-day "paddles," a sunset and sunrise tour, and the "Friday Night Phosphorescence" where you and your dog can take a star-filled paddle with a guide. Rates range from $40 to $105 depending on tour and length. Island stopovers are available so your dog doesn't have to sit still all day. For beginners or experts. Dennett's Wharf; (207) 326-9045.

CUTLER

PARKS, BEACHES, AND RECREATION AREAS

• Cutler 😺 😺 😺 See 🔟 on page 572.

If you want to get a true taste of the tough conditions to be found on the northern Maine coast, visit this Public Reserve Land on any day other than September 1. That seems to be the one day of the year when you don't have to worry about losing a boot in spring mud or a moose pie, a finger to frostbite in a winter coastal storm, or a pint of blood to summer black flies and mosquitoes.

If you do visit this remote and beautiful park on the one good day, you'll find 2,200 acres of pristine, weather-beaten forests and stunning rocky coastline. The main trail starts off on bog bridges through the woods and arrives at the sea and the Coastal Trail after 1.5 miles. The views are fantastic. You can continue along the Coastal Trail and loop back to the parking lot via other inland routes. Now, if they could just do something about the weather and black flies. . .

Dogs must be on leash.

From the center of Cutler, take State Route 191 east for four miles. The park and a parking area are on the right. Open sunrise to sunset. (207) 827-5936.

DEER ISLE

Deer Isle is a lovely place to visit, but not a particularly hospitable island for dogs. On the island, here are several conservation lands managed by the Island Heritage Land Trust, but dogs are only allowed on one. If you do stay here, you will probably do better to walk your dog on the mainland at Holbrook Sanctuary in Brookfield.

PARKS, BEACHES, AND RECREATION AREAS

• Edgar M. Tennis Preserve 🐾🐾 🐕 See 16 on page 572.

This 40-plus acre reserve is located on a finger overlooking Southeast Harbor and, although the trails are not in top shape, you can find your way through a pine forest to some sandy spots along the water. The view from the point is beautiful, and you might wish to stop for a picnic while your dog happily swims in the gentle harbor waters. Managed by the Island Heritage Land Trust, dogs are allowed off leash if under voice command.

From State Route 15, take Fish Creek Road east for a half mile. Turn right at the fork onto Marshall Road/Sunshine Road for three-quarters of a mile, then turn right onto Fire Road 523 for a quarter mile into the park. Roadside pull-outs are along the dirt road. Open sunrise to sunset. (207) 348-2455.

PLACES TO STAY

Eggemoggin Landing: This 20-room motel complex is located on the water-front on Little Deer Isle as you cross the Deer Isle Bridge. The motel rooms are simple but comfortable and look out over the bay. You can rent canoes or swim at the beach when the tide is high. Dogs are welcome for an additional $10 per night, except during the high season of July and August. Rates range from $59 to $65 in the off-season. State Route 15, Deer Isle, ME 04681; (207) 348-6115.

Pilgrim's Inn: This quaint, 12-room bed-and-breakfast is listed on the National Register of Historic Places and offers lovely antique-filled rooms with high ceilings. The two on-site cottages feature large living areas, kitchens, and bedrooms with decks that overlook Northwest Harbor. Dogs are welcome in the cottages, which rent by the night or the week. Rates include breakfast and dinner. Cottage rates are $100 to $220 per night; $600 to $1,320 weekly. Main Street, Box 69, Deer Isle, ME 04681; (207) 348-6615; www.pilgrimsinn.com.

DEDHAM

PARKS, BEACHES, AND RECREATION AREAS

• Bald Mountain Trail 🐾🐾🐾 🐕 See 17 on page 572.

If you haven't been able to get a clear picture of how the islands and bays of Acadia National Park all fit together, then the view from Bald Mountain can help. Granted, it is a good distance away, but at least the exposed granite summit is not as crowded as Acadia's Cadillac Mountain.

The summit is 1,234 feet high and, on a clear day, you can see all the way to Mount Katahdin to the north. The main route to the summit is a half-mile trail from the parking area. Another route, which begins a quarter mile north of the parking area on Dedham Road, follows an old ski trail. The elevation gain for both is 500 feet.

From State Route 46, take Johnson Road into Dedham Road southeast for four miles. Turn left onto Fire Road 62 for a quarter mile into the park on the left on the ledges. Open sunrise to sunset. (207) 287-2631.

EASTPORT
PARKS, BEACHES, AND RECREATION AREAS
• **Shackford Head State Park** 🐾🐾🐾 See **18** on page 572.
This undeveloped state park is a 90-acre peninsula on Cobscook Bay. The park, just next to paradise, has plenty of shoreline, protected coves, and beautiful views. You're really in the far north here. There aren't many specific routes, but a single mile-long hiking trail runs from the parking area through the woods out to the rocky point of Shackford Head.

Dogs need to be leashed in all state parks.

Located off State Route 190, just west of downtown. Open 9 A.M. to sunset. (207) 941-4014.

PLACES TO STAY
Todd House Bed-and-Breakfast: This inn, which dates back to 1775 and the American Revolution, is filled with period antiques and detailing. History buffs will enjoy checking out the library filled with historic artifacts and books. The seven rooms offer casual comfort in a cozy setting. Rates range from $55 to $95 per night. Breakfast is included. 1 Capen Avenue, Eastport, ME 04631; (207) 853-2328.

EDMUNDS TOWNSHIP
PARKS, BEACHES, AND RECREATION AREAS
• **Cobscook Bay State Park** 🐾🐾🐾 See **19** on page 572.
Is there anything more beautiful than a secluded, sparkling bay with a shoreline of majestic pines nestled along the rocky coast of Maine? Probably, but we doubt wet dogs and tennis balls are welcome. Plus, you can find the highest tides in the continental U.S. here with a difference of 24 feet between high tide and low tide. That's an awful lot of beach for you and your pup to explore.

This 888-acre state park has plenty of hiking trails which are open for exploring and and for cross-country skiing in the winter.

The 125 scenic campsites are right on the bay or in the thick pine forest. Services include hot showers and pit toilets. Camping rates range from $16 to $20; the day-use fee is $2. Dogs are required to be on leash in all state parks.

The park is located on U.S. Route 1, four miles south of Dennysville. Open from 9 A.M. to sunset. (207) 726-4412.

PLACES TO STAY
Cobscook Bay State camping: See above.

ELLSWORTH
RESTAURANTS
Blueberry Hill Dairy Farm: For farm-fresh ice cream and more flavors than you could possibly count, stop at this popular summer spot. Located on your way to and from Acadia National Park, you'll find this a convenient place to quench those sugar cravings. State Route 3; (207) 457-1151.

Cap'n Cook's: Catch a big fish at this seasonal seafood restaurant. You and your dog can enjoy lobster, steamers, or fish and chips at this local roadside eatery. Plenty of picnic tables welcome all of you. State Route 3; (207) 633-2127.

PLACES TO STAY

Colonial Travelodge: This 68-room motel offers comfortable suites or efficiencies to weary travelers. Dogs are allowed with advance reservations. Rates range from $65 to $130 per night. 321 High Street, Ellsworth, ME 04605; (207) 667-5548.

Holiday Inn: This standard hotel offers what you would expect from a Holiday Inn. A restaurant is on-site for room orders to go, plus coffee makers are in every room. Dogs are allowed in certain rooms. Rates run from $65 to $140 per night. 215 High Street, Ellsworth, ME 04605; (207) 667-9341, (800) 401-9341; www.holiday-inn.com.

Jasper's Motel and Restaurant: This cheerful 33-room hotel is conveniently located on State Route 3 in the heart of the business area. Clean, comfortable, and roomy, well-behaved dogs are welcome. Rates range from $49 to $109. 200 High Street, Ellsworth, ME 04605; (207) 667-5318.

HANCOCK

PLACES TO STAY

Crocker House Country Inn: Stay in style at this secluded 11-room bed-and-breakfast. All rooms have private baths and tasteful furnishings, and some have refrigerators. Both dinner and breakfast are included in your room rate. Dogs are allowed with prior approval. Rates range from $75 to $150. Hancock Point Road, Hancock, ME 04640; (207) 422-3146.

LAMOINE

PARKS, BEACHES, AND RECREATION AREAS

• Lamoine State Park 🐾 🐾 See **20** on page 572.

The 55 acres here on the rocky coast of Frenchman Bay are a bit overlooked being so close to Acadia National Park. In our opinion, that's all the better for dogs. Your pup is welcome throughout the park even in the busy summer months. A swim is a possibility on a hot summer day, but you do need to pick your spots along the rough shoreline.

Dogs need to be leashed in all state parks. There is a $2 day-use fee.

From Lamoine Center, take State Route 184 east for eight miles. The park is on the right. Open 9 A.M. to sunset. Call (207) 667-4778 May 15 to October 15, (207) 941- 4014 off-season.

LUBEC

PARKS, BEACHES, AND RECREATION AREAS

• Quoddy Head State Park 🐾 🐾 🐾 See **21** on page 572.

Quoddy Head is the easternmost point of the United States and a great place to view the adjacent Quoddy Head Lighthouse. It's also a good place for some coastal hiking. This 481-acre coastal park has trails along the rocky shoreline (complete with 80-foot cliffs), through a thick evergreen forest, and over a peat bog via a boardwalk.

Dogs need to be leashed in all state parks. There is a day-use fee of $1.

From State Route 189, take South Lubec Road south for four miles into the park. Open 9 A.M. to sunset. Call (207) 733-0911 May 15 to October 15, (207) 941-4014 off-season.

ORLAND

PARKS, BEACHES, AND RECREATION AREAS

• **Craig Brook Fish Hatchery/Great Pond Mountain** 🐾🐾🐾 🐕
See **22** on page 572.

This unique salmon hatchery fosters the preservation of the Atlantic salmon, or Skwamekw, as the Penobscot Native Americans called them. By artificially harvesting salmon eggs and then releasing them into the wild, the hatchery is providing a chance for the salmon, whose numbers have dropped dangerously low in recent years, to rebound. This novel hatchery, first started in 1871, offers special exhibits on the salmon, picnic areas along Craig Brook, and hiking trails for dogs and people.

The Craig Brook Nature Trail is a one-mile interpretive walk along boulder-strewn Craig Brook. A map is available at the visitors center to guide you along the way. The trail starts a half mile north of the hatchery off the Don Fish Trail. Dogs must be on leash.

The Great Pond Mountain Trail begins one mile north of the hatchery. Follow the Don Fish Trail to a gate and brochure kiosk. Hike one mile to the summit of Great Pond Mountain, which towers 1,038 feet and offers lookouts of Penobscot Bay, Mount Desert Island, and Camden Hills. Dogs are allowed off leash on this trail.

From State Route 15, take U.S. Route 1 north for 1.5 miles. Turn left onto Hatchery Road for a mile to the end and the park. Parking is available. Open 8 A.M. to 8 P.M. (207) 469-2803.

PROSPECT

PARKS, BEACHES, AND RECREATION AREAS

• **Fort Knox State Historic Site** 🐾🐾 🐕 See **23** on page 572.
This fort, built in 1844, never experienced enemy fire. But one tour of the massive, granite structure and you'll understand why no one wanted to mess with her. The fort, which sits on the cliffs overlooking the Penobscot River and Bucksport, protected Maine's valuable North Woods and lumber industry.

You are your dog are welcome to walk the state grounds and the fort itself, including the barracks, cannon stations, and parade ground.

Dogs need to be leashed in all state parks. There is a $2 fee to walk the grounds.

From U.S. Route 1, take State Route 174 north for a quarter mile. The park entrance is on the right. Open 9 A.M. to sunset. The grounds are open year-round, and the fort is open May to November 1. (207) 469-7719.

ROQUE BLUFFS

PARKS, BEACHES, AND RECREATION AREAS

• **Roque Bluffs State Park** 🐾🐾🐾 See **24** on page 572.
Ho hum. Just another one of those gorgeous pieces of land along the Maine coast. When you're on the eastern coast of Maine, every acre is breathtaking, and Roque Bluffs is just another example. The 274-acre park offers woodlands and fresh- and saltwater swimming.

There is a day-use fee of $1. Dogs must be leashed.

From State Route 1 in Machias, take Roque Bluffs Road south for six miles to the park. Open from 9 A.M. to sunset May through September. (207) 255-3475.

STOCKTON SPRINGS

PARKS, BEACHES, AND RECREATION AREAS

• **Fort Point State Park** 🐾🐾 See **25** on page 572.
This 154-acre state park was the site of a 1626 British trading post until it became the British Fort Pownall in 1759. The colonists took it over in 1775 in the War of Independence. Today it is as peaceful as it once was turbulent; you can wander the scenic grounds at your leisure and picnic on the point. A few short trails lead to and overlook the water, but this is not a park for running or romping. If your dog needs more exercise, you might want to visit this park after you've already worn him out elsewhere.

Dogs need to be leashed in all state parks. There is a day-use fee of $1.

From Main Street (off of U.S. Route 1), take Jellison Road south for a mile. Turn left onto East Cape Road for a mile, then left onto Fort Point Road into the park. Parking is available. Open 9 A.M. to sunset. (207) 941-4014.

• **Meadow Farm Wildlife Sanctuary** 🐾🐾 See **26** on page 572.
If this place didn't have a sign, you'd swear you were in the wrong place. It's a secret we'll share only with you.

This beautiful meadow is filled with wildflowers and teeming with wild-life. Take the two-mile loop trail around the circumference of the meadow and through the woods; a shorter one-mile trail cuts a swath through the meadow. But we can't predict how fresh the trails will be on your visit; this park is only sporadically maintained and the grass does grow quickly! There is a wooden map board at the trailhead to help you find your way. Dogs must be on leash.

From U.S. Route 1, take Meadow Road a mile west. Turn right onto Ryan Road into the park. Parking is available. Open dawn to dusk. There is no contact.

• **Sandy Point Beach** 🐾🐾🐾 See **27** on page 572.
A trip to Sandy Point is a great day at the beach for everyone. The sandy beach

is 1,370 yards long and sits on one of the widest points of the Penobscot River, just before it empties into the Penobscot Bay.

Access to the shore is through a thin meadow of beach grass. The remains of the old Steamboat Wharf make for a good place to sniff around.

From U.S. Route 1, take Sandy Point Road a quarter mile east. Turn right onto Hersey Retreat Road for a quarter mile, then left onto Steamboat Wharf Road into the park. Parking is available. Open 7 A.M. to 10 P.M. Sunday to Thursday and to 12 A.M. Friday and Saturday. (207) 990-4642.

RESTAURANTS

Just Barb's: Until we taste every clam in the state of Maine, we're still skeptical of Barb's clam claim of "Best in Maine," but we can say they taste pretty darn good. We'll get back to you when we've tried all the rest. The outdoor picnic tables make it easy for your dog to cast a vote. U.S. Route 1; (207) 567-3886.

SURRY

PARKS, BEACHES, AND RECREATION AREAS

• **Carter Nature Preserve** 🐾🐾 See **28** on page 572.

This small half-mile trail on the northern corner of Surry Neck overlooks Morgan Bay. The view is lovely here, and you may want to make it a picnic spot, but the trail isn't really long enough to tire out most dogs. Your dog will want to swim at high tide, but during low tide a swim will end up with him looking more like a pig in mud than a dog in water. The preserve is managed by the Blue Hill Heritage Trust. Dogs need to be leashed.

From the intersection of State Routes 172 and 176, take State Route 176 south for 1.5 miles. Turn left onto Cross Road for a quarter mile. The park is on the right. Open dawn to dusk. (207) 374-5118.

VERONA

RESTAURANTS

Lunch Box and Ice Box: A convenient and tasty stop, this roadside eatery offers shakes, burgers, and clams. Located on Verona Island just outside of Bucksport. U.S. Route 1; (207) 469-6519.

PLACES TO STAY

The Flying Dutchman Campground: This campground offers full amenities along the scenic Penobscot River just across from Fort Knox. A swimming pool, nightly movies, and wooded or riverfront sites are a few of the amenities. Dogs need to be leashed and well behaved. Rates range from $12 to $18 for tents and from $14 to $23 for RVs. U.S. Route 1, Verona. P.O. Box 1639, Bucksport, ME 04416; (207) 469-3256, (888) 541-2267.

GRRRRR

18
NORTH WOODS

It seems you can't go anywhere in the world these days without running into the familiar bumper sticker "NORTH WOODS NATIONAL PARK." The green-and-white stickers are part of a grass-roots campaign to have the northern portion of the Pine Tree State become a preserved wilderness of millions of acres of Maine's natural beauty with endless recreational opportunities for all.

In many ways the North Woods, which is also called the Maine Woods or the Great North Woods, already is a spectacular parkland, but in far too many ways it is not. Some of the largest state parks in the country are found here, including Baxter State Park and thousands of square miles of public reserve lands. But the general concern of national park advocates is that most of the vast woods are privately owned by lumber and paper companies.

Whatever your opinion is on the matter, you will be happy to know that the majority of the commercial land is open to the public and dogs. Hiking, camping, canoeing, and hunting are the biggest public activities on these lands, and they all come with fees and permits ranging from $4 to $7 for day-use fees and $5 for camping. For more information on the private lands, contact the North Maine Woods, an organization responsible for the management of recreational use on commercial forest land in the North Woods. (207) 435-6213.

In this condensed chapter, we've listed some of the public and private highlights of this area that covers the four largest and northernmost counties in Maine. But don't let us limit you—throw a stone and just about anywhere it lands will be a new adventure for you and your dog to explore. There are limited hotels and services here, however, and most visitors start their explorations from the Bangor/Orono and Millinocket/Medway areas.

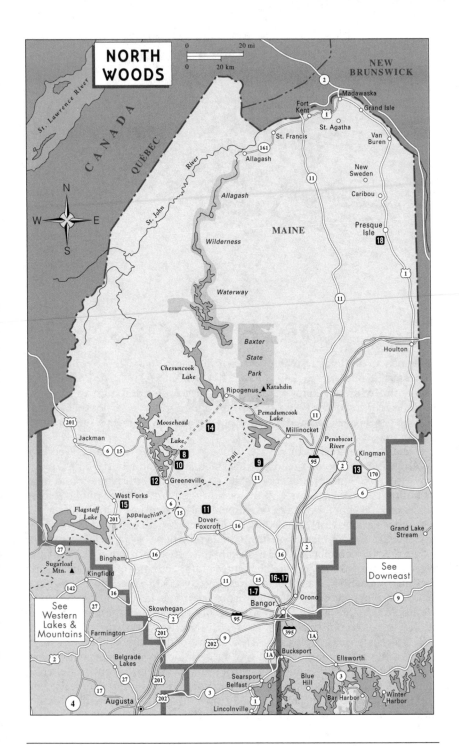

One final note, the centerpiece of the North Woods, Baxter State Park, does not allow dogs.

For more information about public lands, contact Maine's Bureau of Parks and Lands at (207) 287-3821.

Allagash Wilderness Waterway: The Allagash Wilderness Waterway encompasses over 22,800 acres and flows for 92 miles through Aroostook and Piscataquis Counties. Some people say a canoe or kayak trip through this system of lakes and rivers is the only way to experience the North Woods. Not that you have to do all 92 miles of it; there are numerous places to put in along the waterway. You will probably want to log some significant miles on the water, however, both because of its breathtaking beauty and because the only way to get to the remote Allagash is through miles of commercial forests on private, gravel, toll roads. Let's just say, "Are we there yet?" will become a familiar refrain.

The timing of your trip is another factor to consider. Long winters and the spring bug season limit appealing conditions to late summer and early fall.

Note that there are very limited services along the way to the Allagash and nothing once you dip your canoe in the river. For a well-planned trip, contact the Maine Bureau of Parks and Recreation for maps and brochures on the river, suppliers, and recommended gear. (207) 941-4014.

Most first-timers on the river and many returnees prefer to use guides and outfitters to help with their Allagash adventure, especially for shuttling services. A list of these guides and outfitters is available from the North Maine Woods at (207) 435-6213.

BANGOR

PARKS, BEACHES, AND RECREATION AREAS

• Bangor Mental Health Institute Walking Trails and Cascade Park
🐾🐾🐾🐾 🐕 See ❶ on page 590.

Don't be fooled! The expensive dog behaviorists don't want you to know that 99 percent of the time when your dog acts strangely or misbehaves, it's because he's pulling the most common canine ploy in the book: pretending to have some kind of mental disorder so that, before you can shake a stick, you're spending the afternoon at the Bangor Mental Health Institute (and roaming on the spectacular hilltop walking trails!). The green, winding trails are freshly cut through the meadow grass that grows waist high in early summer. The property is about a square mile in size but the crisscrossing, looping trails offer more than four miles to walk and romp.

Cascade Park borders the institute and is a good way to access the meadow trails.

Dogs need to be under voice control.

From downtown Bangor, take U.S. Route 2 north for 1.5 miles. Cascade Park is on the left; the entrance to the Bangor Mental Health Institute is just past the park on the left. The trails leave from the left side of the property. Parking is available at both areas. Open 6 A.M. to 10 P.M. (207) 941-4000.

• Bass Park 🐾🐾 See **2** on page 590.

You won't miss this one-acre town park located at the gateway to Bangor. Towering over the grass and the street beyond is a statue of Paul Bunyan, lumberjack of the Great North Woods. This isn't a big park, but it's worth a stop for a car break. Plus, the visitor's center is located here, so why not hop out and gaze at Paul and his gigantic size 89 shoes? Dogs must be on leash.

The park is located off State Routes 1A, 9, and 202 between Buck and Dutton Streets. Open 6 A.M. to 10 P.M. (207) 947-1018.

• Brown Woods 🐾🐾🐾 See **3** on page 590.

This quiet, 28-acre forest has wide-open trails that run through a cool pine forest. Picnic tables are available at the trailhead and, from there, you can take the 1.5-mile loop trail on a soft pine-covered footpath. Your dog will like this place—plenty of trees to sniff and easy trails on which to kick up his canine heels. You'll like this forest for its solitude and the feeling of being away from it all, even though you won't be far from the busy urban center. Dogs must be on leash.

From downtown Bangor on U.S. Route 2, take Ohio Street north for 2.75 miles (past Griffin Street). The park and a parking lot are on the left. Open 6 A.M. to 10 P.M. (207) 947-1018.

• Chapin Park 🐾🐾 See **4** on page 590.

This two-city-block sized neighborhood park is a well-maintained, grassy, green space that gets its share of local dogs. The park has a few trees for shade and a playground facility where dogs are not permitted.

From downtown Bangor, take U.S. Route 2 north a quarter mile. Turn left onto Forest Avenue for two blocks. The park is on the right. Street parking is available. Open 6 A.M. to 10 P.M. (207) 947-1018.

• Essex Woods 🐾🐾🐾 See **5** on page 590.

This 70-acre park offers plenty of variety for the dog who can't decide what he wants. Several winding trails weave their way through an open meadow and lead down to the bike trail for a longer hike. Go in the opposite direction and you can sample a woodland walk. These trails aren't long, but collectively you can walk over a mile.

Dogs must be on leash.

From downtown Bangor, take U.S. Route 2 north a quarter mile. Turn left onto Essex Street for 1.5 miles, then left onto Watchmaker Street and into the park. Parking is available. Open 6 A.M. to 10 P.M. (207) 947-1018.

• Kendudkeag Stream Parkway 🐾🐾🐾 See **6** on page 590.

This crushed-gravel pathway runs right through the middle of town, following the Kendudkeag Stream and Penobscot River for 1.25 miles. Along the way are numerous scenic, green spaces and water access points. The southern half of the trail is in the busy downtown section and crosses many city streets. The northern half offers more opportunities for a dog to frolic. The city is currently in the process of expanding the waterfront and parkway southward along the Penobscot. Currently it is called the Penobscot River Trail. Dogs need to be leashed.

The trail is easily accessible anywhere along the Kendudkeag Stream corridor, and parking is available at the current southern terminus at the Bangor Landing on Front Street or at numerous parking areas along Valley Road along the northern half of the path. The path is open 24 hours a day, and the parking lots are open 6 A.M. to 10 P.M. (207) 947-1018.

• **Prentiss Woods** 🐾 🐾 🐾 See **7** on page 590.

This tall, dark, pine forest park is right next to Bangor High School and is part of the city's Recreation, Wildlife, and Forest Management program. The park comprises about 30 acres; a half-mile loop trail runs through it.

From downtown Bangor on U.S. Route 2, take State Route 15 (Broadway) north for two miles. Turn right onto Grandview Avenue for a quarter mile. The park and a parking lot are on the left. Open 6 A.M. to 10 P.M. (207) 947-1018.

PLACES TO STAY

Comfort Inn: This 95-room hotel offers the comfortable lodging you would expect at this chain inn. A restaurant is on-site, and continental breakfast is included each morning. Small pets are allowed with a $5 fee. Rooms range from $60 to $110 per night. 750 Hogan Road, Bangor, ME 04401; (207) 942-7899 or (800) 221-2222; www.comfort.inn.com.

Days Inn: This newly renovated motel, only a short drive from downtown, is located near the Bangor Airport. The rooms are standard corporate fare, but they're clean and comfortable. Pets are welcome for an additional $6 per night. Rooms range from $55 to $98. 50 Odlin Road, Bangor, ME 04401; (207) 942-8272 or (800) 325-2525; www.daysinn.com.

Main Street Inn: This convenient downtown inn is located in the heart of the business district of Bangor. Although the streets are fairly quiet, once the sun goes down, you're still in the thick of the pack here. There are 64 simple rooms, and continental breakfast is included. Rooms range from $50 to $85. Small pets are welcome. 480 Main Street, Bangor, ME 04401; (207) 942-5282.

Motel 6: All Motel 6 locations allow dogs, as long as you don't leave them unattended. One dog is welcome per room. Room rates are $59. 1100 Hammond Street, Bangor, ME 04401; (207) 947-6921, (800) 4-MOTEL6; www.motel6.com.

The Phenix Inn: This comfortable city hotel is located on a quiet street downtown, and you'll be pleasantly surprised by the spacious rooms and friendly service. The hotel was built in the late 19th century, but all the rooms have been updated to include every modern convenience while preserving the charm of an old-world hotel. We stayed here while exploring the Great North Woods and definitely recommend it. Rooms range from $79 to $139, breakfast included. 20 West Market Square, Bangor, ME 04401; (207) 947-3850; www.mainguide.com/bangor/phenixinn.

Ramada Inn: This motel is nothing fancy, but they do welcome dogs, and it's conveniently located just off Exit 45B off Interstate 95. So if you're looking for a quick place to stop on your way elsewhere, you will be comfortable here. Rates range from $55 to $89. 357 Odlin Road, Bangor, ME 04401; (207) 947-6961.

White House Inn—Best Western: This full-service hotel is located just south of Bangor on 40 acres. There are 66 rooms and three suites to choose from, plus plenty of room to walk your dog on the grounds. Rooms range from $55 to $85 per night. 155 Littlefield Avenue, Bangor, ME 04401; (207) 862-3737.

DIVERSIONS

Paws on Parade: Strike up the band for the annual Paws on Parade walk to benefit the Bangor Humane Society. This two-mile stroll on some of the town trails is a great way for you and your grand marshall to meet the local canines, get some exercise, and raise money for the shelter. The event also includes canine games, prizes, and Painting with Paws. Find out once and for all, is your pet a Picasso? The walk is held the first Sunday in October and begins at the United Technologies Center on Hogan Road. Call the Bangor Humane Society for more information at (207) 942-8902.

Holiday Hounds: Each December you can join the holiday celebrations at the Bangor Humane Society and bring some good cheer to our less fortunate four-legged friends. You can help decorate the Tree of Hope or sponsor an animal while raising badly need funds. There are treats for everyone in attendance and a visit from Santa, too. Call the Bangor Humane Society for more information at (207) 942-8902.

Walk with a Purpose: You and your dog can join the tens of thousands across America who walk to find a cure for diabetes. The American Diabetes Association sponsors America's Walk for Diabetes at over 300 sites in the United States held simultaneously the first weekend in October. The walk is five- to six-miles long, and walkers are asked to raise funds through sponsors and donations. The walk begins and ends at the YMCA on Hammond Street. (800) 254-9255.

BEAVER COVE

PARKS, BEACHES, AND RECREATION AREAS

• Lily Bay State Park 🐾🐾🐾 See 🎱 on page 590.

Lily Bay State Park is 924 wooded acres on the eastern shore of spectacular and spacious Moosehead Lake. Although most visitors come to the park to enjoy the lake, there are miles of interconnected hiking trails here, as well. Swimming, boating, and other water sports are the most popular activities.

A shore path runs out to a small peninsula in this corner of the lake, and another trail runs to the fire tower atop a 750-foot rocky cliff that rises above the water. Pick up maps at the park headquarters for a vast array of hiking options.

The park has two camping areas for a total of 91 well-spaced campsites. Many of the sites overlook the lake, with places to tie your canoe or boat near your camping area. Reservations are recommended, and you must pay in full when you confirm your dates. Sites are $12 per night for residents of Maine; all others pay $16. For reservations, call (207) 695-2700. Some sites are on a first-come, first-served basis.

Canoe and boat rentals are available in the park; we recommend that you don't stay landlocked on a visit to this fabulous lake.

Dogs are not permitted in the beach area and are required to be on a leash in all state parks. There is a day-use fee of $2.

From State Routes 6 and 15 in Greenville, take Lily Bay Road north for nine miles into Beaver Cove. The park is on the left. Open from 9 A.M. to sunset. Call (207) 695-2700 May 15 to October 1, (207) 941-4014 off-season.

PLACES TO STAY
Lily Bay State Park camping: See pages 594–595.

BOWDOIN COLLEGE GRANT EAST
PARKS, BEACHES, AND RECREATION AREAS

•Gulf Hagas 🐾🐾🐾🐾 🐕 See 9 on page 590.
"Hagas," native for "evil place," is not the word we would choose to describe this wondrously beautiful canyon. Known as the "Grand Canyon of the East," Gulf Hagas, part of the Katahdin Iron Works (KI)/Jo-Mary Multiple Use Management Forest, has breathtaking views at every turn. The gorge is over three miles long and over a hundred feet deep in places with waterfalls, ancient forests, and sheer drops to the raging river below.

The heavily wooded gorge is cut by the Pleasant River, and you'll have plenty of opportunities to see the power of this river. The waterfalls are endless and have names like Buttermilk Falls and Screw Auger Falls. The different canyon formations created by the rivers also have names like The Jaws and Hammond Street Pitch.

But George will tell you a visit here does not come easy. To get to Gulf Hagas via the main trailhead, you and your dog must ford the Pleasant River. Most times, it's a difficult crossing and not worth the risk. A second gulf trailhead only requires a forging of Hay Brook, but, because of poor road conditions, it's very trying on vehicles without four-wheel drive.

Dogs need to be leashed, and land managers are considering restricting dogs from the gulf. There is a $7 fee, payable at the toll gate.

From Brownville Junction, take State Route 11 north for 5.5 miles. Turn left onto a dirt road, known as KI Road, at the Katahdin Iron Works sign. Continue for seven miles to the toll gate (where you can get a trail map for a $1) and the main trailhead. Open 24 hours a day. (207) 435-6213.

BOWDOIN COLLEGE GRANT WEST
PARKS, BEACHES, AND RECREATION AREAS

•Elephant Mountain 🐾🐾🐾 🐕 🐕 See 10 on page 590.
Elephant Mountain is a great example of the struggle between man and nature. Although a true scenic wilderness area, there are signs of man's dominance and nature's cruelty at several turns.

As an example of the capriciousness of Mother Nature, a B-52 bomber crashed on the mountainside in 1963, killing seven. The plane and a memorial are still there on the mountain as reminders of the harsh conditions in this area.

If you continue on the trail beyond the crash site to Baker Pond, you come to a vast wasteland of clear-cut logging. The emptiness is horrifying and creates a different memorial to the vast indifference of man to nature's own kingdom.

The one-mile loop trail to the bomber is relatively easy, but you are sure to have a muddy start and finish. You may want to have some tall boots and plenty of big towels for this trip.

For water dogs, take the 1.5-mile Baker Pond Trail from the crash site—that is, if you can find it. The route is poorly marked because of the clear-cutting, but the clearings do offer some impressive views.

From State Routes 6 and 15 in Greenville, take Lily Bay Road north for seven miles. Turn right onto Prong Pond Road (a dirt road). Continue for six miles following signs to B-52—Baker Pond Trail. The trailhead is on the right. Open 24 hours a day. There is no contact.

CARIBOU

PLACES TO STAY

Caribou Inn and Convention Center: This deluxe conference center offers 70 rooms and suites—northern Maine's premier hotel. Although a relatively conventional modern hotel, they do offer pet-walking services and a pet doggie bag on check-in. Rates are $50 to $130. Box 25, U.S. Route 1, Caribou, ME 04736; (207) 498-3733; www.mainerec.com/cnvntion.html.

DOVER-FOXCROFT

PARKS, BEACHES, AND RECREATION AREAS

• **Peaks-Kenny State Park** 🐾🐾🐾 See **11** on page 590.
Many people think the real North Woods begins here, and there is some basis to that claim. With no paved roads from this park on Sebec Lake to the Canadian border, there isn't much out here but the great outdoors. Sebec Lake, a lovely mountain lake, is as pristine as it is difficult to access. The park's 839 acres offer hiking trails that you could walk for days and never see another person.

Take advantage of the myriad wet and wonderful lake opportunities for dogs. You can even rent canoes here for $2.50 an hour or $10 a day.

This park offers 56 fully equipped camping sites with running water, showers, picnic tables, laundry facilities, and a small general store. Sites are $15 per night for Maine residents; $18 for all others. Reservations are recommended and can be made by calling (207) 564-2003.

Dogs are not permitted on the beach area and are required to be on leash in all state parks. There is a day-use fee of $2.

From the center of town at the intersection of State Routes 6, 7, 15, 16, and 153, take State Route 153 (Greeley's Landing Road) north for six miles. Turn left onto Park Road and into the park. Open from 9 A.M. to sunset. Call (207) 564-2003 May 15 to October 1, (207) 941-4014 off-season.

PLACES TO STAY

Peaks-Kenny State Park camping: See above.

LITTLE SQUAW TOWNSHIP

PARKS, BEACHES, AND RECREATION AREAS

• Little Squaw 🐾🐾🐾 🐕 See **12** on page 590.

Just in case you couldn't find a place to walk your dog simply by stepping outside anywhere in northern Maine, the Public Reserve Land of Little Squaw gives you an official destination of leash-free bliss.

Located just outside Greenville off Moosehead Lake, the many footpaths, forest roads, mountains, streams, and ponds on this 15,000-acre state property will keep you and your dog occupied for eons—or at least year-round. The peaks of Big and Little Squaw Mountains are good hiking destinations and have excellent views of Moosehead Lake.

The most popular hike is the three-mile route to the summit of Big Squaw. The rocky peak is 3,196 feet high and towers over the lake. The trail has a 2,000-foot elevation gain but doesn't get difficult until the top. The endless flatter paths, especially the ones to Big Squaw and Little Squaw Ponds, are also attractive, even in winter.

Dogs must be under voice control.

From Greenville, take State Routes 6 and 15 north for three miles. The park access road is on the left. Open sunrise to sunset. (207) 778-8231.

MATTAWAMKEAG

PARKS, BEACHES, AND RECREATION AREAS

• Mattawamkeag Wilderness Park 🐾🐾🐾 See **13** on page 590.

This town-owned recreation area has 1,000 acres of wonderful woodlands on the Mattawamkeag River. The park offers lots of hiking opportunities on 15 miles of trails, but the majority of visitors stick to the routes along the scenic river, especially the ones to Lower and Upper Gordon Falls and Sleugundy Heater Gorge.

A full-service campground is open mid-May to October 15 and has a broad range of camping sites for tents, RVs, and shelters. The rates for the 50 wooded sites are $13 to $17. The park also offers great fishing and canoeing opportunities.

Dogs need to be leashed, and there is a day-use fee of $1 per person.

From Interstate 95, take exit 56 to State Route 157 east for 12 miles. Turn right onto U.S. Route 2 south, then make a quick left at the Wilderness Park sign. (207) 736-2465, (888) 724-2465; www.mwpark.com.

RESTAURANTS

Keag Market and Café: Traveling through the remote North Woods you never know where your next meal is coming from. Luckily, you can stock up on Keag's full menu, box lunches, and homemade breads. U.S. Route 2; (207) 736-7333.

PLACES TO STAY

Mattawamkeag Wilderness Park camping: See above.

MEDWAY

PLACES TO STAY

Gateway Inn: Located at the foot of Mount Katahdin (where dogs can't go!) this modest, but comfortable inn has 39 rooms. Some units have kitchenettes and private decks. Rooms range from $55 to $110 per night. Pets are welcome with prior permission. State Route 157, P.O. Box 360, Medway, ME 04460; (207) 746-3193.

MILLINOCKET

RESTAURANTS

Mountain Village Coffee Shop: Once Inu and George realized that Mountain Village is one of the few restaurants in the North Woods that offers outdoor seating, they were quick to stop complaining about the bagels—the worst we have ever eaten. But what can you expect this far north of New York City? Luckily, the muffins, sandwiches, and ice cream scored higher with our finicky pets. It's not like there is a lot of competition up here. 112 Central Street; (207) 723-9712.

PLACES TO STAY

Best Western—Heritage: This 49-room hotel offers full-service amenities and welcomes your pet with only the request that you not leave your dog in the room unattended. Rates range from $55 to $100. 935 Central Street, Millinocket, ME 04462; (207) 723-9777, (800) 528-1234.

Pamola Motor Lodge: This 29-room motel on the road to the North Woods has an outdoor pool and access to the hiking/snowmobile trails outback. Your stay includes a continental breakfast. The room rate is $50. 973 Central Street, Millinocket, ME 04462; (207) 723-9746.

MONSON

PARKS, BEACHES, AND RECREATION AREAS

• **Nahmakanta Maine Public Reserve Land/100-Mile Wilderness**
🐾 🐾 🐾 🐾 🐕 See **14** on page 590.

If you need to get away from it all, and we mean really get away, this is the place. In all of New England, there isn't a more remote hiking area than this 100-mile stretch of the Appalachian Trail. It runs from Monson to just south of Baxter State Park and Mount Katahdin, and it doesn't cross a single public road or facility. So be sure to pack a couple of extra biscuits for the trip.

However, if you like civilization and don't necessarily want to be gone for days, you can still enjoy this wilderness because it's a great place for day hiking, too. From either end of the trail there are plenty of short destinations to head for.

From the southern end, the trail is relatively flat and, within the first two miles, passes three ponds—in order, they are Spectacle, Bell, and Lily—great for cooling off a hot trail dog.

From the northern end, much of your hike is filled with fine views of Mount Katahdin (the state's highest point) and the numerous rivers and streams that run down from it.

A good side trail begins just 200 feet east of the northern trailhead. It's the Abol Falls Trail, and it follows the West Branch of the Penobscot River for a mile to—you guessed it—Abol Falls. The falls follow a gradual drop to the river.

Dogs need to be leashed on the Appalachian Trail and under voice control in other areas.

The southern terminus is in Monson off State Routes 6 and 15, 3.5 miles north of the town center. Look for the Appalachian Trailhead and a parking area.

To get to the northern terminus from State Route 11 in Millinocket, take Katahdin Road north for eight miles (follow signs for Baxter State Park). At the North Woods Trading Post, turn left and then make an immediate right onto Golden Road (this is a toll road, and you will also see the toll gate at this intersection, but the fee is no longer collected). Continue for another nine miles. The dirt parking area and Appalachian Trailhead are on the left, just across the Abol Bridge. Open all the time. (304) 535-6331.

MOXIE GORGE

PARKS, BEACHES, AND RECREATION AREAS

•**Moxie Falls** 🐾🐾🐾 🐕 See **15** on page 590.

With a 90-foot drop, Moxie Falls is one of the highest waterfalls in Maine and one of the most impressive. A path runs a half mile from the parking area to the falls on the Moxie Stream, and, if you really want a closer look, there are some steep trails and boardwalks around the falls. Venturing near the falls is refreshing on a warm summer day because the roaring, plunging water gives off a broad spray. For the same reason, the trails are treacherous on cold days when everything ices over.

Dogs must be under voice control.

From The Forks on State Route 201, take Lake Moxie Road east for three miles. Turn left (at the sign for Moxie Falls) onto a dirt road for a half mile to the trailhead and a small parking area. Open 24 hours a day. There is no contact for this park.

ORIENT

PLACES TO STAY

Sweet Water Inn: This country bed-and-breakfast is nestled beside a spruce forest on an apple orchard. Enjoy home cooking and free musical concerts each night. The six rooms range from $50 to $100 per night plus a $50 refundable deposit for your pet. HC 61, Box 4750, Orient, ME 04471; (207) 523-6840.

ORONO

PARKS, BEACHES, AND RECREATION AREAS

• **Jeremiah Colburn Natural Area** 🐾🐾🐾 See **16** on page 590.
This conservation property has two primary looping trails that make for an engaging outing through a thick forest. The 55-acre parcel, with its three miles of trails, is popular year-round—especially in the winter when the mud and bugs are gone and the snow-covered pines glisten in fleeting rays of cherished sunshine.

Just in from the trailhead, you will find a carved wooden trail map to make it easier to plan your route.

The property is managed by the Orono Land Trust, and dogs need to be leashed.

From U.S. Route 2, take Forest Avenue west for a half mile. Turn right onto Forest Hill Terrace to the end and the park. Park at the end of the street. Open sunrise to sunset. (207) 866-0023.

• **University of Maine Forest Trails** 🐾🐾🐾 See **17** on page 590.
Now this is the kind of classroom we all enjoy. Miles of thickly wooded trails right on campus might get your dog thinking about getting another degree.

The endless hiking possibilities include an assortment of loops on footpaths, forest roads, and even a two-mile-long paved bike path that runs out to Old Town through the northern end of the forest. We like the 1.25-mile-long loop around the corn field near Concert Park.

Dogs need to be leashed and should avoid the animals at the University of Maine Dairy Farm in the middle of the woods. Campus visitors are required to get a free, one-day parking permit at the University Visitor's Center (Chadburne Hall). Trail maps are available at the Visitor's Center and at the Memorial Union.

From U.S. Route 2, take State Route 2A (College Avenue) into the University of Maine. Turn right onto Munson Road. The Visitor's Center is on the left. The forest trails are at the north end of campus. Continue on Munson Road. Make a right onto Long Road and a left onto Gannett Road for the bike path and trails, or turn left onto Rangeley Road for more trails. Open sunrise to sunset. (207) 581-3740.

RESTAURANTS

Bear Brew Pub: Kick back on the back porch with any number of local microbrew beers and tasty pub food. 36 Main Street; (207) 866-2739.

PLACES TO STAY

Black Bear Inn: This full-service, 66-room hotel offers all the amenities in a modern, if predictable, setting. The rooms are spacious and tasteful, and the inn will provide you with most anything you forget to pack. Free continental breakfast is included. Rooms range from $60 to $140 per night. There's no extra charge for Rover. 4 Godfrey Drive, Orono, ME 04473; (207) 866-7120, (800) 528-1234.

University Motel: Small pets are welcome at this motel, but since we stayed here and Inu is 65 pounds and George weighs 35, we aren't sure how "small" small should be. In any event, our hunch is that "too big" really means "rude and unruly," so let them know you'll be traveling with a pet and make sure your pooch is on best behavior. Rooms range from $50 to $80 per night. Breakfast is included. College Avenue, Orono, ME 04473; (207) 866-4921.

PRESQUE ISLE

PARKS, BEACHES, AND RECREATION AREAS

• **Aroostook State Park** 🐾 🐾 See **18** on page 590.
Aroostook is Maine's northernmost state park. It's also its first state park, established in 1939, thanks to the good citizens of Presque Isle who came up with the idea and donated the land, totaling over 600 acres.

There are two prominent features of Aroostook. The first is twin-peaked Quaggy Jo Mountain, which towers over the surrounding flat farmlands. You can climb both peaks; each has a summit trail about two miles in length, but the easiest route and best views are on the north peak. Additionally, there are four miles of level trails popular with cross-country skiers in winter that your dog will enjoy all year round.

The other noticeable feature here is Echo Lake. If you've climbed both peaks and your French poodle is still looking to run for the Quebec border, take her out on the water! You can rent canoes here for $2.50 an hour or $10 a day.

The park also offers 30 campsites; fees are $15 per night for residents and $18 per night for out-of-staters. For reservations, call the state campground reservation system at (800) 332-1501 (within Maine) or (207) 287-3824 (out of state).

Dogs are required to be on leash in all Maine state parks. There is a day-use fee of $1.00 per adult and $.50 per child (5–11 years of age).

The park is located five miles south of Presque Isle center on U.S. Route 1. Open from 9 A.M. to sunset. (207) 768-8341.

PLACES TO STAY
Aroostook State Park camping: See above.

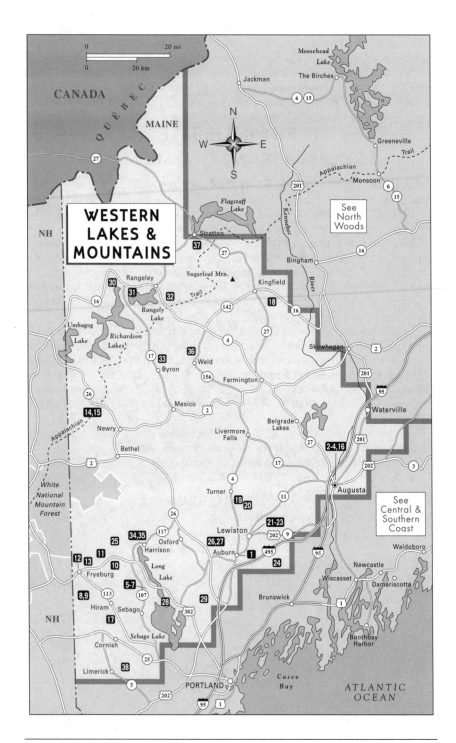

WESTERN
LAKES &
MOUNTAINS

CANADA

QUÉBEC

MAINE

NH

20 mi
20 km

N
W E
S

Jackman

Moosehead
Lake

The Birches

6 15

Greeneville
Trail

Appalachian

Monsoon

6

15

See
North
Woods

27

201

Flagstaff
Lake

Stratton
37

27

Sugarloaf Mtn.

Rangeley

30

31

32

Trail

142

18

16

Kingfield

Bingham

16

Kennebec

River

Rangely
Lake

Umbagog
Lake

Richardson
Lakes

16

17

33

Byron

Weld

36

4

27

156

Farmington

Skowhegan

2

201

95

Waterville

26

14,15

Appalachian

Newry

Mexico

2

Livermore
Falls

Belgrade
Lakes

27

2-4,16

201

202

3

Bethel

2

17

Augusta

White
National
Mountain
Forest

4

Turner

19 20

11

See
Central &
Southern
Coast

26

Lewiston

21-23

202

9

Waldoboro

25

34,35

117

Oxford

26,27

495

Newcastle

12

11

Harrison

Auburn

1

24

Wiscasset

13

10

Fryeburg

Long
Lake

5-7

107

29

Brunswick

1

Damariscotta

8,9

113

28

302

Sebago

17

Hiram

Cornish

Sebago Lake

25

Limerick

38

5

PORTLAND

202

95

1

Casco
Bay

Boothbay
Harbor

ATLANTIC
OCEAN

19

WESTERN LAKES AND MOUNTAINS

As one might suppose, this region of the Pine Tree State is dominated by water and mountains. The Saco and Androscoggin Rivers travel through much of Maine's landscape here, just as the White Mountains and the Mahoosuc Range dominate on the western border. Augusta, the capital city located along the great Kennebec River, has been a major center since the Pilgrims established a trading post here in the 17th century.

Wherever you go, you'll have countless opportunities to experience the Great Outdoors. Whether you hike, bike, canoe, or swim, you and your happy pup will find more activities here than you can shake a stick at.

Appalachian Trail: The Appalachian Trail, administered by the National Park Service, runs for over 2,000 miles from Mount Springer in Georgia to Mount Katahdin in Maine. In Maine, the Appalachian Trail covers 276 miles from the New Hampshire border in the White Mountains to Mount Katahdin in Baxter State Park, where dogs are not permitted. But the rest of the trail is open to leashed dogs, and it's packed with boundless adventure.

For more information, including maps and guidebooks, contact the Appalachian Trail Conference at (304) 535-6331, or locally the Maine Appalachian Trail Club, P.O. Box 283, Augusta, ME 04330.

AUBURN

PARKS, BEACHES, AND RECREATION AREAS

• **Mount Apatite Recreation Area** 🐾 🐾 🐾 See **1** on page 602.
The historic riverside mills and industrial downtown neighborhoods of Auburn and Lewiston don't offer a lot of recreational green spaces for man or dog. But here on the western end of Maine's Twin Cities is a quick wilderness

getaway that should whet any dog's appetite. The park comprises 325 acres of woods, ponds, and marshes with three miles of trails and forest roads. The remains of a quarry are also found within the park boundary where the mineral apatite was mined. A map display at the park entrance will help orient you on the looping trails and leave you hungry for more.

Dogs need to be leashed and are not permitted on the ball fields.

From State Routes 11 and 121 (Minot Avenue), take Garfield Road north for a half mile. The park entrance is on the left. To get to the trailhead, continue on the park road beyond the ball fields and the National Guard base. Open dawn to dusk. (207) 784-0191.

RESTAURANTS

Mac's Grill: Steak, seafood, and spirits plus an outdoor patio make Mac's a mouthwatering stop. 1052 Minot Avenue; (207) 783-6885.

PLACES TO STAY

The Auburn Inn: This in-town hotel has 114 remodeled and modern rooms. Your small pet is welcome with a $25 refundable deposit. Rates range from $65 to $85. 1777 Washington Street, Auburn, ME 04210; (207) 777-1777.

FESTIVALS

Pup, Pup, and Away: If you want a day where the sky's the limit or where everything is looking on the upside, be sure to catch the Twin Cities' Great Falls Balloon Festival. Thousands of pups and people come out to see the skies over the Androscoggin River filled with the colorful "floatilla." The mid-August Auburn-Lewiston festival is Maine's biggest ballooning event with about 45 to 50 balloons. For more information, call (207) 783-2249.

Walk with a Purpose: You and your dog can join the tens of thousands across America who walk to find a cure for diabetes. The American Diabetes Association sponsors America's Walk for Diabetes at over 300 sites in the United States held simultaneously the first weekend in October. The walk is five- to six-miles long, and walkers are asked to raise funds through sponsors and donations. In Auburn, the walk begins and ends at the Central Maine Technical College on Turner Street. (800) 254-9255.

AUGUSTA

PARKS, BEACHES, AND RECREATION AREAS

• **Capitol Park** 🐾 🐾 See **2** on page 602.

This blockwide city park is located in the shadow of the State House and offers a lovely green space in the midst of the surrounding concrete. Stretched between Capitol and Union Streets, you are welcome to walk your leashed dogs on the footpaths that crisscross the grass.

The park is located next to the State House between State Routes 27 and 201 and Capitol and Union Streets. Open 8 A.M. to 8 P.M. (207) 626-2352.

• **Pine Tree State Arboretum** 🐾 🐾 🐾 🐾 🐾 See **3** on page 602.

Well, what can we say about this park that will do it justice? Perhaps the best thing we can offer is that you should go and see it for yourself. There are over

224 wooded acres of meadows, forest, and ponds, five miles of trails, and 300 varieties of trees, shrubs, and plants to dazzle the eye. In every season it has a different beauty, and, if you're like the other dog lovers in Augusta, this will be your daily stop.

From the main parking area, take the one-mile Viles Pond Loop to lovely Viles Pond (where else?). Along the way you'll pass through the Visitor's Center gardens and some freshly cut meadows. If you wish to take a longer hike, continue past Viles Pond to the Woodland Loop. This path takes you by Whitney Brook, a vernal pool, and some diverse woods, tacking on an additional half mile to your hike.

Currently the Arboretum has a leash law that is only loosely enforced once you are past the main Visitor's Center. But in an ongoing attempt to both protect the arboretum from unleashed dogs, and please the dogs' walkers and non–dog lovers alike, Director Steven Oliveri is trying to negotiate a compromise that will encourage dog owners to police ill-behaved dogs (and their owners). He plans to set up a special off-leash dog area to reduce the infractions in the rest of the arboretum. This sounds reasonable to us, and we hope the dog owners in Augusta are willing to figure something out so they won't lose their privileges at this beautiful park altogether. Needless to say, dogs must be on leash.

From the East Rotary and State Routes 9, 17, 100, 201, and 202, take State Route 9 (Hospital Street) south for one mile. The park entrance is on the left. Open dawn to dusk. (207) 621-0031.

•Waterfront Park ☘ ☘ See ▨ on page 602.

This park runs along both sides of the Kennebec River offering picnic spots, a bike trail, and a view of the river flowing by. The main access to the park is on the western side next to Fort Western. Picnic tables, a grassy area, water access, and a gravel walking trail leading south along the river make this a great place to take a break.

The eastern side has a few picnic tables and the bike trail and is a popular luncheon spot for area business people. Dogs must be on leash on both sides.

From the East Rotary and State Routes 9, 17, 100, 201, and 202, take Bridge Street west one block. Turn left onto Arsenal Street. The park is on the right. Open 8 A.M. to 8 P.M. (207) 626-2352.

NATURE HIKES AND URBAN WALKS

Augusta—Gardiner Bike Path: This planned 6.5-mile bike path is a work in progress. The stone-dust trail is scheduled to open in the year 2001 and will run along the Kennebec River and the riverside railroad tracks from the Capitol to Gardiner. (207) 626-2352.

PLACES TO STAY

Best Western Senator Inn and Spa: This full-service hotel offers 80 rooms and 20 suites with efficiencies for travelers on the go. The rooms are fully equipped and spacious, and the staff is very accommodating to your dog. Rates range from $69 to $139 per night. No extra charge or deposit is required for Fido. 284 Western Avenue, Augusta, ME 04330; (207) 622-5804; www.bestwestern.com.

Motel 6: All Motel 6 locations allow dogs, as long as you don't leave them unattended. One dog is welcome per room. Room rates are $59. 18 Edison Drive, Augusta, ME 04330; (207) 622-0000, (800) 4-MOTEL6; www.motel6.com.

DIVERSIONS

Marching Mutts of Maine: This annual two-mile walk is a fundraiser for the Kennebec Valley Humane Society. The mid-May event starts at Youth Memorial Park, and participants are asked to make a donation or to raise pledges. Prizes and goodie bags follow the walk. Contact KVHS for more information at (207) 626-3491.

Holiday Tree: Brighten your holidays with a visit to the Kennebec Valley Humane Society's Holiday Tree. The festive lighting ceremony takes place in the beginning of December, and visitors can place a light on the Christmas tree in honor of their pets for a $10 donation. For more information, contact the Kennebec Valley Humane Society. Pet Haven Lane; (207) 626-3491.

BETHEL

PARKS, BEACHES, AND RECREATION AREAS

• **Bethel Town Forest and Mount Will** 🐾🐾🐾 See **5** on page 602.
This is a pleasant 165-acre forest on the slopes on Mount Will. The park, managed by the Bethel Conservation Commission, has a single three-mile loop trail to the summit at 1,704 feet. It's a moderate climb with a couple of steep sections, and the views of the Androscoggin River Valley are very rewarding. Along the trail are interpretive signs about the interesting history, flora, and fauna of the area.

Dogs need to be leashed.

From downtown Bethel, take State Route 2 east for two miles. The trailhead and roadside parking are on the left (across from the Bethel Transfer Station). Open sunrise to sunset. (207) 824-2669.

PLACES TO STAY

Bethel Inn and Country Club: This classic luxury inn features four different buildings housing deluxe rooms and spacious townhouses on a large estate property. The townhouses are fully equipped apartments with fireplaces and sunny decks; the rooms have living rooms and private baths. All rooms are priced to include dinner and breakfast daily. Rates range from $99 to $209, plus an additional $10 fee for Fido. Broad Street, Box 49, Bethel, ME 04217; (800) 654-0125, (207) 824-2175; www.bethelinn.com.

BRIDGTON

PARKS, BEACHES, AND RECREATION AREAS

• **Bald Pate Mountain** 🐾🐾🐾 See **6** on page 602.
Although the hard times have past, you can still see some of the scars across this land when you climb to the top of Bald Pate Mountain. The mountainside forest was once logged extensively, but it wasn't until the threat of a summit television tower that town folks rallied to buy Bald Pate and preserve it for-

ever. You can take a fairly easy one-mile trail to the summit or explore the other lower woodland trails around the 450-acre preserve now managed by Loon Echo Land Trust. Dogs must be on leash.

From State Route 117, take State Route 107 south for four miles. The park's trailhead and small parking area are on the left. Open sunrise to sunset. (207) 647-2538.

• **Holt Pond Nature Area** 🐾 🐾 🐾 See **7** on page 602.

This conservation area on Holt Pond has a boardwalk trail system that traverses a diverse wetland of swamps and bogs. There are two loop trails; the longest, at a mile in length, is the Dolly Holt Trail which goes to the edge of the wetland surrounding the bog pond. The Swamp Trail is about three-quarters of a mile long and goes through more of the area's woodlands.

Eventually, the Lakes Environmental Association hopes to connect the bog trails with the trails on Bald Pate Mountain, two miles away.

Dogs need to be leashed. And, if you want to keep any of your blood and skin, use bug spray.

From State Route 117, take State Route 107 south for 2.5 miles. Turn left onto Fosterville Road for 1.5 miles, then left onto Fire Lane 228 (Mosquito Roost Road), a dirt road, for a half mile. Parking is on the left and the trailhead is on the right. Open sunrise to sunset. (207) 647-8580.

RESTAURANTS

Adams Bakery: Whether you are strolling through town or heading out on the trail, you can get your morning fix of caffeine and sugar here. There's outdoor seating too. 114 Main Street; (207) 647-2302.

The Gazebo: Great seafood, burgers, ice cream, and sandwiches make this one of the best take-out places in town. 26 Portland Street; (207) 647-2231.

Ruby Food: They say that the Chinese food in Maine is the best in New England. We aren't sure if our tail is being pulled, but the only way to know is to pay a visit to Ruby Food. You can enjoy any of the Szechuan, Hunan, and Cantonese dishes at their outdoor tables. 78 Main Street; (207) 647-8890.

PLACES TO STAY

The First and Last Resort: This motel complex has 12 basic rooms on five acres. Pets are welcome in select rooms for an additional $10 per night, and, for a definite last resort, there is a kennel on site if needed. Continental breakfast is served each morning. Rates range from $45 to $75. Route 302, Bridgton, ME 04009; (207) 647-2200.

Pleasant Mountain Inn: This great getaway inn is located on the shores of Beaver Pond overlooking Shawnee Peak. Rates range from $49 to $100, and guests with pets are asked to sign a damage waiver (which they have never had to call upon). P.O. Box 246, West Bridgton, ME 04009; (207) 647-4505; www.mainegiude.com\bridgeton\pmi.

DIVERSIONS

An Apple a Dog: Let your dog join in a New England autumn tradition with a trip to Five Fields Farm for apple picking. You can pick your own Macouns, Cortlands, and Delicious, or enjoy the ready-picked fruit. This farm dates back to 1776, but, as far as we know, the apples are a bit fresher than that. Apple season is from September through October, and the farm is located on State Route 107 in South Bridgton. For more information, call (207) 647-2425.

Snow Dog: Winter doesn't mean the dog walks stop. In fact this is a great time to get out and do some cross-country skiing or snowshoeing at Five Fields Farm. Five Fields' trails encompass 70 acres of orchards and 450 acres in the surrounding woodlands. The farm is located on State Route 107 in South Bridgton. Skiing rates are $8 per day or $6 for a half day. Dogs can go leash free but must be under control, and trails must be kept clean. For more information, call (207) 647-2425.

BROWNFIELD

PARKS, BEACHES, AND RECREATION AREAS

• Burnt Meadow Mountain 🐾🐾🐾 🐕 See 🎇 on page 602.

Follow an abandoned ski slope to the peak of Burnt Meadow Mountain for a steep climb that will energize the hearty hound but may not be suitable for all dogs. But even if you decide hiking to the summit isn't for you, you still may wish to venture part of the way up the slope. It is a little over a mile to the highest point at 1,624 feet, and along the way are wild blueberries and some rocky ledges that provide fine viewing areas.

Dogs need to be under voice control.

From State Routes 5 and 113, take State Route 160 west for 1.5 miles. Turn right onto Fire Lane 32 for a quarter mile to the trailhead and a small parking area. Open 24 hours a day. There is no contact.

• Peary Mountain 🐾🐾🐾 🐕 See 🎇 on page 602.

The granite summit may only be 958 feet high, but a hike up Peary Mountain can give you that top-of-the-world feeling. The panoramic views from the open granite top include the White Mountains and nearby Burnt Meadow Mountain. The trail itself begins at the Little Saco River, where mosquitoes and black flies always seem to get us off to a fast pace into the woods. Luckily, it's only about a mile to the cool, insect-free breezes of the peak. Even paradise has a few bugs to work out.

Dogs need to be under voice control.

From State Route 160, take State Routes 5 and 113 north for two miles. Turn left onto Farnsworth Road (Fire Lane 100), a dirt road, for 1.5 miles. Just before the one-lane bridge, parking is on the right and the trailhead is on the left. Open 24 hours a day. There is no contact.

PLACES TO STAY

Woodland Acres Camp 'N' Canoe: This campground offers a great two-in-one camp 'n' canoe experience. The full-service campground is located right on the scenic Saco River, and their canoe and shuttle services allow you to explore the covered bridges and many nooks and crannies of the river. Tent and RV rates range from $20 to $30 per night, plus a $5 fee for Buster. Dogs need to be leashed. Route 160, RFD 1, Box 445, Brownfield, ME 04010; (207) 935-2529; www.woodlandacres.com.

DIVERSIONS

Tip a Canoe and Your Dog Too: The western part of Maine is dominated by beautiful lakes and rivers, so don't waste any time getting out there with your paddling pet. Renting a canoe from River Run Canoe Rental on the Saco River makes a good start. This river outfitter offers canoes, shuttle service, and riverside camping from mid-May through September. They are located off State Route 160. For information and reservations, call (207) 452-2500.

DENMARK

PARKS, BEACHES, AND RECREATION AREAS

• **Pleasant Mountain** 🐾🐾🐾 🐕 See **10** on page 602.

Five summit trails, a long, open granite ridge above the Saco River Valley, a 2,009-foot peak, great views of the White Mountains and western lakes, and even a few blueberries along the trails make Pleasant Mountain more than just a pleasant outing.

The most popular hikes to the top are the Fire Warden's Trail from the west and the Moose (Ledges) Trail from the east. The 2.5-mile Fire Warden's Trail follows active logging roads and has an elevation gain of about 1,600 feet. The two-mile Moose Trail is a bit steeper, going over some passable but rocky ledges. In spring and summer, look for wild blueberries along the trail.

Other trailheads include the Bald Peak Trail, the most difficult route to the top. If you decide to tackle this trail, wild strawberries and waterfalls are perks; the Southwest Ridge Trail offers fine views all the way up and not much foot traffic.

Dogs need to be under voice control.

To get to the eastern trailheads from U.S. Route 302 in West Bridgton (just west of Moose Pond), take Mountain Road south for two miles or for 3.5 miles. The trailheads are on the right. To get to the western trailhead from U.S. Route 302 in Fryeburg (at the Bridgton border), take Warren Road (Fire Lane 37) south for a mile over a little wooden bridge. The trailhead (a forest road) and roadside parking are on the left before the yellow Victorian house. Open 24 hours. There is no contact available.

FRYEBURG

PARKS, BEACHES, AND RECREATION AREAS

• **Hemlock Bridge** 🐾🐾 🐕 See **11** on page 602.

Naming a bridge after a poison that causes instant death seems like a risky proposition to us. With so many bridges in New England succumbing to floods, fire, weather, and neglect, we just don't see the logic behind this name. Why risk the bad karma? But the covered Hemlock Bridge was built in 1857 and is still going strong today. Clearly the name hasn't affected its durability, although in this remote location on a channel of the Saco River, it probably hasn't seen much traffic in recent years.

Still, it's impressive to see this wooden structure still in use after so many years. The covered bridge was fashionable in the 19th century because the cover or roof helped protect the wooden trusses from the harsh elements; that is, until iron and steel found a way to do the job better. So enjoy this old relic from the past.

Around the Hemlock Bridge are plenty of places to relax and go in for a dip. Dogs must be under voice control.

From State Route 5, take U.S. Route 302 east for five miles. Turn left onto Hemlock Bridge Road for three miles to the bridge. Parking is available on the right before the bridge. Open 24 hours a day. (207) 287-2551.

• Jockey Cap Trail 🐾 🐾 🐾 See **12** on page 602.

Although the ledge or cap brim that gave this giant boulder its name broke off years ago, it's still a good place for a short hike. The trail is four-tenths of a mile long through a pine forest to the top of Jockey Cap on an easy climb to the massive boulder. At the top, you'll find views of Mount Washington and a monument to Admiral Peary who once lived in Fryeburg.

Dogs must be under voice control and on leash in the parking area. Watch for broken glass at the boulder.

From State Route 5, take U.S. Route 302 east for a mile. The trailhead is on the left behind the Jockey Cap Country Store. Open dawn to dusk. (207) 935-2306 and (207) 935-3933.

• Mount Tom 🐾 🐾 🐕 See **13** on page 602.

This 1.5-mile hike follows a forest road to the somewhat wooded summit of Mount Tom (1,073 feet). We can't call it exciting, but it's a good way to avoid the crowds on the more popular Jockey Cap (see above) and there *are* those luscious wild berries along the way to distract you from the boredom of the road. The trail begins on a private farm that is open to public access.

Dogs need to be under voice control and on leash in the parking area.

From State Route 5, take U.S. Route 302 east for two miles. Turn left onto Old Mountain Road/Menotomy Road (Fire Lane 31) for two miles. The trailhead and limited parking are on the right at the farm with a "Welcome Hikers" sign. Open sunrise to sunset. (207) 287-2631.

RESTAURANTS

Jockey Cap Country Store: In this neck of the woods supplies are tough to come by. So you had better stock up on drinks and sandwiches at the Country Store. There's outdoor seating, too, to rest your legs for the long haul. 16 Bridgton Road; (207) 935-2306.

DIVERSIONS

Doggie Day Care: The new facilities at the Conway Area Humane Society offer short- and long-term care for your dog. For those of you traveling through the area, take advantage of the one-hour and half-day options for doggie day care. Located on 25 acres, your pet will be pampered and played with while you are shopping or taking advantage of the many activities in the Mount Washington Valley. This is not just a kennel, but a home away from home. (207) 935-4358.

Doggie Paddle?: If you really want to see how good of a paddler your dog is, rent a canoe from Saco River Canoe and Kayak and get out on the water.

The scenic river winds it's way through the Fryeburg area at a safe, relaxing pace. Shuttle service is available too. Located off State Route 5. For information and reservations, call (207) 935-2369.

GRAFTON

PARKS, BEACHES, AND RECREATION AREAS

• **Grafton Notch State Park** 🐾🐾🐾🐾 See **14** on page 602.
With 3,112 acres on the northern end of the Mahoosuc Mountain Range, Grafton Notch is one of the largest and most scenic state parks in Maine.

You and your dog will have countless options when it comes to picking a hiking destination. Some of the more popular places in the park are Screw Auger Falls, an impressive waterfall and swimming hole, and Mother Walker Falls, which drops through a narrow gorge. Both are accessible via hikes less than a quarter-mile long. If you are looking for a longer hike with views that will knock the socks off Socks, try the 2.5-mile loop to Table Rock via the Appalachian Trail. You'll find impressive outlooks from the precariously perched flat rock.

Dogs need to be leashed in all state parks. There is a day-use fee of $1.

The park is located off State Route 26. Open 9 A.M. to sunset. Call (207) 824-2912 May 15 to October 15, (207) 624-6080 off-season.

• **Mahoosuc Maine Public Reserve Land** 🐾🐾🐾🐾 See **15** on page 602.
If you want to experience some of the most remote, breathtaking mountain ranges in the Pine Tree State without getting too far up into the Great North Woods, then the Mahoosuc Range, offering a wilderness experience without the long drive, is for you. This state-owned land is comprised of 27,000 acres on the eastern end of the White Mountains, bordering on Grafton Notch State Park and accessed via the Appalachian Trail. Hiking here, especially at the numerous high altitudes, is considered challenging but rewarding. Popular destinations are Speck Pond, Maine's highest body of water, and Cataracts Gorge. Older dogs probably won't be up to the task, but active trail hounds should love this unlimited terrain.

On all Maine Public Reserve Lands dogs must be kept on leash in camping areas and under voice control outside of camping areas.

Hiking trails can be accessed through Grafton Notch State Park or, from State Route 26 a mile north of the park exit sign, take Success Pond Road (a private gravel road) southwest for seven miles to the trailheads. Other trailheads are off Sunday River Road off State route 26 in Bethel. Open 24 hours a day. (207) 778-8231.

HALLOWELL

PARKS, BEACHES, AND RECREATION AREAS

• **Vaughan Woods** 🐾🐾🐾🐾 🐕 See **16** on page 602.
What a find! This 166 acres isn't on any map, and trying to find it proved to

be a case fit for Sherlock Holmes, but, golly, was it worth the effort. With beautiful trails sweeping through open meadows filled with wildflowers, scenic woodlands, and babbling brooks, this preserve will probably show up on every dog's wish list once the word gets out.

The main trail winds through a glade of trees before opening up onto a lovely meadow. Our dogs romped through the tall grasses while we blew dandelions across the open field. Soon the trail leads back into the forest as the path eases slowly along the ridge down to Vaughn Brook.

Plenty of flat rocks make great seats from which to dangle your feet in the brook. If you want a swim, go up the hill towards the stone dam, and the woods will open onto a scenic pond where your dog can take a dip.

From the brook, the trail continues into the woods on the other side. Take the left fork which leads into another meadow and woodland trail. The trail to the right leads to another parking area behind Hallowell High School.

These woods are privately owned but managed by the Kennebec Land Trust, and dogs are allowed off leash. The owners have recently purchased another nearby parcel of land where a pair of bald eagles is breeding.

From State Route 201 in the center of town, take Center Road west for two blocks. Turn left onto Middle Road for a quarter mile to the intersection with Litchfield Road. The unidentified park and a dirt parking lot are straight ahead. Open dawn to dusk. (207) 933-2220.

HIRAM

PARKS, BEACHES, AND RECREATION AREAS

• **Mount Cutler Trail** 🐾🐾🐾 🐕 See **17** on page 602.

This is a short but fairly steep hike to the summit of Mount Cutler (1,180 feet). The route is about 1.5 miles and starts with a trip through a pine forest ascending some rocky ledges and traversing the open ridges of Mount Cutler.

For dogs that might have difficulty with the ledges, you may prefer venturing along some of the snowmobile trails that cross the Mount Cutler Trail. A good one starts at the beginning of the trailhead. Take the side trail on your left to an overgrown, abandoned mine.

From Hiram center at the intersection of State Routes 5, 113, and 117, cross the concrete bridge over the Saco River. Make an immediate left and then right onto Mountain View Road for a tenth of a mile to a small parking area by the railroad tracks. Open sunrise to sunset. (207) 287-2631.

KINGFIELD

PARKS, BEACHES, AND RECREATION AREAS

• **Mount Abraham** 🐾🐾🐾🐾 🐕 See **18** on page 602.

Mount Abraham, at 4,049 feet high, is one of 12 peaks over 4,000 feet in the Pine Tree State and arguably one of Maine's most beautiful. It also has one of the largest summits above the timberline, offering you acres of wide-open views including 4,237-foot Sugarloaf Mountain, the region's tallest peak.

Although this four-mile climb of 3,000 feet is not for every dog, we list it here because it is one of the more scenic areas we've encountered, and it is perfectly fine for dogs used to full-day outings.

Dogs need to be under voice control.

From State Route 27, take West Kingfield Road west for six miles (it becomes a dirt road). Bear left across Rapid Stream and turn right on the other side for a half mile to a T intersection and the unidentified trailhead in front of you. Roadside parking is available. Open 24 hours. No contact.

PLACES TO STAY

The Herbert: This historic 1918 beaux-arts hotel offers old-world European charm with modern conveniences. This recently renovated jewel has 40 comfortable rooms, many with Jacuzzis, brass beds, and wood trim. Spa facilities and a restaurant are available on-site. Rooms range from $65 to $180; pets are allowed in select rooms. Main Street, Kingfield, ME 04947; (207) 265-2000, (800) 843-4372; www.byme.com/theherbert.

LEEDS

PARKS, BEACHES, AND RECREATION AREAS

• Androscoggin River—Twin Bridges 🐾 🐾 🐕 See **19** on page 602.

The Androscoggin and Saco Rivers dominate the landscape of western Maine so we had better be able to find a place to go in for a dip. Not that this island in the middle of the Androscoggin is paradise (a lot of natural debris, such as logs and branches, pile up around it), but on the south side of the wooded island there is a half-mile trail and enough water access to cool off a hot dog.

Dogs must be under voice control.

From State Route 108, take State Route 219 east for a tenth of a mile over the first bridge. The trail and roadside parking are on the right. Open sunrise to sunset. There is no contact.

• Monument Hill Trail 🐾 🐾 🐕 See **20** on page 602.

Monument Hill gets its name from the Civil War monument at its partially wooded summit. You will also find, after a moderate climb, fine views of the White Mountains and Androscoggin Lake. We can't wax poetic over the trail; the main trek leads a half mile through some dense woods on an overgrown trail. But once you come out of the woods, literally and figuratively, it's like a breath of fresh air.

Dogs need to be under voice control.

From State Route 108, take State Route 219 east for 1.5 miles. Turn right onto North Road for two miles. The trailhead is on the left, and a very small parking area is on the right. Open sunrise to sunset. (207) 287-2631.

LEWISTON

PARKS, BEACHES, AND RECREATION AREAS

• Kennedy Park 🐾🐾 See **21** on page 602.

For a two-block downtown city park, Kennedy Park has a lot going on. Most of the action centers around the band shell, pool, and playground, but the other half of the park lies on a grassy lawn with lovely walkways that will please upper-crust pups.

Dogs need to be leashed.

The park is located at Park and Pine Streets. Street parking is available. Open 5 A.M. to 1 A.M. (207) 783-6702.

• Railroad Park 🐾🐾 See **22** on page 602.

George thinks it must have been an impressive sight to see one of the many steam engines that used to rumble across the Androscoggin River near the Great Falls. We agree, but it's much more enjoyable crossing the 1909 historic railroad bridge now that it has been converted to a pedestrian/bike bridge. The bridge and bike path, connecting the downtown areas of Auburn and Lewiston, are part of Lewiston's Railroad Park running north along the river for a half mile. The park is a former train yard that now offers grassy fields, views of the river and falls, and some water access.

Dogs need to be leashed.

The main parking is at the end of Beech Street off of Lincoln Street (State Route 196). Additional parking is available at Mill Street off of Main Street (State Routes 11 and 100) just east of Longley Memorial Bridge. Open 5 A.M. to 1 A.M. (207) 783-6702.

• Thorncrag Bird Sanctuary 🐾🐾🐾🐾 See **23** on page 602.

This 310-acre property has been a popular escape for city residents since the land was first protected by Dr. Alfred Anthony and the Stanton Bird Club back in 1921. It's easy to see why. The park has 10 miles of trails and bridle paths, 310 acres of rolling hills covered with a variety of plants, and enough ponds and streams to make a Portuguese water dog apply for citizenship. Picnic on one of the well-placed stone benches situated along gravel paths through pine and maple trees, or stop and throw sticks in the water for your retriever to fetch.

This park is actively managed to promote bird and wildlife. The bird club also plans to cut down a few select hilltop trees to open up the view to the White Mountains. So be respectful of the wildlife, but also go and enjoy one of the better parks in this corner of Maine.

Dogs need to be leashed.

From Main Street (State Routes 11, 100, and 202), take Sabattus Street (State Route 126) east for a mile. Turn left onto East Avenue for 1.5 miles to the park and parking. Open sunrise to sunset. (207) 782-5238.

NATURE HIKES AND URBAN WALKS

Historical Walking Tour of Lewiston-Auburn: This six-mile route covers the downtown areas of the Twin Cities, both historic mill towns along the Androscoggin River. The walk includes the Railroad Bridge, the Lewiston

Canal, the Great Falls, and the many brick and brownstone mills that line the river and canal. Railroad Park is a good place to park and start the walk. For more information, call (207) 783-2249.

PLACES TO STAY

Main Motel and Cabins: Owners Don and Penny Pitt welcome pets at their friendly 16-unit motel and cabin complex. Six motel rooms and 10 rustic cabins are available, varying from a single room to a two-bedroom cottage. Some of the larger cabins have small kitchen facilities, and all motel rooms are air-conditioned. The motel is open all year; cabins are available seasonally for daily or weekly rentals. Dogs are welcome in all rooms as long as they are not left unattended. Rates range from $40 to $65 per day. 1101 Main Street, Lewiston, ME 04240; (207) 784-7925.

Morning Star Motel: This no-frills motel is located on seven grassy acres offering plenty of room to walk your dog. The 25 newly renovated rooms range from $38 to $48 per night. Dogs are welcome in select rooms for an additional $10 per night. 1905 Lisbon Road, Lewiston, ME 04240; (207) 783-2277.

Motel 6: All Motel 6 locations allow dogs, as long as you don't leave them unattended. One dog is welcome per room. Room rates are $59. 516 Pleasant Street, Lewiston, ME 04240; (207) 782-6558; www.motel6.com.

DIVERSIONS

Walk a Mile in My Shoes: Join the 100–150 dogs who participate each year in the Dog Walk and Fun Day, a furry fundraiser for the Greater Androscoggin Humane Society. Held the first Sunday in May, this mile-long sponsored walk provides maximum fun for a good cause. There are agility demonstrations and local vendor booths; get your dog's photo made into a festive key chain. Call for exact date and time. (207) 783-2311.

LISBON

PARKS, BEACHES, AND RECREATION AREAS

• Beaver Park 🐾 🐾 🐾 🐕 See **24** on page 602.
This town park is 330 acres in size and a bit of a mixed bag when it comes to dogs. Although your pooch is permitted leash free, she is not allowed around the ponds. Our dogs look at us with those melted chocolate eyes as we lead them past the water, and, although it's hard to resist the beckoning ponds, them's the rules, so please abide.

If your dog can resist the temptation to tiptoe to the pond's edge, five miles of hiking trails are available to ease the pain, offering an excellent walk through a rich pine forest. And, for dogs who can never get enough water, a few stream and brook crossings allow a splash of the paws.

Dogs need to be under voice control and are not permitted at the picnic areas or beaches. There is a day-use fee of $1 for residents and $3 for nonresidents. Yearly passes are also available.

From State Route 196, take Village Street south for a half mile. Turn right onto Pinewoods Road for a mile, then make a right onto Cotton Road for a quarter mile. The park is on the right. Open sunup to sundown. (207) 353-9075.

LOVELL

PARKS, BEACHES, AND RECREATION AREAS

• **Sabattus Mountain** 🐾🐾🐾 🐕 See **25** on page 602.

The trail to the summit of Sabattus Mountain is one of the more popular short hikes in western Maine. George and Inu like it because the trail is wide enough so that two alpha dogs can both lead the way, side by side. It's also a relatively easy ascent over three-quarters of a mile, yet once you "top out" you'll have impressive views of nearby Fryeburg and the White Mountains from this 1,200-foot peak. And you may just happen to notice the dramatic drop-offs at the summit cliffs. Phobics beware! Keep your dog close.

Dogs need to be under voice control.

From State Route 5, take Sabattus Road east for 1.5 miles. Bear right onto Sabattus Mountain Road (a dirt road) for a half mile. The trailhead and roadside parking are on the right. Open sunrise to sunset. There is no contact.

PLACES TO STAY

Hewnoaks Cottages: This six-cottage complex lies on lovely Kezar Lake where you and your dog can fish, boat, or work on those tan lines. They offer small kitchens in a fairly simple but comfortable setting. Dogs are welcome in most units. Rooms range from $75 to $110 per night. RR 1, Box 65, Center Lovell, ME 04016; (207) 925-6051.

MECHANICS FALLS

PARKS, BEACHES, AND RECREATION AREAS

• **Androscoggin River** 🐾🐾 🐕 See **26** on page 602.

This riverside green space gives your pet some access to a meandering section of the Androscoggin River and a trail that runs a half mile through the forest. For a quick and easy place to get a little exercise, you could do worse. Note that the site is also used as a boat launch, and the trail is an extension of a snowmobile route.

Dogs must be under voice control.

From State Route 121, take State Route 11 south for a quarter mile. The park is on the right just before the bridge. Parking is available. Open sunrise to sunset. (207) 287-2631.

• **True Farm Living Forest** 🐾🐾 🐕 See **27** on page 602.

This park's tote roads, the only way to get around this 150-acre preserve, are quite overgrown, but we think that makes for an interesting hike through the knee-high grass. Although scruffy, the roads are easy to follow, and the dogs seem to like the rustic environment. The forest is a rich mix of pines and hardwoods, although the vegetation is often so dense it's difficult to see for any distance into the woods. But you can log at least two miles of hiking on these roads which should tire out the friskiest of Fidos.

The park is managed and owned by the New England Forestry Foundation. Dogs must be under voice control.

From State Route 11, take State Route 26 north for one mile. Turn right onto an abandoned road across from Edwards Road. The entrance is on the left. Open dawn to dusk. (978) 448-8380.

NAPLES

PARKS, BEACHES, AND RECREATION AREAS

• Sebago Lake State Park 🐾 🐾 See 28 on page 602.

This is a good-sized state park with 1,300 acres right on Sebago Lake. But we've found out the hard way that no matter how much lake frontage there is, dogs are not permitted on any of it. After being shooed away from the unmarked shoreline on a visit here, we discovered that this popular lake wants to keep all the water fun for the two-legged folk.

Dogs are permitted in the picnic areas and on the short woodland trails, but with the lake so close and so inviting, it's hard to be content with just a view.

Dogs are not permitted in the campground or in the water and must be on leash in the rest of the park. There is a $2 day-use fee.

The park is located off State Routes 35 and 302 on the Casco town line. Open June 20 through Labor Day, 9 A.M. to sunset. (207) 693-6613.

PLACES TO STAY

Fern Hill Farm Bed-and-Breakfast: Stay in the guest room of this historic 1870 farmhouse and enjoy seeing a working farm in action. Your room, with private bath, is decorated tastefully with antiques and a tin bathtub. Rates include a full breakfast. Pets are allowed with prior notice. The room rate is $75. RR 1, Box 416C, Wiley Road, Naples, ME 04055; (207) 693-4320; www.mainefarmvacation.com/fernhill.

POLAND

PARKS, BEACHES, AND RECREATION AREAS

• Range Ponds State Park 🐾 🐾 🐾 See 29 on page 602.

These 750 scenic acres are on the shores of Lower Range Pond. The park gets a bit crowded during summer weekends, but for most of the year it is a pleasant stop for Spot. The park has a looping 1.5-mile trail that runs the length of the waterfront. Be sure to check out the southern end of the pond where the trail follows an old railroad bed along a marsh.

Dogs are required to be on leash in all Maine state parks. They are not permitted on the bathing beaches but may go in the water at more discreet areas. There is a day-use fee of $2.

From State Route 26, take State Route 122 east for one mile. Turn left onto Empire Road for a half mile into the park. Open from 9 A.M. to 8 P.M. Call (207) 998-4104 May 15 to September 15, (207) 624-6080 off-season.

PLACES TO STAY

Country Abundance Bed-and-Breakfast: You may think you are getting away for the weekend, but once you arrive at Country Abundance, you'll feel as if you've gone home again. This relaxing, dog-friendly bed-and-breakfast has three private rooms on 11 acres of land near Tripp Pond. The property's hiking trails lead right from the back porch to the pond. Open year-round, rates range from $65 to $85. Mary, one of our favorite dog-friendly hosts, also offers dog-sitting services. 509 White Oak Hill Road, Poland Spring, ME 04274; (207) 998-2132.

RANGELEY

PARKS, BEACHES, AND RECREATION AREAS

• Bald Mountain 🐾🐾🐾🐾 🐕 See 30 on page 602.

These wooded, mountainous 1,873 acres wedged between Rangeley Lake to the east and Mooselookmeguntic Lake to the west are a great destination for you and your trail dog.

The one-mile moderate climb up Bald Mountain (2,443 feet high) is the park's most-used trail. The granite top has great views and gives new meaning to the term "a breath of fresh air."

On all Maine Public Reserve Lands dogs must be kept on leash in camping areas and must be under voice control on the trails.

From the intersection of State Routes 4, 16, and 17, take State Route 4 west one mile. Turn left onto Bald Mountain Road. The trailhead and a parking turnout are a half mile down on the left. Open 24 hours a day. (207) 778-4111.

• Rangeley Lake State Park 🐾🐾🐾 See 31 on page 602.

This remote parkland on Rangeley Lake, surrounded by Maine's western mountains, offers some of the best scenery in the state park system. Miles of shoreline are included on these 691 acres, plus enough hiking trails to make each visit a new experience. Although your dog will have to avoid the bathing beaches, he is permitted on the shoreline path where plenty of access points will allow him to practice his version of the cannonball.

Dogs must be on leash. There is a day-use fee of $2.

From Rangeley center at the intersection of State Routes 4 and 16, take State Route 4 south for four miles. Turn right onto South Shore Drive for five miles. The park is on your right. Open from 9 A.M. to sunset. Call (207) 864-3858 May 15 to October 1, (207) 624-6080 off-season.

SANDY RIVER PLANTATION

PARKS, BEACHES, AND RECREATION AREAS

• Appalachian Trail—Piazza Rock and The Caves 🐾🐾🐾 See 32 on page 602.

The dogs are always ready to hit the trail, but when Chris told them they were going to Pizza Rock, they were especially excited. Unfortunately, Chris's Italian accent deserted him at an inopportune moment, and when he explained that we were actually hiking Piazza Rock, they still wanted to go. We just had to stop for olives and pepperoni on the way.

But whether it's Pizza or Piazza, the giant rock formation jutting out of the cliffs and the nearby caves are a great rocky playground. Take a two-mile hike with a steady climb to the cliffs across the Sandy River.

Super hikers and super dogs can continue on the Appalachian Trail to Saddleback Mountain and The Horn. Both are over 4,000 feet high, and the one-way, 10-mile journey is strenuous, waterless, and a challenge for most canines. (Humans too but we'll never admit it!)

Dogs must be on leash.

The trailhead and turnout for parking are located at the intersection of the Appalachian Trail and State Route 4, about 10 miles south of Rangeley center and the intersection of State Routes 4 and 12. Open 24 hours a day. (304) 535-6331.

STANDISH
PLACES TO STAY

Acres of Wildlife: This full-service campground at the southern end of Sebago Lake has 200 sites on Rainbow Lake and Chub Pond. With five miles of hiking trails, you may never leave the camping area. Dogs need to be leashed. Tent and RV sites range from $25 to $35 with a $5 fee per dog per night on holiday weekends. P.O. Box 2, Steep Falls, ME 04085; (207) 675-3211.

TOWNSHIP 6 NORTH OF WELD
PARKS, BEACHES, AND RECREATION AREAS

• **Tumbledown Mountain** 🐾 🐾 🐾 🐾 🐕 See **33** on page 602.

Old age is setting in with Inu, and he seems to be dealing with it just fine. Chris, on the other hand, is having a difficult adjustment period. Long, rocky trails are just not the same without the old boy. Gone are the days when they would push each other to the outer limits and back on just an old potato, half a biscuit, and some lake water along the way.

Don't be misled, the team still does get "out there." They just take to easier trails now and then, and one of those routes is on Tumbledown Mountain.

There are three trails up Tumbledown Mountain, but the Brook Trail up to Tumbledown Pond is a doable doggie hike for anyone at 1.5 miles. And the alpine pond provides a good base camp from which to reach one or two of the three peaks of Tumbledown Mountain.

Dog must be under voice control.

From the center of Weld at the intersection of State Routes 142 and 156, take State Route 146 north for 2.5 miles. Turn left onto West Road for a half mile, then bear right onto Byron Road (a dirt road) for 2.25 miles. Turn right onto the second dirt road on your right for 1.5 miles to the turnout and Brook Trailhead. Open 24 hours a day. There is no contact.

WATERFORD
PARKS, BEACHES, AND RECREATION AREAS

• **Hawk Mountain** 🐾 🐾 🐾 🐕 See **34** on page 602.

Take this three-quarter-mile-long trail through woodlands to the granite peak of Hawk Mountain. The forest road is fairly easy to follow; just stay to the right at the forks. Once at the summit you will have earned yourself top-shelf views over Bear Pond.

Dogs need to be under voice control. Watch out for broken glass.

From State Routes 35 and 37 (two miles south of Waterford center), take Mill Hill east and make a quick right onto Fire Lane 95 for 1.25 miles. The forest road trailhead is on the right, and roadside parking is on the left at the end of the pavement. Open sunrise to sunset. There is no contact for this hike.

•Mount Tire'm 🐾🐾🐾 🐕 See **35** on page 602.

Sometimes it seems your dog will always have more energy than you. No matter what the hour, just say, "You wanna go for a walk?" and they are always ready to go. So when we heard about a mountain that would "tire'm," well, we had to check it out.

Although we can't promise this relatively easy hike will exhaust the perkiest of pups, it will certainly take the top off all that energy. The Daniel Brown Trail is about a mile to the top of Mount Tire'm from which there are fine views of nearby Bear Pond and Long Lake. So how about it? You wanna go for a walk?

Dogs need to be under voice control.

From the intersection of State Routes 35 and 37, take Plummer Hill Road northwest for a quarter mile. The trailhead and roadside parking are on the left (just after the Wilkins Community House). Open sunrise to sunset. There is no contact for this hike.

PLACES TO STAY

Waterford Inne: With 25 acres to explore and eight antique-filled rooms with fireplaces, you'll be sure to remember your stay at this lovely bed-and-breakfast. This inn has true country charm with urban elegance and service. A full breakfast is served each morning. Pets are welcome for an additional $10 per night in select rooms. Box 149, Chadbourne Road, Waterford, ME 04088; (207) 583-4037; www.innbook.com/water.html.

WATERVILLE AND WINSLOW
NATURE HIKES AND URBAN WALKS

"When a boy and girl, hand in hand, walk across the span,
A spark of love fills their hearts forever."

Ticonic Two-Cent Bridge: This footbridge, spanning the Kennebec River at the Waterville-Winslow border, has an illustrious history for a bridge that was never used much. Built in 1835 to compete with the ferries across the river, it was originally named the Ticonic Bridge but washed away in a flood 22 years later in 1857.

Rebuilt in 1901, it was renamed the Two-Cent Bridge, reflecting the crossing toll. Disaster struck again a few months later when this new bridge also washed away in a flood. (Not such a great place for a bridge, one might think.) Determined not to be overcome by nature, city leaders rebuilt the bridge again in 1903, and this time it was operational (at two cents a crossing) until 1973.

The bridge was restored in 1997 by the National Park Service, and you and your dog can walk across and experience this wrought-iron bit of history.

The bridge and the green spaces on each side are accessible from Front and Temple Streets in Waterville and from Benton Avenue near State Routes 100 and 201 in Winslow.

RESTAURANTS

Jorgensen's Café: This charming little café in the heart of Waterville has a few tables outside where you and your dog can dine. A full bistro menu is available. 201 Main Street; (207) 872-8711.

WELD

PARKS, BEACHES, AND RECREATION AREAS

• **Mount Blue State Park** 🐾🐾🐾 See **36** on page 602.

This 5,000-acre state park is so big they had to split it into two sections. The southern half is right on beautiful Webb Lake where you'll find plenty of places to practice the doggie paddle. A few miles north is the Center Hill area of the park where there are a number of good hiking trails through the wooded hills and mountains on the north side of the lake. The climb to Mount Blue is a popular destination. It's a steep 1.75-mile hike, but it's a doggie doable climb to the summit at 3,187 feet.

Camping with hot showers is also available at the lake section of the park from May 15 to October 1. Rates range from $8 to $17 for the tents and non-hookup RV sites. Hot showers and flush toilets are provided.

Dogs must be on leash. There is a day-use fee of $2.

From the intersection of State Routes 142 and 156, take Maxwell Road north one mile into the park. Open from Memorial Day to Labor Day, 9 A.M. to sunset. (207) 585-2347.

PLACES TO STAY

Kawanhee Inn Lakeside Lodge and Cabins: This charming 1930s log cabin hearkens back to the days when hunting lodges were hideaways for the rich. There are 21 rooms and luxury wood-lined cabins here along gorgeous Webb Lake. You and your dog can enjoy the beach and many water activities from your lakeside lodging. The lodge lies directly across from Mount Blue State Park. Rooms range from $75 to $150 per night. Route 142, Box 119, Weld, ME 04285; (207) 585-2000; www.lakeinn.com.

Mount Blue State Park camping: See above.

WINDHAM

NATURE HIKES AND URBAN WALKS

Babb's Bridge: At this site over the Presumpscot River between the towns of Gorham and Windham, there once stood Maine's oldest covered bridge, dating back to 1843. Sadly, Babb's Bridge was destroyed by arsonists in 1973. However, you can still enjoy the area and a few water spots on the river for your pet because the bridge was rebuilt in 1976. Local teens hang out here at night, so you'll have to step over the occasional beer can. Dogs must be under voice control. The bridge is on Covered Bridge Road off River Road. Open 24 hours a day. (207) 287-2551.

RESTAURANTS

O'Malley's Diner: Enjoy your favorite diner foods, from chicken-in-a-basket to burgers and BLTs, all with outdoor seating. 862 Roosevelt Trail; (207) 892-3630.

PLACES TO STAY

Sebago Lake Lodge and Cottages: Located right on the water, these one- and two-bedroom cottages offer all the water activities you can imagine—from lakefront swimming to free use of canoes, row boats, and kayaks. Rates range from $68 to $250, plus a $15-per-night pet fee. White's Bridge Road, Windham, ME 04062; (207) 892-2698; www.sebagolakelodge.com.

WYMAN

PARKS, BEACHES, AND RECREATION AREAS

• Bigelow Preserve 🐾🐾🐾🐾 See **37** on page 602.

The Bigelow Preserve is 35,027 acres of true Maine Woods—rugged, demanding, beautiful, and rewarding.

Miles of trails offer a wide variety of terrain, from 21 miles of shoreline at Flagstaff Lake to forests leading to wind-swept, alpine peaks. The highest peak here is West Peak at 4,150 feet.

And since our dogs wouldn't know a ski from a pull toy, they were happy to note that, thanks to public outcry, this pristine land did not become a ski resort in 1976, but instead became part of the Maine Public Reserve Land system.

Dogs must be under voice control.

From the northern intersection of State Routes 16 and 27 in the village of Stratton, go east and south respectively for 5.25 miles and look for the Appalachian Trailhead. Open 24 hours a day. (207) 778-8231.

APPENDIX

PICK OF THE LITTER

DOG DAY AFTERNOONS: THE BEST FOUR-PAW PARKS

- **Amethyst Brook Conservation Area,** Amherst, MA
- **Beaver Brook Association Land,** Hollis, NH
- **Big River Management Area,** West Greenwich, RI
- **Chase Farms Park,** Lincoln, RI
- **Estabrook Woods,** Concord, MA
- **Goose Pond Preserve,** Keene, NH
- **Great Brook Farm,** Carlisle, MA
- **Harriman Reservoir,** Wilmington, VT
- **Hazen's Notch,** Montgomery Center, VT
- **Madame Sherri's Forest,** Chesterfield, NH
- **Pine Tree State Arboretum,** Augusta, ME
- **Pittsfield State Forest,** Pittsfield, MA
- **Rocky Mountain and Highland Park,** Greenfield, MA
- **Rocky Woods,** Medfield, MA
- **Sanford Farm/Ram Pasture/The Woods,** Nantucket, MA
- **Salt Bay Farm Heritage Center,** Damariscotta, ME
- **Taylor Farm,** Norwalk, CT
- **Vaughn Woods,** Hallowell, ME
- **Wagon Hill Farm,** Durham, NH
- **Winslow Park,** Westport, CT

DOGGY DIGS:
TOP DOG-FRIENDLY LODGINGS

- **Country Abundance Bed-and-Breakfast,** Poland, ME
- **Four Seasons Hotel,** Boston, MA
- **The Hanover Inn,** Hanover, NH
- **Harbor Village,** Hyannisport, MA
- **Hilltop Inn,** Sugar Hill, NH
- **Inn at East Hill Farm,** Troy, NH
- **Inn By The Sea,** Cape Elizabeth, ME
- **Jared Coffin House,** Nantucket, MA
- **Jericho Valley Inn,** Williamstown, MA
- **Old Riverton Inn,** Riverton, CT
- **PowderHound Inn,** Warren, VT
- **Publick House Historic Resort,** Sturbridge, MA
- **Sanford-Covell Mansion,** Newport, RI
- **Silvermine Tavern,** Norwalk, CT
- **Whitney's Inn,** Jackson, NH

JAUNTS JUST FOR DOGS

- **All Dogs Gym,** Manchester, NH
- **Camp Gone To The Dogs,** Putney, VT
- **Doggie Dash,** South Kingston, RI
- **Easter Bonnets and Bones,** Mystic, CT
- **Fur 'n' Foliage,** Rockport, ME
- **Walk for the Animals,** Easton, MA

GO, DOG, GO!

- **Boston Harbor Lunch Cruises,** Boston, MA
- **Interstate Aviation,** Southington, CT
- **Lake Champlain Ferries,** Burlington, VT
- ***Margaret Todd* Schooner,** Bar Harbor, ME
- **Southland Riverboat,** Narragansett, RI
- **Winnipesaukee Scenic Railroad,** Meredith, NH

INDEX

ACCOMMODATIONS

Boston Harbor Hotel 271
Bradley Ramada Inn 47
Braeside Motel 417
Branbury State Park camping 368
Brandon Motor Lodge 359
Brandt House, The 169
Breezemere Farm Inn 576
Brentwood Motor Inn 236
Brown's Landing 235
Buck Hill Family Campground 115
Budget Inn of North Kingstown 145
Burgundy Rose Motor Inn 394
Burkehaven Resort Motel 486
Burton Farm Lodge Bed-and-Breakfast 415

C

Cabot Cove Cottages 543
Caddy House 126
Camden Hills State Park camping 534
Camp Annisquam 298
Candlelight Inn 169
Cape Ann Motor Inn 298
Capital Hill Ramada Inn 29
Captain Jefferds Inn, The 543
Caribou Inn and Convention Center 596
Cascades Lodge 370
Castine Harbor Lodge 581
Cavendish Pointe Hotel 409
Centennial Inn, The 26
Chamberlain-Reynolds Memorial Forest camping 427
Channel Inn & Cottages 439
Charlemont Inn 161
Charles Hotel, The 279–280
Chesterfield Inn 458
Chez Gabrielle 167
Chocorua Camping Village 516–517
Claremont Motor Lodge 458
Clarion Inn (Griswold, CT) 57
Clarion Suites Inn (Manchester, CT) 32
Clark Tavern Inn Bed-and-Breakfast 170
Clarksburg State Park camping 163
Clearwater Campground 440

Clipper Ship Lodge 339
Cobscook Bay State camping 584
Colonial Comfort Inn 507
Colonial Hotel 197
Colonial House Inn 236
Colonial Motel 403
Colonial Travelodge 585
Colonnade Hotel, The 271
Colony Hotel 543–544
Combes Family Inn 409
Comfort Inn (Bangor, ME) 593
Comfort Inn (Concord, NH) 460
Comfort Inn (Cromwell, CT) 24
Comfort Inn Airport (Warwick, RI) 129
Commodore's Inn 394
Coolidge State Park camping 410
Copley Plaza, The 271
Cornwall Inn 79
Cortina Inn 370
Country Abundance Bed-and-Breakfast 617–618
Country Fair Motel 537
Country Inn at Bartlett, The 499
Country Lake Resort 450
Country View Motel and Guesthouse 569–570
Courtyard by Marriott 102
Covered Bridge Campground 498
Cozy Corner Motel 187
Crawford Notch General Store and Campground 508
Crestwood Chapel and Pavilion 494
Crocker House Country Inn 585
Crown 'N' Anchor Inn 559
Crowne Plaza (Hartford, CT) 29
Crowne Plaza (Pittsfield, MA) 180
Crowne Plaza at the Crossings (Warwick, RI) 129
Cut Leaf Maple Motel 358

D

D. K. Motel 434
Dana Place Inn 508–509
Danforth Inn 247
Danforth, The 554
Darling Family Inn 415

Highlander Motel 367
Hill Farm Inn 358
Hilltop Acres 517
Hilltop Inn 516
Hilltop Motel 161
Hilton and Towers 80
Hilton Back Bay 271
Historic Valley Campground 176
Hivue Bed-and-Breakfast 359
Holiday Acres Campground 119
Holiday Inn (Bridgeport, CT) 76
Holiday Inn (Concord, NH) 460
Holiday Inn (Danbury, CT) 80
Holiday Inn (East Hartford, CT) 25
Holiday Inn (Ellsworth, ME) 585
Holiday Inn (Falmouth, MA) 225
Holiday Inn (Holyoke, MA) 171
Holiday Inn (North Haven, CT) 67
Holiday Inn (Provincetown, MA) 231
Holiday Inn (Randolph, MA) 333
Holiday Inn (RutlandVT) 368
Holiday Inn (Salem, NH) 447
Holiday Inn (Springfield, MA) 182
Holiday Inn Express (Rockland, MA) 334
Holiday Inn Express (Springfield, VT) 412
Holiday Inn Select (Stamford, CT) 98
Homespun Farm B&B 56
Homestead Inn, The 516
Homewood Suites (Farmington, CT) 26
Homewood Suites Hotel (Windsor Locks, CT) 47
Horseneck Beach State Reservation 348
House on the Hill Bed-and-Breakfast 102
Howard Johnson (Rutland, VT) 368
Howard Johnson (Vernon, CT) 44
Howard Johnson Cambridge 280
Howard Johnson Hotel (Portland ME) 554
Howard Johnson Hotel (South Portland, ME) 564
Howard Johnson Inn (Hadley, MA) 170

Howard Johnson Inn (Mystic, CT) 63
Howard Johnson Inn—Newport (Middletown, RI) 141
Howard Johnson Kenmore (Boston, MA) 271
Huttleston Motel, The 293

I

Inn at Bath, The 524
Inn at Chester 51
Inn at Crotched Mountain, The 463
Inn at East Hill Farm, The 488
Inn at Highview 401–402
Inn at Iron Masters 94–95
Inn at Maplemont Farm, The 376
Inn at Mystic, The 63
Inn at Plymouth Bay 308
Inn at Quail Run 372
Inn at St. John 554
Inn On Bellevue 142
Inn on the Hill 200
Inn-By-The-Sea, The 536–537
Iron Horse Inn 40
Isaac Randall House, The 540–541
Island Inn (Oak Bluffs, MA) 241
Island Inn, The (Monhegan Island, ME) 546
Ivanhoe Country House 181

J

Jamaica State Park camping 363
Jared Coffin House 247
Jasper's Motel and Restaurant 585
Jenkins Inn 193
Jericho Valley Inn 187
Josselyn's "Getaway" Log Cabins 509
Joy Cottages 425

K

Kawanhee Inn Lakeside Lodge and Cabins 621
Kedron Valley Inn 417–418
Kennebunk Inn 542
King's Inn 37
Knotty Pine Motel 359
Kona Mansion Inn 441

RESTAURANTS

MAIN INDEX

A

X, Y, Z

ACKNOWLEDGMENTS

The authors would like to thank the dog constables, conservation commissioners, parks and recreation directors, and town clerks and officials who proved to be indispensable in the writing of this book. Many of the parks listed herein are located on conservation properties not detailed on most public maps, so we especially appreciate the hard work of the many volunteers who made the maps, tended the trails, and answered our endless questions about these beautiful parks.

We would also like to commend young Connor Lau for his countless uncomplaining hours strapped into his car seat while we researched this book. He was a real trooper—a hard thing to be at any age, let alone the age of three.

ABOUT THE AUTHORS

Inu and George consider taking care of their owners, Chris Lau and JoAnna Downey, to be a very serious, full-time job. It's their duty to wake them up, ensure they get plenty of exercise, see the world in a different way, and make new friends. They decided that writing this book was a way to accomplish all these tasks with one big swat of the paw.

George is a "cannardly" dog (which means you can hardly tell what kind of dog he is), but people who insist on more limiting categories claim he must be a bearded collie, a Tibetan terrier, a Puli, a Portuguese water dog—in other words, a cannardly. For the most part, George shuns these labels and just considers himself a *Canis familiaris* (commonly known as a "dog"). While residing at Buddy Dog, an animal shelter, he picked JoAnna out of the multitudes, decided she looked like the perfect meal ticket, and hitched a ride home. When he's not out sniffing trails and gathering information for his budding writing career, George likes to chase squirrels and bark at weird people.

Inu is proud of his heritage and carries his golden retriever lineage with style. Although an enormously social animal, Inu loves the solitude of the Great Outdoors—a taste he developed while living in the Berkshires for the first three years of his life. Then, needing a home and deciding city life would provide the attention he so dearly loves, he traveled to Boston and adopted Chris Lau. Although Inu loves calling the streets of Beacon Hill his own, he still heeds the call of the wild and is ready to travel at a moment's notice. When not out swimming or riding the surf, Inu can be found in the Boston Common working the crowd, looking for free pats, food, and adulation.

JoAnna and Chris have been friends ever since George and Inu introduced them in the Boston Common over eight years ago. When they aren't arguing about the demise of baseball and whether or not the Red Sox will ever win a World Series, JoAnna is a playwright/screenwriter and Chris works as a systems analyst. They are the authors of the *Boston Dog Lover's Companion*.

Beth Rogers is a consultant and part-time writer who lives in Boston with her Shetland sheepdog, Rocky.

THE DLC ANIMAL PARTNERSHIP PROGRAM

The Dog Lover's Companion series is pleased to promote animal rescue and adoption organizations nationwide. In an effort to create an awareness of these worthy causes, we ask you to support your local nonprofit animal rescue and adoption organization, Humane Society, or SPCA, such as:

MASSACHUSETTS SOCIETY FOR THE
PREVENTION OF CRUELTY TO ANIMALS
AMERICAN HUMANE EDUCATION SOCIETY

The MSPCA/AHES is one of the country's oldest and largest humane organizations founded in 1868 by Boston attorney, George Thorndike Angell. The Society's mission is to protect animals, relieve their suffering, advance their welfare, prevent cruelty, and work for a just and compassionate society. The Society works towards this mission through many local, national and international programs and services including the following;

- **ANIMAL HOSPITALS:** The Society's hospitals include world-renowned Angell Memorial Animal Hospital in Boston, Rowley Memorial Animal Hospital in Springfield, Carlee Memorial Animal Hospital on Nantucket Island and The American Fondouk, a charitable animal hospital in Fez, Morocco.
- **ANIMAL SHELTERS:** The MSPCA's eight animal shelters take in and care for more than 30,000 animals each year. The Nevins Farm & Equine Centre provides refuge and adoption services for neglected, abandoned and surrendered large animals including horses, cows, sheep, goats and others. The society's small animal shelters, which care for dogs, cats, and other small animals are located in Boston, Brockton, Centerville, Edgartown, Methuen, Nantucket, and Springfield.
- **ADVOCACY:** The MSPCA lobbies for animal protection legislation as well as provides community programs including "Phinney's Friends, a volunteer program which assists pet owners living with HIV/AIDS and the "Pets In Housing" program which serves as a resource for housing managers and pet owners living in rental housing.
- **LAW ENFORCEMENT:** Authorized to enforce the state's animal anti-cruelty laws, the Society's Law Enforcement Department investigates cruelty complaints throughout the state and inspects pet shops, circuses, rodeos, fairs and other animal exhibits and businesses. To report cruelty call MSPCA Law Enforcement at (800) 628-5808 or within 617 area code, call 522-6008.
- **HUMANE SERVICES:** In addition to overseeing the MSPCA's shelters and the Animal Hall of Fame, this division coordinates a statewide low-cost spay/neuter program and participates in a national council on pet overpopulation.
- **ANIMAL HALL OF FAME:** Launched in 2001, the MSPCA's Animal Hall of Fame is a traveling exhibit providing lessons in compassion, heroism and history.
- **INTERNATIONAL ANIMAL PROTECTION:** The MSPCA assists animal protection and disaster relief efforts all over the world sending staff, supplies or funds to areas where the animal population has been affected by natural or man-made disasters or inhumane conditions.

The MSPCA/AHES is a private, non-profit organization which relies on donations and fees for services to fund its programs. For information about membership, volunteering or other MSPCA/AHES programs, contact MSPCA/AHES, 350 South Huntington Ave., Boston, MA 02130. (617) 522-7400 or visit online at www.MSPCA.org.

**AVALON
TRAVEL**
p u b l i s h i n g

How far will our travel guides take you? As far as you want.

Discover a rhumba-fueled nightspot in Old Havana, explore prehistoric tombs in Ireland, hike beneath California's centuries-old redwoods, or embark on a classic road trip along Route 66. Our guidebooks deliver solidly researched, trip-tested information—minus any generic froth—to help globetrotters or weekend warriors create an adventure uniquely their own.

And we're not just about the printed page. Public television viewers are tuning in to Rick Steves' new travel series, Rick Steves' Europe. On the Web, readers can cruise the virtual black top with Road Trip USA author Jamie Jensen and learn travel industry secrets from Edward Hasbrouck of The Practical Nomad. With Foghorn AnyWare eBooks, users of handheld devices can place themselves "inside" the content of the guidebooks.

In print. On TV. On the Internet. In the palm of your hand.
We supply the information. The rest is up to you.

Avalon Travel Publishing
Something for everyone

www.travelmatters.com

Avalon Travel Publishing guides are available at your favorite book or travel store.

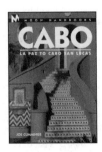

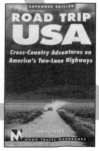

FOGHORN OUTDOORS guides are for campers, hikers, boaters, anglers, bikers, and golfers of all levels of daring and skill. Each guide focuses on a specific U.S. region and contains site descriptions and ratings, driving directions, facilities and fees information,and easy-to-read maps that leave only the task of deciding where to go.

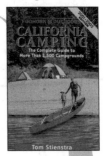

"Foghorn Outdoors has established an ecological conservation standard unmatched by any other publisher."
~Sierra Club

WWW.FOGHORN.COM

TRAVEL SMART guidebooks are accessible, route-based driving guides focusing on regions throughout the United States and Canada. Special interest tours provide the most practical routes for family fun, outdoor activities, or regional history for a trip of anywhere from two to 22 days. Travel Smarts take the guesswork out of planning a trip by recommending only the most interesting places to eat, stay, and visit.

"One of the few travel series that rates sightseeing attractions. That's a handy feature. It helps to have some guidance so that every minute counts."
~San Diego Union-Tribune

CiTY·SMaRT™ guides are written by local authors with hometown perspectives who have personally selected the best places to eat, shop, sightsee, and simply hang out. Thehonest, lively, and opinionated advice is perfect for business travelers looking to relax with the locals or for longtime residents looking for something new to do Saturday night.

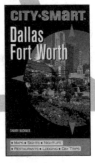